Operating Systems
Principles and Practice

Beta Edition

Thomas Anderson
Michael Dahlin

Operating Systems: Principles and Practice (Beta Edition) by Thomas Anderson and Michael Dahlin

ISBN 978-0-9856735-1-2

Publisher:	Recursive Books, Ltd.
	http://RecursiveBooks.com/
Printer:	Lightning Source

SUGGESTIONS, COMMENTS, and ERRORS. We welcome suggestions, comments and error reports, by email to suggestions@RecursiveBooks.com

Version 0.4

Contents

Memory Management

Persistent Storage

Index and References

Preface

Why We Wrote This Book

Many of our students tell us that their operating systems courses were both the best courses they took as undergraduates, and that they were also the most important for their careers. We are not alone — many of our colleagues report a similar feedback from their students. Our goal with this book is simple: to write a textbook that meets the high standards of how operating systems are taught in practice.

The material in an operating systems class is both exciting and highly relevant. There has been a huge amount of innovation in both the principles and practice of operating systems over the past two decades. The pace of innovation in operating systems has, if anything, increased over the past few years, with the introduction of the iOS and Android operating systems for smartphones, the shift to multicore computers, and the advent of cloud computing.

Perhaps even more importantly, the core ideas in a modern operating system — protection, concurrency, virtualization, resource allocation, and reliable storage — have become widely applied throughout computer science. Whether you get a job at Facebook, Google, Microsoft, or any other leading-edge technology company, it is impossible to build resilient, secure, and flexible computer systems without the ability to apply operating systems concepts in a variety of settings. In a modern world, nearly everything a user does is distributed, nearly every computer is multi-core, security threats abound, and many applications such as web browsers have become mini-operating systems in their own right.

It should be no surprise that for many computer science students, an undergraduate operating systems class has become a *de facto* requirement: a ticket to an internship and eventually to a full-time position.

Unfortunately, many operating systems textbooks are stuck in the past, failing to keep pace with rapid technological change. Many topics are covered as if technology stopped in the 60's and 70's. Even when new topics are added, they are treated as an afterthought, without pruning material that has become less important. The result are textbooks that are very long, yet provide students only a passing familiarity of important concepts.

Our goal is to help students gain mastery over modern operating systems concepts, while still fitting in a quarter or semester long course.

Our approach is to be selected and deep, focusing on how real systems work today, down to the specifics so that students can build these systems for themselves.

We believe it is important to teach students both *principles* and *practice*, concepts and implementation, rather than either alone. At Texas and Washington, we have been teaching these topics for years and winning awards for our teaching. Precisely because operating systems concepts are among the most difficult in all of computer science, we need to take concepts all the way down to the level of working code. In our experience, this is the only way students will really understand and master the material.

We use a rigorous operating systems course project in our classes; there are several to choose from, such as Nachos, Pintos, OS/161, or JOS. Our aim is to be deep enough that instructors will be able to use any of these projects without a large amount of additional material.

This implies a tradeoff: we can go deeper because we do not spend time on discarded approaches. Neither do we try to describe any specific operating system in complete detail. Rather, it is our goal for students to understand the key concepts found in common across the major commercial operating systems; Linux, Windows, Android and MacOS share more than they differ.

For those familiar with other operating systems textbooks, our treatment has several important differences:

- **Top down chapters.** Each chapter orients the student by posing a systems design challenge. We start by presenting the conceptual tools needed to solve the challenge, and then we show how those concepts work in real systems.

- **Protection.** The concept of safe execution of untrusted code has become central to many types of computer systems. Yet existing textbooks treat protection as a side effect of UNIX processes, never clearly explaining the requirements for safe execution of untrusted code, or how those concepts can be applied in the operating system kernel, virtual machines, or web browser sandboxes.

- **Concurrency.** With the advent of multi-core architectures, most students today will spend much of their careers writing concurrent code. Existing textbooks provide a blizzard of concurrency alternatives, most of which were abandoned decades ago as impractical. Instead, we focus on providing students a *single* methodology that will enable students to write correct concurrent programs — this methodology is by far the dominant approach used in industry.

- **Reliable storage.** Reliable storage in the presence of failures is central to almost all computer systems. Existing textbooks survey the history of file systems, spending time on the diverse set of ad hoc approaches to reliability. Instead, we focus on how modern systems use journalling and other techniques to achieve reliability.

By taking a fresh start, we have been able to include the best ideas from how different faculty approach the material. That remains our commitment. We welcome and encourage suggestions for how the material could be better presented; please send any comments to suggestions@recursivebooks.com.

A Guide to Instructors

We believe a rigorous operating systems course should be taken early in an undergraduate's course of study. Many students use this course as a springboard to an internship and a career. To that end, we have designed this textbook to assume minimal pre-requisites: a course on data structures and one on basic machine structures. In particular, we have designed the book to interface well with either the Bryant and O'Halloran or Patterson and Hennessey textbooks on machine structures. Since some machine structures courses only get through the first half of these books, this book reviews and covers in much more depth the material from the second half of those books.

The textbook is organized to allow each instructor to choose an appropriate level of depth for each topic. Each chapter begins at a conceptual level, with implementation details and the more advanced material towards the end. A more conceptual course will skip the back parts of several of the chapters; a more advanced or more implementation-oriented course will need to go into chapters in more depth. No single semester course is likely to be able to cover every topic we have included, but we think it is a good thing for students to come away from an operating systems course with an appreciation that there is *always* more to learn.

Because students better understand what they are learning by using the concepts to solve problems, we have integrated selected homework questions into the body of each chapter. This provides students a way of judging whether they understood the material covered to that point. A more complete set of sample assignments is given at the end of each chapter.

The book is divided into five parts: an introduction (Chapter 1), kernels and processes (Chapters 2-3), concurrency, synchronization, and scheduling (Chapters 4-7), memory management (Chapters 8-10), and persistent storage (Chapters 11-14).

The goal of chapter 1 is to introduce the recurring themes found in the later chapters. We define some common terms, and we provide a bit of the history of the development of operating systems.

Chapter 2 covers kernel-based process protection — the concept and implementation of executing a user program with restricted privileges. is a key concept to most modern computer systems, Given the increasing importance of computer security issues, we believe protected execution and safe transfer across privilege levels are worth treating in depth. For a quick introduction to the concepts, students need only read through 2.3.2. The chapter then dives into the mechanics of system calls, exceptions and interrupts in some detail. Some instructors launch directly into concurrency, and cover kernels and kernel protection afterwards, as a lead-in to address translation and virtual memory. While our textbook can be used that way, we have found that students benefit from a basic understanding of the role of operating systems in executing user programs, before introducing concurrency.

Chapter 3 is intended as an impedance match for students of differing backgrounds. Depending on student background, it can be skipped or covered in depth. The chapter covers the operating system from a programmer's perspective: process creation and management, device-independent input/output, interprocess communication, and network sockets. Our goal is that students should understand at a detailed level what happens between a user clicking on a link in a web browser, and that request being transferred through the operating system kernel on each machine to the web server running at user-level, and back again. The second half of Chapter 3 dives into the organization of the operating system itself: how device drivers and the hardware abstraction layer work in a modern operating system; the difference between a monolithic and a microkernel operating system; and how policy and mechanism can be separated in modern operating systems.

Chapter 4 motivates and explains the concept of threads. Because of the increasing importance of concurrent programming, and its integration with Java, many students will have been introduced to multi-threaded programming in an earlier class. This is a bit dangerous, as students at this stage are prone to writing programs with race conditions, problems that may or may not be discovered with testing. Thus, the goal of this chapter is to provide a solid conceptual framework for understanding the semantics of concurrency, as well as how concurrent threads are implemented in both the operating system kernel and in user-level libraries. Instructors needing to go more quickly can omit Section 3.4 and 3.5.

Chapter 5 discusses the synchronization of multi-threaded programs, a central part of all operating systems and increasingly important in many other contexts. Our approach is to describe one effective method for structuring concurrent programs (monitors), rather than to cover in depth every proposed mechanism. In our view, it is important for students to master one methodology, and monitors are a particularly robust and simple one, capable of implementing most concurrent programs efficiently. The implementation of synchronization primitives are covered in Section 5.5; this should be included if there is time, so students see that there is no magic.

Chapter 6 discusses advanced topics in concurrency, including deadlock, synchronization across multiple objects, and advanced synchronization techniques like read-copy-update (RCU). This material is important for students to know, but some courses may need to go quickly through this chapter.

Chapter 7 covers the concepts of resource allocation in the specific context of processor scheduling. With the advent of data center computing and multi-core architectures, the principles and practice of resource allocation have renewed importance. After a quick tour through the tradeoffs between response time and throughput for uniprocessor scheduling, the chapter covers a set of more advanced topics in affinity and multiprocessor scheduling, power-aware and deadline scheduling, as well as basic queueing theory and overload management. We conclude these topics by walking students through a case study of server-side load management.

Chapter 8 explains mechanisms for hardware and software address translation. The first part of the chapter covers how hardware and operating systems cooperate to provide flexible, sparse address spaces through multi-level segmentation and paging. Section 8.3 then considers how to make flexible memory management efficient with translation lookaside buffers (TLBs) and virtually addressed caches. We consider how to keep TLBs consistent when the operating system makes changes to its page tables. We conclude with a discussion of modern software-based protection mechanisms such as those found in the Microsoft Common Language Runtime and Google's NativeClient.

Chapter 9 covers caching and virtual memory. Caches are central to many different types of computer systems. Most students will have seen the concept of a cache in an earlier class machine structures, so our goal here is to cover the theory and implementation of caches: when they work and when they don't, and how they are implemented in hardware and software. We then show how these ideas are applied in the context of memory-mapped files and virtual memory.

Chapter 10 discusses advanced topics in memory management. Address translation is a powerful tool in system design, and we show how it can be used for zero copy I/O, virtual machines, process checkpointing, and recoverable virtual memory. As this is more advanced material, it can be skipped by those classes pressed for time.

Chapter 11 frames the file system portion of the book, starting top down with the challenges of providing a useful file abstraction to users. We then discuss the UNIX file system interface, the major internal elements inside a file system, and how disk device drivers are structured.

Chapter 12 surveys block storage hardware, specifically magnetic disks and flash memory. The last two decades have seen rapid change in storage technology affecting both application programmers and operating systems designers; this chapter provides a snapshot for students, as a building block for the next two chapters. If students have previously seen this material, this chapter can be skipped.

Chapter 13 discusses file system layout on disk. Rather than survey all possible file layouts — something that changes rapidly over time — we use this a case study to introduce the concept of mapping complex data structures onto block storage devices to achieve flexibility and performance.

Chapter 14 explains the concept and implementation of reliable storage, using file systems as a concrete example. Starting with the ad hoc techniques in UNIX fsck for implementing a reliable file system, the chapter explains checkpointing and write ahead logging as alternate implementation strategies for building reliable storage, and it discusses how redundancy such as checksums and replication are used to improve reliability and availability.

Acknowledgments

We have been incredibly fortunate to have the help of a large number of people in the conception, writing, editing, and production of this book. We started on the journey of writing this book over dinner at the USENIX/ACM NSDI conference in 2010. At the time, we thought perhaps it would take us the summer to complete the first version. We were very wrong! It is no exaggeration to say that it would have taken us a lot longer without the help we've received from the people we mention below.

Perhaps most important have been our early adopters — the instructors who agreed to use partial and incomplete versions of this textbook during the 2011-2012 school year:

ETH Zurich	Mothy Roscoe
New York University	Laskshmi Subramanian
University of California Riverside	Harsha Madhyastha
University of Texas Austin	Mike Dahlin and Lorenzo Alvisi
University of Washington	Ed Lazowska

We appreciate their patience with us, and we especially would like to thank their students for their patience as we revised some of the chapters in real-time. The book has benefitted tremendously from both the faculty and student feedback we have received from these offerings.

In developing our approach to teaching operating systems, both before we started writing and afterwards as we tried to put our thoughts to paper, we made extensive use of lecture notes and slides developed by other faculty. Of particular help were the materials created by Pete Chen, Peter Druschel, Steve Gribble, Eddie Kohler, John Ousterhout, Mothy Roscoe, and Geoff Voelker. We thank them all.

We are grateful to Lorenzo Alvisi, Adam Anderson, Pete Chen, Steve Gribble, Sam Hopkins, Ed Lazowska, Harsha Madhyastha, John Ousterhout, Mark Rich, Mothy Roscoe, Will Scott, Gun Sirer, Ion Stoica, Lakshmi Subramanian, and John Zahorjan for their helpful comments and suggestions as to how to improve the book.

We thank Jeff Dean, Garth Gibson, Mark Oskin, Simon Peter, Dave Probert, Amin Vahdat, and Mark Zbikowski for their help in explaining the internal workings of some of the commercial systems mentioned in this book.

We would like to thank Dave Wetherall, Dan Weld, Michael Walfish, Dave Patterson, Olav Kvern, Dan Halperin, Robin Briggs, Katya Anderson,

Sasha Anderson, Lorenzo Alvisi, and William Adams for their help and advice on textbook economics and production.

The Helen Riaboff Whiteley Center as well as Don and Jeanne Dahlin were kind enough to lend us a place to escape when we needed to get chapters written.

Finally, we thank our families, our colleagues, and our students for supporting us in this larger-than-expected effort.

All I really need to know I learned in kindergarten.

Robert Fulgham

1 Introduction

How do we construct reliable, portable, efficient and secure computer systems? An essential component is the computer's operating system — the software that manages a computer's resources.

First, the bad news: operating systems concepts are among the most complex topics in computer science. A modern general-purpose operating system can run to over 50 million lines of code, or in other words, more than a thousand times as long as this textbook. New operating systems are being written all the time. If you use an e-book reader, tablet, or smartphone, there is an operating system managing the device. Since we will not be able to cover everything, our focus will be on the essential concepts for building computer systems, ones that every computer scientist should know.

Now the good news: operating systems concepts are also among the most accessible topics in computer science. Most of the topics in this book will seem familiar to you — if you have ever tried to do two things at once, or picked the wrong line at a grocery store, or tried to keep a roommate or sibling from messing with your things, or succeeded at pulling off an April Fool's joke. Each of these has an analogue in operating systems, and it is this familiarity that gives us hope that we can explain how operating systems do their work in a single textbook. All we will assume of the reader is a basic understanding of the operation of a computer and the ability to read pseudo-code.

We believe that understanding how operating systems work is essential for any student interested in building modern computer systems. Of course, everyone who uses a computer or a smartphone or even a modern toaster uses an operating system, so understanding the function of an operating

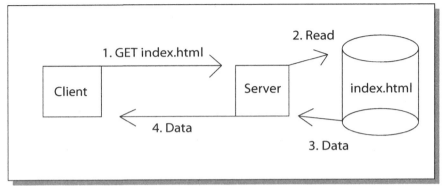

Figure 1.1: The operation of a web server.

system is useful to most computer scientists. Our goal in this book is to go much deeper than that, to explain the technologies used inside operating systems, technologies many of us rely on every day without realizing it.

Software engineers often encounter challenges similar to those faced by operating systems when building other complex systems, and they use many of the same technologies and design patterns. Whether your goal is to work on the internals of an operating system kernel, or to build the next generation of software for cloud computing, secure web browsers, game consoles, graphical user interfaces, media players, databases, or multicore software, the concepts and abstractions needed for reliable, portable, efficient and secure software are much the same. In our experience, the best way to learn these concepts is to study how they are used in operating systems, but we hope you will apply these concepts to a much broader range of computer systems.

To get started, consider the web server in Figure 1.1. Its behavior is amazingly simple: it receives a packet containing the name of the web page from the network. The web server decodes the packet, fetches the file from disk, and sends the contents back over the network to the user.

Part of an operating system's job is to make it easy to write applications like web servers. But if we dig a bit deeper, this simple story quickly raises as many questions as it answers:

- Many web requests involve both data and computation. For example, the Google home page presents a simple text box, but each search query entered in that box consults data spread over literally thousands of machines. To keep their software manageable, web servers often invoke helper applications, e.g., to manage the actual search function. The main web server needs to be able to communicate with the helper applications for this to work. How does the operating system enable multiple applications to commmunicate with each other?

- What if two users (or a million) try to request a web page from the server at the same time? A simple approach might be to handle each request in turn. If any individual request takes a long time, however, this approach would mean that everyone else would need to wait for it to complete. A faster, but more complex, solution is to *multitask*: to juggle the handling of multiple requests at once. Multitasking is especially important on modern multicore computers, as it provides a way to keep many processors busy. How does the operating system enable applications to do multiple things at once?

- For better performance, the web server might want to keep a copy, sometimes called a *cache*, of recently requested pages, so that the next user to request the same page can be returned the results from the cache, rather than starting the request from scratch. This requires the application to synchronize access to the cache's data structures by the thousands of web requests being handled at the same time. How does the operating system support application synchronization to shared data?

- To customize and animate the user experience, it is common for web servers to send clients scripting code, along with the contents of the web page. But this means that clicking on a link can cause someone else's code to run on your computer. How does the client operating system protect itself from being compromised by a computer virus surreptitiously embedded into the scripting code?

- Suppose the web site administrator uses an editor to update the web page. The web server needs to be able to read the file that the editor wrote; how does the operating system store the bytes on disk so that later on the web server can find and read them?

- Taking this a step further, the administrator probably wants to be able to make a consistent set of changes to the web site, so that embedded links are not left dangling, even temporarily. How can the operating system enable users to make a set of changes to a web site, so that requests either see the old pages or the new pages, but not a mishmash of the two?

- What happens when the client browser and the web server run at different speeds? If the server tries to send the web page to the client faster than the client can draw the page, where are the contents of the file stored in the meantime? Can the operating system decouple the client and server so that each can run at its own speed, without slowing the other down?

- As demand on the web server grows, the administrator is likely to want to move to more powerful hardware, with more memory, more processors, faster network devices, and faster disks. To take advantage of this new hardware, does the web server need to be re-written from scratch, or can it be written in a hardware-independent fashion? What about the operating system — does it need to be re-written for every new piece of hardware?

We could go on, but you get the idea. This book will help you understand the answers to these questions, and more.

Goals of this chapter

The rest of this chapter discusses three topics in detail:

- **OS Definition.** What is an operating system and what does it do?

- **OS Challenges.** How should we evaluate operating systems, and what are some of the tradeoffs their designers face?

- **OS Past, Present and Future.** What is the history of operating systems, and what new functionality are we likely to see in future operating systems?

1.1 | What is an operating system?

operating system

An *operating system* is the layer of software that manages a computer's resources for its users and their applications. Operating systems run in a wide range of computer systems. Sometimes they are invisible to the end user, controlling embedded devices such as toasters, gaming systems, and the many computers inside modern automobiles and airplanes. Operating systems are also an essential component of more general-purpose systems such as smartphones, desktop computers, and servers.

Our discussion will focus on general-purpose operating systems, because the technologies they need are a superset of the technologies needed for embedded systems. Increasingly though, technologies developed for general-purpose computing are migrating into the embedded sphere. For example, early mobile phones had simple operating systems to manage the hardware and to run a handful of primitive applications. Today, smartphones — phones capable of running independent third party applications — are the fastest growing part of the mobile phone business. These new devices require much more complete operating systems, with sophisticated resource management, multi-tasking, security and failure isolation.

Likewise, automobiles are increasingly software controlled, raising a host of operating system issues. Can anyone write software for your car? What if the software fails while you are driving down the highway? How might the operating system of your car be designed to prevent a computer virus from hijacking control of your car's computers? Although this

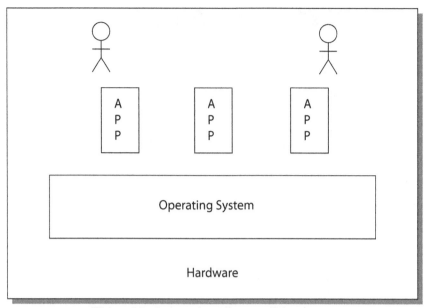

Figure 1.2: A general-purpose operating system

might seem far fetched, researchers recently demonstrated that they could remotely turn off a car's braking system through a computer virus introduced into the car's computers through a hacked car radio. A goal of this book is to explain how to build more reliable and secure computer systems in a variety of contexts.

For general-purpose systems, users interact with applications, applications execute in an environment provided by the operating system, and the operating system mediates access to the underlying hardware (Figure 1.2, and expanded in Figure 1.3). What do we need from an operating system to be able to run a group of programs? Operating systems have three roles:

- Operating systems play *referee* — they manage shared resources between different applications running on the same physical machine. For example, an operating system can stop one program and start another. Operating systems isolate different applications from each other, so that if there is a bug in one application, it does not corrupt other applications running on the same machine. The operating system must protect itself and other applications from malicious computer viruses. And since the applications are sharing physical resources, the operating system needs to decide which applications get which resources.

- Operating systems play *illusionist* — they provide an abstraction of physical hardware to simplify application design. To write a "hello world" program, you do not need (or want!) to think about how much

An Expanded View of an Operating System

Figure 1.3 shows the structure of a general-purpose operating system, as an expansion on the simple view presented in Figure 1.2. At the lowest level, the hardware provides processor, memory, and a set of devices for providing the user interface, storing data and communicating with the outside world. The hardware also provides primitives that the operating system can use to provide fault isolation and synchronization. The operating system runs as the lowest layer of software on the computer, with a device-specific layer interfaces to the myriad hardware devices, and a set of device-independent services provided to applications. Since the operating system needs to be able to isolate malicious and buggy applications from affecting other applications or the operating system itself, much of the operating system runs in a separate execution environment protected from application code. A portion of the operating system can also run as a library linked into each application. In turn, applications run in an execution context provided by the operating system. The application context is much more than a simple abstraction on top of hardware devices: applications execute in a virtual environment that is both more constrained (to prevent harm), more powerful (to mask hardware limitations), and more useful (via common services), than the underlying hardware.

physical memory the system has, or how many other programs might be sharing the computer's resources. Instead, operating systems provide the illusion of a nearly infinite memory, as an abstraction on top of a limited amount of physical memory. Likewise, operating systems provide the illusion that each program has the computer's processors entirely to itself. Obviously, the reality is quite different! These illusions enable applications to be written independently of the amount of physical memory on the system or the physical number of processors. Because applications are written to a higher level of abstraction, the operating system is free to change the amount of resources assigned to each application as applications start and stop.

- Operating systems provide *glue* — a set of common services between applications. An important benefit of common services is to facilitate sharing between applications, so that, for example, cut and paste works uniformly across the system and a file written by one application can be read by another. Many operating systems provide a common set of user interface routines to help applications provide a common "look and feel." Perhaps most importantly, operating systems provide a layer separating applications from hardware input and output devices, so that applications can be written independently of which specific keyboard, mouse or disk drive is being used on a particular computer.

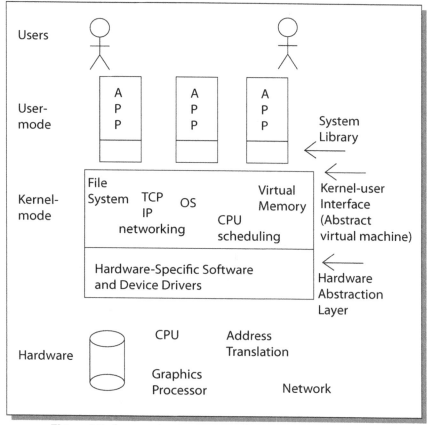

Figure 1.3: A general-purpose operating system: expanded view

We next discuss these three roles in a bit more detail.

Resource sharing: Operating system as referee

Sharing is central to most uses of computers. Right now, my laptop is running a browser, podcast library, text editor, email program, document viewer, and newspaper. The operating system must somehow keep all of these activities separate, yet allow each the full capacity of the machine if the others aren't running. At a minimum, when one program stops running, the operating system should let me run another. Better, the operating system should allow multiple applications to run at the same time, as when I read email while I am downloading a security patch to the system software.

Even individual applications can be designed to do multiple things at once. For instance, a web server will be more responsive to its users if it can handle multiple requests at the same time rather than waiting for each to complete before the next one starts running. The same holds for the browser — it is more responsive if it can start drawing a page while the rest of the page is still being transferred. On multiprocessors, the computation inside a parallel application can be split into separate units that can be run independently for faster execution. The operating system itself is an example of software written to be able to do multiple things at once. As we will describe later, the operating system is a customer of its own abstractions.

Sharing raises several challenges for an operating system:

- **Resource Allocation.** The operating system must keep all of the simultaneous activities separate, allocating resources to each as appropriate. A computer usually has only a few processors and a finite amount of memory, network bandwidth, and disk space. When there are multiple tasks to do at the same time, how should the operating system choose how many resources to give to each? Seemingly trivial differences in how resources are allocated can have a large impact on user-perceived performance. As we will see later, if the operating system gives too little memory to a program, it will not only slow down that particular program, it can dramatically hurt the performance of the entire machine.

  As another example, what should happen if an application executes an infinite loop:

```
while ( true ) {
      ;
}
```

Figure 1.4: An infinite loop, illustrating the difference between execution on the physical machine versus the abstract machine provided by the operating system.

  If programs ran directly on the raw hardware, this code fragment would lock up the computer, making it completely non-responsive to user input. If the operating system ensures each program gets its own slice of the computer resources, the specific application might lock up, but other programs can proceed unimpeded. Additionally, the user can ask the operating system to force the looping program to exit.

- **Isolation.** An error in one application should not disrupt other applications, or even the operating system itself. This is called *fault isolation*. Anyone who has taken an introductory computer science class knows the value of an operating system that can protect itself and other applications from programmer bugs. Debugging would be vastly harder if an error in one program could corrupt data structures in other applications. Likewise, downloading and installing a screen saver or other application should not crash other unrelated programs,

fault isolation

nor should it be a way for a malicious attacker to surreptitiously install a computer virus on the system. Nor should one user be able to access or change another's data without permission.

Fault isolation requires restricting the behavior of applications to less than the full power of the underlying hardware. Given access to the full capability of the hardware, any application downloaded off the web, or any script embedded in a web page, would have complete control of the machine. Thus, it would be able to install spyware into the operating system to log every keystroke you type, or record the password to every website you visit. Without fault isolation provided by the operating system, any bug in any program might cause the disk to become irretrievably corrupted. Erroneous or malignant applications would cause all sorts of havoc.

- **Communication.** The flip side of isolation is the need for communication between different applications and between different users. For example, a web site may be implemented by a cooperating set of applications: one to select advertisements, another to cache recent results, yet another to fetch and merge data from disk, and several more to cooperatively scan the web for new content to index. For this to work, the various programs need to be able to communicate with one another. If the operating systems is designed to prevent bugs and malicious users and applications from affecting other users and their applications, how does the operating system support communication to share results? In setting up boundaries, an operating system must also allow for those boundaries to be crossed in carefully controlled ways as the need arises.

In its role as a referee, an operating system is somewhat akin to that of a government, or perhaps a particularly patient kindergarten teacher, balancing needs, separating conflicts, and facilitating sharing. One user should not be able to hog all of the system's resources or to access or corrupt another user's files without permission; a buggy application should not be able to crash the operating system or other unrelated applications; and yet applications also need to be able to work together. Enforcing and balancing these concerns is the role of the operating system.

Exercises

Take a moment to speculate. We will provide answers to these questions throughout the rest of the book, but given what you know now, how would you answer them? Before there were operating systems, someone needed to develop solutions, without being able to look them up! How would you have designed the first operating system?

1. Suppose a computer system and all of its applications are completely bug free. Suppose further that everyone in the world is completely

honest and trustworthy. In other words, we do not need to consider fault isolation.

    a) How should the operating system allocate time on the processor? Should it give all of the processor to each application until it no longer needs it? If there are multiple tasks ready to go at the same time, should it schedule the task with the least amount of work to do or the one with the most? Justify your answer.

    b) How should the operating system allocate physical memory between applications? What should happen if the set of applications do not all fit in memory at the same time?

    c) How should the operating system allocate its disk space? Should the first user to ask be able to grab all of the free space? What would the likely outcome be for that policy?

2. Now suppose the computer system needs to support fault isolation. What hardware and/or operating support do you think would be needed to accomplish this goal?

    a) For protecting an application's data structures in memory from being corrupted by other applications?

    b) For protecting one user's disk files from being accessed or corrupted by another user?

    c) For protecting the network from a virus trying to use your computer to send spam?

3. How should an operating system support communication between applications?

    a) Through the file system?

    b) Through messages passed between applications?

    c) Through regions of memory shared between the applications?

    d) All of the above? None of the above?

Mask hardware limitations: Operating system as illusionist

A second important role of operating systems is to mask the restrictions inherent in computer hardware. Hardware is necessarily limited by physical constraints — a computer has only a limited number of processors and a limited amount of physical memory, network bandwidth, and disk. Further, since the operating system must decide how to split the fixed set of resources among the various applications running at each moment, a particular application will have different amounts of resources from time to

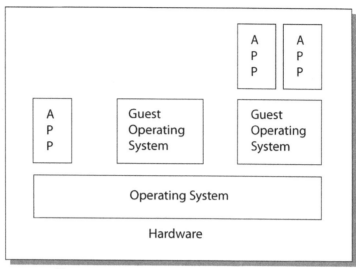

Figure 1.5: An operating system virtual machine

time, even when running on the same hardware. While a few applications might be designed to take advantage of a computer's specific hardware configuration and their specific resource assignment, most programmers want to use a higher level of abstraction.

We have just discussed one example of this: a uniprocessor can run only one program at a time, yet most operating systems allow multiple applications to appear to the user to be running at the same time. The oper-

virtualization ating system does so through a concept called *virtualization*. Virtualization provides an application with the illusion of resources that are not physically present. For example, the operating system can present to each application the abstraction that it has an entire processor dedicated to it, even though at a physical level there may be only a single processor shared among all the applications running on the computer. With the right hardware and operating system support, most physical resources can be virtualized: examples include the processor, memory, screen space, disk, and the network. Even the type of processor can be virtualized, to allow the same, unmodified application to be run on a smartphone, tablet, and laptop computer.

Pushing this a step further, some operating systems virtualize the entire computer, to run the operating system as an application running on top of another operating system (see Figure 1.5). This is called creating a *virtual*

virtual *machine*. The operating system running in the virtual machine, called the
machine *guest operating system*, thinks it is running on a real, physical machine, but

guest this is an illusion presented by the true operating system running under-
operating neath. One reason for the operating system to provide a virtual machine
system is for application portability. If a program only runs on an old version of an operating system, then we can still run the program on a new system

running a virtual machine. The virtual machine hosts the application on the old operating system, running on top of the new operating system. Another reason for virtual machines is as an aid in debugging. If an operating system can be run as an application, then the operating system developers can set breakpoints, stop, and single step their code just as they would an application.

In addition to virtualization, operating systems mask many other limitations inherent in physical hardware, by providing applications with the illusion of hardware capabilities that are not physically present. For example, on a computer with multiple processors sharing memory, each processor can update only a single memory location at a time. The memory system in hardware ensures that any updates to the same memory word are *atomic*, that is, the value stored in memory is the last value stored by one of the processors, not a mixture of the updates of the different processors. Atomicity at the level of a memory word is preserved in hardware even if more than one processor attempts to write to memory at exactly the same time. While this might seem sufficient, applications (and the operating system itself) need to be able to update larger data structures, ones spread over many memory locations. What happens when two processors attempt to update the same data structure at roughly the same time? As we'll discuss later, the results can be quite unexpected and quite different from what would have happened had each of the processors updated the data structure in turn. Ideally, the programmer would like to have the abstraction of an atomic update to the entire data structure, not just to a single memory word. As we will discuss, the illusion of atomic updates to data structures is provided by the operating system using some specialized mechanisms provided in hardware.

Persistent block storage devices, such as magnetic disk or flash RAM, provide another example. At a physical level, these systems support block writes to storage, where the size of the block depends on physical device characteristics. If the computer crashes in the middle of a block write, it could leave the disk in an unknown state, with neither the old nor the new value stored at that location. Of course, applications need to be able to store data on disk that is variable in size, possibly spanning multiple disk blocks. And users want their data to be preserved even — or especially — if there is a machine failure while the disk is being updated.

We will discuss techniques that the operating system uses to accomplish these and other illusions. In each of these cases, the operating system provides a more convenient and flexible programming abstraction than what is provided by the underlying hardware.

Margin note: atomic memory

Exercises

Take a moment to speculate; to build the systems we use today, someone needed to answer these questions. Consider how you might answer them, before seeing how others solved these puzzles.

4. How would you design combined hardware and software support to provide the illusion of a nearly infinite virtual memory on a limited amount of physical memory?

5. How would you design a system to run an entire operating system as an application running on top of another operating system?

6. How would you design a system to update complex data structures on disk in a consistent fashion despite machine crashes?

Common services: Operating system as glue

Operating system also play a third role: providing a set of common, standard services to applications to simplify and regularize their design. We saw an example of this with the web server outlined at the beginning of this chapter. The operating system hides the specifics of how the network and disk devices work, providing a simpler abstraction to applications based on receiving and sending reliable streams of bytes, and reading and writing named files. This allows the web server to focus on its core task of decoding incoming requests and filling them, rather than on the formatting of data into individual network packets and disk blocks.

An important reason for the operating system to provide common services, rather than leaving it up to each application, is to facilitate sharing between applications. The web server needs to be able to read the file that the text editor wrote. If applications are to share files, they need to be stored in a standard format, with a standard system for managing file directories. Likewise, most operating systems provide a standard way for applications to pass messages, and to share memory, to facilitate sharing.

The choice of which services an operating system should provide is often a matter of judgment. For example, computers can come configured with a blizzard of different devices: different graphics co-processors and pixel formats, different network interfaces (WiFi, Ethernet, and Bluetooth), different disk drives (SCSI, IDE), different device interfaces (USB, Firewire), and different sensors (GPS, accelerometers), not to mention different versions of each of those standards. Most applications will be able to ignore these differences, using only a generic interface provided by the operating system. For other applications, such as a database, the specific disk drive may matter quite a bit. For those applications that can operate at a higher level of abstraction, the operating system serves as an interoperability layer, so that both applications, and the devices themselves, can be independently evolved without requiring simultaneous changes to the other side.

Another standard service in most modern operating systems is the graphical user interface library. Both Microsoft's and Apple's operating systems provide a set of standard user interface widgets. This facilitates

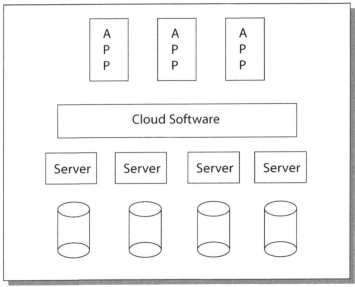

Figure 1.6: Cloud computing

a common "look and feel" to users, so that frequent operations such as pull down menus and "cut" and "paste" are handled consistently across applications.

Most of the code of an operating system is to implement these common services. However, much of the complexity of operating systems is due to resource sharing and masking hardware limits. Because the common service code is built on the abstractions provided by the other two operating system roles, this book will focus primarily on those two topics.

Operating system design patterns

The challenges that operating systems address are not unique — they apply to many different computer domains. Many complex software systems have multiple users, run programs written by third party developers, and/or need to coordinate many simultaneous activities. These pose questions of resource allocation, fault isolation, communication, abstractions of physical hardware, and how to provide a useful set of common services for software developers. Not only are the challenges the same, but often the solutions are as well: these systems use many of the design patterns and techniques described in this book.

For now, we focus on the challenges these systems have in common with operating systems:

- Cloud computing (Figure 1.6) is a model of computing where large-scale applications are run on shared computing and storage infrastruc-

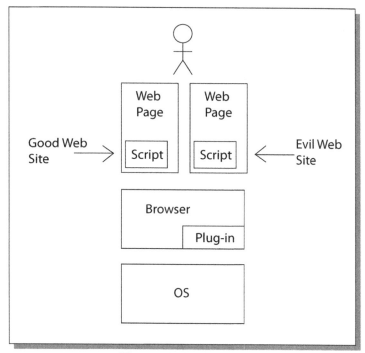

Figure 1.7: Web browser

ture in data centers, instead of on the user's own desktop computer. A similar approach is to run compute-intensive applications in the idle cycles of remote desktop computers. In both cases, many of the same issues arise as in operating systems, in terms of sharing, abstraction, and common services.

- **Referee.** How are resources allocated between competing applications running in the cloud? How are buggy or malicious applications prevented from disrupting other applications?

- **Illusionist.** The computing resources in the cloud are continually evolving; what abstractions are provided to isolate application developers from changes in the underlying hardware?

- **Glue.** Cloud services often distribute their work across different machines. What abstractions should the cloud software provide to help services coordinate and share data between their various activities?

- Web browsers (Figure 1.7) such as Chrome, Internet Explorer, Firefox, and Safari each play a role similar to an operating system. Browsers load and display web pages, but as we mentioned earlier, many web pages embed scripting programs that the browser must execute. These scripts are often buggy and sometimes malicious; hackers have used them to take over vast numbers of home computers. Like an operating system, the browser must isolate the user, other web sites, and even the browser itself from errors or malicious activity by these scripts. Similarly, most browsers have a plug-in architecture for supporting extensions, and these extensions also need to be isolated from causing harm.

- **Referee.** How can a browser ensure responsiveness, when a user has multiple tabs open and each tab is running a script from a different web site? How can we sandbox web scripts and plug-ins to prevent bugs from crashing the browser, and to prevent malicious scripts from accessing sensitive user data?

- **Illusionist.** Many web services are geographically distributed for better fault tolerance. This way, if one server crashes or if its network connection has problems, the browser can connect to a different site. The user in most cases doesn't notice the difference, even when updating a shopping cart or web form. How does the browser mask server changes transparently to the user?

- **Glue.** How does the browser achieve a portable execution environment for scripts that works consistently across operating systems and hardware platforms?

- Media players, such as Flash and Silverlight, are often packaged as browser plug-ins, but they themselves provide an execution environment for scripting programs. Thus, these systems face many of the same issues as both the browsers and the operating systems on which they run: isolation of buggy or malicious code, concurrent background and foreground tasks, and plug-in architectures.

- Multi-user database systems (Figure 1.8) such as Oracle and Microsoft's SQL Server provide the ability for large organizations to store, query, and update large data sets, such as detailed records of every purchase ever made at Walmart. Large scale data analysis provides a huge benefit to optimizing business operations, but a consequence is that databases face many of the same challenges as operating systems. Databases are simultaneously accessed by many different users in many different locations. Databases therefore need to allocate resources among different user requests, isolate concurrent updates to shared data, and ensure data is stored consistently on disk. In fact, several of the file system storage techniques we will discuss for operating systems, were originally developed for database systems.

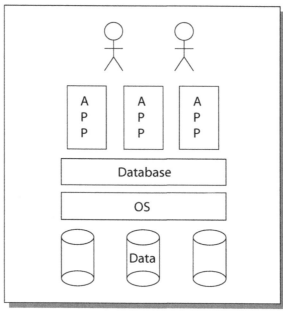

Figure 1.8: Database

- **Referee.** How should resources be allocated among the various users of a database? How does the database enforce data privacy so that only authorized users access relevant data?

- **Illusionist.** How does the database mask machine failures so that data is always stored consistently regardless of when the failure occurs?

- **Glue.** What common services make it easier for database users to develop their programs?

- Parallel applications (Figure 1.9) are programs that have been designed to take advantage of multiple processors on a single computer. Each application divides its work onto a fixed number of processors and needs to ensure that accesses to shared data structures are coordinated to preserve consistency. While some parallel programs directly use the services provided by the underlying operating system, others need more careful control of the assignment of work to processors to achieve good performance. These systems interpose a runtime system on top of the operating system to manage user-level parallelism, essentially building a mini-operating system on top of the operating system.

- On the Internet (Figure 1.10), multiple users share the underlying physical network, posing the challenge of how the system should

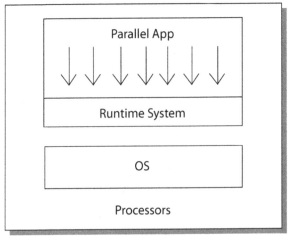

Figure 1.9: Parallel Application

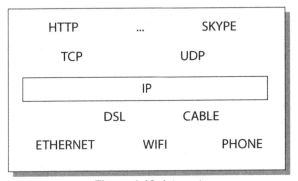

Figure 1.10: Internet

handle resource contention. The Internet is rife with malicious behavior, such as denial-of-service attacks that flood traffic on certain links to prevent legitimate users from communicating. Various attempts are underway to design solutions to allow the Internet to continue to function despite such attacks.

- **Referee.** Should the Internet treat all users identically (e.g., network neutrality) or should ISPs have the ability to favor some uses over others? Can the Internet be re-designed to prevent denial-of-service, spam, phishing, and other malicious behavior?

- **Illusionist.** The Internet provides the illusion of a single worldwide network, with the ability to deliver a packet from any machine on the Internet to any other machine. However, network hardware is in fact a large number of discrete network elements, with the ability to transmit limited size packets over a limited distance, and with some chance that the packet is garbled in the process. The Internet transforms the network into something more useful for applications like the web — a facility to reliably transmit data of arbitrary length, anywhere in the world.

– **Glue.** The Internet protocol suite was explicitly designed to act as an interoperability layer, to allow network applications to evolve independently of changes in network hardware, and vice versa. Does the success of the Internet hold any lessons for operating system design?

Many of these systems use the same techniques and design patterns as operating systems to address these challenges; studying operating systems is a great way to understand how these others systems work. In a few cases, different mechanisms are used to achieve the same goals, but even here, the boundary can be fuzzy. For example, browsers often use compile-time checks to prevent scripts from gaining control over the browser, while most operating systems use hardware-based protection to limit application programs from taking over the machine. More recently, however, some smartphone operating systems have begun to use the same compile-time techniques as browsers, but for protecting the smartphone operating system. In turn, some browsers have begun to use operating system hardware-based protection to improve the isolation they provide.

To avoid spreading our discussion too thinly, we focus this book on how operating systems work. Just as it is easier to learn a second computer programming language after you are fluent in the first, it is better to see how these operating systems principles are applied in one context before moving on to how these concepts are applied in other settings. We hope and expect however, that you will be able to apply the concepts in this book more widely than just operating system design.

Exercises

7. Society must also grapple with managing resources. What ways do we use for allocating resources, isolating misuse, and fostering sharing in real life?

1.2 | Evaluation Criteria

Having defined what an operating system does, how should we choose among alternative approaches to the design challenges posed by operating systems? We next discuss several desirable criteria for operating systems. In many cases, tradeoffs between these criteria are inevitable — improving a system along one dimension will hurt it along another. We conclude with a discussion of some concrete examples of tradeoffs between these considerations.

Reliability

reliability

Perhaps the most important characteristic of an operating system is its reliability. *Reliability* is that a system does exactly what it is designed to do. As the lowest level of software running on the system, errors in operating system code can have devastating and hidden effects. If the operating system breaks, the user will often be unable to get any work done, and in some cases, may even lose previous work, e.g., if the failure corrupts files on disk. By contrast, application failures can be much more benign, precisely because operating systems provides fault isolation and a rapid and clean restart after an error.

Making the operating system reliable is challenging. Operating systems often operate in a hostile environment, where computer viruses and other malicious code may often be trying to take control of the system for their own purposes by exploiting design or implementation errors in the operating system's defenses.

Unfortunately, the most common ways for improving software reliability, such as running test cases for common code paths, are less effective when applied to operating systems. Since malicious attacks can target a specific vulnerability precisely to cause execution to follow a rare code path, literally everything has to work correctly for the operating system to be reliable. Even without malicious attacks that trigger bugs on purpose, extremely rare corner cases can occur regularly in the operating system context. If an operating system has a million users, a once in a billion event will eventually occur to someone.

availability

A related concept is *availability*, the percentage of time that the system is usable. A buggy operating system that crashes frequently, losing the user's work, is both unreliable and unavailable. A buggy operating system that crashes frequently, but never loses the user's work and cannot be subverted by a malicious attack, would be reliable but unavailable. An operating system that has been subverted, but continues to appear to run normally while logging the user's keystrokes, is unreliable but available.

mean time to failure

mean time to repair

Thus, both reliability and availability are desirable. Availability is affected by two factors: the frequency of failures, called the *mean time to failure (MTTF)*, and the time it takes to restore a system to a working state after a failure (for example, to reboot), the *mean time to repair (MTTR)*. Availability can be improved by increasing the MTTF or reducing the MTTR, and we will present operating systems techniques that do each.

Throughout this book, we will present various approaches to improving operating system reliability and availability. In many cases, the abstractions may seem at first glance overly rigid and formulaic. It is important to realize this is done on purpose! Only precise abstractions provide a basis for constructing reliable and available systems.

Exercises

8. Suppose you were tasked with designing and implementing an ultra-reliable and ultra-available operating system. What techniques would you use? What tests, if any, might be sufficient to convince you of the system's reliability, short of handing your operating system to millions of users to serve as beta testers?

9. MTTR, and therefore availability, can be improved by reducing the time to reboot a system after a failure. What techniques might you use to speed up booting? Would your techniques always work after a failure?

Security

security

privacy

Two concepts closely related to reliability are security and privacy. *Security* is the property that the computer's operation cannot be compromised by a malicious attacker. *Privacy* is a part of security — that data stored on the computer is only accessible to authorized users.

Alas, no useful computer is perfectly secure! Any complex piece of software has bugs, and even otherwise innocuous bugs can be exploited by an attacker to gain control of the system. Or the hardware of the computer might be tampered with, to provide access to the attacker. Or the computer's administrator might turn out to be untrustworthy, using their privileges to steal user data. Or the software developer of the operating system might be untrustworthy, inserting a backdoor for the attacker to gain access to the system.

Nevertheless, an operating system can, and should, be designed to minimize its vulnerability to attack. For example, strong fault isolation can prevent third party applications from taking over the system. Downloading and installing a screen saver or other application should not provide a

computer virus

way for a malicious attacker to surreptitiously install a *computer virus* on the system. A computer virus is a computer program that modifies an operating system or application to provide the attacker, rather than the user, control over the system's resources or data. An example computer virus is a keylogger: a program that modifies the operating system to record every keystroke entered by the user and send those keystrokes back to the attacker's machine. In this way, the attacker could gain access to the user's passwords, bank account numbers, and other private information. Likewise, a malicious screen saver might surreptiously scan the disk for files containing personal information or turn the system into an email spam server.

Even with strong fault isolation, a system can be insecure if its applications are not designed for security. For example, the Internet email standard provides no strong assurance of the sender's identity; it is possible to form an email message with anyone's email address in the "from" field, not necessarily the actual sender. Thus, an email message can appear to be from someone (perhaps someone you trust), when in reality it is from someone else (and contains a malicious virus that takes over the computer when the attachment is opened). By now, you are hopefully suspicious of clicking on any attachment in an email. If we step back, though, the issue could instead be cast as a limitation of the interaction between the email system and the operating system — if the operating system provided a cheap and easy way to process an attachment in an isolated execution environment with limited capabilities, then even if the attachment contained a virus, it would be guaranteed not to cause a problem.

Complicating matters is that the operating system must not only prevent unwanted access to shared data, it must also *allow* access in many cases. We want users and programs to interact with each other, to be able to cut and paste text between different applications, and to read or write data to disk or over the network. If each program was completely standalone, and never needed to interact with any other program, then fault isolation by itself would be enough. However, we not only want to be able to isolate programs from one another, we also want to be able to easily share data between programs and between users.

enforcement

security policy

Thus, an operating system needs both an enforcement mechanism and a security policy. *Enforcement* is how the operating system ensures that only permitted actions are allowed. The *security policy* defines what is permitted — who is allowed to access what data and who can perform what operations. Malicious attackers can target vulnerabilities in either enforcement mechanisms or security policy.

Portability

portability

All operating systems provide applications an abstraction of the underlying computer hardware; a *portable* abstraction is one that does not change as the hardware changes. A program written for Microsoft's Windows 7 should run correctly regardless of whether a specific graphics card is being used, whether persistent storage is provided via flash memory or rotating magnetic disk, or whether the network is Bluetooth, WiFi, or gigabit Ethernet.

Portability also applies to the operating system itself. Operating systems are among the most complex software systems ever invented, so it is impractical to re-write them from scratch every time some new hardware is produced or every time a new application is developed. Instead, new operating systems are often derived, at least in part, from old ones. As one example, iOS, the operating system for the iPhone and iPad, is derived from the OS X code base.

As a result, most successful operating systems have a lifetime measured in decades: the initial implementation of Microsoft Windows 8 began with the development of Windows NT starting in 1990, when the typical computer was more than 10000 times less powerful and had 10000 times less memory and disk storage, than is the case today. Operating systems that last decades are no anomaly: Microsoft's prior operating system code base, MS/DOS, was first introduced in 1981. It later evolved into the early versions of Microsoft Windows before finally being phased out around 2000.

This means that operating systems need to be designed to support applications that have not been written yet and to run on hardware that has yet to be developed. Likewise, we do not want to have to re-write applications as the operating system is ported from machine to machine. Sometimes of course, the importance of "future-proofing" the operating system is discovered only in retrospect. Microsoft's first operating system, MS/DOS, was designed in 1981 assuming that personal computers had no more than 640 KB of memory. This limitation was acceptable at the time, but today, even a cellphone has orders of magnitude more memory than that.

How might we design an operating system to achieve portability? We will discuss this in more depth, but an overview is provided above in Figure 1.3. For portability, it helps to have a simple, standard way for applications to interact with the operating system, through the abstract machine interface. The *abstract machine interface (AMI)* is the interface provided by operating systems to applications. A key part of the AMI is the *application programming interface (API)*, the list of function calls the operating system provides to applications. The AMI also includes the memory access model and which instructions can be legally executed. For example, an instruction to change whether the hardware is executing trusted operating system code, or untrusted application code, needs to be available to the operating system but not to applications.

abstract machine interface

application programming interface

A well-designed operating system AMI provides a fixed point across which both application code and hardware can evolve independently. This is similar to the role of the Internet Protocol (IP) standard in networking — distributed applications such as email and the web, written using IP, are insulated from changes in the underlying network technology (Ethernet, WiFi, optical). Equally important is that changes in applications, from email to instant messaging to file sharing, do not require simultaneous changes in the underlying hardware.

This notion of a portable hardware abstraction is so powerful that operating systems use the same idea *internally*, so that the operating system itself can largely be implemented independently of the specifics of the hardware. This interface is called the *hardware abstraction layer (HAL)*. It might seem at first glance that the operating system AMI and the operating system HAL should be identical, or nearly so — after all, both are portable layers designed to hide unimportant hardware details. The AMI needs to do more, however. As we noted, applications execute in a restricted, virtualized context and with access to high level common services, while the operating system itself is implemented using a procedural abstraction much closer to the actual hardware.

hardware abstraction layer

Today, Linux is an example of a highly portable operating system. Linux has been used as the operating system for web servers, personal computers, tablets, netbooks, e-book readers, smartphones, set top boxes, routers, WiFi access points, and game consoles. Linux is based on an operating system called UNIX, originally developed in the early 1970's. UNIX was written by a small team of developers, and because they could not afford to write very much code, it was designed to be very small, simple to program against, and highly portable, at some cost in performance. Over the years, UNIX's and Linux's portability and convenient programming abstractions have been keys to its success.

Performance

While the portability of an operating system can become apparent over time, the performance of an operating system is often immediately visible to its users. Although we often associate performance with each individual application, the operating system's design can have a large impact on the application's perceived performance because it is the operating system that decides when an application can run, how much memory it can use, and whether its files are cached in memory or clustered efficiently on disk. The operating system also mediates application access to memory, the network, and the disk. The operating system needs to avoid slowing down the critical path while still providing needed fault isolation and resource sharing between applications.

efficiency

overhead

Performance is not a single quantity, but rather it can be measured in several different ways. One performance metric is the *efficiency* of the abstraction presented to applications. A related concept to efficiency is *overhead*, the added resource cost of implementing an abstraction. One way to measure efficiency (or inversely, overhead) is the degree to which the abstraction impedes application performance. Suppose the application were designed to run directly on the underlying hardware, without the overhead of the operating system abstraction; how much would that improve the application's performance?

Operating systems also need to allocate resources between applications, and this can affect the performance of the system as perceived by the end

fairness

user. One issue is *fairness*, between different users of the same machine, or between different applications running on that machine. Should resources be divided equally between different users or different applications, or should some get preferential treatment? If so, how does the operating system decide what tasks get priority?

response
time

Two related concepts are response time and throughput. *Response time*, sometimes called *delay*, is how long it takes for a single specific task from when it starts until it completes. For example, a highly visible response time for desktop computers is the time from when the user moves the hardware mouse until the pointer on the screen reflects the user's action. An operating

throughput

system that provides poor response time can be unusable. *Throughput* is the rate at which a group of tasks can be completed. Throughput is a measure of efficiency for a group of tasks rather than a single one. While it might seem that designs that improve response time would also necessarily improve throughput, this is not the case, as we will discuss later in this book.

predictability

A related consideration is performance *predictability*, whether the system's response time or other metric is consistent over time. Predictability can often be more important than average performance. If a user operation sometimes takes an instant, and sometimes much longer, the user may find it difficult to adapt. Consider, for example, two systems. In one, the user's keystrokes are almost always instantaneous, but 1% of the time, a keystroke takes 10 seconds to take effect. In the other system, the user's keystrokes always take 0.1 seconds to be reflected on the screen. Average response time may be the same in both systems, but the second is more predictable. Which do you think would be more user-friendly?

For a simple example illustrating the concepts of efficiency, overhead, fairness, response time, throughput, and predictability, consider a car driving to its destination. If there were never any other cars or pedestrians on the road, the car could go quite quickly, never needing to slow down for stop lights. Stop signs and stop lights enable cars to share the road, at some cost in overhead and response time for each individual driver. As the system becomes more congested, predictability suffers. Throughput of the system is improved with carpooling. In congested situations and especially with dedicated carpool lanes, carpooling can also improve latency even though carpoolers need to coordinate their pickups. Predictability, throughput, and arguably fairness can all be improved by scrapping the car and installing mass transit.

Adoption

In addition to reliability, portability and performance, the success of an operating system depends on two factors outside its immediate control: the (wide) availability of applications ported to that operating system, and the (wide) availability of hardware that the operating system can support. An iPhone runs iOS, but without the preinstalled applications and the contents of the App Store, the iPhone would be just a cellphone with (allegedly) bad phone reception.

network effect   The *network effect* occurs when the value of some technology depends not only on its intrinsic capabilities, but also on the number of other people who have adopted that technology. Application and hardware designers spend their efforts on those operating system platforms with the most users, while users favor those operating systems with the best applications or the cheapest hardware. If this sounds circular, it is! More users imply more applications and cheaper hardware; more applications and cheaper hardware imply more users, in a virtuous cycle.

Consider how you might design an operating system to take advantage of the network effect, or at least to avoid being crushed by it. An obvious step would be designing the system to make it easy to accommodate new hardware, and to make it easy for applications to be ported across different versions of the same operating system.

A more subtle issue is the choice of whether the operating system programming interface (API), or the operating system source code itself, is open or proprietary. A *proprietary* system is one under the control of a single company, so it can be changed at any time by its provider to meet the needs of its customers. An *open system* is one where the system's source code is public, allowing anyone the ability to inspect the code and change it. Often, an open system will have an API that can only be changed with the agreement of a public standards body. Adherence to standards provides assurance to the application developer that the API will not be changed except by general agreement; on the other hand, standards bodies can make it difficult to quickly add new, desired features.

proprietary system

open system

Neither open systems nor proprietary ones are obviously better for widespread adoption. Windows 7 and MacOS are examples of proprietary operating systems; Linux is an example of an open operating system. All three are widely used! Open systems are easier to adapt to a wide variety of hardware platforms, but risk fragmentation, impairing the network effect. Purveyors of proprietary operating systems argue that their systems are more reliable and better adapted to the needs of their customers. Interoperability problems are reduced if both the hardware and software are controlled by the same company, but limiting an operating system to one hardware platform impairs the network effect.

Making it easy to port applications from existing systems to a new operating system can help a new system become established, and conversely, designing an operating system API to make it difficult to port applications away from the operating system can help prevent competition from becoming established. Thus, there are often commercial pressures for operating system interfaces to become idiosyncratic. Throughout this book, we will discuss operating systems issues at a conceptual level, but it is important to realize that the details will vary quite a bit for any specific operating system, due to important, but also somewhat chaotic, commercial interests.

Android vs. iPhone

One avenue to improving system reliability might be to limit third party applications, or to vet them in some way. Of course, limiting applications can hurt adoption. Two operating systems vendors taking opposite positions on this recently are Apple and Google. For the iPhone, Apple requires pre-approval before any application can be loaded on the iPhone, possibly enhancing reliability. In practice, however, it can be difficult to verify all aspects of application behavior, e.g., to prevent a game application from downloading telephone numbers stored on the smartphone for telemarketing purposes. Thus, it is unclear how much benefit users will have in practice. Google takes the opposite approach: it gives the users control over which applications can be installed on Android phones, possibly enhancing wider user adoption, but potentially hurting system reliability. It will be interesting to see which approach is more successful.

Tradeoffs

Most practical operating system designs need to strike a balance between the goals of reliability, security, portability, performance, and adoption. Design choices that improve portability — for example, by preserving legacy interfaces — often make the system as a whole less reliable and less secure. Similarly, there will often be ample room for breaking an abstraction to tweak some added performance out of the system. However, such performance optimizations come at a cost of added complexity and therefore potentially decreased reliability. The operating system designer must carefully weigh these competing goals.

To illustrate the tradeoff between performance and complexity, we relate the following true story. An operating system was designed and implemented in the late 1980's, using a type-safe language to reduce the incidence of programmer errors. For speed, the most frequently used routines at the core of the operating system were implemented in assembly code. In one of these routines, the implementers decided to use a sequence of instructions that shaved a single instruction off a very frequently used code path, but that would sometimes break if the operating system exceeded a particular size. At the time, the operating system was nowhere near this limit. After a few years of production use, however, the system started mysteriously crashing, apparently at random, and only after many days of execution. Many weeks of painstaking investigation revealed the problem: the operating system had grown beyond the limit assumed in the assembly code implementation. The fix was easy, once the problem was found, but the question for the reader is: do you think the original optimization was worth the risk?

	1981	1996	2011	factor
MIPS	1	300	10000	10K
MIPS/$	$100K	$30	$0.50	200K
DRAM	128 KB	128 MB	10 GB	100K
Disk	10 MB	4 GB	1 TB	100K
Home Internet	9.6 Kbps	256 Kbps	5 Mbps	500
Local area network	3 Mbps (shared)	10 Mbps	1 Gbps	300
Ratio of users to computers	100:1	1:1	1:few	100+

Figure 1.11: Computer performance over time. MIPS stands for "millions of instructions per second," a measure of processor performance.

Exercises

10. For the computer you are currently using, how should the operating system designers prioritize among reliability, security, portability, performance, and adoption? Explain why.

1.3 | A brief history of operating systems

We conclude this chapter with a discussion of the origins of operating systems, as a way of illustrating where operating systems are headed in the future. As the lowest layer of software running on top of computer hardware, operating systems have been around nearly as long as the first computers, and they have evolved nearly as rapidly as computer hardware.

Impact of technology trends on operating systems

Moore's Law

The most striking aspect of the last fifty years in computing technology has been the cumulative effect of Moore's Law, and the comparable advances in related technologies such as memory and disk storage. *Moore's Law* states that transistor density increases exponentially over time; similar exponential improvements have occurred in many other component technologies. Figure 1.11 provides an overview of the past thirty years of technology improvements in computer hardware. The cost of processing has decreased by over five orders of magnitude over the past thirty years; the cost of memory and disk capacity has followed a similar trajectory. Of course, not all technologies have improved at the same rate; disk latency has improved over time, but at a much slower rate than disk capacity. These relative changes have radically altered both the use of computers and the tradeoffs faced by the operating system designer.

It is hard to imagine how things used to be. Today, we are able to carry smartphones with incredibly powerful computers around in our pockets. Thousands of server computers wait patiently for a user to type in a search query; when the query arrives, the servers can synthesize a response in a fraction of a second. In the early years of computing, however, the computers were more expensive than the salaries of the people who used them. Users would queue up, often for days, for their turn to run a program. A similar progression from expensive to cheap devices occurred with telephones over the past hundred years. Initially, telephone lines were very expensive, so that a single line was shared among everyone in a neighborhood. Over time, of course, both computers and telephones have become cheap enough to sit idle until we need them.

Despite these changes, operating systems still face the same conceptual challenges as they did fifty years ago. To manage computer resources for applications and users, operating systems must allocate resources among applications, provide fault isolation and communication services, abstract hardware limitations, and so forth. Tremendous progress has been made towards improving the reliability, security, efficiency, and portability of operating systems, but much further progress is still needed. Despite the fact we do not know how computing technology or application demand will evolve over the next 10-20 years, it is highly likely we will continue to need to address these fundamental operating system challenges in the future.

Early operating systems

The first operating systems were runtime libraries, intended to simplify programming early computer systems. Rather than the tiny, inexpensive yet massively complex hardware and software systems we have today, the first computers often took up an entire floor of a warehouse, cost millions of dollars, yet were only capable of being used by a single person at a time. The user would first reset the computer, load in their program, and hit go, producing output that could be pored over while the next user took their turn. If the user made an error, they needed to wait their turn to try the run over again, often the next day.

Although it might seem like there was no need for an operating system in this setting, if computers are enormously expensive, anything that reduces the likelihood of programmer error is extremely valuable. The first operating systems were seen as a way of reducing errors by providing a standard set of common services. For example, early operating systems provided standard routines to perform input/output (I/O) processing, which each user could link into their program. By using these services, a user's program would be more likely to run correctly and produce useful output.

Even though these initial operating systems were a huge step forward, the result was still horribly inefficient. It was around this time that the CEO of IBM famously predicted that there would only ever be a market for five computers in the world. If computers still cost millions of dollars and could only be used to run the tiny applications of the time by a single person at a time, he would probably have been proven right!

Multi-user operating systems

The next step forward was sharing, introducing many of the advantages, and challenges, that we see from operating systems today. If processor time is incredibly valuable, restricting the system to one user at a time is incredibly wasteful. The processor is idle while the program is being loaded and as the data in being input or the results being output, even though there was usually a long line of people waiting their turn to use the processor.

batch operating systems
With *batch operating systems*, one program can be using the processor while another is being loaded into memory. The batch operating system was installed in the system's memory, and ran a simple loop: load, run, and unload each job in turn. While one job was running, the operating system would set up the I/O devices to do background transfers for the next/previous job using a process called *direct memory access (DMA)*. With DMA, the I/O device transfers its data directly into memory at a location specified by the operating system. When the I/O transfer completes, the hardware interrupts the processor, transferring control to the operating system interrupt handler. The operating system starts the next DMA transfer and then resumes execution of the application. The interrupt appears to the application as if nothing had happened, except for some delay between one instruction and the next.

direct memory access

multitasking
Batch operating systems were soon extended to run multiple applications at once, that is, *multitasking*, or what is also sometimes called *multiprogramming*. Multiple programs were loaded into memory at the same time, each ready to use the processor if for any reason the previous task needed to pause, for example, to read some additional input or produce some output. Multitasking improves processor efficiency essentially to 100%; provided the queue of tasks is long enough, and there are a sufficient number of I/O devices to keep feeding the processor, there is never a need for the processor to wait for work.

multi-programming

However, processor sharing raises the problem that programs need to be isolated from one another, if only to protect against a bug in one program crashing or corrupting another. During this period, computer designers added hardware memory protection, as a way of reducing the overhead of fault isolation.

A practical challenge with batch computing, however, was how to debug the operating system itself. Unlike an application program, a batch operating system assumes it is in direct control of the hardware. New versions could only be tested by stopping every application and rebooting the system, essentially turning the computer back into a single user system. Needless to say, this was an expensive operation, and so it typically was scheduled for the dead of the night.

Virtual machines were developed to address this limitation (see Figure 1.5). Instead of running a test operating system directly on the hardware, with virtual machines an operating system can be run just like any another

host operating system

application. The *host operating system*, also called a *virtual machine monitor*, exports an abstract machine interface (AMI) that is identical to the underlying hardware. The test operating system running on top of the virtual machine does not need to know that it is running in a virtual environment — it executes instructions, accesses hardware devices, restores application state after an interrupt just as it would running on real hardware.

Virtual machines have become widely used for operating system development, backward compatibility, and cross-platform support. Old application software that runs only on an old version of an operating system can share hardware with entirely new applications. The virtual machine monitor runs two virtual machines — one for the new operating system for up to date applications and a separate one for any legacy applications. As another example, MacOS users wanting to run Windows applications can do so by running them inside a virtual machine.

Time-sharing operating systems

Eventually, the cumulative effect of Moore's Law meant that the cost of computing dropped to where we could start designing systems optimized for users, rather than optimized for efficient use of the processor. UNIX, for example, was developed in the early 70's on a spare computer that no one was using at the time. UNIX became the basis of Apple's MacOS X, Linux, widely used for servers at Google and Facebook, VMware, a widely used virtual machine monitor, and Google Android, a smartphone operating system. Figure 1.12 provides a sketch of the history of some of today's commercial operating systems.

time-sharing

A *time-sharing* operating system, such as Windows, MacOS, and Linux, is one designed to support interactive use of the computer, rather than the batch mode processing of earlier systems. With time-sharing, the user types input on a keyboard or other input device directly connected to the computer. Each keystroke or mouse action causes an interrupt to the processor signalling the event; the interrupt handler reads the event from the device and queues it inside the operating system. When the user's word

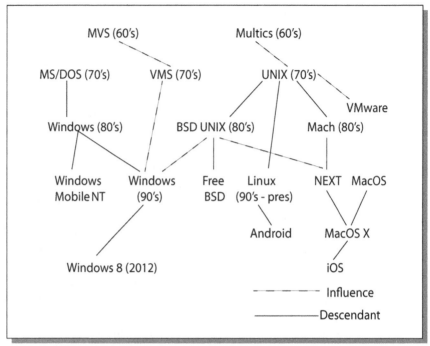

Figure 1.12: Genealogy of several modern operating systems.

processor, game, or other application resumes, it fetches the event from the operating system, processes the event, and alters the display appropriately, before fetching the next event. Hundreds or even thousands of such events can be processed per second, requiring both the operating system and the application to be designed for frequent, very short bursts of activity, rather than the sustained execution model of batch processing.

The basic operation of a web server is similar to a time-sharing system. The web server waits for a packet to arrive, requesting a web page or to perform an action such as search the web or purchase a book. The network hardware copies the arriving packet into memory using DMA. Once the transfer is complete, it signals the arrival of a packet by interrupting the processor, triggering the server to perform the requested task. Likewise, the processor is interrupted as each block of the web page is read from disk into memory. Like a time-sharing system, server operating systems need to be designed to handle very large numbers of short actions per second.

The earliest time-sharing systems supported many simultaneous users, but even this was only a phase. Eventually, computers became cheap enough that people could afford their own dedicated "personal" computers, which would sit patiently unused for much of the day. Instead, access to shared data became paramount, cementing the shift to client-server computing.

Modern operating systems

Today, we have vast diversity of computing devices, and many different operating systems running on those devices. The tradeoffs faced by an operating system designer depend on the physical capabilities of the hardware, and on the application and user demand for that hardware. Here are some examples of operating systems that the reader might have used recently:

- **Desktop, laptop, and netbook operating systems.** Examples include Windows 7, MacOS, and Linux. These systems are characterized by having a single user at a time, many applications, and many I/O devices. One might think that with only one user, there is no need to design the system to support sharing, and indeed the initial personal computer operating systems took this approach. They had very limited ability to isolate different parts of the system from one another. Over time, however, it became clear that stricter fault isolation was needed to improve system reliability and resilience against computer viruses.

- **Smartphone operating systems.** A smartphone is a cellphone with an embedded computer capable of running third party applications. Examples of smartphone operating systems include iOS, Android, Symbian, WebOS, Blackberry OS and Windows Phone. Obviously smartphones have only one user, but they still must support many applications. Because applications downloaded off the Internet might have viruses that attempt to surreptitiously take control over the phone, the operating system must be designed to protect itself from misbehaving applications and to protect applications from each other.

- **Embedded systems.** Over time, computers have become cheap enough to integrate into any number of consumer devices, from cable TV set top boxes, to microwave ovens, to the control systems for automobiles and airplanes, to LEGO robots, and to medical devices such as MRI machines and WiFi based intravenous titration systems. Embedded devices typically run a customized operating system bundled with the task-specific software to control the device. Although you might think these systems as too simple to merit much attention, software errors can have quite devastating effects. One of the earliest documented examples of a computer causing human deaths was the Therac-25 in the mid-1980's. The problem occurred because of programming errors in the operating system code for a medical device, errors that could have been prevented had the system developers followed the design paradigms outlined in this book.

- **Virtual machines.** As we mentioned, a virtual machine monitor is an operating system that can run another operating system as if it were an application. Example virtual machine monitors include VMWare, Xen, and Windows Virtual PC. Virtual machine monitors face many of the same challenges as other operating systems, with the added challenge posed by coordinating a set of coordinators. The operating system running inside a virtual machine makes resource allocation and fault isolation decisions as if it is in complete control of its resources, even though it is in fact sharing the system with other operating systems and applications.

- **Server operating systems.** Search engines, web media, e-commerce sites, and email systems are hosted on computers in data centers; each of these computers runs an operating system, often an industrial strength version of one of the desktop systems described above. Usually, only a single application, such as a web server, runs per machine, but the operating system needs to coordinate thousands of simultaneous incoming network connections onto that application. Servers operate in a hostile environment, sometimes receiving many thousands of packets per second attempting to subvert or block the service. At the same time, there is a premium on responsiveness. Amazon and Google both report that adding even less than 100 milliseconds of delay to each web request can dramatically reduce their revenue per user.

- **Server clusters.** For fault tolerance and scale, many web sites are implemented on distributed clusters of computers housed in one or more geographically distributed data centers. If one computer fails due to a hardware fault, software crash, or power failure, another computer can take over its role. If demand for the web site exceeds what a single computer can accommodate, web requests can be partitioned among multiple machines. As with normal operating systems, server cluster applications run on top of an abstract cluster interface to isolate the application from hardware changes and to isolate faults in one application from affecting other applications in the same data center. Likewise, resources can be shared between various applications on the same web site (such as Google search, Google earth, and gmail), and resources can be shared between multiple web sites hosted on the same cluster hardware (such as with Amazon's Elastic Compute Cloud).

Future operating systems

Where do operating systems go from here over the next decade? Operating systems have become dramatically better at resisting malicious attacks over the past decade, but they still have quite a ways to go. Provided security and reliability challenges can be met, there are huge potential benefits from having computers tightly control and coordinate physical infrastructure such as the power grid, the telephone network, and a hospital's medical devices and medical record systems. Thousands of lives are lost annually through traffic accidents that could potentially be prevented through computer control of automobiles. If we are to rely on computers for these critical systems, we need greater assurance that operating systems are up to the task.

Beyond mission critical systems, whenever the underlying hardware changes, there is work to do for the operating system designer. The future of operating systems is also the future of hardware:

- Very large scale data centers, coordinating hundreds of thousands or even millions of computers to support some essential online service.

- Very large scale multicore systems. Computer architectures have already switched to providing multiple processors per chip; this trend will continue, potentially yielding systems with hundreds or possibly even thousands of processors per machine.

- Ubiquitous portable computing devices, including smartphones, tablets, and e-book readers. Computers are likely to become untethered from the keyboard and the screen, responding to voice, gestures, and perhaps even brain waves.

- Very heterogeneous systems, as every device becomes programmable, from supercomputers to refrigerators down to individual light switches.

- Very large scale storage: everything that can be stored, will be, and needs to be stored reliably so that it can be retrieved at any point, even decades later.

Managing all this is the job of the operating system.

Exercises

For convenience, the exercises from the body of the chapter are repeated here.

1. Suppose a computer system and all of its applications are completely bug free. Suppose further that everyone in the world is completely honest and trustworthy. In other words, we do not need to consider fault isolation.

    a) How should the operating system allocate time on the processor? Should it give all of the processor to each application until it no longer needs it? If there are multiple tasks ready to go at the same time, should it schedule the task with the least amount of work to do or the one with the most? Justify your answer.

b) How should the operating system allocate physical memory between applications? What should happen if the set of applications do not all fit in memory at the same time?

c) How should the operating system allocate its disk space? Should the first user to ask be able to grab all of the free space? What would the likely outcome be for that policy?

2. Now suppose the computer system needs to support fault isolation. What hardware and/or operating support do you think would be needed to accomplish this goal?

a) For protecting an application's data structures in memory from being corrupted by other applications?

b) For protecting one user's disk files from being accessed or corrupted by another user?

c) For protecting the network from a virus trying to use your computer to send spam?

3. How should an operating system support communication between applications?

a) Through the file system?

b) Through messages passed between applications?

c) Through regions of memory shared between the applications?

d) All of the above? None of the above?

4. How would you design combined hardware and software support to provide the illusion of a nearly infinite virtual memory on a limited amount of physical memory?

5. How would you design a system to run an entire operating system as an application running on top of another operating system?

6. How would you design a system to update complex data structures on disk in a consistent fashion despite machine crashes?

7. Society must also grapple with managing resources. What ways do we use for allocating resources, isolating misuse, and fostering sharing in real life?

8. Suppose you were tasked with designing and implementing an ultra-reliable and ultra-available operating system. What techniques would you use? What tests, if any, might be sufficient to convince you of the system's reliability, short of handing your operating system to millions of users to serve as beta testers?

9. MTTR, and therefore availability, can be improved by reducing the time to reboot a system after a failure. What techniques might you use to speed up booting? Would your techniques always work after a failure?

10. For the computer you are currently using, how should the operating system designers prioritize among reliability, security, portability, performance, and adoption? Explain why.

Part I

Kernels and Processes

Strong fences make good neighbors.

17th century proverb

2 The Kernel Abstraction

protection   A central role of operating systems is *protection* — the isolation of potentially misbehaving applications and users so that they do not corrupt other applications or the operating system itself. Protection is essential to achieving several of the goals we listed for operating systems in the previous chapter:

- **Reliability.** Protection is needed to prevent bugs in one program from causing crashes in other programs or in the operating system. To the user, a system crash will appear to be the operating system's fault, even if the root cause of the problem was some unexpected behavior by an application or user. Thus, for high system reliability, an operating system must bullet proof itself so that it operates correctly regardless of whatever an application or user might do.

- **Security.** Some users or applications on a system may be less than completely trustworthy and therefore the operating system needs to limit the scope of what they can do. Without protection, a malicious user might surreptitiously change application files or even the operating system itself, leaving the user none the wiser. For example, if a malicious application is permitted to write directly to the disk, it could modify the file containing the operating system's code, so that the next time the system starts, the modified operating system

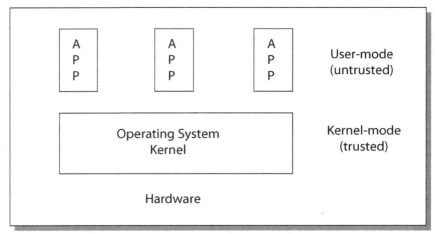

Figure 2.1: User-mode and kernel-mode operation.

will boot instead, installing spyware and disabling virus protection. For security, an operating system must prevent untrusted code from modifying system state.

- **Privacy.** On a multi-user system, each user must be limited to just the data that she is permitted to access. Without protection provided by the operating system, any user or application running on a system could access any of the data stored on the system, without the knowledge or approval of the data's owner. For example, hackers often use popular applications such as screen savers as a way to gain access to personal emails, telephone numbers, and credit card data stored on the system. For privacy, an operating system must prevent untrusted code from accessing unauthorized data.

- **Efficiency.** Protection is also needed for effective resource allocation. Without protection, an application can gather any amount of processing time, memory, or disk space that it wants. On a single-user system, this means that a buggy application can prevent other applications from running, or simply make them run so slowly that they appear to be stalled. On a multi-user system, one user could grab all of the system's resources for herself. Thus, for efficiency and fairness, an operating system must be able to limit the amount of resources assigned to each application or user.

operating
system
kernel

Implementing protection is the job of the *operating system kernel*. The kernel is the lowest level of software running on the system, with full access to all of the capabilities of the hardware. The kernel is necessarily *trusted* to do anything that can be done with the hardware. Everything else — that is, the untrusted software running on the system — is run in a restricted environment, with less than complete access to the full power of the hardware. Figure 2.1 illustrates this difference between kernel-level and user-level execution.

In turn, applications themselves often need to safely execute untrusted third party code. An example is a web browser executing embedded Javascript to draw a web page. Without protection, a script with an embedded virus can take control of the browser, making the user think they are interacting directly with the web when in fact their web passwords are being forwarded to an attacker. This design pattern — extensible applications running third party scripts — occurs in many different domains. Applications become more powerful and more widely used if third party developers and users can customize them, but that raises the issue of how to protect the application itself from rogue extensions. In this chapter we focus on how the operating system protects the kernel from rogue applications, but the principles also apply at the application level.

process
A *process* is the abstraction for protection provided by the operating system kernel: the execution of an application program with restricted rights. A process needs permission from the operating system kernel before accessing the memory of any other process, before reading or writing to the disk, before changing hardware settings, and so forth. In other words, a process's access to hardware is mediated and checked by the operating system kernel. In this chapter, we explain the process concept and how the kernel implements process isolation.

A key consideration is that we need to provide protection while still running application code at high speed. The operating system kernel runs directly on the processor with unlimited rights. The kernel can perform any operation available on the hardware. What about applications? They need to run on the processor with all potentially dangerous operations disabled. To make this work, we will need a bit of assistance from hardware, which we will describe shortly. Throughout the book we will see examples of this — small amounts of carefully designed hardware can help make it much easier for the operating system to provide what users want.

Of course, both the operating system kernel and application processes running with restricted rights are in fact sharing the same machine — the same processor, the same memory, and the same disk. When reading this chapter, it is helpful to keep these two perspectives in mind: sometimes, when we are running the operating system, the system can do anything, and at other times, when we're running an application process on behalf of a user, the behavior is restricted.

Thus, a processor running an operating system is somewhat akin to someone with a split personality in charge of their own insane asylum. When running the operating system kernel, the processor is like a warden with complete access to everything. At other times, the processor runs application code in a process — the processor becomes the inmate, wearing a straightjacket locked in a padded cell by the warden, protected from

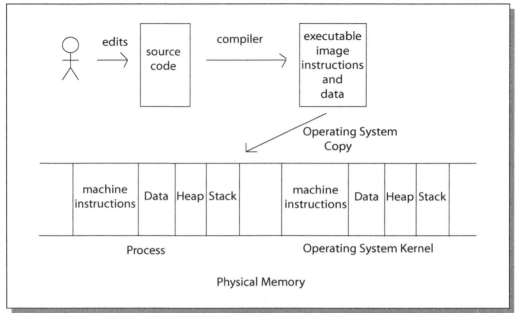

Figure 2.2: A user edits, compiles, and runs a user program. Other programs can also be stored in physical memory, including the operating system itself.

harming anyone else. Of course, it is the same processor in both cases, sometimes completely trustworthy and at other times completely untrusted.

Protection raises several important questions which we will answer in the rest of the chapter:

- **The process abstraction.** What is a process and how does it differ from a program?

- **Dual-mode operation.** How does the operating system implement processes? What hardware is needed for efficient restricted execution?

- **Safe control transfer: exceptions, interrupts, and system calls.** How do we switch safely across the boundary between processes at user-level and the kernel?

- **Booting the kernel.** What steps are needed to start running an operating system kernel, up to the point where it can create a process?

2.1 | The process concept

In the model you are likely familiar with, illustrated in Figure 2.2, a programmer types up some code in some appropriately high-level language. A compiler converts that code into a sequence of machine instructions, and stores those instructions into a file, called the *executable image* of the program. The compiler also defines any static data the program needs, along with their initial values, and includes them in the executable image.

executable image

To start the program running, the operating system copies the program instructions and data from the executable image into physical memory. The operating system sets aside some memory for the execution stack to store the state of local variables during procedure calls. The operating system also sets aside a region of memory, called the heap, for any dynamically allocated data structures or objects the program might need. Of course, in order to copy the program into memory, the operating system itself must already be loaded into memory, with its own stack and heap.

Ignoring protection, once a program is loaded into memory, the operating system can start running the program by setting the stack pointer and jumping to the first instruction of the program. The compiler itself is just a regular program: the operating system starts the compiler by copying the compiler's executable image into memory and jumping to its first instruction.

If the user wants to run multiple copies of the same program, the operating system can do that by making multiple copies of the program's instructions, static data, heap and stack in memory. As we will describe in a later chapter, most operating systems are designed to reuse memory wherever possible: they store only a single copy of a program's instructions when multiple copies of the program are executed at the same time. Even so, a separate copy of the program's data, stack and heap are needed. For now, we will keep things simple and make a separate copy of the entire program each time we run a process.

Thus, the difference between a process and a program is that a process is an *instance* of a program, in much the same way that an object is an instance of a class in object-oriented programming. At any point in time, each program can have zero, one or more processes executing it. For each instance of a program, there is a process with its own copy of the program in memory.

The operating system keeps track of the various processes on the computer using a data structure called the *process control block*. The process control block stores all the information the operating system needs about a particular process: where it is stored in memory, where its executable image is on disk, which user asked it to start executing, what privileges the process has, and so forth.

process control block

Earlier, we defined a process to be the execution of a program with

Processes, lightweight processes, and threads

The word "process", like many terms in computer science, has evolved over time. Although you will often be able to ignore this history, it can sometimes trip up the unwary as systems built at different times will use the same word in significantly different ways.

A "process" was originally coined to mean what we now call a "thread" – some logical sequence of instructions, executing either operating system or application code. The concept of a process was developed as a way of simplifying the correct construction of operating systems, for early systems that provided no protection between application programs.

Organizing the operating system as a cooperating set of processes proved immensely successful, and soon virtually every new operating system was built this way, including systems that also provided protection against malicious or buggy user programs. At the time, almost all user programs were simple single-threaded programs with only one program counter and one stack, so there was no confusion. A process was what was needed to run a program, that is, a single sequential execution stream with a protection boundary.

As parallel computers became more popular, though, we once again needed a word for a logical sequence of instructions. A multiprocessor program can have multiple instruction sequences running in parallel, each with their own program counter, but all cooperating together within a single protection boundary. For a time, these were called "lightweight processes" (each a sequence of instructions cooperating inside a protection boundary), but eventually the word "thread" became more widely used.

This leads to the current naming convention used in almost all modern operating systems: a process executes a program, consisting of one or more threads running inside a protection boundary.

restricted rights. Each of these roles — execution and protection — is important enough that we will devote several chapters to each concept. In this chapter, we will focus on protection, and so we will limit our discussion to simple processes, each with one program counter, code, data, heap, and stack.

Some programs consist of multiple concurrent activities, or threads. A web browser, for example, might need to be able to receive user input at the same time it is also drawing the screen or receiving input from the network. Each of these separate activities has its own program counter and stack but operates on the same code and data as the other threads. The operating system multiplexes threads running in a process, in much the same way that the operating system multiplexes processes into physical memory. We will generalize on the process abstraction to allow multiple activities in the same protection domain in the next chapter.

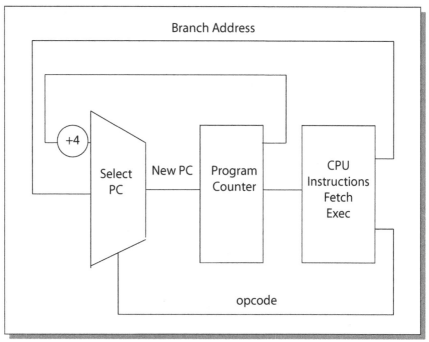

Figure 2.3: The basic operation of a CPU.

2.2 | Dual-mode operation

Once a program is loaded into memory, and the operating system starts the process, the processor will fetch each instruction in turn, decode, and execute it. Some instructions compute values, say, by multiplying two registers and putting the result into another register. Some instructions read or write locations in memory. Still other instructions like branches or procedure calls change the program counter and thus determine the next instruction to execute. The basic operation of a processor is illustrated in Figure 2.3.

How does the operating system kernel prevent a process from doing any harm to other processes or to the operating system itself? After all, if multiple programs are loaded into memory at the same time, what is to keep one process from overwriting another process' data structures, or for that matter, overwriting the operating system image stored on disk?

If we step back from any consideration of performance, a very simple, safe, and entirely hypothetical approach would be to have the operating system kernel simulate, step by step, every instruction in every user process. Instead of the processor directly executing instructions, each instruction in a user program would be fetched, decoded, and executed by a software interpreter. Before each instruction is executed, the interpreter could check to see if the process had permission to do the operation in question: is it referencing part of its own memory, or someone else's? Is it trying to branch into someone else's code? Is it directly accessing the disk, or is it using the correct routines in the operating system to do so? The interpreter could allow all legal operations while halting any application that overstepped its bounds.

Now suppose we want to speed up our hypothetical simulator. Most instructions are perfectly safe, such as adding two registers together and storing the result into a third register. Can we modify the processor in some way to allow safe instructions to execute directly on the hardware?

To accomplish this, we can implement the same checks as in our hypothetical interpreter, but we do so in hardware rather than software. This is called *dual-mode operation*, represented by a single bit in the processor status register to signify which mode the processor is currently executing in. In *user-mode*, the processor checks each instruction before executing it to verify that the instruction is permitted to be performed by that process. (We will describe the specific checks next.) In *kernel-mode*, the operating system executes with protection checks turned off.

Figure 2.4 shows the operation of a processor with a mode bit; the program counter and the mode control the operation of the processor. In turn, the mode bit is modified by some instructions, in the same way that the program counter is modified by some instructions.

What hardware is needed to allow the operating system kernel to protect applications and users from one another, yet also allow user code to run directly on the processor? At a minimum, the hardware must support three things:

- **Privileged instructions.** All potentially unsafe instructions are prohibited when executing in user-mode.

- **Memory protection.** All memory accesses outside of a process's valid memory region are prohibited when executing in user-mode.

- **Timer interrupts.** Regardless of what the process does, the kernel must have a way to periodically regain control from the current process.

In addition, the hardware must also provide a way to safely transfer control from user-mode to kernel-mode and back. As the mechanisms to do this are relatively involved, we defer the discussion of that topic to the following section of this chapter.

Privileged instructions

Process isolation is only possible if there is a way to limit programs running in user-mode from directly changing their privilege level. We will see later that processes can indirectly change their privilege level by executing a

dual-mode operation

user-mode

kernel-mode

The operating system kernel vs. the rest of the operating system

The operating system kernel is a crucial piece of an operating system, but it is only a portion of the overall operating system. In most modern operating systems, a portion of the operating system runs in user-mode as a library linked into each application. An example is library code to manage an application's menu buttons. To encourage a common user interface across applications, most operating systems provide a library of user interface widgets. Applications are free to write their own user interface of course, but most developers will choose to reuse the routines provided by the operating system. This code could run in the kernel but does not need to do so. If the application crashes, it won't matter if that application's menu buttons stop working. The library code (but not the operating system kernel) *shares fate* with the rest of the application: a problem with one has the same effect as a problem with the other.

Likewise, parts of the operating system can run in their own user-level processes. A window manager is one example. The window manager directs mouse actions and keyboard input that occurs inside a window to the correct application, and the manager also ensures that each application modifies only that application's portion of the screen, and not the operating system's menu bar or any other application's window. Without this, a malicious application could grab user input to itself, potentially inducing the user to disclose their password to the application, allowing it to take control of the machine.

Why not include the entire operating system — the library code and any user-level processes — in the kernel itself? While that might seem more natural, one reason is that it is often easier to debug user-level code than kernel code. The kernel can use low-level hardware to implement debugging support such as breakpoints and single step for user-level code; to single step the kernel requires an even lower-level debugger running underneath the kernel. The difficulty of debugging operating system kernels was the original motivation behind the development of virtual machines.

Further, the kernel must be trusted, as it has the full power of the hardware. Any error in the kernel may corrupt the disk, the memory of some unrelated application, or simply crash the system. By separating out code that does not need to be in the kernel, the operating system can become more reliable — a bug in the window system is bad enough, but it would be even worse if it could corrupt the disk. This is an illustration of the *principle of least privilege*, that security and reliability are enhanced if each part of the system has exactly the privileges it needs to do its job, and no more.

special instruction called a *system call* to transfer control into the kernel at a fixed location specified by the operating system. Other than transferring control into the operating system kernel (that is, in effect, becoming the kernel) at these fixed locations, an application process cannot be allowed to change its privilege level.

Other instructions are also prohibited to application code. The applica-

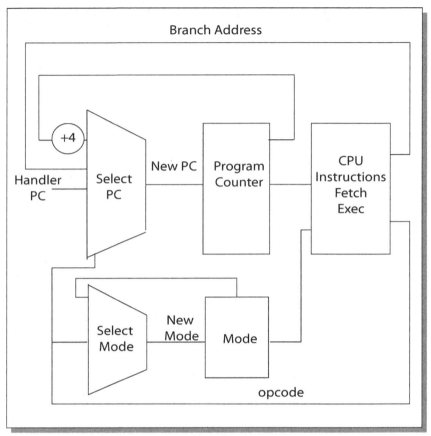

Figure 2.4: The operation of a CPU with kernel and user modes.

tion cannot be allowed to change the set of memory locations it can access; as we will see shortly, limiting an application to being able to access only its own memory is essential to preventing an application from either intentionally, or accidentally, corrupting or misusing the data or code from other applications or the operating system itself. Another limitation on applications is that they cannot disable processor interrupts, for reasons that we we will also describe shortly.

Instructions available in kernel-mode, but not in user-mode, are called, **privileged instruction** naturally enough, *privileged instructions*. The operating system kernel needs to be able to execute these instructions to be able to do its work — it needs to be able to change privilege levels, adjust memory access, and disable and enable interrupts. But if these instructions were available to applications, then a rogue application would in effect have the power of the operating system kernel.

Thus, while application programs can use only a subset of the full instruction set, the operating system executes in kernel-mode with the full

The processor status register and privilege levels

Conceptually, the kernel/user mode is a one bit register. When set to 1, the processor is in kernel mode and can do anything. When set to 0, the processor is in user mode and is restricted. On most processors, the kernel/user mode is stored in the *processor status register*. This register contains flags that control the operation of the processor. The register is typically not directly accessible to application code. Rather, flags are set or reset as a by product of executing instructions. For example, the status register is automatically saved to memory by hardware during an interrupt, because executing instructions during the interrupt will overwrite its contents.

The kernel/user mode bit is one flag in the processor status register, set whenever the kernel is entered and reset whenever the kernel is exited. Other flags include condition codes, set as a side effect of arithmetic operations, to allow a more compact encoding of conditional branch instructions. Still other flags can specify whether the processor is executing with 16-bit, 32-bit, or 64-bit addresses. The specific contents of the processor status register is processor architecture dependent.

Some processor architectures, including the Intel x86, support more than two privilege levels in the processor status register (the x86 supports four privilege levels). The original reason for this was to allow the operating system kernel to be separated into layers: a core with unlimited access to the machine, while other portions of the operating system would be restricted from certain operations, but with more power than completely unprivileged application code. This way, bugs in one part of the operating system kernel might not crash the entire system. However, to our knowledge, neither MacOS, Windows, nor Linux make use of this feature.

A potential future use for multiple privilege levels is to simplify running an operating system as an application, or virtual machine, on top of another operating system. Applications running on top of the virtual machine operating system would run at user-level, the virtual machine would run at some intermediate level, while the true kernel would run in kernel-mode. Of course, with only four levels, this doesn't work for a virtual machine running on a virtual machine running on a virtual machine. For the purposes of our discussion, we will assume the simpler case of two levels of hardware protection.

power of the hardware.

What happens if an application attempts to access memory it shouldn't or attempts to change its privilege level? Such actions cause a processor *exception*. Unlike taking an exception in a programming language where the exception is handled by the language runtime, a processor exception causes the processor to transfer control to an exception handler in the operating system kernel. (We will describe in detail how exception handling works a bit later in the chapter, as exceptions can occur for many reasons beyond privilege violations.) Usually, the operating system kernel simply halts the process on privilege violations, as it often means that the application's code has encountered a bug.

MS/DOS and memory protection

As an illustration of the power of memory protection, MS/DOS was an early Microsoft operating system that did not provide memory protection. Instead, user programs were permitted to read and modify any memory location in the system, including operating system data structures. While this was seen as acceptable for a personal computer that was only ever used by a single person at a time, there were a number of downsides. One obvious problem was system reliability: application bugs frequently crashed the operating system or corrupted other applications. The lack of memory protection also made the system more vulnerable to computer viruses.

Over time, some applications were written to take advantage of the ability to change operating system data structures, for example, to change certain control parameters or to directly manipulate the frame buffer for controlling the display. As a result, changing the operating system became quite difficult; either the new version couldn't run the old applications, limiting its appeal, or it needed to leave these data structures in precisely the same place as they were in the old version. In other words, memory protection is not only useful for reliability and security, it is also helpful as a way of enforcing a well-defined interface between applications and the operating system kernel, to aid future evolvability and portability.

Memory protection

In order to run an application process, both the operating system and the application must be resident in memory at the same time. The application needs to be in memory in order to execute, while the operating system needs to be in memory to be able to start the program, as well as to handle any system calls, interrupts, or exceptions. More generally, there are often several application processes with code and data stored in memory; for example, you may read email, download songs, Skype, instant message, and browse the web at the same time.

To make this memory sharing work, the operating system must be able to configure the hardware so that each application process can read and write only its own memory and not the memory of the operating system or any other application. If an application could modify the operating system kernel's code or data, it could potentially do so in a way that would give the application complete control over the machine. For example, it could change the login program to give the attacker full system administrator privileges. While it might seem that read-only access to memory is harmless, recall that we want to provide both security and privacy. Kernel data structures — such as the file system buffer — may contain data that is private to one user and not permitted to be seen by another. Likewise, user passwords may be stored in kernel memory while they are being verified.

How does the operating system prevent a user program from accessing

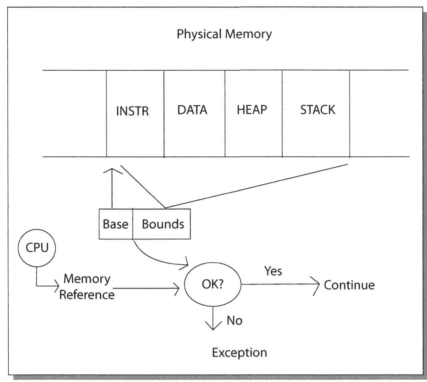

Figure 2.5: Base and bounds memory protection.

parts of physical memory? We will discuss a wide variety of different approaches in a later chapter, but early computers pioneered a very simple mechanism that was sufficient for providing protection. We describe it as an illustration of the general principle.

base and bounds

In these systems, a processor has two extra registers, called *base and bounds*. The base specifies the start of the process's memory region, while the bound gives its length. This is illustrated in Figure 2.5. These registers can only be changed by privileged instructions, that is, by the operating system executing in kernel-mode. User-level code cannot change their values.

Every time the processor fetches an instruction, the address of the program counter is checked to see if it lies between the base and the bound registers. If so, the instruction fetch is allowed to proceed; otherwise, the hardware raises an exception, the program is halted, and control is transferred back to the operating system kernel. Although it might seem extravagant to do two extra comparisons for each instruction, the value of memory protection makes it worth the cost. In fact, we will see much more sophisticated and "extravagant" memory protection schemes later.

Likewise, for instructions that read or write data to memory, each mem-

Memory-mapped devices

On most computers, the operating system controls input/output devices such as the disk, network, or keyboard by reading and writing to special memory locations. Each device monitors the memory bus for the address assigned to that device, and when it sees its address, the device triggers the desired I/O operation. The operating system sets things so that it can access these special memory locations, but user-level processes cannot. Thus, memory protection has the added advantage of limiting direct access to input/output devices by user code. By limiting each process to just its own memory locations, the kernel prevents it from directly reading or writing to the disk controller or other devices. This way, a buggy or malicious application cannot modify the operating system's image stored on disk, and a user cannot gain access to another user's files without first going through the operating system to check file permissions.

ory reference is also checked against the base and bounds registers, and an exception generated if the boundaries are violated. Complex instructions, such as the x86 block copy instruction, must check every location touched by the instruction, to ensure that the application does not inadvertently or maliciously read or write to a buffer that starts in its own region but that extends into the kernel's region. Doing so might enable the application to read or overwrite key parts of the operating system code or data and thereby gain control of the physical hardware.

The operating system kernel executes without the base and bounds registers, allowing it to access any memory on the system — the kernel's memory or the memory of any application process running on the system. Because applications can only touch their own memory, the kernel must explicitly copy any input or output into or out of the application's memory region. For example, a simple program might print "hello world". The kernel must copy the string out of the application's memory region into the screen buffer.

Although the base and bounds mechanism is sufficient for implementing protection, it is unable to provide some important features:

- **Expandable heap and stack.** With a single base and bound per process, the memory allocated to a process's heap and stack must be fixed at the time the program is loaded into physical memory.

- **Memory sharing.** Base and bounds does not allow memory to be shared between different processes, as would be useful for sharing code between multiple processes running the same program.

- **Non-relative memory addresses.** For base and bounds, the location of procedures and data within a program are determined at runtime, when the program is copied from disk to memory. Thus, any instruction with an absolute physical address (such as a procedure call) would need to be changed as part of loading a program into memory.

- **Memory fragmentation.** Once a program has started, it becomes nearly impossible to relocate it, as its physical addresses may be stored in registers or on the program's execution stack, for example, as return addresses. Over time, as applications start and finish at irregular times, if memory cannot be re-compacted, it will become increasingly fragmented. Potentially, memory fragmentation may reach a point where there is not enough contiguous space to start a new process, even when there is enough memory in aggregate.

virtual address

For these reasons, most modern processors introduce a level of indirection, called *virtual addresses*. With virtual addresses, every process's memory starts at the same place, e.g., zero. Each process thinks that it has the entire machine to itself, although obviously that is not the case in reality. The hardware translates these virtual addresses to physical memory locations. A very simple algorithm would be to add the base register to every virtual address, so that the process can use virtual addresses starting from zero.

In practice, modern systems use much more complex algorithms for translating between virtual and physical addresses. The layer of indirection provided by virtual addresses gives operating systesm an enormous amount of flexibility to efficiently manage its physical memory. For example, many systems with virtual addresses allocate physical memory in fixed-sized, rather than variable-sized chunks, reducing fragmentation.

Virtual addresses can also allow the heap and the stack to start at separate ends of the virtual address space, so that they can grow according to the particular needs of each program. We illustrate this in Figure 2.6. If the stack or heap grow beyond their initially allocated regions, the operating system can allocate them more space in physical memory, but leave them in the same location in virtual memory. The expansion is completely transparent to the user process. We will discuss virtual addresses in more depth in Chapter 8.

As another example, the operating system kernel needs to manage many different concurrent activities, each with its own execution stack. Because we need to grow these stacks dynamically, most commercial operating system kernels use virtual addresses for some of their kernel memory.

Figure 2.7 is a simple test to verify that your computer supports virtual addresses. Suppose we write a program with a static variable and a procedure local variable allocated on the stack. The program updates the value of each variable, waits for a bit, and then prints the locations of the variables and their values.

If we start multiple copies of this program running simultaneously on a modern operating system with virtual addressing, each prints exactly

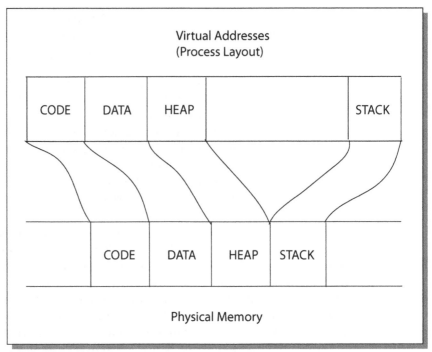

Figure 2.6: Virtual addresses allow the stack and heap regions of a process to grow independently.

```
int staticVar = 0;        // a static variable
main () {
    int localVar = 0;     // a procedure local variable

    staticVar += 1;
    localVar += 1;

    // sleep causes the program to wait for x seconds
    sleep (10);
    printf ("static address: %x, value: %d\n", &staticVar, staticVar);
    printf ("procedure local address: %x, value: %d\n", &localVar, localVar);
}

Produces:
    static address: 5328, value: 1
    procedure local address: fffffe2 , value: 1
```

Figure 2.7: A simple program whose output illustrates the difference between execution in physical memory versus virtual memory.

the same result. That would be impossible if the programs were directly addressing physical memory locations. In other words, each instance of the program appears to have its own complete copy of memory, so that when it stores a value to a memory location, it is the only one that sees its changes to that location. Other processes change their own copy of the memory location. This way, a process cannot alter any other process's memory, because it has no way of referencing the other process's memory. Instead, only the kernel can read or write the memory of a process other than itself.

This is very much akin to a set of television shows, each occupying their own universe, even though they all appear on the same television. Events in one show do not (normally) affect the plot lines of other shows. Sitcom characters are blissfully unaware that Jack Bauer has just saved the world from nuclear Armageddon. Of course, just as television shows can from time to time share characters, processes can also communicate if the kernel allows it. We will discuss how this happens in Chapter 3.

Timer interrupts

Process isolation also requires that the hardware provide a way for the operating system kernel to periodically regain control of the processor. When the operating system starts a user-level program, the process is free to execute any user-level (non-privileged) instructions it chooses, call any function in the process's memory region, load or store any value to its memory, and so forth. To the user program, it appears to have complete control of the hardware, within the limits of its memory region.

However, this too is only an illusion. If the application enters an infinite loop, or if the user simply becomes impatient and wants the system to stop the application, then the operating system needs to be able to regain control. Of course, the operating system needs to be able to execute instructions to be able to decide if it should stop the application, but if the application controls the processor, the operating system by definition is not running. A similar issue occurs in more normal circumstances. Suppose you are listening to music on your computer, downloading a file, and typing at the same time. To be able to smoothly play the music, and to respond in a timely way to user input, the operating system needs to be able regain control promptly when it needs to switch to a new task.

hardware
timer
Almost all computer systems include a device called a *hardware timer* which can be set to interrupt the processor after a specified delay, either in time or after some number of instructions have been executed. The operating system might set the timer to expire every ten milliseconds. (Human reaction time is measured in the hundreds of milliseconds.) Resetting the timer is a privileged operation, accessible only within the kernel, so that the user-level process cannot inadvertently or maliciously disable the timer.

When the timer interrupt occurs, control is transferred by the hardware from the user process to the operating system kernel running in kernel-mode. Other hardware interrupts, such as to signal the processor that an I/O device has completed its work, likewise cause control to be transferred

---

MacOS and preemptive scheduling

Until 2002, Apple's MacOS operating system lacked the ability to force a process to yield the processor back to the kernel. Instead, all application programmers were told to design their systems to periodically call into the operating system to check if there was other work to be done. The operating system would then save the state of the original process, switch control to another application, and return back only when it again became the original process's turn. This has a drawback: if a process fails to yield, e.g., because it has a bug and enters an infinite loop, the operating system kernel has no recourse. The user needed to reboot the machine to give control back to the operating system. This happened frequently enough that it was given its own name: the "spinning cursor of death."

---

from the user process to the operating system kernel. A timer or other interrupt does not imply that the program has done anything wrong — in most cases, after resetting the timer, the operating system will resume execution of the process, with the mode, program counter and registers set back to the values they had immediately before the interrupt occurred. We will discuss the hardware and operating system kernel mechanisms for implementing interrupts in the next section.

Exercises

1. We mentioned that for the "Hello world" program, the kernel must copy the string from the user program into the screen memory. Why must the screen's buffer memory be protected? Explain what might happen if a (malicious) application could alter any pixel on the screen, not just those within its own window.

2. For each of the three mechanisms for supporting dual mode operation — privileged instructions, memory protection, and timer interrupts — explain what might go wrong without that mechanism, assuming the system still had the other two.

3. Suppose we had a perfect object-oriented language and compiler, so that only an object's methods could access the internal data inside an object. If the operating system only ran programs written in that language, would it still need hardware memory address protection?

4. Suppose you are tasked with designing the security system for a new web browser that supports rendering web pages with embedded web page scripts. What checks would you need to ensure that executing buggy or malicious scripts could not corrupt or crash the browser?

2.3 | Safe control transfer

Once the kernel has placed a user process in a carefully constructed sandbox, the next question is how do we safely transition from executing a user process to executing the kernel and the reverse. These transitions are not rare events. A high-performance web server, for example, might switch between user-mode and kernel-mode hundreds or thousands of times per second. Thus, the mechanism needs to be both fast and safe, leaving no room for a malicious or buggy program to intentionally or inadvertently corrupt the kernel.

User to kernel mode

We first focus on transitions from user-mode to kernel-mode; as we'll see, transitioning in the other direction works by "undo"ing the transition from the user process into kernel.

There are three reasons for why the kernel will take control from a user process: exceptions, interrupts, and system calls. While interrupts occur asynchronously, exceptions and system calls are synchronous events triggered by the execution of the process. We use the term *trap* to refer to any synchronous transfer of control from user-mode to the kernel; some systems use the term more generically for any transfer of control from a less privileged level to a more privileged level.

trap

exception

- **Exceptions.** A processor *exception* is any unexpected condition caused by user program behavior. On an exception, the hardware will stop the currently executing process and start running the kernel at a specially designated exception handler. As we mentioned earlier, a processor exception will be triggered whenever a process attempts to perform a privileged instruction or accesses memory outside of its own memory region. Other exceptions occur when a process divides an integer by zero, accesses a word of memory with a non-aligned address, attempts to write to read-only memory, and so forth. In these cases, the operating system simply halts the process and returns an error code to the user.

  Exceptions can also be triggered by a number of other, more benign, program events. For example, to set a breakpoint in a program, the kernel replaces the machine instruction in memory with a special instruction that invokes an exception. When the program reaches that point in its execution, the hardware switches into the kernel. The kernel restores the old instruction and transfers control to the debugger. The debugger can then examine the program's variables, set a new breakpoint, and resume the program at the instruction causing the exception.

Exceptions and virtualization

Exceptions are a particularly powerful tool for virtualization — the emulation of hardware that does not actually exist. As one example, it is common for different versions of a processor architecture family to support some parts of the instruction set and not others, such as when an inexpensive low power processor does not support floating point operations. At some cost in performance, the operating system can use exceptions to make the difference completely transparent to the user process. When the program issues a floating point instruction, an exception is raised, trapping into the operating system kernel. Instead of halting the process, the operating system can *emulate* the missing instruction, and on completion, return to the user process at the instruction immediately after the one that caused the exception. This way, the same program binary can run on all the different versions of the processor.

More generally, exceptions are used to transparently emulate a virtual machine. When a guest operating system is running as a user-level process on top of an operating system, it will attempt to execute privileged instructions as if it were running on physical hardware. These instructions will cause privilege violations, trapping into the host operating system kernel. To maintain the illusion of physical hardware, the host kernel then performs the requested instruction of behalf of the user-level virtual machine, and restarts the guest operating system at the instruction immediately following the one that caused the exception.

As a final example, exceptions are a key building block for memory management. With most types of virtual addressing, the processor can be set up to take an exception whenever it reads or writes inside a particular virtual address range. This allows the kernel to treat addressing as *virtual* — a virtual address need not always correspond to a physical memory location. Whenever the program touches a missing address, the operating system takes an exception and fills in the data from disk before resuming the program. In this way, the operating system can execute programs that require more memory than can ever be physically on the machine at any one time.

---

interrupt

- **Interrupts.** An *interrupt* is an asynchronous signal to the processor that some external event has occurred that may require its attention. An interrupt operates much as an exception does: the processor stops the currently executing process and starts running in the kernel at a specially designated interrupt handler. Each different type of interrupt requires its own handler. For timer interrupts, the handler checks if the current process is being responsive to user input, to detect if the process has gone into an infinite loop. The timer handler can also periodically switch the processor to run a different process, to ensure each process gets a turn. If there is no other work to do, the timer handler resumes execution at the interrupted instruction, transparently to the user process.

Buffer descriptors and high-performance I/O

In early computer systems, the key to good performance was to keep the processor busy; particularly for servers, the key to good performance today is to keep I/O devices such as the network and disk device busy. Neither Internet nor disk bandwidth has kept pace with the rapid improvement in processor performance over the past four decades, leaving them relatively more important to system performance.

If only one network or disk request is outstanding at a time, interrupt handling can be the limiting factor. When a device completes a request, it raises an interrupt, triggering the operating system to make a new request. In the meantime, while the processor is handling the interrupt, the device is idle, when it could be putting the next request on the network or sending it to disk.

The solution in modern systems is for the operating system to set up a circular queue of requests, one for incoming and outgoing, for each device to handle. Each entry in the queue, called a *buffer descriptor*, specifies one I/O operation: where to find the buffer to put the incoming data or fetch the outgoing data, whether to take an interrupt on every packet or only every few packets, and so forth. This decouples the processor and the I/O devices, so that each only needs to keep up with the average rate of I/O events.

Buffer descriptors are stored in memory, accessed by the device using DMA (direct memory access). An implication is that each logical I/O operation can involve several DMA requests: one to download the buffer descriptor from memory into the device, then to copy the data in or out, and then to store the success/failure of the operation back into buffer descriptor.

In addition to timer events, interrupts are also used to inform the kernel of the completion of input/output requests. For example, the mouse device hardware will trigger an interrupt every time the user moves or clicks on the mouse. The kernel in turn will notify the appropriate user process — the one the user was mousing across. Virtually every input/output device — the Ethernet, WiFi, hard disk, thumb drive, keyboard, mouse — generates an interrupt whenever some input arrives for the processor and whenever a request completes.

polling   An alternative to interrupts is *polling*: the kernel could loop, checking each input/output device to see if an event has occurred which required handling. Needless to say, if the kernel is polling, it is not available to run user-level code.

Interprocessor interrupts are another source of interrupts. On a multiprocessor, a processor can cause an interrupt to occur on any of the other processors. The kernel uses these interrupts to coordinate actions across the multiprocessor; for example, if one processor takes a fatal exception, the kernel will normally send an interrupt to stop any of the other processors who might be running the failed program.

system call

- **System calls.** User processes can also transition into the operating system kernel voluntarily, to request that the kernel do some operation on the user's behalf. A *system call* is any procedure provided by the kernel that can be called from user-level. Most processors implement system calls with a special *trap* instruction. However, a special instruction is not strictly required; on some systems, a process triggers a system call by executing an instruction with a specific invalid opcode.

  As with an interrupt or an exception, the trap instruction changes the processor mode from user to kernel and starts executing in the kernel at a pre-defined handler. As we will explain shortly, to protect the kernel from misbehaving user programs, it is essential that the hardware transfers control on a system call to a pre-defined address — user processes can *not* be allowed to jump to arbitrary places in the kernel.

  Operating systems provide a substantial number of system calls. Examples include ones to establish a connection to a web server, to send or receive packets over the network, to create or delete files, to read or write data into files, and to create a new user process. To the user program, these are called just like normal procedures, with parameters and return values. Like any good abstraction, the caller only needs to be concerned with the interface; they do not need to know that the routine is actually being implemented by the kernel rather than by a library. The kernel handles all of the details of checking and copying arguments, performing the operation, and copying any return values back into the process's memory. When the kernel is done with the system call, it resumes user-level execution at the instruction immediately after the trap.

Kernel to user mode

Just as there are several different causes for transitions from user-mode to kernel-mode, there are also several causes for transitions from kernel-mode to user-mode:

- **New process.** To start a new process, the kernel copies the program into memory, sets the program counter to be the first instruction of the process, sets the stack pointer to be the base of the user stack, and switches to user-mode.

- **Resume after an exception, interrupt or system call.** When the kernel finishes handling the request, it resumes execution of the interrupted process by restoring its program counter, restoring its registers, and changing the mode back to user-level.

- **Switch to a different process.** In some cases, such as on a timer interrupt, the kernel will decide to switch to running a different process than the one that had been running before the interrupt, exception, or system call. Since the kernel will eventually want to resume the old process, the kernel needs to save the process's state — its program counter, registers, and so forth — in the process's control block. The kernel can then resume a different process, by loading its state — its program counter, registers, and so forth — from the process's control block into the processor, and then switching to user-mode.

- **User-level upcall.** Many operating systems provide user programs the ability to receive asynchronous notification of events. The mechanism, which we will describe shortly, is very similar to kernel interrupt handling, except at user-level.

Safe mode switch

Whether transitioning from user to kernel mode, or in the opposite direction, care must be taken to ensure that a buggy or malicious user program cannot corrupt the kernel. Although the basic idea is simple, the low-level implementation can be a bit gnarly: we need the processor to save its state and switch what it is doing, all while it continues to execute instructions that might alter the state that is in the process of saving. This is akin to rebuilding a car's transmission while it barrels down the road at 60 mph.

The context switch code must be carefully crafted, and it relies on some amount of hardware support. To avoid confusion and reduce the possibility of error, most operating systems have a common sequence of instructions for entering the kernel — whether due to interrupts, exceptions or system calls — and a common sequence of instructions for returning to user level, again regardless of the cause.

At a minimum, this common sequence must provide:

- **Limited entry.** To transfer control to the operating system kernel, the hardware must ensure that the entry point into the kernel is one set up by the kernel. User programs cannot be allowed to jump to arbitrary locations in the kernel. For example, the kernel code for handling a system call to read a file will first check whether the user program has permission to do so, and if not, the kernel should return an error. Without limited entry points into the kernel, a malicious program could simply jump immediately after the code to perform the check, allowing any user access to any file in the file system.

- **Atomic changes to processor state.** In user mode, the program counter and stack point to memory locations in the user process; memory protection prevents the user process from accessing any memory outside of its region. In kernel mode, the program counter and stack point to memory locations in the kernel; memory protection is changed to allow the kernel to access both its own data and that of the user process. Transitioning between the two must be done atomically, so that the mode, program counter, stack, and memory protection are all changed at the same time.

- **Transparent, restartable execution.** A running user-level process may be interrupted at any point, between any instruction and the next one. For example, the processor could have calculated a memory address, loaded it into a register, and be about to store a value to that address. The key to making interrupts work is that the operating system must be able to restore the state of the user program exactly as it was before the interrupt occurred. To the user process, an interrupt is invisible, except that the program temporarily slows down. A "hello world" program does not need to be written to understand interrupts! But an interrupt might still occur while it is running. Thus, on an interrupt, the processor saves its current state to memory, temporarily defers further events, and sets the processor to execute in kernel-mode, before jumping to the interrupt or exception handler. When the handler completes, the steps are reversed: the processor state is restored from its saved location, with the interrupted program none the wiser.

With that context, we first describe the hardware and software mechanism for handling an interrupt, exception, or system call, followed by how we can reuse this same basic mechanism as a building block for system calls, starting a new process, and user-level signals.

Interrupt vector

When an interrupt, exception or system call trap occurs, the operating system must take different actions depending on whether the event is a divide by zero exception, a file read system call, or a timer interrupt. How does the processor know what code to run?

To identify the code to run on a context switch, the processor will include a special register that points to an area of kernel memory called the *interrupt vector*. The interrupt vector is an array of pointers, with each entry pointing to the first instruction of a different handler procedure in the kernel. An *interrupt handler* is term used for the procedure called by the kernel on an interrupt. As Figure 2.8 illustrates, some entries might point to various interrupt handlers such as for the timer interrupt or keyboard interrupt. Another might point to the system call handler. Still other entries might point to various exception handlers like the handler for a divide-by-zero exception.

interrupt vector

interrupt handler

When an interrupt, system call, or exception occurs, the hardware determines which hardware device caused the interrupt, whether the trap instruction was executed, or what exception condition occurred. Thus, the

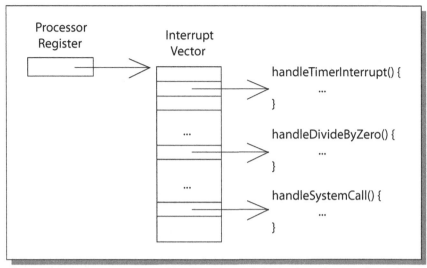

Figure 2.8: An interrupt vector identifies the code in the kernel to handle various hardware interrupts, system calls, and exceptions.

hardware can select the right entry from the interrupt vector and invoke the appropriate handler.

The format of the interrupt vector is processor-specific. On the x86, for example, the interrupt vector entries 0 - 31 are for different types of hardware exceptions, entries 32 - 255 are for different types of interrupts, and by convention, entry 64 points to the system call trap handler.

Of course, the interrupt vector must be stored in protected kernel memory; otherwise a process could, for example, hijack the network by directing all network interrupts to its own code. Similarly, the hardware register that points to the interrupt vector must be a protected register that can only be set when in kernel-mode.

Interrupt stack

Where should the interrupted process's state be saved and what stack should the kernel's code use?

On most processors, there is a special, privileged hardware register pointing to a region of kernel memory called the *interrupt stack*. When an interrupt, exception, or system call trap causes a context switch into the kernel, the hardware changes the stack pointer to point to the base of the kernel's interrupt stack. The hardware automatically saves some of the interrupted process's registers by pushing them onto the interrupt stack, before calling the kernel's handler.

When the kernel handler runs, it can then push any remaining registers onto the stack before performing the work of the handler. When returning from the interrupt, exception or system call trap, the reverse occurs: first we

interrupt
stack

pop the registers saved by the handler, and then the hardware restores the registers it saved onto the interrupt stack, returning to the point where the process was interrupted. (In the case of returning from a system call, the value of the saved program counter needs to be incremented, so that the hardware returns to the instruction immediately after the one that caused the trap.)

You might think you could use the process's user-level stack to store its state. We use a separate kernel-level interrupt stack for two reasons.

- First, having a dedicated stack is necessary for reliability: even if the process is buggy and its stack pointer is not a valid memory address, kernel handlers can continue to work properly.

- Second, having a protected stack is necessary for security: on a multi-processor machine if the kernel handler stored some of its variables on the user-level process's stack (for example, if the kernel handler did a procedure call), other threads in that process might read or write the kernel's return address, potentially causing the kernel to jump to arbitrary code within the kernel.

If the kernel is running on a multiprocessor system, each processor needs to have its own interrupt stack in the kernel so that, for example, we can handle simultaneous system calls and exceptions across multiple processors. For each processor, the kernel allocates a separate region of memory to be used as that processor's interrupt stack.

Most operating system kernels go one step further and allocate a kernel interrupt stack for every user-level process (and as we'll see in the next chapter, every user-level thread). When a user-level process is running, the hardware interrupt stack points to that process's kernel stack. Note that when a process is running at user-level, it is not running in the kernel so its kernel stack is empty.

Allocating a kernel stack per process makes it easier to switch to a new process inside an interrupt or system call handler. For example, when the timer interrupt handler runs, it might decide to give the processor to a different process. Likewise, a system call might need to wait for an I/O operation to complete, and meanwhile we would want to give the processor to someone else. With per-process stacks, to suspend a process, we simply store a pointer to its kernel stack in the process control block, and switch to running on the stack of the new process. We will describe this mechanism in much more detail in the next chapter,

Figure 2.9 summarizes the various states of a process's user and kernel stacks:

- If the process is running on the processor in user-mode, its kernel stack is empty, ready to be used for an interrupt.

Multiprocessors and interrupt routing

On a multiprocessor, which of the various processors should take an interrupt? Some early multiprocessors dedicated a single processor ("processor 0") to take all external interrupts. If an event required a change to what one of the other processors was doing, processor 0 could send an interprocessor interrupt to trigger that processor to switch to a new process.

For systems needing to do a large amount of input and output, such as a web server, directing all I/O through a single processor can become a bottleneck. In modern systems, interrupt routing is increasingly programmable, under control of the kernel. Often, each processor has its own, asynchronous, timer, so that different processors take interrupts at different times, reducing contention for shared data structures. Likewise, disk I/O events can be sent directly to the processor that requested the I/O operation, rather than to a random processor. Modern multicore systems can run as much as 1000 times faster if their data is already loaded into the processor cache versus if code and data needs to be transferred from some other processor.

Efficient delivery of network I/O packets is even more challenging. A high performance server might send and receive more than 100,000 packets per second, representing thousands of different connections. From a processing perspective, it is best to deliver incoming packets to the processor responsible for handling that connection; this requires the network interface hardware to demultiplex the incoming packet based on the contents of its header. Recent network controllers accomplish this by supporting multiple buffer descriptor rings for the same device, choosing which ring to use, and therefore which processor to interrupt, based on the arriving packet header.

- If the process is running on the processor in kernel-mode, e.g., due to an interrupt, exception or system call trap, its kernel stack is in use, containing the saved registers from the suspended user-level computation, as well as the current state of the kernel handler.

- If the process is available to run but is waiting for its turn on the processor, its kernel stack contains the registers and state to be restored when the process is resumed.

- If the process is waiting for an I/O event to complete, its kernel stack contains the suspended computation to be resumed when the I/O finishes.

Interrupt masking

Interrupts arrive asynchronously, so the processor might be executing either user or kernel code when an interrupt arrives. There are certain regions of the kernel (such as inside interrupt handlers themselves, or inside the

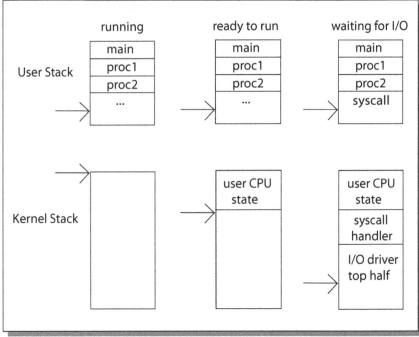

Figure 2.9: Kernel and user stacks for various states of a process. When a process is running in user-mode, its kernel stack is empty. When a process has been preempted (ready but not running), its kernel stack will contain the user-level processor state at the point when the user process was interrupted. When a process is inside a system call waiting for I/O, the kernel stack contains the context to be resumed when the I/O interrupt occurs, and the user stack contains the context to be resumed when the system call returns.

UNIX and kernel stacks

In the original implementation of UNIX, kernel memory was at a premium, because main memory was roughly one million times more expensive per byte than it is today. The initial system could run with only 50KB of main memory. Instead of allocating an entire interrupt stack per process, UNIX allocated just enough memory in the process control block to store the user-level registers saved on a mode switch. This way, UNIX could suspend a user-level process with the minimal amount of memory. UNIX still needed a few kernel stacks: one to run the interrupt handler and one for every system call waiting for an I/O event to complete, but that is much less than one for every process.

Of course, now that memory is much cheaper, most systems keep things simple and allocate a kernel stack per process or thread.

Interrupt handlers: Top and bottom halves

When a machine invokes an interrupt handler because some hardware event occurred (e.g., a timer expired, a key was pressed, a network packet arrived, or a disk I/O completed), the processor hardware typically masks interrupts while the interrupt handler executes. While interrupts are masked, if another hardware event occurs, it will not trigger another invocation of the interrupt handler until the interrupt is reenabled.

Some interrupts can trigger a large amount of processing, and it is undesirable to leave interrupts masked for too long. Hardware I/O devices have a limited amount of buffering, and this can lead to dropped events if interrupts are not processed in a timely fashion. For example, the keyboard hardware will drop keystrokes if the keyboard buffer is full. Interrupt handlers are therefore often divided into a *top half* and a *bottom half.* Unfortunately, this terminology can differ a bit from system to system, so in this book we use the more common usage.

The interrupt handler's bottom half is invoked by the hardware and executes with interrupts masked. It is designed to complete quickly. The bottom half typically saves the state of the hardware device, resets it so that it can receive a new event, and notifies the scheduler that the top half needs to run. At this point, the bottom half is done, and it can re-enable interrupts and return to the interrupted task, or (if the event is high priority) switch to the top half but with interrupts enabled. When the top half runs, it can do more time consuming things, such as parsing the arriving packet, delivering it to the correct user-level process, sending an acknowledgment, and so forth.

As we will explain in a later chapter, while the bottom half must always be able to run to completion in a bounded amount of time, the top half can do operations that require waiting, and therefore can synchronize access to shared kernel data structures.

Be aware, however, that on Linux, the terms are reversed: the bottom half is called the top half and vice versa.

CPU scheduler) where taking an interrupt might cause confusion. If we are running an interrupt handler when another interrupt occurs, we cannot just set the stack pointer to point to the base of the kernel's interrupt stack — doing so would obliterate the state of the first handler.

interrupt disable

interrupt enable

To simplify the design of the kernel, the hardware provides a privileged instruction to temporarily defer delivery of an interrupt until it is safe to do so. On the x86 and several other processors, this instruction is called *disable interrupts.* However, this is a misnomer: the interrupt is only deferred (masked), and not ignored. Once a corresponding *enable interrupt.* instruction is executed, any pending interrupts are delivered to the processor. The instructions to mask and unmask interrupts must be privileged — otherwise, user code could inadvertently or maliciously disable the hardware timer, allowing the machine to freeze.

If the processor is running in kernel-mode with interrupts enabled, then if an interrupt occurs, it is safe to simply use the current stack pointer rather than resetting it to the base of the exception stack. This approach can recursively push a series of handlers' states onto the stack; then, as each one completes, its state is popped from the stack and the earlier handler is resumed where it left off.

Hardware support for saving and restoring registers

The interrupted process's registers must be saved before the handler changes any of them so that the process can be restarted exactly as it left off. This is tricky because we have to save the registers without changing them in the process. Typically, the hardware provides some support to help with this process.

To make this concrete, consider the x86 architecture. First, rather than relying on the handler software to save all of the registers, when a context switch occurs the x86 hardware:

- If in user-mode, pushes the interrupted process's stack pointer onto the kernel's exception stack, and switches to the kernel stack.

- Pushes the interrupted process's instruction pointer.

- Pushes the x86 *processor status word*. The processor status word includes control bits such as whether the most recent arithmetic operation in the interrupted code resulted in a positive, negative, or zero value (needed for the correct behavior of any subsequent conditional branch instruction).

This hardware feature is needed because it is essential to save these *before* running the handler software: once the handler software starts running, the stack pointer, instruction pointer, and processor status word will be those of the handler, not those of the interrupted process.

Once the handler starts running, it can use the pushad instruction to save the remaining registers onto the stack. pushad saves the x86 integer registers; because the kernel does not typically do floating point operations, those do not need to be saved unless the kernel switches to a new process.

x86 has complementary features for restoring state: a popad instruction to pop an array of integer register values off the stack into the registers and an iret (return from interrupt) instruction that loads a stack pointer, instruction pointer, and processor status word off of the stack into the appropriate processor registers.

Putting it all together: Mode switch on the x86

As noted above, the high level steps needed to handle an interrupt, system call trap, or exception are simple, but the details require some care.

Architectural support for fast mode switches

Some processor architectures are able to execute user and kernel mode switches very efficiently, while other architectures are much slower at performing these switches.

The SPARC architecture is in the first camp. SPARC defines a set of *register windows* that operate like a hardware stack. Each register window includes a full set of the registers defined by the SPARC instruction set. When the processor performs a procedure call, it shifts to a new window, so the compiler never needs to save and restore registers across procedure calls, making them quite fast. (At a deep enough level of recursion, the SPARC will run out of its register windows; it then takes an kernel exception that saves half the windows and resumes execution. Another exception is taken when the processor pops its last window, allowing the kernel to reload the saved windows.)

Mode switches can be quite fast on the SPARC. On a mode switch, the processor switches to a different register window. The kernel handler can then run, using the registers from the new window and not disturbing the values stored in the interrupted process's copy of its registers. Unfortunately, this comes at a cost: switching between different processes is quite expensive on the SPARC, as the kernel needs to save and restore the entire register set of every active window.

The Motorola 88000 was in the second camp. The 88000 was an early pipelined architecture; for improved performance, multiple instructions were in various stages of execution at the same time. For example, one instruction might be fetching the instruction while another is doing a floating point operation and yet another is finishing a store to memory. When an interrupt or exception occurred on the 88000, the pipeline operation was suspended, and the operating system kernel was required to save and restore the entire state of the pipeline to preserve transparency.

Most modern processors with deep execution pipelines, such as the x86, instead provide *precise interrupts*: in hardware, all instructions that occur before the interrupt or exception, according to the program execution, are completed by the hardware before the interrupt handler is invoked. Any instruction is annulled if it occurs in the program after the interrupt or exception, even if the instruction is in progress when the processor detects the exception.

To give a concrete example of how such "carefully crafted" code works, we now describe one way to implement interrupt-triggered context switch on the x86 architecture. Different operating systems on the x86 follow this basic approach, though details differ. Similarly, different architectures handle the same types of issues, but they may do so with different hardware support.

First, a bit of background on the x86 architecture. The x86 is segmented, and so pointers come in two parts: a segment, such as code, data or stack, and an offset within that segment. The current user-level instruction is based on a combination of the code segment (cs register plus the instruction pointer eip). Likewise, the current stack position is based on the stack

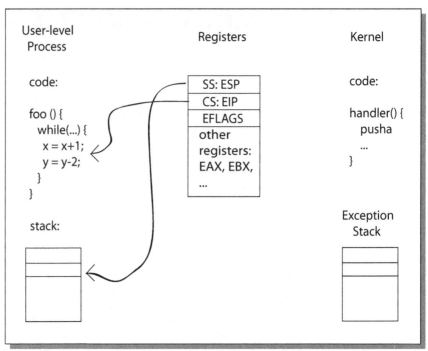

Figure 2.10: State of the system before an interrupt handler is invoked on the x86 architecture. The program counter and stack point to locations in the user process.

segment ss and the stack pointer within the stack segment esp. The current privilege level is stored as the low order bits in the cs register, rather than the processor status word eflags. The eflags register has condition codes that are modified as a by-product of executing instructions; the eflags register also has other flags that control the processor's behavior such as whether interrupts are masked or not.

When a user-level process is running, the current state of the processor, stack, and kernel interrupt vector and kernel stack is illustrated in Figure 2.10. When an exception or system call trap occurs, the hardware carefully saves a small amount of the interrupted thread state, as illustrated in Figure 2.11:

1. **Save three key values.** The hardware saves the value of the stack pointer (the x86 esp and ss registers), the execution flags (the x86 eflags register), and the instruction pointer (the x86 eip and cs registers) to internal, temporary hardware registers.

2. **Switch onto the kernel exception stack.** The hardware then switches the stack pointer to the base of the kernel exception stack, specified in a special hardware register.

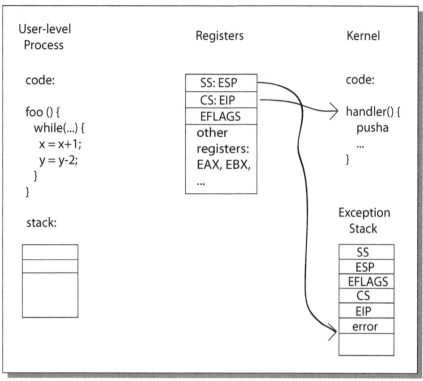

Figure 2.11: State of the system after the hardware has jumped to the interrupt handler on the x86 architecture. The hardware saves the user context on the kernel interrupt stack, and changes the program counter and stack to point to locations in kernel memory.

3. **Push the three key values onto the new stack.** The hardware then stores the internally saved values onto the stack.

4. **Optionally save error code.** Certain types of exceptions such as page faults generate an error code to provide more information about the event; for these exceptions, the hardware pushes this code as the last item on the stack. For other types of events, the software interrupt handler typically pushes a dummy value onto the stack so that the stack format is identical in both cases.

5. **Invoke the interrupt handler.** Finally, the hardware changes the program counter to the address of the interrupt handler procedure, specified via a special register in the processor that is accessible only to the kernel. This register contains a pointer to an array of exception handler addresses in memory. The type of interrupt is mapped to an index in this array, and the program counter is set to the value at this index.

Notice that changing the program counter to start of the interrupt handler means that the next thing that happens is that the interrupt handler software begins to run.

The first thing the handler needs to do is save the rest of the interrupted process's state—it needs to save the other registers before it changes them! So, the handler pushes the rest of the registers, including the current stack pointer, onto the stack. The x86 pushad instruction, which pushes the contents of all general purpose integer registers onto the stack, is convenient here.

As Figure 2.12 indicates, at this point the kernel's exception stack holds (1) the stack pointer, execution flags, and program counter saved by the hardware, (2) an error code or dummy value, and (3) a copy of all of the general registers (including the stack pointer but not the instruction pointer or eflags register) as they were after the hardware pushed the stack pointer, execution flags, and program counter onto the exception stack.

Once the handler has saved the interrupted thread's state to the stack, it is free to use the registers as it pleases, and it can also push additional items onto the stack. So, the handler can now do whatever work it needs to do.

When the handler completes, it can resume the interrupted process. To do this, the handler pops all of the registers saved by the software from the stack, thereby restoring all registers except the execution flags, program counter, and stack pointer (which was changed by the hardware when the hardware pushed the execution flags and program counter onto the stack.) For the x86 instruction set, the popad instruction is commonly used. The handler also pops the error value off the stack

Finally, the handler executes the x86 iret instruction to pop the program counter, execution flags, and stack pointer from the kernel's exception stack stack into their respective registers.

Thus, the interrupted thread's state has been restored to exactly what it was before the interrupt, and it continues execution, as if nothing happened.

A small but important detail occurs when the operating system returns from an exception, where the instruction is emulated by the kernel, e.g., for emulating floating point hardware. If we return back to the instruction that caused the exception, another exception will instantly recur! To prevent an infinite loop, the exception handler modifies the program counter stored at the base on the stack to point to the instruction immediately after the one causing the mode switch. The iret instruction will then return to the user process at the correct location.

In the case of a system call trap, the hardware does the increment for us — the program counter for the instruction after the trap is saved on the kernel's interrupt stack.

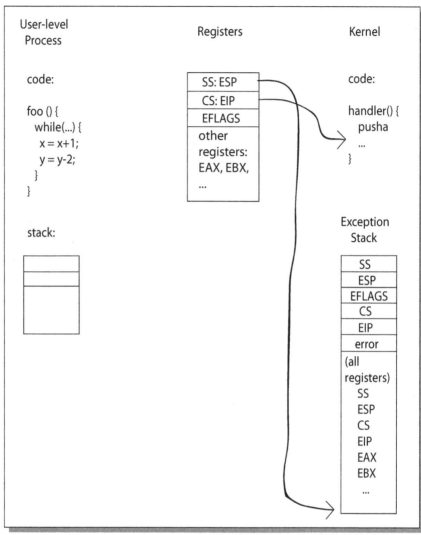

Figure 2.12: State of the system after the interrupt handler has started executing on the x86 architecture. The first thing the handler does is to save the current state of the processor registers, as the handler may overwrite them.

System calls

The operating system kernel constructs a restricted environment for process execution to limit the consequences of erroneous and malicious programs on the reliability of the rest of the computer system. Any time a process needs to do anything that operates outside of its protection domain, such as create a new process, read from the keyboard, or write a disk block, the process must ask the operating system to do the action on its behalf, via a system call.

System calls provide the illusion that the operating system kernel is simply a set of library routines available for use by user programs. To the user program, there are a set of system call procedures, each with arguments and return values, that can be called like any other routine. The user program need not concern itself with how the operating system implements the system call.

This requires us to define a *calling convention* for naming system calls, passing arguments, and receiving return values across the user/kernel boundary. Any convenient calling convention will do, such as putting arguments on the user stack, passing them in registers, and so forth. Typically, the operating system defines a common convention that is used by both compilers and the operating system kernel.

Once the arguments are in the right format, the user level program can issue a system call by executing the trap instruction to transfer control to the operating system kernel, as described above. System calls share much of the same mechanism for switching between user and kernel mode as interrupts and exceptions. In fact, one frequently used Intel x86 instruction to trap into the kernel on a system call is called int, for "software interrupt."

Inside the operating system kernel there is a procedure to implement each system call. This procedure is exactly as if the call was made from within the kernel with one notable exception. The kernel must implement its system calls in a way that protects itself from all errors and attacks that might be launched by the misuse of the interface. Of course, most applications will use the interface correctly! But we do not want an error in an application program to crash the kernel, and we definitely do not want a computer virus to be able to use the system call interface to be able to take over control of the kernel. One can think of this as an extreme version of defensive programming: the kernel should assume the parameters to each system call are intentionally designed to be as malicious as possible.

stub   A short procedure that mediates between two execution contexts, often paired with another stub in the other context, e.g., between two processes using interprocess communication or between the user program and the kernel. We meld these two views — the user program calling the system call, and the kernel implementing the system call — with a pair of stubs. A *pair of stubs* are two short procedures that mediate between two environments, in this case between the user program and the kernel. As we will see later, stubs are also used to mediate procedure calls between computers in a distributed system.

The system call stubs are illustrated in Figure 2.13. The user program calls the user stub in the normal way, oblivious to the fact the implementation of the procedure is in fact in the kernel. The user stub calls the trap instruction. The hardware transfers control to the kernel, vectoring to the system call handler. The handler acts as a stub on the kernel side, calling the implementation of the routine in the kernel. The return path follows

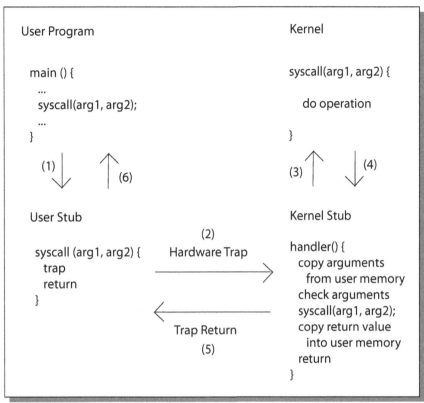

Figure 2.13: Stubs mediate between the user-level caller and the kernel implementation of system calls. The user process makes a normal procedure call to a stub linked with the process. The stub executes the trap instruction. This transfers control to the kernel trap handler. The trap handler copies and checks its arguments and then calls a routine to do the operation. Once the operation completes, the code returns to the trap handler, which returns to the user stub, which returns to the user-level caller.

the reverse sequence.

We illustrate the behavior of the user-level stub in Figure 2.14 for the x86. For each system call, the operating system provides a library routine for that system call. This library routine takes its arguments, reformats them according to the calling convention defined by the operating system kernel, and executes a trap instruction. When the kernel returns, the stub can return the result provided by the kernel. Of course, the user program need not use the library routine — it is free to trap directly to the kernel; in turn, the kernel needs to protect itself from misbehaving programs that do not format arguments correctly.

The system call calling convention is arbitrary, so here we pass arguments on the user stack, with a code indicating the type of system call in

```
// we assume the caller put the filename onto the stack already,
// using the standard calling convention for the x86

open:
    movl #SysCallOpen, %eax // put the code for the system call we want into %eax

    int #TrapCode // trap into the kernel

    ret          // return to the caller; the kernel puts return value in %eax
```

Figure 2.14: User level library stub for the file system open system call. SysCallOpen is the code for the system call we want the kernel to run. TrapCode is the hardware code for the system call handler entry in the kernel interrupt vector table.

the register %eax. The return value comes back in %eax so there is no work to do on the return.

The int instruction operates as described earlier, saving the program counter, stack pointer, and eflags on the kernel stack, before calling the system call handler through the interrupt vector. Depending on the calling convention, the kernel handler saves any additional registers that must be preserved across function calls. It then examines the system call integer code in %eax, verifies that it is a legal opcode, and calls the correct stub for that system call.

The kernel stub has four tasks:

- **Locate system call arguments.** Unlike a regular procedure, the arguments to a system call are stored in user memory. In the example code above, they were stored on the process's user stack. Of course, the user stack pointer could be corrupted! Even if it is valid, it is a virtual address, not a physical address. Any address provided by a user program to a system call must be checked (to verify it is a legal address within the user domain) and converted to a physical address that the kernel can use to access the memory. In the example above, the pointer to the string representing the file name is stored on the stack, so both the stack address must be (checked and) translated, and then the value of the string pointer stored on the stack must be (checked and) translated.

- **Validate parameters.** The operating system kernel must also protect itself against malicious or accidental errors in the format or content of its arguments. A file name will normally be a zero-terminated string, but the kernel cannot trust the user code to always work correctly. The file name may be corrupted, it may point to memory outside the application's region, it may start inside the application's memory region but extend beyond it, the application may not have permission to access the file, and so forth. If an error is detected, the kernel returns to the user program with an error; otherwise the kernel performs the operation on behalf of the application.

- **Copy before check.** In most cases, the kernel copies system call parameters into kernel memory before performing the necessary checks. The difficulty arises if the application can modify the user memory holding a system call parameter (such as a file name), *after* the check is performed, but *before* the parameter is used in the actual implementation of the routine. This is called a *Time of Check vs. Time of Use* (TOCTOU) attack. This is not a new attack — the first occurrence dates from the mid-1960's. While it might seem that a process necessarily stops whenever it does a system call, this can be misleading. For example, if one process shares a memory region with another process, then the two processes working together can launch the TOCTOU attack. Similarly, on a multiprocessor, one processor can launch the TOCTOU attack while the other processor traps into the kernel with the system call.

Time of Check vs. Time of Use attack

- **Copy back any results.** If the system call reads data into a buffer in user memory, the stub needs to copy the data from the kernel buffer into user memory so that the program can access it. Again, the kernel must first check the user address and convert it to a kernel address before use.

Putting this together, the kernel stub for the system call "open" is given in Figure 2.15.

When the system call completes, it returns back to the stub which returns back to the system call handler. At this point, the stub takes steps to pass the results of the system call back to the user process. In the example, the return value fits in a register so the stub can return directly; in the case of a file read, the stub would need to ensure that the data is placed in the buffer pointed to by the user, that is, in the user program's memory.

In turn, the system call handler pops any saved registers (except %eax) and uses the iret instruction to return back to the user stub immediately after the trap, allowing the user stub to return to the user program.

Starting a new process

So far, we have described how we transfer control from a user-level process to the kernel on an interrupt, exception, or system call, and how the kernel resumes execution at user-level when done.

With that context, we can complete the description of how we start running at user-level in the first place. The mechanism is straightforward, if a bit backhanded. The kernel needs to:

- Allocate and initialize the process control block.

```
int KernelStub_Open() {
    char *localCopy[MaxFileNameSize + 1];

// check that the stack pointer is valid and that the arguments are
// stored at valid addresses

    if (!validUserAddressRange(userStackPointer,
            userStackPointer + size of arguments on stack))
        return error_code;

// fetch pointer to file name from user stack, and convert to a kernel pointer

    filename = VirtualToKernel(userStackPointer);

// Make a local copy of the filename, inside the OS.  This prevents the
// application from changing the name surreptitiously, after the check,
// but before the read!

// The string copy needs to check each address in the string before use
// to make sure every address in the string is valid

// The string copy terminates after it copies MaxFileNameSize
// to ensure we don't overwrite our internal buffer

    if (!VirtualToKernelStringCopy(filename, localCopy,
            MaxFileNameSize))
        return error_code;

// let's make sure our local copy is null terminated

    localCopy[MaxFileNameSize] = 0;

// we can now check if the user is permitted to access this file

    if (!UserFileAccessPermitted(localCopy, current_process)
        return error_code;

// finally we can call the actual routine to open the file
// this returns a file handle on success, or an error_code on failure

    return Kernel_Open(localCopy);
}
```

Figure 2.15: Stub routine for the open system call inside the kernel. The kernel must validate all parameters to a system call before it uses them.

- Allocate memory for the process.

- Copy the program from disk into the newly allocated memory.

- Allocates a user-level stack for user-level execution.

- Allocate a kernel-level stack for handling system calls, interrupts and exceptions.

To start the program running, we need two additional steps:

- **Copy arguments into user memory.** When starting a program, the user sometimes gives it arguments, much like calling a procedure. For example, when you click on a file icon in MacOS or Windows, the window manager asks the kernel to start the application associated with the file, passing it the file name to open. The system call to create a process then copies the file name from the memory of the window manager process to a special region of memory in the new process. By convention, arguments to a process are typically copied to the base of the user-level stack, and the user's stack pointer is incremented so those addresses are not overwritten when the program starts running.

- **Transfer control to user-mode.** When we start a new process, there is no saved state to restore. While we could special-case the code to transfer to a new process, most operating systems re-use the same code to exit the kernel for starting a new process and for returning from a system call. When we create the new process, we allocate it a kernel stack, and we reserve room at the bottom of the kernel stack for the initial values of its user-space registers, program counter, stack pointer, and processor status word. To start the new program, we can then switch to the new stack and jump to the end of the interrupt handler. When the handler executes popad and iret, the processor "returns" to the start of the user program.

Finally, although you can think of a user program as starting with a call to main, in fact the compiler inserts one level of indirection. It generates a stub, at the location within the process's memory where the kernel will jump on process start. The stub's job is to call main and then if main returns, calls exit. Without this, a user program that returned from main would try to pop the return program counter from main, and since there wasn't any such address on the stack, the processor would start executing random code. exit() is a system call that terminates the process.

```
start(arg1, arg2) {
    main(arg1, arg2);    // call user's main
    exit();              // if main returns, call exit
}
```

Upcalls

We can use system calls for most of the communication between applications and the operating system kernel. When a program needs to request some protected operation, it can trap to ask the kernel to perform the operation on its behalf. Likewise, if there is data inside the kernel that the application needs, the program can simply perform a system call to retrieve it.

If we want to allow applications to be able to implement operating system-like functionality, we need something more. For many of the reasons that operating system kernels need interrupt-based event delivery, applications can also benefit from being told when some event that deserves its immediate attention has occurred. Throughout this book, we will see this pattern repeatedly: the need to *virtualize* some part of the operating system kernel, so that applications can behave more like operating systems. **upcall** We call virtualized interrupts and exceptions *upcalls*. In UNIX, they are called *signals*, and in Windows they are called *asynchronous events*.

Here are some cases where immediate event delivery with upcalls are useful:

- **Preemptive user-level thread package.** Just as the operating system kernel multiplexes processes onto a processor, an application may want to multiplex its tasks, or threads, onto a process. A user-level thread package can assume all of its tasks run to completion or at least cooperatively yield the processor from time to time, but another approach is to to use a periodic timer upcall as a trigger to switch tasks. This is helpful to share the processor more evenly among user-level tasks. It is also helpful for stopping a runaway task, e.g., if the application needs to run third party code, such as when a web browser executes an embedded web page script.

- **Asynchronous I/O notification.** A system call is designed to wait until the requested operation is complete and then return. What if the process has other work it could have done in the meantime? One approach is *asynchronous I/O*: a system call starts the request and **asynchronous I/O** returns immediately; later on, the application can poll the kernel for I/O completion, or a separate notification can be sent via an upcall to the application when the I/O completes.

- **Interprocess communication.** Most interprocess communication can be handled with system calls — one process writes data, while the other reads it sometime later. A kernel upcall is needed if a process generates an event that needs the instant attention of another process. As an example, UNIX will send an upcall to notify a process when the debugger wants to suspend or resume the process. Another use is for logout — to notify applications that they should save file data and cleanly terminate.

- **User-level exception handling.** Earlier, we described a mechanism where hardware exceptions, such as divide by zero errors, are handled by the operating system kernel. However, many applications have their own exception handling routines, e.g., to ensure that files

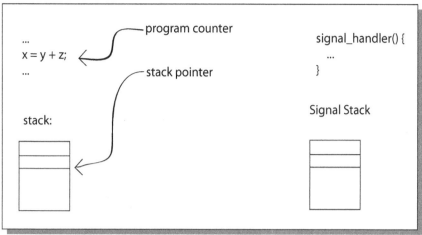

Figure 2.16: The state of the user program and signal handler before a UNIX signal. UNIX signals behave analogously to hardware exceptions, but at user-level.

are saved before the application shuts down, or in some cases, to terminate an offending script, while the rest of the application continues to work. For this, the operating system needs to inform the application when it receives an exception, so the application runtime, rather than the kernel, handles the event.

- **User-level resource allocation policy.** One of the tasks of an operating system is resource allocation — deciding which users or which processes get how much CPU time, how much memory, and so forth. In turn, many applications are resource adaptive — able to optimize their behavior to differing amounts of CPU time or memory. An example is a garbage collected system like the Java runtime. Within limits, a Java process can adapt to different amounts of available memory by changing the frequency of how often it runs its garbage collector. The more memory, the less time Java needs to run its collector, speeding up execution. This only works if the operating system somehow is able to inform the process when its allocation needs to change, e.g., because some other process needs more memory or less at the moment.

We should note that upcalls from kernels to user processes are not always needed. Many applications are more simply structured around an event loop that polls for events, and then processes each event in turn. In this model, the kernel can pass data to the process by sending it events, provided they do not need to be handled immediately. In fact, until recently, Windows lacked support for the immediate delivery of upcalls to user-level programs.

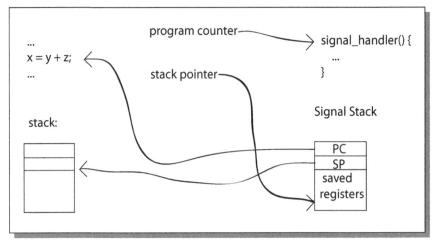

Figure 2.17: The state of the user program and signal handler during a UNIX signal. The signal stack stores the state of the hardware registers at the point where the process was interrupted, with room for the signal handler to execute on the signal stack.

We next describe UNIX signals as a concrete example of kernel support for upcalls. As shown in Figure 2.16 and Figure 2.17, most of the features in UNIX signals have a direct analogue with hardware interrupts:

- **Types of signals.** In place of hardware-defined interrupts and exceptions, the kernel defines a limited number of types of signals that can be received by a process.

- **Handlers.** Each process defines its own handlers for each signal type, much as the kernel defines its own interrupt vector table. If a process does not define a handler for a specific signal, then the kernel calls a default handler instead.

- **Signal stack.** Applications have the option to run UNIX signal handlers either on the process's normal execution stack or on a special signal stack allocated by the user process in user memory. Running signal handlers on the normal stack can reduce the flexibility of the signal handler in manipulating the stack, e.g., to cause a language-level exception to be raised.

- **Signal masking.** A UNIX signal handler automatically masks further delivery of that type of signal until the handler returns. The program can mask other signals, either all together or individually, as needed.

- **Processor state.** The kernel provides the UNIX signal handler a data structure containing the saved state of the program counter, stack pointer, and general purpose registers when the program was interrupted. Normally, when the handler returns, the kernel reloads the saved state back into the processor to resume execution of the program. However, the handler can also modify the state to be restored, e.g., if it wants to switch to another user-level task.

The mechanism for delivering UNIX signals to user processes requires only a small modification to what we have already described for transferring control across the kernel-user boundary. For example, on a timer interrupt, the hardware and the kernel interrupt handler save the state of the user-level computation. To deliver the timer interrupt to user-level, the kernel copies that saved state to a user-level buffer, resets the saved state to point to the signal handler and signal stack, and then exits the kernel handler. The reti instruction will then resume execution at the signal handler, rather than the original program counter. When the signal handler returns, these steps are unwound: the processor state is copied back from the signal handler into kernel memory, and the reti then returns back to the original computation.

Exercises

5. Define three styles of switching from user-mode to kernel-mode, and four styles of switching from kernel-mode to user-mode.

6. A typical hardware architecture provides an instruction called return from interrupt, abbreviated by something like iret. This instruction switches the mode of operation from kernel-mode to user-mode. This instruction is usually only available while the machine is running in kernel-mode.

   a. Explain where in the operating system this instruction would be used.

   b. Explain what happens if an application program executes this instruction.

7. A hardware designer argues that there are enough transistors on the chip to provide 1024 integer registers and 512 floating point registers, so that the compiler almost never needs to store anything on the stack. You have been invited as the operating system guru to give an opinion on the new design.

   a. What is the effect of having such a large number of registers on the operating system?

   b. What additional hardware features you would recommend adding to the design above?

> c. What happens if the hardware designer also wants to add a 16-station pipeline into the CPU, with precise exceptions. How would that affect the user-kernel switching overhead?

2.4 | Case Study: Booting an operating system kernel

When a computer initially starts, it sets the machine's program counter to start executing at a pre-determined position in memory. As the computer has not started running at this point, the initial machine instructions must be ready to be fetched and executed immediately when the power is turned on. For this, systems typically use a special read-only hardware **Boot ROM** memory (*Boot ROM*) to store these boot instructions. On most x86 personal computers, the boot program is called the BIOS, for "Basic Input/Output System".

What does the BIOS need to do? We could try to store the machine instructions for the entire operating system in ROM, but this has several drawbacks. The most significant problem is that this would make the operating system difficult to update. The instructions stored in ROM are fixed at the time the computer is manufactured and (except in rare cases) never changed. If an error occurs while the BIOS is being updated, the machine can be left in a permanently unusable state — unable to boot and unable to complete the update of the BIOS.

By contrast, operating systems are updated quite frequently, as bugs and security vulnerabilities are discovered and fixed. ROM storage is also relatively slow and expensive.

Instead, the BIOS provides a level of indirection, as illustrated in Figure 2.18. The BIOS reads a fixed size block of bytes from a fixed position on disk (or flash RAM) into a fixed position in memory. This block of bytes is **bootloader** called the *bootloader*. Once the BIOS has copied the bootloader into memory, it then jumps to the first instruction in the block. On some newer machines, the BIOS also checks that the bootloader has not been corrupted by a virus. (Needless to say, if a virus is able to overwrite the bootloader and get the BIOS to jump to it, the virus can then do whatever it wants with the machine.) As a check, the bootloader is stored with a cryptographic signature. A *cryptographic signature* is a hash function of the bytes in a file, such that it **cryptographic** is computationally intractable for an attacker to create a different file that **signature** matches the signature of the true file. The BIOS checks the signature before jumping to the code, verifying its authenticity.

The bootloader in turn loads the actual operating system kernel into memory, and jumps to it. Again, the bootloader can check the cryptographic signature of the operating system to verify that it has not been corrupted by a virus. The operating system kernel executable image is usually stored in

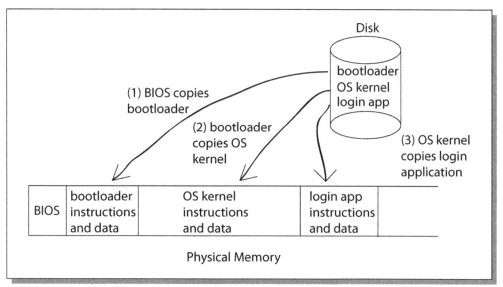

Figure 2.18: The boot ROM copies the bootloader image from disk into memory, and the bootloader copies the operating system kernel image from disk into memory.

the file system. Thus, to find the bootloader, the BIOS needs to know how to read a block of raw bytes from disk. The bootloader needs to know how to read bytes from the file system to find and read the operating system image.

When the operating system kernel starts running, it can initialize its data structures, including setting up the interrupt table to point to the various interrupt, exception and system call handlers. The kernel then starts the first process, typically the user login page. To run this process, the operating system reads the code for the login program from where it is stored on disk, and jumps to the first instruction in the program, using the start process procedure described above to safely transition control to user-level. The login process in turn can trap into the kernel using a system call whenever it needs the kernel's services, e.g., to render the login prompt on the screen. We will discuss what system calls are needed for processes to do useful work in the next chapter.

2.5 | Case Study: Virtual machines

Some operating system kernels provide the abstraction of an entire virtual machine at user-level. How do interrupts, exceptions, and system calls work in this context? To avoid confusion when discussing virtual machines, we need to remind you of some terminology we introduced in Chapter 1. The operating system providing the virtual machine abstraction is called

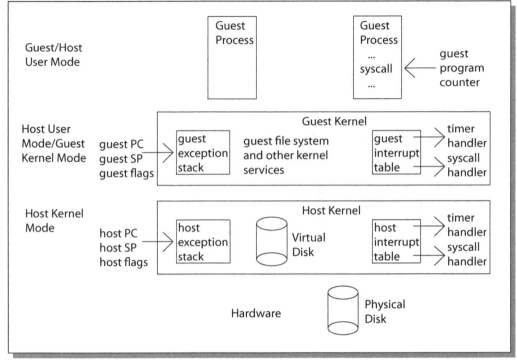

Figure 2.19: Emulation of user/kernel mode transfer for processes running inside a virtual machine. Both the guest kernel and the host kernel have their own copy of an interrupt vector table and interrupt stack.

host operating system

guest operating system

the *host operating system*. The operating system running inside the virtual machine is called the *guest operating system*.

The guest operating system needs to be able to do everything a real operating system would do. For example, to provide a guest disk, the host operating system simulates a virtual disk as a file on the physical disk. To provide network access to the guest operating system, the host operating system simulates a virtual network using physical network packets. Likewise, the host operating system needs to manage memory to provide the illusion that the guest operating system is managing its own memory protection, even though it is running with virtual addresses. We will discuss address translation for virtual machines in more detail in a later chapter.

Here we focus on how the host operating system manages the control transfer between processes running on the guest operating system and the guest OS itself. During boot, the host operating system initializes its interrupt table to point to its own interrupt handlers in the host kernel memory region. When the host operating system starts the virtual machine, the guest operating system starts running as if it is being booted:

- The host operating system loads the guest bootloader from the virtual disk and starts it running.

- The guest bootloader loads the guest operating operating system from the virtual disk into memory and starts it running.

- The guest operating system then initializes its own interrupt tables to point to the interrupt handlers within the guest kernel.

- The guest operating system loads a process from the virtual disk into memory.

- To start a process, the guest operating system issues instructions to resume execution at user-level, e.g., using reti on the x86. As changing the privilege level is a privileged operation, this instruction will trap into the host operating system kernel.

- The host operating system simulates the requested mode switch as if the processor had directly executed it, restoring the program counter, stack pointer, and processor status word exactly as the guest operating system had intended. Note that the host operating system needs to protect itself from bugs in the guest operating system, and so it also needs to check the validity of the mode switch — e.g., that the guest operating system is not surreptitiously attempting to get the host kernel to "switch" to an arbitrary point in the kernel code.

Next, consider what happens when the guest user process does a system call, illustrated in Figure 2.19. To the hardware, there is only one kernel, the host operating system. Thus, the trap instruction will trap into the host kernel's system call handler. Of course, the system call was not for the host! Rather, the host kernel simulates what would have happened had the system call instruction occurred on real hardware running the guest operating system:

- The host kernel saves the instruction counter, processor status register, and user stack pointer in the exception stack of the guest operating system.

- The host kernel transfers control to the guest kernel at the beginning of the interrupt handler, but with the guest kernel running with user-mode privilege.

- The guest kernel performs the system call.

- When the guest kernel attempts to return from the system call back to user-level, this will cause a privilege exception, dropping back into the host operating system kernel.

- The host kernel can then restore the state of the user process, running at user level, as if the guest operating system had been able to return there directly.

Exceptions are handled similarly, with one caveat. Some exceptions generated by the virtual machine are due to the user process; these are forwarded to the guest kernel for handling. Other exceptions are generated by the guest kernel itself (e.g., when it tries to execute privileged instructions); these must be handled by the host kernel. Thus, the host kernel needs to keep track of whether the virtual machine is executing in virtual user mode or virtual kernel mode.

Hardware interrupts are vectored by the hardware to the host kernel. Special handling is needed for time: time can elapse in the host without elapsing in the guest. When a timer interrupt occurs, it may be that enough virtual time has passed that the guest kernel is due a timer interrupt; in that case, the host kernel returns from the interrupt to the interrupt handler for the guest kernel. The guest kernel may in turn switch guest processes; its return from interrupt will cause a privilege exception, returning back to the host kernel, which can then resume the correct guest process.

Handling input/output interrupts is even simpler, as the simulation of the virtual device does not need to be anything like a real device. When the guest kernel makes a request to a virtual disk, it writes instructions to the buffer descriptor ring for the disk device; the host kernel will need to translate these instructions into operations on the virtual disk. The host kernel can simulate the disk request however it likes — e.g., through regular file reads and writes, copied into the guest kernel memory as if there was true DMA hardware. The guest kernel will expect to receive an interrupt when the virtual disk completes its work; this can be triggered by the timer interrupt as described above, but vectored to the guest disk interrupt handler instead of the guest timer interrupt handler.

Exercises

8. Virtualization uses a hypervisor running in privileged mode to create a virtual machine that runs in unprivileged mode. Then, unmodified guest operating systems can run in the virtual machine. The hypervisor can provide the illusion that each guest operating system is running on its own machine in privileged mode.

   Early versions of the x86 architecture (pre-2006) were not *completely virtualizable* – these system could not guarantee to run unmodified guest operating systems properly. One problem was the popf "pop flags" instruction. When popf was run in privileged mode, it could change both the ALU flags (e.g., ZF) and the systems flags (e.g., IF, which controls interrupt delivery), and when popf was run in unprivileged mode, it could change just the ALU flags.

   Why do instructions like popf prevent transparent virtualization of the (old) x86 architecture?

   How would you change the (old) x86 hardware to fix this problem?

Hardware support for operating systems

In this chapter, we have described a number of hardware mechanisms to support operating systems:

- Privilege levels: user and kernel
- Privileged instructions: instructions available only in kernel mode
- Memory translation: to prevent user programs from accessing kernel data structures, and to aid in memory management
- Exceptions: trap to the kernel on a privilege violation or other unexpected event
- Timer interrupts: return control to the kernel on time expiration
- Device interrupts: return control to the kernel to signal I/O completion
- Interprocessor interrupts: cause another processor to return control to the kernel
- System calls: trap to the kernel to perform a privileged action on behalf of a user program
- Return from interrupt: switch from kernel-mode to user-mode, to a specific location in a user program
- Boot ROM: fixed code to load startup routines from disk into memory

To support threads, we will need one additional mechanism, described in a later chapter:

- Atomic instructions: instructions to atomically read and modify a memory location, used to implement synchronization in multithreaded programs

---

2.6 | Conclusion and future directions

The process concept – the ability to execute arbitrary user programs with restricted rights – has been remarkably successful. With the exception of devices that run only a single application at a time (such as embedded systems and game consoles), every commercially successful operating system started in the past two decades has provided process isolation and several existing systems have switched over.

The reason for this success is obvious. Without process isolation, computer systems would be much more fragile and less secure. As recently as a decade ago, it was common for personal computers to crash on a daily basis. Today, it is not unusual for laptops to remain working for weeks at a time without rebooting. This has occurred even though the operating system and application software on these systems has become more complex.

While some of the improvement is due to factors such as better hardware reliability and automated bug tracking, process isolation has been a key technology in constructing more reliable systems software.

Process isolation is also essential to building more secure computer systems. Without isolation, computer users would be forced to trust everything loaded onto the computer — not just the operating system code, but every application installed on the system. In practice, however, complete process isolation is still more of an aspiration than a reality. Most operating systems are vulnerable to malicious applications, because the attacker can exploit any vulnerability in the implementation. Although keeping your system up to date with the latest patches provides some level of defense, it is still inadvisable to download and install untrusted software off the web.

In the future, we are likely to see three complementary trends:

- **Operating system support for fine-grained protection.** Process isolation is evolving to be more flexible and fine-grained, to reflect different levels of trust in different applications. Even if the operating system is successfully hardened against rogue applications, it is typical for an application invoked by a user to have the permissions of that user. In other words, a virus masquerading as a screen saver does not need to compromise the operating system to steal or corrupt that user's data. Smartphone operating systems have been the first to add these types of controls — to prevent certain applications without a "need to know" from accessing sensitive information, such as the smartphone's location or the list of frequently called telephone numbers.

- **Operating system support for application-layer sandboxing.** Increasingly, many applications are becoming mini-operating systems in their own right, capable of safely executing third party software to extend and improve the user experience. Scripts embedded in web pages have become increasingly sophisticated; web browsers need to be able to efficiently and completely isolate these scripts so that they cannot steal the user's data or corrupt the browser. Other applications such as databases and desktop publishing systems are also moving in the direction of needing application-layer sandboxing. Google's NativeClient and Microsoft's AppDomains are two example systems that provide general-purpose safe execution of third party code at the user-level.

- **Hardware support for virtualization.** Virtual machines provide an extra layer of protection beneath the operating system. Even if a malicious process run by a guest operating system on a virtual machine is able to corrupt the kernel, its impact will be limited to just that virtual machine. Below the virtual machine interface, the host operating system needs to provide isolation between different virtual machines;

this is much easier in practice because the virtual machine interface is much simpler than the operating system kernel's system call interface. For example, in a data center, virtual machines provide users the flexibility to run any application, without compromising the data center operation.

For this to be practical, processor architectures are being re-designed to reduce the cost of running a virtual machine. For example, on some new processors, guest operating systems can directly handle their own system calls, interrupts and exceptions, without those events needing to be mediated by the host operating system implementing the virtual machine. Likewise, I/O devices are being re-designed to do direct transfers to and from the guest operating system, without the need to go through the host kernel.

Exercises

For convenience, the exercises from the body of the chapter are repeated here, along with several additional problems.

1. We mentioned that for the "Hello world" program, the kernel must copy the string from the user program into the screen memory. Why must the screen's buffer memory be protected? Explain what might happen if a (malicious) application could alter any pixel on the screen, not just those within its own window.

2. For each of the three mechanisms for supporting dual mode operation — privileged instructions, memory protection, and timer interrupts — explain what might go wrong without that mechanism, assuming the system still had the other two.

3. Suppose we had a perfect object-oriented language and compiler, so that only an object's methods could access the internal data inside an object. If the operating system only ran programs written in that language, would it still need hardware memory address protection?

4. Suppose you are tasked with designing the security system for a new web browser that supports rendering web pages with embedded web page scripts. What checks would you need to ensure that executing buggy or malicious scripts could not corrupt or crash the browser?

5. Define three styles of switching from user-mode to kernel-mode, and four styles of switching from kernel-mode to user-mode.

6. A typical hardware architecture provides an instruction called return from interrupt, abbreviated by something like iret. This instruction switches the mode of operation from kernel-mode to user-mode. This instruction is usually only available while the machine is running in kernel-mode.

   a. Explain where in the operating system this instruction would be used.

   b. Explain what happens if an application program executes this instruction.

7. A hardware designer argues that there are enough transistors on the chip to provide 1024 integer registers and 512 floating point registers, so that the compiler almost never needs to store anything on the stack. You have been invited as the operating system guru to give an opinion on the new design.

    a. What is the effect of having such a large number of registers on the operating system?

    b. What additional hardware features you would recommend adding to the design above?

    c. What happens if the hardware designer also wants to add a 16-station pipeline into the CPU, with precise exceptions. How would that affect the user-kernel switching overhead?

8. Virtualization uses a hypervisor running in privileged mode to create a virtual machine that runs in unprivileged mode. Then, unmodified guest operating systems can run in the virtual machine. The hypervisor can provide the illusion that each guest operating system is running on its own machine in privileged mode.

    Early versions of the x86 architecture (pre-2006) were not *completely virtualizable* – these system could not guarantee to run unmodified guest operating systems properly. One problem was the popf "pop flags" instruction. When popf was run in privileged mode, it could change both the ALU flags (e.g., ZF) and the systems flags (e.g., IF, which controls interrupt delivery), and when popf was run in unprivileged mode, it could change just the ALU flags.

    Why do instructions like popf prevent transparent virtualization of the (old) x86 architecture?

    How would you change the (old) x86 hardware to fix this problem?

9. Which of the following components is responsible for loading the initial value in the program counter for an application program before it starts running: the compiler, the linker, the kernel, or the boot ROM?

10. We described how the operating system kernel mediates access to I/O devices for safety. Some newer I/O devices are *virtualizable* — they permit safe access from user-level programs, such as a guest operating system running in a virtual machine. Explain how you might design the hardware and software to get this to work. (Hint: For this, the device needs much of the same hardware support as the operating system kernel.)

11. System Calls vs. Procedure Calls: How much more expensive is a system call than a procedure call? Write a simple test program to compare the cost of a simple procedure call to a simple system call (getpid() is a good candidate on UNIX; see the man page.) To prevent the optimizing compiler from "optimizing out" your procedure calls, do not compile with optimization on. You should use a system call such as the UNIX gettimeofday() for time measurements. Design your code such that the measurement overhead is negligible. Also, be

aware that timer values in some systems have limited resolution (e.g., millisecond resolution).

Explain the difference (if any) between the time required by your simple procedure call and simple system call by discussing what work each call must do.

12. Suppose you have to implement an operating system on hardware that supports interrupts and exceptions but that does not have a trap instruction. Can you devise a satisfactory substitute for traps using interrupts and/or exeptions? If so, explain how. If not, explain why.

13. Suppose you have to implement an operating system on hardware that supports exceptions and traps but that does not have interrupts. Can you devise a satisfactory substitute for interrupts using exceptions and/or traps? If so, explain how. If not, explain why.

14. Explain the steps that an operating system goes through when the CPU receives an interrupt.

15. When an operating system receives a system call from a program, a switch to the operating system code occurs with the help of the hardware. In such a switch, the hardware sets the mode of operation to kernel-mode, calls the operating system trap handler at a location specified by the operating system, and allows the operating system to return back to user mode after it finishes its trap handling.

Consider the stack on which the operating system must run when it receives the system call. Should this be a different stack from the one that the application uses, or could it use the same stack as the application program? Assume that the application program is blocked while the system call runs.

16. Write a program to verify that the operating system on your computer protects itself from rogue system calls correctly. For a single system call such as file system open, try all possible illegal calls: e.g., an invalid system call number, an invalid stack pointer, an invalid pointer stored on the stack, etc. What happens?

From a programmer's point of view, the user is a peripheral that types when you issue a read request.

Peter Williams

3 The Programming Interface

The previous chapter concerned the mechanisms needed in the operating system kernel to implement the process abstraction. A process is an instance of a program — the kernel provides an efficient sandbox for executing untrusted code at user-level, running user code directly on the processor.

This chapter concerns how we choose to use the process abstraction: what functionality does the operating system provide applications, and what should go where — what functionality should be put in the operating system kernel, what should be put into user-level libraries, and how should the operating system itself be organized?

There are as many answers to this as there are operating systems. Describing the full programming interface and internal organization for even a single operating system would take an entire book. Instead, in this chapter we explore a subset of the programming interface for UNIX, the foundation of Linux, MacOS, iOS, and Android. We also touch on how the same issues are addressed in Windows.

First, we need to answer "what" — what functions do we need an operating system to provide applications?

- **Process management.** Can a program create an instance of another program? Wait for it to complete? Stop or resume another running program? Send it an asynchronous event?

- **Input/output.** How do processes communicate with devices attached to the computer and through them to the physical world? Can processes communicate with each other?

- **Thread management.** Can we create multiple activities or threads that share memory or other resources within a process? Can we stop and start threads? How do we synchronize their use of shared data structures?

- **Memory management.** Can a process ask for more (or less) memory space? Can it share the same physical memory region with other processes?

- **File systems and storage.** How does a process store the user's data persistently so that it can survive machine crashes and disk failures? How does the user name and organize their data?

- **Networking and distributed systems.** How do processes communicate with processes on other computers? How do processes on different computers coordinate their actions despite machine crashes and network problems?

- **Graphics and window management.** How does a process control pixels on its portion of the screen? How does a process make use of graphics accelerators?

- **Authentication and security.** What permissions does a user or a program have, and how are these permissions kept up to date? On what basis do we know the user (or program) is who they say they are?

In this chapter, we focus on just the first two of these topics: process management and input/output. We will cover thread management, memory management, and file systems in detail in later chapters in this book. We expect to add chapters on networks, distributed systems and security in later releases of this book. Typically, the graphics systems is covered in a specialized course on that topic, and so we do not plan to include it here.

Remarkably, we can describe a functional interface for process management and input/output with just a dozen system calls, and the rest of the system call interface with another dozen. Even more remarkably, these calls are nearly unchanged from the original UNIX design. Despite being first designed and implemented in 1973, most of these calls are still in wide use in systems today!

Second, we need to answer "where" — for any bit of functionality the operating system provides to user programs, we have several options for where it lives, illustrated in Figure 3.1:

- We can put the functionality in a user-level program. In both Windows and UNIX, for example, there is a user program for managing a user's login and another for managing a user's processes.

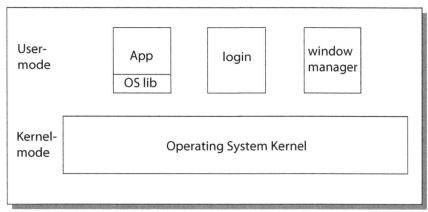

Figure 3.1: Operating system functionality can be implemented in user-level programs, in user-level libraries, in the kernel itself, or in a user-level server invoked by the kernel.

- We can put the functionality in a user-level library linked in with each application. In Windows and MacOS, user interface widgets are part of user-level libraries, included in those applications that need them.

- We can put the functionality in the operating system kernel, accessed through a system call. In Windows and UNIX, low level process management, the file system and the network stack are all implemented in the kernel.

- We can access the function through a system call, but implement the function in a standalone server process invoked by the kernel. In many systems, the window manager is implemented as a separate server process.

How do we make this choice? It is important to realize that the choice can be (mostly) transparent to both the user and the application programmer. The user wants a system that works; the programmer wants a clean, convenient interface that does the job. As long as the operating system provides that interface, where each function is implemented is up to the operating system, based on a tradeoff between flexibility, reliability, performance and safety.

- **Flexibility.** It is much easier to change operating system code that lives outside of the kernel, without breaking applications using the old interface. If we create a new version of a library, we can just link that library in with new applications, and over time convert old applications to use the new interface. However, if we need to change the system call interface, we must either simultaneously change both the kernel and all applications, or we must continue to support both

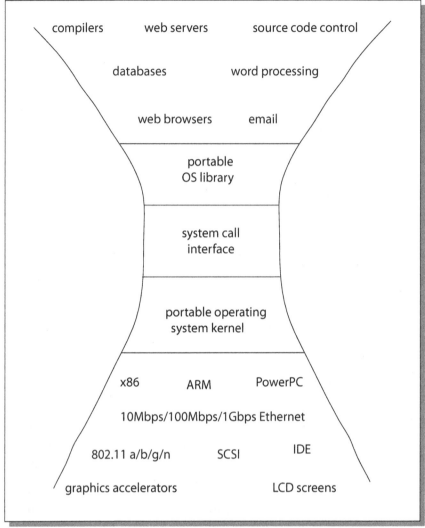

Figure 3.2: The kernel system call interface can be seen as a "thin waist", enabling independent evolution of applications and hardware.

the old and the new versions until all old applications have been converted. Since many applications may be written by third party developers, outside of the control of the operating system vendor, changing the system call interface is a huge step, often requiring coordination across many companies.

One of the key ideas in UNIX, responsible for much of its success, was to design its system call interface to be simple and powerful, so that almost all of the innovation in the system could happen in user code without changing the interface to the operating system. The

The Internet and the "thin waist"

The Internet is another example of the benefit of designing interfaces to be simple and portable. The Internet defines a packet-level protocol that can run on top of virtually any type of network hardware and can support almost any type of network application. Creating the World Wide Web required no changes to the Internet packet delivery mechanism; likewise, the introduction of wireless networks required changes in hardware devices and in the operating system, but no changes in network applications. Although the Internet's "thin waist" can sometimes lead to inefficiencies, the upside is to foster innovation in both applications and hardware by decoupling changes in one from changes in the other.

UNIX system call interface is also highly portable — the operating system could be ported to new hardware without needing to rewrite application code. As shown in Figure 3.2, the kernel can be seen as a "thin waist", enabling innovation at the application-level, and in the hardware, without requiring simultaneous changes in the other parts of the system.

- **Safety.** However, resource management and protection must be implemented in the operating system kernel, or in a specially privileged process called by the kernel. As we explained in the previous chapter, if applications can directly execute instructions on the processor, they can skip any protection code in a user-level library, so protection checks cannot be implemented at that level.

- **Reliability.** Improved reliability is another reason to keep the operating system kernel minimal. Kernel code needs the power to set up hardware devices, such as the disk, and to control protection boundaries between applications. However, kernel modules are typically not protected from one another, and so a bug in kernel code (whether sensitive or not) may corrupt user or kernel data. This has led some systems to use a philosophy of "what can be at user level, should be." An extreme version of approach is to isolate privileged, but less critical, parts of the operating system such as the file system or the microkernel   window system, from the rest of the kernel. This is called a *microkernel* design. In a microkernel, the kernel itself is kept small, and instead most of the functionality of a traditional operating system kernel is put into a set of user-level processes, or servers, accessed from user applications via interprocess communication.

- **Performance.** Finally, transferring control into the kernel is more expensive than a procedure call to a library, and transferring control to a user-level file system server via the kernel is still even more costly.

Application-level sandboxing and operating system functionality

Applications that support executing third-party code or scripts in a restricted sandbox must address many of these same questions, with the sandbox playing the role of the operating system kernel. In terms of functionality: Can the scripting code start a new instance of itself? Can it do input/output? Can it perform work in the background? Can it store data persistently, and if it can, how does it name that data? Can it communicate data over the network? How does it authenticate actions?

For example, in web browsers, HTML5 not only allows scripts to draw on the screen, communicate with servers, and save and read cookies, it also has recently added programming interfaces for offline storage and cross-document communication. The Flash media player provides scripts with the ability to do asynchronous operations, file storage, network communication, memory management, and authentication.

Just as with system calls, these interfaces must be carefully designed to be bullet-proof against malicious use. A decade ago, email viruses became widespread because scripts could be embedded in documents that were executed on opening; the programming interfaces for these scripts would allow them to discover the list of correspondents known to the current email user and to send them email, thereby propagating and expanding the virus with a single click. The more fully featured the interface, the more convenient it is for developers, and the more likely that some aspect of the interface will be abused by a hacker.

Modern processor hardware has added various support to reduce the cost of these boundary crossings, but the performance issue remains important. Microsoft Windows NT, a precursor to Windows 7, was initially designed as a microkernel, but over time much of its functionality has been migrated back into the kernel for performance reasons.

There are no easy answers! We will investigate the question of how to design the system call interface and where to place operating system functionality through case studies of UNIX and other systems:

- **Process management.** What is the system call interface for process management?

- **Input/output.** What is the system call interface for performing I/O and interprocess communication?

- **Case study: Implementing a shell.** We will illustrate these interfaces by using them to implement a user-level job control system called a *shell*.

- **Case study: Interprocess communication.** How does the communication between a client and server work?

- **Operating system structure.** Can we use the process abstraction to simplify the construction of the operating system itself and to make it more secure, more reliable, and more flexible?

3.1 | Process management

On a modern computer, when a user clicks on a file or application icon, the application starts up. How does this happen and who gets called? Of course, we could implement everything that needs to happen in the kernel — draw the icon for every item in the file system, map mouse positions to the intended icon, catch the mouse click, and start the process. In early batch processing systems, the kernel was in control by necessity. Users submitted jobs, and the operating system took it from there, instantiating the process when it was time to run the job.

A different approach is to allow user programs to create and manage their own processes. This has fostered a blizzard of innovation. Today, programs that create and manage processes include window managers, web servers, web browsers, shell command line interpreters, source code control systems, databases, compilers, and document preparation systems. We could go on, but you get the idea. If creating a process is something a process can do, then anyone can build a new version of any of these applications, without recompiling the kernel or forcing anyone else to use it.

An early motivation for user-level process management was to allow
shell   developers to write their own shell command line interpreters. A *shell* is a job control system; both Windows and UNIX have a shell. Many tasks involve a sequence of steps to do something, each of which can be its own program. With a shell, you can write down the sequence of steps, as a sequence of programs to run to do each step. Thus, you can view it as a very early version of a scripting system.

For example, to compile a C program from multiple source files, you might type:

```
cc −c sourcefile1.c
cc −c sourcefile2.c
ln −o program sourcefile1.o sourcefile2.o
```

Figure 3.3: This shell program compiles sourcefile1.c and sourcefile2.c and then links the results together into an executable program.

If we put those commands into a file, the shell reads the file and executes it, creating, in turn, a process to compile sourcefile1.c, a process to compile

User-level process management is another way of saying "there is an app for that." Instead of a single program that does everything, we can create specialized programs for each task, and mix and match what we need. The formatting system for this textbook uses over fifty separate programs.

The web is a good example of the power of composing complex applications from more specialized services. A web page does not need to do everything itself: it can mash up the results of many different web pages, and it can invoke process creation on the local server to generate part of the page. The flexibility to create processes was extremely important early on in the development of the web. HTML was initially just a way to describe the formatting for static information, but it included a way to escape to a process to, say, do a lookup in a database or to authenticate a user. Over time, HTML has added support for many different features that were first prototyped via execution by a separate process. And of course, HTML still retains the ability to execute a process for everything not supported by the standard.

sourcefile2, and a process to link them together. Once a shell script is a program, we can create other programs by combining scripts together. In fact, on UNIX, the C compiler is itself a shell program! The compiler first invokes a process to expand header include files, then a separate process to parse the output, another process to generate (text) assembly code, and yet another to convert assembly into executable machine instructions.

Windows process management

One approach to process management is to just add a system call to create a process, and other system calls for other process operations. This turns out to be simple in theory and complex in practice. In Windows, there is a routine called, unsurprisingly, CreateProcess, in simplified form below:

```
boolean CreateProcess(char *prog, char *args)
```

Figure 3.4: Simplified version of the Windows call to create a process with arguments.

parent process

child process

We call the process creator the *parent* and the process being created the *child*.

What steps does CreateProcess take? As we explained in the previous chapter, the kernel needs to:

- Create and initialize the process control block (PCB) in the kernel

- Create and initialize a new address space

```
// Start the child process
if (!CreateProcess(NULL,      // No module name (use command line)
       argv[1],               // Command line
       NULL,                  // Process handle not inheritable
       NULL,                  // Thread handle not inheritable
       FALSE,                 // Set handle inheritance to FALSE
       0,                     // No creation flags
       NULL,                  // Use parent's environment block
       NULL,                  // Use parent's starting directory
       &si,                   // Pointer to STARTUPINFO structure
       &pi )                  // Pointer to PROCESS_INFORMATION structure
)
```

Figure 3.5: Excerpt from an example of how to use the Windows CreateProcess system call. The first two arguments specify the program and its arguments; the rest concern aspects of the process runtime environment.

- Load the program prog into the address space

- Copy arguments args into memory in the address space

- Initialize the hardware context to start execution at "start"

- Inform the scheduler that the new process is ready to run

Unfortunately, there are quite a few aspects of the process that the parent might like to control, such as: its privileges, where it sends its input and output, what it should store its files, what to use as a scheduling priority, and so forth. We can't trust the child process itself to set its own privileges and priority, and it would be inconvenient to expect every application to include code for figuring out its context. So the real interface to CreateProcess is quite a bit more complicated in practice, given in Figure 3.5.

UNIX process management

UNIX takes a different approach to process management, one that is complex in theory and simple in practice. UNIX splits CreateProcess in two steps, called fork and exec, illustrated in Figure 3.6.

UNIX fork

UNIX fork creates a complete copy of the parent process, with one key exception. (We need some way to distinguish between which copy is the parent and which is the child.) The child process sets up privileges, priorities, and I/O for the program that is about to be started, e.g., by closing some files, opening others, reducing its priority if it is to run in the background, etc. Because the child runs exactly the same code as the parent, it can be trusted to set up the context for the new program correctly.

UNIX exec

Once the context is set, the child process calls *UNIX exec*. UNIX exec brings the new executable image into memory and starts it running. It may seem wasteful to make a complete copy of the parent process, just

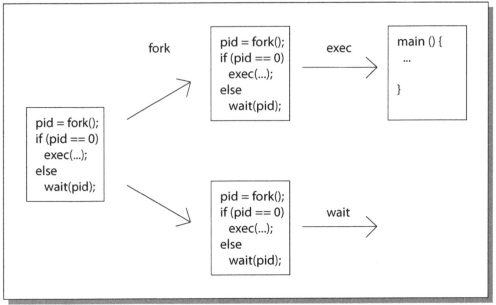

Figure 3.6: The operation of the UNIX fork and exec system calls. UNIX fork makes a copy of the parent process; UNIX exec changes the child process to run the new program.

to overwrite that copy when we bring in the new executable image into memory using exec. It turns out that fork and exec can be implemented efficiently, using a set of techniques we will describe in Chapter 8.

With this design, UNIX fork takes no arguments and returns an integer. UNIX exec takes two arguments (the name of the program to run and an array of arguments to pass to the program). This is in place of the ten parameters needed for CreateProcess. In part because of the simplicity of UNIX fork and exec, this interface has remained nearly unchanged since UNIX was designed in the early 70's. (Although the interface hasn't changed, the word fork is now a bit ambiguous. It is used for creating a new copy of a UNIX process, and in thread systems for creating a new thread. To disambiguate, we will always use the term "UNIX fork" to refer to UNIX's copy process system call.)

UNIX fork

The steps for implementing UNIX fork in the kernel are:

- Create and initialize the process control block (PCB) in the kernel

- Create a new address space

- Initialize the address space with a copy of the entire contents of the address space of the parent

```
int child_pid = fork();
if (child_pid == 0) {              // I'm the child process
    printf("I am process #%d\n", getpid());
    return 0;
} else {                           // I'm the parent process
    printf("I am parent of process #%d\n", child_pid);
    return 0;
}

Possible output:
  I am parent of process 495
  I am process 495

Another less likely but still possible output:
  I am process 456
  I am parent of process 456
```

Figure 3.7: Example UNIX code to fork a process, and some possible outputs of running the code. getpid is a system call to get the current process' ID.

- Inherit the execution context of the parent (e.g., any open files)

- Inform the scheduler that the new process is ready to run

A strange aspect of UNIX fork is that the system call returns *twice*: once to the parent and once to the child. To the parent, UNIX returns the process ID of the child; to the child, it returns 0 indicating success. Just as if you made a clone of yourself, you would need some way to tell who was the clone and who was the original, UNIX uses the return value from fork to distinguish the two copies. Some sample code to call fork is given in Figure 3.7.

If we run the program in Figure 3.7, what happens? If you have access to a UNIX system, you can try it and see for yourself. UNIX fork returns twice, once in the child, with a return value of 0, and once in the parent with a return value of the child's process ID. However, we do not know whether the parent will run next or the child. The parent had been running, and so it is likely that it will reach its print statement first. However, a timer interrupt could intervene between when the parent forks the process and when it reaches the print statement, so that the processor is reassigned to the child. Or we could be running on a multicore, where both the parent and child are running simultaneously. In either case, the child could print its output before the parent. We will talk in much more depth about the implications of different orderings of concurrent execution in the next chapter.

UNIX exec and wait

The UNIX system call exec completes the steps needed to start running a new program. UNIX exec is typically called by the child process after it has

UNIX fork and the Chrome Web browser

Although UNIX fork is normally paired with a call to exec, in some cases UNIX fork is useful on its own. A particularly interesting example is in Google's Chrome web browser. When the user clicks on a link, Chrome forks a process to fetch and render the web page at the link, in a new tab on the browser. The parent process continues to display the original referring web page, while the child process runs the same browser, but in its own address space and protection boundary. The motivation for this design is to isolate the new link, so that if the web site is infected with a virus, it won't infect the rest of the browser. Closing the infected browser tab will then remove the link and the virus from the system.

Some security researchers take this a step further. They set up their browsers and email systems to create a new *virtual machine* for every new link, running a copy of the browser in each virtual machine; even if the web site has a virus that corrupts the guest operating system running in the virtual machine, the rest of the system will remain unaffected. In this case, closing the virtual machine cleans the system of the virus.

Interestingly, on Windows, Google Chrome does not use CreateProcess to fork new copies of the browser on demand. The difficulty is that if Chrome is updated while Chrome is running, CreateProcess will create a copy of the new version, and that may not interoperate correctly with the old version. Instead, they create a pool of helper processes that wait in the background for new links to render.

returned from UNIX fork and configured the execution environment for the child. We will describe more about how this works when after we discuss UNIX pipes in the next section.

UNIX exec does the following steps:

- Load the program prog into the current address space

- Copy arguments args into memory in the address space

- Initialize the hardware context to start execution at "start"

Note that exec does not create a new process!

On the other side, often the parent process needs to pause until the child process completes, e.g., if the next step depends on the output of the previous step. In the shell example we started the chapter with, we need to wait for the two compilations to finish before it is safe to start the linker.

UNIX wait   UNIX has a system call, naturally enough called *wait*, that pauses the parent until the child finishes, crashes, or is terminated. Since the parent could have created many child processes, wait is parameterized with the process ID of the child. With wait, a shell can create a new process to perform some step of its instructions, and then pause for that step to complete before

Kernel handles and garbage collection

As we discussed in the previous chapter, when a UNIX process finishes, it calls the system call exit. Exit can release various resources associated with the process, such as the user stack, heap, and code segments. It must be careful, however, in how it garbage collects the process control block (PCB). Even though the child process has finished, if it deletes the PCB, then the parent process will be left with a dangling pointer if later on it calls UNIX wait. Of course, we don't know for sure if the parent will ever call wait, so to be safe, the PCB can only be reclaimed when both the parent and the child have finished or crashed.

Generalizing, both Windows and UNIX have various system calls that return a handle to some kernel object; these handles are used in later calls as an ID. The process ID returned by UNIX fork is used in later calls to UNIX wait; we'll see below that UNIX open returns a file descriptor that is used in other system calls. It is important to realize that these handles are *not* pointers to kernel data structures; otherwise, an erroneous user program could cause havoc in the kernel by making system calls with fake handles. Rather, they are specific to the process and checked for validity on each use.

Further, in both Windows and UNIX, handles are reference counted. Whenever the kernel returns a handle, it bumps a reference counter, and whenever the process releases a handle (or exits) the reference counter is decremented. UNIX fork sets the process ID reference count to two, one for the parent and one for the child. The underlying data structure, the PCB, is reclaimed only when the reference count goes to zero, that is, when both the parent and child terminate.

proceeding to the next step. It would be hard to build a usable shell without wait.

However, the call to wait is optional in UNIX. For example, the Chrome browser does not need to wait for its forked clones to finish. Likewise, most UNIX shells have an option to run operations in the background, signified by appending an '&' to the command line. (As with fork, the word wait is now a bit ambiguous. It is used for pausing the current UNIX process to wait for another process to complete; it is also used in thread synchronization, for waiting on a condition variable. To disambiguate, we will always use the term "UNIX wait" to refer to UNIX's wait system call. Oddly, waiting for a thread to complete is called "thread join", even though it is most analogous to UNIX wait. Windows is simpler, with a single function called "WaitForSingleObject" that can wait for process completion, thread completion, or on a condition variable.)

Finally, as we outlined in the previous chapter, UNIX provides a facility for one process to send another an instant notification, or upcall. In UNIX, the notification is sent by calling *signal*. Signals are used for terminating an application, suspending it temporarily for debugging, resuming after a suspension, timer expiration, and a host of other reasons. In the default

UNIX signal

case, where the receiving application did not specify a signal handler, the kernel implements a standard one on its behalf.

Exercises

1. Can UNIX fork return an error? Why or why not?
   Note: You can answer this question by looking at the manual page for fork, but before you do that, think about what the fork system call does. If you were designing this call, would you need to allow fork to return an error?
   Note: A manual page (or "man page") is a standard way of documenting Unix system calls and utility programs. On a Unix machine, you can access a manual page by running the man command (e.g., man fork). Another way to find manual pages is via web search (e.g., search for man fork and many of the top results will be manual pages for the fork system call.)

2. Can UNIX exec return an error? Why or why not?
   Note: You can answer this question by looking at the manual page for exec, but before you do that, think about what the exec system call does. If you were designing this call, would you need to allow it to return an error?

3. What happens if we run the following program on UNIX?
   ```
   main () {
       while (fork () >= 0)
           ;
   }
   ```

4. Explain what must happen for UNIX wait to return (successfully and) immediately.

3.2 | Input/output

Computer systems have a wide diversity of input and output devices: keyboard, mouse, disk, USB port, Ethernet, WiFi, display, hardware timer, microphone, camera, accelerometer, and GPS, to name a few.

To deal with this diversity, we could specialize the application programming interface for each device, customizing it to the device's specific characteristics. After all, a disk device is quite different from a network and both are quite different from a keyboard: a disk is addressed in fixed sized chunks, while a network sends and receives a stream of variable sized packets, and the keyboard returns individual characters as keys are pressed.

While the disk only returns data when asked, the network and keyboard provide data unprompted. Early computer systems took the approach of specializing the interface to the device, but it had a significant downside: every time a new type of hardware device is invented, the system call interface has to be upgraded to handle that device.

One of the primary innovations in UNIX was to regularize all device input and output behind a single common interface. In fact, UNIX took this one giant step further: it uses this same interface for reading and writing files and for interprocess communication. This approach was so successful that it is almost universally followed in systems today. We will sketch the interface in this section, and then in the next section, show how it can be used to build a shell.

The basic ideas in the UNIX I/O interface are:

- **Uniformity.** All device I/O, file operations, and interprocess communication use the same set of system calls: open, close, read and write.

- **Open before use.** Before an application does I/O, it must first call open on the device, file, or communication channel. This gives the operating system a chance to check access permissions and to set up any internal bookkeeping. Some devices, such as a printer, only allow one application access at a time — the open call can return an error if the device is in use.

UNIX file
descriptor
Open returns a handle to be used in later calls to read, write and close to identify the file, device or channel; this handle is somewhat misleadingly called a *file descriptor*, even when it refers to a device or channel so there is no file involved. For convenience, the UNIX shell starts applications with open file descriptors for reading and writing to the terminal.

- **Byte-oriented.** All devices, even those that transfer fixed-size blocks of data, are accessed with byte arrays. Similarly, file and communication channel access is in terms of bytes, even though we store data structures in files and send data structures across channels.

- **Kernel-buffered reads.** Stream data, such as from the network or keyboard, is stored in a kernel buffer and returned to the application on request. This allows the UNIX system call read interface to be the same for devices with streaming reads as those with block reads, such as disks and Flash memory. In both cases, if no data is available to be returned immediately, the read call blocks until it arrives, potentially giving up the processor to some other task with work to do.

- **Kernel-buffered writes.** Likewise, outgoing data is stored in a kernel buffer for transmission when the device becomes available. In the normal case, the system call write copies the data into the kernel buffer and returns immediately. This decouples the application from the device, allowing each to go at their own speed. If the application generates data faster than the device can receive it (as is common when spooling data to a printer), the write system call blocks in the kernel until there is enough room to store the new data in the buffer.

- **Explicit close.** When an application is done with the device or file, it calls close. This signals to the operating system that it can decrement the reference-count on the device, and garbage collect any unused kernel data structures.

For interprocess communication, we need a few more concepts:

UNIX pipe

- **Pipes.** A *UNIX pipe* is a kernel buffer with two file descriptors, one for writing (to put data into the pipe) and one for reading (to pull data out of the pipe), as illustrated in Figure 3.8. Data is read in exactly the same sequence it is written, but since the data is buffered, the execution of the producer and consumer can be decoupled, reducing waiting in the common case. The pipe terminates when either endpoint closes the pipe or exits.

  The Internet has a similar facility to UNIX pipes called TCP (Transmission Control Protocol). Where UNIX pipes connect processes on the same machine, TCP provides a bi-directional pipe between two processes running on different machines. In TCP, data is written as a sequence of bytes on one machine, and read out as the same sequence on the other machine. We plan to discuss the implementation of TCP in detail in a chapter to be added to the next revision of this textbook.

- **Replace file descriptor.** By manipulating the file descriptors of the child process, the shell can cause the child to read its input from, or send its output to, a file or a pipe instead of from a keyboard or to the screen. This way, the child process does not need to be aware of who is providing or consuming its I/O. The shell does this redirection using a special system call named dup2(from, to) that replaces the to file descriptor with a copy of the from file descriptor.

- **Wait for multiple reads.** For client-server computing, a server may have a pipe open to multiple client processes. Normally, read will block if there is no data to be read, and it would be inefficient for the server to poll each pipe in turn to check if there is work for it to do. The UNIX system call select(fd[], number) addresses this. Select allows the server to wait for input from any of a set of file descriptors; it returns the file descriptor that has data, but it does not read the data. Windows has an equivalent function, called WaitForMultipleObjects.

Figure 3.9 summarizes the dozen UNIX system calls discussed in this section.

Open vs. creat vs. stat

By default, the UNIX open system call returns an error if the application tries to open a file that does not exist; as an option (not shown above), a parameter can tell the kernel to instead create the file if it does not exist. Since UNIX also has system calls for creating a file (creat) and for testing whether a file exists (stat), it might seem like open could be simplified to always assume that the file already exists.

However, UNIX often runs in a multi-user, multi-application environment, and in that setting the issue of system call design can become more subtle. Suppose instead of the UNIX interface, we had completely separate functions for testing if a file exists, creating a file, and opening the file. Assuming that the user has permission to test, open, or create the file, does this code work?

```
if (!exists(file)) {     // if the file doesn't exist create it
// are we guaranteed the file doesn't exist?
    create(file);
}
// are we guaranteed the file does exist?
open(file)
```

The problem is that on a multi-user system, some other user might have created the file in between the call to test for its existence, and the call to create the file. Thus, call to create must also test the existence of the file. Likewise, some other user might have deleted the file between the call to create and the call to open. So open also needs the ability to test if the file is there, and if not to create the file (if that is the user's intent).

UNIX addresses this with an all-purpose, atomic open: test if the file exists, optionally create it if it doesn't, and then open it. Because system calls are implemented in the kernel, the operating system can make open (and all other I/O systems calls) non-interruptable with respect to other system calls. If another user tries to delete a file while the kernel is executing an open system call on the same file, the delete will be delayed until the open completes. The open will return a file descriptor that will continue to work until the application closes the file. The delete will remove the file from the file system, but the file system does not actually reclaim its disk blocks until the file is closed.

3.3 | Case Study: Implementing a shell

The dozen UNIX system calls listed above are enough to build a flexible and powerful command line shell, one that runs entirely at user-level with no special permissions. As we mentioned, the process that creates the shell is responsible for providing it an open file descriptor for reading commands for its input (e.g., from the keyboard), called *stdin* and for writing output (e.g., to the display), called *stdout*.

UNIX stdin

UNIX stdout

Figure 3.10 illustrates the code for the basic operation of a shell. The

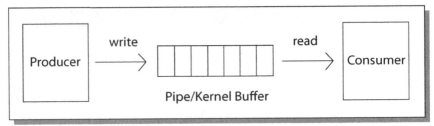

Figure 3.8: A pipe is a temporary kernel bufer connecting a process producing data with a process consuming the data.

shell reads a command line from the input, and it forks a process to execute that command. UNIX fork automatically duplicates all open file descriptors in the parent, incrementing the kernel's reference counts for those descriptors, so the input and output of the child is the same as the parent. The parent waits for the child to finish before it reads the next command to execute.

Because the commands to read and write to an open file descriptor are the same whether the file descriptor represents a keyboard, screen, file, device, or pipe, UNIX programs do not need to be aware of where their input is coming from, or where their output is going. This is helpful in a number of ways:

- **A program can be a file of commands.** Programs are normally a set of machine instructions, but on UNIX a program can be a file containing a list of commands for a shell to interpret. To disambiguate, shell programs signified in UNIX by putting "#! interpreter" as the first line of the file, where "interpreter" is the name of the shell executable.

  The UNIX C compiler is structured this way. When it is exec'ed, the kernel recognizes it as a shell file and starts the interpreter, passing it the file as input. The shell reads the file as a list of commands to invoke the pre-processor, parser, code generator and assembler in turn, exactly as if it was reading text input from the keyboard. When the last command completes, the interpreter exits to inform the kernel that the program is done.

- **A program can send its output to a file.** By changing the stdout file descriptor in the child, the shell can redirect the child's output to a file. In the standard UNIX shell, this is signified with a "greater than" symbol. Thus, "ls > tmp" lists the contents of the current directory into the file "tmp". After the fork and before the exec, the shell can replace the stdout file descriptor for the child using dup2. Because the parent has been cloned, changing stdout for the child has no effect on the parent.

Creating and managing processes	
fork()	Create a child process as a clone of the current process. Fork() returns to both the parent and child.
exec(prog, args)	Run the application "prog" in the current process.
exit()	Tell the kernel the current process is complete, and its data structures should be garbage collected.
wait(processID)	Pause until the child process has exited.
signal(processID, type)	Send an interrupt of "type" to a process.
I/O operations	
fileDescriptor = open(name)	Open a file or hardware device, specified by "name"; returns a file descriptor that can be used by other calls.
pipe(fileDescriptor[2])	Create a one-directional pipe between two processes. pipe() returns two file descriptors, one for reading and one for writing.
dup2(fromFileDesc, toFileDesc)	Replace the toFileDesc file descriptor with a copy of from-FileDesc. Used for replacing stdin/stdout in a child process before calling exec().
int read(fileDesc, buffer, size)	Read up to "size" bytes into buffer, from the device, file, or channel. read() returns the number of bytes actually read. For streaming devices this will often be less than "size". For example, a read from the keyboard device will (normally) return all of its queued bytes.
int write(fileDesc, buffer, size)	Analogous to "read", write up to "size" bytes into kernel output buffer for a device, file or channel. "write" normally returns immediately, but may stall if there is no space in the kernel buffer.
fileDescriptor = select(fileDescArray[], arraySize)	Return when any of the file descriptors in the array have data available to be read. Returns the file descriptor with data pending.
close(fileDescriptor)	Tell the kernel the process is done with this device, file, or channel.

Figure 3.9: List of UNIX system calls discussed in this section.

- **A program can read its input from a file.** Likewise, by using dup2 to change the stdin file descriptor, the shell can cause the child to read its input from a file. In the standard UNIX shell, this is signified with a "less than" symbol. Thus, "zork < solution" plays the game "zork" with a list of instructions stored in the file "solution."

- **The output of one program can be the input to another program.** The

```
main() {
    char *prog = NULL;
    char **args = NULL;

    // Read the input a line at a time, and parse each line into the program
    // name and its arguments. End loop if we've reached the end of the input.
    while (readAndParseCmdLine(&prog, &args)) {

        // create a child process to run the command
        int child_pid = fork();

        if (child_pid == 0) {
            // I'm the child process.
            // Run program with the parent's input and output
            exec(prog, args);
            // NOT REACHED
        } else {
            // I'm the parent; wait for the child to complete
            wait(child_pid);
            return 0;
        }
    }
}
```

Figure 3.10: Example code for a simple UNIX shell.

producer-
consumer
communica-
tion

shell can use a pipe to connect two programs together, so that the output of one is the input of another. This is called a *producer-consumer* relationship. For example, in the C-compiler, the output of the pre-processor is sent to the parser, and the output of the parser is sent to the code-generator and then to the assembler. In the standard UNIX shell, a pipe connecting two programs is signified by a "|" symbol, as in: "cpp file.c | cparse | cgen | as > file.o". In this case the shell creates four separate child processes, each connected by pipes to its predecessor and successor. Each of the phases can run in parallel, with the parent waiting for all of them to finish.

Exercises

5. Suppose you were the instructor of a very large introductory programming class. Explain (in English) how you would use UNIX system calls to automate testing of submitted homework assignments.

6. What happens if you run "exec csh" in a UNIX shell? Why?

7. What happens if you run "exec ls" in a UNIX shell? Why?

3.4 | Case Study: Interprocess communication

For many of the same reasons it makes sense to construct complex applications from simpler modules, it often makes sense to create applications that can specialize on a specific task, and then combine those applications into more complex structures. We gave an example above with the C compiler, but many parts of the operating system are structured this way. For example, instead of every program needing to know how to coordinate access to a printer, UNIX has a printer server, a specialized program for managing the printer queue.

For this to work, we need a way for processes to communicate with each other. Three widely used forms of interprocess communication are:

- **Producer-consumer.** In this model, programs are structured to accept as input the output of other programs. Communication is one-way: the producer only writes, and the consumer only reads. As we explained above, this allows chaining: a consumer can be in turn a producer for a different process. Much of the success of UNIX was due to its ability to easily compose many different programs together in this fashion.

- **Client-server.** An alternative model is to allow two-way communication between processes, as in client-server computing. The server implements some specialized task, such as managing the printer queue or managing the display. Clients send requests to the server to do some task, and when the operation is complete, the server replies back to the client.

- **File system.** Another way programs can be connected together is through reading and writing files. A text editor can import an image created by a drawing program, and the editor can in turn write an HTML file that a web server can read to know how to display a web page. A key distinction is that, unlike the first two modes, communication through the file system can be separated in *time*: the writer of the file does not need to be running at the same time as the file reader. Therefore data needs to be stored persistently on disk or other stable storage, and the data needs to be named so that you can find the file when needed later on.

All three models are widely used both on a single system and over a network. For example, the Google MapReduce utility is a central part of many of Google's services, and it operates over a network in a producer-consumer fashion: the output of the map function is sent to the machines running the reduce function. The web is an example of client-server computing, and many enterprises and universities run centralized file servers to connect a text editor on one computer with a compiler running on another.

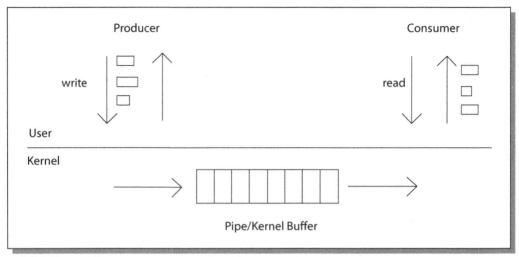

Figure 3.11: Interprocess communication between a producer application and a consumer. The producer uses the system call write to put data into the buffer; the consumer uses the system call read to take data out of the buffer.

As persistent storage, file naming, and distributed computing are each complex topics in their own right, we defer the discussions of those topics to later chapters. Here we focus on interprocess communication, where both processes are running simultaneously on the same machine.

Producer-consumer communication

Figure 3.11 illustrates how two processes communicate through the operating system in a producer-consumer relationship. Via the shell, we establish a pipe between the producer and the consumer. As one process computes and produces a stream of output data, it issues a sequence of write system calls on the pipe into the kernel. Each write can be of variable size. Assuming there is room in the kernel buffer, the kernel copies the data into the buffer, and returns immediately back to the producer.

At some point later, the operating system will schedule the consumer process to run. (On a multicore, the producer and consumer could be running at the same time.) The consumer issues a sequence of read calls. Because the pipe is just a stream of bytes, the consumer can read the data out in any convenient chunking — the consumer can read chunks in 1 KB chunks, while the producer wrote its data in 4 KB chunks, or vice versa. Each system call read made by the consumer returns the next successive chunk of data out of the kernel buffer. The consumer process can then compute on its input, sending its output to the display, a file, or onto the next consumer.

The kernel buffer allows each process to run at its own pace. There is

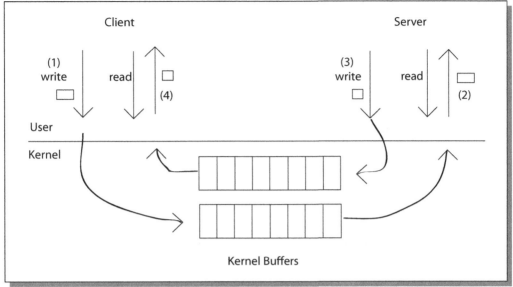

Figure 3.12: Interprocess communication between a client process and a server process. Once the client and server are connected, the client sends requests to the server by writing them into a kernel buffer. The server reads the requests out of the buffer, and returns the results by writing them into a separate buffer read by the client.

no requirement that each process have equivalent amounts of work to do. If the producer is faster than the consumer, the kernel buffer fills up, and when the producer tries to write to a full buffer, the kernel stalls the process until there is room to store the data. Equivalently, if the consumer is faster than the producer, the buffer will empty and the next read request will stall until the producer creates more data.

In UNIX, when the producer finishes, it closes its side of the pipe, but there may still be data queued in the kernel for the consumer. Eventually, the consumer reads the last of the data, and the read system call will return an "end of file" marker. Thus, to the consumer, there is no difference between reading from a pipe and reading from a file.

Decoupling the execution of the producer and consumer through the use of kernel buffers reduces the number and cost of context switches. Modern computers make extensive use of hardware caches to improve performance, but caches are ineffective if a program only runs for a short period of time before it must yield the processor to another task. The kernel buffer allows the operating system to run each process long enough to benefit from reuse, rather than alternating between the producer and consumer on each system call.

```
Client:
    char request[RequestSize];
    char reply[ReplySize]

    // ..compute..

    // put the request into the buffer

    // send the buffer to the server
    write(output, request, RequestSize);

    // wait for response
    read(input, reply, ReplySize);

    // ..compute..
Server:
    char request[RequestSize];
    char reply[ReplySize];

    // loop waiting for requests
    while (1) {
        // read incoming command
        read(input, request, RequestSize);

        // do operation

        // send result
        write(output, reply, ReplySize);
    }
```

Figure 3.13: Example code for client-server interaction.

Client-server communication

We can generalize the above to illustrate client-server communication, shown in Figure 3.12. Instead of a single pipe, we create two, one for each direction. To make a request, the client writes the data into one pipe, and reads the response from the other. The server does the opposite: it reads requests from the first pipe, performs whatever is requested (provided the client has permission to make the request), and writes the response onto the second pipe.

The client and server code are shown in Figure 3.13. To simplify the code, we assume that the requests and responses are fixed size.

Frequently, we want to allow many clients to talk to the same server. For example, there is one server to manage the print queue, although there can be many processes that want to be able to print. For this, the server uses the select system call, to identify the pipe containing the request to be read, as shown in Figure 3.14. The client code is unchanged.

Streamlining client-server communication

Client-server communication is a common pattern in many systems, and so one can ask: how can we improve its performance? One step is to recognize that both the client and the server issue a write immediately followed by a read, to wait for the other side to reply; at the cost of adding a system call, these can be combined to eliminate two kernel crossings per round trip. Further, the client will always need to wait for the server, so it makes sense for it to donate its processor to run the server code, reducing delay. Microsoft added support for this optimization to Windows in the early 1990's when it converted to a microkernel design (explained a bit later in this chapter). However, as we noted earlier, modern computer architectures make extensive use of caches, so for this to work we need code and data for both the client and the server to be able to be in cache simultaneously. We will talk about mechanisms to accomplish that in a later chapter.

We can take this streamlining even further. On a multicore system, it is possible or even likely that both the client and server each have their own processor. If the kernel sets up a shared memory region accessible to both the client and the server and no other processes, then the client and server can (safely) pass requests and replies back and forth, as fast as the memory system will allow, without ever traversing into the kernel or relinquishing their processors.

```
Server:
    char request[RequestSize];
    char reply[ReplySize];
    FileDescriptor clientInput[NumClients];
    FileDescriptor clientOutput[NumClients];

    // loop waiting for a request from any client
    while (fd = select(clientInput, NumClients) {

        // read incoming command from a specific client
        read(clientInput[fd], request, RequestSize);

        // do operation

        // send result
        write(clientOutput[fd], reply, ReplySize);
    }
```

Figure 3.14: Server code for communicating with multiple clients.

3.5 | Operating system structure

We started this chapter with a list of functionality that users and applications need from the operating system. We have shown that by careful design of the system call interface, we can offload some of the work of the operating system to user programs, such as to a shell or to a print server.

In the rest of this chapter, we ask how should we organize the remaining parts of the operating system? There are many dependencies among the modules inside the operating system, and there is often quite frequent interaction between these modules:

- Many parts of the operating system depend on synchronization primitives for coordinating access to shared data structures with the kernel.

- The virtual memory system depends on low level hardware support for address translation, support that is specific to a particular processor architecture.

- Both the file system and the virtual memory system share a common pool of blocks of physical memory. They also both depend on the disk device driver.

- The file system can depend on the network protocol stack if the disk is physically located on a different machine.

This has led operating system designers to wrestle with a fundamental tradeoff: by centralizing functionality in the kernel, performance is improved and it makes it easier to arrange tight integration between kernel modules. However, the resulting systems are less flexible, less easy to change, and less adaptive to user or application needs. We discuss these tradeoffs by describing several options for the operating system architecture.

Monolithic kernels

monolithic
kernel

Almost all widely used commercial operating systems, such as Windows, MacOS, and Linux, take a similar approach to the architecture of the kernel — a monolithic design. As shown in Figure 3.15, with a *monolithic kernel*, most of the operating system functionality runs inside the operating system kernel. In truth, the term is a bit of a misnomer, because even in so-called monolithic systems, there are often large segments of what users consider the operating system that runs outside the kernel, either as utilities like the shell, or in system libraries, such as libraries to manage the user interface.

Internal to a monolithic kernel, the operating system designer is free to develop whatever interfaces between modules that make sense, and so there is quite a bit of variation from operating system to operating system in those internal structures. However, two common themes emerge across systems: to improve portability, almost all modern operating systems have both a hardware abstraction layer and dynamically loaded device drivers.

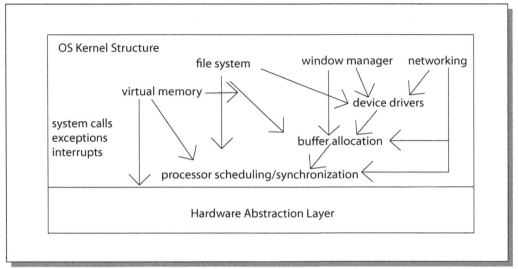

Figure 3.15: In a monolithic operating system kernel, most of the operating system functionality is linked together inside the kernel. Kernel modules directly call into other kernel modules to perform needed functions. For example, the virtual memory system uses buffer management, synchronization, and the hardware abstraction layer.

Hardware abstraction layer

hardware abstraction layer

A key goal of operating systems is to be portable across a wide variety of hardware platforms. To accomplish this, especially within a monolithic system, requires careful design of the *hardware abstraction layer*. The hardware abstraction layer (HAL) is a portable interface to machine configuration and processor-specific operations within the kernel. For example, within the same processor family, such as an Intel x86, different computer manufacturers will require different machine-specific code to configure and manage interrupts and hardware timers.

Operating systems that are portable across processor families, say between an ARM and an x86 or between a 32-bit and a 64-bit x86, will need processor-specific code for process and thread context switches. The exception, interrupt, and system call trap handling is also processor-specific; all systems have those functions, but the specific implementation will vary. As we will see in a later chapter, machines differ quite a bit in their architecture for managing virtual address spaces; most kernels provide portable abstractions on top of the machine-dependent routines, such as to translate virtual addresses to physical addresses or to copy memory from applications to kernel memory and vice versa.

With a well-defined hardware abstraction layer in place, most of the operating system is machine- and processor-independent. Thus, porting an operating system to a new computer is just a matter of creating new

The Hardware Abstraction Layer in Windows

As a concrete example, Windows has a two-pronged strategy for portability. To allow the same Windows kernel binary to be used across personal computers manufactured by different vendors, the kernel is dynamically linked at boot time with a set of library routines specifically written for each hardware configuration. This isolates the kernel from the specifics of the motherboard hardware.

Windows also runs across a number of different processor architectures. Typically, a different kernel binary is produced for each type of processor, with any needed processor-specific code; sometimes conditional execution is used to allow a kernel binary to be shared across closely related processor designs.

---

implementations of these low level HAL routines and relinking.

Dynamically installed device drivers

A similar consideration leads to operating systems that can easily accommodate a wide variety of physical I/O devices. Although there are only a handful of different instruction set architectures in wide use today, there are a huge number of different types of physical I/O devices, manufactured by a large number of companies. There is diversity in the hardware interfaces to devices as well as in the hardware chip sets for managing the devices. A recent survey found that approximately 70% of the code in the Linux kernel was in device-specific software.

To keep the rest of the operating system kernel portable, we want to decouple the operating system source code from the specifics of each device. For instance, suppose a manufacturer creates a new model a printer — what steps are needed by the operating system manufacturer to accommodate that change?

The key innovation, widely adopted today, is a *dynamically loadable device driver*. A dynamically loadable device driver is software to manage a specific device or interface or chipset, that is added to the operating system kernel after the kernel starts running, to handle the devices that are present on a particular machine. The device driver code is typically written by the device manufacturer, using a standard interface provided by the kernel. The operating system kernel calls into the driver whenever it needs to read or write data to the device.

dynamically loadable device driver

At boot, the operating system starts with a small number of device drivers – e.g., for the disk (to read the operating system binary into memory). For the devices physically attached to the computer, the computer manufacturer bundles those drivers into a file it stores along with the boot-loader. When the operating system starts up, it queries the I/O bus for which devices are attached to the computer and then loads those drivers from the file on disk. Finally, for any network-attached devices, such as a network printer, the operating system can load those drivers over the Internet.

While dynamically loadable device drivers solve one problem, they pose a different one. Errors in a device driver can corrupt the operating system kernel and application data structures; just as with a regular program, errors may not be caught immediately, so that user may be unaware that their data is being silently modified. Even worse, a malicious attacker can use device drivers to introduce a computer virus into the operating system kernel, and thereby silently gain control over the entire computer. Recent studies have found that 90% of all system crashes were due to bugs in device drivers, rather than in the operating system itself.

Operating system developers have taken five approaches to dealing with this issue:

- **Code inspection.** Operating system vendors typically require all device driver code to be submitted in advance for inspection and testing, before being allowed into the kernel.

- **Bug tracking.** After every system crash, the operating system can collect information about the system configuration and the current kernel stack, and sends this information back to a central database for analysis. Microsoft does this on a wide scale. With hundreds of millions of installed computers, even a low rate of failure can yield millions of bug reports per day. Many crashes happen inside the device driver itself, but even those that do not can sometimes be tracked down. For example, if failures are correlated with the presence of a particular device driver, or increase after the release of a new version of the driver, that can indicate the source of a problem.

- **User-level device drivers.** Both Apple and Microsoft strongly encourage new device drivers to be written at user-level rather than in the kernel. Each device driver runs in a separate user-level process, using system calls to manipulate the physical device. This way, a buggy driver can only affect its own internal data structures and not the rest of the operating system kernel; if the device driver crashes, the kernel can restart it easily.

  Although user-level device drivers are becoming more common, it can be time-consuming to port existing device drivers to run at user-level. Unfortunately, there is a huge amount of existing device driver code that makes use of the ability to directly address internal kernel data structures; drawing a boundary around these drivers has proven difficult. Of course, supporting legacy drivers is less of a problem as completely new hardware and operating system platforms, such as smartphones and tablets, are developed.

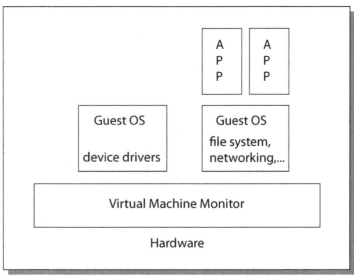

Figure 3.16: Legacy device drivers can be run inside a guest operating system on top of a virtual machine in order to isolate the effect of implementation errors in driver code.

- **Virtual machine device drivers.** To handle legacy device drivers, one approach that has gained some traction is to run device driver code inside a guest operating system running on a virtual machine, as shown in Figure 3.16. The guest operating system loads the device drivers as if it was running directly on the real hardware, but when the devices attempt to access the physical hardware, the underlying virtual machine monitor regains control to ensure safety. Device drivers can still have bugs, but they can only corrupt the guest operating system and not other applications running on the underlying virtual machine monitor.

- **Driver sandboxing.** A further challenge for both user-level device drivers and virtual machine drivers is performance. Some device drivers need frequent interaction with hardware and the rest of the kernel. Some researchers have proposed running device drivers in their own restricted execution environment inside the kernel. This requires lightweight sandboxing techniques, a topic we'll return to at the end of Chapter 8.

Microkernel

An alternative to the monolithic kernel approach is to run as much of the operating system as possible in one or more user-level servers. The window manager on most operating systems is implemented this way:

individual applications draw items on their portion of the screen by sending requests to the window manager. The window manager adjudicates which application window is in front or in back for each pixel on the screen, and then renders the result. If the system has a hardware graphics accelerator present, the window manager can use it to render items more quickly. Some systems have moved other parts of the operating system into user-level servers: the network stack, the file system, device drivers, and so forth.

The difference between a monolithic and a microkernel design is often transparent to the application programmer. The location of the service can be hidden in a user-level library — calls go to the library, which casts the requests either as system calls or as reads and writes to the server through a pipe. The location of the server can also be hidden inside the kernel — the application calls the kernel as if the kernel implements the service, but instead the kernel reformats the request into a pipe that the server can read.

A microkernel design offers considerable benefit to the operating system developer, as it easier to modularize and debug user-level services than kernel code. Aside from a potential reliability improvement, however, microkernels offer little in the way of visible benefit to end users and can slow down overall performance by inserting extra steps between the application and the services it needs. Thus, in practice, most systems adopt a hybrid model where some operating system services are run at user-level and some are in the kernel, depending on the specific tradeoff between code complexity and performance.

3.6 | Conclusion and future directions

In this chapter, we have seen how system calls can be used by applications to create and manage processes, perform I/O, and communicate with other processes. Every operating system has its own unique system call interface; describing even a single interface in depth would be beyond the scope of this book. In this chapter, we focused parts of the UNIX interface because it is both compact and powerful. A key aspect of the UNIX interface are that creating a process (with fork) is separate from starting to run a program in that process (with exec); another key feature is the use of kernel buffers to decouple reading and writing data through the kernel.

Operating systems use the system call interface to provide services to applications and to aid in the internal structuring of the operating system itself. Almost all general-purpose computer systems today have a user-level shell and/or a window manager that can start and manage applications on behalf of the user. Many systems also implement parts of the operating system as user-level services accessed through kernel pipes.

As we've noted, a trend is for applications to become mini-operating systems in their own right, with multiple users, resource sharing and allocation, untrusted third-party code, processor and memory management, and so forth. The system call interfaces for Windows and UNIX were not designed with this in mind, and an interesting question is how they will change to accommodate this future of powerful meta-applications.

In addition to the fine-grained sandboxing and process creation we described at the end of the last chapter, a trend is to re-structure the system call interface to make resource allocation decisions explicit and visible to applications. Traditionally, operating systems make resource allocation decisions — when to schedule a process or a thread, how much memory to give a particular application, where and when to store its disk blocks, when to send its network packets — transparently to the application, with a goal of improving end user and overall system performance. Applications are unaware of how many resources they have, appearing to run by themselves, isolated on their own (virtual) machine.

Of course, the reality is often quite different. An alternate model is for operating systems to divide resources among applications and then allow each application to decide for itself how best to use those resources. One can think of this as a type of federalism. If both the operating system and applications are governments doing their own resource allocation, they are likely to get in each other's way if they aren't careful. As a simple example, consider how a garbage collector works; it assumes it has a fixed amount of memory to manage. However, as other applications start or stop, it can gain or lose memory, and if the operating system does this reallocation transparently, the garbage collector has no hope of adapting. Later in the book, we will see examples of this same design pattern in many different areas of operating system design.

Exercises

For convenience, the exercises from the body of the chapter are repeated here.

1. Can UNIX fork return an error? Why or why not?
   Note: You can answer this question by looking at the manual page for fork, but before you do that, think about what the fork system call does. If you were designing this call, would you need to allow fork to return an error?
   Note: A manual page (or "man page") is a standard way of documenting Unix system calls and utility programs. On a Unix machine, you can access a manual page by running the man command (e.g., man fork). Another way to find manual pages is via web search (e.g., search for man fork and many of the top results will be manual pages for the fork system call.)

2. Can UNIX exec return an error? Why or why not?
   Note: You can answer this question by looking at the manual page

for exec, but before you do that, think about what the exec system call does. If you were designing this call, would you need to allow it to return an error?

3. What happens if we run the following program on UNIX?

```
main () {
    while (fork () >= 0)
        ;
}
```

4. Explain what must happen for UNIX wait to return (successfully and) immediately.

5. Suppose you were the instructor of a very large introductory programming class. Explain (in English) how you would use UNIX system calls to automate testing of submitted homework assignments.

6. What happens if you run "exec csh" in a UNIX shell? Why?

7. What happens if you run "exec ls" in a UNIX shell? Why?

8. Consider the following program:

```
main (int argc, char ** argv) {
    forkthem (5)
}

void forkthem (int n) {
    if (n > 0) {
        fork ();
        forkthem (n−1);
    }
}
```

How many processes are created if the above piece of code is run?

9. Consider the following program:

```
main (int argc, char ** argv) {
    int child = fork ();
    int x = 5;

    if (child == 0) {
        x += 5;
    } else {
        child = fork ();
        x += 10;
        if (child) {
            x += 5;
        }
    }
}
```

How many different copies of the variable x are there? What are their values when their process finishes?

10. What is the output of the following programs? (Please try to solve the problem without compiling and running the program.)

```
// Program 1
main () {
      int val = 5;

      if (fork ())
            wait (& val );
      val ++;
      printf ( "%d\n", val );
      return val ;
}
```

```
// Program 2:
main () {
      int val = 5;

      if (fork ())
            wait (& val );
      else
            exit ( val );
      val ++;
      printf ( "%d\n", val );
      return val ;
}
```

11. Implement a shell using UNIX system calls. Features of your shell can include pipes, background and foreground tasks, and job control (suspend, resume, and kill).

Part II

Concurrency

Many hands make light work.

anon

4 Concurrency and Threads

In the real world — outside of computers — different activities often proceed at the same time: five jazz musicians play their instruments while reacting to each other; one car drives north while another drives south; one part of a drug molecule is attracted to a cell's receptor while another part is repelled; a humanoid robot walks, raises its arms, and turns its head; I fetch one article from the *The New York Times* website while you fetch another; or millions of people make long distance phone calls on Mother's Day.

Internally, computers also harness concurrency. For example, a modern server might have 8 processors, 10 disks, and 4 network interfaces; a workstation might have a dozen active IO devices including a screen, a keyboard, a mouse, a camera, a microphone, a speaker, a wireless network interface, a wired network interface, an internal disk drive, an external disk drive, a printer, and a scanner; today, even mobile phones can have dual-core processors.

However, programmers are used to thinking sequentially. For example, when reading or writing the code for a procedure, we identify an initial state and a set of preconditions, think through how each successive statement changes the state, and from that determine the postconditions. How would one even think about a program where dozens of things are happening at once?

To simulate or interact with the real world, to manage hardware resources, and to map parallel applications to parallel hardware, computer systems must provide programmers with abstractions for expressing and managing *concurrency*. These abstractions are used both by applications and within the operating system, itself.

Threads: A core abstraction for concurrency. This chapter will focus on the powerful concurrency abstraction of *threads*. Threads let us define a set of tasks that should run at the same time, but they let us write the code for each task as if the task were standard, sequential code.

Threads are used within the operating system and within user-level processes.

EXAMPLE   **Threads in an operating system.** For example an operating system kernel may have one thread that writes modified file blocks from memory to disk, another thread that encrypts (or decrypts) blocks as they are written to (or read from) an encrypted disk, another thread that monitors system load and manages the processor's power-saving features, and another thread that scans the cache of disk blocks and frees old entries.

EXAMPLE   **Threads in an application.** Consider an Earth Visualizer application similar to Google Earth (http://earth.google.com/). This application allows a user to virtually fly anywhere in the world, to see aerial images at different resolutions, and to view other information associated with each location. A key part of the design is that the user's controls are always operable so that as the user mouses to a new location, the image is redrawn in the background at successively better resolutions while the program continues to allow the the user to adjust the view, to select additional information about the location for display, or to enter search terms.

To implement this application, as Figure 4.1 illustrates the programmer might write code to draw a portion of the screen, code to draw user interface (UI) widgets and process user inputs, and code to fetch higher resolution images for newly-visible areas. In a sequential program, these functions would run in turn. With threads, these can run concurrently so that the user interface is responsive even while new data is being fetched and the screen is being redrawn

Chapter overview. The rest of this chapter discusses three topics in detail:

- **Thread abstraction.** What are threads and what do they do?

- **Thread internals.** What building blocks are needed so that we can construct threads?

- **Thread implementation.** Given these building blocks, how can we implement threads?

4.1 | Threads: Abstraction and interface

As Figure 4.2 illustrates, threads *virtualize the processor*, providing the illusion that programs run on machines with an infinite number of virtual

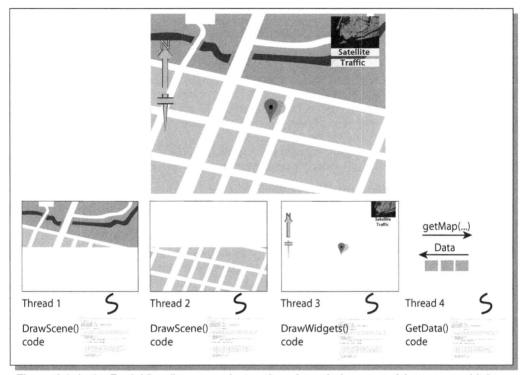

Figure 4.1: In the Earth Visualizer example, two threads each draw part of the scene, a third thread manages the user interface widgets, and a fourth thread fetches new data from a remote server. Satellite Image Credit: NASA Earth Observatory.

processors. The programs can then create however many threads they need without worrying about the exact number of physical processors, and each thread runs on its own virtual processor.

Of course, the physical reality is that a given system only has so many processors. The operating system's job is to multiplex all of the system's threads on the actual physical processor present in the system. It does this by transparently suspending and resuming threads so that at any given time only a subset of the threads are actively running.

Multi-threaded programs. The intuition for using the thread abstraction is simple: in a program, we can represent each concurrent task as a *thread*. Each thread provides the abstraction of a sequential execution similar to the traditional programming model. In fact, we can think of a traditional program as *single-threaded* with one logical sequence of steps as each instruction follows the previous one. The program executes statements, iterates through loops, and calls/returns from procedures one after another.

A *multi-threaded program* is a generalization of the same basic programming model. Each individual thread follows a single sequence of steps as it

Deja vu all over again?

Threads are widely used and modern programming languages often make it easy to use threads. You may have programmed with threads before or may have taken classes that talk about using threads. What is new here?

The discussions in this chapter and the next are designed to make sense even if you have never seen threads before. If you have seen threads before, great! But we think you will find the discussions useful.

Beyond describing the basics threads abstractions, we emphasize two points in our discussions in this chapter and the next the next one.

- **Implementation.** We will describe how operating systems implement threads both for their own use and for use by user-level applications. It is important to understand how threads really work so that you can understand their costs and performance characteristics and use them effectively.

- **Practice.** We will present a methodology for writing correct multi-threaded programs. Concurrency is increasingly important in almost all significant programming projects, but writing correct multi-threaded programs requires much more care and discipline than writing correct single-threaded programs. That said, following a few simple rules that we will describe can greatly simplify the process of writing robust multi-threaded code.

Multithreaded programming has a reputation for being difficult, and we believe the ideas in this chapter and the next can help almost anyone become better at programming with threads.

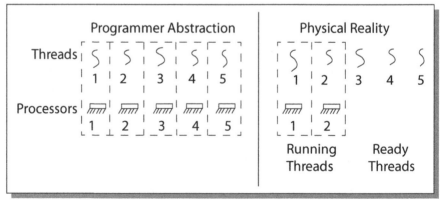

Figure 4.2: Threads virtualize the processor, providing the illusion that the system has an infinite number of processors. Then, programmers can create as many threads as they need, and each thread runs on a virtual processor. In reality, of course, a machine only has a finite number of processors, and it is the operating system's job to transparently multiplex threads on the actual processors.

executes statements, iterates through loops, calls/returns from procedures, etc. However, a program can now have several such threads executing at the same time.

Uses for threads. A programmer—whether programming the operating system or an outside application—uses threads to address three issues:

- **Program structure: Expressing logically concurrent tasks.** Programs often interact with or simulate real world applications that have concurrent activities. Threads allow the programmer to express an application's concurrency by writing each concurrent task as a separate thread.

EXAMPLE **Threads for program structure.** In our Earth Visualizer application, threads allow different activities—updating the screen, fetching additional data, and receiving new user inputs—to run in at the same time. For example, we do not want to freeze the user interface widgets while we fetch data and redraw the screen.

Programmers are used to thinking sequentially, and threads allow them to write the code for each task as a separate, sequential program rather than requiring them to write one program that somehow interleaves all of these activities. Although one could imagine manually writing a program that interleaves these activities (e.g., draw a few pixels on the screen, then check to see if the user has moved the mouse, then check to see if new image data have arrived on the network, ...), using threads can make things much simpler.

- **Performance: Exploiting multiple processors.** If programs can use multiple processors to do their processing in parallel, they can run faster—doing the same work in less time or doing more work in the same time. Today, a server may have over a dozen processors, a desktop or laptop machines may include two to eight processor cores, and even some cell phones are multicore machines. Looking forward, Moore's law makes it likely that the number of processors per system will continue to increase.

An important property of the threads abstraction is that the number of threads used by the program need not match the number of processors in the hardware on which it is running. The operating system transparently switches which threads are running on which processors.

EXAMPLE **Threads for parallel processing.** If our Earth Visualizer application runs on an 8-processor machine, the programmer might parallelize the demanding job of rendering different portions of the image on the screen across seven threads. Then, the operating system might run those seven rendering threads on seven processors and run the remaining threads on the remaining processor to update the on-screen navigation widgets, to construct the network messages needed to fetch additional images from the distant servers, and to parse the reply messages that come back.

- **Performance: Coping with high-latency I/O devices.** To do useful work, computers must interact with the outside world via Input/Output (I/O) devices. By running tasks as separate threads, when one task is waiting for I/O, the processor can make progress on a different task.

  We do not want the processor to be idle while waiting for I/O to complete for two reasons.

  First, processors are often much faster than the I/O systems with which they interact, so it is useful for a programmer to multiplex the processor among multiple tasks. For example, the latency to read from disk can be tens of milliseconds, so after requesting a block from disk, an operating system switches to doing other work until the disk has copied that block to the machine's main memory.

  Second, I/O provides a way for the computer to interact with external entities like users pressing keys on a keyboard or a remote computer sending network packets. The arrival of this type of I/O event is unpredictable, so we want the processor to be able to work on other things while still responding quickly to these events.

EXAMPLE   **Threads for I/O performance.** In our Earth Visualizer application, a snappy user interface is essential, but much of the imagery is stored on remote servers and fetched by the application only when needed. The application still provides a responsive experience when a user changes location by simultaneously drawing a low-resolution view of the new location while fetching higher-resolution images from the distant servers. The application then progressively updates the view as the higher-resolution images arrive.

Threads: Definition and properties

Above, we sketched what a thread is, how it is used, and why it is useful. To go further, we must define a thread and its properties more precisely.

thread   A *thread* is *a single execution sequence* that represents *a separately schedulable task*.

- **Single execution sequence.** By *single execution sequence* we mean that each thread executes a sequence of instructions—assignments, conditionals, loops, procedures, and so on—just as in the familiar programming model.

- **Separately schedulable task.** By *separately schedulable task* we mean that the operating system can run, suspend, or resume a thread at any time.

Running, suspending, and resuming threads.   Threads provide the illusion of an infinite number of processors. How does the operating system implement this illusion? It needs to be able to execute instructions from each thread so that each thread makes progress, but the underlying hardware has only a limited number of processors—maybe only one!

To map an arbitrary set of threads to a fixed set of processors, operating systems include a *scheduler* that can switch which threads are running and which are ready but not running. For example, in Figure 4.2, a scheduler might suspend thread 1 from processor 1, move it to the list of ready threads, and then resume thread 5 by moving it from the ready list to run on processor 1.

Switching between threads is transparent to code being executed by the threads. Remember that the point of the abstraction is to make each thread appear to be a single stream of execution, so a programmer should only have to worry about the sequence of instruction within a thread and not have to worry about where that sequence may be (temporarily) suspended to let another thread run.

Threads thus provide an execution model in which *each thread runs on a dedicated virtual processor with unpredictable and variable speed*. From the point of view of a thread's code, each instruction appears to execute immediately after the preceding instruction. However, the scheduler may suspend a thread between one instruction and the next and resume running it later. It is as if the thread was continually running on a processor that sometimes becomes very slow.

For example, Figure 4.3, illustrates a programmer's view of a simple program and three (of many) possible ways that program might be executed, depending on what the scheduler does. From the point of view of the thread, other than the speed of execution, all of these ways are equivalent. Indeed, the thread would typically not even know which of these (or other) executions actually occurred.

Of course, a thread's speed of execution and its interleavings with other threads will be affected by how it is scheduled. Figure 4.4, shows a handful of the many possible interleavings of a three thread program. Thread programmers should therefore not make any assumptions about the relative speed that different threads execute.

Why "unpredictable speed"?   It may seem strange to assume that a thread's virtual processor runs at a completely unpredictable speed and to assume that any interleavings with other threads are possible. Surely some interleavings are more likely than others?

Cooperative multithreading

Although most thread systems include a scheduler that can—at least in principle—run any thread at any time, some systems provide the abstraction of *cooperative threads.* In these systems, a thread runs without interruption until it explicitly relinquishes control of the processor to another thread. An advantage of cooperative multithreading is increased control over the interleavings among threads. For example, in most cooperative multithreading systems, only one thread runs at a time, so while a thread is running, no other thread can run and affect the system's state.

Unfortunately, cooperative multithreading has significant disadvantages. For example, a long-running thread can monopolize the processor, starving other threads and making the system's user interface sluggish or nonresponsive. Additionally, modern multiprocessor machines run multiple threads at a time, so one would still have to reason about the interleavings of threads even if cooperative multithreading were used. Thus, although cooperative multithreading was used in some significant systems in the past, including early versions of Apple's MacOS operating system, cooperative multithreading is less often used today.

The alternative we describe in the main body is sometimes called *preemptive multithreading* since a running thread can be preempted without explicitly relinquishing the processor. In the rest of this book, when we talk about multithreading, we are talking about preemptive multithreading unless we explicitly state otherwise.

Programmer's View	Possible Execution #1	Possible Execution #2	Possible Execution #3
.	.	.	.
.	.	.	.
.	.	.	.
$x = x + 1$;	$x = x + 1$;	$x = x + 1$	$x = x + 1$
$y = y + x$;	$y = y + x$;	....	$y = y + x$
$z = x + 5y$;	$z = x + 5y$;	thread is suspended	....
.	.	other thread(s) run	thread is suspended
.	.	thread is resumed	other thread(s) run
.	.	....	thread is resumed
		$y = y + x$	....
		$z = x + 5y$	$z = x + 5y$

Figure 4.3: Threads virtualize the underlying hardware's fixed number of processors to allow programmers to use any number of threads.

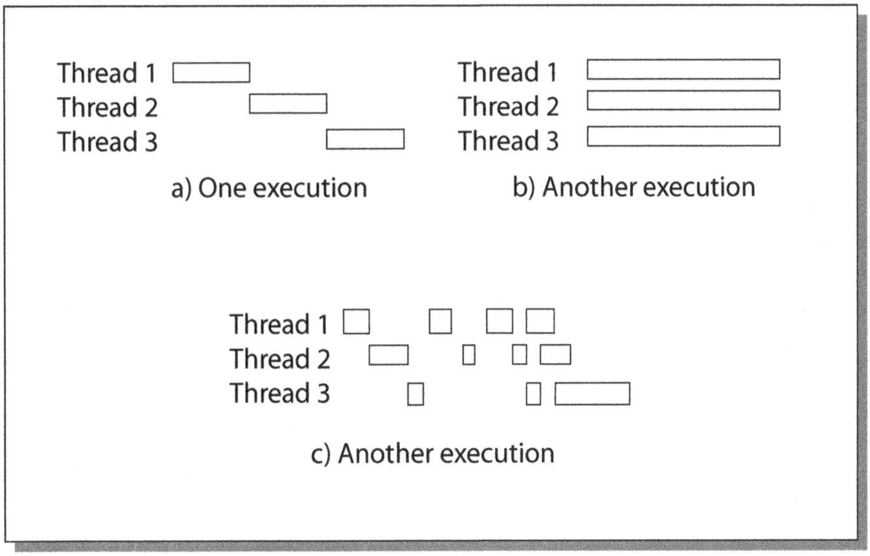

Figure 4.4: A handful of the many possible ways that three threads might be interleaved at runtime. Threads runs at unpredictable speeds due to many factors including policy decisions by the scheduler, the number of available processors, the physical characteristics of the processors, other programs competing for resources, and the arrival of I/O events.

The reason the threads programming model adopts this assumption is to guide programmers when reasoning about correctness. As Chapter 5 describes, rather than assuming that one thread at the same speed as another (or faster or slower) and trying to write programs that coordinate threads based on their relative speeds of execution, multi-threaded programs use explicit synchronization to control how threads interact with one another.

The physical reality is that the relative execution speeds of different threads are significantly affected by many factors outside their control. For example, on a modern processor, accessing memory can stall a processor for hundreds or thousands of cycles if there is a cache miss. Other factors include how frequently the scheduler preempts the thread, how many physical processors are present on a machine, how large the caches are, how fast the memory is, how the energy-saving firmware adjusts the processors' clock speeds, what network messages arrive, or what input is received from the user. As a result, execution speeds for the different threads of a program are hard to predict, can vary on different hardware, and can even vary from run to run on the same hardware.

sthreads API	
void **sthread_create(thread, func, arg)**	Create a new thread, storing information about it in **thread**. The thread will execute the function **func**, which will be called with the argument **arg**.
void **sthread_yield()**	The calling thread voluntarily gives up the processor to let some other thread(s) run. The scheduler can resume running the calling thread whenever it chooses to do so.
int **sthread_join(thread)**	Wait for the specified thread **thread** to finish if it has not already done so; then return the value passed to **sthread_exit()** by the specified thread **thread**. Note that **sthread_join()** may be called only once for each **thread**.
void **sthread_exit(ret)**	Finish the current thread. Store the the value ret in the current thread's data structure and, if another thread is already waiting in a call to **sthread_join()**, then wake it up so that it can run and return this value.

Figure 4.5: Simple API for using threads called sthreads ("simple threads.")

4.2 | Simple API and example

Figure 4.5 shows our simple thread API called sthreads ("simple threads.") Sthreads is based on the Posix standard pthreads API, but it simplifies things by omitting some options and error handling. Although the sthreads API is based on Posix, most other threads packages are quite similar; if you understand how to program with sthreads, you will find it easy to write code with most standard APIs for threads.

A simple multi-threaded program

Figure 4.6 shows a simple multi-threaded program written in 'C' using sthreads.

The main() function uses sthread_create() to create 10 threads. The interesting arguments are the second and third.

- The second argument, go, is a pointer to the function go(), which is the function in which the newly-created thread should begin execution.

- The third argument, ii, is the argument that should be passed to that function.

Thus, sthread_create() will initialize the iith thread's state so that it is prepared to call the function go() with the argument ii.

```
#include <stdio.h>
#include "sthread.h"

static void go(int n);

#define NTHREADS 10
static sthread_t threads[NTHREADS];

int main(int argc, char **argv)
{
  int ii;

  for(ii = 0; ii < NTHREADS; ii++){
    sthread_create(&(threads[ii]), &go, ii);
  }
  for(ii = 0; ii < NTHREADS; ii++){
    long ret = sthread_join(threads[ii]);
    printf("Thread %d returned %ld\n", ii, ret);
  }
  printf("Main thread done.\n");
  return 0;
}

void go(int n)
{
  printf("Hello from thread %d\n", n);
  sthread_exit(100 + n);
  // Not reached
}
```

Figure 4.6: Simple multi-threaded program.

When the scheduler runs the iith thread, the thread runs the function go() with the value ii as an argument and prints Hello from thread ii\n. The thread then returns a value (ii + 100) by calling sthread_exit(ii+100). This call stores the specified value in a field in the sthread_t object so that it can be retrieved by the initial thread's call to sthread_join().

The main() function uses sthread_join() to wait for each of the threads it created to finish. As each thread finishes, code in main() reads the thread's exit value and prints it.

Figure 4.7 shows the output of one possible run of this program. Of course, other runs may give different interleavings of the output lines.

Exercises

To complete the following problems, download the sthread library from http://www.cs.utexas.edu/users/dahlin/osbook/code/sthread.h, and http://www.cs.utexas.edu/users/dahlin/osbook/code/sthread.c. The comment at the top of threadHello.c explains how to compile and run a program that uses this library.

1. Download this example code http://www.cs.utexas.edu/users/dahlin/osbook/

```
bash-3.2$ ./threadHello
Hello from thread 0
Hello from thread 1
Thread 0 returned 100
Hello from thread 3
Hello from thread 4
Thread 1 returned 101
Hello from thread 5
Hello from thread 2
Hello from thread 6
Hello from thread 8
Hello from thread 7
Hello from thread 9
Thread 2 returned 102
Thread 3 returned 103
Thread 4 returned 104
Thread 5 returned 105
Thread 6 returned 106
Thread 7 returned 107
Thread 8 returned 108
Thread 9 returned 109
Main thread done.
```

Figure 4.7: Output of one possible run of the program in Figure 4.6.

code/threadHello.c, compile it, and run it several times. What do you get if you run it? Do you get the same thing if you run it multiple times? What if you are also running some other demanding processes (e.g., compiling a big program, playing a Flash game on a website, or watching streaming video) when you run this program?

2. For the threadHello program in Figure 4.6, what is the *maximum* number of threads that could exist while the program is running? *(Be careful.)*

3. For the threadHello program in Figure 4.6, suppose that we delete the second for loop so that the main routine simply creates NTHREADS threads and then prints "Main thread done." What are the possible outputs of the program now. **Hint:** Fewer than NTHREADS+1 lines may be printed in some runs. Why?

4. How expensive are threads? Write a program that times how long it taks to create and then join 1000 threads, where each thread simply calls sthread_exit(0) as soon as it starts running.

5. Write a program that has two threads. The first thread a simple loop that continuously increments a counter and prints a period (".") whenever the value of that counter is divisible by 10,000,000. The second thread repeatedly waits for the user to input a line of text and then prints "Thank you for your input." On your system, does the operat-

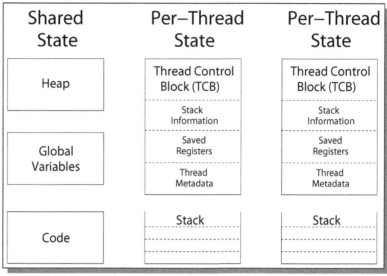

Figure 4.8: A multi-threaded process or operating system's state is divided into *per thread state* and *shared state*. The thread control block is the object that stores per-thread state. The per-thread state includes the state needed to represent the thread's computation (e.g., the processor registers, the stack, and thread-local variables.) The per-thread state also included metadata—data about the thread used by the operating system in managing the thread (e.g., the thread's ID, scheduling priority, owner, and resource consumption.) In addition to per-thread state, a multi-threaded process (or the operating system kernel) includes shared state, shared by all threads running in that process (or kernel). For example, this shared state includes the program's code, global static variables, and the heap.

ing system do a good job of making sure that the first thread makes rapid progress and that the second thread responds quickly?

4.3 | Thread internals

Each thread represents a sequential stream of execution, and the operating system provides the illusion that each thread runs on its own virtual processor by transparently suspending and resuming threads.

To understand how the operating system implements the threads abstraction, we must define the state needed to represent a thread. Then, we can understand a thread's lifecycle—how the operating system can create, start, stop, and delete threads to provide the abstraction.

Thread control block (TCB) and per-thread state

The operating system needs a data structure to represent a thread's state; a thread is like any other object in this regard. The data structure that hold the thread's state is called the *thread control block (TCB)*. For every thread the operating system creates, it will create one TCB.

thread control block (TCB)

A thread's TCB holds two types of information:

- The state of the computation being performed by the thread

- Metadata about the thread that is used to manage the thread

Per-thread computation state.   Each thread represents its own sequentially-executed computation, so to create multiple threads, we must allocate per-thread state to represent the current state of each thread's computation. Each thread's TCB therefore contains two elements of per-thread computation state:

1. **Stack.**

   A thread's stack is the same as the stack for a single-threaded computation — it stores information needed by the nested procedures the thread is currently running. For example, if a thread calls foo(), foo() calls bar(), and bar() calls bas(), then the stack would contain a *stack frame* for each of these three procedures, and each stack frame might contain the local variables used by the procedure, the parameters the procedure was called with, and the return address to jump to when the procedure completes.

   Because at any given time, each thread can be in a different state in its sequential computation — it can be in a different place in a different procedure called with different arguments from a different nesting of enclosing procedures — each thread needs its own stack. Typically, when a new thread is created, a new stack is allocated for it, and a pointer to that stack is stored in the thread's TCB.

2. **Copy of processor registers.** A processor's registers include not only general purpose registers for storing values for ongoing computations but also special purpose registers like the instruction pointer and stack pointer.

   Because the operating system needs to be able to suspend a thread, run another thread, and then later resume the original thread, the operating system needs somewhere to store a thread's registers when that thread is not actively running on a processor. So, the TCB contains fields in which the operating system can store a copy of all of the processor's registers.

Other per-thread state: Thread-local variables

In addition to the per-thread state that corresponds to execution state in the single-threaded case, some systems include additional *thread-local variables*. These variables are similar to global variables in that their scope spans different procedures, but they differ in that each thread has its own copy of these variables.

EXAMPLE   **Errno.** In UNIX programs a variable called errno stores information about any errors that occurred in the most recently executed system call. In a multi-threaded program, multiple threads can perform system calls concurrently. Thus, to retrieve the status of the current thread's most recent library call, errno is typically a macro that maps to a thread-local variable.

EXAMPLE   **Heap internals.** Although a program's heap is logically shared — it is OK for one thread to allocate an object on the heap and then pass a pointer to that object to another thread — for performance reasons heaps may internally subdivide their space into per-thread regions. The advantage of subdividing the heap this way is that multiple threads can each be allocating objects at the same time without interfering with one another, and cache hit rates may be better. For this to work, each subdivision of the heap has some thread-local variables that keep track of what parts are allocated, what parts are free, and so on. Then, the code that allocates new memory (e.g., malloc() and new()) are written to use these thread-local data structures.

Thread-local variables are useful, but for simplicity, the rest of our discussion focuses on just the TCB, registers, and stack as the core pieces of per-thread state.

Per-thread metadata.   The TCB also includes include *per-thread metadata—* information about each thread. This information is used by the operating system to manage the thread. For example, each thread might have a thread ID, scheduling priority, and any other information the operating system wants to remember about the thread.

Shared state.   In addition to per-thread state that is allocated for each thread, as Figure 4.8 illustrates, other state is *shared* by different threads in a multi-threaded process or multi-threaded operating system.

In particular, the program *code* is shared by all of the threads in a process. Additionally, statically-allocated *global variables* and dynamically-allocated *heap variables* can store information that is accessible to all threads.

Warning.   Note that although there is an important logical division between per-thread state and shared state, nothing in the operating system

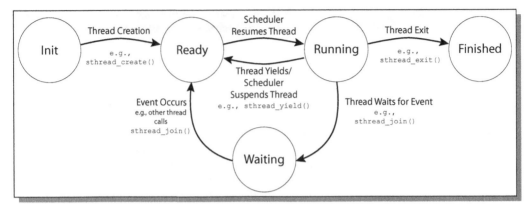

Figure 4.9: The states occupied by a thread during its life cycle.

typically *enforces* this division, and nothing protects a program from bugs when one thread accesses another thread's (conceptually private) per thread state.

So, writing to a bad pointer in one thread might corrupt the stack of another, or a careless programmer might pass a pointer to a local variable on one thread's stack to another thread, giving the second thread a pointer to a stack location whose contents may change as the first thread calls and returns from various procedures. Because they can depend on the specific interleavings of the threads' executions, such bugs can be diabolically hard to find.

It is therefore important when writing multi-threaded programs to know what variables are designed to be shared across threads (global variables, objects on the heap) and what variables are designed to be private (local/automatic variables) in order to avoid unexpected behaviors.

Thread life cycle

Figure 4.9 shows the states occupied by a thread during its lifetime.

INIT.   Thread creation puts a thread into its initial INIT state and allocates and initializes per-thread data structures. Once that is done, the thread creation code puts the thread into the READY state by adding the thread to a list of READY threads called the *ready list*.

READY.   A thread in the READY state is available to be run but it is not currently running. Its TCB is on the ready list and the values of its registers are stored in the thread control block. At any time, the scheduler can cause a a thread to transition from the READY to RUNNING by copying the thread's register values from its TCB to a processor's registers.

The idle thread.

If a system has k processors, then there will normally be exactly k RUNNING threads; the operating system typically keeps a low priority *idle thread* per processor and runs it if there is nothing else to run.

In old machines, the idle thread would spin in a tight loop doing nothing.

Today, to save power, the idle thread is typically a loop that on each iteration puts the processor into a low-power sleep mode in which the processor stops executing instructions until a hardware interrupt occurs. Then, when a hardware interrupt occurs, the processor wakes up and handles it in the normal way — saving the state of the currently running thread (the idle thread) and running the handler. After running the handler, if a thread other than the idle thread is READY, the scheduler runs that thread next; otherwise, the idle thread resumes execution, putting the processor to sleep again.

RUNNING.   A thread in the RUNNING state is running on a processor. When a thread is RUNNING, its register values are stored on a processor rather than in the TCB data structure. A RUNNING thread can transition to the READY state in two ways.

- The scheduler can preempt a running thread and move it to the READY state at any time by saving the thread's registers to its TCB and switching the processor to running the next thread on the ready list.

- A running thread can voluntarily relinquish the processor go from RUNNING to READY by calling yield() (e.g., sthread_yield() in the sthreads library.)

Notice that a thread can transition between READY and RUNNING and back many times while it runs. Since the operating system saves and restores the thread's registers exactly, only the speed of the the thread's execution is affected by these transitions.

WAITING.   A thread in the WAITING state is waiting for some event. Whereas a thread in the READY stage is eligible to be moved the RUNNING state by the scheduler, a thread in the WAITING state is not eligible to be run until some action by another thread moves it from the WAITING state to the READY state.

EXAMPLE   **A WAITING thread.** We saw an example of this earlier in the multi-threaded program shown in Figure 4.6 on page 149. After creating a number of threads, the main thread receives the exit value for each of the other threads thread, so it calls sthread_join() once for each of the child

State of Thread	Location of Thread Control Block (TCB)	Location of Registers
INIT	Being Created	TCB
READY	Ready List	TCB
RUNNING	Running List	Processor
WAITING	Synchronization Variable's Waiting List	TCB
FINISHED	Finished List then Deleted	TCB

Figure 4.10: Location of thread's per-thread state for different life cycle stages.

threads. If the child thread is not done yet, the main thread waits for it to finish so it can learn the exit value the child passed to sthread_exit(). In this case, the main thread goes from RUNNING to WAITING until the child's exit value is available.

While a thread is waiting for an event, it cannot make progress, so it is not useful to run it. Therefore, rather than continuing to run the thread or storing the TCB on the scheduler's ready list, the TCB is stored on the *waiting list* of some *synchronization variable* associated with the event. Then, when the event occurs, the TCB can be moved from the synchronization variable's waiting list to the scheduler's ready list, thus transitioning the thread from the WAITING state to the READY state. We will describe synchronization variables in the next chapter.

FINISHED.   Finally, a thread in the FINISHED state will never run again. The system can free some or all of its state for other uses, though it may keep some remnants of the thread in the FINISHED state for some time by putting the TCB on a *finished list*. For example, our sthread_exit() call allows a thread to pass its exit value to its parent thread via sthread_join(). Eventually, when a thread's state is no longer needed (e.g., after its exit value has been read by a join() call), the thread's state can be deleted and reclaimed by the system.

Follow the bouncing TCB.   As Figure 4.10 summarizes, one way to understand these stages is to think about where a thread's TCB and registers are stored. For example, all of the threads in the READY state have their TCBs on the ready list and their registers in the TCB, all threads in the RUNNING state have their TCBs on the running list and their registers on the processors, and all threads in the WAITING state have their TCBs on various synchronization variables' waiting lists.

Exercises

6. For the threadHello program in Figure 4.6, when pthread_join() returns for thread ii, in which of the states shown in Figure 4.9 is thread ii?

7. For the threadHello program in Figure 4.6 the procedure go() has the parameter np and the local variable n. Are these variables *per thread* or *shared* state? Where does the compiler store these variables' states?

8. For the threadHello program in Figure 4.6 the procedure main() has local variables such as ii, err, and status. Are these variables *per thread* or *shared* state? Where does the compiler store these variables' states?

9. In the sidebar on page 153, we describe *thread-local variables*, which are another piece of per-thread state present in many thread systems.

   Describe how you would implement thread-local variables. Each thread should have an array of 1024 pointers to its thread-local variables.

   - What would you add to the TCB?

   - How would you change the thread creation procedure? (For simplicity, assume that when a thread is created, all 1024 entries should be initialized to NULL.)

   - How would a running thread allocate a new thread-local variable?

   - In you design, how would a running thread access a particular thread-local variable?

4.4 | Implementation details

In the discussion above, we sketched the basic operation of threads. To make things concrete, we now describe how to implement threads in more detail.

Types of threads. Operating systems use threads internally—the operating system kernel can be multi-threaded—and they also provide the abstraction of threads to user-level processes so that processes can be multi-threaded.

The implementation of these two cases is almost identical. For simplicity we initially focus on how to implement *in-kernel threads*. This case is the simplest one because all of the scheduling and thread-switching actions occur in one place—the kernel. We will then discuss the small changes needed to extend the threads abstraction to support multi-threaded processes.

```
// func is a pointer to a procedure we want the thread to run
// arg is the argument to be passed to that procedure
void
thread_create(sthread_t *thrd, void (*func)(int), int arg)
{
    // Allocate TCB and stack
    TCB *tcb = new TCB();
    thrd->tcb = tcb;
    tcb->stack_size = INITIAL_STACK_SIZE;
    tcb->stack_base = new Stack(INITIAL_STACK_SIZE);

    // Initialize register values
    tcb->setStackPointer(stack);
    tcb->setInstructionPtr(stub);   // Don't call func() directly
    tcb->setArg0Register(func);     // Tell stub to call func()
    tcb->setArg1Register(arg);      // Tell stub to use arg to call func()
    ...

    // Put thread in READY state
    readyList->add(tcb);            // Put tcb on ready list
}

void
stub(void (*func)(int), int arg)
{
    (*func)(arg);                   // Execute the function func()
    thread_exit(0);                 // If func() doesn't call exit, call it here
}
```

Figure 4.11: Pseudo-code for thread creation. For convenience, we assume that the stack grows from low addresses to high ones and that arguments to functions are passed in registers. The code would be somewhat different for the x86 architecture, where the stack grows down and arguments are passed on the stack.

Creating a thread

Figure 4.11 shows the pseudo-code to allocate a new thread. Since we have to say what we want the thread to do, when we call sthread_create() we hand it a pointer to a procedure func() and an argument that we would like to pass to that procedure arg. Then, when the thread we create runs, it will execute func(arg).

Allocating per-thread state.   To allocate a thread, we must first allocate its per-thread state. As the pseudo-code illustrates, the thread constructor therefore allocates a *thread control block* (TCB) and *stack*. The TCB is just a data structure with fields for the state we want to be able to maintain for a thread. The stack is just an area of memory like any other data structure allocated in memory.

Note that we must choose some size for the allocated stack. Some implementations allocate a fixed-sized stack, and it is a bug for a thread's stack to overflow the fixed-sized stack. Other systems allocate an initial stack of some size and dynamically grow it if needed.

Initializing per-thread state.   When we initialize the thread control block, we need to set the new thread's registers to some sensible initial values. In the pseudocode, we first the thread's stack pointer to the base of the newly allocated stack. Then, we initialize the thread's instruction pointer and argument registers so that when it runs it will call func(arg).

Note that rather than having the thread call func(arg) directly, we initialize the thread's state so that the thread will first call the function stub() with two arguments: func, the function to run, and arg, the arguments to that function. The function stub() then calls func(arg) to run the function specified by the caller. We add this extra step so that if the func() procedure returns (rather than calling thread_exit() when it is done), it has somewhere to return to. If func() does return to stub(), stub() calls thread_exit() itself to finish this thread.

Deleting a thread

To delete a thread, we need to (1) remove it from the ready list so that it will never run again and (2) free the per-thread state we allocated for it.

There is one subtlety: if a thread removes itself from the ready list and frees its own per-thread state, then the constructs we've described will break. For example, if a thread removes itself from the ready list but an interrupt occurs before the thread finishes deallocating its state, we have a memory leak since the thread will never resume to finish deallocating its state. Worse, suppose that a thread frees its own state; what does it do then? How can it continue running the rest of the code in sthread_exit() if it does not have a stack? What happens if an interrupt occurs after the running thread's state has been deallocated? If the context switch code tries to save the current thread's state to its TCB, it will be writing to freed memory, possibly corrupting memory and causing a subtle bug.

There is a simple fix. A thread does not delete its own state. Instead, a thread transitions to the FINISHED state by moving its TCB from the ready list to a list of *finished* threads the scheduler should never run. Then, any time the thread library code runs (e.g., when some other thread calls yield() or when an interrupt occurs), the thread library can call a method to free the state of any threads on the finished list.

Thus, sthread_delete() merely moves the current thread to the finished list and then yields to some thread on the ready list. Later on, it is safe for some *other* thread to free the state of the threads on the finished list.

Thread context switch

When the kernel has multiple threads, we need a mechanism to switch which threads are RUNNING and which are READY.

thread
context
switch

A *thread context switch* suspends execution of the currently running thread and resumes execution of some other thread. This is done by copying the currently running thread's registers from the processor to the thread's TCB and then copying the other thread's registers from that thread's TCB to the processor.

The more things change, the more they stay the same.   We've already seen in Chapter 2 how an interrupt, an exception, or a system call trap can cause a *mode switch* that suspends a running process, runs a kernel handler, and returns to running the original process.

Recall that to implement a mode switch, the hardware saves some of the registers of the currently running process, switches to kernel mode, and starts running the handler. Then the handler software saves the remaining registers, handles the event, and finally restores the suspended process's registers and mode to resume running the suspended process exactly where it left off.

The mechanism for switching between threads in the kernel is almost identical. For example, if an interrupt or exception occurs: the hardware saves some of the registers of the currently running process and starts running a handler; the handler then saves the remaining registers, and begins running the main body of the handler.

Then, when the handler is done running, instead of resuming the interrupted process, it can invoke the scheduler to choose a different thread to run rather than restoring the thread that was interrupted. This is easy to do: we have already saved the state of the interrupted thread and we have a ready list of other threads whose state has already been saved. We can copy the interrupted thread's state to its TCB and copy the state of some ready thread from its TCB to the registers; then our thread switch is done.

The devil is in the details.   There are some small differences between the two cases, but they amount to implementation details rather than changes in the big picture. We describe these details below by discussing

- What triggers a context switch?

- How does context switch work?

The rest of this section discusses these issues.

Note that we defer discussing one issue

- Which READY thread should the scheduler choose to run next?

Separating mechanism from policy

Separating mechanism from policy is a useful and widely-applied principle in operating system design. When mechanism and policy are cleanly separated, it is easier to introduce new policies to optimize a system for a new workload or new technology.

For example, the thread context switch abstraction cleanly separates mechanism (how to switch between threads) from policy (which thread to run) so that the mechanism works no matter what policy is used. Then, some systems can elect to do something simple (e.g., FIFO scheduling), while other systems can optimize scheduling to meet their goals (e.g., a periodic scheduler to smoothly run real-time multimedia streams for a media device, a round-robin scheduler to balance responsiveness and throughput for a server, or a priority scheduler that devotes most resources to the visible application on a smartphone.)

We will see this principle many times in this book. For example, thread synchronization mechanism are also designed to work regardless of the scheduling policy, file metadata mechanisms for locating a file's blocks are designed to work regardless of the policy for choosing where to place the file's blocks on disk, and page translation mechanisms for mapping virtual page addresses to physical page addresses work regardless of which ranges of virtual addresses a process uses and which physical pages the operating system assigns to it.

The *mechanisms* we discuss work regardless of what *policy* the scheduler uses when choosing threads.

As for the *policy* for choosing which READY to run next, there are trade-offs among different scheduling policies, and different operating systems use different approaches. We therefore defer discussing scheduling policy to Chapter 7 where we can discuss these policy trade-offs in depth.

For now, you can assume that the scheduler's ready list is a simple FIFO list; most schedulers do something more sophisticated — they may prioritize some threads over others, optimize for throughput or responsiveness, or run ensure that multimedia threads run at a regular interval — but nothing we talk about here depends on these details.

What triggers a kernel thread context switch?

When a thread in the kernel is running, two things can cause a thread context switch.

First, the thread may *call a thread library function* that triggers a context switch. For example, many thread libraries provide a thread_yield() call that allows the currently running thread to voluntarily give up the processor and context switch the processor to some other thread that is ready to run. Similarly, the thread_join() and thread_exit() calls can suspend execution of the current thread and start running a different one.

Second, an *interrupt* or *exception* may invoke an interrupt handler, which must save the state of the running thread, execute the handler's code, and switch to some thread that is ready to run (or it may just restore the state and resume running the thread that was just interrupted.)

For example, many thread libraries switch threads when a timer interrupt occurs. In particular, thread libraries typically want to ensure that no thread can monopolize the processor, so they arrange for a hardware timer to periodically (e.g., every 10ms) cause a *timer interrupt.* The handler for the timer interrupt saves the state of the running thread, chooses another thread to run, and runs that thread by restoring its state to the processor.

Other hardware events (e.g., a keyboard key is pressed, a network packet arrives, or a disk operation completes) also invoke interrupt handlers. In all cases, these handlers save the state of the currently running thread so that it can be restored later. They then execute the handler code, and when the handler is done, they restore the state of some ready thread. If the interrupt caused a high priority thread to become ready, then the scheduler will set things up so that the interrupt returns to that thread instead of the interrupted one.

How does a kernel thread context switch work?

Regardless of whether a switch between kernel threads is triggered via an interrupt or an explicit call to the threads library, what needs to be done is conceptually simple:

1. Copy the running thread's registers from the processor to the thread's TCB

2. Copy a ready thread's registers from the thread's TCB to the processor

The implementation details differ slightly depending on whether the thread switch is caused by an interrupt or a explicit library call by the thread. Still, the cases are more the same than different—we want to make sure that all of the threads on the ready list have their state saved in the same way so that we can restore them in the same way.

Hardware-triggered thread switch.   We saw what happens when an interrupt, exception, or trap interrupts a running user-level process in Chapter **??**: hardware and software work together to save the state of the interrupted process, run the kernel's handler, and restore the state of the interrupted process.

The mechanism is almost identical when an interrupt or trap triggers a thread switch among threads in the kernel. We tweak the three steps described in Chapter **??** for handling a context switch from a user-level process to a kernel handler as follows (changes are written in italics):

1. **Save the state.** Save the currently running *thread's* registers so that the handler can run code without disrupting the interrupted *thread*.

   Recall that this is done with a combination of hardware saving some state when the interrupt or exception occurs and software saving the rest of the state when the handler runs.

2. **Run the kernel's handler.** Run the kernel's handler code to handle the interrupt or exception.

   Since we are already in kernel mode, we do not need to change from user to kernel mode in this step.

   We also do not need to change the stack pointer to the base of the kernel's exception stack. Instead, we can just push and pop saved state or handler variables onto the current stack starting from the current stack pointer.

3. **Restore the state.** Restore the *next ready thread's* registers so that it can resume running where it left off.

In short, comparing this approach to what happens on a mode switch from a user-level process, the only significant changes are (1) we do not need to switch modes (and therefore do not need to switch stacks) and (2) we can resume any thread on the ready list rather than always resuming the thread or process that was just suspended.

Library-call-triggered thread switch. When a thread calls a library function such as thread_yield() that triggers a thread switch, the steps are similar to what an interrupt or exception does. We need to

1. **Save the state.** Save the currently running thread's registers so that the kernel can later resume this thread.

   Here there is no hardware event; the running thread just calls the kernel handler with a regular procedure call. So, the library procedure must save all of the state on its own.

   That said, the library software should save the state to the thread's TCB using the same format as used in the interrupt- or exception-triggered case so that we can restore threads the same way regardless of what caused the thread to be suspended.

2. **Run the called library procedure.** Run the code to handle the library call.

3. **Restore the state.** Restore the next ready thread's registers so that it can resume running where it left off.

   As you can see, these steps are quite similar to the steps for an interrupt- and exception-triggered thread context switch. This is no accident!

```
void thread_yield()
{
    // Make stack look similar to the interrupt case (e.g., Fig. ??)
    push eflags;  // Push processor execution flags onto stack
    push LABEL;    // Push address of LABEL instruction (below)
                   // instead of current instruction pointer. In x86
                   // the pushed address needs to include both the
                   // code segment (cs) and program counter (eip).
    pushad;        // Push general purpose registers

    // Copy the current thread's saved state to TCB data structure
    memcopy(&(currentThread->TCB.savedRegisters), stackPointer, STATE_SIZE);

    // Choose another TCB from the ready list
    chosenTCB = readyList->getNextThread();

    //
    // Restore state of the chosen thread
    //
    // First, set stack pointer to point to area of TCB data structure
    // that stores the saved state. Then, restore the rest of the
    // state as if we were just popping it off the stack.
    stackPointer = &(chosenTCB->savedRegisters);
    popad;         // Pop other thread's general purpose registers
    iret;          // Pop other thread's instruction pointer and execution flags

    // This line is never executed!
    assert(0);

    // When calling thread is resumed, it will start here
LABEL:
    return;
}
```

Figure 4.12: Pseudo-code for thread_yield() for in-kernel threads on x86 architecture.

EXAMPLE   **thread_yield() on x86.** To make this software-based approach concrete, Figure 4.12 shows pseudo-code for a simple implementation of thread_-yield() for in-kernel threads for the x86 hardware architecture. A thread calls thread_yield() to voluntarily relinquish the processor to another thread. The calling thread's registers are copied to its TCB on the ready queue, and that thread resumes running later, when the scheduler chooses it.

In this code, the calling thread first saves its state to its stack. In our pseudo-code we take care to ensure the stack we construct here looks like the one constructed when an interrupt triggers the context switch (Figure ?? on page ??).

So, we first push the x86 eflags register, which includes the mode bit (user v. kernel) and a flag indicating whether interrupts are masked or enabled. Then, we push an instruction pointer. Notice that — perhaps surprisingly — the instruction pointer we push is not the address of the current instruction. Instead, we save the address of the instruction at LABEL, near the end of the thread_yield() procedure. We need to do this to avoid an endless loop. In particular, if we instead stored a pointer to the current instruction, then

One small difference.

You may notice that in Chapter 2, for a mode switch the x86 hardware saved not just the instruction pointer and eflags register but also the the *stack pointer* of the interrupted process before starting the handler. In the mode switch case, the hardware changed the stack pointer to the kernel's exception stack, so it must save the original stack pointer.

In contrast, when we switch from a kernel thread to a kernel handler — as we do for a thread context switch initiated by either a library call or an interrupt — the hardware does not switch stacks. Instead, the handler runs on the current stack not a separate exception stack. Therefore, the hardware does not need to save the original stack pointer; the handler just saves the stack pointer with the other registers as part of the pushad instruction.

Thus, x86 hardware thus works a bit differently when switching between a kernel thread and a kernel handler than when doing a mode switch.

- **Entering the handler.** When an interrupt or exception occurs, if the processor detects that it is already in kernel mode (by inspecting the eflags register), it just pushes the instruction pointer and eflags registers (but not the stack pointer) onto the existing stack.

  On the other hand, if the hardware detects that it is switching from user mode to kernel mode, then the processor also changes the stack pointer to the base of the exception stack and pushes the original stack pointer along with the instruction pointer and eflags registers onto the new stack.

- **Returning from the handler.** When the iret instruction is called, it inspects both the current eflags register and the value on the stack that is will use to restore the earlier eflags register. If the mode bit is identical, then iret just pops the instruction pointer and eflags register and continues to use the current stack.

  On the other hand, if the mode bit differs, then the iret instruction pops not only the instruction pointer and eflags register, but also the saved stack pointer, thus switching the processor's stack pointer to the saved one.

To be compatible with this x86 hardware behavior, our software implementation of thread_yield for in-kernel threads simulates the hardware case, saving only the instruction pointer and eflags register before calling pushad to save the general-purpose registers (including the stack pointer.) Now, iret will work properly whether the kernel thread it is resuming was suspended by a hardware event or a software call.

later, when this thread is restored, it would continue where it left off (e.g., it would finish saving its state to the stack, copy its saved state to its TCB, and run another thread.)

Finally, we save the remaining registers to the stack using the x86 pushad instruction.

Once the calling thread saves its state to its stack, it copies its saved state to its TCB, chooses another thread to run, and runs it by restoring its state in three steps: (1) change the stack pointer to point to the other thread's saved registers; (2) pop the other thread's general purpose registers; and (3) pop the other thread's instruction pointer and execution flags. After step (3), the current thread is no longer executing, and the assert(0) in the pseudo-code is never reached.

When the original thread is eventually restored, its stack, stack pointer, and all registers except the instruction pointer are the same as they were when the pushad call saved the registers. The instruction pointer is now LABEL, and the first thing the thread does upon being resumed is to execute the return. In essence, thread_yield() appears to the caller as an empty procedure that does nothing but immediately return. Of course, behind the scenes a lot is happening.

Processor's point of view.   From the processor's point of view, one instruction follows the next, but now the instructions from different threads are interleaved (as they must be if we are to support multiplexing!)

This interleaving can seem a bit unusual — thread_yield() deliberately violates the procedure call conventions compilers normally follow by manipulating the stack and program counter to switch between threads. For example, Figure 4.13 shows the interleaving when two threads each execute a simple endless loop:

```
while (1){
   thread_yield ();
}
```

One way to view Figure 4.13 is that from the processor's point of view — because of the way a context switch manipulates the registers — thread_-yield() is called by one thread but returns in a different thread.

But, once the operating system has the needed mechanisms to switch between threads, the threads, themselves, get to ignore this complexity. From their point of view, they each just run this loop on their own (variable-speed) virtual processor.

Multi-threaded processes

So far, we have described how to implement multiple threads in a kernel. Threads are also a useful abstraction for applications, so modern operating systems support *multi-threaded processes.*

We will describe how operating systems provide the abstraction of multi-threaded processes in two steps.

- First, we will describe how single-threaded processes mesh with the mechanisms we've just described for implementing a multi-threaded operating system.

Logical View	
Thread 1	Thread 2
while(1){	while(1){
thread_yield()	thread_yield()
}	}

Physical Reality		
Thread 1's instructions	Thread 2's instructions	**Processor's instructions**
call thread_yield		call thread_yield
save state to stack		save state to stack
save state to TCB		save state to TCB
choose another thread		choose another thread
load other thread state		load other thread state
	call thread_yield	call thread_yield
	save state to stack	save state to stack
	save state to TCB	save state to TCB
	choose another thread	choose another thread
	load other thread state	load other thread state
return thread_yield		return thread_yield
call thread_yield		call thread_yield
save state to stack		save state to stack
save state to TCB		save state to TCB
choose another thread		choose another thread
load other thread state		load other thread state
	return thread_yield	return thread_yield
	call thread_yield	call thread_yield
	save state to stack	save state to stack
	save state to TCB	save state to TCB
	choose another thread	choose another thread
	load other thread state	load other thread state
return thread_yield		return thread_yield
...	...	...

Figure 4.13: Interleaving of instructions when two threads loop and call thread_yield().

- Then, we will describe a few small additions needed to support multi-threaded processes.

Multi-threaded kernel with single-threaded processes

Figure 4.14 illustrates two single-threaded user-level processes running on a multi-threaded kernel with three kernel threads. Notice that each user-level process includes the process's thread. But, each process is more than just a thread because each process has its own address space — process 1 has its own view of memory, its own code, its own heap, and its own global variables that differ from those of process 2 (and differ from those of the kernel).

A zero-thread kernel

Not only can we have a single-threaded kernel or a multi-threaded kernel, it is actually possible to have a kernel with no threads of its own — a zero-threaded kernel! In fact, this used to be quite common.

Consider the simple picture of an operating system we sketched in Chapter 2. Once the system has booted, initialized its device drivers, and started some user-level processes like a login shell, everything else the kernel does is event-driven — done in response to an interrupt, exception, or trap.

In a simple operating system like this, there is no need for a "kernel thread" or "kernel thread control block" to keep track of an ongoing computation. Instead, when an interrupt, trap, or exception occurs, the stack pointer gets set to the base of the exception stack, the instruction pointer gets set to the address of the handler. Then the handler executes and either returns immediately to the interrupted user-level process or suspends the user-level process and "returns" to some other user-level process. In either case, the next event (interrupt, trap, or exception) starts this process anew.

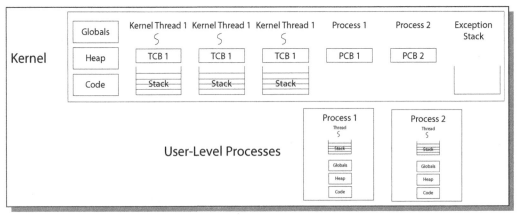

Figure 4.14: A multi-threaded kernel with 3 kernel threads and 2 single-threaded user-level processes.

Because a process is more than just a thread, each process's *process control block* (PCB) needs more information than a thread control block (TCB) for a kernel thread, and switching between processes — or between a kernel thread and a user-level process — needs to do a bit more work.

PCB v. TCB. The a kernel thread's TCB and a user-level process's PCB are similar, but it has some additional information. Like a TCB, a PCB must store the processor registers when the process's thread is not running. In addition, the PCB has information about the process's address space so that when we context switch from one process to another or between a process and the kernel, the right virtual memory mappings are used. We discuss virtual memory in Chapter ??.

With respect to concurrency and threads, the PCB and TCB each represents one thread, and the kernel's ready list contains a mix of PCBs for processes and TCBs for kernel thread. When the scheduler chooses the next thread to run, it can pick either kind.

Process switch v. thread switch. At a high level, thread switch is nearly identical whether we are switching between kernel threads or switching between a process's thread and a kernel thread. In all cases, we save the state of the currently running thread and restore the state of the next thread to run.

The difference is that when switching from a user-level thread, we need to switch from operating in user mode to to kernel mode. Leaving aside the additional work needed to change the virtual memory mappings (which we'll discuss in Chapter ??), the mode change can also slightly change the low-level implementation details for saving and restoring thread state.

- **Hardware-triggered (interrupts and exceptions.).** When an interrupt or exception causes a hardware-triggered thread switch, the hardware and software work together to save the state of the suspended thread. Exactly what state gets saved by the hardware may differ slightly depending on whether the interrupted thread is running in user mode or kernel mode, but these changes are relatively small implementation details. For example, we saw that for the x86 architecture, the hardware saves the stack pointer when it switches from user to kernel mode but not when it stays in kernel mode, and the iret instruction to resume a suspended thread has to account for this difference.

- **Software-triggered (library calls v. system calls).** When an in-kernel thread accesses the threads library to create or delete a thread or to suspend, resume, or switch threads it can use a simple procedure call, but when a user-level thread accesses the threads library to do these things, it needs to use a system call; because the PCBs are in the kernel's memory, a user-level process's threads must invoke kernel code to save their state.

Multi-threaded kernel with multi-threaded processes

The basic infrastructure just described for running a mix of kernel threads and single-threaded user processes needs little change to run multithreaded user processes such as the mix shown in Figure ??. The kernel's ready list includes kernel thread TCBs and one or more PCBs for each user-level process, and the thread context switch mechanisms work as described in

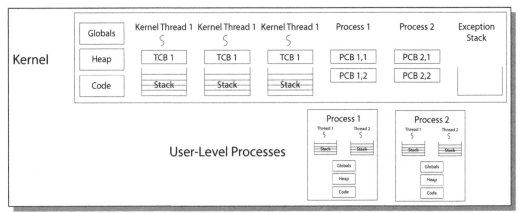

Figure 4.15: A multi-threaded kernel with 3 kernel threads and 2 user-level processes, each with 2 threads.

the previous subsection to allow switching between kernel threads, between a kernel thread and a process thread, between threads from different processes, or between threads from the same process.

A process can now use system calls to create multiple threads. Notice that for each thread, the thread's PCB is created in the kernel, but the thread's stack is allocated in the process's memory. But, the process's threads share other state such as the process's code, heap, and globals.

A process can create multiple threads for the reasons listed at the start of the chapter.

1. **Program structure.** A program that needs to do multiple things at the same time can create a thread for each one and rely on the operating system to transparently switch among these threads so that each makes progress.

2. **Exploiting multiple processors.** If a program can divide its work into independent pieces, it can create a thread for each piece. If multiple processors are available — this depends on what hardware the program is running on and on what other kernel threads and other processes are active — the operating system may spread this program's threads across multiple processors, allowing it to finish its work more quickly.

EXAMPLE   **Parallel processing.** Suppose a program running on a 16-processor machine needs to multiply two large matrices together. For matrix multiply $C = A * B$, result entry $C_{(i,j)}$ is computed by taking the dot product of the ith row of A and the jth column of B: $C_{i,j} = \Sigma_{k=0}^{N-1} A_{(i,k)} B_{(k,j)}$. So, we can divide the work of computing C into 16 parts, and create one thread to compute each part, and then compute those parts on different processors in parallel. For example, thread 0 running on one processor might compute the upper left square:

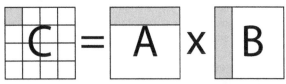

3. **Coping with high latency I/O devices.** If a program has multiple threads, then when some are waiting for I/O to complete, others can be running.

   User-level programs typically access I/O devices such as keyboards, screens, disks, and networks via system calls. If a system call blocks because it needs to wait for the I/O device, then the calling thread goes from the RUNNING state to the WAITING state, and the scheduler chooses another thread to run.

EXAMPLE   **Overlapping I/O and processing.** For example, if a process running on a single-processor machine needs to encrypt 100 files, it might create two threads, each of which iterates through 50 files, reading one file, encrypting it, reading the next, and so on. Then, while one thread is waiting for a file to be read from disk, the other one can be using the processor to encrypt the file it read from disk.

Threads without kernel support

In the body of the text, we describe how a an operating system can provide system calls so that a process can create multiple threads and have multiple schedulable PCBs in the kernel.

It is also possible to implement threads as a library completely at user level, without any operating system support.

The basic idea is simple. The threads library instantiates all of its data structures within the process: TCBs, the ready list, the finished list, and the waiting lists all are just data structures in the process's address space. Then, calls to the threads library are just procedure calls (similar to how the same functions are implemented within a multi-threaded kernel as described above.)

What about interrupts and exceptions? Can we implement something like a timer interrupt so that we can suspend a long-running thread so that it does not monopolize the processor? Yes; on most operating systems, we can. Most operating systems implement *signal handlers* or something similar, which allows the operating system to trigger execution of specified handler code within a user-level process when a specified event like a timer interrupt or memory exception occurs.

So, first the user-level threads library for some process P uses a system call to register a signal handler with the kernel. When a hardware timer interrupt occurs, the hardware and kernel software save P's register state and run the kernel's handler. Rather than restoring P's register state and resuming P where it was interrupted, kernel's handler copies P's saved registers into P's address space (e.g., onto a signal stack that P has registered or onto P's existing stack) and restore a slightly modified state with the a stack pointer changed to point to where this state was saved and the instruction pointer changed to point to the signal handler code that P registered. Thus, P's signal handler is invoked with the state of the previously running thread stored on its stack. It can then save that state to a TCB within the process and restore the state of some other TCB on the process's ready list.

This approach essentially virtualizes interrupts and exceptions, providing a user-level process with a very similar picture to the one the kernel gets when these events occur.

Why would you do this? Early libraries for threads often took this pure user-level approach for the simple reason that few operating systems supported multi-threaded processes. Even once operating system support for threads became widespread, pure user-level threads were sometimes used to minimize dependencies on the operating systems and to maximize portability; for example the earliest implementations of Sun's Java Virtual Machine (JVM) implemented what were called *green threads*, a pure user-level implementation of threads.

Why wouldn't you do this? From the kernel's point of view, a process that uses a library to implement pure user-level threads appears to be single-threaded no matter how many threads the user-level library creates.

As a result, pure user-level threads do not meet all of the goals of threads outlined at the start of this chapter. In particular, although pure user-level threads can be used for *program structure*, they do not help with *performance (parallel processing)* because the kernel only sees one "thread" that it can schedule. Similarly, they do not help with *performance (coping with high-latency I/O)* because if one thread blocks due to a long-running system call, the kernel does not have access to (and is unaware of) other TCBs that it could enable.

Today, most programs make use of kernel-supported threads rather than pure user-level threads. Major operating systems support threads and support them using fairly standard abstractions, so the past motivations are seldom compelling enough to compensate for the significant performance disadvantages.

Hybrid implementations. Although today few threads packages operate completely at user level, many split their work between the user-level library and the operating system kernel to reduce overheads by avoiding mode switches into the kernel for some of their operations.

EXAMPLE   **Hybrid thread join.** As a simple example, rather than always having thread_join() make a system call to wait for the target thread to finish and return its exit value, we can have thread_exit() store its exit value in a data structure in the process's address space. Then, if the call to thread_join() happens after the targeted has exited, it can immediately return that stored value without having to make a system call and mode switch into the kernel. However, if the call to thread_join() precedes the call to thread_exit(), then the call to thread_exit() would make a system call to transition to the WAITING state and let some other thread run.

EXAMPLE   **Scheduler activations.** A more sophisticated example is *scheduler acti-*
vations. Like the full user-level threads package described at the start of
this sidebar, a thread system based on scheduler activations maintains
its ready list and other data structures within the process and handles
most thread management functions — thread_create(), thread_destroy(),
thread_yield(), thread_exit(), and thread_join(), as well as the synchronization functions described in the next chapter — as procedure calls within
the process.

Scheduler activations address the two problems noted above for pure
user-level threads packages: they allow a process to run multiple threads
in parallel on a multiprocessor, and they allow a process to hide I/O latency
by running other threads when one thread blocks for I/O.

Scheduler activations solve these problems by allowing the kernel to
activate the user-level scheduler when it wants to start running another one
of the process's threads. Initially, the process does a system call to register
its scheduler with the kernel; this is similar to registering a signal handler.
Then, if the kernel is running on a multiprocessor machine and notices
that a processor is available or if one of the process's threads blocks in
a system call, the kernel can activate the process's scheduler in a way
similar to how it would invoke a signal handler. The user-level scheduler
activation code can then transition to running any of the process's READY
threads.

Exercises

10. Using sthreads, write a program that creates several threads and
    that then determines whether the threads package on your system
    allocates a fixed size stack for each thread or whether each thread's
    stack starts at some small size and dynamically grows as needed.

    Hints: You will probably want to write a recursive procedure that
    you can use to consume a large amount of stack memory. You may
    also want to examine the addresses of variables allocated to different
    threads' staks. Finally, you may want to be able to determine how
    much memory has been allocated to your process; most operating sys-
    tems have a command or utility that an show resource consumption
    by currently running processes (e.g., top in Linux, Activity Monitor
    in OSX, or Task Manager in Windows.)

4.5 | Asynchronous I/O and event-driven programming

Although threads are a common way to express concurrency, they are not the only way. Asynchronous I/O and event-driven programming are one popular alternative. This approach allows a single-threaded program to cope with high-latency I/O devices by overlapping I/O with processing and other I/O.

The basic idea is to allow a process to make a system call to issue and I/O request but not wait for the result. At a later time the operating system provides the result to the process by calling a signal handler, by making a callback to code in the process, by placing the result in a queue in the process's memory, or by storing the result in kernel memory until the process makes another system call to retrieve it.

EXAMPLE   **Asynchronous disk read.** Reading from disk can take tens of milliseconds, so in Linux, rather than issuing a read() system call that blocks until the requested blocks have been read from disk, a process can issue an aio_read() (asynchronous I/O read) system call, which tells the operating system to initiate the read from disk but which then immediately returns. Later, the process can call aio_error() to determine if the disk read has finished and aio_return() to retrieve the read's results. E.g.,

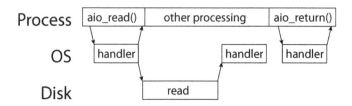

One common design pattern allows a single thread to interleave several different I/O-bound tasks by waiting for several different I/O events.

EXAMPLE   **Web server.** Consider a web server with 10 active clients. Rather than create one thread per client and have each thread do a blocking read() on the network connection, an alternative is for the server to have one thread that does a select() call that blocks until *any* of the 10 network connections has data available to read; when the select() call returns, it provides the thread with an identifier for a connection that has data available, and the thread can then read() from that connection, knowing that the read will immediately return. After processing the data, the thread then calls select() again to wait for the next message.

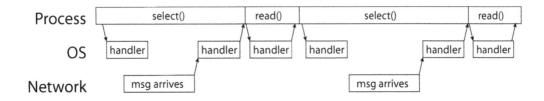

In servers, asynchronous I/O allows many concurrent tasks to be in progress at once. This gives rise to an *event-driven programming pattern* where a thread spins in a loop, and on each iteration it gets and processes the next I/O event. In order to be able to process each event, the thread typically maintains for each task a *continuation*, a data structure that keeps track of a task's current state and next step.

event-driven program-ming pattern

continuation

EXAMPLE   **Web server.** Handling a web server request can involve a series of I/O steps: making a network connection, reading a request from the network connection, reading the requested data from disk, and writing the re-quested data to the network connection. If a single thread is handling requests from multiple different clients at once, it needs to keep track of the state of its processing for each request. For example, the network may divide a client's request into several packets so that the server needs to make several read() calls to assemble the full packet. The server may be doing this request assembly for multiple clients at once, so it needs to keep several per-client variables (e.g., a request buffer, the number of bytes expected, and the number of bytes received so far). When new data arrives, the thread uses the network connection's port number to identify which client sent the request and retrieves the appropriate client's variables using this port number/client ID. It can then process the data.

Event-driven programming v. threads.   Although superficially different, overlapping I/O with computation and other I/O is fundamentally the same whether you use asynchronous I/O and event-driven programming or use synchronous I/O and threads. In either case, we block until the next I/O can be done, restore the state of the task that can make progress, exe-cute the next step of that task, and save the task's state until it can take its next step. The differences are whether the state is stored in a continuation or thread control block and whether the state save/restore is done explicitly by the application or automatically the threads system.

EXAMPLE   **Receiving from multiple connections.** Consider a simple server that just collects incoming data from several clients. The pseudocode for the event-driven and thread-per-client cases are similar:

```
// Event−driven
Hashtable<Buffer*> *hash;
while (1){
   connection = use select() to find a
              readable connection ID
   buffer = hash.remove(connection);
   got = read(connection,
            tmpBuf,
            TMP_SIZE);
   buffer −>append(tmpBuf, got);
   buffer = hash.put(connection,
            buffer);
}
```

```
// Thread−per−client
Buffer *b;
while (1){
   got = read(connection,
            tmpBuf,
            TMP_SIZE);
   buffer −>append(tmpBuf, got);
}
```

When these programs execute, the system does essentially the same things. However, in the first case, it explicitly saves and restores each connection's state, while in the second case, the thread system saves and restores this state transparently.

The state in both cases is also essentially the same. In both cases, the application needs to keep one buffer per client connection. In the event-driven case, the application maintains a data structure (e.g., hash in the pseudocode) to keep track of the different clients' data structures. In the thread-per-client case, each thread has just one buffer to keep track of, and the operating system keeps track of the different threads' states.

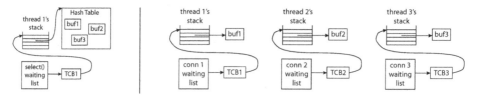

To compare the event-driven and threads approaches, consider the three goals for threads discussed at the start of this chapter.

- **Performance: Coping with high-latency I/O devices.** Either approach — event-driven or threads — can be used to overlap I/O and processing. Which provides better performance?

  In the past, the common wisdom has been that the event-driven approach could often be significantly faster for two reasons. First, the space and context switch overheads of the approach can be lower because a thread system must use generic code that allocates a stack for each thread's state and that saves and restores all registers on each context switch, but the event-driven approach allows programmers to allocate and save/restore just the state needed for each thread. Second, some past operating systems had inefficient or unscalable implementations of their thread systems, making it important not to create too many threads for each process.

  Today, the comparison is less clear cut. Many systems now have large memories, so the cost of allocating a thread stack for each task is less critical. For example, allocating 1000 threads with a 16KB stack for each thread on a machine with 4GB of memory would consume 0.4% of the machine's memory. Also, most operating systems now have efficient and scalable threads libraries. For example, where the Linux 2.4 kernel had poor performance when processes had many threads, Linux 2.6 revamped the thread system, improving its scalability and absolute performance.

Anecdotal evidence suggests that the performance gap between the two approach has at least greatly narrowed and that for some applications the highly-optimized thread management code and synchronous I/O paths can beat the often less-optimized application code and asynchronous I/O paths. Performance has probably reached the point that for most application other factors (e.g., code simplicity and ease of maintenance) may be more important than raw performance. If performance is critical for a particular application, then — as is often the case — tere is no substitute for careful benchmarking and measurements in making your decision.

- **Performance: Exploiting multiple processors.** The event-driven approach does not help a program exploit multiple processors. Note, however, that the event-driven and thread approaches can be combined: a program that wants to use n processors can have n threads, each of which uses the event-driven pattern to multiplex multiple I/O-bound tasks on each thread.

- **Program structure: Expressing logically concurrent tasks.** Whenever one compares two viable programming styles, one can find strong advocates for each approach. The situation is no different here, with some advocates of event-driven programming arguing that the synchronization required when threads share data makes threads more complex than events and advocates for threads arguing that threads provide a more natural way to express the control flow of a program than having to explicitly store a computation's state in a continuation.

In our opinion, there remain cases where both styles are appropriate, and we use both in our own programs. That said, it seems to us that for most I/O-intensive programs, threads are preferable: they are often more natural, sufficiently efficient, and able to exploit multiple processors.

4.6 | Conclusion and future directions

Concurrency is ubiquitous — many smartphones and the vast majority of servers, desktops, laptops, and tablets and have 2 or more cores. Multithreaded programming is a skill that every professional programmer needs to master.

Technology trends suggest that concurrent programming will only get more important over time. After several decades in which computer architects were able to make individual processor cores run faster and faster, we have reached an era where individual cores are not getting much faster and where speedups will have to come from parallel processing.

Threads and event-driven programming are important models, but they are not the only ways to write parallel programs. Other approaches are also highly effective, particularly for certain classes of applications.

Data parallel programming

SIMD (single instruction multiple data) programming

- **Data parallel programs.** *Data parallel programming* or *SIMD (single instruction multiple data) programming* models allow a programmer to describe a computation that should be performed in parallel on many different pieces of data. Rather than having the programmer divide work among threads, the runtime system decides how to map the parallel work across the hardware's processors.

  For example, to divide each element in an N-element array in half, you might write

  ```
  forall(i in 0:N−1) array[i] = array[i]/2
  ```

  and the runtime system would divide the array among processors to execute this computation in parallel.

  Data parallel programming is frequently used in large data-analysis tasks. For example, the Hadoop system is widely-used, open source system that can process and analyze terabytes of data spread across hundreds or thousands of servers. As another example, SQL (Structured Query Language) is a standard language for accessing databases in which programmers specify the database query to perform and the database maps the query to lower-level operations and schedules those operations on its processors and disks.

  Multimedia streams (e.g., audio, video, and graphics) often have large amounts of data on which similar operations are repeatedly performed, so data parallel programming is frequently used for media processing, and specialized hardware to support this type of parallel processing is common. Because they can be optimized for regular, data parallel programs, GPUs (Graphical Processing Units) can provide significantly higher rates of data processing. For example, in 2011 a Radeon HD5870 GPU is capable of 544 GFLOPS (billion (Giga) Floating Point Operations Per Second (double-precision)); for comparison, an Intel Core i7 980 XE CPU (a high end, general purpose processor) is capable of 109 double-precision GFLOPS.

  Considerable research and development effort is currently going towards developing and using *General Purpose GPUs (GPGPUs)*, GPUs that have been extended to better support a wider-range of programs. It is still not clear what classes of programs can work well with

GPGPUs and which require more traditional CPU architectures, but for those programs that can be ported to the more restrictive GPGPU programming model, the performance gains can be dramatic.

- **Distributed and parallel processing.** Many of the services we rely on today are implemented by large scale distributed systems. For example, when you use your browser to do a web search, hundreds or thousands of servers may work together to process your request and produce your search results, all in a few hundredths of a second.

  Similarly, parallel scientific computations such as drug discovery, climate simulation, and geologic modeling can run on clusters of hundreds or thousands of machines, with threads on different machines coordinating their work by sending messages to each other over a high speed network.

There are entire courses devoted to parallel programming or and even to some of these individual techniques, and improving techniques for parallel programming is seen as an important research challenge. Over your career, all of these techniques will evolve and new ones are likely to appear.

Exercises

For convenience, the exercises from each section are repeated here.
To complete the following problems, download the sthread library from http://www.cs.utexas.edu/users/dahlin/osbook/code/sthread.h, and http://www.cs. utexas.edu/users/dahlin/osbook/code/sthread.c. The comment at the top of threadHello.c explains how to compile and run a program that uses this library.

1. Download this example code http://www.cs.utexas.edu/users/dahlin/osbook/code/threadHello.c, compile it, and run it several times. What do you get if you run it? Do you get the same thing if you run it multiple times? What if you are also running some other demanding processes (e.g., compiling a big program, playing a Flash game on a website, or watching streaming video) when you run this program?

2. For the threadHello program in Figure 4.6, what is the *maximum* number of threads that could exist while the program is running? *(Be careful.)*

3. For the threadHello program in Figure 4.6, suppose that we delete the second for loop so that the main routine simply creates NTHREADS threads and then prints "Main thread done." What are the possible outputs of the program now. **Hint:** Fewer than NTHREADS+1 lines may be printed in some runs. Why?

4. How expensive are threads? Write a program that times how long it taks to create and then join 1000 threads, where each thread simply calls sthread_exit(0) as soon as it starts running.

5. Write a program that has two threads. The first thread a simple loop that continuously increments a counter and prints a period (".") whenever the value of that counter is divisible by 10,000,000. The second thread repeatedly waits for the user to input a line of text and then prints "Thank you for your input." On your system, does the operating system do a good job of making sure that the first thread makes rapid progress and that the second thread responds quickly?

6. For the threadHello program in Figure 4.6, when pthread_join() returns for thread ii, in which of the states shown in Figure 4.9 is thread ii?

7. For the threadHello program in Figure 4.6 the procedure go() has the parameter np and the local variable n. Are these variables *per thread* or *shared* state? Where does the compiler store these variables' states?

8. For the threadHello program in Figure 4.6 the procedure main() has local variables such as ii, err, and status. Are these variables *per thread* or *shared* state? Where does the compiler store these variables' states?

9. In the sidebar on page 153, we describe *thread-local variables*, which are another piece of per-thread state present in many thread systems.

   Describe how you would implement thread-local variables. Each thread should have an array of 1024 pointers to its thread-local variables.

   • What would you add to the TCB?
   • How would you change the thread creation procedure? (For simplicity, assume that when a thread is created, all 1024 entries should be initialized to NULL.)
   • How would a running thread allocate a new thread-local variable?
   • In you design, how would a running thread access a particular thread-local variable?

10. Using sthreads, write a program that creates several threads and that then determines whether the threads package on your system allocates a fixed size stack for each thread or whether each thread's stack starts at some small size and dynamically grows as needed.

    Hints: You will probably want to write a recursive procedure that you can use to consume a large amount of stack memory. You may also want to examine the addresses of variables allocated to different threads' staks. Finally, you may want to be able to determine how much memory has been allocated to your process; most operating systems have a command or utility that an show resource consumption by currently running processes (e.g., top in Linux, Activity Monitor in OSX, or Task Manager in Windows.)

It is not enough to be industrious. So are the ants. The question is: What are we industrious about?

Henry David Thoreau

5 Synchronizing Access to Shared Objects

Multi-threaded programs extend the traditional, single-threaded programming model so that each thread provides a single sequential stream of execution composed of familiar instructions. If we only have *independent threads* that operate on completely separate subsets of state, then we can reason about each thread separately. In this case, writing and reasoning about independent threads differs little from writing and reasoning about a series of independent, single-threaded programs.

independent threads

However, most multi-threaded programs have both both *per-thread* state (e.g., a thread's stack and registers) and *shared* state (e.g., shared variables on the heap). *Cooperating threads* read and write shared state.

Cooperating threads

Sharing state among threads is useful because it allows threads to communicate, to coordinate work, and to share information. For example, in our Earth Visualizer example in the previous chapter, once one thread has finished downloading a detailed image from the network, it needs to share that image data with a rendering thread that draws the new image on the screen.

Unfortunately, when cooperating threads use shared state, writing correct multi-threaded programs becomes much more difficult. Most programmers are used to thinking "sequentially" when reasoning about programs. For example, we often reason about the series of states traversed by a program as a sequence of instructions is executed. But this sequential model of reasoning breaks down in programs with cooperating threads for three reasons.

1. Program execution depends on the interleavings of threads' access to

shared state.

For example, if two threads write a shared variable, one thread with the value 1 and the other with the value 2, the final value of the the variable depends on which of the threads' writes finishes last.

Although this example is simple, the problem is severe because programs need to work for *any possible interleaving*. In particular, recall that thread programmers should not make any assumptions about the relative speed at which their threads operate.

Worse, as programs grow, there is a combinatorial explosion in the number of possible interleavings.

How can we reason about all possible interleavings of threads' actions in a multi-million line program.?

2. Program execution can be nondeterministic.

Different runs of the same program may produce different results. For example, the scheduler may make different scheduling decisions, the processor may run at a different frequency, or another concurrently running program may affect the cache hit rate. Even common debugging techniques — such as running a program under a debugger, recompiling with the -g option instead of -O, or adding a printf() — can change how a program behaves.

Jim Gray, the 1998 ACM Turing Award winner, coined the term *Heisenbugs* for bugs that disappear or change behavior when you try to examine them. Multi-threaded programming is a common source of Heisenbugs. In contrast *Bohrbugs* are deterministic and generally much easier to diagnose.

How can we debug programs whose behaviors change across runs?

3. Compilers and architectures reorder instructions.

Modern compilers and hardware will reorder instructions to improve performance. This reordering is generally invisible to single-threaded programs; compilers and processors take care to ensure that dependencies within a sequence of instruction are preserved. However, this reordering can become visible when multiple threads interact and observe intermediate states.

For example, consider the following code to compute q as a function of p.

Thread 1

```
p = someComputation ();
pIsInitialized = true;
```

Thread 2

```
while (!pIsInitialized)
    ;
q = anotherComputation (p);
```

Although it might appear that this code ensures that p is initialized before anotherComputation(p) is called to compute q, it does not. To maximize instruction level parallelism, the hardware or compiler may set pIsInitialized = true before the computation to compute p has completed, and anotherComputation(p) may be computed using an unexpected value.

How can we reason about thread interleavings when compilers and hardware may reorder a thread's operations?

Structured synchronization. Given all of these challenges, multi-threaded code can introduce subtle, non-deterministic, and unreproducible bugs. This chapter describes a *structured synchronization* approach to sharing state in multi-threaded programs. Rather than scattering access to shared state throughout the program and attempting *ad hoc* reasoning about what happens when the threads' accesses are interleaved in various ways, we structure the program to facilitate reasoning about it and we use a set of standard synchronization primitives to control access to shared state. This approach gives up some freedom, but if you consistently follow the rules we describe, then reasoning about programs with shared state becomes much simpler.

The first part of this section elaborates on the challenges faced by multi-threaded programmers and on why it is futile to try to reason about all possible thread interleavings in the general, unstructured case.

- **Challenges.** Why are unstructured multi-threaded programs difficult to reason about?

The rest of the chapter describes how to structure shared objects in multi-threaded programs so that we can reason about them. We will describe aspects of this structure. First, we will structure a multi-threaded program's shared state as a set of *shared objects* that encapsulate the shared state and that define and limit how the state can be accessed. Second, to avoid *ad hoc* reasoning about the interleavings of access to the state variables within a shared object, we will describe how shared objects include a small set of *synchronization primitives* like locks and condition variables to coordinate access to their state by different threads. Third, to simplify reasoning about the code in shared objects, we will describe a set of *best practices* for writing the code that implements each shared object. Because the first two issues are so closely tied together, we address these two issues in two main sections:

- **Shared objects and synchronization variables.** How do we use synchronization variables like locks and condition variables to construct shared objects that encapsulate shared state?

- **Best practices.** Given the building blocks provided by synchronization variables, what is a systematic way to write and reason about the code for shared objects?

Finally, it is important to understand how the tools we use actually work, so we dive into the details of how synchronization primitives are implemented.

- **Implementing synchronization primitives.** How are locks and condition variables implemented?

Multi-threaded programming has a reputation for being difficult. We agree that it takes care. But, this chapter provides a set of simple rules that anyone can follow to implement objects that can be shared by multiple threads.

5.1 | Challenges

The start of this section outlined the core challenge of multi-threaded programming: a multi-threaded program's execution depends on the interleavings of different threads' access to shared memory, which can make it difficult to reason about or debug these programs. In particular, cooperating threads' execution may be affected by *race conditions.*

Race conditions

race
condition

A *race condition* is when the behavior of a program depends on the interleaving of operations of different threads. In effect, the threads run a race between their operations, and the results of the program execution depends on who wins the race.

Reasoning about even simple programs with race conditions can be difficult. To appreciate this, we will look at several extremely simple multi-threaded programs.

The world's simplest cooperating-threads program. Suppose we run a program with two threads that do the following:

$$\begin{array}{cc} \text{Thread 0} & \text{Thread 1} \\ x = 1; & x = 2; \end{array}$$

Q: What are the possible final values of x?
A: x = 1 or x = 2 depending on which thread wins or loses the "race" to set x. That was easy, so let's try one that is a bit more interesting.

The world's second-simplest cooperating-threads program. Suppose that initially y = 12 and we run a program with two threads that do the following:

> Thread 0   Thread 1
> x = y + 1;   y = y * 2;

Q: What are the possible final values of x?
A: We can get x = 13 if Thread 0 executes first or x = 25 if Thread 1 executes first. More precisely, we get x = 13 if Thread 0 reads y before Thread 1 updates y or we get x = 25 if Thread 1 updates y before Thread 0 reads y.

The world's third-simplest cooperating-threads program. Suppose that initially x = 0 and we run a program with two threads that do the following:

> Thread 0   Thread 1
> x = x + 1;   x = x + 2;

Q: What are the possible final values of x?
A: Obviously, we can get x = 3. For example, Thread 0 can run to completion and then Thread 1 can start and run to completion. However, we can also get x = 2 or x = 1. In particular, when we write a single statement like x = x + 1, compilers on many processors produce multiple instructions such as (1) load memory location x into a register, (2) add 1 to that register, and (3) store the result to memory location x. If we mentally disassemble the above program into simple pseudo-assembly-code, we can see some of the possibilities.

One Interleaving	Another Interleaving	Yet Another Interleaving
load r1, x	load r1, x	load r1, x
add r2, r1, 1	load r1, x	load r1, x
store x, r2	add r2, r1, 1	add r2, r1, 1
load r1, x	add r2, r1, 2	add r2, r1, 2
add r2, r1, 2	store x, r2	store x, r2
store x, r2	store x, r2	store x, r2
final: x == 3	final: x == 2	final: x == 1

Already, for this 2-line program, the complexity of reasoning about race conditions and interleavings is beginning to grow: not only would one have to reason about all possible interleavings of statements, but one would have to mentally disassemble the programs and reason about all possible interleavings of assembly instructions. (And if the compiler and hardware can reorder those instructions, things are even worse.)

Atomic operations

atomic operations

When we mentally disassembled the code in last example, we were able to reason about *atomic operations*, indivisible operations that cannot be interleaved or split with or by other operations.

On most modern architectures a load or store of a 32-bit word from or to memory is an atomic operation. So, our above analysis reasoned about interleaving of atomic loads and stores to memory.

Conversely, a load or store is not always an atomic operation. Depending on the implementation of the hardware, if two threads store the value of a a 64-bit floating point register to a memory address, the final result might be the first value, the second value, or a mix of the two.

In the next subsection, we will give an example of reasoning about a program based on its atomic loads and stores to memory. Because of these challenges, we then move on to a better approach that raises the level of abstraction by constructing *shared objects* using *synchronization variables*.

Too much milk

Although one could, in principle, reason carefully about the possible interleavings of different threads' atomic loads and stores, doing so is tricky. To illustrate this, we will present three solutions to a simple problem called "Too much milk."

The too much milk problem models two roommates who share a refrigerator and who—as good roommates—make sure the refrigerator is always well stocked with milk. With such responsible roommates, the following scenario is possible:

Roommate 1's actions	Roommate 2's actions
3:00 Look in fridge; out of milk	
3:05 Leave for store	
3:10 Arrive at store	Look in fridge; out of milk
3:15 Buy milk	Leave for store
3:20 Arrive home; put milk away	Arrive at store
3:25	Buy milk
3:30	Arrive home; put milk away
3:35	Oh no!

We can model each roommate as a thread, and we can model the number of bottles of milk in the fridge with a variable in memory. The question is, if the only atomic operations on shared state are atomic loads and stores to memory, can we devise a solution to the too much milk problem that ensures both *safety* (the program never enters a bad state) and *liveness* (the program eventually enters a good state.) Here, we strive for the following properties:

safety

liveness

1. **Safety:** Never more than one person buys milk.

2. **Liveness:** If milk is needed, eventually somebody buys milk.

Simplifying assumption.   Throughout our analysis in this section, we assume that the instructions are executed in exactly the order written—neither the compiler nor the architecture reorders instructions. Such an assumption is crucial for reasoning about the order of atomic load and store operations, but many modern compilers and architectures will violate it, so be careful about using this approach.

With modern machines and compilers, in addition to the challenges discussed in this section, one would also have to use *memory barriers* to constrain such reordering, further complicating the problem. We discuss memory barriers later.

Solution 1.   We first present solution 1 of 3.[1]

The basic idea is for a roommate to leave a note on the fridge before leaving for the store. The simplest way to leave this note—given our programming model that we have shared memory on which we can perform atomic loads and stores—is to set a flag when going to buy milk and to check this flag before going to buy milk. We might have each thread run the following code:

```
if (milk ==0){          // if no milk
    if (note ==0){       // if no note
        note = 1;        // leave note
        milk ++;         // buy milk
        note = 0;        // remove note
    }
}
```

Unfortunately, this implementation can violate safety. For example, the first thread could execute everything up to and including the check of the milk value and then get context switched. Then the second thread could run through all of this code and buy milk. Finally, the first thread could be rescheduled, see that note == 0 is true, leave the note, buy more milk, and remove the note, leaving the system with milk == 2.

---

[1]Two more solutions are coming. The reader should be suspicious.

```
if (milk==0){
                                    if (milk==0){
                                        if (note==0){
                                            note = 1;
                                            milk++;
                                            note = 0;
                                        }
                                    }
        if (note==0){
            note = 1;
            milk++;
            note = 0;
        }
}
```

Oh no!

This "solution" makes the problem worse. The above code will usually work, but it may fail occasionally when the scheduler does just the right (or wrong) thing. We have created a Heisenbug that will cause the program to occasionally fail in ways that may be really hard to reproduce (e.g., probably only when the grader is looking at it or when the CEO is demonstrating the prototype to an important investor!).

Solution 2. We now present solution 2 of 3.[2]

In the above solution, we had to check the note before setting it, which led to the possibility of bad interleavings where one roommate had already made a decision to buy milk before notifying the other roommate of that decision. If we use two variables for the notes, a roommate can create a note before checking the other note and the milk and making a decision to buy. For example, we can do the following:

Path A				Path B			
noteA = 1;	// leave note			noteB = 1;	// leave note		
if (noteB==0){	// if no note	A1		if (noteA==0){	// if no note	B1	
if (milk==0){	// if no milk	A2		if (milk==0) {	// if no milk	B2	
milk++;	// buy milk	A3		milk++;	// buy milk	B3	
}				}	//	B4	
}				}	//	B5	
noteA = 0;	// remove note A			noteB = 0;	// remove note		

If the first thread executes the Path A code and the second thread executes the Path B code, this protocol is safe; by having each thread write a note ("I might buy milk") before deciding to buy milk, we ensure that we can never heave both threads buy milk.

Although this intuition is solid, proving safety without enumerating all possible interleavings requires a bit of care.

---

[2]The odds that this one will work also seem low, don't they?

Safety Proof. Assume for the sake of contradiction that the algorithm is *not* safe — both A and B buy milk. Consider the state of the two variables (noteB, milk) when thread A is at the line marked **A1** at the moment when the atomic load of noteB from shared memory to A's register occurs. There are three cases to consider:

- Case 1: (1, *). Impossible because this state contradicts the assumption that thread A buys milk and reaches **A3**.

stable
property

- Case 2: (0, > 0). Impossible because in this simple program the property milk > 0 is a *stable property* — once it becomes true, it remains true forever. Thus, if milk > 0 is true when A is at **A1**, A's test at line **A2** will fail, and A will not buy milk, contradicting our assumption.

- Case 3: (0, 0). We know that thread B must not currently be executing any of the lines marked **B1-B5**. We also know that either noteA == 1 or milk > 0 will be true from this time forward (noteA OR milk is also a stable property.) But, this means that B can not buy milk in the future (either the test at B1 or B2 must fail), which contradicts our assumption that both A and B buy milk. □

Liveness. Unfortunately, solution 2 does not ensure liveness. In particular, it is possible for both threads to set their respective notes, for each thread to check the other thread's note, and for both threads to decide not to buy milk.

This brings us to solution 3.

Solution 3. We now present solution 3 of 3.[3]

Solution 2 was safe because a thread would avoid buying milk if there was any chance that the other thread *might* buy milk. For solution 3, we will make sure that at least one of the threads determines whether the other thread has bought milk or not before deciding whether or not to buy. In particular, we do the following:

```
          Path A                                    Path B

noteA = 1;         // leave note A     noteB = 1;         // leave note B
while(noteB==1){   // wait for no note B  if(noteA==0){    // if no note A
   ;               // spin                 if(milk==0) {  // if no milk
}                                              milk++;    // buy milk
if(milk==0){       // if no milk M         }              //
   milk++;         // buy milk           }                //
}                                        noteB = 0;       // remove note B
noteA = 0;         // remove note A
```

We can show that solution 3 is safe using a similar argument to the one we used for solution 2.

---

[3]This one will work, but even better answers come in the next section.

To show that solution 3 is live, observe that code path B has no loops, so eventually thread B must finish executing the listed code and eventually, noteB == 0 becomes true and remains true. Therefore, eventually thread A must reach line **M** and decide whether to buy milk. If it finds M == 1, then milk has been bought, and we are live. If it finds M == 0, then it will buy milk, and we are live.

Discussion

The above discussion shows that—assuming that instructions are executed in program order—it is possible to devise a solution to "Too much milk" that is both safe and live using nothing but atomic load and store operations on shared memory. However, the solution we developed is not terribly satisfying.

- The solution is complex, and it requires careful reasoning to convince oneself that it works.

- The solution is asymmetric. Thread A executes slightly different code than Thread B. If we added more threads, more variations would be needed.

  Note that this limitation is not fundamental. For example, Peterson defined a symmetric solution to a more general version of "Too Much Milk" that works for any fixed number n of threads attempting to access a resource. More details on Petersen's algorithm can be found elsewhere (e.g., http://en.wikipedia.org/wiki/Peterson's_algorithm.)

- The solution is inefficient. While thread A is waiting, it is *busy-waiting* and consuming CPU resources.

- The solution may fail if the compiler or hardware reorders instructions.

  This limitation can be addressed through the use of memory barriers, but the need to add memory barriers further increases the complexity of trying to implement and reason about this type of algorithm; barriers also do not address the other limitations just mentioned. See the sidebar for a discussion of memory barriers.

A better solution

The next section will describe a better approach to writing programs in which multiple threads access shared state. We will write *shared objects* that use *synchronization objects* to coordinate different threads' access to shared state.

Suppose, for example, we had a primitive called a *lock* that ensures that only one thread at a time can own a lock. Then, we can solve the too much

Memory barriers

Suppose you are writing low-level code that must reason about the ordering of memory operations. How can this be done on modern hardware and with modern compilers?

A *memory barrier* instruction prevents the compiler and hardware from reordering memory accesses across the barrier — no accesses before the barrier will be moved after the barrier and no accesses after the barrier will be moved before the barrier. One can add memory barriers to the "too much milk" solution or to Peterson's algorithm to get code that works on modern machines with modern compilers. Of course, that may make such code even more complex.

Details of how to issue a memory barrier instruction depend on hardware and compiler details, but a good example is gcc's __sync_synchronize() builtin, which tells the compiler not to reorder memory accesses across the barrier and to issue architecture-specific instructions that the underlying hardware will treat as a memory barrier.

milk problem by defining the class for a Kitchen object with the following method:

```
Kitchen :: buyIfNeeded (){
    lock.acquire ();
    if (milk == 0){      // if no milk
        milk++;          // buy milk
    }
    lock.release ();
}
```

We will define locks and condition variables (another type of synchronization object) in the next section.

Exercises

1. Show that solution 3 to the Too Much Milk problem is safe — that it guarantees that at most one roommate buys milk.

5.2 | Shared objects and synchronization variables

The above discussion should convince you that it is unappealing to try to write multi-threaded programs using just atomic loads and stores. Fortunately, decades of work have developed a much simpler approach that extends the modularity of object oriented programming to multi-threaded

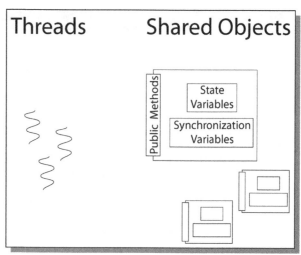

Figure 5.1: In a multi-threaded program, threads are separate from and operate on shared objects.

programs: as Figure 5.1 illustrates, a multi-threaded program is build using *shared objects* and a set of threads that operate on them.

shared object   *Shared objects* are objects that can safely be accessed by multiple threads. All shared state in a program—including variables allocated on the heap (e.g., objects allocated with malloc() or new()) and static, global variables—should be encapsulated in one or more shared objects.

Shared objects extend traditional object-oriented programming in which objects hide their implementation details behind a clean interface. In the same way, shared objects hide the details of synchronizing the actions of multiple threads behind a clean interface. The threads using shared objects just need to understand the interface, they don't need to know how the shared object internally handles synchronization.

Just like regular objects, the shared objects are completely general—programmers implement shared objects for whatever modules, interfaces, and semantics their application needs. Each shared object's class defines a set of public methods on which threads operate. Then, to assemble the overall program out of these shared objects, each thread executes some "main loop" written in terms of actions on public methods of shared objects.

Note that since the shared objects encapsulate the program's shared state, the main-loop code that defines a thread's high-level actions doesn't concern itself with the details of synchronization. The programming model thus looks very much like it does for single-threaded code.

Implementing shared objects.   Of course, internally the shared objects must handle the details of synchronization. As Figure 5.2 shows, shared objects are implemented in three layers.

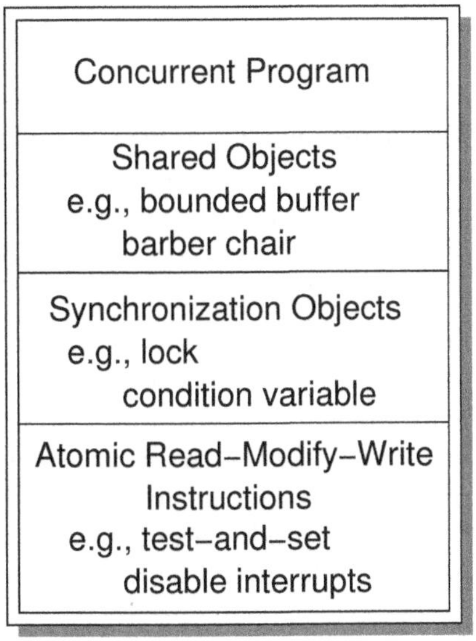

Figure 5.2: Multi-threaded programs are built with shared objects, shared objects are built using synchronization objects, and synchronization objects are implemented using atomic read-modify-write instructions.

- **Shared objects.** As in standard object-oriented programming, the shared objects define the application-specific logic and hide the internal implementation details. Externally, shared objects appear essentially the same as objects you define for single-threaded programs.

- **Synchronization variables.** Rather than trying to implement shared objects directly with carefully interleaved atomic loads and stores, shared objects include *synchronization variables* as member variables. Synchronization variables are stored in memory just like any other object, so they can be included in any data structure.

synchronization variable

Synchronization variables are instances of carefully designed classes that provide broadly-useful primitives for synchronization. In particular, we build shared objects using two types of synchronization variables: *locks* and *condition variables*. We define these and describe how to construct them later.

state variable

Synchronization variables coordinate access to *state variables*, which are just the normal member variables of an object that you are familiar with from single-threaded programming (e.g., integers, strings, arrays, pointers, etc.)

Using synchronization variables simplifies implementing shared objects. In fact, not only do shared objects externally appear quite similar to traditional single-threaded objects, by implementing them with synchronization variables, we can also make their internal implementations quite similar to what you are used to from implementing single-threaded programs.

- **Atomic read-modify-write instructions.** Although the layers above benefit from a simpler programming model, it is not turtles all the way down. Internally, synchronization variables must manage the interleavings of different threads' actions.

Rather than implementing synchronization variables such as locks and condition variables using only atomic loads and stores as we attempted to do for the Too Much Milk problem, modern implementations build synchronization variables using *atomic read-modify-write instructions*. An atomic read-modify-write instruction allows one thread to have exclusive access a memory location while the instruction's read, modification, and write of that location are guaranteed not to be interleaved with any other thread's access to that memory.

atomic read-
modify-write
instructions

Scope and roadmap. As Figure 5.1 indicates, concurrent programs are built on top of shared objects. The rest of this chapter focuses on the three bottom layers of the figure — how to build shared objects using synchronization objects and how to build synchronization objects out of atomic read-modify-write instructions. Chapter **??** discusses issues that arise when composing multiple shared objects into a larger program.

5.3 | Lock: Mutual Exclusion

lock

A *lock* is a synchronization variable that provides *mutual exclusion* — when one thread holds a lock, no other thread can hold the lock (other threads are *excluded*.)

A program associates each lock with some subset of shared state and requires a thread to hold the lock when accessing that state. Then, only one thread can be accessing the shared state at a time.

Mutual exclusion greatly simplifies reasoning about programs because a thread can perform an arbitrary set of operations while holding a lock, and those operations *appear to be atomic* from the point of view of other threads. In particular, because a lock enforces mutual exclusion and because threads must hold the lock to access the shared state, no other thread will be able to observe an intermediate — they can only observe the state left after the lock has been released.

EXAMPLE

Locking to group multiple operations. Consider, for example, a bank account object that includes a list of transactions and a total balance. To add a new transaction, we would acquire the account's lock, append the new transaction to the list, read the old balance, modify it, write the new balance, and release the lock. To query the balance and list of recent

Shared objects, monitors, and syntactic sugar

We focus on *shared objects* because object-oriented programming provides a good way to think about shared state: hide shared state behind public methods that provide a clean interface to threads and that handle the details of synchronization.

Although we use object-oriented terminology in our discussion, the ideas are equally applicable in non-object-oriented languages. For example, where a C++ program might define a class for shared objects that defines public methods to manipulate its private state variables and member variables in a well-defined way, a C program might define a struct that includes synchronization variables and state variables as fields, and — rather than having code that accesses the struct's fields scattered about — it might define a fixed set of functions that operate on the struct's fields

Conversely, some programming languages build in even more support for shared objects than we describe here. When a programming language includes support for shared objects, a shared object is often called a *monitor*. Early languages with built-in support for monitors included Brinch Hansen's Concurrent Pascal and Xerox PARC's Mesa; today, Java includes built in monitor support via the synchronized keyword.

We regard the distinctions between procedural languages, object-oriented languages, and languages with built-in support for monitors as relatively unimportant syntactic sugar. We use the terms "shared objects" or "monitors" broadly to refer to a conceptual approach to constructing shared state that can and should be used regardless of the level of built in support in a particular programming language.

That said, for this book, our code and pseudo-code are based on C++'s syntax, which we believe provides the right level of detail for teaching the shared objects/-monitors approach. We prefer teaching with C++ to, say, Java because we want to explicitly show where locks and condition variables are allocated and accessed rather than relying on operations hidden by a language's built in monitor syntax. Conversely, we prefer C++ to, say, C because we think C++'s support for object-oriented programming may help readers internalize the underlying philosophy of the shared object approach.

transactions, we would acquire the account's lock, read the recent transactions from the list, read the balance, and release the lock. Using locks this way would guarantee that one update or query completes before the next one starts so that a query always shows a balance that reflects the set of recent transactions shown.

It is much easier to reason about interleavings of atomic groups of operations rather than interleavings of individual operations for two reasons. First, there are (obviously) fewer interleavings to consider, so reasoning about interleavings on a coarser-grained basis reduces the sheer number of cases we have to worry about. Second, and more important, we can make each atomic group of operations correspond to the logical structure of the program, which allows us to reason about *invariants* not specific *interleavings.*

In particular, with shared objects we usually use one lock to guard all of an object's state, and we usually have each public method acquire the lock on entry and release the lock on exit. Then, reasoning about a shared class's code is similar to reasoning about a traditional class's code: we assume a set of invariants when a public method is called and reestablish those invarients before a public method returns. If we do a good job of defining our invariants, we can then reason about each method largely independently.

Lock: API and properties

A lock enables mutual exclusion by providing two methods: Lock::acquire() and Lock::release(). These operations are defined as follows:

- A lock can be in one of two states: BUSY or FREE.

- A lock is initially in the FREE state.

- Lock::acquire() waits until the lock is FREE , and then it atomically makes the lock BUSY.

  Checking the state to see if it is FREE and setting the state to BUSY are together an *atomic operation.* Een if multiple thread are trying to acquire the lock, at most one thread will succeed — only one thread will observe that the lock is FREE and set it to BUSY; the other threads will just see that the lock is BUSY and wait.

- Lock::release() makes the lock FREE. If there are pending acquire() operations, then this state change causes one of them to proceed.

We will describe how to implement locks with the above properties in Section 5.5. But, assuming we can implement such a lock, solving the Too Much Milk problem is trivial. Both threads run the following code:

```
lock.acquire();
if(milk == 0){      // if no milk
    milk++;         // buy milk
}
lock.release();
```

Formal properties.   The above definition describes the basic operation of a lock. A lock can be defined more precisely as follows.

We say that a thread *holds a lock* if it has returned from a lock's acquire() method more often than it has returned from a lock's release() method. We say that a thread *is attempting to acquire* a lock if it has called but not yet returned from a call to acquire() on the lock.

A lock should ensure the following three properties:

1. **Mutual Exclusion.** At most one thread holds the lock.

2. **Progress.** If no thread holds the lock and any thread attempts to acquire the lock, then eventually some thread succeeds in acquiring the lock.

3. **Bounded waiting.** If thread T attempts to acquire a lock, then there exists a bound on the number times other threads successfully acquire the lock before T does.

The first property is a safety property. It says that we can use locks to enforce mutual exclusion on access to shared state.

The second and third properties are liveness properties. The second says that if a lock is FREE, *some* thread must be able to acquire it. The third defines a fairness property: any *particular* thread that wants to acquire the lock must eventually succeed in doing so. If the definitions above sound a bit stilted, it is because they are carefully crafted to avoid introducing subtle corner cases. For example, if a thread holding a lock never releases it, other threads can't make progress, so the *bounded waiting* condition is defined in terms of successful acquire() operations.

Non-property: Thread ordering.   The *bounded waiting* fairness property defined above for locks is very weak. It guarantees that eventually a thread will get a chance to acquire the lock, but it does not, for example, promise that the threads will acquire the lock in FIFO order.

Locks and shared objects

As in standard object oriented programming, each shared object is an instance of a class that defines the class's state and the methods that operate on that state.

That state includes both state variables (e.g., ints, floats, strings, arrays, and pointers) and synchronization variables (e.g., locks). Thus, every time we use a class's constructor to produce another instance of a shared object, we allocate both a new lock and new instances of the state protected by that lock.

Figure 5.3 defines a simple shared object, a *thread-safe bounded queue*. Our implementation allows any number of threads to safely insert and remove items from it. As Figure 5.4 illustrates, a program can allocate multiple such queues (e.g., queue1, queue2, and queue3), each of which includes its own lock and state variables.

Notice that our queue stores only a bounded number of items. If the queue is full, an insert request returns an error flag. Similarly, if the queue is empty, a remove request returns an error flag. In the next section, we will show how *condition variables* would allow us to instead wait until the queue has room on insert or wait until an item is available on remove.

```
const int MAX = 10;

class TSQueue{
  // Synchronization variables
  Lock lock;

  // State variables
  int items[MAX];
  int nFull;
  int firstFull;
  int nextEmpty;

public:
  TSQueue();
  ~TSQueue(){};
  bool tryInsert(int item);
  bool tryRemove(int *item);
```

```
// Try to nsert an item. If the queue
// is full return false; otherwise true
bool
TSQueue::tryInsert(int item)
{
  bool ret = false;
  lock.Acquire();
  if(nFull < MAX){
    items[nextEmpty] = item;
    nFull++;
    nextEmpty = (nextEmpty + 1) % MAX;
    ret = true;
  }
  lock.Release();
  return ret;
}

// Try to remove an item. If the queue
// is empty, return false; otherwise true
bool
TSQueue::tryRemove(int *item)
{
  bool ret = false;
  lock.Acquire();
  if(nFull > 0){
    *item = items[firstFull];
    nFull--;
    firstFull = (firstFull + 1) % MAX;
    ret = true;
  }
  lock.Release();
  return ret;
}
```

Code from http://www.cs.utexas.edu/ users/dahlin/osbook/code/TSQueue.h   Code from http://www.cs.utexas.edu/users/dahlin/ osbook/code/TSQueue.cc

Figure 5.3: The class definition for a simple shared object (a thread-safe queue.)

Also, to keep the example as simple as possible, we only allow items of type int to be stored in and removed from the queue, but the pattern can be used for queuing anything.

The TSQueue implementation defines a circular queue that stores data in an array, items[]. We maintain a number of simple invariants on the state. nFull indicates how many items are currently stored in the queue. If nFull is nonzero, then firstFull is the index of the oldest item in the queue. If nFull is less than MAX, then nextEmpty is the index where the next item to be inserted should be placed.

All of these variables are as they would be for a single-threaded version of this object. The lock allows tryInsert() and tryRemove() to atomically read and write multiple variables just as a single-threaded version would.

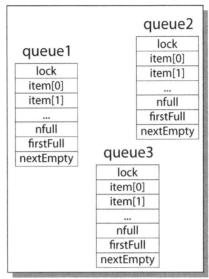

Figure 5.4: Three shared objects, each an instance of class TSQueue

Critical sections.   A sequence of code that operates on shared state is
critical a critical section. A *critical section* is a sequence of code that atomically
section accesses shared state. By ensuring that an object's lock is held while any of
its critical sections is executed, we can ensure that each critical section on a
collection of shared state appears to execute atomically.

EXAMPLE   For the TSQueue class in Figure 5.3, the methods tryInsert() and tryRe-
move() each include a critical section that manipulates several of a TSQueue
object's state variables (items, nFull, firstFull, and nextEmpty.)

Notice two things:

- Each class may define multiple methods that operate on the shared
  state defined by the class, so there may be *multiple critical sections per
  class*. However, for each instance of the class (i.e., for each object) only
  one thread holds the object's lock, *only one thread is actively executing
  any of the critical sections per shared object instance.*

EXAMPLE   For the TSQueue class in Figure 5.3, if one thread calls queue1.tryInsert()
and another thread calls queue1.tryRemove(), either the insert() will occur
before the remove() or vice versa; these functions' accesses to object
queue1's state variables will not be interleaved.

- A program may create *multiple instances of a class.* Each instance is a
  shared object, and each shared object has its own lock. Thus, multiple

```
int main(int argc, char **argv)
{
  TSQueue *queues[3];
  sthread_t workers[3];
  int ii, jj, ret;
  bool got;

  // Start the worker threads
  for(ii = 0; ii < 3; ii++){
    queues[ii] = new TSQueue();
    sthread_create_p(&workers[ii],          void *putSome(void *tsqueuePtr)
                     putSome,                {
                     queues[ii]);              int ii;
  }                                            TSQueue *queue = (TSQueue *)tsqueuePtr;

  sthread_join(workers[0]);                    for(ii = 0; ii < 100; ii++){
                                                 queue->tryInsert(ii);
  // Remove from the queues                    }
  for(ii = 0; ii < 3; ii++){                   return NULL;
    printf("Queue %d:\n", ii);             }
    for(jj = 0; jj < 20; jj++){
      got = queues[ii]->tryRemove(&ret);
      if(got){
        printf("Got %d\n", ret);
      }
      else{
        printf("Nothing there\n");
      }
    }
  }
}
```

Figure 5.5: This code creates three TSQueue objects and adds and removes some items from these queues. The full code is in http://www.cs.utexas.edu/users/dahlin/osbook/code/TSQueueMain.cc. Note that rather than creating threads using the sthread_create() function introduced earlier, we use the sthread_create_p() variation so that we can pass an argument to the newly created thread; in this case, we pass each newly created thread a pointer to the queue it will use.

threads may be active in the critical sections for different shared object instances.

EXAMPLE   For the TSQueue class in Figure 5.3 and instances of that class in Figure 5.4, if one thread calls queue1.tryInsert(), another thread calls queue2.tryRemove(), and a third thread calls queue3.tryInsert(), all three threads may be simultaneously executing critical section code operating on *different instances* of the TSQueue class.

Using shared objects.   Shared objects are allocated the same ways other objects — they can be dynamically allocated from the heap using malloc()

and new() or they can be statically allocated in global memory by declaring static variables in the program.

Multiple threads need to be able to access shared objects. If shared objects are global variables, then a thread's code can just refer to an objects global name to reference it; the compiler computes the corresponding address. If shared objects are dynamically allocated, then each thread that uses an object needs a pointer or reference to it. Two common ways to provide a pointer to a shared object to a thread are (1) providing a pointer to the shared object when the thread is created and (2) storing references to shared objects in other shared objects (e.g., containers). For example, a program might have a global, shared (and synchronized!) hash table that threads can use to store and retrieve references to other shared objects.

EXAMPLE   **Using the queue.** Figure 5.5 shows a simple program that creates three queues and then creates some threads that insert into these queues. Finally, it removes 20 items out of each of the queues and prints the values it removes. The initial, main thread allocates the shared queues on the heap using new(), and each of the worker threads is provided a pointer to a shared queue when it is created.

Warning: Nothing prevents you from writing a program that allocates a shared object as an automatic variable in a procedure or method, but you should not write programs that do this. Automatic variables (sometimes called "local variables" with good reason) are allocated on the stack as part of a procedure invocation. If one thread passes a pointer or reference to one of its automatic variables to another thread and later returns from the procedure where the automatic variable was allocated, then that second thread now has a pointer into a region of the first thread's stack that may now be used for other purposes.

You might be tempted to argue that for a particular program, you know that the a procedure won't return until all of the threads with which it is sharing an object are done using that object and that sharing one of the procedure's local variables is safe. The problem with this argument is that someday the code may change, introducing a dangerous and subtle bug. When sharing dynamically-allocated variables, it is best to stay in the habit of only sharing variables from the heap and never sharing variables from the stack across threads.

Exercises

2. Precisely describe the set of possible outputs that could occur when the program shown in Figure 5.5 is run.

3. Suppose that a programmer mistakenly creates an automatic (aka local) variable v in one thread $t1$ and passes a pointer to v to another thread $t2$. Is it possible for a write by $t1$ to some variable other than v

```
// Naive, polling-based implementation of
// remove that waits so it can always return
// an item.
int
TSQueue::remove()
{
   int ret;
   bool empty;
   do{
      empty = tryRemove(&ret);
   } until(!empty);
   return ret;
}
```

Figure 5.6: A naive, polling-based implementation of remove() from a bounded queue that retries in a loop until it succeeds in removing an item. The method tryRemove() is defined in Figure 5.3.

will change the state of v as observed by $t2$? If so, explain how this can happen and give an example. If not, explain why not.

4. Suppose that a programmer mistakenly creates an automatic (aka local) variable v in one thread $t1$ and passes a pointer to v to another thread $t2$. Is it possible for a write by $t2$ to v will cause $t2$ to execute the wrong code? If so, so, explain how. If not, explain why not.

5.4 | Condition variables: Waiting for a change

Condition variables provide a way for one thread to wait for another thread to take some action. For example, in the thread safe queue example in Figure 5.3, rather than returning an error when we try to remove an item from an empty queue, we might want to wait until the queue is non-empty and always return an item.

Similarly, a web server might want to wait until a new request arrives, a word processor might want to wait for a key to be pressed, a weather simulator's coordinator thread might wait for the worker threads calculating temperatures in each region to finish, or in our Earth Visualizer example, a thread in charge of rendering part of the screen might wait either for a user input that shifts the scene or for new data to update the view.

Broadly speaking, what we want to do in all of these cases is have a thread wait for something else to change the state of the system so that it can make progress.

One way to have a thread wait for another thread to act would be to **poll** *poll* — repeatedly check the state of interest. For example, TSQueue could wrap tryRemove() in a polling loop to provide a remove() method that always returns an item as shown in Figure 5.6. Unfortunately, such an approach can be inefficient because waiting threads continually loop, consuming CPU cycles without making useful progress. Worse, it might delay the scheduling of the other threads — perhaps exactly the ones for which the looping threads are waiting.

A "fix" to the polling-based approach is to add a delay. For example, in Figure 5.6, we might sleep, yielding the processor, for 100ms after each unsuccessful tryRemove() call so that there is a 100ms delay after a failed attempt.

This approach has two problems. First, although it reduces the inefficiency of polling, it does not eliminate it. Suspending and scheduling a thread imposes nontrivial overheads, and if a program has a large collection of threads polling every few tens or hundreds of milliseconds, they may still consume significant resources. Second, periodic polling adds latency. In our hypothetical Google Earth example, if the thread waiting for keyboard input waited 100ms between each check, the application might become noticeably more sluggish.

As an extreme example, one of the authors once had an employee implement a network server that provided several layers of processing, where each layer had a thread that received work from the layer above and sent the work to the layer below. Measurements of the server showed surprisingly bad performance; we expected each request to take a few milliseconds but instead each request was taking half a second. Fortunately, the performance was so horrible that it was easy to track down the problem: layers were passing work to each other through queues much like the TSQueue shown above, and remove() was implemented as a polling loop with a 100ms delay. With five such layers of processing, the server became unusably slow. Fortunately, the fix was simple: use condition variables, which we will now define.

Condition variable definition

condition
variable

A *condition variable* is a synchronization object that enables a thread to efficiently wait for a change to shared state that is protected by a lock. A condition variable has three methods:

- CV::wait(Lock *lock) atomically *releases the lock* and *suspends execution of the calling thread*, placing the calling thread on the condition variable's waiting queue. Later, when the calling thread is reenabled, it *reacquires the lock* before returning from the wait() call.

- CV:signal() takes one waiting thread off the condition variable's waiting queue and marks it as eligible to run (i.e., it puts the thread on the scheduler's ready list.)

```
SharedObject :: someMethodThatWaits ()
{
    lock.acquire ();
    // ... read and/or write shared state here ...
    while (! testOnSharedState ()){
        cv.wait(&lock);
    }
    assert (testOnSharedState ());
    // ... read and/or write shared state here ...
    lock.release ();
}
```

Figure 5.7: Design pattern for a method that wait()'s using a condition variable.

```
SharedObject :: someMethodThatSignals ()
{
    lock.acquire ();
    // ... read and/or write shared state here ...

    // If state has changed in a way that could
    // allow another thread to make progress,
    // signal (or broadcast).
    cv.signal ();

    lock.release ();
}
```

Figure 5.8: Design pattern for a method that signal()'s using a condition variable. The pattern for broadcast() is similar.

- CV::broadcast() takes all waiting threads off the condition variable's waiting queue and marks them as eligible to run.

Notice that a condition variable is always associated with a lock. One uses a condition variable to wait for a change to shared state, and updates to shared state are protected with a lock. Thus, the condition variable API is carefully designed to work in concert with mutual exclusion locks.

In particular, the standard design pattern is for a shared object to include a lock and zero or more condition variables. Then, a method that waits using a condition variable will work as shown in Figure 5.7. In this code, the calling thread first acquires the lock and then can read and write the shared object's state variables. To wait until testOnSharedState() passes, the thread calls wait() on the shared object's condition variable cv. Later, once the calling thread runs again and sees testOnSharedState() pass, it can do whatever it is it wants to do, release the lock, and return.

Figure 5.8 shows complementary code that changes the shared object's state in a way that might allow a waiting thread to make progress and then signals that thread with the condition variable.

Condition variables integrate with locks. Notice that a waiting thread is always waiting for the state of a shared object to change, so it must inspect the object's state in a loop. So, the condition variable's wait() method releases the lock (to let other threads change the state of interest) and then reacquires the lock (to check that state again.)

Similarly, the only reason for a thread to signal() (or broadcast()) is that it just changed the state in a way that may be of interest to a waiting thread. In order to make such a change to shared state, the thread must hold the lock, so signal() and broadcast() are always called while holding a lock on the state that was just changed.

Discussion. As just indicated, condition variables have been carefully designed to work in tandem with mutual exclusion locks and shared state. The precise definition of condition variables therefore includes three properties worth additional comment:

1. A condition variable is *memoryless*; the condition variable, itself, has no internal state other than a queue of waiting threads.

   Condition variables do not need state of their own because they are always used within shared objects that define their own state. Condition variables therefore provide a way to wait for changes to the enclosing object's state, but they do not have interesting state of their own.

   If no threads are currently on the condition variable's waiting queue, a signal() or broadcast() call has no effect. In particular, the condition variable does not "remember" an earlier call to signal() or broadcast(), and a later call to wait() will still block until signal() or broadcast() is called again.

2. *Wait() atomically releases the lock.*

   A thread always calls wait() while holding a lock, and the call to wait *atomically* releases the lock and puts the thread on the condition variable's waiting queue. The atomicity ensures that there is no separation between checking the shared object's state, deciding to wait, adding the waiting thread to the condition variable's queue, and releasing the lock so that the other thread can access the shared object to change its state and signal.

   Conversely, if threads released the lock before calling wait(), we would have to contend with the possibility that a thread misses a signal or broadcast and waits forever.

   Because wait() releases the lock, any invariants that should be true for the object must be reestablished before calling wait(). Similarly, code must not assume more than the normal invariants that are always true for an object when wait() returns; other than that, just because something was true before wait() was called does not mean it remains true when wait() returns — because wait() releases the lock, other threads may access the object and change its state during a call to wait(). In practice most methods that wait() are simple enough that they follow these restrictions naturally, but be aware of the potential pitfall.

EXAMPLE   **A missed signal.** For example, consider the case where thread T_1 checks an object's state and decides to wait, so it releases the lock in anticipation of calling cv.wait() on the shared object's condition variable cv. Then thread T_2 changes the object's state to what T_1 wants and calls cv.signal(), but cv has no waiting threads so the call to signal() has no effect. Finally T_1 calls cv.wait(), has its execution suspended, and is put on cv's list of waiting threads. Unfortunately, the lack of atomicity means that T_1 missed the signal and is now waiting even though T_2 has already changed the state to what T_1 wants.

3. When a waiting thread is reenabled via signal() or broadcast(), it may not run immediately.

   When a waiting thread is re-enabled, it is moved to the scheduler's ready queue with no special priority, and the scheduler may run it at some later time. Furthermore, when the thread finally does run, it must reacquire the lock, which means that other threads may have acquired and released the lock in the meantime. Therefore, even if the desired predicate was true when signal() or broadcast() was called, it may no longer be true when wait() returns. This may seem like a small window of vulnerability, but we need to design concurrent programs to work with all possible schedules. Otherwise, programs may fail sometimes, but not always, making debugging very difficult. See the sidebar on *Hansen v. Hoare semantics* on page 211 for a discussion of the history behind this property.

Note to programmers.   The points above have an important implication for programmers: *wait() must always be called from within a loop.*
   Because wait() releases the lock and because there is no guarantee of atomicity between signal()/broadcast() and the return of a call to wait(), when a thread returns from wait(), there is no guarantee that the checked-for state holds. Therefore, a waiting thread must always wait in a loop, rechecking the state until the desired predicate holds. Thus, the design pattern is

```
. . .
while (predicateOnStateVariables (...)){
    wait(&lock);
}
. . .
```

and not

```
...
if(predicateOnStateVariables(...)){
    wait(&lock);
}
...
```

There are fundamentally two reasons why condition variables are designed to impose this requirement: *simplifying implementation* and *improving modularity*.

Implementation: As noted above, when a waiting thread is reenabled, it may not run immediately, other threads may access the shared state before it runs, and the desired predicate on the shared state may no longer hold when wait() finally does return.

This definition simplifies the implementation of condition variables without hurting the complexity of the code that uses them. No special code is needed for scheduling — we just put a signalled thread onto the scheduler's ready list and let it run whenever the scheduler chooses it. Similarly, no special code is needed for acquiring the lock — we just have the thread call Lock::acquire() when it is rescheduled; just as with any attempt to acquire a lock, it may succeed immediately, or it have to wait while other threads acquire and release the lock.

Some implementations go even further and warn that a call to wait() may return even if no thread has called *signal()* or *broadcast()*. So, not only is it possible that the desired predicate on the state *is no longer true*, it is possible that the desired predicate on the state *was never true*. For example, Sun's Java JDK1.5's interface to condition variables allows for "spurious wakeups":

> When waiting upon a Condition, a "spurious wakeup" is permitted to occur, in general, as a concession to the underlying platform semantics. This has little practical impact on most application programs as a Condition should always be waited upon in a loop, testing the state predicate that is being waited for. An implementation is free to remove the possibility of spurious wakeups but it is recommended that applications programmers always assume that they can occur and so always wait in a loop. (From http://download.oracle.com/docs/cd/E17476_01/javase/1.5.0/docs/api/index.html)

Modularity: Waiting in a loop that checks the shared state makes shared objects' code more modular because we can reason about when the thread will continue by looking just at the wait() loop; in particular, we do not need to examine the rest of the shared object's code to understand where and why calls to signal() and broadcast() are done to know the postcondition for wait() loop. For example, in Figure 5.7, we know the assert() call will never fail without having to look at any other code.

Not only does always waiting in a loop simplify writing and reasoning about the code that waits, it simplifies writing and reasoning about the code that signals or broadcasts because you never have to worry that signaling at the wrong time will cause a waiting thread to proceed when it shouldn't. Signal() and broadcast() can be regarded as *hints* that it *might* be a good time to try to proceed, but if the hints turn out to be wrong, no damage is done. You can always convert a signal() to a broadcast() add any number of signal() or broadcast() calls without changing the semantics of the object. Avoiding extra signal() and broadcast() calls may matter for performance, but not for correctness.

Bottom line: Given the range of implementations that are possible and given the modularity benefits, wait() must always be done from within a loop that tests the desired predicate.

Thread life cycle revisited

In Chapter 4 on page 154, we discussed how a thread can switch between the READY, WAITING, and RUNNING states. We can now explain the WAITING state in more detail.

A RUNNING thread that calls Cond::wait() is put in the WAITING state. This is typically implemented by moving the thread's thread control block (TCB) from the scheduler's ready queue to a queue of waiting threads associated with that condition variable. Later, when some other RUNNING thread calls Cond::signal() or Cond::broadcast() on that condition variable, one (if signal() or all (if broadcast() of the TCBs on that condition variable's waiting queue are moved to the scheduler's ready list. This changes those threads from the WAITING state to the READY state. At some later time, the scheduler selects a READY thread and runs it by moving it to the RUNNING state.

Locks are similar. Lock::acquire() on a busy lock puts caller into the WAITING state, with the caller's TCB on a list of waiting TCBs associated with the lock. Sometime later, when the lock owner calls Lock::release(), the TCB is moved to the ready list and the thread transitions to the READY state.

Notice that threads that are RUNNING or READY have their state located at a pre-defined, "global" location like the CPU (for a RUNNING thread) or the scheduler's list of ready threads (for a READY thread). However,

Hansen v. Hoare semantics

In modern condition variables, signal() or broadcast() calls take waiting threads from a condition variable's waiting queue and put them on the scheduler's ready list. Later, when these threads are scheduled, they may block for some time while they try to reacquire the lock. Thus, modern condition variables implement what are sometimes called *Hansen semantics* (for Brinch Hansen, who first defined such condition variables) or *Mesa Semantics* (for Mesa, an early programming language at Xerox PARC that implemented these semantics.)

C.A.R. "Tony" Hoare proposed a different definition for condition variables. Under *Hoare semantics*, when a thread calls signal(), execution of the signaling thread is suspended, the ownership of the lock is immediately transferred to one of the waiting threads, and execution of that thread is immediately resumed. Later, when that resumed thread releases the lock, ownership of the lock reverts to the signaling thread, whose execution continues.

Thus, under Hoare semantics, signaling is atomic with the resumption of a waiting thread, and a signaled thread may assume that the state has not changed since the signal that woke it up was issued. So, where under Hansen semantics, waiting is always done in a loop (e.g.,while(predicate()){cv.wait();}), under Hoarse semantics, waiting can be done with a simple conditional (e.g., if(predicate()){cv.wait();})

There are debates about which semantics are better. Some argue that the atomicity of signaling and resuming a waiting process makes it easier to prove liveness properties of programs under Hoare semantics. For example, if I know that one thread is waiting on a condition, and I do a signal, I know that waiting thread will resume and make progress (and not some other late-arriving thread.)

For what it is worth, the authors of this book come down strongly on the side of Hansen supporters. The modularity advantages of Hansen semantics greatly simplify reasoning about an object's core safety properties. For the properties we care most about (i.e., the safety properties that the threads only proceed when they are supposed to) and for large programs where modularity matters, Hansen semantics seem vastly preferable to us Furthermore, in cases where liveness is a concern, you can implement explicit queuing to manage the order that waiting threads access an object (we leave this as an exercise for the reader.)

Regardless of which semantics are better, as a practical matter the debate has been settled: essentially all systems use Hansen semantics, and we know of no widely-used system that implements Hoare semantics. This resolution of the debate may be due as much to a desire for simpler implementations than to a universal consensus regarding the "right" semantics. Furthermore, programmers that program assuming the weaker Hansen semantics (e.g., always writing while(predicate()) cv.wait(&lock);) will write programs that will work under either definition. (And note that the overhead from the "extra" check of the predicate upon return from wait() in a while loop rather than an if conditional is unlikely to be significant compared to the signaling and scheduling overheads being paid in any event.) In any event, as a programmer, you won't go wrong if you write your code assuming Hansen semantics.

```
#include "Cond.h"

const int MAX = 10;

class BBQ{
 private:
  // Synchronization variables
  Lock lock;
  Cond itemAdded;
  Cond itemRemoved;

  // State variables
  int items[MAX];
  int nFull;
  int firstFull;
  int nextEmpty;

 public:
  BBQ();
  ~BBQ() {};
  void insert(int item);
  int remove();

 private:
  // Private methods are called with lock already held
  inline bool isFull() {return (nFull == MAX ? true : false);};
};
```

Figure 5.9: BBQ.h defines the interface and member variables for our blocking bounded queue.

threads that are WAITING typically have their state located on some per-lock or per-condition-variable queue of waiting threads. Then, a Cond::signal(), Cond::broadcast(), or Lock::release() call can easily find and reenable a waiting thread for that particular condition variable or lock.

Example: Blocking bounded queue

As an example, consider the bounded queue described in Section 5.3. Suppose we change the interface so that insert() blocks until there is room to insert an item and remove() blocks until there is an item to remove. BBQ.h in Figure 5.9 defines the *blocking bounded queue's* interface and public methods. BBQ.cc in Figure 5.10 defines the queue's implementation.

Notice that as in TSQueue, we acquire and release the lock at the beginning and end of the public methods (e.g., insert() and remove()). Now, however, we can (atomically) release the lock and wait if there is no room in insert() or there is no item in remove(). Before returning, insert() signals on itemAdded since a thread waiting in remove() may now be able to proceed; similarly, remove() signals on itemRemoved before it returns.

We signal() rather than broadcast() because each insert() allows at most one remove() to proceed and vice versa.

```
/*
 * BBQ.cc — Blocking Bounded Queue.
 */
#include <assert.h>
#include <pthread.h>
#include "BBQ.h"

BBQ::BBQ()
{
  nFull = 0;
  firstFull = 0;
  nextEmpty = 0;
}
```

```
// Wait until there is room           // Wait until there is an item
// then insert an item.               // then remove an item.
void                                  int
BBQ::insert(int item)                 BBQ::remove(void)
{                                     {
  lock.Acquire();                       int ret;
                                        lock.Acquire();
  while(isFull()){
    itemRemoved.Wait(&lock);            while(isEmpty()){
  }                                       itemAdded.Wait(&lock);
  assert(!isFull());                    }
  items[nextEmpty] = item;              assert(!isEmpty());
  nFull++;                              ret = items[firstFull];
  nextEmpty = (nextEmpty + 1) % MAX;    nFull--;
                                        firstFull = (firstFull+1)%MAX;
  itemAdded.Signal(&lock);
  lock.Release();                       itemRemoved.Signal(&lock);
  return;                               lock.Release();
}                                       return ret;
                                      }
```

Figure 5.10: BBQ.cc defines the implementation of our blocking bounded queue.

Semaphores considered harmful

During system conception it transpired that we used the semaphores in two completely different ways. The difference is so marked that, looking back, one wonders whether it was really fair to present the two ways as uses of the very same primitives. On the one hand, we have the semaphores used for mutual exclusion, on the other hand, the private semaphores.

(From Dijkstra "The structure of the 'THE'-Multiprogramming System" *Communications of the ACM* v. 11 n. 5 May 1968.)

In this book we focus on constructing shared objects using locks and condition variables for synchronization. Another widely used type of synchronization variable is a *semaphore*.

Semaphores were introduced by Dijkstra to provide synchronization in the THE operating system, which (among other advances) explored structured ways of using concurrency in operating system design.

Semaphores are defined as follows:

- A semaphore has a non-negative value
- When a semaphore is created, value can be set to any non-negative integer
- Semaphore::P() waits until value is positive. When value is positive, it atomically decrements value by 1.
- Semaphore::V() increments the value by 1, and if any threads are waiting in P(), one such thread is atomically enabled with its call to P() succeeding in decrementing the value and returning.

Note that P() is an atomic operation — the read that observes the positive value is atomic with the update that decrements it. Also note that if V() enables a thread in P(), then P()'s increment and V()'s decrement of value are atomic — no other thread can observe the incremented value, and the thread in P() is guaranteed to decrement the value and return.

The names P() and V() are historical artifacts. Sorry.

Given this definition, semaphores can be used for either mutual exclusion (like locks) or waiting for another thread to do something (like condition variables.)

To use a semaphore like a mutual exclusion lock, initialize it to 1. Then Semaphore::P() is equivalent to Lock::acquire() and Semaphore::V() is equivalent to Lock::release().

Using a semaphore for more general waiting is trickier. Normally (but not always), you initialize the semaphore to 0. Then Semaphore::V() is *similar to* Cond::wait(&lock) and Semaphore::P() is *similar to* Cond::signal(). However, there are important differences. First, Cond::Wait(&lock) atomically releases a lock, so you can check a shared object's state while holding the lock and then atomically suspend execution; conversely Semaphore::V() does not release an associated mutual exclusion lock, so you have to carefully construct the program so that you can release the lock and then call V() without allowing intervening operations to cause confusion. Second, whereas a condition variable is stateless, a semaphore has a value, so if no threads are waiting, a call to Cond::signal() has no effect, while a call to Semaphore::P() increments the value, which will cause the next call to Semaphore::V() to proceed without blocking.

Semaphores considered harmful.[4]   Our view is that programming with locks and condition variables is superior to programming with semaphores, and we advise you to always write your code using those synchronization variables for two reasons.

---

[4]Edsger Dijkstra is the author of the short note "Go To Statement Considered Harmful", *Communications of the ACM*, v. 11 n. 3, March 1968, pp 147–148.

First, using separate lock and condition variable classes makes code more self-documenting and easier to read. As the quote from Dijkstra above notes, there really are two abstractions here, and code is clearer when the role of each synchronization variable is made clear through explicit typing.

Second, a stateless condition variable bound to a lock turns out to be a better abstraction for generalized waiting than a semaphore. By binding a condition variable to a lock, we can conveniently wait on any arbitrary predicate on an object's state. In contrast, semaphores rely on carefully mapping the object's state to the semaphore's value so that a decision to wait or proceed in P() can be made entirely based on the value, without holding a lock or examining the rest of the shared object's state.

Although we do not recommend writing new code with semaphores, code based on semaphores are not uncommon, especially in operating systems. So, it is important to understand the semantics of semaphores and be able to read and understand semaphore-based code written by others.

One exception.   There is one situation in which semaphores are often superior to condition variables and locks: synchronizing communication between an I/O device and threads running on the processor. In this situation, there is often a data structure shared by the hardware device and the operating system software, and it is often not possible to require the hardware to acquire a lock on that data structure before updating it. Instead, the data structure, hardware, and device drivers are designed to work with carefully-ordered atomic memory operations.

If a hardware device needs attention, it updates the shared data structure and then may need to cause some waiting operating system thread to run.

To trigger this waiting thread, one might consider using a condition variable and calling Signal() without holding the lock (this is sometimes called a *naked notify*.) Unfortunately, there is a corner case: suppose that the operating system thread first checks the data structure, sees that no work is currently needed, and is just about to call Wait() on the condition variable. At that moment, the hardware updates the data structure with the new work and calls Signal(). Thus, when the thread calls Wait(), the signal has already occurred and the thread waits — possibly for a long time.

The solution is for devices to enable operating system threads using semaphores instead. Because semaphores are stateful, a Signal() (or V()) cannot be lost. A common approach is for the hardware to send information to the software thread via a bounded queue that is synchronized using semaphores.

Exercises

5. Assuming Hansen semantics for condition variables, our implementation of the blocking bounded queue in Figure 5.10 does not guarantee freedom from starvation: if a continuous stream of threads

makes insert() (or remove()) calls, it is possible for a waiting thread to wait forever. For example, a thread may call insert() and wait in the while(isFull()) loop; then, every time another thread calls remove() and signals on the itemRemoved condition variable, a *different* thread might call insert(), see that the queue is not full, and insert an item before the waiting thread resumes. Then, when the waiting thread resumes, it will retest the isFull() predicate, see that the queue is full, and wait().

Prove that under Hoare semantics and assuming that when a signal occurs, it is the longest-waiting thread that is resumed, our implementation of BBQ ensures freedom from starvation. That is, that if a thread waits in insert(), then it is guaranteed to proceed after a bounded number of remove() calls complete, and vice versa.

6. As noted in the previous problem, our implementation of the blocking bounded queue in Figure 5.10 does not guarantee freedom from starvation. Modify the code to ensure freedom from starvation so that if a thread waits in insert(), then it is guaranteed to proceed after a bounded number of remove() calls complete, and vice versa. **Note:** Your implementation must work under *Hansen/Mesa semantics* for condition variables.

5.5 | Implementing synchronization objects

We have described two types of synchronization variables, locks and condition variables. Given these synchronization variables, we can implement shared objects to coordinate access to shared state. In this section, we describe how to implement these important building blocks.

Recall from Chapter 4 that threads can be implemented for the kernel or for user-level processes. We will initially describe how to implement locks for in-kernel threads; at the end of this section we discuss the changes needed to support these abstractions for threads in user-level processes.

Implementing locks

Recall from Section 5.3 that a lock allows us to group an arbitrary sequence of operations on shared state into an atomic unit by calling Lock::acquire() at the start of the sequence and Lock::release() at the end. To enable this abstraction, each lock has a state (FREE or BUSY) and a queue of zero or more threads waiting for the lock to become FREE.

The discussion of Too Much Milk showed that it is both complex and costly to implement locks with just memory reads and writes, so modern implementations use more powerful hardware primitives that allow us to atomically read, modify, and write pieces of the lock's state. We will look at locks based on two primitives: *disabling interrupts*, which can make a sequence of instructions atomic with respect to a single processor, and *atomic read-modify-write* instructions, which allow a single instruction to atomically read and update a word of memory with respect to every processor on a multiprocessor.

Implementing uniprocessor locks by disabling interrupts

On a uniprocessor machine, any sequence of instructions by one thread will appear atomic to other threads if there is no context switch in the middle of the sequence. So, *on a uniprocessor machine* a thread can make a sequence of actions atomic by disabling interrupts (and refraining from calling thread library functions that can trigger a context switch) during the sequence.

This observation suggests a trivial—but seriously limited—approach to implementing locks on a uniprocessor machine:

```
Lock :: acquire (){  disableInterrupts (); }
Lock :: release (){  enableInterrupts (); }
```

This implementation does provide the mutual exclusion property we need from locks, and some uniprocessor kernels use this simple approach. However, it does not suffice as a general implementation for locks. If the code sequence the lock protects runs for a long time, interrupts will be disabled for a long time; this will prevent other threads from running for a long time, and it will make the system unresponsive to handling user inputs or other real-time tasks. Furthermore, although this approach can work within the kernel where all code is (presumably) carefully crafted and trusted to release the lock quickly, we cannot let untrusted user-level code run with interrupts turned off, since a malicious or bugger program could then monopolize a processor.

Implementing uniprocessor queuing locks

A more general solution is to briefly disable interrupts to protect the lock's data structures, but to reenable them once a thread has acquired the lock or determined that the lock is busy. In the latter case, there is no point in running the thread until the lock is free, so we suspend the thread by moving its thread control block (TCB) from the ready list to a queue of threads waiting for the lock.

This approach is illustrated in the Lock implementation shown in Figure 5.11. In this pseudo-code, if a lock is BUSY when a thread tries to acquire it, the thread moves its thread control block (TCB) off of the ready list and onto the lock's waiting list; the thread then suspends itself using a call similar to yield(); since the thread's TCB is off the ready list, this suspend() call

```
class Lock{
    private:
      int value = FREE;
      Queue waiting;

    public:
      void Lock::Acquire(){
          disableInterrupts();
          if(value == BUSY){
              waiting.add(current thread's TCB); // This thread off
                                                 // ready list
              suspend();  // Like yield(), but current thread's TCB
                          // is on waiting list rather than ready list
          }
          else {
              value = BUSY;
          }
          enableInterrupts();
      }

      void Lock::Release(){
          disableInterrupts();
          if(waiting.notEmpty()){
              move one TCB from waiting to ready;
          }
          else{
              value = FREE;
          }
          enableInterrupts();
      }
}
```

Figure 5.11: Pseudocode for uniprocessor lock implementation via disabling interrupts.

will not return until some calls Lock::Release() and moves the suspended thread's TCB to the ready list.

An optimization.   Notice that if a thread is waiting for the lock, a call to Lock::Release() does not set value to FREE. Instead, it leaves value as BUSY. Then, the thread whose TCB is moved to the ready list is guaranteed to be the one that acquires the lock and returns next. This arrangement allows an implementation to ensure freedom from starvation: assuming that TCBs are removed from the waiting list in FIFO order, then a thread waiting for a lock is guaranteed to succeed in acquiring the lock within a bounded number of Release() calls on that lock.

This feature is an optimization of this specific implementation of the lock primitive. Users of locks should not assume anything about the order that waiting threads will acquire a lock.

Interrupt discipline and invariants.   You may notice that a thread calls suspend() with interrupts turned off. Who turns them back on?

The next thread to run will turn interrupts back on. In particular, when we implement a thread system, we typically enforce the invariant that a thread always disables interrupts before performing a context switch and always assumes that interrupts are disabled when they run again after a context switch. So, whenever a thread returns from a context switch, it must reenable interrupts. For example, just as the Lock::Acquire() code in Figure 5.11 reenables interrupts before returning, the yield() code in Figure 4.12 on page 164 disables interrupts before the context switch and reenables interrupts before returning, and the interrupt handling approach described for context switches (Section 4.4) disables interrupts in the handler but restores interrupts when the interrupted thread is resumed.

Multiprocessor spinlocks

On a multiprocessor machine, however, disabling interrupts is insufficient. Even if interrupts are turned off, a sequence of operations by a thread on one processor can be interleaved with operations by another thread on another processor.

Atomic read-modify-write instructions. Since turning off interrupts is insufficient, most processor architectures provide *atomic read-modify-write* instructions to support synchronization. These instructions can read a value from a memory location to a register, modify the value, and write the modified value to memory atomically with respect to all instructions on other processors.

As an example, some architectures provide a *test_and_set* instruction, which atomically reads a value from memory to a register and writes a "1" to that memory location.

We can implement a spinlock that works on a multiprocessor (or a uniprocessor) using test_and_set as follows:

```
class SpinLock{
    private :
        int value = 0;  // 0 = FREE; 1 = BUSY

    public :
        void SpinLock :: Acquire (){
            while (test_and_set(&value))  // While busy
                ; // spin
        }

        void SpinLock :: Release (){
            value = 0;
        }
}
```

spinlock   Such a lock is called a *spinlock* because a thread waiting for a BUSY lock "spins" in a tight loop until some other lock makes it FREE. This approach

```
class Lock{
    private:
      SpinLock spinlock;
      int value = FREE;
    Queue waiting;

    public:
      void Lock::Acquire(){
          spinlock.acquire();
          if(value != FREE){
              disableInterrupts();    // Must finish what I start
              readyList->removeSelf(myTCB);
              waiting.add(myTCB);
              spinlock.release();
              suspend();  // Like yield(), but current  thread's TCB
                          // is on waiting list or ready list
              enableInterrupts();
          }
          else{
              value = BUSY;
              spinlock.release();
          }
    }

      void Lock::Release(){
          spinlock.Acquire()
          if(waiting.notEmtpy()){
                otherTCB = waiting.removeOne();
                readyList->add(otherTCB);  // Ready list protected by
                                           // its own spinlock
          }
            else{
                  value = FREE;
            }
            spinlock.Release();
      }
}
```

Figure 5.12: Pseudo-code for a queuing lock that suspends threads that try to acquire the lock when it is BUSY.

will be inefficient if locks are held during long operations on shared data, but if locks are known to only be held for short periods (i.e., less time than a context switch would take), spinlocks make sense. So, spinlocks are frequently used in multiprocessor kernels for shared objects whose methods all run fast.

Multiprocessor queuing locks

Often we need to support critical sections of varying length. For example, we may want a general solution to locks that does not make assumptions about the running time of methods that hold locks.

We cannot completely eliminate busy-waiting, but we can minimize it using the same approach as we did for uniprocessor locks based on disabling interrupts. Figure 5.12 shows an implementation of locks that uses a spinlock to guard the (short) sequences of instructions that manipulate the lock's state but that suspends threads that try to acquire the lock when it is busy.

The basic idea is simple. A SpinLock called spinlock protects the lock's data structures. Once the spinlock is acquired a thread can inspect and update the lock's state. If a thread finds that the lock is BUSY, it removes itself from the ready list, adds itself to the lock's waiting list, and then suspends its execution to allow another thread to run. Later, when the lock is released, if any threads are waiting, then one of them is moved off the lock's waiting list to the scheduler's ready list.

Belt and suspenders.   Why do we both acquire a spinlock and disable interrupts in the case where we suspend or resume a thread?

The basic issue is that we want to prevent a context switch during a context switch. Note that we must access two shared data structures—the lock and the scheduler's ready list. If the current thread is suspended after removing itself from the ready list but before adding itself to the lock's waiting list, then it will never be resumed. Turning off interrupts before beginning this sequence ensures that both operations occur before the thread is suspended.

Notice that turning off interrupts in this case does *not* ensure mutual exclusion. Instead, the lock and the ready list each have their own (spin-) locks to protect their own data structures.

Case study: Linux 2.6 kernel mutex lock

The pseudo-code above may seem a bit abstract, but real implementations closely follow this approach. For example, in Linux 2.6 the file include/linux/-mutex.h defines a mutex's data structure as follows[5]:

```
struct mutex {
    /* 1: unlocked, 0: locked, negative: locked, possible waiters */
    atomic_t                count;
    spinlock_t              wait_lock;
    struct list_head        wait_list;
};
```

This structure is similar to what we sketched in Figure 5.12. wait_lock and wait_list correspond to the waiting queue and spinlock's state; the count field is similar to the value field.

---

[5]For simplicity, throughout this example we include excerpts of the code and omit code for debugging code and for coordinating with signal handing, and we omit compiler/linker directives.

However, Linux provides an optimized path to acquire a free lock or release a lock with no waiting threads.

In particular, a lock can be in one of three main states as defined by count. If count is 1 the lock is unlocked. If count is 0, the lock is locked, but the wait_list is empty. Finally, if count is negative, the lock is locked and there may be threads on the wait_list.

Note that to coordinate the fast and slow paths, the implementation uses atomic operations whenever it needs to manipulate count. Then, as long as a lock stays in the first two states, lock() and unlock() stay on their fast paths.

Acquiring the lock.   To acquire a lock, a thread calls mutex_lock(), which is defined in kernel/mutex.c:

```
void mutex_lock(struct mutex *lock)
{
        __mutex_fastpath_lock(&lock->count, __mutex_lock_slowpath);
}
```

On a 32-bit x86 machine, __mutex_fastpath_lock() is defined in arch/x_- 86/include/asm/mutex_32.h:

```
/**
 * Change the count from 1 to a value lower than 1, and call <fn> if it
 * wasn't 1 originally. This function MUST leave the value lower than 1
 * even when the "1" assertion wasn't true.
 */
#define  __mutex_fastpath_lock(count, fail_fn)                    \
do {                                                              \
  unsigned int dummy;                                            \
  asm volatile(LOCK_PREFIX "    decl (%%eax)\n"                  \
               "    jns 1f \n"                                    \
               "    call " #fail_fn "\n"                          \
               "1:\n"                                             \
               : "=a" (dummy)                                     \
               : "a" (count)                                      \
               : "memory", "ecx", "edx");                         \
} while (0)
```

The syntax of this inline assembly is a bit baroque, but the function itself is simple. Near the end, the notation :"a" (count) says that before running this assembly code, the x86 eax register should be initialized to hold the parameter count; notice from above that count holds the address of the mutex's atomic_t count field. Thus, the first x86 assembly instruction LOCK_- PREFIX decl(%%eax) is an atomic read-modify-write instruction that reads the old value of count from memory, decrements it, and stores the new value back to memory; the LOCK_PREFIX directive tells the assembler to use a version of the decrement instruction that executes atomically.

The second instruction jns 1f ("jump if not signed") implements the fast path. If the new value of count is zero, then this conditional jump instruction jumps to the end of the assembly code snippet (to the 1: label), and __mutex_fastpath_lock() returns. In this case, the lock is acquired in just two instructions!

On the other hand, if the new value of count is negative, the jns instruction falls through, and the call #fail_fn instruction calls the __mutex_lock_slowpath() function.

The slowpath function is implemented by __mutex_lock_common(), as described in the following excerpts from kernel/mutex.c.

```
/*
 * Lock a mutex (possibly interruptible), slowpath:
 */
static inline int __sched
__mutex_lock_common(struct mutex *lock)
{
    struct task_struct *task = current;
    struct mutex_waiter waiter;
    unsigned long flags;

    preempt_disable();
    spin_lock_mutex(&lock->wait_lock, flags);

    /* add waiting tasks to the end of the waitqueue (FIFO): */
    list_add_tail(&waiter.list, &lock->wait_list);
    waiter.task = task;
```

As shown in the excerpt above, the thread first disables interrupts, grabs the lock's wait_lock guard, and adds itself to the locks's wait_list.

Next in __mutex_lock_common() is the main loop:

```
for (;;) {
        /*
         * Lets try to take the lock again — this is needed even if
         * we get here for the first time (shortly after failing to
         * acquire the lock), to make sure that we get a wakeup once
         * it's unlocked. Later on, if we sleep, this is the
         * operation that gives us the lock. We xchg it to −1, so
         * that when we release the lock, we properly wake up the
         * other waiters:
         */
        if (atomic_xchg(&lock->count, −1) == 1)
                break;

        /* didn't get the lock, go to sleep: */
        spin_unlock_mutex(&lock->wait_lock, flags);
        preempt_enable_no_resched();
        schedule();
        preempt_disable();
        spin_lock_mutex(&lock->wait_lock, flags);
}
```

In this loop, the thread atomically swaps the value of the lock with -1 using an atomic read-modify-write atomic_xchg instruction. If the previous state was 1 (free), the lock is now owned by the calling thread, and it breaks out of the loop. Otherwise, the thread clears the wait_lock spinlock guard, moves itself off the ready queue, reenables interrupts (preempt_enable_- no_resched()), and suspends its own execution to switch the processor to another thread (schedule()).

Later, when the thread runs again, it returns from schedule(), disables interrupts, and reacquires the lock's guard.

Eventually, the thread breaks out of the loop, which means that it found a moment when the lock was in the free state (the lock's count was 1), and at that moment it set the lock to the "busy, possible waiters" state (by setting count = -1.) The thread now has the lock, and it cleans up before exiting the acquire slow path as follows:

```
/* got the lock – rejoice! */
mutex_remove_waiter(lock, &waiter, current_thread_info());

/* set it to 0 if there are no waiters left: */
if (likely(list_empty(&lock->wait_list)))
    atomic_set(&lock->count, 0);

spin_unlock_mutex(&lock->wait_lock, flags);
preempt_enable();

return 0;
}
```

Here, the thread removes itself from the list of waiting threads. If there are no other waiting threads, it resets lock's state to "locked" (count = 0) so that when it releases the lock it can use the fast path if nothing has changed. Finally, the thread releases the lock's guard and reenables interrupts.

Releasing the lock. Lock release is similar. The function mutex_unlock() in kernel/mutex.c first tries a fast path and falls back on a slow path if needed:

```
void __sched mutex_unlock(struct mutex *lock)
{
        __mutex_fastpath_unlock(&lock->count, __mutex_unlock_slowpath);
}
```

And the fast path for unlock follows a similar path to that of lock. Here are the relevant excerpts from arch/x86/include/asm/mutex_32.h, for example:

```
#define __mutex_fastpath_unlock(count, fail_fn)           \
do {                                                      \
  unsigned int dummy;                                     \
  asm volatile(LOCK_PREFIX "    incl (%%eax)\n"           \
```

```
"       jg       1f\n"                                    \
"         call  " #fail_fn "\n"                            \
"1:\n"                                                     \
: "=a" (dummy)                                             \
: "a" (count)                                              \
: "memory", "ecx", "edx");                                \
} while (0)
```

Here, when we atomically increment count, if we find that the new value is 1, then the previous value must have been 0, so there can be no waiting threads and we're done. Otherwise, fall back to the slowpath by calling fail_fn, which corresponds to the following function in kernel/mutex.c.

```
static inline void
__mutex_unlock_common_slowpath(atomic_t *lock_count, int nested)
{
    struct mutex *lock = container_of(lock_count, struct mutex, count);
    unsigned long flags;

    spin_lock_mutex(&lock->wait_lock, flags);
    /*
     * Unlock lock here
     */
    atomic_set(&lock->count, 1);
    if (!list_empty(&lock->wait_list)) {
        struct mutex_waiter *waiter =
                        list_entry(lock->wait_list.next,
                                   struct mutex_waiter, list);
        wake_up_process(waiter->task);
    }
    spin_unlock_mutex(&lock->wait_lock, flags);
}
```

Notice that this function always sets count to 1, even if there are waiting threads. As a result, a new thread this is not waiting may swoop in and acquire the lock on its fast path, setting count = 0. However, in this case, the waiting thread will still eventually run, and when it does, the main loop above will set count = -1.

Discussion: Mutex fast path. An important thing to remember from this example is that many implementations of locks include a fast path so that acquiring and releasing an uncontended lock is cheap. Programmers will sometimes go to great lengths to convince themselves that they can avoid acquiring a lock in a particular situation. However, the reasoning in such cases can be subtle, and omitting needed locks is dangerous. In cases where there is little contention, avoiding locks is unlikely to significantly improve performance, so it is usually better just to keep things simple and rely on locks to ensure mutual exclusion when accessing shared state.

Locks for user-level and kernel-supported threads

The discussion above focused on implementing locks for in-kernel threads. In that case everything—code, shared state, lock data structures, thread control blocks, and the ready list–is in kernel memory, and all threads run in kernel mode. Fortunately, although some details change, the basic approaches work when we implement locks for threads that run within user-level processes.

Kernel-supported threads.   In a kernel-supported threads library, the kernel provides multiple threads to a process. In this situation, the kernel scheduler needs to know when a thread is waiting for the lock so that it can suspend the waiting thread and run a different one.

In the simplest case, we can place the lock data structure, including all of a lock's state (e.g., value, waiting, and the spinlock in the kernel's address space and replace each method call on the lock object with a system call. Then, the implementations described above for kernel-level locks can be used without significant changes.

A more sophisticated approach splits the lock's state and implementation into a fast path and slow path similar to the Linux lock described above. For example, each lock has two data structures: one in the process's address space that holds something similar to the count field and one in the kernel with the spinlock and wait_list queue.

Then, acquiring a free lock or releasing a lock that has no waiting threads can be done with a few instructions executed by the user-level thread and without a system call. A system call is still needed when the fast path fails (e.g., when the thread needs to remove itself from the ready list, add itself to the waiting list, and suspend execution.) We leave the details of such an implementation as an exercise for the reader.

User-level threads.   In a threads library that operates completely at user level, the kernel provides just one thread to a process, and the process multiplexes user-level threads over that one virtual processor. The situation is similar to the kernel-level threads case, except everything operates in a process's address space rather than in the kernel's address space. In particular, all of the code, shared state, lock data structures, thread control blocks, and the ready list are in the process's address space.

Lock implementations based on disabling interrupts change only slightly. A user-level threads package cannot disable interrupts; the kernel can not allow an untrusted process to disable interrupts and potentially run forever. Instead, it can disable signals from the operating system, which effectively accomplishes the same thing: just as a thread in a kernel-level threads package running on a uniprocessor machine can make a set of operations atomic by disabling interrupts before the operations and enabling them at the end, a thread in a user-level threads package that multiplexes user-level threads

```
class Cond{
   private:
    SpinLock spinlock;
    Queue waiting;

   public:
     void Cond:Wait(Lock *lock){
          spinlock.Acquire();
          disableInterrupts();       // Must finish what I start
          readyList ->removeSelf(myTCB);
          waiting.add(myTCB);
          lock ->Release();
          spinlock.Release();
          suspend();  // Like yield(), but current thread's TCB
                          // may be on the waiting list or the ready list
          enableInterrupts();
          lock ->Acquire();
     }

     void Cond::Signal(){
          disableInterrupts();
          if(waiting.notEmpty()){
              move one TCB from waiting to ready;
          }
          enableInterrupts();
     }

     void Cond::Broadcast(){
          disableInterrupts();
          while(waiting.notEmpty()){
              move all TCBs from waiting to ready;
          }
          enableInterrupts();
     }
}
```

Figure 5.13: Pseudocode for condition variable implementation via atomic read-modify-write instructions.

over one kernel thread can make a set of operations atomic by disabling signals before the operations and disabling them at the end.

Implementations based on atomic read-modify-write instructions need no changes at all.

Implementing condition variables

We can implement condition variables using the same techniques we use to implement locks.

To illustrate the similarity, Figure **??** shows a implementation of condition variables for a kernel-level threads based on atomic read-modify-write instructions. There are few changes from the lock implementation for that environment shown in Figure 5.12 on page 220. For example, as in the lock implementation, we still disable interrupts to ensure that once a thread removes itself from the ready list it puts itself onto the waiting list.

This implementation provides Hansen semantics — when we signal a waiting thread, that thread becomes READY, but it may not run immediately, and it still must reacquire the lock. It is possible for another thread to acquire the lock first and to change the state guarded by the lock before the waiting thread returns from Cond::Wait().

Exercises

7. Wikipedia provides an implementation of Peterson's algorithm to provide mutual exclusion using loads and stores at http://en.wikipedia. org/wiki/Peterson's_algorithm. Unfortunately, this code is not guaranteed to work with modern compilers or hardware. Update the code to include memory barriers where necessary. (Of course you could add a memory barrier before and after each instruction; your solution should instead add memory barriers only where necessary for correctness.)

8. Linux provides a sys_futex() system call to assist in implementing hybrid user-level/kernel-level locks and condition variables.

A call to long sys_futex(void *addr1, FUTEX_WAIT, int val1, NULL, NULL, 0 checks to see if the memory at address addr1 has the same value as val1. If so, the calling thread is suspended. If not, the calling thread returns immediately with the error return value EWOULDBLOCK. In addition, the system call will return with the value EINTR if the thread receives a signal.

A call to long sys_futex(void *addr1, FUTEX_WAKE, 1, NULL, NULL, 0) causes one thread waiting on addr1 to return.

Consider the following (too) simple implementation of a hybrid user-level/kernel-level lock.

```
class TooSimpleFutexLock{
   private:
       int val;

   public:

      TooSimpleMutex() : val (0) { }   // Constructor

      void Acquire () {
         int c;
         // atomic_inc returns *old* value
         while ((c = atomic_inc (val)) != 0){
             futex_wait (&val, c + 1);
         }
      }
```

```
void Release () {
    val = 0;
    futex_wake (&val , 1);
}
};
```

There are three problems with this code.

(a.) **Performance.** The goal of this code is to avoid making (expensive) system calls in the uncontested case when an Acquire() tries to acquire a free lock or a Release() call releases a lock with no other waiting threads. This code fails to meet this goal. Why?

(b.) **Performance.** There is a subtle corner case when multiple threads try to acquire the lock at the same time that can show up as occasional slowdowns and bursts of CPU usage. What is the problem?

(c.) **Correctness.** There is a corner case that can cause the mutual exclusion correctness condition to be violated, allowing two threads to both believe they hold the lock. What is the problem?

5.6 | Designing and implementing shared objects

Although multi-threaded programming has a reputation for being difficult, shared object provide a basis for writing simple, safe code for multi-threaded programs. In this section, we first define a high-level approach to designing shared objects. Then, we define some specific rules that you should follow when you implement them. Our experience is that following this approach and these rules makes it much more likely that you will write code that is not only correct but also easy for others to read, understand, and maintain.

Of course, writing individual shared objects is not enough. Most programs have multiple shared objects, and new issues arise when combining them. But, before trying to compose multiple shared objects, we must make sure that each individual object works. Chapter **??** discusses the issues that arise when programs use multiple shared objects.

High level design

In the discussion above, observe that a shared object has public methods, private methods, state variables, and synchronization variables, where a shared object's synchronization variables are a lock and one or more condition variables. At this level, shared object programming is basically like standard object oriented programming, except we've added synchronization variables to each shared object. This similarity is deliberate: synchronization variables are carefully defined so that we can continue to apply familiar techniques for programming and reasoning about objects.

So, most of high level design challenges for a shared object's class are the same as for class design in single-threaded programming:

- Decompose the problem into objects

- For each object

  - Define a clean interface
  - Identify the right internal state and invariants to support that interface
  - Implement methods with appropriate algorithms to manipulate that state.

All of these steps require creativity and good engineering judgement and intuition. Going from single-threaded to multi-threaded programming does not make these these steps particularly more difficult.

Compared to what you do to implement a class in a single-threaded program, the new steps needed for the multi-threaded case for shared objects are straightforward.

- Add a lock

- Add code to acquire and release the lock

- Identify and add condition variables

- Add loops to wait using the condition variable(s)

- Add signal() and broadcast() calls

We will talk about each of these issues in turn.

Other than these fairly-mechanical changes, writing the rest of the code for your proceeds as it does in the single-threaded case.

Add a lock

Add a lock as a member variable for each object in the class to enforce mutual exclusion on access to each object's shared state.

Note that in this chapter, we focus on the simple case where each shared object includes exactly one lock. Later, we will talk about more advanced variations such as an ownership design pattern where higher-level program structure enforces mutual exclusion by ensuring that at most one thread at a time owns and can access an object and fine grained locking where a single object may subdivide its state into multiple parts, each protected by its own lock.

Acquiring and releasing the lock

All code that accesses the object's state that is shared across more than one thread must hold the object's lock. Typically, all of an object's member variables are shared state.

The simplest and most common thing to do is to acquire the lock at the start of each public method and release it at the end of each public method. If you do this, it is easy to inspect your code to verify that a lock is always held when needed. Also, if you do this, then the lock is already held when each private method is called, and you don't need to reacquire it.

Warning. You may be tempted to try to avoid acquiring the lock in some methods or some parts of some methods. Do not be tempted by this "optimization" until you are a very experienced programmer and have done sufficient profiling of the code to verify that the optimization you are considering will significantly speed up your program.

Remember that acquiring an uncontended lock is a relatively inexpensive operation. Also, remember from the Too Much Milk problem that reasoning about memory interleavings can be quite difficult — and the instruction reordering done by modern compilers and processors makes it even harder. The sidebar discusses one commonly used (and abused) "optimization."

Identifying condition variables

How should a programmer decide what condition variables a shared object needs?

A systematic way to approach this problem is to consider each method and ask, *"When can this method wait?"* Then, you can map each situation in which a method can wait to a condition variable.

A programmer has considerable freedom in deciding how many condition variables a class should have and what each should represent. One option is to add add a condition variable corresponding to each situation in which a call to the method must wait — perhaps creating a distinct condition variable for each method that can block.

EXAMPLE   **Blocking Bounded Queue with two condition variables.** In our blocking bounded queue example, if the queue is full insert() must wait until someone removes an item, so we create a condition variable itemRemoved. Similarly, if the queue is empty remove() must wait until someone inserts an item, so we create a condition variable itemAdded. It is fairly natural in this case to create two condition variables, itemAdded to wait until the queue has items and itemRemoved to wait until the queue has space.

Alternatively, a single condition variable can often suffice. In fact, early versions of Java defined a single condition variable per object and did not allow programmers to allocate additional ones, so this approach was effectively mandated by the language. Under this approach, any thread that waits for any reason uses that condition variable; if the condition variable is used by different threads waiting for different reasons, then any thread that makes a state change that could allow one or more other threads to proceed broadcasts on that variable.

EXAMPLE   **Blocking Bounded Queue with one condition variable.** It is also possible to implement the blocking bounded queue with a single condition variable somethingChanged on which both threads in insert() or threads in remove() can wait. If we choose this approach, insert() andremove() will need to Broadcast() rather than Signal() to ensure that the right threads get a chance to run.

More complex programs make these trade-offs more interesting.

EXAMPLE   **ResourceManager.** For example, imagine a ResourceManager class that allows a calling thread to request exclusive access of any subset of n distinct resources. One could imagine creating 2^n condition variables so that a requesting thread could wait on a condition variable representing exactly its desired combination and the signaling on all affected condition variables when a resource becomes free. However, it may be simpler in this case to have a single condition variable on which requesting threads wait and to broadcast on that condition whenever a resource is freed.

The bottom line here is that there is no hard and fast rule for how many condition variables to use in a shared object or selecting the conditions that map to each condition variable. Selecting condition variables requires some thought, and different designers may group blocking situations differently and end up with different condition variables for a class. Like many other design decisions, these decisions are a matter of programmer taste, judgement, and experience. The point is that asking "When can this method wait" may help you identify what is for you a natural way of thinking about the condition variables for a shared object.

Waiting using condition variables

Add a while(...) {cv.Wait()} loop into each method that you just identified as potentially needing to wait before returning.

Remember that every call to Condition::Wait() must be enclosed in a while loop that tests an appropriate predicate — modern implementations almost invariably enforce Hansen semantics and often allow for spurious wakeups (a thread can return from Wait() even if no thread called Signal() or Broadcast(). Therefore, a thread must always check the condition before proceeding — even if the condition was true when the Signal() or Broadcast() call occurred, it my no longer be true when the waiting thread resumes execution.

Modularity benefits. Notice that if you always wait in a while loop, your code becomes highly modular. You can look at the code that waits and know what is true when it proceeds *without* examining any other code or understanding when calls to Signal() or Broadcast() are made. Even erroneous calls to Signal() or Broadcast() will not change how the waiting code behaves.

For example, consider the assertion in the following code:

```
...
while (!workAvailable ()){
    cond.wait(&lock );
}
assert(workAvailable ());
...
```

We know that the assertion holds by local inspection *without knowing anything about the more distant code that calls Signal() or Broadcast().*

Waiting in a while loop also makes the signal and broadcast code more robust. Adding an extra Signal() or changing a Signal() to a Broadcast() will not introduce bugs.

Hint: Top-down design. As you start writing your code, you may know that a method needs to include a wait loop, but you may not know exactly what the predicate should be. In this situation, we often find it useful to name a private method function that will perform the test (e.g., workAvailable() in the above example) and write the code that defines the details for that test later.

Signal() and Broadcast() calls

Just as you must decide when methods can wait, you must decide when methods can let other waiting threads proceed. It is usually easy to ask "Can a call to this method allow another thread to proceed?" and then add a Signal() or Broadcast() call if the answer is yes. But which call should you use?

Signal() is appropriate when (1) at most one waiting thread can make progress and (2) any thread waiting on the condition variable can make progress. In contrast, Broadcast() is needed when (1) multiple waiting threads may all be able to make progress or (2) different threads are using the same condition variable to wait for different predicates, so some of the waiting threads can make progress but others can't.

EXAMPLE   **Resource Manager.** As an example of the latter case, suppose that we use a single condition variable the n-resource ResourceManager sketched above. Whenever a resource is freed, we must broadcast() on the condition variable: we don't know which thread(s) can make progress, so we tell them all to check. If, instead, we just signalled, then the "wrong" thread might receive the signal, and a thread that could make progress might remain blocked.

It is always safe to use Broadcast(). Even in cases where signal would suffice, at worst all of the waiting threads would run and check the condition in the while loop, but only one would continue out of the loop. Compared to signal(), such a case consumes some additional resources, but would not introduce any bugs.

Double Checked Locking

The body of the text advises holding a shared object's lock across any method that accesses the object's member variables. Programmers are often tempted to avoid some of these lock acquire and release operations. Unfortunately, such efforts often result in code that is complex, wrong, or both.

To illustrate the challenges, consider the *double checked locking* design pattern. The canonical example[6] is for an object Singleton that provides access to an object that is allocated lazily the first time it is needed by any thread.

The "optimization" is to avoid acquiring the lock if the object has not already been allocated, but to avoid allocating the object multiple times by acquiring the lock and rechecking the status before allocating the object:

```
class Singleton {
  public:
    static Singleton* instance();
    Lock lock;
    ...
  private:
    static Singleton* pInstance;
};
```

Singleton.h header file

```
Singleton* Singleton::pInstance = NULL;
// BUG!  Don't do this!
Singleton* Singleton::instance() {
  if (pInstance == NULL) {
    lock->Acquire();
    if(pInstance == NULL){
      pInstance = new Instance();
    }
    lock->Release();
  }
  return pInstance;
}
```

Singleton.cc implementation file

Although the intuition is appealing, **this code does not work.** The problem is that the statement pInstance = new Instance() is not an an atomic operation; in fact, it comprises at least three steps:

1. Allocate memory for a Singleton object
2. Initialize the Singleton object's memory by running the constructor
3. Make pInstance point to this newly constructed object

The problem is that, modern compilers and hardware architectures can reorder these events. Thus, it is possible for thread 1 to execute the first step and then the third step; then thread 2 can call instance(), see that pInstance is non-null, return it, and begin using this object before thread 1 initializes it.

---

[6]The example and analysis is taken from Meyers and Alexandrescu's TBD"C++ and the Perils of Double-Checked Locking"

Discussion.   This is just an example of dangers that lurk when you try to elide locks; the lesson applies more broadly. This example is extremely simple — fewer than 10 lines of code with very simple logic — yet a number of published solutions have ben wrong. For example, TBDMeyers and Alexandrescu's "C++ and the Perils of Double-Checked Locking" notes, some tempting solutions using temporary variables and the volatile keyword don't work.[7] http://www.cs.umd.edu/ pugh/java/memoryModel/DoubleCheckedLocking.htmlBacon et al.'s "The 'Double-Checked Locking is Broken' Declaration" discusses a wide range of non-working solutions in Java.

This type of optimization is risky and often does not end up providing significant performance gains in program. Most programmers should not consider them. Even expert programmers should habitually stick to simpler programming patterns like the ones we discuss in the body of the text and should consider optimizations like double-checked locking only rarely and only when performance measurements and profiling indicate that the optimizations will matter for overall performance.

Implementation best practices:
Writing simple, safe code with shared objects

Above we described the basic thought process you will follow when including and using locks and condition variables in a shared object. To make things more concrete, this section describes five simple rules that we strongly advocate as a set of best practices for writing code for shared objects.

Consistent structure.   At the core of many of these rules is a simple principle: *follow a consistent structure.* This is a meta-rule that underlies the other rules. Although programming with a clean, consistent structure is always useful, it is particularly important to strictly follow tried and true design patterns for shared objects.

At a minimum, even if one way is not better than another, following the same strategy every time (a) frees you to focus on the core problem because the details of the standard approach become a habit and (b) makes it easier for the people who follow you and have to review, maintain, or debug your code understand your code. (Of course, often the person that has to debug the code is you!)

As an analogy, electricians follow standards for the colors of wire they use for different tasks. White is neutral. Black or red is hot. Copper is

---

[7]There are (non-portable) solutions in C/C++, but we won't give them here. If you want to try these advanced techniques, then you should read the literature for more in-depth discussions so that you deeply understand the issues and why various appealing "solutions" fail.

Coding standards, soap boxes, and preaching

Some people rebel against coding standards. We do not understand the logic. For concurrent programming in particular, there are a few good solutions that have stood the test of time (and many unhappy people who have departed from these solutions.) For concurrent programming, *debugging will not work.* You must rely on (a) writing correct code and (b) writing code that you and others can read and understand — not just for now, but also over time as the code changes. Following the rules below will help you write correct, readable code.

When we teach multithreaded programming, we treat the six rules described in this section as *required coding standards* for all multi-threaded code that students write in the course. We say, "We can't control what you do when you leave this class, but while you are in this class, any solution that violates these standards is, by definition, *wrong.*"

In fact, we feel so strongly about these rules that one of us actually presents them in class by standing on a table and pronouncing these as the Six Commandments of multi-threaded programming:

1. Thou shalt always do things the same way

etc.

The particular formulation (and presentation) of these rules evolved from our experience teaching multi-threaded programming dozens of times to hundreds of students and identifying common mistakes. We have found that when we insist that students follow these rules (adding a bit of drama to drive home the point), the vast majority find it easy to write clear and correct code for shared objects. Conversely, in earlier versions of the course when we were more subtle and phrased these items as "strong suggestions," many students found themselves adrift, unable to write code for even the simplest shared objects.

Our advice to those learning multi-threaded programming is to treat these rules as a given and follow them strictly for a semester or so, until writing shared objects is easy. At that point, you understand things well enough to decide whether to continue to follow them.

We also believe that experienced programmers benefit from adhering closely to these rules. Since we began teaching these rules in their current form, we have also disciplined ourselves to follow them unless there is a very good reason not to. We have found exceptions few and far between. Conversely, the vast majority of the time when we catch ourselves being tempted to deviate from the rules and then force ourselves to rewrite the code to follow them, the code improves.

We should note that although these rules may come across as opinionated (and they are), they are far from novel. For example, over three decades ago, Lampson and Redell's paper "Experience with Processes and Monitors in Mesa" (*Communications of the ACM* v. 23 n. 2 Feb 1980) provided similar advice (albeit in a much more measured tone.)

ground. An electrician doesn't have to decide "Hm. I have a bit more white on my belt today than black, should I use white or black for my grounds?" When an electrician walks into a room she wired last month, she doesn't have to spend 2 minutes trying to remember which color is which. If an electrician walks into a room she has never seen before, she can immediately figure out what the wiring is doing (without having to trace it back into the switchboard.) Similar advantages apply to following coding standards.

However, for concurrency programs, the evidence is that in fact the abstractions we describe *are* better than almost all others. Until you become a *very* experienced concurrent programmer, you should take advantage of the hard-won experience of those that have come before you. Once you are a concurrency guru, you are welcome to invent a better mousetrap.

Sure, you can cut corners and occasionally save a line or two of typing by departing from the standards, but you'll have to spend a few minutes thinking to convince yourself that you are right on a case-by-case basis (and another few minutes typing comments to convince the next person to look at the code that you're right), and a few hours or weeks tracking down bugs when you're wrong. It's just not worth it.

Five rules. These five rules are designed to help you avoid common pitfalls we see in multi-threaded code from students and experienced programmers.

1. **Always synchronize with locks and condition variables.**

   Either locks and condition variables or semaphores could be used to implement shared objects. We recommend that you be able to read and understand semaphores so you can understand legacy code, but that you only write new code using locks and condition variables.

   99% of the time code with locks and condition variables is more clear than the equivalent semaphore code because it is more "self-documenting". If the code is well-structured, it is usually clear what each synchronization action is doing. Admittedly, occasionally semaphores seem to fit what you are doing perfectly because you can map the object's invariants onto the internal state of the semaphore exactly — for example you can write an extremely concise version of our blocking bounded queue using semaphores — but what happens when the code changes a bit next month? Will the fit be as good? For consistency and simplicity, you should choose one of the two styles and stick with it, and in our opinion, the right one to pick is to use locks and condition variables.

2. **Always acquire the lock at the beginning of a method and release it right before the return.**

This is mainly an extension of the principle of consistent structure: pick one way of doing things and always follow it. The benefit here is that it is easy to read code and see where the lock is held and where it isn't because synchronization is structured on a method-by-method basis. Conversely, if Lock::Acquire() and Lock::Release() calls are buried in the middle of a method, it is harder to quickly inspect and understand the code.

Taking a step back, if there is a logical chunk of code that you can identify as a set of actions that require a lock, then that section should probably be its own procedure — it is a set of logically related actions. If you find yourself wanting to grab a lock in the middle of a procedure, that is usually a red flag that you should break the piece you are considering into a separate procedure. We are all sometimes lazy about creating new procedures when we should. Take advantage of this signal, and you will write clearer code.

3. **Always hold the lock when operating on a condition variable.**

   The reason you signal on a condition variable because you just got done manipulating shared state — some other thread is waiting in a loop for some test on shared state become to true. Condition variables are useless without shared state and shared state should only be accessed while holding a lock.

   Many libraries enforce this rule — you cannot call any condition variable methods unless you hold the corresponding lock. But some run-time systems and libraries allow sloppiness, so take care.

4. **Always wait in a while() loop**

   E.g., the pattern is always

   ```
   while ( predicateOnStateVariables ( ... ) ) ) {
       condition ->Wait (& lock ) ;
   }
   ```

   never

   ```
   if ( predicateOnStateVariables ( ... ) ) ) {
       condition ->Wait (& lock ) ;
   }
   ```

   Here, predicateOnStateVariables(...) is code that looks at the state variables of the current object to decide if it is OK to proceed.

   One is sometimes tempted to guard a wait() call with an if conditional rather than a while loop when one knows exactly what threads are taking what actions and one can deduce from the global structure of the program that despite Hansen semantics, any time a thread returns from wait(), it can proceed. Avoid this temptation.

While works any time if does, and it works in situations when if doesn't. By the principle of consistent structure, you should do things the same way every time. But there are three additional issues.

First, if breaks modularity. In the example sketched above, one needs to consider the global structure of the program — what threads are there, where is signal() called, etc — to determine whether if will work. The problem is that a change in code in one method (say, adding a signal()) can then cause a bug in another method (where the wait() is). While code is also self-documenting — one can look at the wait() and see exactly when a thread may proceed.

Second, when you always use while, you are given incredible freedom about where you put the signals(). In fact, signal() becomes a hint — you can add more signals to a correct program in arbitrary places and it remains a correct program.

Third, if breaks portability. Some implementations of condition variables may allow *spurious wakeups*, where wait() returns even though no thread called signal() or broadcast(). For example, implementations of condition variables in both Java and the Posix pthreads library are allowed to have spurious wakeups.

5. **(Almost) never sleep().**

Many threads libraries have a sleep() function that suspends execution of the calling thread for some period of wall clock time. Once that time passes, the thread is returned to the scheduler's ready queue and can run again.

Never use sleep() to have one thread wait for another thread to do something. The correct way to wait for a condition to become true is to wait() on a condition variable.

In general, sleep() is only appropriate when there is a particular real-time moment when you want to perform some action. If you catch yourself writing while(testOnObjectState() {sleep();}, treat this is a big red flag that you are probably making a mistake.

Similarly, if a thread needs to wait for an object's state to change, it should wait on a condition variable, not just call yield(). Instead, yield() is appropriate when a low priority thread that could make progress instead yields the processor to let higher-priority threads run.

Two pitfalls in Java

Java is a modern type-safe language that included support for threads from its inception. This built-in support makes multi-threaded programming in Java convenient. However, some aspects of the language are *too* flexible and can encourage bad practices. We highlight two pitfalls here.

1. Avoid defining a synchronized block in the middle of a method

   Java provides built in language support for shared objects ("monitors.") The base Object class, from which all classes inherit, includes a lock and a condition variable as members. Then, any method declaration can include the keyword synchronized to indicate that the object's lock is to be automatically acquired on entry to the method and automatically released on any return from the method. E.g.,

   ```
   public synchronized foo(){
       // Do something; lock is automatically acquired/released.
   }
   ```

   This syntax is useful — it follows rule #2 above, and it frees the programmer from having to worry about details like making sure the lock is released before every possible return point including exceptions. The pitfall is that Java also allows a *synchronized block* in the middle of a method. E.g.,

   ```
   public bar(){
       // Do something without holding the lock
       synchronized{
           // Do something while holding the lock
       }
       // Do something without holding the lock
   }
   ```

   This construct violates rule #2 from Section 5.6 and suffers from the disadvantages listed there. The solution is the same as discussed above: when you find yourself tempted to write a synchronized block in the middle of a Java method, treat that as a strong hint that you should define a separate method to more clearly encapsulate the logical chunk you have identified.

2. Keep *shared state classes* separate from *thread classses*

   Java defines a class called Thread that implements an interface called Runnable that other classes can implement in order to be treated as threads by the runtime system. To write the code that represents a thread's "main loop", you typically extend the Thread class or implement a class that implements Runnable.

   The pitfall is that when extending the Thread class (or writing a new class that implements Runnable) programmers can be tempted to include not only the thread's main loop but also state that will be shared across multiple threads, blurring the lines between the threads and the shared objects. This is almost always confusing.

   For example, for a blocking bounded queue, rather than defining two classes, BBQ for the shared queue and WorkerThread for the threads, programmers are sometimes tempted to combine the two into a single class — for example, a queue with an associated worker thread. If this sounds confusing, it is, but it is a pitfall we frequently see among students.

The solution is simple — always make sure threads and shared objects are defined in separate classes. State that can be accessed by multiple threads, locks, and condition variables should never appear in any Java class that extends Thread or implements Runnable.

Example: Readers/writers

Multithreaded programming is an important skill, and we anticipate that almost everyone who reads this book will be frequently called on to write multithreaded programs. This section and the next walk through two substantial examples that illustrate how to implement shared objects.

First, we will solve the classic *readers/writers* problem. In this problem, we have a database that can have records that can be read and written. To maximize performance, we will allow multiple threads to simultaneously read a record. However, for correctness, if any thread is writing a record, no other thread may simultaneously read or write that record.

Thus, we need to generalize our mutual exclusion Lock into readers-writers lock. We will do this by implementing a new kind of a new kind of shared object, RWLock, to guard access to each record and enforce these rules. The RWLock will be implemented using our standard synchronization building blocks: mutual exclusion locks and condition variables.

Then, a thread that wants to read a record will proceed as follows:

```
rwLock->startRead();
// Read database entry
rwLock->doneRead();
```

Similarly, a thread that wants to write a record will do the following:

```
rwLock->startWrite();
// Write database entry
rwLock->doneWrite();
```

To design a class, we begin by defining its interface (already done in this case) and the state needed for the interface. For the latter, it is important to keep enough state in the shared object to allow a precise characterization of the state — it is usually better to have too much state than to little. Here, the object's behavior is fully characterized by the number of threads reading or writing and the number of threads waiting to read or write, so we have

```
class RWLock{                              public:
 private:                                   RWLock();
  // Synchronization variables              ~RWLock() {};
  Lock lock;                                void startRead();
  Cond readGo;                              void doneRead();
  Cond writeGo;                             void startWrite();
                                            void doneWrite();
  // State variables
  int activeReaders;                        private:
  int activeWriters;                         bool readShouldWait();
  int waitingReaders;                        bool writeShouldWait();
  int waitingWriters;                      };
```

Figure 5.14: The interface and member variables for our readers/writers solution.

chosen to keep four integers to track these values. Figure 5.14 shows the members of and interface to the RWLock class.

Next, we add synchronization variables by asking "When can methods wait?" First, we add a mutual exclusion lock since a method must wait if another thread is accessing shared state. Next, we observe that startRead() or startWrite() may have to wait, so we add a condition variable for each case: readGo and writeGo.

DoneRead() and doneWrite() do not wait (other than to acquire the mutual exclusion lock), so these methods do not suggest the need for any additional condition variables.

We can now implement RWLock. Figure 5.15 shows the complete solution, which we develop in a few simple steps.

Much of what we need to do is almost automatic.

- Since we always acquire/release mutual exclusion locks at the beginning/end of a method (never in the middle), we can write calls to acquire and release the mutual exclusion lock at the start and end of each public method before even thinking in detail about what these methods do.

At this point, startRead() and doneRead() look like this:

```
void RWLock::startRead()        void RWLock::doneRead()
{                               {
   lock.Acquire();                 lock.Acquire();



   lock.Release()                  lock.Release()
}                               }
```

startWrite() and doneWrite() are similar. So far, we can write all of these without much thought.

- Since we know startRead() and startWrite() may have to wait, we can write a while(...){wait(...);} loop in the middle of each. In fact, we can defer thinking too hard about the details by making the predicate for the while loop be a call to a private method that checks a condition to be defined later (e.g., readShouldWait() and writeShouldWait()).

At this point, startRead() looks like this:

```
void RWLock::startRead()
{
    lock.Acquire();

    while(readShouldWait()){
        readGo.Wait(&lock);
    }

    lock.Release();
}
```

StartWrite() looks similar.

Now we do need to think a bit. We can add code to maintain the invariants that activeReaders, activeWriters, waitingReaders, and waitingWriters track the state of the threads as expected from their names; since we hold mutual exclusion locks in all of the public methods, this is easy to do. For example, a call to startRead() initially increments the number of waiting readers; then when the thread gets past the while loop, the number of waiting readers is decremented but the number of active readers is incremented.

When reads or writes finish, it may become possible for waiting threads to proceed. We therefore need to add some signal() or broadcast() calls to doneRead() and doneWrite(). The easiest thing to do would be to broadcast on both readGo and writeGo in each method, but that would both be inefficient and (to our taste) be less clear about how the class actually works.

Instead, we observe that in doneRead() when a read completes, there are two interesting cases: (a) no writes are pending and nothing needs to be done since this read cannot prevent other reads from proceeding or (b) a write is pending and this is the last active read, so one write can proceed. In case (b) we signal since at most one write can proceed and since any write waiting on the condition variable can proceed.

Our code for startRead() and doneRead() is now done:

```
void RWLock::startRead()            void RWLock::doneRead()
{                                   {
  lock.Acquire();                     lock.Acquire();
  waitingReaders++;                   activeReaders--;
  while(readShouldWait()){            if(activeReaders == 0
    readGo.Wait(&lock);                  && waitingWriters > 0){
  }                                      writeGo.Signal(&lock);
  waitingReaders--;                   }
  activeReaders++;                    lock.Release();
  lock.Release();                   }
}
```

Code for startWrite() and endWrite() is similar. As Figure 5.15 indicates, for doneWrite(), if there are any pending writes, we signal on writeGo. Otherwise, we broadcast on readGo.

All that is left is to define the readShouldWait()and writeShouldWait() predicates. Here, we implement what is called a *writers preferred* solution: reads should wait if there are any active or pending writes, and writes should wait if there are any active reads or writes. Otherwise, a continuous stream of new reads could starve a write request and prevent if from ever being serviced.

```
bool
RWLock::readShouldWait()
{
  if(activeWriters > 0 || waitingWriters > 0){
    return true;
  }
  return false;
}
```

The code for writeShouldWait() is similar.

Notice that since readShouldWait() and writeShouldWait() are private methods that are always called from public methods that hold the mutual exclusion lock, they do not need to acquire the lock.

Our solution may not be to your taste. You may decide to use more or fewer condition variables, use different state variables to implement different invariants, or tweak when we Signal() or Broadcast(). The shared object approach allows designers freedom in these dimensions.

Example: The sleeping barber

Versions of the Sleeping Barber problem date back to at least Dijkstra in 1965 ("Cooperating sequential processes," EWD 123, 1965, http://userweb. cs.utexas.edu/users/EWD/transcriptions/EWD01xx/EWD123.html). The Sleeping Barber problem is illustrative of a system where several threads need to rendezvous with another thread that provides some service to them (e.g., several document editor threads printing documents via a printer driver thread.)

```
// Wait until no active or waiting          // Wait until no active readers or writers
// writers, then proceed.                    // then proceed.
void RWLock::startRead()                     void RWLock::startWrite()
{                                            {
  lock.Acquire();                              lock.Acquire();
  waitingReaders++;                            waitingWriters++;
  while(readShouldWait()){                     while(writeShouldWait()){
    readGo.Wait(&lock);                          writeGo.Wait(&lock);
  }                                            }
  waitingReaders--;                            waitingWriters--;
  activeReaders++;                             activeWriters++;
  lock.Release();                              lock.Release();
}                                            }

// Done reading. If no other active          // Done writing. A waiting write or read
// readers, a write may proceed.             // may proceed.
void RWLock::doneRead()                      void
{                                            RWLock::doneWrite()
  lock.Acquire();                            {
  activeReaders--;                             lock.Acquire();
  if(activeReaders == 0                        activeWriters--;
     && waitingWriters > 0){                    assert(activeWriters == 0);
    writeGo.Signal(&lock);                     if(waitingWriters > 0){
  }                                              writeGo.Signal(&lock);
  lock.Release();                              }
}                                              else{
                                                 readGo.Broadcast(&lock);
// Read waits if any active or waiting        }
// writer ("writers preferred")               lock.Release();
bool RWLock::readShouldWait()                }
{
  if(activeWriters > 0                        // Write waits if any active reader or writer
     || waitingWriters > 0){                  bool
    return true;                              RWLock::writeShouldWait()
  }                                           {
  return false;                                 if(activeWriters > 0 || activeReaders > 0){
}                                                 return true;
                                               }
                                               return false;
                                             }
```

Figure 5.15: A solution to the readers/writers problem.

In our version, there is a barbershop with one barber chair and a waiting room with NCHAIRS chairs. The barber arrives every morning. When the shop is open, while there are customers in the shop, the barber cuts one customer's hair at a time. While the shop is empty of customers, the barber naps in the barber chair. At closing time, a clock rings an alarm, the barber hangs a "closed" sign, cuts the hair of anyone already in the shop, and then departs when the shop is empty.

When a customer arrives at the shop, if the shop is closed, the customer departs. Otherwise, the customer enters the shop. Then, if the barber is asleep, the customer wakes the barber, if there is a free waiting room chair, the customer sits down to wait, but if all waiting room chairs are full, the customer leaves. Waiting customers are served in FIFO order.

Figures 5.16 and 5.17 show our solution.

```
class BarberShop{
 private:
  Lock lock;
  Cond wakeBarber;
  Cond nextCustomer;

  bool timeToClose;
  bool open;
  int  arrivalCount;
  int  cutCount;
  int  fullCount;

 public:
  BarberShop();
  ~BarberShop() {};
  void barberDay(); // Main loop for barber thread
  bool getHairCut(); // Called by customer thread
  void clockRingsClosingTime(); // Called by clock thread

 private:
  void openStore();
  int  waitForCustomer();
  void doneCutting();
  void printFinalStats();

  bool emptyAndOpen();
  bool stillNeedHaircut(int custId);
  bool waitingRoomFull();
};
```

Figure 5.16: The interface and member variables for our Sleeping Barber solution.

We represent the barber shop as a shared object BarberShop and the barber, quitting-time clock, and each customer as a thread. The barber will call BarberShop::barberDay() to open the shop. Each customer will call Barber-Shop::getHairCut(), which returns true if the customer succeeds in getting a haircut or false if the customer fails because the shop is closed or full. Finally, at some point the clock thread will call BarberShop::clockRingsClosingTime() to tell the barber to close shop.

As you can see in Figure 5.17, a barber's day is not an atomic action. In particular, customers can continue to arrive while the barber is cutting hair (we're using the Sleeping Barber problem to model a system where we have a worker thread doing work that arrives and lands in a queue.) So, rather than holding the lock across barberDay(), we break barberDay() into three pieces, openStore(), waitForCustomer(), and doneCutting(), each of which (as per rule #2) holds the lock from start to finish. The barber "cuts hair" by printing a message using printf(); this step represents IO or some CPU-intensive calculation in a more realistic problem.

These openStore(), waitForCustomer(), and doneCutting() actions by the barber and getHairCut() action by customers are straightforward manipulations

```
void BarberShop :: barberDay ()
{
  // BarberDay is not an atomic action.
  // No lock. Only touch object's state
  // by calling methods that lock.
  int cust;
  printf ("Opening for the day\n");
  openStore ();
  while (1){
    cust = waitForCustomer ();
    if (cust == NO_CUST_CLOSING_TIME){
      printf ("Closing for the day\n");
      printFinalStats ();
      return;
    }
    printf ("Cut hair %d\n", cust);
    sthread_sleep (1, 0); // Time to cut
    doneCutting ();
  }
}

void BarberShop :: openStore ()
{
  lock . Acquire ();
  open = true;
  lock . Release ();
  return;
}

int BarberShop :: waitForCustomer ()
{
  int custId;
  lock . Acquire ();
  while (emptyAndOpen ()){
    wakeBarber . Wait (&lock);
  }
  if (timeToClose){
    open = false; // Stop new arrivals
  }
  if (arrivalCount > cutCount){
    custId = cutCount;
  }
  else {
    custId = NO_CUST_CLOSING_TIME;
  }
  lock . Release ();
  return custId;
}

void BarberShop :: doneCutting ()
{
  lock . Acquire ();
  cutCount++;
  nextCustomer . Broadcast (&lock);
  lock . Release ();
  return;
}

void BarberShop :: printFinalStats ()
{
  lock . Acquire ();
  printf ("Stats: arr=%d cut=%d full=%d\n",
          arrivalCount, cutCount, fullCount);
  assert (arrivalCount == cutCount);
  lock . Release ();
}
```

```
bool BarberShop :: getHairCut ()
{
  int myNumber;
  bool ret;
  lock . Acquire ();
  if (!open || waitingRoomFull ()){
    ret = false;
  }
  else {
    // "Take a number" for FIFO service
    myNumber = ++arrivalCount;
    wakeBarber . Signal (&lock);
    while (stillNeedHaircut (myNumber)){
      nextCustomer . Wait (&lock);
    }
    ret = true;
  }
  lock . Release ();
  return ret;
}

void BarberShop :: clockRingsClosingTime ()
{
  lock . Acquire ();
  timeToClose = true;
  wakeBarber . Signal (&lock);
  lock . Release ();
}

// Internal functions for checking status.
//   Always called with lock already held.
bool BarberShop :: emptyAndOpen ()
{
  if ((timeToClose
        || (arrivalCount > cutCount))){
    return false;
  }
  else {
    return true;
  }
}

bool BarberShop :: stillNeedHaircut (int custId)
{
  // Ensure FIFO order by letting customers
  // leave in order they arrive
  if (custId > cutCount){
    return true;
  }
  else {
    return false;
  }
}

bool BarberShop :: waitingRoomFull ()
{
  // +1 b/c barber chair
  if (arrivalCount−cutCount == NCHAIRS+1){
    return true;
  }
  else {
    return false;
  }
}
```

Figure 5.17: A solution to the Sleeping Barber problem.

of shared state while holding the lock and waiting as appropriate. Notice that in waitForCustomer() we use a variation of wait() that not only returns when signalled but also if some specified wallclock time is reached; we use this timeout to close the shop at the end of the day.

In doneCutting() we use broadcast() rather than signal() since several customers can be waiting, but only the customer with custId == cutCount can proceed.

Exercises

9. In the readers-writers lock example for the function RWLock::doneRead(), why do we use writeGo.Signal() rather than writeGo.Broadcast()?

10. Show how to implement a semaphore by generalizing the the multiprocessor lock implementation shown in Figure 5.12.

11. On page page 193, we sketched part of a solution to the Too Much Milk problem. To make the problem more interesting, we will also allow roommates to drink milk.

    Implement in C++ or Java a Kitchen class with a drinkMilkAndBuyIfNeeded(). This method should randomly (with a 20% probability) change the value of milk from 1 to 0. Then, if the value just became 0, it should buy milk (incrementing milk back to 1. The method should return 1 if the roommate bought milk and 0 otherwise.

    Your solution should use locks for synchronization and it should work for any number of roommates. Test your implementation by writing a program that repeatedly creates a Kitchen object and varying numbers of roommate threads; each roommate thread should call drinkMilkAndBuyIfNeeded() multiple times in a loop.

    Hint: You will probably write a main() thread that creates a Kitchen object, creates multiple roommate threads, and then waits for all of the roommates to finish their loops. If you are writing in C++ with the Posix threads library, you can use pthread_join() to have one thread wait for another thread to finish. If you are writing in Java with the java.lang.Thread class, you can use the join() method.

12. For the solution to Too Much Milk suggested in the previous problem, each call to drinkMilkAndBuyIfNeeded() is atomic and holds the lock from the start to the end even if one roommate goes to the store. This solution is analogous to the roommate padlocking the Kitchen while going to the store, which seems a bit unrealistic.

    Implement a better solution to drinkMilkAndBuyIfNeeded() using both locks and condition variables. Since a roommate now needs to release the lock to the kitchen while going to the store, you will no longer acquire the lock at the start of this function and release it at the end. Instead, this function will call two helper-functions, each of which acquires/releases the lock. E.g.,

```
int
Kitchen :: drinkMilkAndBuyIfNeeded (){
       int iShouldBuy = waitThenDrink ();
       if (iShoudBuy){
           buyMilk ();
       }
}
```

In this function, waitThenDrink() should (if there is no milk) wait (using a condition variable) until there is milk, drink the milk, and if the milk is now gone, return a nonzero value to flag that the caller should buy milk. BuyMilk() should buy milk and then broadcast to let the waiting threads know that they can proceed.

Again, test your code with varying numbers of threads.

13. Before entering a *priority critical section*, a thread calls Priority-Lock::enter(priority) and when the thread exits such a critical section it calls PriorityLock::exit(). If several threads are waiting to enter a priority critical section the one with the numerically highest priority should be the next one allowed in. Implement PriorityLock using monitors (locks and condition variables) and following the multi-threaded programming standards defined for the class.

   a) Define the state and synchronization variables and describe the purpose of each.

   b) Implement PriorityLock::enter(int priority)

   c) Implement PriorityLock::exit()

14. Implement a *priority condition variable.* A priority condition variable (PCV) has 3 public methods:

```
void PCV :: wait (Lock *enclosingLock , int priority );
void PCV :: signal (Lock *enclosingLock );
void PCV :: broadcast (Lock *enclosingLock , int priority );
```

These methods are similar to those of a standard condition variable. The one difference is that a PCV enforces both *priority* and *ordering*.

In particular, signal(Lock *lock) causes the currently waiting thread with the highest priority to return from wait(); if multiple threads with the same priority are waiting, then the one that is waiting the longest should return before any that have been waiting a shorter amount of time.

Similarly, broadcast(Lock *lock, int priority) causes all currently waiting threads whose priority equals or exceeds priority to return from wait().

For full credit, you must follow the *thread coding standards* discussed in class.

5.7 | Conclusions

Using well-structured shared objects to share state among threads makes reasoning about multithreaded programs vastly simpler than it would be if we tried to reason about the possible interleavings of individual loads and stores.

Furthermore, if we follow a systematic approach, it is not difficult to write code for shared objects that is easy for us to reason about and for others to read, understand, maintain, and change.

In short, this chapter defines a set of core skills that almost any programmer will use over and over again during the coming decade or longer.

That is not the whole story. As the next chapter will discuss, as systems grow to include many shared objects and threads, new challenges arise: synchronizing operations that span multiple shared objects, avoiding deadlocks in which a set of threads are all waiting for each other to do something, and maximizing performance when large numbers of threads are contending for a single object. Sadly, solutions to these problems are not as cut and dried.

Exercises

For convenience, the exercises from the body of the chapter are repeated here.

1. Show that solution 3 to the Too Much Milk problem is safe — that it guarantees that at most one roommate buys milk.

2. Precisely describe the set of possible outputs that could occur when the program shown in Figure 5.5 is run.

3. Suppose that a programmer mistakenly creates an automatic (aka local) variable v in one thread $t1$ and passes a pointer to v to another thread $t2$. Is it possible for a write by $t1$ to some variable other than v will change the state of v as observed by $t2$? If so, explain how this can happen and give an example. If not, explain why not.

4. Suppose that a programmer mistakenly creates an automatic (aka local) variable v in one thread $t1$ and passes a pointer to v to another thread $t2$. Is it possible for a write by $t2$ to v will cause $t2$ to execute the wrong code? If so, so, explain how. If not, explain why not.

5. Assuming Hansen semantics for condition variables, our implementation of the blocking bounded queue in Figure 5.10 does not guarantee freedom from starvation: if a continuous stream of threads makes insert() (or remove()) calls, it is possible for a waiting thread to wait forever. For example, a thread may call insert() and wait in the while(isFull()) loop; then, every time another thread calls remove() and signals on the itemRemoved condition variable, a *different* thread might call insert(), see that the queue is not full, and insert an item before the waiting thread resumes. Then, when the waiting thread resumes, it will retest the isFull() predicate, see that the queue is full, and wait().

Prove that under Hoare semantics and assuming that when a signal occurs, it is the longest-waiting thread that is resumed, our implementation of BBQ ensures freedom from starvation. That is, that if a thread waits in insert(), then it is guaranteed to proceed after a bounded number of remove() calls complete, and vice versa.

6. As noted in the previous problem, our implementation of the blocking bounded queue in Figure 5.10 does not guarantee freedom from starvation. Modify the code to ensure freedom from starvation so that if a thread waits in insert(), then it is guaranteed to proceed after a bounded number of remove() calls complete, and vice versa. **Note:** Your implementation must work under *Hansen/Mesa semantics* for condition variables.

7. Wikipedia provides an implementation of Peterson's algorithm to provide mutual exclusion using loads and stores at http://en.wikipedia.org/wiki/Peterson's_algorithm. Unfortunately, this code is not guaranteed to work with modern compilers or hardware. Update the code to include memory barriers where necessary. (Of course you could add a memory barrier before and after each instruction; your solution should instead add memory barriers only where necessary for correctness.)

8. Linux provides a sys_futex() system call to assist in implementing hybrid user-level/kernel-level locks and condition variables.

A call to long sys_futex(void *addr1, FUTEX_WAIT, int val1, NULL, NULL, 0 checks to see if the memory at address addr1 has the same value as val1. If so, the calling thread is suspended. If not, the calling thread returns immediately with the error return value EWOULDBLOCK. In addition, the system call will return with the value EINTR if the thread receives a signal.

A call to long sys_futex(void *addr1, FUTEX_WAKE, 1, NULL, NULL, 0) causes one thread waiting on addr1 to return.

Consider the following (too) simple implementation of a hybrid user-level/kernel-level lock.

```
class TooSimpleFutexLock{
  private:
    int val;

  public:

    TooSimpleMutex() : val (0) { }   // Constructor

    void Acquire () {
      int c;
      // atomic_inc returns *old* value
      while ((c = atomic_inc (val)) != 0){
        futex_wait (&val, c + 1);
      }
    }

    void Release () {
      val = 0;
      futex_wake (&val, 1);
    }
};
```

There are three problems with this code.

(a.) **Performance.** The goal of this code is to avoid making (expensive) system calls in the uncontested case when an Acquire() tries to acquire a free lock or a Release() call releases a lock with no other waiting threads. This code fails to meet this goal. Why?

(b.) **Performance.** There is a subtle corner case when multiple threads try to acquire the lock at the same time that can show up as occasional slowdowns and bursts of CPU usage. What is the problem?

(c.) **Correctness.** There is a corner case that can cause the mutual exclusion correctness condition to be violated, allowing two threads to both believe they hold the lock. What is the problem?

9. In the readers-writers lock example for the function RWLock::doneRead(), why do we use writeGo.Signal() rather than writeGo.Broadcast()?

10. Show how to implement a semaphore by generalizing the the multiprocessor lock implementation shown in Figure 5.12.

11. On page page 193, we sketched part of a solution to the Too Much Milk problem. To make the problem more interesting, we will also allow roommates to drink milk.

   Implement in C++ or Java a Kitchen class with a drinkMilkAndBuy-IfNeeded(). This method should randomly (with a 20% probability) change the value of milk from 1 to 0. Then, if the value just became 0, it should buy milk (incrementing milk back to 1. The method should return 1 if the roommate bought milk and 0 otherwise.

Your solution should use locks for synchronization and it should work for any number of roommates. Test your implementation by writing a program that repeatedly creates a Kitchen object and varying numbers of roommate threads; each roommate thread should call drinkMilkAndBuyIfNeeded() multiple times in a loop.

Hint: You will probably write a main() thread that creates a Kitchen object, creates multiple roommate threads, and then waits for all of the roommates to finish their loops. If you are writing in C++ with the Posix threads library, you can use pthread_join() to have one thread wait for another thread to finish. If you are writing in Java with the java.lang.Thread class, you can use the join() method.

12. For the solution to Too Much Milk suggested in the previous problem, each call to drinkMilkAndBuyIfNeeded() is atomic and holds the lock from the start to the end even if one roommate goes to the store. This solution is analogous to the roommate padlocking the Kitchen while going to the store, which seems a bit unrealistic.

    Implement a better solution to drinkMilkAndBuyIfNeeded() using both locks and condition variables. Since a roommate now needs to release the lock to the kitchen while going to the store, you will no longer acquire the lock at the start of this function and release it at the end. Instead, this function will call two helper-functions, each of which acquires/releases the lock. E.g.,

    ```
    int
    Kitchen :: drinkMilkAndBuyIfNeeded (){
        int iShouldBuy = waitThenDrink ();
        if (iShoudBuy){
            buyMilk ();
        }
    }
    ```

    In this function, waitThenDrink() should (if there is no milk) wait (using a condition variable) until there is milk, drink the milk, and if the milk is now gone, return a nonzero value to flag that the caller should buy milk. BuyMilk() should buy milk and then broadcast to let the waiting threads know that they can proceed.

    Again, test your code with varying numbers of threads.

13. Before entering a *priority critical section*, a thread calls Priority-Lock::enter(priority) and when the thread exits such a critical section it calls PriorityLock::exit(). If several threads are waiting to enter a priority critical section the one with the numerically highest priority should be the next one allowed in. Implement PriorityLock using monitors (locks and condition variables) and following the multi-threaded programming standards defined for the class.

a) Define the state and synchronization variables and describe the purpose of each.

b) Implement PriorityLock::enter(int priority)

c) Implement PriorityLock::exit()

14. Implement a *priority condition variable*. A priority condition variable (PCV) has 3 public methods:

```
void PCV::wait(Lock *enclosingLock, int priority);
void PCV::signal(Lock *enclosingLock);
void PCV::broadcast(Lock *enclosingLock, int priority);
```

These methods are similar to those of a standard condition variable. The one difference is that a PCV enforces both *priority* and *ordering*.

In particular, signal(Lock *lock) causes the currently waiting thread with the highest priority to return from wait(); if multiple threads with the same priority are waiting, then the one that is waiting the longest should return before any that have been waiting a shorter amount of time.

Similarly, broadcast(Lock *lock, int priority) causes all currently waiting threads whose priority equals or exceeds priority to return from wait().

For full credit, you must follow the *thread coding standards* discussed in class.

"When two trains approach each other at a crossing, both shall come to a full stop and neither shall start up again until the other has gone."

A US state law in the 1920s, possibly apocryphal

6 | Advanced Synchronization

The shared objects described in Chapter 5 provide a key building block for writing multi-threaded programs, but many such programs must address additional issues.

The first set of issues arise because many programs comprise multiple shared objects, and we need to reason about the interactions among these pieces. Unfortunately, these interactions can break modularity; in some cases when one module calls another, you literally have to know about the modules' internal implementation details to make sure that both modules' synchronization mesh. There are two issues: safety and liveness.

1. **Safety: Multi-object synchronization.** For programs with multiple shared objects, we face a problem similar to what we faced when reasoning about atomic loads and stores: even if each individual operation on a shared object is atomic, we need to reason about interactions of sequences of operations across objects.

2. **Liveness: Deadlock.** One way to help reason about sequences of operations on multiple objects is to hold multiple locks. This approach raises the issue of deadlock where a set of threads get permanently stuck waiting for each other in a cycle.

The bad news here is that there is no cookbook recipe that always works for dealing with these challenges. In particular, current techniques for addressing these problems have two basic limitations. First, there are engineering trade-offs among them. Some solutions are general but complex or expensive; others are simple but slow; and still others are simple and cheap but not general. Second, many of the solutions are inherently *non-modular*. They require reasoning about the global structure of the system and internal implementation details of modules to understand or restrict how different modules can interact.

In addition to discussing the challenges that arrive when dealing with multiple objects and multiple locks, this chapter discusses one other issue: how to construct shared objects that can be accessed without locks. We emphasize that this is an advanced topic that should only be considered by programmers that have mastered multi-threaded programming. The vast majority of the time, the simple shared objects described in the last chapter will be all that is needed in a multi-threaded program.

3. **Synchronization with reduced locking.** In the part of this chapter, we briefly discuss two techniques for synchronizing access to shared state without locking: *read-copy-update (RCU)* and *lock-free/wait-free data structures.*

6.1 | Multi-object synchronization

Having multiple shared objects in a program raises challenges to reasoning about interactions across objects. For example, consider a system storing a bank's accounts. A reasonable design choice might be for each customer's account to be a shared object with a lock (either a mutual exclusion lock or a readers/writers lock as described in the previous chapter.) Consider, however, transferring $100 from account A to account B as follows:

```
A->subtract(100);
B->add(100);
```

Although each individual action is atomic, the sequence of actions is not. As a result, there may be a time where, say, A tells B that the money has been sent and B gets mad because the money does not appear in B's account.

Similarly, consider a bank manager running a program to answer a question: "How much money does the bank have?" If the program simply reads from each account, the calculation may exclude or double-count money "in flight" between accounts such as in the transfer from A to B.

These examples illustrate a general problem that arises whenever a program contains multiple shared objects accessed by threads. Even if each object has a lock and guarantees that its methods operate atomically, *sequences* of operations by different threads across different objects can be interleaved. For example, you would face the same issues if you tried to solve Too Much Milk with a Note object that has 2 methods, readNote and writeNote, and a Fridge object that has 2 methods, checkForMilk and addMilk.

One big lock v. fine-grained locking. The simplest solution is to include all of a program's data structures in a single shared object with a single lock. Then, all threads operate by calling that object's methods, each of which can operate while holding the object's lock. This approach can yield acceptable performance for some applications, especially if the code is structured so that threads do not hold the lock when they perform high-latency I/O operations.

However, for other applications, a single global lock may restrict parallelism too much. In these cases, different data structures may each have their own lock.

fine-grained
locking

By the same token, although the previous chapter focused on the simple case of a shared object with a single lock protecting all of the object's state, *fine-grained locking* — partitioning an object's state into different subsets protected by different locks — is sometimes warranted.

EXAMPLE

Hash table with fine grained locking. A hash table provides put(key, value), value = get(key), and value = remove(key) methods. A simple coarse-grained locking implementation would use a single lock that is acquired and released at the start and end of each of these methods. If serializing all requests limits performance, a fine-grained alternative is to have one lock per hash bucket and to acquire the lock for bucket b before accessing any record that hashes to bucket b.

There is no fundamental difference between a program with multiple shared objects, each with its own lock, and a shared object that uses fine grained locking and that has multiple locks covering different subsets of its data structures. All of our discussions about issues that arise when accessing multiple shared objects in a program also apply to fine-grained locking within an object.

Complexity v. performance. Beware of premature optimization: dividing an object's state into different pieces protected by different locks can significantly increase the object's complexity and does not always significantly improve performance.

EXAMPLE

Resizable hash table. Suppose we want to implement a hash table whose number of hash buckets grows as the number of objects it stores increases. If we have a single lock, this is easy to do. But, what if we use fine-grained locking? Then the design becomes more complex because we have some operations like put() and get() that operate on one bucket and other operations like resize() that operates across multiple buckets. One solution is to have a readers-writers lock on the overall structure of the table (e.g., the number of buckets and the array of buckets) and a mutual exclusion locks on each bucket. Then, put() and get() acquire the table's readers-writers lock in read mode and also acquire the relevant bucket's mutual exclusion lock, and resize() acquires the readers-writers lock in write mode.

A second solution is to have one mutual exclusion lock for each bucket, for get() and put() to acquire the relevant bucket's mutual exclusion lock, and for resize() to iterate through the buckets, acquiring all of the buckets' locks.

A third solution is to divide the hash key space into r regions, to have a mutual exclusion lock for each region, and to allow each region to be resized independently when that region becomes heavily loaded. Then, get(), put(), and resizeRegion() each acquire the relevant region's mutual exclusion lock.

Which is solution is best? It is not obvious. The first solution is simple and appears to allow good concurrency, but acquiring the readers-writers lock even in read mode often involves writing a cache line that will be shared by many processors, so it may have poor cache performance. The second solution makes resize() expensive, but if resize() is a rare operation, that may be OK. The third solution could balance concurrency for get()/put() against the cost of resize(), but it is more complex and may require tuning the number of groups to get good performance. And, these trade-offs may change as the implementation becomes more complex; for example to trigger resize() at appropriate times, we probably need to maintain an additional nObjects count of the number of objects currently stored in the hash table, so whatever locking approach we use would need to be extended to cover this information.

Often, the best practice is to start simple, often with a single-lock per shared object. If the objects' interfaces are well designed, then refactoring their implementations to increase concurrency and performance can be done once the system is built and performance measurements have identified the bottlenecks. "It is easier to go from a working system to a working, fast system than to go from a fast system to a fast, working system."

EXAMPLE   **Linux evolution.** The first versions of Linux ran only on uniprocessor machines. To allow Linux to run on multiprocessor machines, version 2.0 introduced the Big Kernel Lock (BKL) — a single lock that protected all of the kernel's shared data structures. The BKL allowed the kernel to function on multiprocessor machines, but scalability and performance were limited. So, over time, different subsystems and different data structures got their own locks, allowing them to be accessed without holding the BKL. By version 2.6, Linux has been highly optimized to run well on multiprocessor machines — Linux now has thousands of different locks and TBDresearchers have demonstrated scalability for a range of benchmarks on a 48 processor machine. Still, the BKL remains in use in a few — mostly less performance-critical — parts of the Linux kernel like the reboot() system call, some older file systems, and some device drivers.

Solutions and design patterns

As noted above, there are no completely general solutions for how to structure multi-object and multi-lock programs. However, there are approaches and design patterns that work well in practice. We discuss four examples here and more examples after we have addressed deadlock, which also affects techniques for writing multi-object, multi-lock programs.

Careful class design

It can be easier to reason about sequences of operations on objects than to reason about sequences of atomic reads and writes of memory because we often have control over the interface to those objects. Careful class and interface design can make it feasible to reason about the overall program. This need for careful design includes the design of individual objects (e.g., specifying clean interfaces that expose the right abstractions). It also includes the architecture of how those objects interact (e.g., structuring a system architecture in well-defined layers.)

EXAMPLE   **Too much milk.** For example, as just noted, it would be difficult to solve Too Much Milk with a Note object and Fridge object with interfaces Note::readNote(), Note::writeNote(), Fridge::checkForMilk(), and Fridge::addMilk(). On the other hand, if we refactor the objects so that we have Fridge::checkforMilkAndSetNoteIfNeeded() and Fridge::addMilk(), the problem is straightforward.

This advice is admittedly rather generic and perhaps obvious: of course one should strive for elegant designs for both single- and multi-threaded code. Nonetheless, we emphasize that the choices you make for your interfaces, abstractions, and software architecture can dramatically affect the complexity or feasibility of your designs.

Ownership pattern

ownership
design
pattern

One common synchronization technique in large, multi-threaded programs is an *ownership design pattern* in which a thread removes an object from a container and then may access the object without holding a lock because the program structure guarantees that at most one thread owns an object at a time.

EXAMPLE   **Work queue.** A single web page can contain multiple objects including html frames, style sheets, and images. Consider a multi-threaded web browser whose processing is divided into three stages: receiving an object via the network, parsing the object, and rendering the object (see Figure 6.1.) For the first stage, we have one thread per network connection, and for the other stages we have several worker threads, each of which processes one object at a time.

The work queues between stages coordinate object ownership. Objects in the queues are not being accessed by any thread. When a worker thread in the *parse* stage removes an object from the stage's work queue, it owns the object and has exclusive access to it. When it is done parsing the object, it puts the parsed object into the second queue and stops

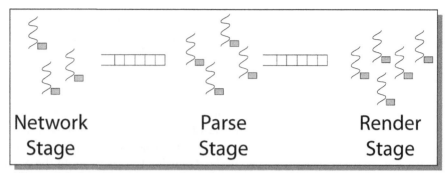

Figure 6.1: A multi-stage server based on the ownership pattern. In the first stage, one thread exclusively owns each network connection. In later stages, one thread is processing a given object at a time.

accessing it. A worker thread from the *render* stage then removes it from the second queue, gaining exclusive access to it to render it to the screen.

Acquire-all/release-all

If a system that processes requests has multiple locks, one way to manage these locks is the *acquire-all/release-all pattern*. To process a request in this pattern, a thread first acquires all of the locks that will be needed at any point during request processing, then the thread processes the request, finally the thread releases all of the locks.

acquire-all/release-all pattern

This approach can allow significant concurrency. If requests touch nonoverlapping subsets of state protected by different locks, then they can proceed in parallel.

This approach can be easy to reason about because it enforces *serializability* across requests — the result of any execution of the program is equivalent to an execution in which requests are processed one at a time in some sequential order. As Figure 6.2 illustrates, requests that access nonoverlapping data can proceed in parallel. The result is the same as it woud have been if, instead, the system first executed one of the requests and then the other. On the other hand, if two requests touch any of the same data, then one will be processed entirely before the other's processing begins. Ensuring serializability thus allows one to reason about multi-step tasks *as if* each task executed alone.

serializability

EXAMPLE   **Hash table.** Consider a hash table with one lock per hash bucket and that supports a changeKey(k1, k2) operation that changes the object that initially has key k1 to have key k2 instead. This function could be implemented to acquire k1 and k2's locks, remove the object using key k1, update the object's key, insert the object using key k2, and then release k1 and k2's locks.

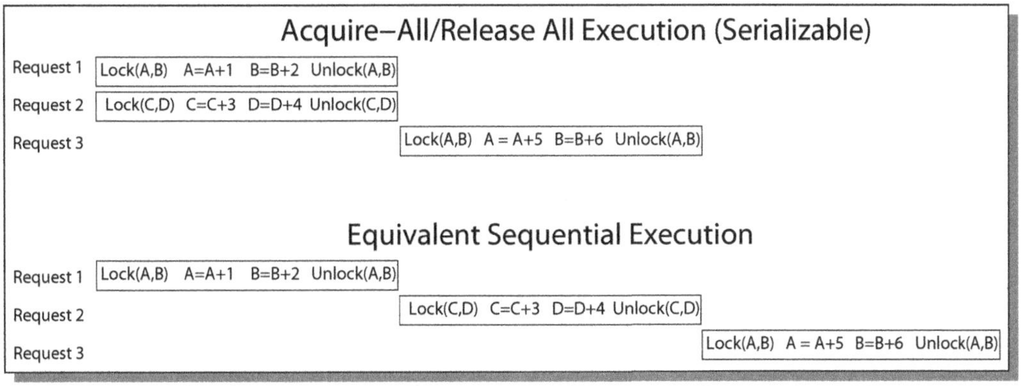

Figure 6.2: Locking multiple objects using an acquire-all/release-all pattern results in a serializable execution that is equivalent to an execution where requests are executed sequentially in some order.

One challenge to using this approach is knowing exactly what locks will be needed by a request before beginning to process it. One solution is to conservatively acquire more locks than needed (e.g., acquire any locks that *may* be needed by a particular request), but this approach can reduce concurrency.

Another challenge is that locks may be held for longer than needed. This aspect of the approach can also reduce concurrency.

Two-phase locking refines the acquire-all/release-all pattern to address these two challenges.

Two-phase locking

two phase locking

In *two phase locking* a multi-step task is divided into two phases. During the *expanding* phase, locks may be acquired but not released. Then, in the *contracting* phase, locks may be released but not acquired.

For some programs, this approach can support more concurrency than the acquire-all/release-all pattern. Because locks can be acquired during the expanding phase, two-phase locking does not require deciding what locks to grab *a priori*, so programs may be able to avoid acquiring locks they do not end up needing, and they may not need to hold some locks for as long.

Two phase locking pattern facilitates reasoning about programs because it also ensures that all executions are serializable. To see this, notice that if two requests access overlapping data, then one of them will lock all of the overlapping data before the other one begins its access to that data; then, once the thread processing the first request begins releasing locks and the thread processing the second request begins acquiring locks, the second request only modifies data that the first request will not access again. The execution thus appears as it would have if the first request finished

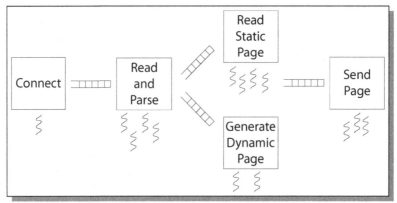

Figure 6.3: A staged architecture for a simple web server.

accessing all of the overlapping data before the second request accesses any of the overlapping data, which, in turn, appears as it would have if the first request finished executing before the second request began executing.

EXAMPLE   **Hash table.** A changeKey(k1, k2) function for a hash table with per-bucket locks could be implemented to acquire k1's lock, remove the object using key k1, update the object's key, acquire k2's lock, release k1's lock, insert the object using key k2, and release k2's lock.

Staged architectures

staged
architecture

One common pattern is the *staged architecture* pattern, illustrated in Figure 6.3. A staged architecture divides a system into multiple subsystems called stages, where each stage includes some state private to the stage and a set of one or more worker threads that operate on that state. Different stages communicate by sending messages to each other via shared producer-consumer queues, and each worker thread repeatedly pulls the next message from a stage's incoming queue and then processes it, possibly producing one or more messages for other stages' queues.

EXAMPLE   **Simple web server.** Figure 6.3 shows a staged architecture for a simple web server that has a first *connect* stage that uses 1 thread to set up network connections and that passes each connections to a second *read and parse* stage.

The *read and parse* stage has several threads, each of which repeatedly gets a connection from the incoming queue, reads a request from the connection, and parses the request to determine what web page is being requested.

If the request is for a static web page (e.g., an HTML file), the *read and parse* stage passes the request and connection to the *read static page* stage, where one of the stage's threads reads the specified page from disk.

Otherwise, the *read and parse* stage passes the request and connection to the *generate dynamic page* stage, where one of the stage's threads runs a program that dynamically generates a page in response to the request. Once the page has been fetched or generated, the page and connection are passed to the *send page* stage, where one of the threads transmits the page over the connection.

The key property of a staged architecture is that the state of each stage is private to that stage. This property improves modularity, making it easier to reason about each stage individually and about interactions across stages.

As an example of the modularity benefits, consider implementing a system where different stages are produced by different teams or even different companies. Each stage can be designed and tested almost independently, and the system is likely to work as expected when the stages are brought together. For example, it is common practice for a web site to use a web server from one company and a database from another company and for the two to communicate via messages.

Another benefit of this approach for some applications is improved cache locality. If a thread on a processor is operating on a subset of the system's state, it may have a better cache hit rate than a thread that must access state from all stages. On the other hand, for some workloads, passing a request from stage to stage will hurt cache hit rates compared to doing all of the processing for a request on one processor.

Also note that for good performance, the processing in each stage must be large enough to amortize the cost of sending and receiving messages.

event processing
The special case when there is exactly one thread per stage is called *event processing*. A special property of event processing architectures is that there is no concurrency within a stage, so no locking is required and each message is processed atomically with respect to that stage's state.

Overload. One challenge with staged architectures is dealing with overload. The throughput of the system will be limited by that of the slowest stage. If the system is overloaded, the slowest stage will fall behind and the queue before it will grow. Depending on the system's implementation, two bad things can happen. First, the queue can grow indefinitely, consuming more and more memory until the system runs out of memory. Second, if the queue is limited to a finite size, once that size is reached, earlier stages must either discard messages they want to send to the overloaded stage or they must block until the queue has room. Notice that if they block, then the backpressure will limit earlier stages' throughput to that of the bottleneck stage, and their queues may begin to grow.

One solution is to dynamically vary the number of threads per stage. If a stage's incoming queue is growing, shift processing resources to it by stopping one of the threads for a stage with a short queue start a new thread for the stage that is falling behind.

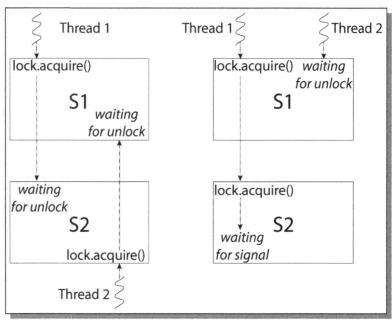

Figure 6.4: Two examples of deadlock: *mutually recursive locking* (left) and *nested waiting* (right).

6.2 | Deadlock

Deadlock

A challenge to constructing programs that include multiple shared objects is deadlock. *Deadlock* is a cycle of waiting among a set of threads where each thread is waiting for some other thread in the cycle to take some action.

mutually recursive locking

Figure 6.4 shows two examples of deadlock. In *mutually recursive locking*, code in each of two shared objects $s1$ and $s2$ holds a lock while calling into a method in the other shared object that uses that object's lock. Then, threads 1 and 2 can deadlock if thread 1 calls a method in $s1$ that holds the lock and tries to call a method in $s2$ that needs a lock while thread 1 calls a method in $s2$ that holds $s2$'s lock and that tries to call a method in $s1$ that needs $s1$'s lock.

nested waiting

In *nested waiting*, code in one shared object $s1$ calls a method of another shared object $s2$, which waits on a condition variable. The condition variable's wait() method releases $s2$'s lock but not $s1$'s, so the thread that would have done a signal in $s2$ may stuck waiting for $s1$'s lock.

EXAMPLE

The Dining Philosophers.

The Dining Philosophers problem is a classic synchronization problem that illustrates the challenge of deadlock. There is a round table with n plates and n chopsticks arranged as illustrated in Figure 6.5. A philosopher sitting at each plate requires two chopsticks to eat. Suppose that each

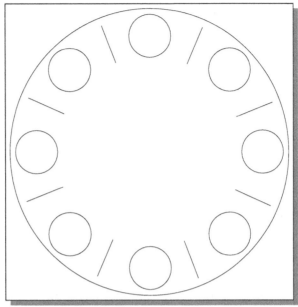

Figure 6.5: In this example of the dining philosophers problem, there are 8 philosophers, 8 plates, and 8 chopsticks.

philosopher proceeds by grabbing the chopstick on the left, grabbing the chopstick on the right, eating, and then replacing both chopsticks. If philosophers follow this approach they can unfortunately, enter a deadlock: each philosopher can grab the chopstick on the left but then be stuck waiting for the philosopher on the right to release the chopstick she holds.

Deadlock v. starvation.   Deadlock and starvation are both liveness con-

starvation   cerns. In *starvation*, some thread fails to make progress for an indefinite period of time. Deadlock is a form of starvation but with the stronger condition that a group of threads form a cycle where none of the threads make progress because each thread is waiting for some other thread in the cycle. Thus, deadlock implies starvation (literally, for the dining philosophers), but starvation does not imply deadlock.

For example, recall the readers/writers example discussed in Section 5.6. If instead of implementing a writers-preferred solution we implement a readers-preferred solution where a reader only waits if a writer is currently active, then writers could starve if the workload includes a large number of readers. Note that such starvation would not be deadlock — the writers are waiting on the readers, but the readers are not waiting on the writers.

Nondeterminism.   Just because a system might suffer a deadlock or might starve a thread does not mean that it always will. A system is *subject to* *starvation* if it is possible for a thread to starve in some circumstances. A system is *subject to deadlock* if it is possible for a group of threads to enter deadlock in some circumstances. Here, the circumstances that affect whether deadlock or starvation occurs may include a broad range of factors such as the choices made by the scheduler, the number of threads running, the workload or sequence of requests processed by the system, which threads win races to acquire locks, and which threads are enabled in what order when signals or broadcasts occur.

A system that is subject to starvation or deadlock may be live in many or most runs and only starve or deadlock for particular workloads or "unlucky" interleavings. For example, in the *mutually recursive locking* example in Figure 6.4, the deadlock only occurs if the threads call the indicated functions at about the same time, and for the Dining Philosophers problem, philosophers may succeed in eating for a long time before hitting the unlucky sequence of events that causes them to deadlock. Similarly, in the readers/writers example, the readers-preferred solution will allow some writes to complete as long as the rate of reads stays below some threshold.

Since testing may not uncover deadlock problems, it is important to construct systems that are deadlock-free by design.

Necessary conditions for deadlock

There are four necessary conditions for deadlock to occur. Knowing these conditions is useful for designing solutions to deadlock: if you can prevent any one of these conditions, then you can eliminate the possibility of deadlock.

1. **Bounded resources.** There are a finite number of threads that can simultaneously use a resource.

2. **No preemption.** Once a thread acquires a resource, the ownership of the resource cannot be revoked until the thread acts to release it.

3. **Wait while holding.** A thread holds one resource while waiting for another. This condition is sometimes called *multiple independent requests* because it occurs when a thread first acquires one resource and then attempts to acquire another resource.

4. **Circular waiting.** There is a set of waiting threads such that each thread is waiting for a resource held by another.

EXAMPLE   **Dining Philosophers.** To illustrate the circular waiting condition, Figure 6.6 maps the state of a deadlocked Dining Philosophers implementation to an abstract graph that shows which resources are *owned by* which threads and which threads *wait for* which resources. In this type of graph, if there is one instance of each type of resource (e.g., a particular

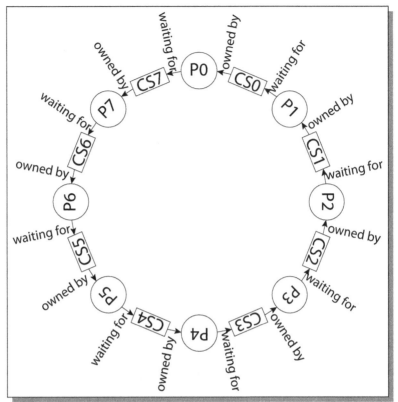

Figure 6.6: Graph representation of the state of a deadlocked Dining Philosophers system. Circles represent threads, boxes represent resources, an arrow from a box/resource to a circle/thread represents an *owned by* relationship and an arrow from a circle/thread to a box/resource represents a *waiting for* relationship.

chopstick), then a cycle implies deadlock (assuming the system does not allow preemption.)

These four conditions are necessary but not sufficient for deadlock. If there are multiple instances of a type of resource, then there can by a cycle of waiting without deadlock because a thread not in the cycle may return resources to the pool.

EXAMPLE   **Dining Philosophers.** Suppose we have a set of 5 philosophers at a table with 5 chopsticks but that the chopsticks are placed in a tray at the center of the table when they are not in use. We could be in the state illustrated in Figure 6.7 where philosopher 1 has two chopsticks, philosophers 2, 3, and 4 each have one chopstick and is waiting for another chopstick, and philosopher 5 has no chopsticks. In this state we have bounded resources (5 chopsticks), no preemption (we cannot forcibly remove a chopstick from a hungry philosopher's hand), wait while holding (philosophers 2,

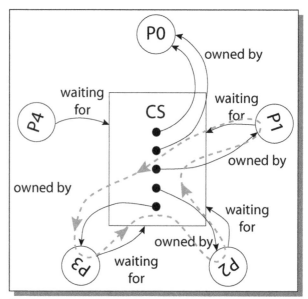

Figure 6.7: Graph representation of the state of a Dining Philosophers system that includes a cycle among waiting threads and resources but that is not deadlocked. Circles represent threads, boxes represent resources, dots within a box represent multiple instances of a resource, an arrow from a dot/resource instance to a circle/thread represents an *owned by* relationship and an arrow from a circle/thread to a box/resource represents a *waiting for* relationship.

3 and 4 are holding a chopstick while waiting for another), and circular waiting (each of philosophers 2, 3, and 4 are waiting for a resource held by another of them.) However, we do not have deadlock; eventually thread 1 will release its two chopsticks, which may, for example, allow threads 2 and 3 to eat and release their chopsticks which would allow threads 4 and 5 to eat.

Although the system shown in Figure 6.7 is not currently deadlocked, it is still subject to deadlock. For example, if philosopher 1 returns two chopsticks, philosopher 5 grabs one, and philosopher 1 grabs the other, then the system would deadlock.

Preventing deadlock

Preventing deadlock can be challenging. For example, consider a system with 3 resources—A, B, and C—and two threads that access them. Thread 1 acquires A then C then B and thread 2 acquires B then C then A. The following sequence can lead to deadlock:

	Thread 1	Thread 2
1	Acquire A	
2		Acquire B
3	Acquire C	
4		Wait for C
5	Wait for B	

How could we avoid this deadlock? The deadlock's circular waiting occurs when we reach step 5, but our fate was sealed much earlier. In particular, once we complete step 2 and thread 2 acquires B, deadlock is inevitable. In this case to prevent the deadlock we have to be smart enough to see the deadlock that will occur at step 5 much earlier; once step 1 completes and thread 1 acquires A, we cannot allow thread 2 to complete step 2 and acquire B or deadlock will follow.

This example illustrates that given an arbitrary program, preventing deadlock can be challenging. Deadlock prevention solutions, therefore, often restrict or take advantage of the structure of a program to avoid such complexity. As a result, no single solution is best in all cases.

Section 6.2 listed four necessary conditions for deadlock. These conditions are useful because they suggest approaches for preventing deadlock: if a system is structured to prevent at least one of the conditions, then the system can not deadlock. Considering these conditions in the context of a given system often points to a viable deadlock prevention strategy. Below, we discuss some commonly-used approaches.

Bounded resources: Provide sufficient resources. One way to ensure deadlock freedom is to have sufficient resources to satisfy all threads' demands. For example, suppose an operating system allows a maximum of 10 open files per process, 10 processes, and 50 open files total; this system could deadlock for some workloads. On the other hand, if this system increases the global limit to 100 open files, then the open files resource cannot cause a deadlock.

No preemption: Preempt resources. Another technique is to allow the runtime system to forcibly reclaim resources held by a thread. For example, an operating system can preempt a page of memory from a running process by copying it to disk in order to prevent applications from deadlocking as they acquire memory pages.

Wait while holding: Abort request. Programs can choose not to wait for resources and abort a request that cannot immediately get all of the resources it needs. Although this approach sounds extreme, it can provide acceptable performance and can be much simpler than other alternatives for engineering deadlock out of a system.

For example, in old-style circuit-switched telephone networks, a call would have to reserve a circuit at a series of switches along its path. If the connection setup fails to find a free circuit at any hop, rather than wait for a circuit at the next hop to become free, it cancels the connection attempt, giving the user an error message ("All circuits are busy. Please try again later.")

Similarly, when a router in the modern Internet is overloaded and runs out of packet buffers, it drops incoming packets. An alternative would be for each router to wait to send a packet until the next router has a buffer for it, but such an approach could deadlock.

Wait while holding: Atomically acquire all resources.   Rather than acquiring resources in a sequence of steps, programs can be structured so that threads wait until all required resources are available and then acquire them all atomically. For example, a dining philosopher might wait until the two neighboring chopsticks are available and then simultaneously grab them both.

A thread may not know exactly which resources it will need to complete its work, but it can still acquire all resources that it *might* need when it begins work. For example, in an operating system for mobile phones where memory is constrained and where memory cannot be preempted by copying it to disk, rather than having applications request additional memory as needed, we might instead have each application state its maximum memory needs and allocate that much memory when each application starts. Disadvantages of this approach include the challenge of having applications accurately estimate their worst-case needs and the cost of allocating significantly more resources than may be necessary in the common case.

Wait while holding: Release lock when calling out of module.   If we have a series of nested modules, each of which has a lock, then waiting on a condition variable in an inner module can lead to a nested waiting deadlock. One solution is to restructure a module's code so that no locks are held when calling other modules. For example, we can change the code on the left to the code on the right:

```
Module :: foo (){                    Module :: foo (){
   lock . acquire ();                   doSomeStuff ();
   doSomeStuff ();                      otherModule –>bar ();
   otherModule –>bar ();                doOtherStuff ();
   doOtherStuff ();                  }
   lock . release ();               Module :: doSomeStuff (){
}                                      lock . acquire ();
Module :: doSomeStuff (){              x  =  x+1;
   x  =  x+1;                           lock . release ();
}                                    }
Module :: doOtherStuff (){           Module :: doOtherStuff (){
   y  =  y–2;                           lock . acquire ();
}                                       y  =  y–2;
                                        lock . release ();
                                     }
```

Circular waiting: Lock ordering. An approach used in many systems is to identify an ordering among locks and to forbid acquiring a lock if any higher-ordered lock is already held.

For example, we can eliminate deadlock among the dining philosophers if—instead of always grabbing the chopstick on the left and then the one on the right, the philosophers number the chopsticks from 1 to n and always grab the lower-numbered chopstick before the higher-numbered one.

Similarly, for our hash table with per-bucket locks that supports a changeKeys(k1, k2) operation, we can avoid deadlock by always grabbing the lock for the lower-numbered bucket before the one for the higher-numbered bucket.

The Banker's Algorithm for avoiding deadlock

The Banker's Algorithm is another deadlock prevention approach. It is more complex to describe than the ones above, and systems seldom use it in its full generality. Nonetheless, we include this discussion both because simplified versions of the algorithm can be useful and because it sheds light on some underlying principles for understanding deadlocks such as the distinction between *safe* and *unsafe* states and how the occurrence of deadlocks often depends on a system's workload and sequence of operations.

Dijkstra defined the *Banker's Algorithm* as an approach that improves upon the *atomically acquire all resources* approach. A thread still *states* its maximum resource requirements when it begins a task, but it then acquires and releases those resources incrementally as the task runs. The runtime system *delays* granting some requests in a way that ensures the system never deadlocks.

The key idea behind the algorithm is that just because a system is capable of deadlock doesn't mean that it must always deadlock: for some interleavings of requests it will deadlock, but for others it won't. By delaying when some resource requests are processed, a system can avoid interleavings that could lead to deadlock.

A deadlock-prone system can be in one of three states: a *safe state*, an *unsafe state*, and a *deadlocked state* (see Figure 6.8.)

safe state
- In a *safe state*, for any possible sequence of resource requests, there exists at least one *safe sequence* of processing the requests that eventually succeeds in granting all pending and future requests.

unsafe state
- In an *unsafe state*, there exists at least one sequence of pending and future resource requests that leads to deadlock no mater what processing order is tried.

deadlocked state
- In a *deadlocked state*, the system has at least one deadlock.

So, as long as the system is in a safe state, it has control of its own destiny: for any workload, it can avoid deadlock by delaying the processing of some

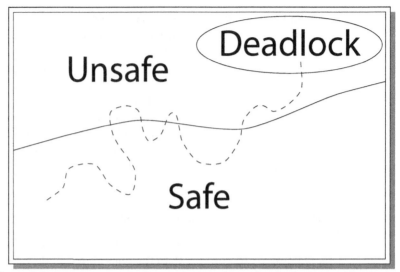

Figure 6.8: A process can be in a *safe*, *unsafe*, or *deadlocked* state. The dashed line illustrates a sequence of states visited by a thread — some are safe, some are unsafe, and the final state is a deadlock.

requests. In particular, the Banker's Algorithm will delay any request that would take it from a safe to an unsafe state because once the system enters an unsafe state, it may not be able to avoid deadlock.

Notice that an unsafe state does not always lead to deadlock. A system in an unsafe state may remain in an unsafe state or return to a safe state, depending on the specific interleaving of resource requests and completions. However, as long as the system is in an unsafe state, a bad workload or unlucky scheduling of requests can force it to deadlock.

The Banker's Algorithm is an approach to keeping a system in a safe state. The algorithm is based on a loose analogy with a small town banker who has a maximum total amount that can be loaned at one time total and a set of businesses that each have a credit line max[i] for business i. A business will borrow and pay back amounts of money as various projects are started and finished, so that the business i will always have an outstanding loan amount between 0 and max[i]. For each business with a credit line, if all of the business's requests are granted, the business will eventually reach a state where all current projects are finished and the loan balance returns to 0.

A conservative banker might only issue credit lines so that the sum of the credit lines is at most total; this approach is analogous to the *atomically acquire all resources* approach or the *provide sufficient resources* approach, and it trivially guarantees that the system remains in a safe state and that eventually all businesses with credit lines will complete their projects.

However, a more aggressive banker can issue more credit as long as the

```
class ResourceMgr{
  private:
    Lock lock;
    Cond cv;
    int r;  // Number of resources
    int t;  // Number of threads
    int avail[];  // avail[i]: instances of resource i available
    int max[][];  // max[i][j]: max of resource i needed by thread j
    int alloc[][];  // alloc[i][j]: current allocation of resource i
                    // to   thread j

  ...
}
```

Figure 6.9: State maintained by banker algorithm's resource manager. Resource manager code is in Figures 6.10 and 6.11.

```
//
// Invariant: the system is in a safe state
//
ResourceMgr::Request(int resourceID, int threadID){
    lock.Acquire();
    assert(isSafe());
    while(!wouldBeSafe(resourceID, threadID)){
        cv.Wait(&lock);
    }
    alloc[resourceID][threadID]++;
    avail[resourceID]--;
    assert(isSafe());
    lock.Release();
}
```

Figure 6.10: High level pseudo-code for banker's algorithm. The state maintained by the algorithm is defined in Figure 6.9 and the method isSafe() is defined in Figure 6.11.

bank can live up to its commitment to each business — to provide a loan of max[i] if business i requests it. The key observation is that the bank can *delay* requests to increase a loan amount within a businesses existing credit line. For example, the bank might lose the paperwork for a few hours, days, or weeks.

By delaying loan requests, the bank can remain in a safe state—a state for which there exists at least one series of loan fulfillments by which every business i can eventually receive its maximal loan max[i], complete its projects, and pay back all of its loan. The bank can then use that repaid money to grant pending loans to other businesses.

Figure 6.10 shows pseudo-code for a version of the banker's algorithm that manages a set of r resources for a set of t threads. To simplify discussion, threads request each unit of resource separately, but the algorithm can be extended to allow multiple resources to be requested at the same time.

```
//
// A state is safe iff there exists a safe sequence of grants
// that would allow all threads to eventually receive their
// maximum resource needs
//
bool
ResourceMgr :: isSafe ()
{
    int j;
    int toBeAvail [] = copy avail [];
    int need [][] = max [][] - alloc [][]; // need[i][j] initialized to
                                           // max[i][j] - alloc[i][j]
    bool finish [] = [false , false , false , ...]; // finish[j] is true
                                                    // if thread j is guaranteed
                                                    // to finish

    while ( true ){
        j = any threadID such that :
            ( (finish [j]==false) && ( forall i: need[i][j] <= toBeAvail [i]));
        if (no such j exists ){
            if (forall j: finish [j] == true ){
                return true ;
            }
            else {
                return false ;
            }
        }
        else {
            // Thread j will eventually finish and return its current
            // allocation to the pool
            finish [j] = true ;
            forall i:   toBeAvail [i] = toBeAvail [i] + alloc [i][j];
        }
    }
}


//
// Hypothetically grant request and see if resulting state
// is safe .
//
bool
ResourceMgr :: wouldBeSafe (int resourceID , int threadID )
{
    bool ret = false ;
    avail [resourceID]--;
    alloc [resourceID ][ threadID ]++;
    if (isSafe ()){
        ret = true ;
    }
    avail [resourceID ]++;
    alloc [resourceID ][ threadID ]--;
    return ret ;
}
```

Figure 6.11: Banker's algorithm test on system state (pseudo-code.) Figure 6.10 provides the high-level pseudo-code of the banker's algorithm and and Figure 6.9 defines the state on which these tests work.

The high-level idea is simple: when a request arrives, wait until it is safe to grant the request before granting it. As Figure 6.9 shows, we can realize this high-level approach by tracking the current allocation of each resource to each thread, the maximum allocation possible for each thread, and the current set of available, unallocated resources.

Figure 6.11 shows how we can test whether a state is safe. Recall that a state is safe if there is some sequence of thread executions that will allow each thread to gain its maximum resource need, finish its work, and release its resources. So, we first see if the currently free resources would allow any thread to finish; if so, then the resources held by that thread would eventually be released to the system. Next, we see if the currently free resources plus the resources held by the thread identified in the first step would allow any other thread to finish; if so, both the first and second threads resources would eventually be released to the system. We continue this process until we have identified all threads that can be guaranteed to finish. If that set includes all of the threads, the state is safe.

EXAMPLE   **Page allocation with the Bankers Algorithm.** Suppose we have a system with 8 pages of memory and three processes: A, B, and C, which may need as many as 4, 5, and 5 pages to complete, respectively.

If they take turns requesting one page each, and the system grants requests in order, the system deadlocks, reaching a state where each process is stuck until some other process releases memory:

Process								Allocation				
A	0	1	1	1	2	2	2	3	3	3	wait	wait
B	0	0	1	1	1	2	2	2	3	3	3	wait
C	0	0	0	1	1	1	2	2	2	wait	wait	wait
Total	0	1	2	3	4	5	6	7	8	8	8	8

On the other hand, if the system follows the Banker's algorithm, then it can delay some processes and guarantee that all processes eventually complete. E.g.,

Process										Allocation									
A	0	1	1	1	2	2	2	3	3	3	4	0	0	0	0	0	0	0	0
B	0	0	1	1	1	2	2	2	wait	wait	wait	wait	3	4	4	5	0	0	0
C	0	0	0	1	1	1	2	2	2	wait	wait	wait	3	3	wait	wait	4	5	0
Total	0	1	2	3	4	5	6	7	7	7	8	4	6	7	7	8	4	5	0

By delaying B and C in the ninth through twelfth steps, the algorithm allows A to complete and release its resources. Then, by delaying C in the fifteenth and sixteen steps, the algorithm allows B to complete and release its resources.

Though not complex in absolute terms, the Banker's Algorithm is noticeably more involved than the other approaches discussed above. It is rarely used in its full generality, but understanding the distinction between *safe, unsafe,* and *deadlock* states and understanding how manifestations of deadlock depend on request ordering are both important for understanding deadlock.

Additionally, an understanding of the Banker's Algorithm can help us design simple solutions for specific problems. For example, if we apply the Banker's Algorithm to the variation of the Dining Philosopher's problem where we place the chopsticks in the middle of the table, then a philosopher taking a chopstick would wait if it would be the last chopstick and no philosopher would have two chopsticks; otherwise, the philosopher would take the chopstick.

Detecting and breaking deadlock

Rather than preventing deadlocks, some systems allow deadlocks to occur and break them when they arise.

Why allow deadlocks to occur at all? Sometimes, it is difficult or expensive to enforce sufficient structure on the system's data and workloads to prevent deadlock. For example, this approach is often used in databases, which provide a general interface that applications can use to access shared data via multi-step *transactions* that can acquire and release locks covering different subsets of data. Because the database is meant as a general tool, there is seldom any way to prevent users from issuing requests that could cause deadlock. Also, because a database is often shared by multiple users, it can not allow bugs in one user's queries or unexpected interactions between two users' queries to create deadlocks that permanently make some data inaccessible.

For this approach to work, we need ways to break deadlocks when they occur, ideally with minimal harm to programs, and we need ways to detect deadlocks so that we know when to invoke the recovery mechanisms. We now talk about each of these challenges:

Breaking deadlocks

Breaking a deadlock once it has occurred generally requires forcibly taking resources away from some or all of the deadlocked threads. Because the resources by definition are not revokable, this process generally damages the victim threads in some way, but it hopefully allows the rest of the system to continue to function.

As a simple example, when some operating systems decide that a process is part of a deadlock, they simply kill the process and release the process's resources. Although this sounds drastic, if a deadlocked process cannot make any progress anyhow, killing it does not make it much worse off.

Notice, however, that under the lock-based shared object programming abstractions we have discussed, it is seldom possible to kill deadlocked threads within a process and allow the other threads sharing the process's shared objects to continue to function. If the deadlocked threads hold locks on shared objects, simply killing the threads and marking the locks as free could leave the objects in an inconsistent state.

Transactions. To allow deadlocks to be broken with minimal disruption in systems that use locks, we would like to do two things.

- First, we would like to ensure that revoking locks from one thread does not leave the system's objects in an inconsistent state. To do this, we would like to be able to *undo* a deadlocked thread's actions. Then, to fix a deadlock, we can choose one or more victim threads, stop them, undo their actions, and let other threads proceed.

- Second, once the deadlock is broken and other threads have completed some or all of their work, we would like to be able to *restart* the victim threads. If these threads can now complete, the system operates as if the victim threads never caused a deadlock but, instead, just had the start of their executions delayed.

Transactions, which we discuss in detail in Chapter ??, are widely used in databases and provide these two properties.

A transaction is like a critical section, and it has beginTransaction and endTransaction statements that are similar to a critical section's Lock::Acquire() and Lock::Release(). In particular, in that transactions are *isolated* so that during a transaction, the one transaction's actions cannot affect other transactions. Isolation can be ensured with appropriate locking. If all of a transaction's actions including the endTransaction complete, then the transaction *commits*, the transaction's locks are released, and the transaction's operations become visible.

One key difference between transactions and critical sections is that transactions can *abort* and *roll back* their actions. If a transaction fails to reach its endTransaction statement (e.g., because of a deadlock or because some other exception occurred), the system can reset all of the state modified by the transaction to what it was when the transaction began. One way to support this is to maintain an *undo log* that keeps track of the initial values of all state modified by each transaction.

So, if a transactional system becomes deadlocked, the system can abort one or more of the deadlocked transactions. Aborting these transactions rolls back the system's state to what it would have been if these transactions had never started and releases the aborted transactions' locks and other resources. If aborting the chosen transactions releases sufficient resources, the deadlock is broken and the remaining transactions can proceed. If not, then the system can abort additional transactions.

Since aborting a transaction rolls back the state of the system to what it would have been had the transaction not begun execution, the system can restart the aborted transactions at some later time. For example, a conservative system might minimize the risk of encountering the same deadlock by waiting for all of the current (non-aborted) transactions to complete and then restarting and completing one aborted victim transaction at a time until all of them complete. Alternatively, a more aggressive system could restart multiple victim transactions at the same time, repeating the recovery process if it gets unlucky and deadlocks again.

Transactions with optimistic concurrency control.   Instead of using trans-actions as a way to let us break deadlocks, we can also use transactions to avoid them. *Optimistic concurrency control* allows transactions to execute in parallel without locking any data, but it only allows a transaction to commit if none of the objects accessed by the transaction have been modified since the transaction began; otherwise, the transaction must abort. Typically, systems then retry the aborted transaction — since each reexecution runs with a different set of concurrent transactions, it should eventually be able to successfully commit.

Optimistic
concurrency
control

One way to implement transactions with optimistic concurrency control is for each transaction to keep track of which versions of which objects it reads and for it to apply its updates to a local copy of each object it modifies. Then, before a transaction commits, it verifies that none of the objects it accessed were modified by other transaction.

Optimistic concurrency control works well for most systems and work-loads, where different transactions usually access different subsets of data. In these cases, the approach not only eliminates deadlock but also maxi-mizes concurrency since threads do not wait for locks. On the other hand, if there are significant numbers of conflicting, concurrent transactions, over-heads from rolling back and reexecuting transactions can be high.

Detecting deadlock

There are various ways to detect deadlock.

One simple approach used in some systems is to assume that any thread that fails to make progress is part of a deadlock. This approach risks false positives where a non-deadlocked thread is incorrectly classified as dead-locked, but for some systems an occasional false positive may be an accept-able price to pay for the simplicity of the approach.

If there are several resources and only one thread can hold each resource at a time (e.g., one printer, one keyboard, and one audio speaker or several mutual exclusion locks), then we can detect a deadlock by analyzing a simple graph where each thread and each resource is represented by a node and where there is a directed edge from a resource to a thread if the resource is owned by the thread and a directed edge from a thread to a resource if the thread is waiting for the resource. See, for example, Figure 6.12-a. There is a deadlock if and only if there is a cycle in such a graph.

If there are multiple instances of some resources, then we represent a resource with k interchangeable instances (e.g., k equivalent printers) as

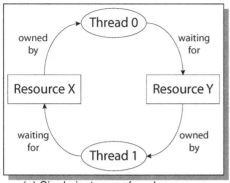

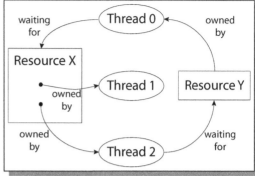

(a) Single instance of each resource   (b) Multiple instances of one of the resources

Figure 6.12: In this graph used for deadlock detection, threads and resources are nodes, and directed edges represent the *owned by* and *waiting for* relationships among them.

a node with k connection points (e.g., see Figure 6.12-b). Now, a cycle is a necessary but not sufficient condition for deadlock.

Another solution, described by Coffman, Elphick, and Shoshani in 1971 is a variation of Dijkstra's Banker's Algorithm. Now, we assume we no longer know max[][], so we cannot assess whether the current state is safe or whether some future sequence of requests can force us to deadlock. However, we can look at the current set of resources, granted requests, and pending requests and ask whether it is possible for the current set of requests to eventually be satisfied assuming no more requests come and all threads eventually complete. If so, there is no deadlock (yet, though we may be in an unsafe state); otherwise, there is a deadlock.

Figure 6.13 shows the pseudocode of the main testIfDeadlocked() method, a variation of the isSafe() method shown in Figure 6.11 for the Banker's Algorithm. We leave the state variables and high level interface (Figures 6.9 and 6.10) as an exercise for the reader.

One might hope that we could avoid deadlock by asking "Will satisfying the current request put us in a deadlocked state?" and then blocking requests that do, but as this algorithm highlights, deadlock is determined not just by what requests we grant but also by what requests are waiting. The request that puts us into a deadlocked state ("circular wait") will be a request that waits, not a request that is granted.

Taking a step back, it is the the lack of knowledge about possible future requests prevents us from using this algorithm to avoid deadlock. As Figure 6.8 illustrates, we can be in an unsafe state long before we reach a deadlock state, and once we reach an unsafe state, there are request sequences that will force us to deadlock.

For example, recall the ACB/BCA example on page 271. Even though we are not yet deadlocked after thread 1 acquires A and thread 2 acquires B, once these two actions occur, deadlock is inevitable given the requests

```
//
// A state is safe iff there exists a safe sequence of grants
// that would allow all threads to eventually receive their
// maximum resource needs
//
bool
ResourceMgr :: isDeadlock ()
{

        // avail [] holds free resource count;
        // alloc [][] holds current allocation
        // request [][] holds currently –blocked requests
        int j;
        int toBeAvail [] = copy avail [];
        bool finish [] = [false , false , false , ...];  // finish [j] is true if thread
                                                          // j is guaranteed to finish

      while ( true ){
         j = any threadID s.t. ( (finish [j]==false)
                                    &&
                                    (forall i: request[i][j] <= toBeAvail[i]));
         if (no such j exists ){
             if (forall j: finish [j] == true ){
                 return false ;
             }
             else {
                 return true ;
             }
         }
         else {
             // Thread j *may* eventually finish and return its current
             // allocation to the pool
             finish [j] = true ;
             forall i: toBeAvail [i] = toBeAvail [i] + alloc [i][j];
         }
      }
   }
}
```

Figure 6.13: Coffman et al.'s algorithm test for deadlock. This algorithm is similar to the isSafe() test of the banker's algorithm shown in Figure 6.11. We omit a detailed description of Coffman's high level design and state declarations; these are straightforward variations of the corresponding pseudo-code for the Banker's Algorithm; see Figure 6.10 and 6.9.

that will arrive in the future.

Exercises

1. Figure 6.2 shows an execution that executes some requests in parallel, and it shows an equivalent sequential execution — request 1 then request 2 then request 3 —. There are two other sequential executions that are also equivalent to the parallel execution shown in the figure. What are these other equivalent sequential executions?

2. Generalize the rules for two phase locking to include both mutual exclusion locks and readers-writers locks. What can be done in the expanding phase? What can be done in the contracting phase?

3. Consider the variation of the Dining Philosophers problem shown in Figure 6.7 where all unused chopsticks are placed in the center of the table and any philosopher can eat with any two chopsticks.

   One way to prevent deadlock in this system is to provide sufficient resources. For a system with n philosophers, what is the minimum number of chopsticks that ensures deadlock freedom? Why?

4. If the queues between stages are finite, Is it possible for a staged architecture to deadlock even if each individual stage is internally deadlock free? If so, give an example. If not, prove it.

5. Suppose you build a system using a staged architecture with some fixed number of threads operating on stage. Assuming each stage is individually deadlock free, describe two ways to guarantee that your system as a whole can not deadlock. Each of the ways should eliminate a different one of the 4 necessary conditions for deadlock.

6. Consider a system with four mutual exclusion locks (A, B, C, and D) and a readers-writers lock (E).

   To ensure serializability of request processing and to avoid deadlock, a programmer follows the following rules:

   a) Processing for each request is divided into two parts.

   b) During the first part, no lock may be released and if E is held in writing mode it cannot be downgraded to reading mode. Furthermore, lock A may not be acquired if any of locks B, C, D, or E are held in any mode; lock B may not be acquired if any of locks C, D, or E are held in any mode; lock C may not be acquired if any of locks D or E are held in any mode; lock D may not be acquired if lock E is held in any mode. Lock E may always be acquired in read mode or write mode, and it can be upgraded from read mode to write mode but not downgraded from write mode to read mode.

   c) During the second part, any lock may be released and lock E may be downgraded from write mode to read mode; releases and downgrades can happen in any order; by the end of part 2, all locks must be released; and no locks may be acquired or upgraded.

   Do these rules ensure serializability? Do they ensure freedom from deadlock? Why?

6.3 | Alternative approaches to synchronization

Chapter 5 described a core abstraction for synchronization — shared objects with one lock per object. This abstraction is the right building block for multi-threaded programs the vast majority of the time. Occasionally, as start of the current chapter indicated, you need to resort to fine grained locking, a variation of this basic approach that divides an object's state among different locks.

Even more rarely programmers resort to alternatives that avoid locks such as *read-copy-update (RCU)* synchronization and *lock-free* and *wait-free data structures*. We emphasize that the cases when these approaches are warranted are rare and that these advanced techniques should only be considered by experienced programmers who have mastered the basic lock-based approaches. Many readers will probably never need to use these techniques. If you do find yourself tempted to do so, take extra care. Be sure to measure the performance of your system to make sure that these techniques yield significant gains, and seek out extra peer review from trusted colleagues to help make sure that the code works as intended.

We caution that programmers are often tempted to assume that acquiring a lock is an expensive operation and to therefore try to reduce locking throughout their programs. The most likely result from this premature optimization mindset is a program that is buggy, hard to maintain, no faster than a clean implementation, and — ironically — harder to tune than a cleanly architected program. On most platforms, acquiring or releasing a lock is a highly tuned primitive — acquiring an uncontended lock is often nearly free (and if there is contention then you probably need that lock!)

That said, although you may not often (or ever) write code that uses these advanced techniques, it is important to understand them because they do get used in critical parts of important systems such as the Linux kernel and some Java Virtual Machine libraries and because in some cases they can provide significant performance gains.

Read-Copy-Update (RCU)

The goal of read-copy-update (RCU) is to provide high performance synchronization for data structures that are frequently read and occasionally updated. In particular, RCU optimizes the read path to have extremely low synchronization costs, even if there are many concurrent readers. However, writes can be delayed for a long time — tens of milliseconds in some implementations.

Why RCU?   We might hope that readers-writers locks would be an adequate solution for read-dominated workloads. Recall that readers-writers locks allow multiple concurrent active readers, but there is an active writer no other writer or reader can be active.

The problem with the readers-writers locks approach is its cache behavior for concurrent reads with short critical sections. Recall that before reading, a reader acquires a readers-writers lock in read mode. To do this, it must read and then update some state in the readers-writers synchronization object. Unfortunately, this access pattern causes a large number of cache misses when there are a large number of concurrent readers.

In particular, on a multiprocessor, when one processor updates a hardware cache line, it invalidates that cache line in all other caches. Then, when another processor wants to read and update the data, it first suffers a cache miss and must fetch the data from the first processor's cache or from main memory; then it must invalidate the cache line in other caches; finally, it can update the data in its cache. On a modern processor, fetching and invalidating a cache line can take hundreds of cycles. If there are a large number of processors trying to read a data structure protected by a readers-writers lock, the average processor may wait thousands of cycles to acquire the lock in read mode, even if there are no writers.

So, for critical sections less than a few thousand cycles and for programs where there may be many threads simultaneously trying to read an object, the standard readers-writers lock can impose significant overheads.

The RCU approach.   How can we let concurrent reads access a data structure that can also be written without having to suffer the cache effects of updating the state of a synchronization variable on each read?

To meet this challenge, RCU weakens its semantics in two ways compared to readers-writers locks.

1. **Relax R/W semantics.** RCU allows up to one read/write critical section to be concurrent with any number of read-only critical sections. A read-only critical section that overlaps a read/write critical section may see the old or new version of the data structure.

   Note that an object that uses RCU for synchronization must maintain multiple versions of its state, and it must guarantee that an old version is not freed until all readers have finished accessing it. The time from when an update occurs until the old version has been freed is called **grace period** the *grace period*, and RCU must provide a way to determine when a grace period ends.

2. **Restrict update rules.** To make a data structure update appear atomic to readers, an RCU update must be *published* to the data structure with a single, atomic memory write (e.g., by updating a single pointer.)

Figure 6.14 shows the timeline for a write critical section that is concurrent with several read critical sections under RCU. If a function that

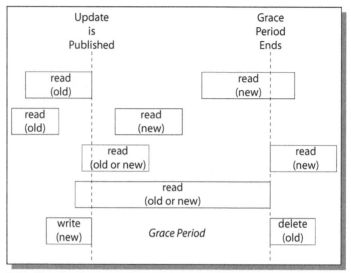

Figure 6.14: Timeline for an update concurrent with several reads for a data structure accessed with read-copy-update (RCU) synchronization.

Reader API	RCU::ReadLock()
	RCU::ReadUnlock()
Writer API	RCU::WriteLock()
	RCU::Publish()
	RCU::WriteUnlock()
	RCU::Synchronize()

Figure 6.15: API for read-copy-update (RCU) synchronization.

reads the data structure completes before a write is published, it will (of course) see the old version of the data structure, and if a read critical section begins after a write is published it will see the new version. But, if a read critical section begins before and ends after a write is published, it may see the old version or the new one; if it reads the updated pointer more than once, it may even first see the old one and then see the new one. Which version it sees depends on which version of the single atomically-updated memory location it observes. Furthermore, the system guarantees that the old version is not deleted until the grace period expires, which means that deletion of the old versions must be delayed until all reads that might be observing the old version have completed.

RCU   **API and use.**   *RCU* is a synchronization abstraction that allows concurrent access to a data structure by multiple readers and a single writer at a time. Figure 6.15 shows a typical API.

A reader calls RCU::ReadLock() and RCU::ReadUnlock() before and after

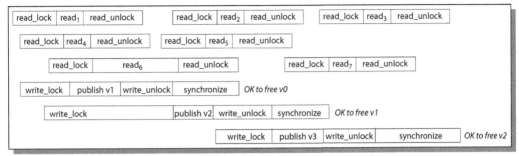

Figure 6.16: RCU allows one write at a time, and it allows reads to overlap each other and writes. The initial version is v0, and overlapping writes update the version to v1, v2, and then v3.

accessing the shared data structure. A writer calls RCU::WriteLock() to exclude other writers, RCU::Publish() to issue the write that atomically updates the data structure so that reads can see the updates, RCU::WriteUnlock() to allow other writers to proceed, and RCU::Synchronize() to wait for the grace period to expire so that the old version of the object can be freed. Notice that as Figure 6.16 illustrates, writes are serialized — only one write can proceed at a time. But also notice that writes can be concurrent with reads and that one write's update can be concurrent with another write's grace period: there may be any number of versions of the object until multiple overlapping grace periods expire.

EXAMPLE   **Overlapping operations.** For each read in Figure 6.16, which version(s) of the shared state can the read observe?

ANSWER   If a read overlaps a publish, it can return the published value or the previous value.

$read_1$	v0 or v1	overlaps publish v1
$read_2$	v2	after publish v2, before publish v3
$read_3$	v3	after publish v3
$read_4$	v0 or v1	overlaps publish v1
$read_5$	v1 or v2	overlaps publish v2
$read_4$	v0, v1, or v2	overlaps publish v1 and v2
$read_7$	v3	after publish v2

Example: RCU linked list. Suppose we have linked list of records, such as the one defined in Figure 6.17. Here, the list comprises an RCU lock rcuLock and a pointer to the head of the list head. Each record has three data fields, key, val1, and val2, and a next pointer to the next record on the list.

Figure 6.19 shows how we implement a search() method that scans down the list until an element with a matching key is found. If such an element is found, the method returns the two value fields by setting the

```
typedef struct ElementS{
    int key;
    int val1;
    int val2;
    struct ElementS *next;
} Element;

class RCULL{
    private:
        RCULock rcuLock;
        Element *head;
    public:
        int search(int key, int *ret1, int *ret2);
        void insert(Element *item);
        void remove(int key);
};
```

Figure 6.17: Declaration of data structures and API for a linked list that uses RCU for synchronization.

```
int
RCULL::search(int key, int *ret1, int *ret2){
    rcuLock.ReadLock();
    int ret = 0;
    Element *current = head;
    while(current != NULL){
        if(current->key == key){
            *ret1 = current->val1;
            *ret2 = current->val2;
            ret = 1;
            current = NULL; // break out of loop
        }
    }
    rcuLock.ReadUnlock();
    return ret;
}
```

Figure 6.18: Implementation of a read-only method for a linked list that uses RCU for synchronization.

two result pointers and providing a nonzero return value. Otherwise, the method returns 0 to indicate that no matching record was found. Since this method does not modify any of the list's state, it acquires and releases the RCU lock in read mode.

Figure 6.19 shows two methods that update the list. Each of them is arranged so that a single pointer update is all that is needed to publish the list update to the readers. In particular, notice that it is important that insert() initialize the data structure *before* updating the head pointer to make the new element visible to readers.

```
void
RCULL::insert(int key,
              int val1,
              int val2){
   // One write at a time
   rcuLock.WriteLock();

   // Initialize item
   Element *item;
   item = (Element*)
          malloc(sizeof(Element));
   item->key = key;
   item->val1 = val1;
   item->val2 = val2;
   item->next = head;

   // Atomically update list
   rcuLock.Publish(&head, item);

   // Allow other writes to proceed
   rcuLock.WriteUnlock();

   // On return, no reader
   // has old version.
   rcuLock.Synchronize();
}
```

```
void
RCULL::remove(int key){
   // One write at a time
   rcuLock.WriteLock();

   int found = 0;
   Element *prev=NULL;
   Element *current = head;
   while(!found && current != NULL){
      if(current->key == key){
         found = 1;
         // Publish update to readers
         if(prev != NULL){
            rcuLock.Publish(&(prev->next),
                            current->next);
         }
         else{
            rcuLock.Publish(&head,
                            current->next);
         }
      }
   }
   // Allow other writes to proceed
   rcuLock.WriteUnlock();
   if(found){
      // Wait until no reader has
      // old version
      rcuLock.Synchronize();
      free(current);
   }
}
```

Figure 6.19: Implementation of two updating methods for a linked list that uses RCU for synchronization.

Implementing RCU.   In implementing RCU, the central goal is to minimize the cost of read critical sections — the cost should be low and should be constant regardless of the number of concurrent readers. Conversely, we are willing to allow writes to have a high *latency* (i.e., we are willing to allow long grace periods, where it might be tens of milliseconds from when an update is published until the system can guarantee that no readers can access the old version), though we would like the *overhead* of writes to stay modest (i.e., the CPU consumption of the write operations should be small, allowing a large numbers of writers to complete their updates quickly, even if old versions may continue to be used by readers for some time, and allowing other threads to run while a thread waits for a grace period to expire.)

A common technique for achieving these goals is to change the scheduler, integrating the RCU implementation with that of the scheduler. In contrast with the synchronization primitives described in the previous chapter, which make no assumptions about the scheduler, this integration

```
class RCULock{
  private:
    // Global state
    Spinlock globalSpin;
    long globalCounter;
    // One per processor
    DEFINE_PER_PROCESSOR(static long, quiescentCount);

    // Per-lock state
    Spinlock writerSpin;

    // Public API omitted
    ...
}
```

Figure 6.20: Global and per-lock data structures for a simple quiescence-based RCU implementation. *Credit*: This pseudocode is based on an implementation by Paul McKenney in "Is Parallel Programming Hard, And, If So, What Can be Done About It?"

allows us to rely on strong assumptions about when reads can occur, which relieves us of the (expensive) responsibility of tracking exactly how many readers are active at any given time. In particular, our implementation will require two things from the scheduler: (1) RCU read critical sections complete without being interrupted and (2) whenever a thread on a processor is interrupted, the scheduler updates some per-processor RCU state. Then, once a write completes, RCULock::Synchronize() simply waits for all processors to be interrupted at least once. At that point, the old version quiescent of the object is known to be *quiescent* — no thread has access to that old version (other than the writer that changed it.)

Figure 6.20 and Figure 6.21 show a simple implementation of RCU based on quiescent states.

The first thing to notice is that ReadLock() and ReadUnlock() are extremely cheap operations — they update no state and merely ensure that the read will not be interrupted; in a nonpreemptable kernel, these functions need to do nothing at all.

WriteLock() and WriteUnlock() simply acquire and release a spinlock. This ensures that at most one write per RCULock can proceed at a time.

Publish() is also simple. It replaces the specified pointer with a new one and then executes a memory barrier so that threads on all processors will observe the update.

Synchronize() and QuiescentState() work together to ensure that when Synchronize() returns, all threads are guaranteed to be done with the old version of the object. Synchronize() increments a global counter globalCounter and then waits until all processors' quiescentCounts match c, the new value of that counter. QuiescentState(), which is called by the scheduler whenever

```
void RCULock::ReadLock(){
    // No-op in nonpreemptable
    // kernel
    DISABLE_INTERRUPTS();
}

void RCULock::ReadUnlock(){
    // No-op in nonpreemptable
    // kernel
    ENABLE_INTERRUPTS();
}

// Called by scheduler
void RCULock::QuiescentState(){
    MEMORY_BARRIER();
    PER_PROC_VAR(quiescentCount)=
        globalCounter;
    MEMORY_BARRIER();
}
```

```
void RCULock::WriteLock(){
    writerSpin.Acquire();    // MEMORY_BARRIER
}

void RCULock::WriteUnlock(){
    writerSpin.Release();   // MEMORY_BARRIER
}

void RCULock::Publish(void **pp1, void *p2){
    *pp1 = p2;
    MEMORY_BARRIER();
}

void
RCULock::Synchronize(){
    int p, c;
    globalSpin.Acquire();   // MEMORY_BARRIER
    c = ++globalCounter;
    globalSpin.Release();   // MEMORY_BARRIER
    FOREACH_PROCESSOR(p){
        while(PER_PROC_VAR(quiescentCount,p)-c<0){
            sleep(10); // Release CPU for 10ms
        }
    }
}
```

Figure 6.21: A simple quiescence-based RCU implementation. Note: We assume that SpinLock::Acquire() and SpinLock::Release() each include a MEMORY_BARRIER(), though such memory barriers are not shown in our earlier SpinLock implementation. *Credit:* This pseudocode is based on an implementation by Paul McKenney in "Is Parallel Programming Hard, And, If So, What Can be Done About It?"

it interrupts a running thread, updates the interrupted processor's quiescentCount by setting it to match the current globalCounter. Thus, once a call to Synchronize() determines that all processors' quiescentCounts are at least as large as c, it knows that all processors have stopped running any read critical sections that could have been concurrent with the update, and that no remaining read critical sections can observe the old version.

Lock-free and wait-free data structures

RCU allows reads to proceed without acquiring a lock or updating shared synchronization state, but it still requires updates to acquire locks. If the thread that holds the lock is interrupted, has a bug that causes it to stop making progress, or becomes deadlocked, other threads can be delayed for a long — perhaps unlimited — period of time.

    It is possible to build data structures that completely avoid locking on both reads and writes. *Lock free* data structures ensure eventual progress: if all threads are allowed to run for some finite number of steps, then at least one of the threads will complete its operation. *Wait free* data structures

lock free

wait free

ensure both eventual progress and fairness: if any thread is allowed to run for some finite number of steps, that thread will complete its operation regardless of the execution speed of the other threads.

Historically the design of efficient lock-free or wait-free data structures has been complex and application-specific. Nonetheless, lock free or wait free algorithms of varying levels of efficiency exist for wide range of data structures including FIFO queues, double-ended queues, LIFO stacks, sets, and hash tables.

Designing efficient wait-free data structures continue to be the domain of experts, and a discussion of the techniques they use is outside the scope of this book. However, some reasonably-efficient and general approaches to implementing lock-free data structures are known and in sufficiently wide use to warrant further comment here.

Lock-free data structures.   Lock free data structures can be implemented by having each operation detect concurrent, conflicting operations. When such updates are detected, the operation waits a finite amount of time for them to finish. If the conflicting operations do not finish, the operation either aborts the conflicting ones (rolling the object's state back to what it was before that conflicting operations began) or it assists them (finishing the updates needed to complete that operation).

Example: Transactions and software transactional memory (STM)   A transactional database with optimistic concurrency control, is an example of a very flexible, lock-free data structure capable of running programs supplied by different users accessing arbitrary data in arbitrary ways without risking deadlock. Recall that optimistic concurrency control allows transactions to proceed without locking the data they access and aborts the transaction if at commit-time any of the accessed data have changed.

To see that such databases are lock free, consider two conflicting transactions executing at the same time. The first one to commit will succeed, and the second one must abort and retry.

On the other hand, the approach is not wait-free since it cannot bound the number of retries needed for a transaction to successfully commit — in the worst case, it is possible for a given transaction to starve forever if it encounters a stream of conflicting transactions that always manage to beat it in the race to commit.

software transactional memory (STM)   Although much work on transactions has been done in the context of databases that store data on disk, *software transactional memory (STM)* is a promising approach to allow transactions on in-memory data structures. Unfortunately, the cost of an STM transaction is often significantly higher than that of a traditional critical section because of the need to maintain the state needed to check dependencies and the state needed either to update the object if there is no conflict or to roll back its state if a conflict is detected.

On the other hand, in situations where STM can be used, it provides a way to compose different modules without having to worry about deadlock.

Exercises

7. In RCUlist::remove(), suppose we attempt to maximize concurrency by replacing the WriteLock() and WriteUnlock() calls with ReadLock() and ReadUnlock() calls and insert new WriteLock() and writeUnlock() calls at beginning and end of the code that is executed only if the if conditional test succeeds. The basic idea is to hold a read lock while searching for the target item an to grab the write lock once it is found. Will this work?

6.4 | Conclusion

The quotes introducing this chapter are intended to emphasize that advanced synchronization techniques should be approached with caution. Your first goal should be to construct a program that works, even it doing so means putting "one big lock" around everything in a data structure or even in an entire program.

Resist the temptation to do complicated fine grained locking (let alone RCU) unless you **know** that doing so is necessary. How do you know? Don't guess. Measure your system's performance. (Measuring the "before" and "after" performance of a program and its subsystems not only helps you make good decisions about the program on which you are working, but it also will help you develop good intuition for the programs you face in the future.)

Spend a lot of time early in the design process developing a clean structure for your program. Given that multi-object synchronization and deadlock are not modular, it is vital to have an overall structure that let's you reason about how the pieces will interact. Often, it is helpful to strive for a strict layering or hierarchy of modules. It is easier to make such programs deadlock free, and it is easier to test them as well.

Performance is important, but it is usually easier to start with a clean, simple, and correct design, measure it to identify its bottlenecks, and then optimize the bottlenecks than to start with a complex design and try to tune its performance (let alone fix its bugs.)

Exercises

1. Figure 6.2 shows an execution that executes some requests in parallel, and it shows an equivalent sequential execution — request 1 then

request 2 then request 3 — . There are two other sequential executions that are also equivalent to the parallel execution shown in the figure. What are these other equivalent sequential executions?

2. Generalize the rules for two phase locking to include both mutual exclusion locks and readers-writers locks. What can be done in the expanding phase? What can be done in the contracting phase?

3. Consider the variation of the Dining Philosophers problem shown in Figure 6.7 where all unused chopsticks are placed in the center of the table and any philosopher can eat with any two chopsticks.

   One way to prevent deadlock in this system is to provide sufficient resources. For a system with n philosophers, what is the minimum number of chopsticks that ensures deadlock freedom? Why?

4. If the queues between stages are finite, Is it possible for a staged architecture to deadlock even if each individual stage is internally deadlock free? If so, give an example. If not, prove it.

5. Suppose you build a system using a staged architecture with some fixed number of threads operating on stage. Assuming each stage is individually deadlock free, describe two ways to guarantee that your system as a whole can not deadlock. Each of the ways should eliminate a different one of the 4 necessary conditions for deadlock.

6. Consider a system with four mutual exclusion locks (A, B, C, and D) and a readers-writers lock (E).

   To ensure serializability of request processing and to avoid deadlock, a programmer follows the following rules:

   a) Processing for each request is divided into two parts.

   b) During the first part, no lock may be released and if E is held in writing mode it cannot be downgraded to reading mode. Furthermore, lock A may not be acquired if any of locks B, C, D, or E are held in any mode; lock B may not be acquired if any of locks C, D, or E are held in any mode; lock C may not be acquired if any of locks D or E are held in any mode; lock D may not be acquired if lock E is held in any mode. Lock E may always be acquired in read mode or write mode, and it can be upgraded from read mode to write mode but not downgraded from write mode to read mode.

   c) During the second part, any lock may be released and lock E may be downgraded from write mode to read mode; releases and downgrades can happen in any order; by the end of part 2, all locks must be released; and no locks may be acquired or upgraded.

Do these rules ensure serializability? Do they ensure freedom from deadlock? Why?

7. In RCUlist::remove(), suppose we attempt to maximize concurrency by replacing the WriteLock() and WriteUnlock() calls with ReadLock() and ReadUnlock() calls and insert new WriteLock() and writeUnlock() calls at beginning and end of the code that is executed only if the if conditional test succeeds. The basic idea is to hold a read lock while searching for the target item an to grab the write lock once it is found. Will this work?

Time is money

Ben Franklin

The best performance improvement is the transition from the non-working state to the working state. That's infinite speedup.

John Ousterhout

7 Scheduling

When there are multiple things to do, how do you choose which one to do first? In the last few chapters, we have described how to create threads, switch between them, and synchronize their access to shared data. At any point in time, some threads are running on the system's processor. Others are waiting their turn for a processor. Still other threads are blocked waiting for I/O to complete, a condition variable to be signalled, or for a lock to be released. When there are more runnable threads than processors, the *processor scheduling policy* determines which threads to run first.

processor scheduling policy

You might think the answer to this question is easy: just do the work in the order in which it arrives. After all, that seems to be the only fair thing to do. Because it is obviously fair, almost all government services work this way. When you go to your local Department of Motor Vehicles (DMV) to get a driver's license, you take a number and wait your turn. Although fair, the DMV often feels slow. There's a reason why: as we'll see later in this chapter, doing things in order of arrival is sometimes the worst thing you can do in terms of improving user-perceived response time. Advertising that your operating system uses the same scheduling algorithm as the DMV is probably not going to increase your sales!

You might think that the answer to this question is unimportant. With the million-fold improvement in processor performance over the past thirty years, it might seem that we are a million times less likely to have anything waiting for its turn on a processor. We disagree! Server operating systems in particular are often overloaded. Parallel applications can create more work than processors, and if care isn't taken in the design of the scheduling policy, performance can badly degrade. There are subtle relationships between scheduling policy and energy management on battery-powered devices such as smartphones and laptops. Further, scheduling issues apply to any scarce resource, whether the source of contention is the processor, memory, disk, or network. We will revisit the issues covered in this chapter throughout the rest of the book.

Scheduling policy is not a panacea. Without enough capacity, performance may be poor regardless of which thread we run first. In this chapter, we will also discuss how to predict overload conditions and how to adapt to them.

Fortunately, you probably have quite a bit of intuition as to impact of different scheduling policies and capacity on issues like response time, fairness, and throughput. Anyone who waits in line probably wonders how we could get the line to go faster. That's true whether we're waiting in line at the supermarket, a bank, the DMV, or at a popular restaurant. Remarkably, in each of these settings, there is a different approach to how they deal with waiting. We'll try to answer why.

There is no one right answer; rather, any scheduling policy poses a complex set of tradeoffs between various desirable properties. The goal of this chapter is not to enumerate all of the interesting possibilities, explore the full design space, or even to identify specific useful policies. Instead, we describe some of the trade-offs and try to illustrate how a designer can approach the problem of selecting a scheduling policy.

Consider what happens if you are running the web site for a company trying to become the next Facebook. Based on history, you'll be able to guess how much server capacity you need to be able to keep up with demand and still have reasonable response time. What happens if your site appears on Slashdot, and suddenly you have twice as many users as you had an hour ago? If you aren't careful, everyone will think your site is terribly slow, and permanently go elsewhere. Google, Amazon, and Yahoo have each estimated that they lose approximately 5-10% of their customers if their response time increases by as little as 100 milliseconds. If faced with overload:

- Would quickly implementing a different scheduling policy help, or hurt?

- How much worse will your performance be if the number of users doubles again?

- Should you turn away some users so that others will get acceptable performance?

- Does it matter which users you turn away?

- If you run out to the local electronics store and buy a server, how much better will performance get?

Performance Terminology

In Chapter 1 we defined some performance-related terms we will use throughout this chapter and the rest of the book; we summarize those terms here.

- **Task.** A user request. A task is also often called a *job*. A task can be any size, from simply redrawing the screen to show the movement of the mouse cursor to computing the shape of a newly discovered protein. When discussing scheduling, we use the term task, rather than thread or process, because a single thread or process may be responsible for multiple user requests or tasks. For example, in a word processor, each character typed is an individual user request to add that character to the file and display the result on the screen.

- **Response time (or delay).** The user-perceived time to do some task.

- **Predictability.** Low variance in response times for repeated requests.

- **Throughput.** The rate at which tasks are completed.

- **Scheduling overhead.** The time to switch from one task to another.

- **Fairness.** Equality in the number and timeliness of resources given to each task.

- **Starvation.** The lack of progress for one task, due to resources given to a higher priority task.

- Do the answers change if you are under a denial-of-service attack by a competitor?

In this chapter, we will try to give you the conceptual and analytic tools to help you answer these questions.

The key topics in this chapter are:

- **Uniprocessor scheduling.** How do uniprocessor scheduling policies affect fairness, response time and throughput?

- **Multiprocessor scheduling.** How do scheduling policies change when we have multiple processor cores per computer?

- **Energy-efficient and deadline scheduling.** Many new computer systems allow energy to be saved by running computations more slowly. How do we make this tradeoff, while still minimizing the impact on user perceived response time? More generally, how do we make sure our jobs finish in time?

- **Queueing theory.** In a server environment, how are response time and throughput affected by the rate at which requests arrive for processing and by the scheduling policy?

- **Overload control.** How do we keep response time reasonable when a system becomes overloaded?

7.1 | Uniprocessor scheduling

We start by considering one processor, generalizing to multiprocessor scheduling policies in the next section. We begin with three simple policies — first-in-first-out, shortest-job-first, and round robin — as a way of illustrating scheduling concepts. Each approach has its own the strengths and weaknesses, and most resource allocation systems (whether for processors, memory, network or disk) combine aspects of all three. At the end of the discussion, we will show how the different approaches are synthesized into a more practical and complete processor scheduler.

workload   Before proceeding, we need to define a few terms. A *workload* is a set of tasks for some system to perform, along with when each task arrives and how long each task takes to complete. In other words, the workload defines the input to a scheduling algorithm. Given a workload, a processor scheduler decides when each task is to be assigned the processor.

We are interested in scheduling algorithms that work well across a wide variety of environments, because workloads will vary quite a bit from system to system and user to user. Some tasks are *compute-bound* and only use the processor. Others, such as a compiler or a web browser, mix I/O and computation. Still others, such as a BitTorrent download, are *I/O-bound*, spending most of their time waiting for I/O and only brief periods computing. In the discussion, we start with very simple compute-bound workloads and then generalize to include mixtures of different types of tasks as we proceed.

compute-bound task

I/O-bound task

Some of the policies we outline are the best possible policy on a particular metric and workload, and some are the worst possible policy. When discussing optimality and pessimality, we are only comparing to policies that are *work-conserving*. A scheduler is work-conserving if it never leaves the processor idle if there is work to do. Obviously a trivially poor policy has the processor sit idle for long periods when there are tasks in the ready queue.

work-conserving policy

preemption   Our discussion also assumes the scheduler has the ability to *preempt* the processor and give it to some other task. Preemption can happen either because of a timer interrupt, or because some task arrives on the ready list with a higher priority than the current task, at least according to some scheduling policy. We explained how to switch the processor between tasks in Chapter 2 and Chapter 4. While much of the discussion is also relevant to non-preemptive schedulers, there are few such systems left, so we leave that issue aside for simplicity.

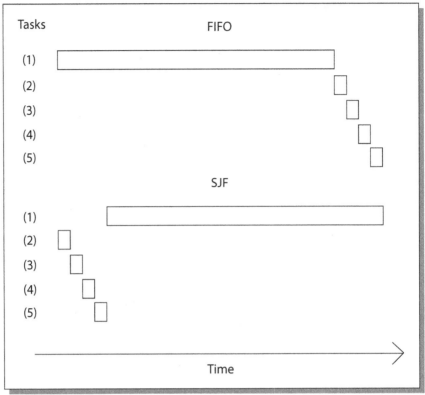

Figure 7.1: Completion times with FIFO (top) and SJF (bottom) scheduling when several short tasks (2-5) arrive immediately after a long task (1).

First In First Out (FIFO)

Perhaps the simplest scheduling algorithm possible is first-in-first-out (FIFO): do each task in the order in which it arrives. (FIFO is sometimes also called first-come-first-served, or FCFS.) When we start working on a task, we keep running it until it is done. FIFO minimizes overhead, switching between tasks only when each one completes. Because it minimizes overhead, if we have a fixed number of tasks, and those tasks only need the processor, FIFO will have the best throughput: it will complete the most tasks the most quickly. And as we mentioned, FIFO appears to be the definition of fairness — every task patiently waits its turn.

Unfortunately, FIFO has a weakness. If a task with very little work to do happens to land in line behind a task that takes a very long time, then the system will seem very inefficient. Figure 7.1 illustrates a particularly bad workload for FIFO; it also shows SJF which we will discuss in a bit. If the first task in the queue takes one second, and the next four arrive an instant later, but each only needs a millisecond of the processor, then they will all need to wait until the first one finishes. The average response time will be

---

FIFO and memcached

Although you may think that FIFO is too simple to be useful, there are some important cases where it is exactly the right choice for the workload. One such example is memcached. Many web services, such as Facebook, store their user data in a database. The database provides flexible and consistent lookups, such as, which friends need to be notified of a particular update to a user's Facebook wall. In order to improve performance, Facebook and other systems put a cache called memcached in front of the database, so that if a user posts two items to her Facebook wall, the system only needs to lookup the friend list once. The system first checks whether the information is cached, and if so uses that copy.

Because almost all requests are for small amounts of data, memcached is designed to reply to requests in FIFO order. This minimizes overhead, as there is no need to time slice between requests. For this workload where tasks are roughly equal in size, FIFO is simple, minimizes average response time, and even maximizes throughput. Win-win!

---

over a second, but the optimal average response time is much less than that. In fact, if we ignore switching overhead, there are some workloads where FIFO is literally the worst possible policy for average response time.

Shortest Job First (SJF)

If FIFO can be a poor choice for average response time, is there an optimal policy for minimizing average response time? The answer is yes: schedule the shortest job first (SJF).

Suppose we could know how much time each task needed at the processor. (In general, we won't know, so this isn't meant as a practical policy! Rather, we use it as a thought experiment; later on, we'll see how to approximate SJF in practice.) If we always schedule the task that has the least remaining work to do, that will minimize average response time. (For this reason, some call SJF shortest-remaining-time-first or SRTF.)

To see that SJF is optimal, consider a hypothetical alternative policy that is not SJF, but that we think might be optimal. Because the alternative is not SJF, at some point it will choose to run a task that is longer than something else in the queue. If we now switch the order of tasks, keeping everything the same, but doing the shorter task first, we will reduce the average response time. Thus, any alternative to SJF cannot be optimal.

Figure 7.1 illustrates SJF on the same example we used for FIFO. If a long task is the first to arrive, it will be scheduled (if we are work-conserving). When a short task arrives a bit later, the scheduler will preempt the current task, and start the shorter one. The remaining short tasks will be processed in order of arrival, followed by finishing the long task.

Starvation and Sample Bias

Systems that might suffer from starvation require extra care when being measured. Suppose you want to compare FIFO and SJF experimentally. You set up two computers, one running each scheduler, and send them the same sequence of tasks. After some period you stop and report the average response time of completed tasks. If some tasks are starved, however, the set of completed tasks will be different for the two policies. We will have excluded the longest tasks from the results for SJF, skewing the average response time even further. Put another way, if you want to manipulate statistics to "prove" a point, this is a good trick to use!

How might you redesign the experiment to provide a valid comparison between FIFO and SJF?

What counts as "shortest" is the remaining time left on the task, not its original length. If we are one nanosecond away from finishing an hour long task, we will minimize average response time by staying with that task, rather than preempting it for a minute long task that just arrived on the ready queue. Of course, if they both arrive at about the same time, doing the minute long task first will dramatically improve average response time.

Does SJF have any other downsides (other than being impossible to implement because it requires knowledge of the future)? It turns out that SJF is pessimal for variance in response time. By doing the shortest tasks as quickly as possible, SJF necessarily does longer tasks as slowly as possible (among policies that are work conserving). In other words, there is a fundamental tradeoff between reducing average response time and reducing the variance in average response time.

Worse, SJF can suffer from starvation and frequent context switches. If enough short tasks arrive, long tasks may never complete. Whenever a task is put on the ready queue that is shorter than the remaining time left on the currently scheduled task, the scheduler will preempt it. If this keeps happening indefinitely, a long task may never finish.

Suppose a supermarket manager reads a portion of this textbook and decides to implement shortest job first to reduce average waiting times. The manager tells herself: who cares about variance! A benefit is that there would no longer be any need for express lanes — if someone has only a few items, they are immediately whisked to the front of the line, interrupting anyone shopping for eighteen kids. Of course, the wait times of the customers with full baskets skyrockets; if the supermarket is open twenty-four hours a day, customers with the largest purchases might have to wait until 3am to finally get through the line. This would probably lead their best customers to go to the supermarket down the street, not exactly what the manager had in mind!

Shortest Job First and bandwidth-constrained web service

Although SJF may seem completely impractical, there are circumstances where it is exactly the right policy. One example is in a web server for static content. Many small-scale web servers are limited by their bandwidth to the Internet, because it is often more expensive to pay for more capacity. Web pages at most sites vary in size, with most pages being relatively short, while some pages are quite large. The average response time for accessing web pages is dominated by the more frequent requests to short pages, while the bandwidth costs are dominated by the less frequent requests to large pages.

This combination is almost ideal for using SJF for managing the allocation of network bandwidth by the server. With static pages, it is possible to predict from the name of the page how much bandwidth each request will consume. By transferring short pages first, the web server can ensure that its average response time is very low. Even if most requests are to small pages, the aggregate bandwidth for small pages is low, so requests to large pages are not significantly slowed down. The only difficulty comes when the web server becomes overloaded, because then the large page requests can be starved. As we will see later, overload situations need their own set of solutions.

Customers could also try to game the system: if you have a lot of items to purchase, simply go through the line with one item at a time — you will always be whisked to the front, at least until everyone else figures out the same dodge.

Exercises

1. For shortest job first, if the scheduler assigns a task to the processor, and no other task becomes schedulable in the meantime, will the scheduler ever preempt the current task? Why or why not?

2. Devise a workload where FIFO is pessimal — it does the worst possible choices — for average response time.

3. Suppose you do your homework assignments in SJF-order. After all, you feel like you are making a lot of progress! What might go wrong?

Round Robin

A policy that addresses starvation is to schedule tasks in a round robin fashion. With Round Robin, tasks take turns running on the processor for a limited period of time. The scheduler assigns the processor to the first task in the ready queue, setting a timer interrupt for some delay, called the *time*

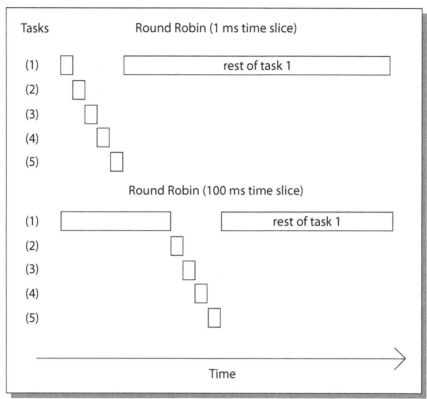

Figure 7.2: Completion times with Round Robin scheduling when short tasks arrive just after a long task, with a time quantum of 1 ms (top) and 100 ms (bottom).

time quantum

quantum. At the end of the quantum, if the task hasn't completed, the task is preempted and the processor is given to the next task in the ready queue. The preempted task is put back on the ready queue where it can wait its next turn. With Round Robin, there is no possibility that a task will starve — it will eventually reach the front of the queue and get its time quantum.

Of course, we need to pick the time quantum carefully. One consideration is overhead: if we have too short a time quantum, the processor will spend all of its time switching and getting very little useful work done. But if we pick too long a time quantum, tasks will have to wait a long time until they get a turn. Figure 7.2 shows the behavior of Round Robin, on the same workload as in Figure 7.1, for two different values for the time quantum.

A good analogy for Round Robin is a particularly hyperkinetic student, studying for multiple finals simultaneously. You won't get much done if you read a paragraph from one textbook, then switch to reading a paragraph from the next textbook, and then switch to yet a third textbook. But if you never switch, you may never get around to studying for some of your courses.

One might think that the cost of switching tasks after a time slice is modest: the cost of interrupting the processor, saving its registers, dispatching the timer interrupt handler, and restoring the registers of the new task. On a modern processor, all these steps can be completed in a few tens of microseconds.

However, we must also include the impact of time slices on the efficiency of the processor cache. Each newly scheduled task will need to fetch its data from memory into cache, evicting some of the data that had been stored by the previous task. Exactly how long this takes will depend on the memory hierarchy, the reference pattern of the new task, and whether any of its state is still in the cache from its previous time slice. Modern processors often have multiple levels of cache to improve performance. Reloading just the first level on-chip cache from scratch can take several milliseconds; reloading the second and third level caches takes even longer. Thus it is typical for operating systems to set their time slice interval to be somewhere between 10 and 100 milliseconds, depending on the goals of the system: better responsiveness or reduced overhead.

One way of viewing Round Robin is as a compromise between FIFO and SJF. At one extreme, if the time quantum is infinite (or at least, longer than the longest task), Round Robin behaves exactly the same as FIFO. Each task runs to completion and then yields the processor to the next in line. At the other extreme, suppose it was possible to switch between tasks with zero overhead, so we could choose a time quantum of a single instruction. With fine-grained time-slicing, tasks would finish in the order of length, as with SJF, but a bit slower: a task A will take as long as it would have under SJF, plus a factor proportional to the number of other tasks as long as $A \times$ the length of A.

Unfortunately, Round Robin has some weaknesses. Figure 7.3 illustrates what happens for FIFO, SJF and Round Robin when several tasks start at roughly same time and are of the same length. Round Robin will rotate through the tasks, doing a bit of each, finishing them all at roughly the same time. This is nearly the worst possible scheduling policy for this workload! FIFO does much better, picking a task and sticking with it until it is done. Not only does FIFO reduce average response time for this workload relative to Round Robin, no task is worse off under FIFO — every task finishes at least as early as it would have under Round Robin. Time slicing added overhead without any benefit. Finally, consider what SJF does on this workload. SJF schedules tasks in exactly the same order as FIFO. The first task that arrives will be assigned the processor, and as soon as it executes a single instruction, it will have less time remaining than all of the other tasks, and so it will run to completion. Since we know SJF is optimal for average response time, this means that both FIFO and Round Robin are

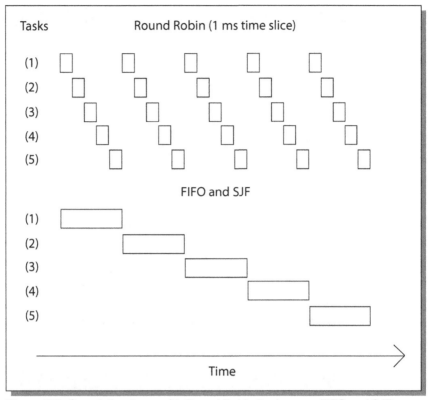

Figure 7.3: Completion times with Round Robin (top) versus FIFO and SJF (bottom) when scheduling equal length tasks.

optimal for some workloads and pessimal for others, just different ones in each case.

Depending on the time quantum, Round Robin can also be quite poor when running a mixture of I/O-bound and compute-bound tasks. I/O-bound tasks often need very short periods on the processor in order to compute the next I/O operation to issue. Any delay to get scheduled onto the processor can lead to system-wide slowdowns. For example, in a text editor, it often takes only a few milliseconds to echo a keystroke to the screen, a delay much faster than human perception. However, if we are sharing the processor between a text editor and several other tasks using Round Robin, the editor must wait several time quanta to be scheduled for each keystroke — with a 100 ms time quantum, this can become annoyingly apparent to the user.

Figure 7.4 illustrates similar behavior with a disk-bound task. Suppose we have a task that computes for 1 ms and then uses the disk for 10 ms, in a loop. Running alone, it can keep the disk almost completely busy. Suppose we also have two compute bound tasks; again, running by themselves, they

---

Simultaneous Multi-Threading

Although zero overhead switching may seem far-fetched, most modern processors do a form of it called *simultaneous multi-threading (SMT)* or *hyperthreading*. With SMT, each processor simulates two (or more) virtual processors, alternating between them on a cycle by cycle basis. Since most threads need to wait for memory from time to time, another thread can use the processor during those gaps, or vice versa. In normal operation, neither thread is significantly slowed when running on an SMT.

You can test whether your computer implements SMT by testing how fast the processor operates when it has one or more tasks, each running a tight loop of arithmetic operations. (Note that on a multicore, you will need to create enough tasks to fill up each of the cores, or physical processors, before the system will begin to use SMT.) With one task per physical processor, each task will run at the maximum rate of the processor. With an SMT of two, and two tasks per processor, each task will run at somewhat less than the maximum rate, but each task will run at approximately the same uniform speed. As you increase the number of tasks beyond the SMT level, however, the operating system will begin to use coarse-grained time-slicing, so tasks will progress in spurts — alternating time on and off the processor.

Round Robin and streaming video

There are some circumstances under which Round Robin is the best policy, even when all tasks are roughly the same size. An example is managing the server bandwidth for streaming video. When streaming, response time is much less of a concern than achieving a predictable, stable rate of progress. For this, Round Robin is nearly ideal: all streams progress at the same rate. As long as Round Robin serves the data as fast or faster than the viewer consumes the video stream, the time to completely download the stream is unimportant.

---

can keep the processor busy. What happens when we run the disk-bound and compute-bound tasks at the same time? With Round Robin and a time quantum of 100 ms, the disk-bound task slows down by nearly a factor of twenty — each time it needs the processor, it must wait nearly 200 ms for its turn. SJF on this workload would perform well — prioritizing short tasks at the processor keeps the disk-bound task busy, while only modestly slowing down the compute-bound tasks.

If you have ever tried to surf the web while doing a large BitTorrent download over a slow link, you can see that network operations visibly slow during the download. This is even though your browser may need to

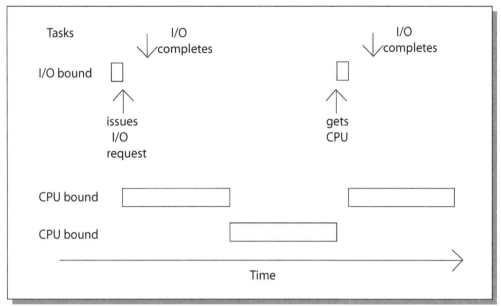

Figure 7.4: Scheduling behavior with Round Robin when running a mixture of I/O-bound and compute-bound tasks. The I/O-bound task yields the processor when it does I/O. Even though the I/O completes quickly, the I/O-bound task must wait to be reassigned the processor until the compute-bound tasks both complete their time quanta.

transfer only a very small amount of data to provide good responsiveness. The reason is quite similar. Browser packets get their turn, but only after being queued behind a much larger number of packets for the bulk download. Prioritizing the browser's packets would have only a minimal impact on the download speed and a large impact on the perceived responsiveness of the system.

Exercises

4. Given the following mix of tasks, task lengths, and arrival times, compute the completion and response time for each task, along with the average response time for the FIFO, RR, and SJF algorithms. Assume a time slice of 10 milliseconds and that all times are in milliseconds.

Max-Min Fairness

In many settings, a fair allocation of resources is as important to the design of a scheduler as responsiveness and low overhead. On a multi-user machine or on a server, we do not want to allow a single user to be able to monopolize the resources of the machine, degrading service for other users.

Task	Length	Arrival Time	Completion Time	Response Time
0	85	0		
1	30	10		
2	35	10		
3	20	80		
4	50	80		
		Average:		

While it might seem that fairness has little value in single-user machines, individual applications are often written by different companies, each with an interest in making their application performance look good even if that comes at a cost of degrading responsiveness for other applications.

Another complication arises with whether we should allocate resources fairly among users, applications, processes, or threads. Some applications may run inside a single process, while others may create many processes, and each process may involve multiple threads. Round robin among threads can lead to starvation if applications with only a single thread are competing with applications with hundreds of threads. We can be concerned with fair allocation at any of these levels of granularity: threads within a process, processes for a particular user, users sharing a physical machine. For example, we could be concerned with making sure that every thread within a process makes progress. For simplicity, however, our discussion will assume we are interested in providing fairness among processes — the same principles apply if the unit receiving resources is the user, application or thread.

Fairness is easy if all processes are compute-bound: Round Robin will give each process an equal portion of the processor. In practice, however, different processes consume resources at different rates. An I/O-bound process may need only a small portion of the processor, while a compute-bound process is willing to consume all available processor time. What is a fair allocation when there is a diversity of needs?

One possible answer is to say that whatever Round Robin does is fair — after all, each process gets an equal chance at the processor. As we saw above, however, Round Robin can result in I/O-bound processes running at a much slower rate than they would if they had the processor to themselves, while compute-bound processes are barely affected at all. That hardly seems fair!

While there are many possible definitions of fairness, a particularly useful one is called *max-min fairness*. Max-min fairness iteratively maximizes the minimum allocation given to a particular process (user, application or thread) until all resources are assigned.

max-min fairness

If all processes are compute-bound, the behavior of max-min is simple: we maximize the minimum by giving each process exactly the same share of the processor — that is, by using Round Robin.

The behavior of max-min fairness is more interesting if some processes cannot use their entire share, for example, because they are short-running or are I/O-bound. If so, we give those processes their entire request and redistribute the unused portion to the remaining processes. Some of the processes receiving the extra portion may not be able to use all of their revised share, and so we must iterate, redistributing any unused portion. When no remaining requests can be fully satisfied, we divide the remainder equally among all remaining processes.

Consider the example in the previous section. The disk-bound process needed only 10% of the processor to keep busy, but Round Robin only gave it 0.5% of the processor, and each of the two compute-bound processes received nearly 50% of the processor. Max-min fairness would assign 10% of the processor to the I/O-bound process, and it would split the remainder equally among the two compute-bound processes, with 45% each.

A hypothetical but completely impractical implementation of max-min would be to give the processor at each instant to whichever process has received the least portion of the processor. In the example above, the disk-bound task would always be instantly scheduled, preempting the compute-bound processes. However, we've already seen why this wouldn't work well. With two equally long tasks, as soon as we execute one instruction in one task, it would have received more resources than the other one, so to preserve "fairness" we would need to instantly switch to the next task.

We can approximate a max-min fair allocation by relaxing this constraint — to allow a process to get ahead of its fair allocation by one time quantum. Every time the scheduler needs to make a choice, it chooses the task for the process with the least accumulated time on the processor. If a new process arrives on the queue with much less accumulated time, such as the disk-bound task, it will preempt the process, but otherwise the current process will complete its quantum. Tasks may get up to one time quantum more than their fair share, but over the long term the allocation will even out.

The algorithm we just described was originally defined for network, and not processor, scheduling. If we share a link between a browser request and a long download, we will get reasonable responsiveness for the browser if we have approximately fair allocation — the browser needs few network packets, and so under max-min its packets will always be scheduled ahead of the packets from the download.

Even this approximation, though, can be computationally expensive, since it requires tasks to be maintained on a priority queue. For some server environments, there can be tens or even hundreds of thousands of scheduling decisions to be made every second. To reduce the computational overhead of the scheduler, most commercial operating systems use a somewhat different algorithm, to the same goal, which we describe next.

Case Study: Multi-level Feedback

Multi-level
Feedback
Queue
(MFQ)

Most commercial operating systems, including Windows, MacOS, and Linux, use a scheduling algorithm called *Multi-level Feedback Queue (MFQ)*. MFQ is designed to achieve several simultaneous goals:

- **Responsiveness.** Run short tasks quickly, as in SJF.

- **Low Overhead.** Minimize the number of preemptions, as in FIFO, and minimize the time spent making scheduling decisions.

- **Starvation-Freedom.** All tasks should make progress, as in Round Robin.

- **Background Tasks.** Defer system maintenance tasks, such as disk defragmentation, so they do not interfere with user work.

- **Fairness.** Assign (non-background) processes approximately their max-min fair share of the processor.

As with any real system that must balance several conflicting goals, MFQ does not perfectly achieve any of these goals. Rather, it is intended to be a reasonable compromise in most real-world cases.

MFQ is an extension of Round Robin. Instead of only a single queue, MFQ has multiple Round Robin queues, each with a different priority level and time quantum. Tasks at a higher priority level preempt lower priority tasks, while tasks at the same level are scheduled in Round Robin fashion. Further, higher priority levels have *shorter* time quanta than lower levels.

Tasks are moved between priority levels to favor short tasks over long ones. A new task enters at the top priority level. Every time the task uses up its time quantum, it drops a level; every time the task yields the processor because it is waiting on I/O, it stays at the same level (or is bumped up a level); and if the task completes it leaves the system.

Figure 7.5 illustrates the operation of an MFQ with four levels. A new compute-bound task will start as high priority, but it will quickly exhaust its time-quantum and fall to the next lower priority, and then the next. Thus, an I/O-bound task needing only a modest amount of computing will almost always be scheduled quickly, keeping the disk busy. Compute-bound tasks run with a long time-quantum to minimize switching overhead while still sharing the processor.

So far, the algorithm we've described does not achieve starvation freedom or max-min fairness. If there are too many I/O-bound tasks, the compute-bound tasks may receive no time on the processor. To combat this, the MFQ scheduler monitors every process to ensure it is receiving its fair share of the resources. At each level, Linux actually maintains two queues — tasks whose processes have already reached their fair share are only scheduled if all other processes at that level have also received their

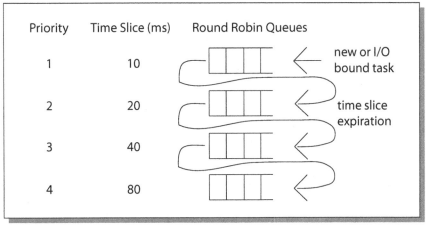

Figure 7.5: Multi-level Feedback Queue when running a mixture of I/O-bound and compute-bound tasks. New tasks enter at high priority with a short quantum; tasks that use their quantum are reduced in priority.

fair share. Periodically, any process receiving less than its fair share will have its tasks increased in priority; equally, tasks that receive more than their fair share can be reduced in priority.

Adjusting priority also addresses strategic behavior. From a purely selfish point of view, a task can attempt to keep its priority high by doing a short I/O request immediately before its time quantum expires. Eventually the system will detect this and reduce its priority to its fair-share level.

Our previously hapless supermarket manager reads a bit farther into the textbook and realizes that supermarket express lanes are a form of multi-level queue. By limiting express lanes to customers with a few items, the manager can ensure short tasks complete quickly, reducing average response time. The manager can also monitor wait times, adding extra lanes to ensure that everyone is served reasonably quickly.

Summary

We summarize the lessons from this section:

- FIFO is simple and minimizes overhead.

- If tasks are variable in size, then FIFO can have very poor average response time.

- If tasks are equal in size, FIFO is optimal in terms of average response time.

- Considering only the processor, SJF is optimal in terms of average response time.

- SJF is pessimal in terms of variance in response time.

- If tasks are variable in size, Round Robin approximates SJF.

- If tasks are equal in size, Round Robin will have very poor average response time.

- Tasks that intermix processor and I/O benefit from SJF and can do poorly under Round Robin.

- Max-min fairness can improve response time for I/O-bound tasks.

- Round Robin and Max-min fairness both avoid starvation.

- By manipulating the assignment of tasks to priority queues, an MFQ scheduler can achieve a balance between responsiveness, low overhead, and fairness.

In the rest of this chapter, we extend these ideas to multiprocessors, energy-constrained environments, real-time settings, and overloaded conditions.

7.2 | Multiprocessor scheduling

Today, most general-purpose computers are multiprocessors. Physical constraints in circuit design make it easier to add computational power by adding processors, or cores, onto a single chip, rather than making individual processors faster. Many high-end desktops and servers have multiple processing chips, each with multiple cores, and each core with hyperthreading. Even smartphones have 2-4 processors. This trend is likely to accelerate, with systems of the future having dozens or perhaps hundreds of processors per computer.

This poses two questions for operating system scheduling:

- How do we make effective use of multiple cores for running sequential tasks?

- How do we adapt scheduling algorithms for parallel applications?

Scheduling Sequential Applications on Multiprocessors

Consider a server handling a very large number of web requests. A common software architecture for servers is to allocate a separate thread for each user connection. Each thread consults a shared data structure to see which portions of the requested data are cached, and fetches any missing elements from disk. The thread then spools the result out across the network.

How should the operating system schedule these server threads? Each thread is I/O-bound, repeatedly reading or writing data to disk and the network, and therefore makes many small trips through the processor. Some requests may require more computation; to keep average response time low, we will want to favor short tasks.

A simple approach would be to use a centralized multi-level feedback queue, with a lock to ensure only one processor at a time is reading or modifying the data structure. Each idle processor takes the next task off the MFQ and runs it. As the disk or network finishes requests, threads waiting on I/O are put back on the MFQ and executed by the network processor that becomes idle.

There are several potential performance problems with this approach:

- **Contention for the MFQ lock.** Depending on how much computation each thread does before blocking on I/O, the centralized lock may become a bottleneck, particularly as the number of processors increases.

- **Cache Coherence Overhead.** Although only a modest number of instructions are needed for each visit to the MFQ, each processor will need to fetch the current state of the MFQ from the cache of the previous processor to hold the lock. On a single processor, the scheduling data structure is likely to be already loaded into the cache. On a multiprocessor, the data structure will be accessed and modified by different processors in turn, so the most recent version of the data is likely to be cached only by the processor that made the most recent update. Fetching data from a remote cache can take two to three orders of magnitude longer than accessing locally cached data. Since the cache miss delay occurs while holding the MFQ lock, the MFQ lock is held for longer periods and so can become even more of a bottleneck.

- **Limited Cache Reuse.** If threads run on the first available processor, they are likely to be assigned to a different processor each time they are scheduled. This means that any data needed by the thread is unlikely to be cached on that processor. Of course, some of the thread's data will have been displaced from the cache during the time it was blocked, but on-chip caches are so large today that much of the thread's data will remain cached. Worse, the most recent version of the thread's data is likely to be in a remote cache, requiring even more of a slowdown as the remote data is fetched into the local cache.

For these reasons, commercial operating systems such as Linux use a *per-processor* data structure: a separate copy of the multi-level feedback queue for each processor. Figure 7.6 illustrates this approach.

affinity
scheduling

Each processor uses *affinity scheduling*: once a thread is scheduled on a processor, it is returned to the same processor when it is rescheduled,

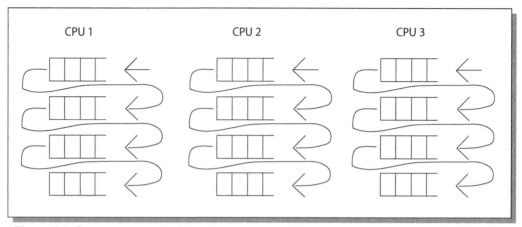

Figure 7.6: Per-processor scheduling data structures. Each processor has its own (multi-level) queue of ready threads.

maximizing cache reuse. Each processor looks at its own copy of the queue for new work to do; this can mean that some processors can idle while others have work waiting to be done. Rebalancing occurs only if the queue lengths are persistent enough to compensate for the time to reload the cache for the migrated threads. Because rebalancing is possible, the per-processor data structures must still be protected by locks, but in the common case the next processor to use the data will be the last one to have written it, minimizing cache coherence overhead and lock contention.

Scheduling Parallel Applications

A different set of challenges occurs when scheduling parallel applications onto a multiprocessor. There is often a natural decomposition of a parallel application onto a set of processors. For example, an image processing application may divide the image up into equal size chunks, assigning one to each processor. While the application could divide the image into many more chunks than processors, this comes at a cost in efficiency: less cache reuse and more communication to coordinate work at the boundary between each chunk.

If there are multiple applications running at the same time, the application may receive fewer or more processors than it expected or started with. New applications can start up, acquiring processing resources. Other applications may complete, releasing resources. Even without multiple applications, the operating system itself will have system tasks to run from time to time, disrupting the mapping of parallel work onto a fixed number of processors.

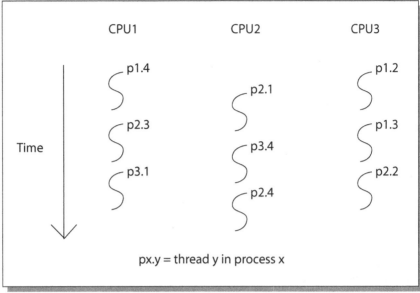

CPU1   CPU2   CPU3

p1.4   p1.2

p2.1

p2.3   p1.3

Time   p3.4

p3.1   p2.2

p2.4

px.y = thread y in process x

Figure 7.7: With oblivious scheduling, threads are time-sliced by the multiprocessor operating system, with no attempt to ensure threads from the same process run at the same time.

Oblivious Scheduling

One might imagine that the scheduling algorithms we've already discussed can take care of these cases. Each thread is time-sliced onto the available processors; if two or more applications create more threads in aggregate than processors, multi-level feedback will ensure that each thread makes progress and receives a fair share of the processor. This is often called *oblivious scheduling*, as the operating system scheduler operates without knowledge of the intent of the parallel application — each thread is scheduled as a completely independent entity. Figure 7.7 illustrates oblivious scheduling.

oblivious scheduling

Unfortunately, several problems can occur with oblivious scheduling on multiprocessors:

- **Bulk synchronous delay.** A common design pattern in parallel programs is to split work into roughly equal sized chunks; once each chunk is done, the processors synchronize, waiting for every chunk to complete before communicating their results to the next stage of the computation. This *bulk synchronous* parallelism is easy to manage — each processor works independently, sharing its results only with the next stage in the computation. Google MapReduce is a widely used bulk synchronous application.

bulk synchronous

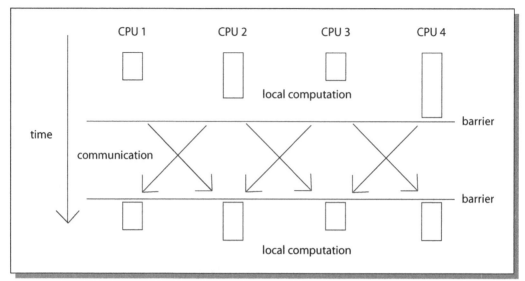

Figure 7.8: Bulk synchronous design pattern for a parallel program; each processor computes on local data and waits for every other processor to complete before proceeding to the next step. Preempting one processor can stall all processors until the preempted process is resumed.

Figure 7.8 illustrates the problem with bulk synchronous computation under oblivious scheduling. At each step, the computation is limited by the slowest processor to complete that step. If a processor is preempted, its work will be delayed, stalling the remaining processors until the last one is scheduled. Even if one of the waiting processors picks up the preempted task, a single preemption can delay the entire computation by a factor of two, and possibly even more with cache effects. Since the application does not know that a processor was preempted, it cannot adapt its decomposition for the available number of processors, so each step is similarly delayed until the processor is returned.

- **Producer-consumer delay.** Some parallel applications use a producer-consumer design pattern, where the results of one thread are fed to the next thread, and the output of that thread is fed onward, as in Figure 7.9. Preempting a thread in the middle of a producer-consumer chain can stall all of the processors in the chain.

critical path
- **Critical path delay.** More general parallel programs have a *critical path* — the minimum sequence of steps for the application to compute its result. Figure 7.10 illustrates the critical path for a fork-join parallel program. Work off the critical path can be done in parallel, but its precise scheduling is less important. Preempting a thread on the critical path, however, will slow down the end result. Although the

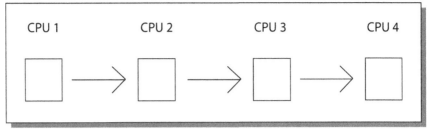

Figure 7.9: Producer-consumer design pattern for a parallel program. Preempting one stage can stall the remainder.

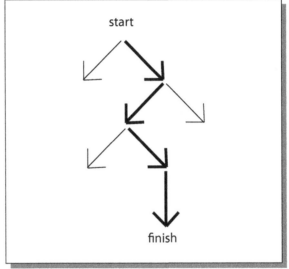

Figure 7.10: Critical path of a parallel program; delays on the critical path increase execution time.

application programmer may know which parts of the computation are on the critical path, with oblivious scheduling, the operating system will not; it will be equally likely to preempt a thread on the critical path as off.

- **Preemption of lock holder.** Many parallel programs use locks and condition variables for synchronizing their parallel execution. Often, to reduce the cost of acquiring locks, parallel programs will use a "spin-then-wait" strategy — if a lock is busy, the waiting thread spin-waits briefly for it to be released, and if the lock is still busy, it blocks and looks for other work to do. This can reduce overhead in the common case that the lock is held for only short periods of time. With oblivious scheduling, however, the lock holder can be preempted — other tasks will spin-then-wait until the lock holder is re-scheduled, increasing overhead.

- **I/O.** Many parallel applications do I/O, and this can also cause problems if the operating system scheduler is oblivious to the application decomposition into parallel work. If a read or write request blocks in the kernel, the thread blocks as well. To reuse the processor while the thread is waiting, the application program must have created more threads than processors, so that the scheduler can have an extra one to run in place of the blocked thread. However, if the thread doesn't block (e.g., on a file read when the file is cached in memory), that means that the scheduler has more threads than processors, and so needs to do time slicing to multiplex threads onto processors — causing all of the problems we have listed above.

Co-scheduling

co-scheduling

One possible approach to some of these issues is to schedule all of the tasks of a program together. This is called *co-scheduling*. The application picks some decomposition of work into some number of threads, and those threads either run together or not at all. If the operating system needs to schedule a different application, if there are insufficient idle resources, it preempts all of the processors of an application to make room. Figure 7.11 illustrates an example of co-scheduling.

Because of the value of co-scheduling, commercial operating systems like Linux, Windows, and MacOS have mechanisms that can be used to co-schedule a single application. This is appropriate when a server is dedicated to a single use, such as a database needing precise control over thread assignment. The application can *pin* each thread to a specific processor and (with the appropriate permissions) mark it to run with high priority. A small subset of the system's processors is reserved to run other applications and system management tasks, multiplexed in the normal way but without interfering with the primary application.

For multiplexing multiple parallel applications, however, co-scheduling can be inefficient. Figure 7.12 illustrates why. It shows the performance of three example parallel programs as a function of the number of processors assigned to the application. While some applications have perfect speedup and can make efficient use of many processors, other applications reach a point of diminishing returns, and still others have a maximum parallelism. For example, if adding processors does not decrease the time spent on the program's critical path, there is no benefit to adding those resources.

An implication of Figure 7.12 is that it is usually more efficient to run two parallel programs each with half the number of processors, than to time slice the two programs, each co-scheduled onto all of the processors. Allocating

space sharing

different processors to different tasks is called *space sharing*, to differentiate it from time sharing, or time slicing — allocating a single processor among

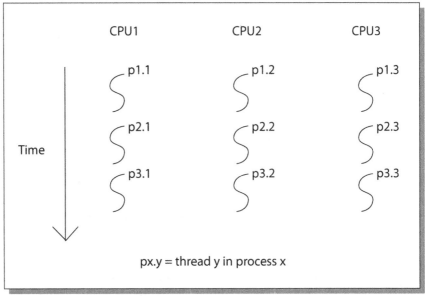

Figure 7.11: With co-scheduling, threads from the same process are scheduled at exactly the same time, and they are time-sliced together to provide a chance for other processes to run.

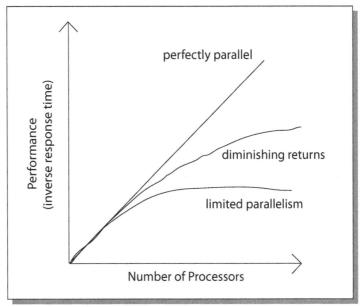

Figure 7.12: Performance as a function of the number of processors, for some typical parallel applications. Some applications scale linearly with the number of processors; others achieve diminishing returns.

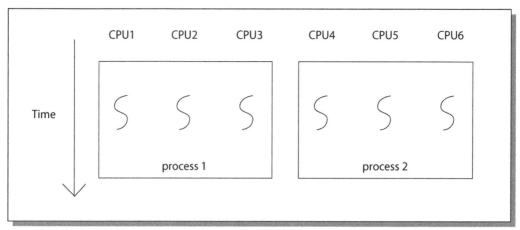

Figure 7.13: With space sharing, each process is assigned a subset of the processors.

multiple tasks by alternating in time when each is scheduled onto the processor. Space sharing on a multiprocessor is also more efficient in that it minimizes processor context switches: as long as the operating system hasn't changed the allocation, the processors don't even need to be time sliced. Figure 7.13 illustrates an example of space sharing.

Space sharing is straightforward if all tasks start and stop at the same time; in that case, we can just allocate evenly. However, the number of available processors is often a dynamic property in a multiprogrammed setting, because tasks start and stop at irregular intervals. How does the application know how many processors to use if the number changes over time?

Scheduler activations

scheduler
activations

A solution, recently added to Windows, is to make the assignment and re-assignment of processors to applications visible to applications. Applications are given an execution context, or *scheduler activation*, on each processor assigned to the application; the application is informed explicitly, via an upcall, whenever a processor is added to its allocation or taken away. Blocking on an I/O request also causes an upcall to allow the application to repurpose the processor while the thread is waiting for I/O.

As we noted in an earlier chapter, user-level thread management is possible with scheduler activations. The operating system kernel assigns processors to applications, either evenly or according to some priority weighting. Each application then schedules its user-level threads onto the processors assigned to it, changing its allocation as the number of processors varies due to external events such as other processes starting or stopping. If no other application is running, an application can use all of the processors of the machine; with more contention, the application must remap its work onto a smaller number of processors.

multiprocessor
scheduling
policy   Scheduler activations defines a *mechanism* for informing an application of its processor allocation, but it leaves open the question of the *multiprocessor scheduling policy*: how many processors should we assign each process? This is an open research question. As we explained in our discussion of uniprocessor scheduling policies, there is a fundamental tradeoff between policies (such as Shortest Job First) that improve average response time and those (such as Max-Min Fairness) that attempt to achieve fair allocation of resources among different applications. In the multiprocessor setting, average response time may be improved by giving extra resources to parallel interactive tasks provided this did not cause long-running compute intensive parallel tasks to starve for resources.

Exercises

5. Is it possible for an application to run slower when assigned 10 processors than when assigned 8? Why or why not?

7.3 | Energy-aware scheduling

Another important consideration for processor scheduling is its impact on battery life and energy use. Laptops and smartphones compete on the basis of battery life, and even for servers, energy usage is a large fraction of the overall system cost. Choices that the operating system makes can have a large effect on these issues.

One might think that processor scheduling has little role to play with respect to system energy usage. After all, each application has a certain amount of computing that needs to be done, computing that requires energy whether we are running on a direct power line or off of a battery. Of course, the operating system should delay background or system maintenance tasks (such as software upgrades) for when the system is connected to power, but this is likely to be a relatively minor effect on the overall power budget.

In part because of the importance of battery life to computer users, modern architectures have developed a number of ways of trading reduced computation speed for lower energy use. In other words, the mental model of each computation taking a fixed amount of energy is no longer accurate. There is quite a bit of flux in the types of hardware support available on different systems, and systems five years from now are likely to make very different tradeoffs than those in place today. Thus, our goal in this section is not to provide a set of widely used algorithms for managing power, but rather to outline the design issues energy management poses for the operating system.

Several power optimizations are possible, provided hardware support:

- **Processor design.** There can be several orders of magnitude difference between one processor design and another with respect to power consumption. Often, making a processor faster requires extra circuitry, such as out of order execution, that itself consumes power; low power processors are slower and simpler. Likewise, processors designed for lower clock speeds can tolerate lower voltage swings at the circuit level, reducing power consumption dramatically. Some systems have begun to put this tradeoff under the control of the operating system, by including both a high power, high performance multiprocessor and a low power, lower performance uniprocessor on the same chip. High power can be used when response time is at a premium, and low power for when power consumption is more important.

- **Processor usage.** For systems with multiple processor chips, or multiple cores on a single chip, lightly used processors can be disabled to save power. Processors will typically draw much less power when they are completely idle, but as we mentioned above, many parallel programs achieve some benefit from using extra processors, yet also reach a point of diminishing returns. Thus, there is a tradeoff between somewhat faster execution (e.g., by using all available resources) and lower energy use (e.g., by turning off some processors even when using them would slightly decrease response time).

- **I/O device power.** Devices not in use can be powered off. Although this is most obvious in terms of the display, devices such as the WiFi or cellphone network interface also consume large amounts of power. Power-constrained embedded systems such as sensors will turn on their network interface hardware periodically to send or receive data, and then go back to quiescence. For this to work, the senders and receivers need to synchronize their periods of transmission, or the hardware needs to have a low power listening mode.

At times, different power optimizations interact in subtle ways. For example, running application code quickly can sometimes improve power efficiency, by enabling the network interface hardware to be turned off more quickly once the application finishes. Because context switching consumes both time and energy to reload processor caches, affinity scheduling improves both performance and energy efficiency.

In most cases, however, there is a tradeoff: how should the operating system balance between competing demands for timeliness and energy efficiency? If the user has requested maximum responsiveness or maximum

Heat Dissipation

A closely related topic to energy use is heat dissipation. In laptop computers, you can save weight by not including a fan to cool the processor. However, a modern multicore chip will consume up to 150 Watts, or more than a very bright incandescent light bulb. Just as with a light bulb, the heat generated has to go somewhere. Making things significantly more complicated, the processor will also break permanently if it is run at too high a temperature. Thus, the operating system increasingly must monitor and manage the temperature of the processor to ensure it stays within its operating region. Much like a cheetah, portable computers are now capable of running at very fast speeds for short periods of time, before they need to take a break to cool down. Or they can amble at much slower speeds for a longer period of time.

The laptop one of us used to write this book illustrates this. Formatting this textbook takes about a minute when the computer is cold, but the same formatting request will stall in the middle of the build for several minutes if run immediately after a previous build request.

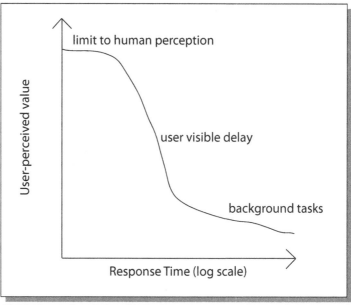

Figure 7.14: Example relationship between response time and user-perceived value. For most applications, faster response time is valuable within a range. Below some threshold, users will not be able to perceive the difference. Above some threshold, users will perform other activities while waiting for the result.

battery life, the choice is easy, but often the user wants a reasonable tradeoff between the two.

One approach would be to consider the value that the user places on fast response time for a particular application: quickly updating the display after a user interface command is probably more important than transferring files quickly in the background. We can capture the relationship between response time and value in Figure 7.14. Although the precise shape and magnitude will vary from user to user and application to application, the curve will head down and to the right — the longer something takes, the less useful it is. Often, the curve is S-shaped. Human perception is unable to tell the difference between a few tens of milliseconds, so adding a short delay will not matter that much for most tasks; likewise, if a protein folding computation has already taken a few minutes, it won't matter much if it takes a few more seconds. Not everything will be S-shaped: in high frequency stock trading, value starts high and plummets to zero within a few milliseconds.

Response time predictability affects this relationship as well. An online video that cuts out for a few seconds every minute is much less watchable than one that is lower quality on average but more predictable.

If we combine Figure 7.14 with the fact that increased energy use often provides diminishing returns in terms of improved performance, this suggests a three prong strategy to spend the system's energy budget where it will make the most difference:

- **Below the threshold of human perception.** Optimize for energy use, to the extent that tasks can be executed with greater energy efficiency without the user noticing.

- **Above the threshold of human perception.** Optimize for response time if the user will notice any slowdown.

- **Long-running or background tasks.** Balance energy use and responsiveness depending on the available battery resources.

7.4 | Real-time scheduling

On some systems, the operating system scheduler must account for process deadlines. For example, the sensor and control software to manage an airplane's flight path needs to be executed in a timely fashion, if it is to be useful at all. Similarly, the software to control anti-lock brakes or anti-skid traction control on an automobile must occur at a precise time if it is to be effective. In a less life critical domain, when playing a movie on a computer, the next frame must be rendered in time or the user will perceive the video quality as poor.

Battery life and the kernel-user boundary

An emerging issue on smartphones is that application behavior can have a significant impact on battery life, e.g., by more intensive use of the network or other power-hungry features of the architecture. If a user runs a mix of applications, how can she know which was most responsible for their smartphone running out of power? Among the resources we will discuss in this book, energy is almost unique in being a *non-virtualizable* resource. When an application drains the battery, the energy lost is no longer available to any other applications.

How can we prevent a misbehaving or greedy application from using more than its share of the battery? One model is to let the user decide: for the kernel to measure and record how much energy was used by each application, so the user can determine if each application is worth it. Apple has taken a different approach with the iPhone. Because Apple controls which applications are allowed to run on the system, it can and has barred applications that (in its view) unnecessarily drain the battery. It will be interesting to see which of these models wins out over time.

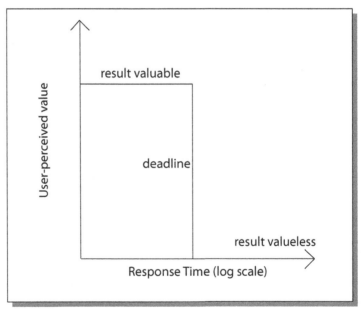

Figure 7.15: With real-time constraints, the value of completing some task drops to zero if the deadline is not met.

real-time
constraint

These systems have *real-time constraints*: computation that must be completed by a deadline if it is to have value. Real-time constraints are a special case of Figure 7.14, shown in Figure 7.15, where the value of completing a task is uniform up to the deadline, and then drops to zero.

How do we design a processor scheduler, and resource allocation in general, to ensure deadlines are met?

We might start by assigning real time tasks a higher priority than any less time critical tasks. We could then run the system under a variety of different of different workloads, and see if the system continues to comfortably meet its deadlines in all cases. If not, the system may need a faster processor or other hardware resources to speed up the real-time tasks.

Unfortunately, testing alone is insufficient for guaranteeing that real-time constraints are met. Recall that the specific ordering of execution events can sometimes lead to different execution sequences – e.g., sometimes a thread will be delayed by a lock being held another thread, and other times it will not.

One option is that threads are the wrong model for this type of computation, and that we should instead use a completely deterministic and repeatable schedule that ensures that the deadlines are met. This can work if the real-time tasks are periodic and fixed in advance, but in more dynamic systems it is difficult to account for all possible variations affecting how long different parts of the computation will take.

Instead, there are three widely used techniques for improving the likelihood that deadlines are met. These approaches are also useful whenever timeliness matters without a strict deadline, e.g., to ensure responsiveness of a user interface.

- **Over-provisioning.** A simple step to increasingly the likelihood that deadlines can be met is to ensure that the real-time tasks, in aggregate, only use a fraction of the system's processing power. This way, the real time tasks will be able to be scheduled quickly, without having to wait for higher-priority, compute-intensive tasks. The equivalent step in college is to avoid signing up for too many hard courses in the same semester!

- **Earliest deadline first.** Careful choice of the scheduling policy can also help meet deadlines. If you have a pile of homework to do, neither shortest job first nor round robin will ensure that the assignment due tomorrow gets done in time. Instead, real time schedulers, mimicking
  earliest deadline first real life, use a policy called *earliest deadline first* (EDF). Tasks are sorted by their deadline, and done in that order. If the required work can be scheduled to meet the deadlines, and the tasks only need the processor (and not I/O, locks or other resources), EDF will ensure that all tasks are done in time.

  Unfortunately, for more complex tasks, EDF can produce anomalous behavior. Consider two tasks. Task A is I/O-bound with a deadline at 12 ms, needing 1 ms of computation followed by 10 ms of I/O. Task B is compute-bound with a deadline at 10 ms, but needing 5 ms of computation. Although there is a schedule that will meet both deadlines (run task A first), EDF will run the compute-bound task first, causing the I/O-bound task to miss its deadline.

This limitation can be addressed by breaking tasks into shorter units, each with its own deadline. In the example, the true deadline for the compute portion of the I/O-bound task is at 2 ms, because if it is not completed by then, the overall task deadline will be missed. If your homework next week needs a book from the library, you need to put that on hold first, even if that slightly delays the homework you have due tomorrow.

- **Priority donation.** Another problem can occur through the interaction of shared data structures, priorities, and deadlines. Suppose we have three tasks, each with a different priority level. The real-time task runs at the highest priority, and it has sufficient processing resources to meet its deadline, with some time to spare. However, the three tasks also access a shared data structure, protected by a lock.

  Suppose the low priority acquires the lock to modify the data structure, but it is then preempted by the medium priority task. The relative priorities imply that we should run the medium priority task first, even though the low priority task is in the middle of a critical section. Next, suppose the real-time task preempts the medium task and proceeds to access the shared data structure. It will find the lock busy and wait. Normally, the wait would be short, and the real-time task would be able to meet its deadline despite the delay. However, in this case, when the high priority task waits for the lock, the scheduler will pick the medium priority task to run next, causing an indefinite *priority inversion* delay. This is called *priority inversion*; it can occur whenever a high priority task must wait for a lower priority task to complete its work.

  priority donation A commonly used solution, implemented in most commercial operating systems, is called *priority donation*: when a high priority task waits on a shared lock, it temporarily donates its priority to the task holding the lock. This allows the low priority task to be scheduled to complete the critical section, at which point its priority reverts to its original state, and the processor is re-assigned to the high priority, waiting, task.

7.5 | Queuing theory

Suppose you build a new web service, and the week before you are to take it live, you test it to see whether it will have reasonable response time. If the your tests show the performance is terrible, what then? Is it because the implementation is too slow? Perhaps you have the wrong scheduler?

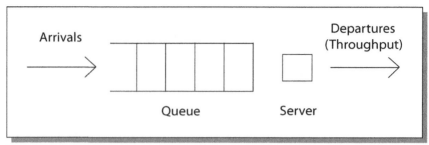

Figure 7.16: An abstract queueing system. Tasks arrive, wait their turn in the queue if necessary, get service, and leave. The response time is the queueing delay plus the service time.

Quick, let's re-implement that linked list with a hash table! And add more levels to the multi-level feedback queue! Our advice: don't panic. In this section, we consider a third possibility, an effect that often trumps all of the others: response time depends non-linearly on the rate that tasks arrive at a system. Understanding this relationship is the topic of *queueing theory*.

Fortunately, if you have ever waited in line (and who hasn't?), you have an intuitive understanding of queueing theory. Its concepts apply whenever there is a queue waiting for a turn, whether it is tasks waiting for a processor, web requests waiting for a turn at a web server, restaurant patrons waiting for a table, cars waiting at a busy intersection, or people waiting in line at the supermarket.

While queueing theory is capable of providing precise predictions for complex systems, our interest is providing you the tools to be able to do back of the envelope calculations for where the time goes in a real system. For performance debugging, coarse estimates are often enough, rather than a precise accounting. For this reason, we make two simplifying assumptions for this discussion. First, we assume the system is work conserving, so that all tasks complete; this will normally be the case except in extreme overload conditions, a topic we'll discuss in the next section of this chapter. Second, although the scheduling policy can affect a system's queueing behavior, we will keep things simple and assume FIFO scheduling.

Definitions

Because queueing theory is concerned with the root causes of system performance, and not just its observable effects, we need to introduce a bit more terminology, A simple abstract queueing system is illustrated by Figure 7.16. In any queueing system, tasks arrive, wait their turn, get service, and finish. If tasks temporarily arrive faster than they can receive service, queues build up. Queues drain over time whenever the processing or service rate exceeds the arrival rate of new tasks. We will introduce more complexity, such as multiple queues and multiple servers, as we proceed.

- **Server.** A server is anything that performs tasks. A web server is obviously a server, performing web requests, but so is the processor on a client machine, since it executes application tasks. The cashier at a supermarket and a waiter in a restaurant are also servers.

  indexarrival rate

- **Arrival process and arrival rate (λ).** The arrival process describes when tasks arrive at the server; as we will see, this can have a large impact on queueing behavior. We define λ to be the average arrival rate over time.

- **Queueing delay (W) and number of tasks queued (Q).** The queueing delay, or wait time, is the total time a task must wait to be scheduled. In a time slicing system, a task might need to wait multiple times for the same server to complete its task; in this case the queuing delay includes all of the time a task spends waiting until it is completed.

- **Service time (S) and service rate (μ).** The service time S, or execution time, is the time to complete a task assuming no waiting. μ is the service rate (the inverse of S), the rate at which the server completes tasks when there is work to do.

- **Response time (R).** The response time is the queueing delay (how long you wait in line) plus the service time (how long it takes once you get to the front of the line). In the web server example we started with, the poor performance can be due to either factor — the system could be too slow even when no one is waiting, or the system could be too slow because each request spends most of its time waiting for service.

$$R = W + S$$

We can improve the response time by focusing on either factor. We can reduce the queueing delay by buying more servers (for example, by having more processors than ready threads or more cashiers than customers). A faster server (or a faster implementation) will reduce response time, even if the queueing delay is already zero, by reducing the service time.

- **Utilization (U).** The utilization is the fraction of time the server is busy. Because having more servers (whether processors on chip or cashiers in a supermarket) or faster servers is costly, you might think that the goal of the system designer is to maximize utilization. However, in most cases, there is no free lunch: as we will see, higher utilization normally implies higher queueing delay and higher response times.

  As a designer, you often need to find an appropriate tradeoff between higher utilization and better response time. Fifty years ago, computer designers made the tradeoff in favor of higher utilization: when computers are wildly expensive, it is annoying but understandable to make people wait for the computer. Now that computers are much cheaper, our lives are better! We now usually make the computer do the waiting.

- **Throughput (X).** Throughput is the number of tasks processed by the system per unit of time. In a work conserving system where all tasks complete, over the long term throughput must be equal to the arrival rate, λ.

$$X = \lambda$$

This is a steady state relationship. In the short term, λ may exceed the rate that the system can process requests; in this case, queues will build up and $\lambda > X$. Conversely, as the queues drain, $X > \lambda$.

Further, some systems have a limited amount of queue space; these systems must discard tasks if too many arrive in too short a period of time. In this case, the throughput may be less than the arrival rate.

- **Number of tasks in the system (N).** The average number of tasks in the system is just the number queued plus the number receiving service:

$$N = Q + U$$

Flow Equations

In steady state and assuming a work conserving system, several of these quantities are related to each other.

For example, throughput is directly related to utilization: utilization is the throughput (tasks per second) times the average service time (seconds per task). If we complete one task per second, and each task takes half a second to complete, the utilization will be 50%.

$$U = X \times S$$

The number of tasks in the system can be derived from the response time and the throughput. If we know that the average Google query takes 100 milliseconds and Google handles an average of 100K queries per second, the average number of pending queries must be 10K. Note that this is true regardless of the internal structure of Google's web service — they may have separate queues for the processor, the disk, and the network, but in aggregate in steady state the number of requests being handled must be equal to the product of the response time and the throughput.

Little's Law

Each of the flow equations can all be derived from a common principle, called Little's Law: the average number of active tasks in a system is equal to average arrival rate multiplied by the average time a task spends in the system. The key is that the definition of "system" can be anything with arriving and departing tasks, provided the system has a steady state.

For example, if we consider just the server, the utilization is the average number of tasks at the server — some number between 0 and 1. The utilization is equal to the arrival rate at the server (λ, or X if we are work-conserving) times the service time.

Likewise, if we consider just the queue, the average queue length is the average number of tasks *in the queue*, and that quantity is equal to the arrival rate times the waiting time, the average amount of time a task spends queued.

$$N = R \times X$$

The algebra works the other way as well: given the average number of requests queued and the average throughput of a system, we can calculate its average wait time:

$$W = \frac{Q}{X}$$

Response time versus utilization

The relationship between a system's response time and utilization (or equivalently, the arrival rate) is more complex. We start with some extreme scenarios as a way of bounding the queueing behavior of the system; we will introduce more realistic scenarios as we proceed.

What is the best case scenario for response time for a given utilization? Suppose we have a set of fixed-sized tasks that arrive equally spaced from one another. As long as the rate at which tasks arrive is less than the rate at which the server completes the tasks, there will be no queueing at all. Perfection! Each server finishes the previous customer in time for the next arrival. The hapless manager of the supermarket from earlier in the chapter is thrilled: if only she can get customers to arrive equally spaced during the day, and she has enough servers, she can keep all of the checkout lines completely busy, without anyone waiting.

Of course, life is usually not so kind. Suppose we take a system where every customer arrives equally spaced and the rate of arrivals precisely balances the rate at which the servers can handle requests. What happens to this system if we add just one extra customer? Obviously, that customer

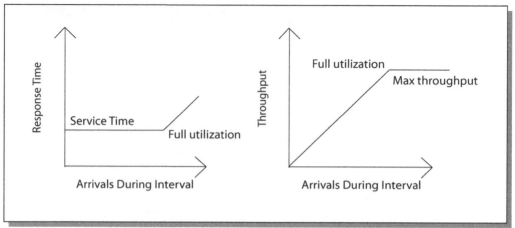

Figure 7.17: Best case response time and throughput as a function of the number of arrivals during an interval. This assumes arrivals are evenly spaced across the interval, service times are fixed-size, and no arrivals occur outside of the interval.

will need to wait. If we serve customers in FIFO order, however, not only does that customer need to wait, *every* customer that arrives afterward will need to wait. (Alternatively, if we serve customers in last-in-first-out order, the customer that arrived just before our extra customer will be the only one to wait — but they will need to wait until the supermarket closes before they can get served. Just as it looks like its their turn, a new request will enter the system and make them wait. The result will be one very unhappy customer!)

A key insight of queueing theory is this: anytime requests arrive faster than the rate at which they can be served, the excess must be queued (or turned away). This extra queueing will last until the servers can process both the waiting requests plus any new arrivals in the meantime. Thus, if utilization is high, the servers will take a very long time to catch up; if utilization is low, the servers will catch up quickly.

Figure 7.17 graphs the best case scenario for response time and through-put, as a function of the rate of arriving work, where we are only consider-ing work that arrives during a specific interval. If there was no queueing to start with, and tasks arrive evenly spaced, the queuing delay will be zero until the work arrives faster than the system can handle. Similarly, throughput and utilization increases with more arrivals, but only up to a point — the system has a maximum rate it can process requests.

Now consider the opposite case. Suppose all the tasks arrive at exactly the same time. The average wait time increases linearly as more tasks arrive together. The throughput also increases linearly up to the maxi-mum throughput of the system. Figure 7.18 graphs the response time and throughput in this case. Our hapless supermarket manager decides to run

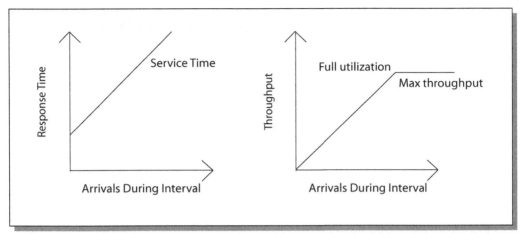

Figure 7.18: Worst case response time and throughput as a function of the number of arrivals during an interval. This assumes arrivals occur at the beginning of the interval, service times are fixed-size, and no arrivals occur outside of the interval.

a promotion, giving away a free iPad to the first five customers in the store. Suddenly, everyone arrives at once, and wait times are very long. Disaster!

Most systems are somewhere in between this best case and worst case. Rather than being perfectly synchronized or perfectly desynchronized, task arrivals in many systems are random: the different customers in a supermarket do not coordinate with each other as to when they arrive. Likewise, service times are not perfectly equal — there's randomness there as well. At a doctor's office, everyone has an appointment, so it may seem like that should be the best case scenario, and no one should ever have to wait. Even so, there is often queueing! Why? If the amount of time the doctor takes with each patient is sometimes shorter and sometimes longer than the appointment length, then random chance will cause queueing.

A particularly useful model for understanding queueing behavior is to use an exponential distribution to describe the time between tasks arriving and the time it takes to service each task. Once you get past a bit of math, the exponential provides a stunningly simple *approximate* description of most real-life queueing systems. We do not claim that all real systems always obey the exponential model in detail; in fact, most don't. However, the model is usually accurate enough for most purposes, and as we will discuss, it is easy to understand the circumstances under which it is inaccurate.

exponential distribution

First, the math. An *exponential distribution* of a continuous random variable with a mean of $\frac{1}{\lambda}$ has the probability density function, shown in Figure 7.19:

$$f(x) = \lambda e^{-\lambda x}$$

Fortunately, you don't need to understand that equation in any detail,

Model vs. Reality

When trying to understand a complex system, it is often useful to try to construct a model of its behavior. A model is a simplification that tries to capture the most important aspects of a more complex system's behavior. Models are neither true nor false. It is often the case that a more complex model will yield a closer approximation; whether the added complexity is useful or gets in the way depends on how the model is being used.

For example, one way of answering what will happen to a system under different load conditions would be to simulate the exact pattern of task arrivals and task service times. This would provide an exact answer for the response time and throughput, assuming that pattern. For a precise answer, it matters exactly when each task arrives and how long each task takes. However, a detailed simulation would not provide any help in understanding the behavior of the system under slightly different conditions, except by re-running the simulation with a different arrival pattern. Since there could be an infinite number of possible arrival patterns, simulation has its limits.

Often, we want to understand the behavior of a system under a range of conditions, and for that a simpler model is often more useful. If after abstracting away detail, we can still provide approximately correct predictions of system behavior under a variety of scenarios, then it is likely the model captures the most important aspects of the system. If the model is inaccurate in some important respect, then it means our explanation for how the system behaves is too coarse, and to improve the prediction we would need to revise the model.

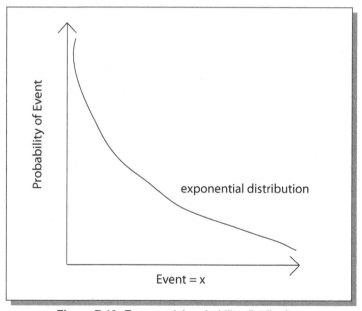

Figure 7.19: Exponential probability distribution.

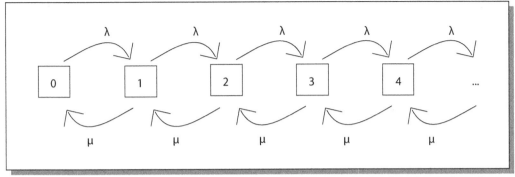

Figure 7.20: State machine representing a queue with exponentially distributed arrivals and departures. λ is the rate of arrivals; μ is the rate at which the server completes each task. With an exponential distribution, the probability of a state transition is independent of how long the system has been in any given state.

except for the following. A very useful property of an exponential distribution is that it is *memoryless*. A memoryless distribution for the time between two events means that the likelihood of an event occurring remains the same, *no matter how long we have already waited* for the event, or what other events may have already happened. For example, on a web server, web requests (usually) arrive independently. Sometimes, two requests will arrive very close together in time; sometimes there will more of a delay. It doesn't matter if the last request arrived 5 ms or 50 ms ago, the time to the next request is (largely) independent.

memoryless property

Not every distribution is memoryless. A Gaussian, or normal, distribution for the time between events is closer to the best case scenario described above — arrivals occur randomly, but they tend to occur at regular intervals, give or take a bit. Some probability distributions work the other way. With a *heavy-tailed distribution*, the longer you have waited for some event, the longer you are likely to still need to wait. This is closer to the worst case behavior above, as it means that most events are clustered together. The line at the Department of Motor Vehicles often *feels* heavy tailed, even if it probably isn't.

heavy-tailed distribution

With a memoryless distribution, the behavior of queueing systems becomes very simple to understand. One can think of the queue as a finite state machine: with some probability, a new task arrives, increasing the queue by one. If the queue length is non-zero, with some other probability, a task completes, decreasing the queue by one. With a memoryless distribution of arrivals and departures, the probability of each transition is constant and independent of the other transitions, as illustrated in Figure 7.20.

Assuming that $\lambda < \mu$, the system is stable; clearly, if tasks arrive faster than they can be processed, the waiting time will become infinite and/or the system will need to discard some requests. Assuming stability and

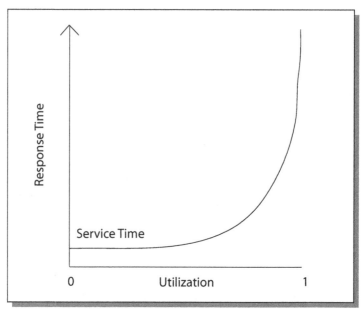

Figure 7.21: Relationship between response time and utilization, assuming exponentially distributed arrivals and departures. Response time goes to infinity as the system approaches full utilization.

exponential distributions for the arrival and departure processes, we can solve the model to determine the average response time as a function of the utilization. Recall that the utilization, the fraction of time that the server is busy, is simply the ratio between λ and μ.

$$R = \frac{S}{1 - U}$$

This equation is illustrated in Figure 7.21. The response time of a system becomes unbounded as the system approaches full utilization. Although it might seem that full utilization is an achievable goal, if there is any randomness in arrivals *or* any randomness in service times, full utilization cannot be achieved in steady state without turning away some tasks. (Or in the case of a doctor's office, this means staying open after hours until you treat the last patient in the queue.)

In most systems, well before a system reaches full utilization, average response time will become unbearably long. Because queue length is directly related to response time by Little's Law, queue lengths increase proportionately as the system approaches full utilization. As no real system has an arbitrary amount of space for queued tasks, tasks must be turned away or some other steps must be taken to reduce load. In the next section, we discuss some of the steps system designers can take in response to overload.

Variance in the response time increases even faster as the system approaches full utilization, proportional to $\frac{1}{(1-U)^2}$. Even with 99% utilization, 1% of the time there is no queue at all; random chance means that while sometimes a large number of customers arrive at nearly the same time, at other times the server will be able to work through all of the backlog. If you are lucky enough to arrive at just that moment, you can receive service with no wait. If you are unlucky enough to arrive immediately after a burst of other customers, your wait will be quite long.

"What if?" questions

Queueing theory is particularly useful for answering "what if?" questions: what happens if we change some design parameter of the system. In this section, we consider a selection of these questions, as a way of providing you a bit more intuition.

Scheduling policy

What happens to the response time curve for other scheduling policies? Assuming exponential service times, the average response time is the exactly the same for Round Robin as for FIFO. With a memoryless distribution, every queued task is equally likely to finish first, so switching among tasks has no impact other than to increase overhead.

If task length can be predicted, however, Shortest Job First can improve average response time. At low to moderate utilization, this will come at a cost of a small increase in response time for long tasks. As utilization becomes high, however, SJF will result in a massive increase in average response time for long tasks.

To see this, note that any server alternates between periods of being idle (when the queue is empty) and periods of being busy (when the queue is non-empty). If we ignore switching overhead, the scheduling discipline has no impact on these periods — they are only affected by when tasks arrive. Scheduling can only affect which tasks we do first.

With SJF, a long task will only complete immediately before an idle period; it is always the last thing in the queue to complete. As utilization increases, these idle periods become increasingly rare. For example, if the server is 99% busy, the server will be idle only 1% of the time. Further, idle periods are *not* evenly distributed — a server is much more likely to be idle if it was idle a second ago. This means that the long jobs may need to wait for a very long time under SJF under high load.

Burstiness

Our analysis so far has assumed exponentially distributed arrival and service times. Many systems have arrival times or service times that are not well-characterized by an exponential distribution. What can we say in these cases? On one side, arrivals and service times can be more evenly distributed about the mean than an exponential; alternately, they can be less evenly distributed, or more *bursty*. A bursty distribution is sometimes called *heavy-tailed* because it has more very long tasks; since the mean rate is the same, this also implies that the distribution has even more very short tasks.

If the distribution of arrivals or service times is less bursty than an exponential (e.g., more like a Gaussian), average response time will be lower under FIFO and higher under Round Robin. This is closer to the best case scenario that we started with; events occur at more predictable intervals. When tasks are more uniform in size, FIFO will be nearly optimal, while Round Robin will perform worse than FIFO.

Many real-world systems, however, exhibit more bursty arrivals or service times than an exponential distribution. For example, web page size is heavy-tailed; so is the processing time per web page. Process execution times on desktop computers are also heavy-tailed. For these types of systems, burstiness results in worse average response time than would be predicted by an exponential distribution. Further, for these types of systems, there is an even greater benefit to approximating SJF to avoid stalling small requests behind long ones, and Round Robin will outperform FIFO.

Arrivals that vary with the queueing delay

What happens if we try to increase load beyond what the system can handle? If new task arrivals are independent of the response time, then the system will de-stabilize: the queueing time will grow indefinitely. In other words, the system will not be in steady state.

In many real systems, however, the rate of arrivals does depend on the system response time. Customers will abandon a web server if the response time is too high. On a single computer, if the processor is so overloaded that it becomes unresponsive, then the user will slow down. This reduces the likelihood that new work arrives when the system is already overloaded, and thus it also reduces the average response time for a given utilization. Of course, this is scant comfort to the operator of the overloaded system: achieving a lower response time because you have scared your customers away is hardly the path to fame and fortune.

Multiple servers

Many real systems have not just one but multiple servers. Does it matter whether there is a single queue for everyone or a separate queue per server? Real systems take both approaches: supermarkets tend to have a separate queue per cashier; banks tend to have a single shared queue for bank tellers. Some systems do both: airports often have a single queue at checkin, but have separate queues for the parking garage. Which is better for response time?

Clearly, there are often efficiency gains from having separate queues. Multiprocessor schedulers use separate queues for affinity scheduling and to reduce switching costs; in a supermarket, it may not be practical to have a single queue. And users often consider a single (FIFO) queue to be more fair than separate queues. It often seems that we always end up in the slowest line at the supermarket, even if that can't possibly be true for everyone.

If we focus on average response time, however, a single queue is always better than separate queues, provided that users aren't allowed to jump lanes. The reason is simple: because of variations in how long each task takes to service, one server can be idle while another server has multiple queued tasks. Likewise, a single fast server is always better for response time than a large number of slower servers of equal aggregate capacity to the fast server. There is no difference when all servers are busy, but the single fast server will process requests faster when there are fewer active tasks than servers.

Secondary bottlenecks

If a processor is 90% busy serving web requests, and we add another processor to reduce its load, how much will that improve average response time? Unfortunately, that's not enough information to say. You might like to believe that it will reduce response time by a considerable amount, from $R = \frac{S}{(1-0.9)} = 10S$ to $R = \frac{S}{(1-0.45)} = 1.8S$.

However, suppose each web request needs not only processing time, but also disk I/O and network bandwidth. If the disk was 80% busy beforehand, it will appear that the processor utilization was the primary problem. Once you add an extra processor, however, the disk becomes the new limiting factor to good performance.

In some cases, queueing theory can make a specific prediction as to the impact of improving one part of a system in isolation. For example, if arrival times are exponentially distributed and independent of the system response time, and if the service times at the processor, disk, and network are also exponentially distributed and independent of one another, then the overall response time for the system is just the sum of the response times of the components:

$$R = \sum_i \frac{S_i}{(1 - U_i)}$$

In this case, improving one part of the system will affect just its contribution to the aggregate system response time. Even though these conditions may not always hold, this is often useful as an approximation to what will occur in real life.

Lessons

To summarize, almost all real-world systems exhibit some randomness in their arrival process or their service times, or both. For these systems:

- Response time increases with increased load.

- System performance is predictable across a range of load factors if we can estimate the average service time per request.

- Burstiness increases average response time. It is mathematically convenient to assume an exponential distribution, but many real-world systems exhibit more burstiness and therefore worse user performance.

- Overload is catastrophic, so we need to design systems to operate with low to moderate load, and we need to have a backup plan in case load spikes too high.

Exercises

6. Suppose your company is considering using one of two candidate scheduling algorithms. One is Round Robin, with an overhead of 1% of the processing power of the system. The second is a wizzy new system that predicts the future and so it can closely approximate SJF, but it takes an overhead of 10% of the processing power of the system.

   Assume randomized arrivals and random task lengths. Under what conditions will the simpler algorithm outperform the more complex, and vice versa?

7.6 | Overload management

Many systems operate without any direct control over their workload. In the previous section, we explained that good response time and low variance in the response time are both predicated on operating well below peak utilization. If your web service is advertised on slashdot, however, you can suddenly receive a ton of traffic from new users. Success! But the flood of new users discover your service has horrible performance. Disaster!

More sophisticated scheduling can help at low to moderate load, but if the load is more than system can handle, response time will spike, even for short tasks.

The key idea in overload management is to design your system do less work when overloaded. This will seem strange! After all, you want your system to work a particular way; how can you cripple the user's experience just when your system becomes popular? Under overload conditions, however, your system is incapable of serving all of the requests in the normal way. The only question is: do you choose what is turned off, or do you let events choose for you?

An obvious step is to simply reject some requests, in order to preserve reasonable response time for the remaining requests. While this can seem harsh, it is also pragmatic. Under overload, the only alternative to giving a few customers good service and others bad or no service is to give all customers bad service. Every long task that is processed under overload conditions means that many shorter tasks will finish much later, if ever. It is better to decide up front to put no effort into a long task rather than to let it accumulate service time if it will never be completed.

The approach of turning away requests under overload conditions is common in streaming video applications. An overloaded movie service will reject requests to start new streams so that it can continue to provide good streaming service to users that have already started. Likewise, during the NCAA basketball tournament or during the Olympics, the broadcaster will turn requests away, rather than giving everyone poor service.

An apt analogy, perhaps, is that of a popular restaurant. Why not set out acres of tables so that everyone who shows up at the restaurant can be seated? If the waiters Round Robin among the various tables, you can be seated, but wait an hour to get a menu, then wait another hour to make an order, and so forth. That is one way of dealing with a persistent overload situation — by making the user experience so unpleasant that none of your customers will return! As absurd as this scenario is, however, it is close to how we allocate scarce space on congested highways — by making everyone wait.

A less obvious step is to somehow reduce the service time per request under overload conditions. A good example of this was that CNN's web page was overwhelmed on 9/11, and so they shifted to a static page that was faster to serve. When experiencing unexpected load, EBay will update its auction listings less frequently, saving work that can be used for processing other requests. A movie service can reduce the video quality/bit rate for everyone in order to serve more simultaneous requests.

Amazon has designed its web site to always return a result quickly, even when the requested data is unavailable due to overload conditions. Every backend service has both a normal interface and a fallback to use if its results aren't ready in time. For example, this means a user can be told that their purchase will be shipped shortly, even when the book is actually out of stock. This is a strategic decision that it is better to give a wrong answer quickly, and apologize later, rather than to wait to give the right answer more slowly.

Unfortunately, many systems have the opposite problem: they do more work per request as load increases. A simple example of this would be using

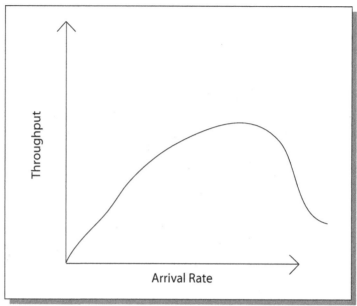

Figure 7.22: Throughput versus load, when the service time increases with added load. At low load, throughput increases linearly; as load increases, throughput drops off due to the added work per task.

a linked list to manage a queue of requests: as more requests are queued, more processing time is used maintaining the queue and not getting useful work done. If amount of work per task increases as the load increases, then response times will soar even faster with increased utilization, and throughput can decrease as we add load. This makes overload management even more important.

A real-life example of this phenomenon is with highway traffic. We sketch a typical graph of throughput versus load for highways in Figure 7.22. As you add cars to an empty highway, it increases the rate that cars traverse the highway. However, at very high loads, the density of cars causes a transition to stop and go traffic, where the rate of progress is much slower than when there were fewer cars. A common solution for highways is to use onramp limiters — to limit the rate that new cars can enter the highway if the system is close to overload.

Time-slicing in the presence of caches has similar behavior. When load is low, there are few time slices, and every task uses its cache efficiently. As more tasks are added to the system, there are more time slices and fewer cache hits, slowing down the processor just when we need it to be running at peak efficiency. In networks, packets are dropped when the network becomes overloaded, and if care is not taken in the protocol design, this can cause the sender to retransmit packets, further overloading the network. TCP congestion control, now a common part of almost every

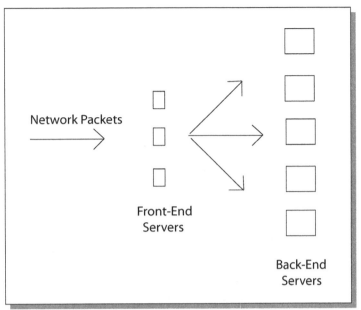

Figure 7.23: A web service often consists of a number of front-end servers who redirect incoming client requests to a larger set of back-end servers.

Internet connection, was developed precisely to deal with this effect.

You may have even experienced this issue. Some students, as homework piles up, become less, rather than more, efficient. After all, it is hard to concentrate on one project if you know that you really ought to be also working on a different one. But if you decide to take the lessons of this textbook to heart and decide to blow off some of your homework to ensure that the rest of your assignments get done, let me suggest that you choose some class other than operating systems!

7.7 | Case Study: Servers in a data center

We can illustrate the application of the ideas discussed in this chapter, by considering how we should manage a collection of servers in a data center to provide responsive web service. Many web services, such as Google, Facebook and Amazon, are organized as a set of front-end machines that redirect incoming requests to a larger set of back-end machines. We illustrate this in Figure 7.23. This architecture isolates clients from the architecture of the back-end systems, so that more capacity can be added to the back-end simply by changing the configuration of the front-end systems. Back-end servers can also be taken off-line, have their software upgraded, and so forth, completely transparently to clients.

To provide good response time to the clients of the web service:

- When clients first connect to the service, the front-end node assigns each customer to a back-end server to balance load. Customers can be spread evenly across the back-end servers or they can be assigned to a node with low current load, much as customers at a supermarket select the shortest line for a cashier.

- Additional requests from the same client can be assigned to the same back-end server, as a form of affinity scheduling. Once a server has fetched client data, it will be faster for it to handle additional requests.

- We need to prevent individual users from hogging resources, because that can disrupt performance for other users. A back-end server can favor short tasks over long ones; they can also keep track of the total resources used by each client, reducing the scheduling priority of any client consuming more than their fair share of resources.

- It is often crucial to the usability of a web service to keep response time small. This requires monitoring both the rate of arrivals and the average amount of computing, disk, and network resources consumed by each request. Back-end servers should be added before average server utilization gets too high.

- Since it often takes considerable time to bring new servers online, we need to predict future load and have a backup plan for overload conditions.

7.8 | Conclusions and Future Directions

Resource scheduling is an ancient topic in computer science. Almost from the moment that computers were first multiprogrammed, operating system designers have had to decide which tasks to do first and which to leave for later. This decision — the system's scheduling policy — can have a significant impact on system responsiveness and usability.

Fortunately, the cumulative effect of Moore's Law has shifted the balance towards a focus on improving response time for users, rather than on efficient utilization of resources for the computer. At the same time, the massive scale of the Internet means that many services need to be designed to provide good response time across a wide range of load conditions. Our goal in this chapter is to give you the conceptual basis for making those design choices.

Several ongoing trends pose new and interesting challenges to effective resource scheduling.

- **Multicore systems.** Although almost all new servers, desktops, laptops and smartphones are multicore systems, relatively few widely used applications have been redesigned to take full advantage of multiple processors. This is likely to change over the next few years as multicore systems become ubiquitous and as they scale to larger numbers of processors per chip. Although we have the concepts in place to manage resource sharing among multiple parallel applications, commercial systems are only just now starting to deploy these ideas. It will be interesting to see how the theory works out in practice.

- **Cache affinity.** Over the past twenty years, processor architects have radically increased both the size and number of levels of on-chip caches. There is little reason to believe that this trend will reverse. Although processor clock rates are improving slowly, transistor density is still increasing at a rapid rate. This will make it both possible and desirable to have even larger, multi-level on-chip caches to achieve good performance. Thus, it is likely that scheduling for cache affinity will be an even larger factor in the future than it is today. Balancing when to respect affinity and when to migrate is still somewhat of an open question, as is deciding how to spread or coalesce application threads across caches.

- **Energy-aware scheduling.** The number of energy-constrained computers such as smartphones, tablets, and laptops, now far outstrips powered computers such as desktops and servers. As a result, we are likely to see the development of hardware to monitor and manage energy use by applications, and the operating system will need to make use of that hardware support. We are likely to see operating systems sandbox application energy use to prevent faulty or malicious applications from running down the battery. Likewise, just as applications can adapt to changing numbers of processors, we are likely to see applications that adapt their behavior to energy availability.

Exercises

For convenience, the exercises from the body of the chapter are repeated here.

1. For shortest job first, if the scheduler assigns a task to the processor, and no other task becomes schedulable in the meantime, will the scheduler ever preempt the current task? Why or why not?

2. Devise a workload where FIFO is pessimal — it does the worst possible choices — for average response time.

3. Suppose you do your homework assignments in SJF-order. After all, you feel like you are making a lot of progress! What might go wrong?

4. Given the following mix of tasks, task lengths, and arrival times, compute the completion and response time for each task, along with the average response time for the FIFO, RR, and SJF algorithms. Assume a time slice of 10 milliseconds and that all times are in milliseconds.

Task	Length	Arrival Time	Completion Time	Response Time
0	85	0		
1	30	10		
2	35	10		
3	20	80		
4	50	80		
		Average:		

5. Is it possible for an application to run slower when assigned 10 processors than when assigned 8? Why or why not?

6. Suppose your company is considering using one of two candidate scheduling algorithms. One is Round Robin, with an overhead of 1% of the processing power of the system. The second is a wizzy new system that predicts the future and so it can closely approximate SJF, but it takes an overhead of 10% of the processing power of the system.

Assume randomized arrivals and random task lengths. Under what conditions will the simpler algorithm outperform the more complex, and vice versa?

7. Most round-robin schedulers use a fixed size quantum. Give an argument in favor of and against a small quantum.

8. Which provides the best average response time when there are multiple servers (e.g., bank tellers, supermarket cash registers, airline ticket takers): a single FIFO queue or a FIFO queue per server? Why? Assume that you can't predict how long any customer is going to take at the server, and that once you have picked a queue to wait in, you are stuck and can't change queues.

9. Three tasks, A, B, and C are run concurrently on a computer system.

   • Task A arrives first at time 0, and uses the CPU for 100 ms before finishing.

   • Task B arrives shortly after A, still at time 0. Task B loops ten times; for each iteration of the loop, B uses the CPU for 2 ms and then it does I/O for 8 ms.

   • Task C is identical to B, but arrives shortly after B, still at time 0.

Assuming there is no overhead to doing a context switch, identify when A, B and C will finish for each of the following CPU scheduling disciplines:

a) FIFO

b) Round robin with a 1 ms time slice

c) Round robin with a 100 ms time slice

d) Multilevel feedback with four levels, and a time slice for the highest priority level is 1 ms.

e) Shortest job first

10. For each of the following processor scheduling policies, describe the set of workloads under which that policy is optimal in terms of minimizing average response time (does the same thing as shortest job first) and the set of workloads under which the policy is pessimal (does the same thing as longest job first). If there are no workloads under which a policy is optimal or pessimal, indicate that.

a) FIFO

b) Round robin

c) Multilevel feedback queues

11. Explain how you would set up a valid experimental comparison between two scheduling policies, one of which can starve some jobs.

12. As system administrator of a popular social networking website, you notice that usage peaks during working hours (10am – 5pm) and the evening (7 – 10pm) on the US east coast. The CEO asks you to design a system where during these peak hours there will be three levels of users. Users in level 1 are the center of the social network, and so they are to enjoy better response time than users in level 2, who in turn will enjoy better response time than users in level 3. You are to design such a system so that all users will still get some progress, but with the indicated preferences in place.

a) Will a fixed priority scheme with pre-emption and three fixed priorities work? Why, or why not?

b) Will a UNIX-style multi-feedback queue work? Why, or why not?

13. Consider the following preemptive priority-scheduling algorithm based on dynamically changing priorities. Larger numbers imply

higher priority. Tasks are preempted whenever there is a higher priority task. When a task is waiting for CPU (in the ready queue, but not running), its priority changes at a rate of a:

$$P(t) = P_0 + a \times (t - t_0)$$

where t_0 is the time at which the task joins the ready queue and P_0 is its initial priority, assigned when the task enters the ready queue or is preempted. Similarly, when it is running, the task's priority changes at a rate b. The parameters a, b and P_0 can be used to obtain many different scheduling algorithms.

    a) What is the algorithm that results from $P_0 = 0$ and $b > a > 0$?

    b) What is the algorithm that results from $P_0 = 0$ and $a < b < 0$?

    c) Suppose tasks are assigned a priority 0 when they arrive, but they retain their priority when they are preempted. What happens if two tasks arrive at nearly the same time and $a > 0 > b$?

    d) How should we adjust the algorithm to eliminate this pathology?

14. For a computer with two cores and a hyperthreading level of two, draw a graph of the rate of progress of a compute-intensive task as a function of time, depending on whether it is running alone, or with 1, 2, 3, or 4 other tasks.

15. Implement a test on your computer to see if your answer to the previous problem is correct.

16. A countermeasure is a strategy by which a user (or an application) exploits the characteristics of the processor scheduling policy to get as much of the processing time as possible. For example, if the scheduler trusts users to give accurate estimates of how long each task will take, it can give higher priority to short tasks. However, a countermeasure would be for the user to tell the system that the user's tasks are short even when they aren't.

Devise a countermeasure strategy for each of the following processor scheduling policies; your strategy should minimize an individual application's response time (even if it hurts overall system performance). You may assume perfect knowledge — for example, your strategy can be based on which jobs will arrive in the future, where your application is in the queue and how long the tasks ahead of you will run before blocking. Your strategy should also be robust — it should work properly even if there are no other tasks in the system, there are only short tasks, or there are only long running tasks. If no strategy will improve your application's response time, then explain why.

a) Last in first out

b) Round robin, assuming tasks are put at the end of the ready list when they become ready to run

c) Multilevel feedback queues, where tasks are put on the highest priority queue when they become ready to run

17. Consider a computer system running a general-purpose workload. Measured utilizations (in terms of time, not space) are:

Processor utilization	20.0%
Disk	99.7%
Network	5.0%

For each of the following changes, say what its likely impact will be on processor utilization, and explain why. Is it likely to significantly increase, marginally increase, significantly decrease, marginally decrease, or have no effect on the processor utilization?

a) Get a faster CPU

b) Get a faster disk

c) Increase the degree of multiprogramming

d) Get a faster network

Part III

Memory Management

There is nothing wrong with your television set. Do not attempt to adjust the picture. We are controlling transmission. If we wish to make it louder, we will bring up the volume. If we wish to make it softer, we will tune it to a whisper. We will control the horizontal. We will control the vertical. We can roll the image, make it flutter. We can change the focus to a soft blur or sharpen it to crystal clarity. For the next hour, sit quietly and we will control all that you see and hear. We repeat: there is nothing wrong with your television set.

Opening narration, The Outer Limits

8 Address Translation

The promise of virtual reality is compelling. Who wouldn't want the ability to travel anywhere without leaving the holodeck? Of course, the promise is far from becoming a reality. In theory, by adjusting the inputs to all of your senses in response to your actions, a virtual reality system could perfectly set the scene. However, your senses are not so easily controlled. We might soon be able to provide an immersive environment for vision, but balance, hearing, taste, and smell will take a lot longer. Touch, prioperception (the sense of being near something else), and g-forces are even farther off. Get a single one of these wrong and the illusion disappears.

Can we create a virtual reality environment for computer programs? We've already seen an example of this with the UNIX I/O interface, where the program doesn't need to know, and sometimes can't tell, if its inputs and outputs are files, devices, or other processes.

From the programmer's perspective, address translation occurs transparently — the program behaves correctly In the next three chapters, we take this idea a giant step further. An amazing number of advanced system features are enabled by putting the operating system in control of *address translation*, the conversion from the memory address the program thinks it is referencing to the physical location of that memory cell. From the programmer's perspective, address translation occurs transparently — the program behaves correctly despite the fact that its memory is stored somewhere completely different from where it thinks it is stored.

address translation

You were probably taught in some early programming class that a memory address is just an address. A pointer in a linked list contains the actual memory address of what it is pointing to. A jump instruction contains the actual memory address of the next instruction to be executed. This is a useful fiction! The programmer is often better off not thinking about how each memory reference is converted into the data or instruction being referenced. In practice, there is quite a lot of activity happening beneath the covers.

Address translation is a simple concept, but it turns out to be incredibly powerful. What can an operating system do with address translation? This is only a partial list:

- **Process isolation.** As we discussed in Chapter 2, protecting the operating system kernel and other applications against buggy or malicious code requires the ability to limit memory references by applications. Likewise, address translation can be used by applications to construct safe execution sandboxes for third party extensions.

- **Interprocess communication.** Often processes need to coordinate with each other, and an efficient way to do that is to have the processes share a common memory region.

- **Shared code segments.** Instances of the same program can share the program's instructions, reducing their memory footprint and making the processor cache more efficient. Likewise, different programs can share common libraries.

- **Program initialization.** Using address translation, we can start a program running before all of its code is loaded into memory from disk.

- **Efficient dynamic memory allocation.** As a process grows its heap, or as a thread grows its stack, we can use address translation to trap to the kernel to allocate memory for those purposes only as needed.

- **Cache management.** As we will explain in the next chapter, the operating system can arrange how programs are positioned in physical memory to improve cache efficiency, through a system called page coloring.

- **Program debugging.** The operating system can use memory translation to prevent a buggy program from overwriting its own code region; by catching pointer errors earlier, it makes them much easier to debug. Debuggers also use address translation to install data breakpoints, to stop a program when it references a particular memory location.

- **Efficient I/O.** Server operating systems are often limited by the rate at which they can transfer data to and from the disk and the network. Address translation enables data to be safely transferred directly between user-mode applications and I/O devices.

- **Memory mapped files.** A convenient and efficient abstraction for many applications is to map files into the address space, so that the contents of the file can be directly referenced with program instructions.

- **Virtual memory.** The operating system can provide applications the abstraction of more memory than is physically present on a given computer.

- **Checkpointing and restart.** The state of a long-running program can be periodically checkpointed so that if the program or system crashes, it can be restarted from the saved state. The key challenge is to be able to perform an internally consistent checkpoint of the program's data while the program continues to run.

- **Persistent data structures.** The operating system can provide the abstraction of a persistent region of memory, where changes to the data structures in that region survive program and system crashes.

- **Process migration.** An executing program can be transparently moved from one server to another, for example, for load balancing.

- **Information flow control.** An extra layer of security is to verify that a program is not sending your private data to a third party; e.g., a smartphone application may need access to your phone list, but it shouldn't be allowed to transmit that data. Address translation can be the basis for managing the flow of information into and out of a system.

- **Distributed shared memory.** We can transparently turn a network of servers into a large-scale shared-memory parallel computer using address translation.

In this chapter, we focus on the mechanisms needed to implement address translation, as that is the foundation of all of these services. We discuss how the operating system and applications use the mechanisms to provide these services in the following two chapters.

For runtime efficiency, most systems have specialized hardware to do address translation; this hardware is managed by the operating system kernel. In some systems, however, the translation is provided by a trusted compiler, linker or byte-code interpreter. In other systems, the application does the pointer translation as a way of managing the state of its own data structures. In still other systems, a hybrid model is used where addresses are translated both in software and hardware. The choice is often an engineering tradeoff between performance, flexibility, and cost. However, the functionality provided is often the same regardless of the mechanism used to implement the translation. In this chapter, we will cover a range of hardware and software mechanisms.

This chapter presents the following main ideas:

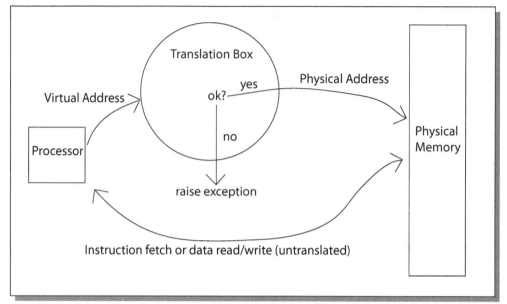

Figure 8.1: Address translation in the abstract. The translator converts (virtual) memory addresses generated by the program into physical memory addresses.

- **Address translation concept.** We start by providing a conceptual framework for understanding both hardware and software address translation.

- **Flexible address translation.** We focus first on hardware address translation; we ask how can we design the hardware to provide maximum flexibility to the operating system kernel?

- **Efficient address translation.** The solutions we present will seem flexible but terribly slow. We next discuss mechanisms that make address translation much more efficient, without sacrificing flexibility.

- **Software address translation.** Increasingly, software compilers and runtime interpreters are using address translation techniques to implement operating system functionality. What changes when the translation is in software rather than in hardware?

8.1 | Address translation concept

Considered as a black box, address translation is a simple function, illustrated in Figure 8.1. The translator takes each instruction and data memory reference generated by a process, checks whether the address is legal, and converts it to a physical memory address that can be used to fetch or store instructions or data. The data itself — whatever is stored in memory — is returned as is; it is not transformed in any way. The translation is usually implemented in hardware, and the operating system kernel configures the hardware to accomplish its aims.

The task of this chapter is to fill in the details about how that black box works. If we asked you right now how you might implement it, your first several guesses would probably be on the mark. If you said we could use an array, a tree, or a hash table, you would be right — all of those approaches have been taken by real systems.

Given that a number of different implementations are possible, how should we evaluate the alternatives? Here are some goals we might want out of a translation box; the design we end up with will depend on how we balance among these various goals.

- **Memory protection.** We need the ability to limit the access of a process to certain regions of memory, e.g., to prevent it from accessing memory not owned by the process. Often, however, we may want to limit access of a program to its own memory, e.g., to prevent a pointer error from overwriting the code region or to cause a trap to the debugger when the program references a specific data location.

- **Memory sharing.** We want to allow multiple processes to share selected regions of memory. These shared regions can be large (e.g., if we are sharing a program's code segment among multiple processes executing the same program) or relatively small (e.g., if we are sharing a common library, a file, or a shared data structure).

- **Flexible memory placement.** We want to allow the operating system the flexibility to place a process (and each part of a process) anywhere in physical memory; this will allow us to pack physical memory more efficiently. As we will see in the next chapter, flexibility in assigning process data to physical memory locations will also enable us to make more effective use of on-chip caches.

- **Sparse addresses.** Many programs have multiple dynamic memory regions that can change in size over the course of the execution of the program: the heap for data objects, a stack for each thread, and memory mapped files. Modern processors have 64-bit address spaces, allowing each dynamic object ample room to grow as needed, but making the translation function more complex.

- **Runtime lookup efficiency.** Hardware address translation occurs on every instruction fetch and every data load and store. It would be impractical if a lookup took, on average, much longer to execute than the instruction itself. At first, many of the schemes we discuss will seem wildly impractical! We will discuss ways to make even the most convoluted translation systems efficient.

- **Compact translation tables.** We also want the space overhead of translation to be minimal; any data structures we need should be small compared to the amount of physical memory being managed.

- **Portability.** Different hardware architectures make different choices as to how they implement translation; if an operating system kernel is to be easily portable across multiple processor architectures, it needs to be able to map from its (hardware-independent) data structures to the specific capabilities of each architecture.

We will end up with a fairly complex address translation mechanism, and so our discussion will start with the simplest possible mechanisms and add functionality only as needed. It will be helpful during the discussion for you to keep in mind the two views of memory: the process sees its own memory, using its own addresses. We will call these *virtual addresses*, because they do not necessarily correspond to any physical reality. By contrast, to the memory system, there are only *physical addresses* — real locations in memory. From the memory system perspective, it is given physical addresses and it does lookups and stores values. The translation mechanism converts between the two views: from a virtual address to a physical memory address.

virtual address

physical address

8.2 | Towards flexible address translation

Our discussion of hardware address translation is divided into two steps. First, we put the issue of lookup efficiency aside, and instead consider how best to achieve the other goals listed above: flexible memory assignment, space efficiency, fine-grained protection and sharing, and so forth. Once we have the features we want, we will then add mechanisms to gain back lookup efficiency.

In Chapter 2, we illustrated the notion of hardware memory protection using the simplest hardware imaginable: base and bounds. The translation box consists of two extra registers per process. The *base* register specifies the start of the process' region of physical memory; the *bound* register specifies the extent of that region. If the base register is added to every address generated by the program, then we no longer need a relocating loader — the virtual addresses of the program start from 0 and go to bound, and the physical addresses start from base and go to base + bound. Figure 8.2 shows an example of base and bounds translation. Since physical memory can contain several processes, the kernel resets the contents of the base and bounds registers on each process context switch to the appropriate values for that process.

Base and bounds translation is both simple and fast, but it lacks many of the features needed to support modern programs. Base and bounds

Address translation in linkers and loaders

Even without the kernel-user boundary, multiprogramming requires some form of address translation. On a multiprogramming system, when a program is compiled, the compiler does not know which regions of physical memory will already in use by other applications and therefore cannot control where in physical memory the program will land. The machine instructions for a program contains both relative and absolute addresses; relative addresses, such as to branch forward or backward a certain number of instructions, continue to work regardless of where in memory the program is located. However, some instructions contain absolute addresses, such as to load a global variable or to jump to the start of a procedure. These will stop working unless the program is loaded into memory exactly where the compiler expects it to go.

Before hardware translation became commonplace, early operating systems dealt with this issue by using a *relocating loader* for copying programs into memory. Once the operating system picked an empty region of physical memory for the program, the loader would modify any instructions in the program that used an absolute address. To simplify the implementation, there was a table at the beginning of the executable image that listed all of the absolute addresses used in the program. In modern systems, this is called a *symbol table*.

Today, we still have something similar. Complex programs often have multiple files, each of which can be compiled independently and then *linked* together to form the executable image. When the compiler generates the machine instructions for a single file, it cannot know where in the executable this particular file will go. Instead, the compiler generates a symbol table at the beginning of each compiled file, indicating which values will need to be modified when the individual files are assembled together.

Most commercial operating systems today support the option of dynamic linking, taking the notion of a relocating loader one step further. With a dynamically linked library (DLL), a library is linked into a running program on demand, when the program first calls into the library. We will explain in a bit how the code for a DLL can be shared between multiple different processes, but the linking procedure is straightforward. A table of valid entry points into the DLL is kept by the compiler; the calling program indirects through this table to reach the library routine.

translation supports only coarse-grained protection at the level of the entire process; it is not possible to prevent a program from overwriting its own code, for example. It is also difficult to share regions of memory between two processes. Since the memory for a process needs to be contiguous, supporting dynamic memory regions, such as for heaps, thread stacks, or memory mapped files, becomes difficult to impossible.

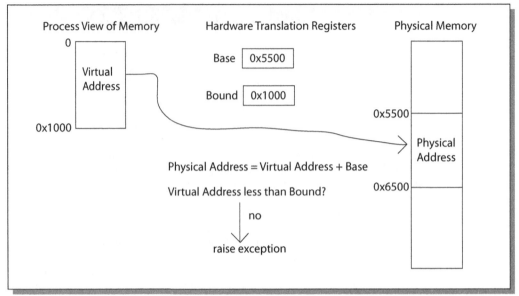

Figure 8.2: Address translation with base and bounds registers. The virtual address is added to the base to generate the physical address; the bound register is checked against the virtual address to prevent a process from reading or writing outside of its allocated memory region.

Segmented Memory

segmentation

Many of the limitations of base and bounds translation can be remedied with a small change: instead of keeping only a single pair of base and bounds registers per process, the hardware can support an array of pairs of base and bounds registers, for each process. This is called *segmentation*. Each entry in the array controls a portion, or *segment*, of the virtual address space. The physical memory for each segment is stored contiguously, but different segments can be stored at different locations. Figure 8.3 shows segment translation in action. The high order bits of the virtual address are used to index into the array; the rest of the address is then treated as above — added to the base and checked against the bound stored at that index. In addition, the operating system can assign different segments different permissions, e.g., to allow execute-only access to code and read-write access to data. Although only three segments are shown in the figure, in general the number of segments is determined by the number of bits for the segment number that are set aside in the virtual address.

It should seem odd to you that segmented memory has gaps; program memory is no longer a single contiguous region, but instead it is a set of regions. Each different segment starts at a new segment boundary. For example, code and data are not immediately adjacent to each other in either the virtual or physical address space.

What happens if a program branches into or tries to load data from one

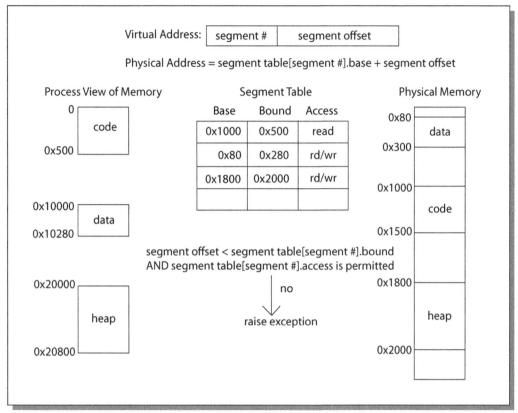

Figure 8.3: Address translation with a segment table. The virtual address has two components: a segment number and a segment offset. The segment number indexes into the segment table to locate the start of the segment in physical memory. The bound register is checked against the segment offset to prevent a process from reading or writing outside of its allocated memory region. Processes can be have restricted rights to certain segments, e.g., to prevent writes to the code segment.

segmentation fault

of these gaps? The hardware will generate an exception, trapping into the operating system kernel. On UNIX systems, this is still called a *segmentation fault*, that is, a reference outside of a legal segment of memory. How does a program keep from wandering into one of these gaps? Correct programs will not generate references outside of valid memory. Put another way, trying to execute code or reading data that doesn't exist is probably an indication that the program has a bug in it.

Although simple to implement and manage, segmented memory is both remarkably powerful and widely used. For example, the x86 architecture is segmented (with some enhancements that we will describe later). With segments, the operating system can allow processes to share some regions of memory while keeping other regions protected. For example, two processes can share a code segment by setting up an entry in their segment

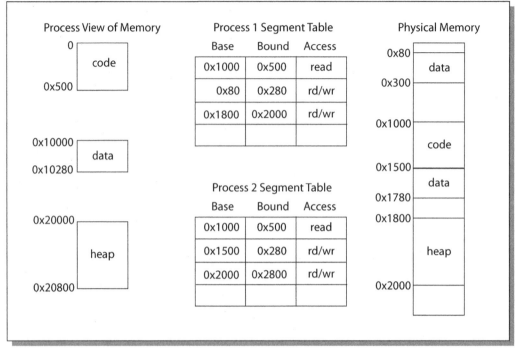

Figure 8.4: Two processes sharing a code segment, but with separate data and stack segments. In this case, each process uses the same virtual addresses, but these virtual addresses map to either the same region of physical memory (if code) or different regions of physical memory (if data).

tables to point to the same region of physical memory — to use the same base and bounds. The processes can share the same code while working off different data, by setting up the segment table to point to different regions of physical memory for the data segment. We illustrate this in Figure 8.4.

Likewise, shared library routines, such as a graphics library, can be placed into a segment and shared between processes. As before, the library data would be in a separate, non-shared segment. This is frequently done in modern operating systems with dynamically linked libraries. A practical issue is that different processes may load different numbers of libraries, and so may assign the same library a different segment number. Depending on the processor architecture, sharing can still work, if the library code uses *segment-local addresses*, addresses that are relative to the current segment.

segment-local address

We can also use segments for interprocess communication, if processes are given read and write permission to the same segment. Multics, an operating system from the 1960's that contained many of the ideas we now find in Microsoft's Windows 7, Apple's Mac OS X, and Linux, made extensive use of segmented memory for interprocess sharing. In Multics, a segment was allocated for every data structure, allowing fine-grained

UNIX fork and copy-on-write

In Chapter 3, we described the UNIX fork system call. UNIX creates a new process by making a complete copy of the parent process; the parent process and the child process are identical except for the return value from fork. The child process can then set up its I/O and eventually use the UNIX exec system call to run a new program. We promised at the time we would explain how this can be done efficiently.

With segments, this is now possible. To fork a process, we can simply make a copy of the parent's segment table; we do not need to copy *any* of its physical memory. Of course, we want the child to have be a copy of the parent, and not just point to the same memory as the parent. If the child changes some data, it should change only its copy, and not its parent's data. On the other hand, most of the time, the child process in UNIX fork simply calls UNIX exec; the shared data is there as a programming convenience.

We can make this work efficiently by using an idea called *copy-on-write*. During the fork, all of the segments shared between the parent and child process are marked "read-only" in both segment tables. If either side modifies data in a segment, an exception is raised and a full memory copy of that segment is made at that time. In the common case, the child process modifies only its stack before calling UNIX exec, and if so, only the stack needs to be physically copied.

---

protection and sharing between processes. Of course, this made the segment table pretty large! More modern systems tend to use segments only for coarser-grained memory regions, such as the code and data for an entire shared library, rather than for each of the data structures within the library.

As a final example of the power of segments, they enable the efficient management of dynamically allocated memory. When an operating system reuses memory or disk space that had previously been used, it must first zero out the contents of the memory or disk. Otherwise, private data from one application could inadvertently leak into another, potentially malicious, application. For example, you could enter a password into one web site, say for a bank, and then exit the browser. However, if the underlying physical memory used by the browser is then re-assigned to a new process, then the password could be leaked to a malicious web site.

Of course, we only want to pay the overhead of zeroing memory if it will be used. This is particularly an issue for dynamically allocated memory on the heap and stack. It is not clear when the program starts how much memory it will use; the heap could be anywhere from a few kilobytes to several gigabytes, depending on the program. The operating system can zero-on-reference address this using *zero-on-reference*. With zero-on-reference, the operating system allocates a memory region for the heap, but only zeroes the first few kilobytes. Instead, it sets the bound register in the segment table to limit the program to just the zeroed part of memory. If the program expands its heap, it will take an exception, and the operating system kernel can zero out additional memory before resuming execution.

Given all these advantages, why can't we stop here? The principal downside of segmentation is the overhead of managing a large number of variable size and dynamically growing memory segments. Over time, as processes are created and finish, physical memory will be divided into regions that are in use and regions that are not, that is, available to be allocated to a new process. These free regions will be of varying sizes. When we create a new segment, we will need to find a free spot for it. Should we put it in the smallest open region where it will fit? The largest open region?

However we choose to place new segments, as more memory becomes allocated, the operating system may reach a point where there is enough free space for a new segment, but the free space is not contiguous. This external frag- is called *external fragmentation*. The operating system is free to compact mentation memory to make room without affecting applications, because virtual addresses are unchanged when we relocate a segment in physical memory. Even so, compaction can be costly in terms of processor overhead: a typical server configuration would take roughly a second to compact its memory.

All this becomes even more complex when memory segments can grow. How much memory should we set aside for a program's heap? If we put the heap segment in a part of physical memory with lots of room, then we will have wasted memory if that program turns out to need only a small heap. If we do the opposite — put the heap segment in a small chunk of physical memory — then we will need to copy it somewhere else if it changes size.

Paged Memory

paged An alternative to segmented memory is *paged memory*. With paging, mem-
memory ory is allocated in fixed-sized chunks called *page frames*. Address translation
page frames is similar to how it works with segmentation. Instead of a segment table whose entries contain pointers to variable-sized segments, there is a page table for each process whose entries contain pointers to page frames. Because page frames are fixed-sized and a power of two, the page table entries only need to provide the upper bits of the page frame address, so they are more compact. There is no need for a "bound" on the offset; the entire page in physical memory is allocated as a unit. Figure 8.5 illustrates address translation with paged memory.

What will seem odd, and perhaps cool, about paging is that while a program thinks of its memory as linear, in fact its memory can be, and usually is, scattered throughout physical memory in a kind of abstract mosaic. The processor will execute one instruction after another using virtual addresses; its virtual addresses are still linear. However, the instruction

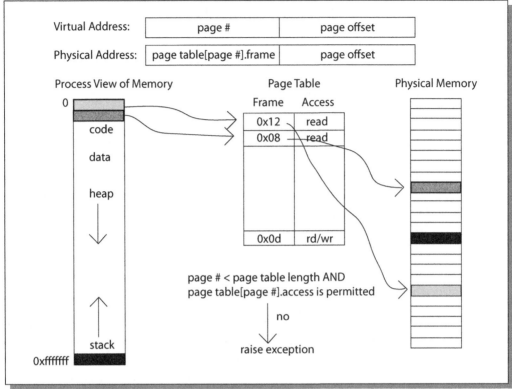

Figure 8.5: Address translation with a page table. The virtual address has two components: a virtual page number and an offset within the page. The virtual page number indexes into the page table to yield a page frame in physical memory. The physical address is the physical page frame from the page table, concatenated with the page offset from the virtual address. The operating system can restrict process access to certain pages, e.g., to prevent writes to pages containing instructions.

located at the end of a page will be located in a completely different region of physical memory from the next instruction at the start of the next page. Data structures will appear to be contiguous using virtual addresses, but a large matrix may be scattered across many physical page frames.

An apt analogy is what happens when you shuffle several decks of cards together. A single process in its virtual address space sees the cards of a single deck in order. A different process sees a completely different deck, but it will also be in order. In physical memory, however, the decks of all the processes currently running will be shuffled together, apparently at random. The page tables are the magician's assistant: able to instantly find the queen of hearts from among the shuffled decks.

Paging addresses the principal limitation of segmentation: free-space allocation is very straightforward. The operating system can represent physical memory as a bit map, with each bit representing a physical page frame that is either free or in use. Finding a free frame is just a matter of finding an empty bit.

Sharing memory between processes is also convenient: we need to set the page table entry for each process sharing a page to point to the same physical page frame. For a large shared region that spans multiple page frames, such as a shared library, this may require setting up a number of page table entries. Since we need to know when to release memory when a finishes, shared memory requires some extra bookkeeping to keep track of whether the shared page is still in use. The data structure for this is called **core map** a *core map*; it records information about each physical page frame such as which page table entries point to it.

Many of the optimizations we discussed under segmentation can also be done with paging. For copy-on-write, we need to copy the page table entries and set them to read-only; on a store to one of these pages, we can make a real copy of the underlying page frame before resuming the process. Likewise, for zero-on-reference, we can set the page table entry at the top of the stack to be invalid, causing a trap into the kernel. This allows us to extend the stack only as needed.

Page tables allow other features to be added. For example, we can start a program running before all of its code and data are loaded into memory. Initially, the operating system marks all of the page table entries for a new process as invalid; as pages are brought in from disk, it marks those pages as read-only (for code pages) or read-write (for data pages). Once the first few pages are in memory, however, the operating system can start execution of the program in user-mode, while the kernel continues to transfer the rest of the program's code in the background. As the program starts up, if it happens to jump to a location that hasn't been loaded yet, the hardware will cause an exception, and the kernel can stall the program until that page is available. Further, the compiler can reorganize the program executable for more efficient startup, by coalescing the initialization pages into a few pages at the start of the program, thus overlapping initialization and loading the program from disk.

data As another example, a *data breakpoint* is request to stop the execution **breakpoint** of a program when it references or modifies a particular memory location. It is helpful during debugging to know when a data structure has been changed, particularly when tracking down pointer errors. Data breakpoints are sometimes implemented with special hardware support, but they can also be implemented with page tables. For this, the page table entry containing the location is marked read-only. This causes the process to trap to the operating system on every change to the page; the operating system can then check if the instruction causing the exception affected the specific location or not.

A downside of paging is that while the management of physical memory becomes simpler, the management of the virtual address space becomes more challenging. Compilers typically expects the execution stack to be contiguous (in virtual addresses) and of arbitrary size; each new procedure call assumes the memory for the stack is available. Likewise, the runtime library for dynamic memory allocation typically expects a contiguous heap. In a single-threaded process, we can place the stack and heap at opposite ends of the virtual address space, and have them grow towards each other, as shown in Figure 8.5. However, with multiple threads per process, we need multiple thread stacks, each with room to grow.

This becomes even more of an issue with 64-bit virtual address spaces. The size of the page table is proportional to the size of the virtual address space, not to the size of physical memory. The more sparse the virtual address space, the more overhead is needed for the page table. Most of the entries will be invalid, representing parts of the virtual address space that are not in use, but physical memory is still needed for all of those page table entries.

We can reduce the space taken up by the page table by choosing a larger page frame. How big should a page frame be? A larger page frame can waste space if a process does not use all of the memory inside the frame. This is called *internal fragmentation*. Fixed-size chunks are easier to allocate, but waste space if the entire chunk is not used. Unfortunately, this means that with paging, either pages are very large (wasting space due to internal fragmentation), or the page table is very large (wasting space), or both. For example, with 16 KB pages and a 64 bit virtual address space, we might need 2^{50} page table entries!

internal fragmentation

Multi-level translation

If you were to design an efficient system for doing a lookup on a sparse keyspace, you probably wouldn't pick a simple array. A tree or a hash table are more appropriate, and indeed, modern systems use both. We focus in this subsection on trees; we discuss hash tables afterwards.

Many systems use tree-based address translation, although the details vary from system to system, and the terminology can be a bit confusing. Despite the differences, the systems we are about to describe have similar properties. They support coarse and fine-grained memory protection and memory sharing, flexible memory placement, efficient memory allocation, and efficient lookup for sparse address spaces, even for 64-bit machines.

Almost all multi-level address translation systems use paging as the lowest level of the tree. The main differences between systems are in how they reach the page table at the leaf of the tree — whether using segments plus paging, or multiple levels of paging, or segments plus multiple levels of paging. There are several reasons for this:

- **Efficient memory allocation.** By allocating physical memory in fixed-size page frames, management of free space can use a simple bitmap.

- **Efficient disk transfers.** Hardware disks are partitioned into fixed-sized regions called sectors; disk sectors must be read or written in their entirety. By making the page size a multiple of the disk sector, we simplify transfers to and from memory, for loading programs into memory, reading and writing files, and in using the disk to simulate a larger memory than is physically present on the machine.

- **Efficient lookup.** We will describe in the next section how we can use a cache called a translation lookaside buffer to make lookups fast in the common case; the translation buffer caches lookups on a page by page basis. Paging also allows the lookup tables to be more compact, especially important at the lowest level of the tree.

- **Efficient reverse lookup.** Using fixed-sized page frames also makes it easy to implement the core map, to go from a physical page frame to the set of virtual addresses that share the same frame. This will be crucial for implementing the illusion of an infinite virtual memory in the next chapter.

- **Page-granularity protection and sharing.** Typically, every table entry at every level of the tree will have its own access permissions, enabling both coarse-grained and fine-grained sharing, down to the level of the individual page frame.

Paged segmentation

paged
segmentation

Let's start a system with only two levels of a tree. With *paged segmentation*, memory is segmented, but instead of each segment table entry pointing directly to a contiguous region of physical memory, each segment table entry points to a page table, which in turn points to the memory backing that segment. The segment table entry "bound" is used to describe the page table length, that is, the length of the segment in pages. Because paging is used at the lowest level, all segment lengths are some multiple of the page size. Figure 8.6 illustrates translation with paged segmentation.

Although segment tables are sometimes stored in special hardware registers, the page tables for each segment are quite a bit larger in aggregate, and so they are normally stored in physical memory. To keep the memory allocator simple, the maximum segment size is usually chosen to allow the page table for each segment to be a small multiple of the page size.

For example, with 32-bit virtual addresses and 4 KB pages, we might set aside the upper ten bits for the segment number, the next ten bits for the page number, and twelve bits for the page offset. In this case, assuming that each page table entry is 4 bytes, the page table for each segment would exactly fit into one physical page frame.

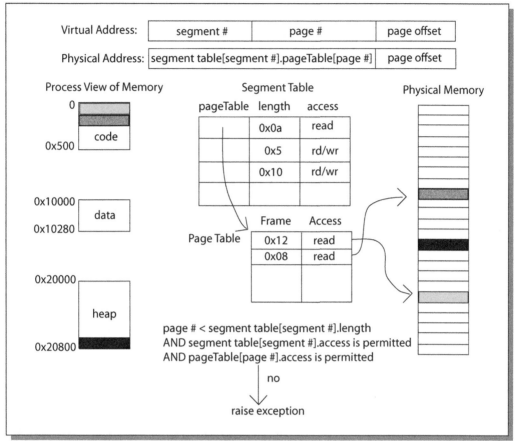

Figure 8.6: Address translation with paged segmentation. The virtual address has three components: a segment number, a virtual page number within the segment, and an offset within the page. The segment number indexes into a segment table that yields the page table for that segment. The page number from the virtual address indexes into the page table (from the segment table) to yield a page frame in physical memory. The physical address is the physical page frame from the page table, concatenated with the page offset from the virtual address. The operating system can restrict access to an entire segment, e.g., to prevent writes to the code segment, or to an individual page, e.g., to implement copy-on-write.

Multi-level paging

A nearly equivalent approach to paged segmentation is to use multiple levels of page tables. On the Sun Microsystems SPARC processor for example, there are three levels of page table. As shown in Figure 8.7, the top-level page table contains entries, each of which points to a second-level page table whose entries are pointers to page tables. On the SPARC, as with most other systems that use multiple levels of page tables, each level of page table is designed to fit in a physical page frame. Only the top-level page

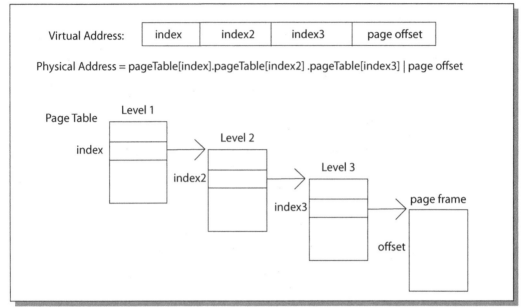

Virtual Address: | index | index2 | index3 | page offset |

Physical Address = pageTable[index].pageTable[index2] .pageTable[index3] | page offset

Figure 8.7: Address translation with three levels of page tables. The virtual address has four components: an index into each level of the page table and an offset within the physical page frame.

table is required to be filled in; the lower levels of the tree are allocated only if those portions of the virtual address space are in use by a particular process. Access permissions can be specified at each level, and so sharing between processes is possible at each level.

Multi-level paged segmentation

We can combine these two approaches by using a segmented memory where each segment is managed by a multi-level page table. This is the approach taken by the x86, for both its 32-bit and 64-bit addressing modes.

We describe the 32-bit case first. The x86 terminology differs slightly from what we have used here. The x86 has a per-process *Global Descriptor* *Table* (GDT), equivalent to a segment table. The GDT is stored in memory; each entry (descriptor) points to the (multi-level) page table for that segment along with the segment length and segment access permissions. To start a process, the operating system sets up the GDT and initializes a register, the *Global Descriptor Table Register (GDTR)*, that contains the address of the GDT and its length.

Because of its history, the x86 uses separate processor registers to specify the segment number (that is, the index into the GDT) and the virtual address for use by each instruction. For example, on the "32-bit" x86, there is both a segment number and 32 bits of virtual address within each segment. On the

Global Descriptor Table

64-bit x86, the virtual address within each segment is extended to 64 bits. Most applications only use a few segments, however, so the per-process segment table is usually short. The operating system kernel has its own segment table; this is set up to enable the kernel to access, with virtual addresses, all of the per-process and shared segments on the system.

For encoding efficiency, the segment register is often implicit as part of the instruction. For example, the x86 stack instructions such as push and pop assume the stack segment (the index stored in the stack segment register), branch instructions assume the code segment (the index stored in the code segment register), and so forth. As an optimization, whenever a code, stack, or data segment register is initialized on the x86, the hardware reads the GDT entry (that is, the top-level page table pointer and access permissions) into the processor, so the processor can go directly to the page table on each reference.

Many instructions also have an option to allow the segment index to be specified explicitly. For example, the ljmp, or long jump, instruction changes the program counter to a new segment number and offset within that segment.

For the 32-bit x86, the virtual address space within a segment has a two-level page table. The first 10 bits of the virtual address index the top level page table, called the *page directory*, the next 10 bits index the second level page table, and the final 12 bits are the offset within a page. Each page table entry takes four bytes and the page size is 4 KB, so the top-level page table and each second-level page table fits in a single physical page. The number of second-level page tables needed depends on the length of the segment; they aren't needed to map empty regions of virtual address space. Both the top-level and second-level page table entries have permissions, so fine-grained protection and sharing is possible within a segment.

The amount of memory per computer is now often well beyond what can be addressed with 32 bits; a top-end server can be configured with two terabytes of physical memory. For the 64-bit x86, virtual addresses within a segment can be up to 64 bits. However, to simplify address translation, current processors only allow 48 bits of the virtual address to be used; this is sufficient to map 128 terabytes, using four levels of page tables. The lower levels of the page table tree are only filled in if that portion of the virtual address space is in use.

As an optimization, the 64-bit x86 has the option to eliminate one or two levels of the page table. Each physical page frame on the x86 is 4 KB. Each page of fourth level page table maps 2 MB of data, and each page of the third level page table maps 1 GB of data. If the operating system places data such that the entire 2 MB covered by the fourth level page table is allocated contiguously in physical memory, then the page table entry one layer up can be marked to point directly to this region instead of to a page table. Likewise, a page of third level page table can be omitted if the operating system allocates the process a 1 GB chunk of physical memory. In addition to saving space needed for page table mappings, this improves translation buffer efficiency, a point we'll discuss in more detail in the next section.

Exercises

1. True or false. A virtual memory system that uses paging is vulnerable to external fragmentation. Why or why not?

2. For systems that use paged segmentation, what translation state does the kernel need to change on a process context switch?

3. For the three-level SPARC page table, what translation state does the kernel need to change on a process context switch?

4. Describe the advantages of an architecture that incorporates segmentation and paging over ones that are either pure paging or pure segmentation. Present your answer as separate lists of advantages over each of the pure schemes.

Portability

The diversity of different translation mechanisms poses a challenge to the operating system designer. To be widely used, we want our operating system to be easily portable to a wide variety of different processor architectures. Even within a given processor family, such as an x86, there are a number of different variants that an operating system may need to support. Main memory density is increasing both the physical and virtual address space by almost a bit per year. In other words, for a multi-level page table to be able to map all of memory, an extra level of the page table is needed every decade just to keep up with the increasing size of main memory.

A further challenge is that the operating system often needs to keep two sets of books with respect to address translation. One set of books is the hardware view — the processor consults a set of segment and multi-level page tables to be able to correctly and securely execute instructions and load and store data. A different set of books is the operating system view of the virtual address space. To support features such as copy-on-write, zero-on-reference, and fill-on-reference, as well as other applications we will describe in later chapters, the operating system must keep track of additional information about each virtual page beyond what is stored in the hardware page table.

This software memory management data structures mirror, but are not identical to, the hardware structures, consisting of three parts:

- **List of memory objects.** Memory objects are logical segments. Whether or not the underlying hardware is segmented, the kernel memory manager needs to keep track of which memory regions represent which underlying data, such as program code, library code, shared data between two or more processes, a copy-on-write region, or a memory-mapped file. For example, when a process starts up, the kernel can check the object list to see if the code is already in memory; likewise, when a process opens a library, it can check if it has already been linked by some other process. Similarly, the kernel can keep reference counts to determine which memory regions to reclaim on process exit.

- **Virtual to physical translation.** On an exception, and during system call parameter copying, the kernel needs to be able to translate from a process' virtual addresses to its physical locations. While the kernel could use the hardware page tables for this, the kernel also needs to keep track of whether an invalid page is truly invalid, or simply not loaded yet (in the case of fill-on-reference) or if a read-only page is truly read-only or just simulating a data breakpoint or a copy-on-write page.

- **Physical to virtual translation.** We referred to this above as the *core map*. The operating system needs to keep track of the processes that map to a specific physical memory location, to ensure that when the status of a page is updated, the kernel can also updated every page table that refers to it.

The most interesting of these are the data structures used for the virtual to physical translation. For the software page table, we have all of the same options as before with respect to segmentation and multiple levels of paging, as well as some others. The software page table need not use the same structure as the underlying hardware page table organization; indeed, if the operating system is to be easily portable, the software data structures may be quite different from the underlying hardware.

In Linux, the operating system's internal address translation data structures are modelled after the x86 architecture of segments plus multi-level page tables. This has made porting Linux to new x86 architectures relatively easy, but porting Linux to other architectures somewhat more difficult.

A different approach, taken first in a research system called Mach and later in Apple OS X, is to use a hash table, rather than a tree, for the software translation data. For historical reasons, the use of a hash table for paged address translation is called an *inverted page table*. Particularly as we move to deeper multi-level page tables, using a hash table for translation can speed up translation.

With an inverted page table, the virtual page number is hashed into a table of size proportional to the number of physical page frames. Each entry

inverted
page table

in the hash table contains tuples of the form (in the figure, the physical page is implicit):

```
inverted page table entry = {
    process or memory object ID,
    virtual page number,
    physical page frame number,
    access permissions
}
```

As shown in Figure 8.8, if there is a match on both the virtual page number and the process ID, then the translation is valid. Some systems do a two stage lookup: they first map the virtual address to a memory object ID, and then do the hash table lookup on the relative virtual address within the memory object. If memory is mostly shared, this can save space in the hash table without unduly slowing the translation.

An inverted page table does need some way to handle hash collisions, when two virtual addresses map to the same hash table entry. Standard techniques can be used for this, such as chaining or rehashing.

hint If the results are still valid, we can use the hint safely; if the results are invalid, there will A particularly useful consequence of having a portability layer for memory management is that the contents of the hardware multi-level translation table can be treated as a *hint*. A hint is a result of some computation whose results may no longer be valid, but where using an invalid hint will trigger an exception. If the results are still valid, we can use the hint safely; if the results are invalid, there will be an exception and we can trigger the recomputation.

With a portability layer, the software page table is the ground truth, while the hardware page table is a hint. The hardware page table can be safely used, provided that the translations and permissions are a *subset* of the translations in the software page table.

8.3 | Towards efficient address translation

At this point you should be getting a bit antsy. After all, most of the hardware mechanisms we have described involve at least two and possibly as many as four memory extra references, on each instruction, before we even reach the intended physical memory location! It should seem completely impractical for a processor to do several memory lookups on every instruction fetch, and even more that for every instruction that loads or stores data.

In this section, we will discuss how to improve address translation performance without changing its logical behavior. In other words, despite the optimization, every virtual address is translated to exactly the same

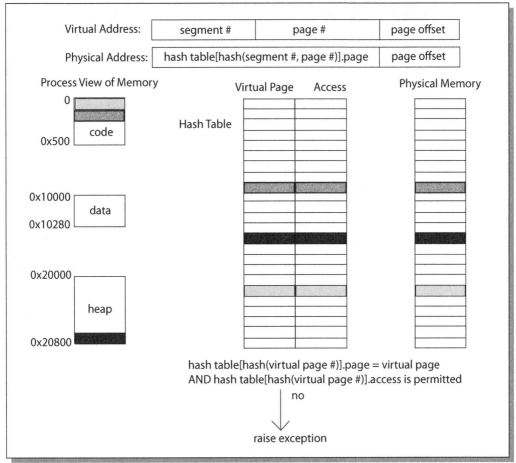

Figure 8.8: Address translation with a software hash table. The hardware page tables are omitted from the picture. The virtual page number is hashed; this yields a position in the hash table that indicates the physical page frame. The virtual page number must be checked against the contents of the hash entry to handle collisions and to check page access permissions.

physical memory location, and every permissions exception causes a trap, exactly as would have occurred without the performance optimization.

cache   For this, we will use a *cache*, a copy of some data that can be accessed more quickly than the original. This section concerns how we might use caches to improve translation performance. Caches are widely used in computer architecture, operating systems, distributed systems, and many other systems; in the next chapter, we discuss more generally when caches work and when they don't. For now, however, our focus is just on the use of caches for reducing the overhead of address translation. There's a reason for this: the very first hardware caches were used to improve translation performance.

Is an inverted page table enough?

The concept of an inverted page table raises an intriguing question: do we need to have a multi-level page table in hardware? Suppose, in hardware, we hash the virtual address. But instead of using the hash value to look up in a table where to find the physical page frame, suppose we just use the hash value *as* the physical page. For this to work, we need the hash table size to have exactly as many entries as physical memory page frames, so that there is a one-to-one correspondence between the hash table entry and the page frame.

We still need a table to store permissions and to indicate which virtual page is stored in each entry; if the process does not have permission to access the page, or if two virtual pages hash to the same physical page, we need to be able to detect this and trap to the operating system kernel to handle the problem. This is why a hash table for managing memory is often called called an *inverted page table*: the entries in the table are virtual page numbers, not physical page numbers. The physical page number is just the position of that virtual page in the table.

The drawback to this approach? Handling hash collisions becomes much harder. If two pages hash to the same table entry, only one can be stored in the physical page frame. The other has to be elsewhere — either in a secondary hash table entry or possibly stored on disk. Copying in the new page can take time, and if the program is unlucky enough to need to simultaneously access two virtual pages that both hash to the same physical page, the system will slow down even further. As a result, on modern systems, inverted page tables are typically used in software to improve portability, rather than in hardware, to eliminate the need for multi-level page tables.

Translation lookaside buffers

If you think about how a processor executes instructions with address translation, there are some obvious ways to improve performance. After all, the processor normally executes instructions in a sequence:

```
. . .
add r1 , r2
mult r1 , 2
. . .
```

The hardware will first translate the program counter for the add instruction, walking the multi-level translation table to find the physical memory where the add instruction is stored. When the program counter is incremented, the processor must walk the multiple levels again to find the physical memory where the mult instruction is stored. If the two instructions are on the same page in the virtual address space, then they will be on the same page in physical memory. The processor will just repeat the same work — the table walk will be exactly the same, and again for the next instruction, and the next after that.

translation lookaside buffer

A *translation lookaside buffer (TLB)* is a small hardware table containing the results of recent address translations. Each entry in the TLB maps a virtual page to a physical page:

```
TLB entry = {
    virtual page number,
    physical page frame number,
    access permissions
}
```

Instead of finding the relevant entry by a multi-level lookup or by hashing, the TLB hardware (typically) checks all of the entries simultaneously against the virtual page. If there is a match, the processor uses that entry to form the physical address, skipping the rest of the steps of address trans-

TLB hit

lation. This is called a *TLB hit*. On a TLB hit, the hardware still needs to check permissions, in case, for example, the program attempts to write to a code-only page or the operating system needs to trap on a store instruction to a copy-on-write page.

TLB miss

A *TLB miss* occurs if none of the entries in the TLB match. In this case, the hardware does the full address translation in the way we described above. When the address translation completes, the physical page is used to form the physical address, and the translation is installed in an entry in the TLB, replacing one of the existing entries. Typically, the replaced entry will be one that has not been used recently.

The TLB lookup is illustrated in Figure 8.9, and Figure 8.10 shows how a TLB fits into the overall address translation system.

Although the hardware cost of a TLB might seem large, it is modest compared to the potential gain in processor performance. To be useful, the TLB lookup needs to be much more rapid than doing a full address translation; thus, the TLB table entries are implemented in very fast, on-chip static memory, situated near the processor. In fact, to keep lookups rapid, many systems now include multiple levels of TLB. In general, the smaller the memory, the faster the lookup, so the first level TLB is small and close to the processor (and often split for engineering reasons into one for instruction lookups and a separate one for data lookups); if the first level TLB doesn't contain the translation, a larger second level TLB is consulted, and the full translation is only invoked if the translation misses both levels. For simplicity, our discussion will assume a single-level TLB.

A TLB also requires an address comparator for each entry to check in parallel if there is a match. Some TLB's are what is called *set associative*; this reduces the number of comparators needed, at some cost in terms of increasing the TLB miss rate. We will discuss set associativity, and its implications for operating system design, in the next chapter.

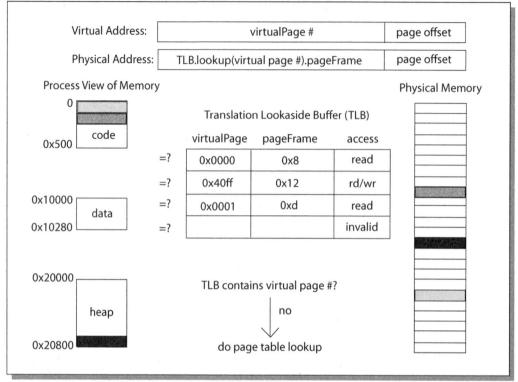

Figure 8.9: Operation of a translation lookaside buffer. In the diagram, each virtual page number is checked against all of the entries in the TLB at the same time; if there is a match, the matching table entry contains the physical page frame and permissions. If not, the hardware multi-level page table lookup is invoked; note the hardware page tables are omitted from the picture.

What is the performance of a TLB lookup? There are two factors: the cost of a successful lookup and the cost of an unsuccessful lookup, times their relative likelihoods. If $P(hit)$ is the likelihood that the TLB has the entry cached:

$$\text{Cost(address translation)} = \frac{\text{Cost(TLB lookup)}}{+\text{Cost(full translation)} \times (1 - P(hit))}$$

In other words, the processor designer needs to include a sufficiently large TLB that most addresses generated by a program will be found in the TLB, so that doing the full translation is the rare event. Even so, TLB misses are a significant cost for many applications.

Superpages

One way to improve the TLB hit rate is using a concept called superpages.
superpage   A *superpage* is a set of contiguous pages in physical memory that map

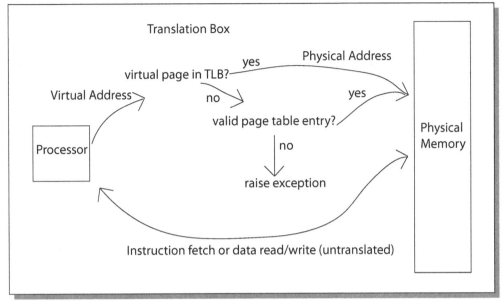

Figure 8.10: Combined operation of a translation lookaside buffer and hardware page tables.

Software-loaded TLB

If the TLB is effective at amortizing the cost of doing a full address translation across many memory references, we can ask a radical question: do we need hardware multi-level page table lookup on a TLB miss? This is the concept behind a software-loaded TLB. A TLB hit works as before, as a fast path. On a TLB miss, instead of doing hardware address translation, the processor traps to the operating system kernel. In the trap handler, the kernel is responsible for doing the address lookup, loading the TLB with the new translation, and restarting the application.

This approach dramatically simplifies the design of the operating system, because it no longer needs to keep two sets of page tables, one for the hardware and one for itself. On a TLB miss, the operating system can consult its own portable data structures to determine what data should be loaded into the TLB.

Although convenient for the operating system, a software-loaded TLB is somewhat slower for executing applications, as the cost of trapping to the kernel is significantly more than the cost of doing hardware address translation. As we will see in the next chapter, the contents of page table entries can be stored in on-chip hardware caches; this means that even on a TLB miss, the hardware can often find every level of the multi-level page table already stored in an on-chip cache, but not in the TLB. For example, a TLB miss on a modern generation x86 can be completed (in the best case) in the equivalent of 17 instructions. By contrast, a trap to the operating system kernel will take several hundred to a few thousand instructions to process, even in the best case.

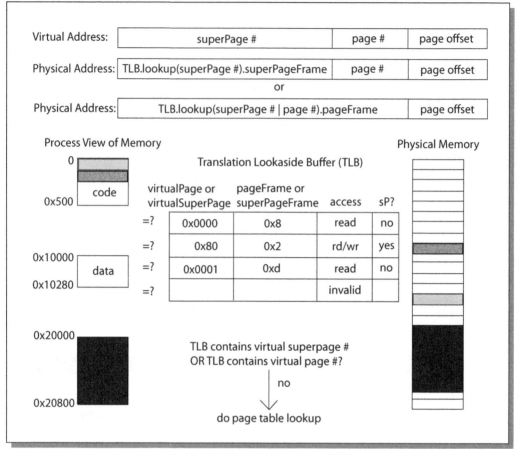

Figure 8.11: Operation of a translation lookaside buffer with superpages. In the diagram, some entries in the TLB can be superpages; these match if the virtual page is in the superpage. The superpage in the diagram covers an entire memory segment, but this need not always be the case.

a contiguous region of virtual memory, where the pages are aligned so that they share the same high-order (superpage) address. For example, an 8 KB superpage would consist of two adjacent 4 KB pages that lie on an 8 KB boundary in both virtual and physical memory. Superpages are at the discretion of the operating system — small programs or memory segments that benefit from a smaller page size can still operate with the standard, smaller page size.

Superpages complicate operating system memory allocation by opening up the possibility that chunks of memory can be allocated in different sizes. However, the upside is that a superpage can drastically reduce the number of TLB entries needed to map large, contiguous regions of memory. Each entry in the TLB has a flag, signifying whether the entry is a page or a superpage. For superpages, the TLB matches the superpage number — that

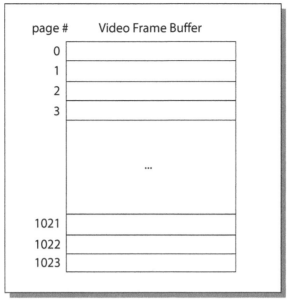

Figure 8.12: Layout of a high-resolution frame buffer in physical memory. Each line of the pixel display can take up an entire page, so that adjacent pixels in the vertical dimension lie on different pages.

is, it ignores the portion of the virtual address that is the page number within the superpage. This is illustrated in Figure 8.11.

To make this concrete, on the x86, a level (or two) of the page table can be skipped whenever there is a 2 MB (or 1 GB) region of physical memory that can be mapped as a unit. When the processor references one of these regions, only a single entry is loaded into the TLB. When looking for a match against a superpage, the TLB only considers the significant bits of the address, ignoring the offset within the superpage. For a 2 MB (1 GB) superpage, the offset is the lowest 21 (30) bits of the virtual address.

A common use of superpages is to more efficiently map the frame buffer for the computer display. When redrawing the screen, the processor may need to touch every pixel; with a high resolution display, this can involve stepping through hundreds of megabytes of memory. If each TLB entry maps a 4 KB page, even a large on-chip TLB with 256 entries would only be able to contain mappings for 1 MB of the frame buffer at the same time. Thus, the TLB would need to repeatedly do page table lookups to pull in new TLB entries is it steps through memory. An even worse case occurs when drawing a vertical line. The frame buffer is a two-dimensional array in row-major order, so that each horizontal line of pixels is on a separate page. Thus, modifying each separate pixel in a vertical line would require loading a separate TLB entry! With superpages, the entire frame buffer can be mapped with a single TLB entry, leaving more room for the other pages

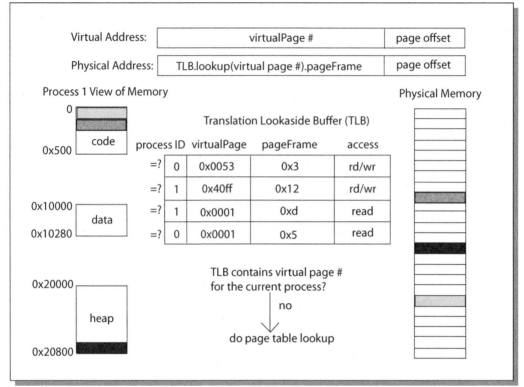

Figure 8.13: Operation of a translation lookaside buffer with process ID's. The TLB contains entries for multiple processes; only the entries for the current process are valid. The operating system kernel must change the current process ID when performing a context switch between processes.

needed by the application.

Similar issues occur with large matrices in scientific code.

TLB consistency

Whenever we introduce any type of cache into a system, we need to consider how best to achieve consistency of the cached copy with the original data it is based on, especially if the data is later modified. A TLB is no exception. To implement a secure protection boundary for application execution, and even simply for the correct execution of programs, the operating system must ensure that the each program sees its memory and no one else's. Any inconsistency between the TLB, the hardware multi-level translation table, and the portable operating system layer is a potential correctness and security flaw.

There are three issues to consider:

- **Process context switch.** What happens on a process context switch?

The virtual addresses of the old process are no longer valid, and should no longer be valid, for the new process. Otherwise the new process will be able to read the old process' data structures, either causing the new process to crash, or potentially allowing it to scavenge sensitive information such as passwords stored in memory.

On a context switch, we need to change the hardware pointer to the top level page table to be the that of the new process. But the TLB contains copies of the old process's page translations and its permissions. One approach is simply to discard the contents of the TLB on every context switch. Since this carries a performance penalty, modern processors have a *tagged TLB*, shown in Figure 8.13. Entries in a tagged TLB contain the process ID that generated each translation:

tagged TLB

```
tagged TLB entry = {
    process ID,
    virtual page number,
    physical page frame number,
    access permissions
}
```

With a tagged TLB, the operating system changes the pointer to the top level page table and the current process ID. This instructs the hardware to ignore translations from other processes sharing the processor, while allowing the hardware to reuse any TLB entries that remain from the last time the process executed.

- **Permission reduction.** What happens when the operating system modifies an entry in a hardware page table? On most processor architectures, special-purpose hardware keeps the copy of data in an on-chip cache consistent with the data stored in memory. However, hardware consistency is (usually) not provided for the TLB; rather keeping the TLB consistent with the hardware page table is the responsibility of the operating system kernel.

  This is for several reasons. First, page table entries can be shared between processes, and if so, a single modification can affect multiple TLB entries (e.g., one for each process sharing the page). Second, the TLB contains only the virtual to physical page mapping — it does not record the page table where the mapping came from. Even if it did, most stores to memory do not affect the page table, and so repeatedly checking each memory store to see if it affected any TLB entry would involve a large amount of overhead that would rarely be needed.

  Instead, the operating system is responsible for ensuring, whenever it changes the page table, that the TLB does not contain an incorrect mapping. One case is that the operating system is *adding permissions* to a portion of the virtual address space. For example, the operating

	process ID	virtualPage	pageFrame	access
Processor 1 TLB =?	0	0x53	0x3	rd/wr
=?	1	0x40ff	0x12	rd/wr
Processor 2 TLB =?	0	0x53	0x3	rd/wr
=?	0	1	0x5	read
Processor 3 TLB =?	1	0x40ff	0x12	rd/wr
=?	0	1	0x5	read

Figure 8.14: Illustration of the need for TLB shootdown to preserve correct translation behavior. In order for processor 1 to change the translation for page 0x53 in process 0 to read-only, it must remove the entry from its TLB, and it must ensure that no other processor has the old translation in its TLB. To do this, it sends an interprocessor interrupt to each processor, requesting it to remove the old translation. The operating system does not know if a particular TLB contains an entry (e.g., processor 3's TLB does not contain page 0x53), so it must remove it from all TLB's. The shootdown is complete only when all processors have verified that the old translation has been removed.

system can dynamically extend the heap or the stack by allocating physical memory and changing invalid page table entries to point to the new memory. In this case, the TLB can be left alone, as it cannot have cached any translations for those pages; any earlier reference to those pages would have caused an exception. Changing a page from read-only to read-write can be treated similarly.

However, if the operating system needs to *reduce permissions* to a page, then the kernel needs to ensure the TLB does not have a copy of the old translation before resuming the process. If the page was shared, the kernel needs to ensure that the TLB does not have the copy for any of the process ID's that might have referenced the page. For example, to mark a region of memory as copy-on-write, the operating system must reduce permissions to the region to read-only, and it must remove any entries for that region from the TLB, since the old TLB entries would still be read-write.

Early computers required the entire contents of the TLB to be discarded whenever there was a change to a page table, but more modern architectures, including the x86 and the ARM, support the removal of individual TLB entries.

- **TLB shootdown.** On a multiprocessor, there is a further complication. Any processor in the system may have a cached copy of a translation in its TLB. Thus, to be safe and correct, whenever a page table entry is modified, the corresponding entry in *every* processor's TLB has to be discarded before the change will take effect. Typically, only the current processor can invalidate its own TLB, so removing the entry from all processors on the system requires that the operating system interrupt each processor, and request it to remove the entry from its TLB.

TLB
shootdown

This heavyweight operation has its own name: it is a *TLB shootdown*, illustrated in Figure 8.14. The operating system first modifies the page table, then sends a TLB shootdown request to all of the other processors. Once another processor has ensured that its TLB has been cleaned of any old entries, it can resume. The original processor can continue only when *all* of the processors have acknowledged removing the old entry from their TLB. Since the overhead of a TLB shootdown increases linearly with the number of processors on the system, many operating systems batch TLB shootdown requests, to reduce the frequency of interprocess interrupts at some increased cost in latency to complete the shootdown.

Virtually addressed caches

Another step to improving the performance of address translation is to include a virtually addressed cache *before* the TLB is consulted, as shown in Figure 8.15. A virtually addressed cache stores a copy of the contents of physical memory, indexed by the virtual address. When there is a match, the processor can use the data immediately, without waiting for a TLB lookup or page table translation to generate a physical address, and without waiting to retrieve the data from main memory. Almost all modern multicore chips include a small, virtually addressed on-chip cache near each processor core. Often, like the TLB, the virtually addressed cache will be split in half, one for instruction lookups and one for data.

The same consistency issues that apply to TLB's also apply to virtually addressed caches:

- **Process context switch.** Entries in the virtually addressed cache must be either tagged with the process ID, or the contents must be invalidated on a context switch to prevent the new process from accessing the old process's data.

- **Permission reduction and shootdown.** When the operating system changes the permission for a page in the page table, the virtual cache will not reflect that change. Invalidating the affected cache entries would require either flushing the entire cache, or finding all memory

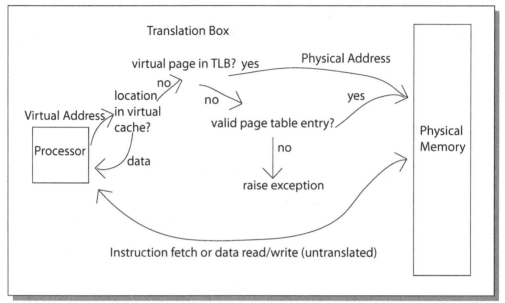

Figure 8.15: Combined operation of a virtually addressed cache, translation lookaside buffer and hardware page table.

locations stored in the cache on the affected page, both relatively heavyweight operations.

Instead, most systems with virtually addressed caches use them in tandem with the TLB. Each virtual address is looked up in both the cache and the TLB at the same time; the TLB specifies the permissions to use, while the cache provides the data if the access is permitted. This way, only the TLB's permissions need to be kept up to date. The TLB and virtual cache are co-designed to take the same amount of time to perform a lookup, so the processor does not stall waiting for the TLB.

A further issue is aliasing. Many operating systems allow processes sharing memory to use different virtual addresses to refer to the same memory location. This is called a *memory address alias*. Each process will have its own TLB entry for that memory, and the virtual cache may also store a separate copy of the memory, one for each process. The problem occurs when one process modifies its copy; how does the system know to update the other copy?

The most common solution to this issue is to store the physical address along with the virtual address in the virtual cache. In parallel with the virtual cache lookup, the TLB is consulted to generate the physical address and page permissions. On a store instruction modifying data in the virtual

memory
address alias

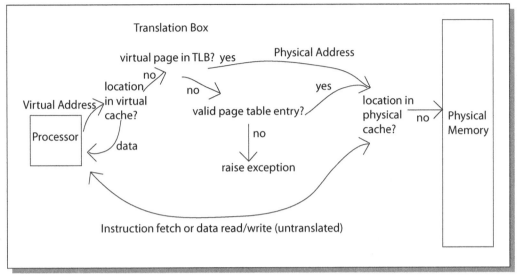

Figure 8.16: Combined operation of a virtually addressed cache, translation lookaside buffer, hardware page table, and physically addressed cache.

cache, the system can do a reverse lookup to find all the entries that match the same physical address, to allow it to update those entries.

Physically addressed caches

Many processor architectures include a physically addressed cache that is consulted as a second-level cache after the virtually addressed cache and TLB, but before main memory. This is illustrated in Figure 8.16. Once the physical address of the memory location is formed from the TLB lookup, the second-level cache is consulted. If there is a match, the value stored at that location can be returned directly to the processor without the need to go to main memory.

With today's chip densities, an on-chip physically addressed cache can be quite large. In fact, many systems include both a second-level and a third-level physically addressed cache. Typically, the second-level cache is per-core and will be optimized for latency; a typical size is 256 KB. The third-level cache is shared among all of the cores on the same chip and will be optimized for size; it can be as large as 2 MB on a modern chip. In other words, the entire UNIX operating system from the 70's, and all of its applications, would fit on a single modern chip, with no need to ever go to main memory.

Together, these physically addressed caches serve a dual purpose:

- **Faster memory references.** An on-chip physically addressed cache will have a lookup latency that is ten times (2nd level) or three times

(3rd level) faster than main memory.

- **Faster TLB misses.** In the event of a TLB miss, the hardware will generate a sequence of lookups through its multiple levels of page tables. Each page table lookup is a memory reference that will be routed through the on-chip physically addressed caches. Because the page tables are stored in physical memory, they can be cached in the same way as physical memory values. Thus, even a TLB miss and full page table lookup may, in fact, be handled entirely on chip.

Exercises

5. Consider the following piece of code which multiplies two matrices:

```
float a[1024][1024], b[1024][1024], c[1024][1024];

multiply() {
    unsigned i, j, k;
    for(i = 0; i < 1024; i++)
        for(j = 0; j < 1024; j++)
            for(k = 0; k < 1024; k++)
                c[i][j] += a[i,k] * b[k,j];
}
```

Assume that the binary for executing this function fits in one page, and the stack also fits in one page. Assume that storing a float (floating point number) takes 4 bytes of memory. If the page size is 4 KB, the TLB has 8 entries, and the TLB always keeps the most recently used pages, compute the number of TLB misses assuming the TLB is empty to begin with.

8.4 | Software protection

An increasing number of systems complement hardware-based address translation with software-based protection mechanisms. Obviously, software-only protection is possible. A machine code interpreter, implemented in software, can simulate the exact behavior of hardware protection. The interpreter could fetch each instruction, interpret it, look each address up in a page table to determine if the instruction is permitted, and if so, execute the instruction. Of course, that would be very slow!

In this section, we ask: are there practical software techniques to execute code within a restricted domain, without relying on hardware address translation? The focus of our discussion will be on using software for providing an efficient protection boundary, as a way of improving computer security. However, the techniques we describe can also be used to provide other operating system services, such as copy-on-write, stack extensibility, recoverable memory, and user-level virtual machines. Once you have the infrastructure to reinterpret references to code and data locations, whether in software or hardware, a number of services become possible.

Hardware protection is nearly universal on modern computers, so it is reasonable to ask, why do we need to implement protection in software?

- **Simplify hardware.** One goal is simple curiosity. Do we really need hardware address translation, or is it just an engineering tradeoff? If software can provide efficient protection, we could eliminate a large amount of hardware complexity and runtime overhead from computers, with a substantial increase in flexibility.

- **Application-level protection.** Even if we need hardware address translation to protect the operating system from misbehaving applications, we often want to run untrusted code within an application. An example is inside a web browser; web pages can contain code to configure the display for a web site, but the browser needs to protect itself against malicious or buggy code provided by web sites.

- **Protection inside the kernel.** We also sometimes need to run untrusted, or at least less trusted, code inside kernel. Examples include third-party device drivers and code to customize the behavior of the operating system on behalf of applications. Because the kernel runs with the full capability of the entire machine, any user code run inside the kernel must be protected in software rather than in hardware.

- **Portable security.** The proliferation of consumer devices poses a challenge to application portability. No single operating system runs on every embedded sensor, smartphone, tablet, netbook, laptop, desktop, and server machine. Applications that want to run across a wide range of devices need a common runtime environment that isolates the application from the specifics of the underlying operating system and hardware device. Providing protection as part of the runtime system means that users can download and run applications without concern that the application will corrupt the underlying operating system.

sandbox The need for software protection is widespread enough that it has its own term: how do we provide a software *sandbox* for executing untrusted code so that it can do its work without causing harm to the rest of the system?

Single language operating systems

A very simple approach to software protection is to restrict all applications to be written in a single, carefully designed programming language. If the

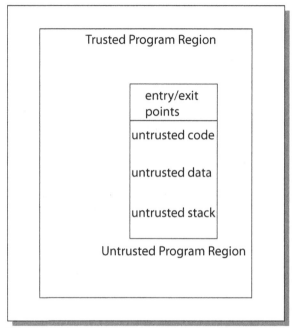

Figure 8.17: Execution of untrusted code inside a region of trusted code. The trusted region can be a process, such as a browser, executing untrusted JavaScript, or the trusted region can be the operating system kernel, executing untrusted packet filters or device drivers.

language and its environment permits only safe programs to be expressed, and the compiler and runtime system are trustworthy, then no hardware protection is needed.

A practical example of this approach that is still in wide use is UNIX packet filters, shown in Figure 8.18. UNIX packet filters allow users to download code into the operating system kernel to customize kernel network processing. For example, a packet filter can be installed in the kernel to make a copy of packet headers arriving for a particular connection and to send those to a user-level debugger.

A UNIX packet filter is typically only a small amount of code, but because it needs to run in kernel-mode, the system can't rely on hardware protection to prevent a misbehaving packet filter from causing havoc to unrelated applications. Instead, the system restricts the packet filter language to permit only safe packet filters. For example, filters may only branch on the contents of packets and no loops are allowed. Since the filters are typically short, the overhead of using an interpreted language is not prohibitive.

Another example of the same approach is the use of JavaScript in modern web browsers, illustrated in Figure 8.19. A JavaScript program customizes the user interface and presentation of a web site; it is provided by

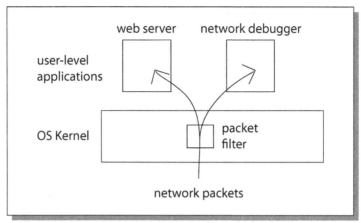

Figure 8.18: Execution of a packet filter inside the kernel. A packet filter can be installed by a network debugger to trace packets for a particular user or application. Packet headers matching the filter are copied to the debugger, while normal packet processing continues unaffected.

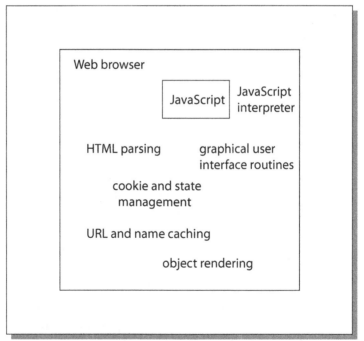

Figure 8.19: Execution of a JavaScript program inside a modern web browser. The JavaScript interpreter is responsible for containing effects of the JavaScript program to its specific page. JavaScript programs can call out to a broad set of routines in the browser, so these routines must also be protected against malicious JavaScript programs.

Language protection and garbage collection

JavaScript, Lisp, and Smalltalk all provide memory-compacting garbage collection for dynamically created data structures. One motivation for this is programmer convenience and to reduce avoidable programmer error. However, there is a close relationship between software protection and garbage collection. Garbage collection requires the runtime system to keep track of all valid pointers visible to the program, so that data structures can be relocated without affecting program behavior. Programs expressible in the language cannot point to or jump to arbitrary memory locations, as then the behavior of the program would be altered by the garbage collector. Every address generated by the program is necessarily within the region of the application's code, and every load and store instruction is to the program's data, and no one else's. In other words, this is exactly what is needed for software protection!

the web site, but it executes on the client machine inside the browser. As a result, the browser execution environment for JavaScript must be carefully designed to prevent malicious Javascript programs from taking control over the browser and possibly the rest of the client machine. Since JavaScript programs tend to be relatively short, they are often interpreted; JavaScript can also call into a predefined set of library routines. If a JavaScript program attempts to call a procedure that does not exist or reference arbitrary memory locations, the interpreter will cause a runtime exception and stop the program before any harm can be done.

Several early personal computers were single language systems with protection implemented in software rather than hardware. Most famously, the Xerox Alto research prototype used software and not hardware protection; the Alto inspired the Apple Macintosh, and the language it used, Mesa, was a forerunner of Java. Other systems included the Lisp Machine, a computer that executed only programs written in Lisp, and computers that executed only Smalltalk (a precursor to Python).

Unfortunately, language-based software protection has some practical limitations, so that on modern systems, it is often used in tandem with, rather than as a replacement for, hardware protection. Using an interpreted language seems like a safe option, but it requires trust in both the interpreter and its runtime libraries. An interpreter is a complex piece of software, and any flaw in the interpreter could provide a way for a malicious program to gain control over the process, that is, to escape its protection boundary. Such attacks are common for browsers running JavaScript, although over time JavaScript interpreters have become more robust to these types of attacks.

Worse, because running interpreted code is often slow, many interpreted systems put most of their functionality into system libraries that can be

Cross-site scripting

Another JavaScript attack makes use of the storage interface provided to JavaScript programs. To allow JavaScript programs to communicate with each other, they can store data in cookies in the browser. For some web sites, these cookies can contain sensitive information such as the user's login authentication. A JavaScript program that can gain access to a user's cookies can potentially pretend to be the user, and therefore access the user's sensitive data stored at the server. If a web site is compromised, it can be modified to serve pages containing a JavaScript program that gathers and exploits the user's sensitive data. These are called *cross-site scripting attacks*, and they are also widespread.

compiled into machine code and run directly on the processor. For example, commercial web browsers provide JavaScript programs a huge number of user interface objects, so that the interpreted code is just a small amount of glue. Unfortunately, this raises the attack surface — any library routine that does not completely protect itself against malicious use can be a vector for the program to escape its protection. For example, a JavaScript program could attempt to cause a library routine to overwrite the end of a buffer, and depending on what was stored in memory, that might provide a way for the JavaScript program to gain control of the system. These types of attacks against JavaScript runtime libraries are widespread.

This leads most systems to use both hardware and software protection. For example, Microsoft Windows runs its web browser in a special process with restricted permissions. This way, if a system administrator visits a web site containing a malicious JavaScript program, even if the program takes over the browser, it cannot store files or do other operations that would normally be available to the system administrator. We know a computer security expert who runs each new web page in a separate virtual machine; even if the web page contains a virus that takes over the browser, and the browser is able to take over the operating system, the original, uninfected, operating system can be automatically restored by resetting the virtual machine.

A related approach is to write all the software on a system in a single, safe language, and then to compile the code into machine instructions that execute directly on the processor. Unlike interpreted languages, the libraries themselves can be written in the safe language. The Xerox Alto took this approach: both applications and the entire operating system were written in the same language, Mesa. Like Java, Mesa had support for thread synchronization built directly into the language. Even with this, however, there are practical issues. You still need to do defensive programming at the trust boundary — between untrusted application code

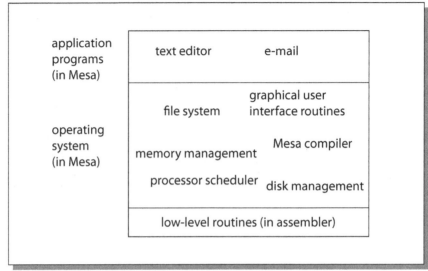

Figure 8.20: Design of the Xerox Alto operating system. Application programs and most of the operating system were implemented in a type-safe programming language called Mesa; Mesa isolated most errors to the code that caused the error.

(written in the safe language) and trusted operating system code (written in the safe language). You also need to be able to trust the compiler to generate correct code that enforces protection; any weakness in the compiler could allow a buggy program to crash the system. The designers of the Alto built a successor system, called the Digital Equipment Firefly, which used a successor language to Mesa, called Modula-2, for implementing both applications and the operating system. However, for an extra level of protection, the Firefly also used hardware protection to isolate applications from the operating system kernel.

Language-independent software fault isolation

A limitation of trusting a language and its interpreter or compiler to provide safety is that many programmers value the flexibility to choose their own programming language, to be suitable to the task at hand. For example, some might use Ruby for configuring web servers, Matlab or Python for writing scientific code, or C++ for large software engineering efforts.

Since it would be impractical for the operating system to trust every compiler for every possible language, can we efficiently isolate application code, in software without hardware support, in a programming language independent fashion?

One reason for considering this is that there are many cases where systems need an extra level of protection within a process. We saw an example of this with web browsers needing to safely execute JavaScript programs, but there are many other examples. With software protection, we could give users the ability to customize the operating system by downloading code into the kernel, as with packet filters, but on a more widespread basis. Kernel device drivers have been shown to be the primary cause of operating system crashes; providing a way for the kernel to execute device drivers in a restricted environment could potentially cut down on the severity of these faults. Likewise, many complex software packages such as databases, spreadsheets, desktop publishing systems, and systems for computer-aided design, provide their users a way to download code into the system to customize and configure the system's behavior to meet the user's specific needs. If this downloaded code causes the system to crash, the user won't be able to tell who is really at fault and is likely to end up blaming the vendor.

Of course, one way to do this is to rely on the JavaScript interpreter. Tools exist to compile code written in one language, like C or C++, into JavaScript. This lets applications written in those languages to run on any browser that supports JavaScript. If executing JavaScript were safe and fast enough, then we could declare ourselves done.

In this section, we discuss an alternate approach: can we take any chunk of machine instructions and modify it to ensure that the code does not touch any memory outside of its own region of data? That way, the code could be written in any language, compiled by any compiler, and directly execute at the full speed of the processor.

Both Google and Microsoft have products that accomplish this: a sandbox that can run code written in any programming language, executed safely inside a process. Google's product is called Native Client; Microsoft's is called AppDomain. These implementations are efficient: Google reports that the runtime overhead of executing code safely inside a sandbox is less than 10%.

For simplicity of our discussion, we'll assume that the memory region for the sandbox is contiguous, that is, the sandbox has a base and bound that needs to be enforced in software. Because we can disallow the execution of obviously malicious code, we can start by checking that the code in the sandbox does not use self-modifying instructions or privileged instructions.

We proceed in two steps. First, we insert machine instructions into the executable to do what hardware protection would have done, that is, to check that each address is legally within the region specified by the base and bounds, and to raise an exception if not. Second, we use control and data flow analysis to remove checks that aren't strictly necessary for the sandbox to be correct. This mirrors what we did for hardware translation — first, we designed a very general-purpose and flexible mechanism, and then we showed how to optimize it using TLB's so that the full translation mechanism wasn't needed on every instruction.

The added instructions for every load and store instruction are simple: just add a check that the address to be used by each load or store instruction is within the correct region of data. In the code, r1 is a machine register.

```
test  r1 ,  data.base
if  less−than ,  branch  to  exception
test  r1 ,  data.bound
if  greater−than ,  branch  to  exception
store  data  at  r1
```

Note that the store instructions must be limited to just the data region of the sandbox; otherwise a store could modify the instruction sequence, e.g., to cause a jump out of the protected region.

We also need to check indirect branch instructions. We need to make sure the program cannot branch outside of the sandbox except for predefined entry and exit points. Relative branches and named procedure calls can be directly verified. Indirect branches and procedure returns jump to a location stored in a register or in memory; the address must be checked before use.

```
test  r1 ,  code.base
if  less−than ,  branch  to  exception
test  r1 ,  code.bound
if  greater−than ,  branch  to  exception
jump  to  r1
```

As a final detail, the above code verifies that indirect branch instructions stay within the code region. This turns out to be insufficient for protection, for two reasons. First, x86 code is byte addressable, and if you allow a jump to the middle of an instruction, you cannot be guaranteed as to what the code will do. In particular, an erroneous or malicious program might jump to the middle of an instruction, whose bytes would cause the processor to jump outside of the protected region. Although this may seem unlikely, remember that the attacker has the advantage; the attacker can try various code sequences to see if that causes an escape from the sandbox. A second issue is that an indirect branch might jump past the protection checks for a load or store instruction. We can prevent both of these by doing all indirect jumps through a table that only contains valid entry points into the code; of course, the table must also be protected from being modified by the code in the sandbox.

Now that we have logical correctness, we can run control and data flow analysis to eliminate many of the extra inserted instructions, if it can be proven that they aren't needed. Examples of possible optimizations include:

- **Loop invariants.** If a loop strides through memory, the sandbox may be able to prove with a simple test at the beginning of the loop that all memory accesses in the loop will be within the protected region.

Virtual machines without kernel support

Modifying machine code to transparently change the behavior of a program, while still enforcing protection, can be used for other purposes. One application is transparently executing a guest operating system inside a user-level process without kernel support.

Normally, when we run a guest operating system in a virtual machine, the hardware catches any privileged instructions executed by the guest kernel and traps into the host kernel. The host kernel emulates the instructions and returns control back to the guest kernel at the instruction immediately after the hardware exception. This allows the host kernel to emulate privilege levels, interrupts, exceptions, and kernel management of hardware page tables.

What happens if we are running on top of an operating system that does not support a virtual machine? We can still emulate a virtual machine by modifying the machine code of the guest operating system kernel. For example, we can convert instructions to enable and disable interrupts to a no op. We can convert an instruction to start executing a user program to take the contents of the application memory, re-write those contents into a user-level sandbox, and start it executing. From the perspective of the guest kernel, the application program execution looks normal; it is the sandbox that keeps the application program from corrupting kernel's data structures and passes control to the guest kernel when the application makes a system call.

Because of the widespread use of virtual machines, some hardware architectures have begun to add support for directly executing guest operating systems in user-mode without kernel support. We will return to this issue in a later chapter, as it is closely related to the topic of stackable virtual machines: how do we manipulate page tables to handle the case where the guest operating system is itself a virtual machine monitor running a virtual machine.

- **Return values.** If static code analysis of a procedure can prove that the procedure does not modify the return program counter stored on the stack, the return can be made safely without further checks.

- **Cross-procedure checks.** If the code analysis can prove that a parameter is always checked before it is passed as an argument to a subroutine, it need not be checked when it is used inside the procedure.

Sandboxes via intermediate code

To improve portability, both Microsoft and Google can construct their sandboxes from intermediate code generated by the compiler. This makes it easier for the system to do the code modification and data flow analysis to enforce the sandbox. Instead of generating x86 or ARM code directly, the various compilers generate their code in the intermediate language, and the sandbox runtime converts that into sandboxed code on the specific processor architecture.

The intermediate representation can be thought of as a virtual machine, with a simpler instruction set. From the compiler perspective, it is as easy to generate code for the virtual machine as it would be to go directly to x86 or ARM instructions. From the sandbox perspective though, using a virtual machine as the intermediate representation is much simpler. The intermediate code can include annotations as to which pointers can be proven to be safe and which must be checked before use. For example, pointers in a C program would require runtime checks while the memory references in a Java program may be able to be statically proven as safe from the structure of the code.

Microsoft has compilers for virtually every commercially important programming language. To avoid trusting all of these compilers with the safety of the system, the runtime is responsible for validating any of the type information needed for efficient code generation for the sandbox. Typically, verifying the correctness of static analysis is much simpler than generating it in the first place.

The Java virtual machine is also a kind of sandbox; Java code is translated into intermediate byte code instructions that can be verified at runtime as being safely contained in the sandbox. Several languages have been compiled into Java byte code, such as Python, Ruby and Javascript. Thus, Java can also be considered a language-independent sandbox. However, because of the structure of the intermediate representation in Java, it is more difficult to generate correct Java byte code for languages such as C or Fortran.

8.5 | Conclusions and future directions

Address translation is a powerful abstraction enabling a wide variety of operating system services. It was originally designed to provide isolation between processes and to protect the operating system kernel from misbehaving applications, but it is more widely applicable. It is now used to simplify memory management, to speed interprocess communication, to provide for efficient shared libraries, to map files directly into memory, and a host of other uses.

A huge challenge to effective hardware address translation is the cumulative effect of decades of Moore's Law: both servers and desktop computers today contain vast amounts of memory. Processes are now able to map their code, data, heap, shared libraries, and files directly into memory. Each of these segments can be dynamic; they can be shared across processes or private to a single process. To handle these demands, hardware systems have converged on a two-tier structure: a multi-level segment and page table to provide very flexible but space-efficient lookup, along with a TLB to provide time-efficient lookup for repeated translations of the same page.

Much of what we can do in hardware we can also do in software; a combination of hardware and software protection has proven attractive in a number of contexts. Modern web browsers execute code embedded in web pages in a software sandbox that prevents the code from infecting the browser; the operating system uses hardware protection to provide an extra level of defense in case the browser itself is compromised.

The future trends are clear:

- **Very large memory systems.** The cost of a gigabyte of memory is likely to continue to plummet, making ever larger memory systems practical. Over the past few decades, the amount of memory per system has almost doubled each year. We are likely to look back at today's computers and wonder how we could have gotten by with as little as a gigabyte of DRAM! These massive memories will require ever deeper multi-level page tables. Fortunately, the same trends that make it possible to build gigantic memories also make it possible to design very large TLBs to hide the increasing depth of the lookup trees.

- **Multiprocessors.** On the other hand, multiprocessors will mean that maintaining TLB consistency will become increasingly expensive. A key assumption for using page table protection hardware for implementing copy-on-write and fill-on-demand is that the cost of modifying page table entries is modest. One possibility is that hardware will be added to systems to make TLB shootdown a much cheaper operation, e.g., by making TLB's cache coherent. Another possibility is to follow the trend towards software sandboxes. If TLB shootdown remains expensive, we may start to see copy-on-write and other features implemented in software rather than hardware.

- **User-level sandboxes.** Applications like browsers that run untrusted code are becoming increasingly prevalent. Operating systems have only recently begun to recognize the need to support these types of applications. Software protection has become common, both at the language level with JavaScript, and in the runtime system with NativeClient and AppDomains. As these technologies become more widely used, it seems likely we may direct hardware support for application-level protection — to allow each application to set up its own protected execution environment, but enforced in hardware. If so, we may come to think of many applications as having their own embedded operating system, and the underlying operating system kernel as mediating between these operating systems.

Exercises

For convenience, the exercises from the body of the chapter are repeated here, along with several additional problems.

1. True or false. A virtual memory system that uses paging is vulnerable to external fragmentation. Why or why not?

2. For systems that use paged segmentation, what translation state does the kernel need to change on a process context switch?

3. For the three-level SPARC page table, what translation state does the kernel need to change on a process context switch?

4. Describe the advantages of an architecture that incorporates segmentation and paging over ones that are either pure paging or pure segmentation. Present your answer as separate lists of advantages over each of the pure schemes.

5. Consider the following piece of code which multiplies two matrices:

```
float a[1024][1024], b[1024][1024], c[1024][1024];

multiply () {
    unsigned i, j, k;
    for (i = 0; i < 1024; i++)
        for (j = 0; j < 1024; j++)
            for (k = 0; k < 1024; k++)
                c[i][j] += a[i,k] * b[k,j];
}
```

   Assume that the binary for executing this function fits in one page, and the stack also fits in one page. Assume that storing a float (floating point number) takes 4 bytes of memory. If the page size is 4 KB, the TLB has 8 entries, and the TLB always keeps the most recently used pages, compute the number of TLB misses assuming the TLB is empty to begin with.

6. Of the following items, which are stored in the thread control block, which are stored in the process control block, and which in neither?

   a) CPU registers

   b) Page table pointer

   c) Page table

   d) Stack pointer

   e) Ready list

   f) Segment table

   g) Program counter

7. Draw the segment and page table for the 32-bit Intel architecture.

8. Draw the segment and page table for the 64-bit Intel architecture.

9. For a computer architecture with multi-level paging, a page size of 4 KB, and 64-bit physical and virtual addresses:

   a) What is the smallest possible size for a page table entry, rounded up to a power of two?

   b) Using your result above, and assuming a requirement that each page table fits into a single page, how many levels of page tables would be required to completely map the 64-bit virtual address space?

10. Suppose you are designing a system with paged segmentation, and you anticipate the memory segment size will be uniformly distributed between 0 and 4 GB. The overhead of the design is the sum of the internal fragmentation and the space taken up by the page tables. If each page table entry uses four bytes per page, what page size minimizes overhead?

11. In an architecture with paged segmentation, the 32-bit virtual address is divided into fields as follows:

4 bit segment number	12 bit page number	16 bit offset

The segment and page tables are as follows (all values in hexadecimal):

Segment Table		Page Table A		Page Table B	
0	Page Table A	0	CAFE	0	F000
1	Page Table B	1	DEAD	1	D8BF
x	(rest invalid)	2	BEEF	2	3333
		3	BA11	x	(rest invalid)
		x	(rest invalid)		

Find the physical address corresponding to each of the following virtual addresses (answer "invalid virtual address" if the virtual address is invalid):

   a) 00000000

   b) 20022002

   c) 10015555

12. Suppose a machine with 32-bit virtual addresses and 40-bit physical addresses is designed with a two-level page table, subdividing the virtual address into three pieces as follows:

10 bit page table number	10 bit page number	12 bit offset

The first 10 bits are the index into the top-level page table, the second 10 bits are the index into the second-level page table, and the last 12 bits are the offset into the page. There are 4 protection bits per page, so each page table entry takes 4 bytes.

   a) What is the page size in this system?

   b) How much memory is consumed by the first and second level page tables and wasted by internal fragmentation for a process that has 64K of memory starting at address 0?

   c) How much memory is consumed by the first and second level page tables and wasted by internal fragmentation for a process that has a code segment of 48K starting at address 0x1000000, a data segment of 600K starting at address 0x80000000 and a stack segment of 64K starting at address 0xf0000000 and growing upward (towards higher addresses)?

13. Write pseudo-code to convert a 32-bit virtual address to a 32-bit physical address for a two-level address translation scheme using segmentation at the first level of translation and paging at the second level. Explicitly define whatever constants and data structures you need (e.g., the format of the page table entry, the page size, and so forth).

Cash is king.

Per Gyllenhammar

9. Caching and Virtual Memory

Cash is king. – Per Gyllenhammar

Some may argue that we no longer need a chapter on caching and virtual memory in an operating systems textbook. After all, most students will have seen caches in an earlier machine structures class, and most desktops and laptops are configured so that they only very rarely, if ever, run out of memory. Maybe caching is no longer an operating systems topic?

We couldn't disagree more. Caches are central to the design of a huge number of hardware and software systems, including operating systems, Internet naming, web clients, and web servers. In particular, smartphone operating systems are often memory constrained and must manage memory carefully. Server operating systems make extensive use of remote memory and remote disk across the data center, using the local server memory as a cache. Even desktop operating systems use caching extensively in the implementation of the file system. Most importantly, understanding when caches work, and why they don't, is essential to every computer systems designer.

Consider a typical Facebook page. It is constructed with information about you, your interests and privacy settings, your posts, and your photos, plus your list of friends, their interests and privacy settings, their posts, and their photos. In turn, your friends' pages are constructed from an overlapping view of much of the same data, and in turn, their friends' pages are constructed the same way.

Now consider how Facebook organizes its data to make all of this work. How does Facebook assemble the data needed to display a page? One option would be to keep all of the data for a particular user's page in one place. However, the information that I need to draw my page overlaps with the information that my friends' friends need to draw their pages. My friends' friends' friends' friends include pretty much the entire planet. We can either store everyone's data in one place or spread the data around. Either way, performance will suffer! If we store all the data in California, Facebook will be slow for everyone from Europe, and vice versa. Equally, integrating data from many different locations is also likely to be slow, especially for Facebook's more cosmopolitan users.

cache   To resolve this dilemma, Facebook makes heavy use of caches; it would not be practical without them. A *cache* is a copy of a computation or data that can be accessed more quickly than the original. While the data underlying my page can change from moment to moment, it usually doesn't. In the common case, Facebook relies on a local, cached copy of the data for my page; it only goes back to the original source if the data is not stored locally or becomes out of date.

Caches work because both users and programs are predictable. You (probably!) don't change your friend list every nanosecond; if you did, Facebook could still cache your friend list, but it would be out of date before it could be used again, and so it wouldn't help. If everyone changed their friends every nanosecond, Facebook would be out of luck! In most cases, however, what users do now is predictive of what they are likely to do soon, and what programs do now is predictive of what they will do next. This provides an opportunity for a cache to save work through reuse.

Facebook is not alone in making extensive use of caches. Almost all large scale computer systems rely on caches. In fact, it is hard to think of any widely used, complex hardware or software system that does *not* include a cache of some sort.

We saw three examples of hardware caches in the previous chapter:

- **TLBs.** Modern processors use a translation lookaside buffer, or TLB, to cache the recent results of multi-level page table address translation. Provided programs reference the same pages repeatedly, translating an address is as fast as a single table lookup in the common case. The full multi-level lookup is needed only in the case where the TLB does not contain the relevant address translation.

- **Virtually addressed caches.** Most modern processor designs take this idea a step farther by including a virtually addressed cache close to the processor. Each entry in the cache stores the memory value associated with a virtual address, allowing that value to be returned more quickly to the processor when needed. For example, the repeated instruction fetches inside a loop are well-handled by a virtually addressed cache.

- **Physically addressed caches.** Most modern processors complement the virtually addressed cache with a second- (and sometimes third-)

level physically addressed cache. Each entry in a physically addressed cache stores the memory value associated with a physical memory location. In the common case, this allows the memory value to be returned directly to the processor without the need to go to main memory.

There are many more examples of caches:

- **Internet naming.** Whenever you type in a web request or click on a link, the client computer needs to translate the name in the link (e.g., amazon.com) to an IP network address of where to send each packet. The client gets this information from a network service, called the Domain Name System (DNS), and then caches the translation so that the client can go directly to the web server in the common case.

- **Web content.** Web clients cache copies of HTML, images, JavaScript programs, and other data so that web pages can be refreshed more quickly, using less bandwidth. Web servers also keep copies of frequently requested pages in memory so that they can be transmitted more quickly.

- **Web search.** Both Google and Bing keep a cached copy of every web page they index. This allows them to provide the copy of the web page if the original is unavailable for some reason. The cached copy may be out of date — the search engines do not guarantee that the copy instantaneously reflects any change in the original web page.

- **Email clients.** Many email clients store a copy of mail messages on the client computer to improve the client performance and to allow disconnected operation. In the background, the client communicates with the server to keep the two copies in sync.

- **Incremental compilation.** If you have ever built a program from multiple source files, you have used caching. The build manager saves and reuses the individual object files instead of recompiling everything from scratch each time.

- **Just in time translation.** Some memory-constrained devices such as smartphones do not contain enough memory to store the entire executable image for some programs. Instead, systems such as the Google Android operating system and the ARM runtime store programs in a more compact intermediate representation, and convert parts of the program to machine code as needed. Repeated use of the same code is fast because of caching; if the system runs out of memory, less frequently used code may be converted each time it is needed.

- **Virtual memory.** Operating systems can run programs that do not fit in physical memory by using main memory as a cache for disk.

Application pages that fit in memory have their page table entries set to valid; these pages can be accessed directly by the processor. Those pages that do not fit have their permissions set to invalid, triggering a trap to the operating system kernel. The kernel will then fetch the required page from disk and resume the application at the instruction that caused the trap.

- **File systems.** File systems also treat memory as a cache for disk. They store copies in memory of frequently used directories and files, reducing the need for disk accesses.

- **Conditional branch prediction.** Another use of caches is in predicting whether a conditional branch will be taken or not taken. In the common case of a correct prediction, the processor can start decoding the next instruction before the result of the branch is known for sure; if the prediction turns out to be wrong, the decoding is restarted with the correct next instruction.

In other words, caches are a central design technique to making computer systems faster. However, caches are not without their downsides. Caches can make understanding the performance of a system much harder. Something that seems like it should be fast — and even something that usually is fast — can end up being very slow if most of the data is not in the cache. Because the details of the cache are often hidden behind a level of abstraction, the user or the programmer may have little idea as to what is causing the poor performance. In other words, the abstraction of fast access to data can cause problems if the abstraction doesn't live up to its promise. One of our aims is to help you understand when caches do and don't work well.

In this chapter, we will focus on the caching of memory values, but the principles we discuss apply much more widely. Memory caching is common in both hardware (by the processor to improve memory latency) and in software (by the operating system to hide disk and network latency). Further, the structure and organization of processor caches requires special care by the operating system in setting up page tables; otherwise, much of the advantage of processor caches can evaporate.

Regardless of the context, all caches face three design challenges:

- **Locating the cached copy.** Because caches are designed to improve performance, a key question is often how to quickly determine whether the cache contains the needed data or not. Because the processor consults at least one hardware cache on every instruction, hardware caches in particular are organized for efficient lookup.

- **Replacement policy.** Most caches have physical limits on how many items they can store; when new data arrives in the cache, the system must decide which data is most valuable to keep in the cache and which can be replaced. Because of the high relative latency of fetching data from disk, operating systems and applications have focused more attention on the choice of replacement policy.

- **Coherence.** How do we detect, and repair, when a cached copy becomes out of date? This question, cache coherence, is central to the design of multiprocessor and distributed systems. Despite being very important, cache coherence beyond the scope of this version of the textbook. Instead, we focus on the first two of these issues.

The main ideas discussed in this chapter are:

- **Cache concept.** What operations does a cache do and how can we evaluate its performance?

- **Memory hierarchy.** What hardware building blocks do we have in constructing a cache in an application or operating system?

- **When caches work and when they don't.** Can we predict how effective a cache will be in a system we are designing? Can we know in advance when caching will *not* work?

- **Memory cache lookup.** What options do we have for locating whether an item is cached? How can we organize hardware caches to allow for rapid lookup, and and what are the implications of cache organization for operating systems and applications?

- **Replacement policies.** What options do we have for choosing which item to replace when there is no more room?

- **Case study: memory mapped files.** How does the operating system provide the abstraction of file access without first reading the entire file into memory?

- **Case study: virtual memory.** How does the operating system provide the illusion of a near-infinite memory that can be shared between applications? What happens if both applications and the operating system want to manage memory at the same time?

9.1 | Cache concept

We start by defining some terms. The simplest kind of a cache is a memory cache. It stores (address, value) pairs. As shown in Figure 9.1, when we need to read value of a certain memory location, we first consult the cache, and it either replies with the value (if the cache knows it) and otherwise

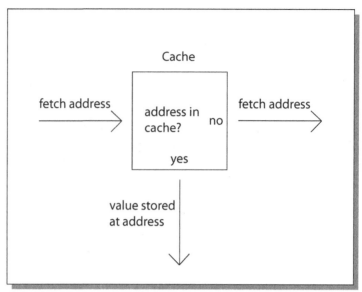

Figure 9.1: Abstract operation of a memory cache on a read request. Memory read requests are sent to the cache; the cache either returns the value stored at that memory location, or it forwards the request onward to the next level of cache.

it forwards the request onward. If the cache has the value, that is called a
cache hit   *cache hit*. If the cache does not, that is called a *cache miss*.

cache miss   For a memory cache to be useful, two properties need to hold. First, the cost of retrieving data out of the cache must be significantly less than fetching the data from memory. In other words, the cost of a cache hit must be less than a cache miss, or we would just skip using the cache.

Second, the likelihood of a cache hit must be high enough to make it
temporal   worth the effort. One source of predictability is *temporal locality*: programs
locality   tend to reference the same instructions and data that they had recently accessed. Examples include the instructions inside a loop, or a data structure that is repeatedly accessed. By caching these memory values, we can improve performance.

spatial   Another source of predictability is *spatial locality*. Programs tend to ref-
locality   erence data near other data that has been recently referenced. For example, the next instruction to execute is usually near to the previous one, and different fields in the same data structure tend to be referenced at nearly the same time. To exploit this, caches are often designed to load a block of data at the same time, instead of only a single location. Hardware memory caches often store 4-64 memory words as a unit; file caches often store data in powers of two of the hardware page size.

A related design technique that also takes advantage of spatial locality
prefetch   is to *prefetch* data into the cache before it is needed. For example, if the file system observes the application reading a sequence of blocks into memory,

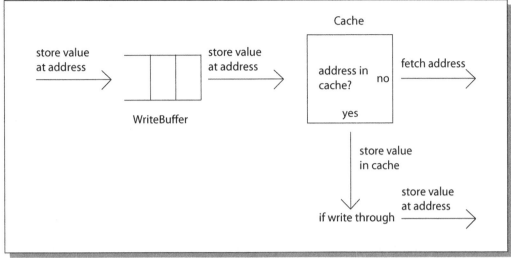

Figure 9.2: Abstract operation of a memory cache write. Memory requests are buffered, and then sent to the cache in the background. Typically, the cache stores a block of data, so each write must first ensure the rest of the block is in the cache, before updating the cache. If the cache is write through, the data is then sent onward to the next level of cache or memory.

it will read the subsequent blocks ahead of time, without waiting to be asked.

Putting these together, the latency of a read request is as follows:

$$\text{Latency}(\text{read request}) = \begin{array}{l} \text{Prob}(\text{cache hit}) \times \text{Latency}(\text{cache hit}) \\ + \text{Prob}(\text{cache miss}) \times \text{Latency}(\text{cache miss}) \end{array}$$

The behavior of a cache on a write operation is shown in Figure 9.2. The operation is a bit more complex, but the latency of a write operation is easier to understand. Most systems buffer writes. As long as there is room in the buffer, the computation can continue immediately while the data is transferred into the cache and to memory in the background. (There are certain restrictions on the use of write buffers in a multiprocessor system, so for this chapter, we are simplifying matters to some degree.) Subsequent read requests must check both the write buffer and the cache — returning data from the write buffer if it is the latest copy.

In the background, the system checks if the address is in the cache. If not, the rest of the cache block must be fetched from memory, and then **write-through cache** updated with the changed value. Finally, if the cache is *write-through*, all updates are sent immediately onward to memory. If the cache is *write-back*, **write-back cache** updates can be stored in the cache, and only sent to memory when the cache runs out of space and needs to evict a block to make room for a new memory block.

Cache	Hit Cost	Size
1st level cache/first level TLB	1 ns	64 KB
2nd level cache/second level TLB	4 ns	256 KB
3rd level cache	12 ns	2 MB
Memory (DRAM)	100 ns	10 GB
Data center memory (DRAM)	100 μs	100 TB
Local non-volatile memory	100 μs	100 GB
Local disk	10 ms	1 TB
Data center disk	10 ms	100 PB
Remote data center disk	200 ms	1 XB

Figure 9.3: Memory hierarchy, from on-chip processor caches to disk storage at a remote data center. On-chip cache size and latency is typical of a high-end processor. The entries for data center DRAM and disk latency assume the access is from one server to another in the same data center; remote data center disk latency if for access to a geographically distant data center.

Since write buffers allow write requests to appear to complete immediately, the rest of our discussion focuses on using caches to improve memory reads.

We first discuss the part of the equation that deals with the latency of a cache hit and a cache miss: how long does it take to access different types of memory? We caution, however, that the issues that affect the likelihood of a cache hit or miss are just as important to the overall memory latency. In particular, we will show that application characteristics are often the limiting factor to good cache performance.

9.2 | Memory hierarchy

When we are deciding whether to use a cache in the operating system or some new application, it is helpful to start with an understanding of the cost and performance of various levels of memory and disk storage.

From a hardware perspective, there is a fundamental tradeoff between the speed, size, and cost of storage. The smaller memory is, the faster it can be; the slower memory is, the cheaper it can be.

This motivates systems to have not just one cache, but a whole hierarchy of caches, from the nanosecond memory possible inside a chip to the multiple exabytes of worldwide data center storage. This hierarchy is illustrated by the table in Figure 9.3. We should caution that this list is just a snapshot; additional layers keep getting added over time.

- **First-level cache.** Most modern processor architectures contain a small first-level, virtually addressed, cache very close to the processor, designed to keep the processor fed with instructions and data at the clock rate of the processor.

- **Second-level cache.** Because it is impossible to build a large cache as fast as a small one, the processor will often contain a second-level, physically addressed cache to handle cache misses from the first-level cache.

- **Third-level cache.** Likewise, many processors include an even larger, slower third-level cache to catch second-level cache misses. This cache is often shared across all of the on-chip processor cores.

- **First- and second-level TLB.** The translation lookaside buffer (TLB) will also be organized with multiple levels: a small, fast first-level TLB designed to keep up with the processor, backed up by a larger, slightly slower, second-level TLB to catch first-level TLB misses.

- **Main memory (DRAM).** From a hardware perspective, the first-, second-, and third- level caches provide faster access to main memory; from a software perspective, however, main memory itself can be viewed as a cache.

- **Data center memory (DRAM).** With a high-speed local area network such as a data center, the latency to fetch a page of data from the memory of a nearby computer is much faster than fetching it from disk. In aggregate, the memory of nearby nodes will often be larger than that of the local disk. Using the memory of nearby nodes to avoid the latency of going to disk is called *cooperative caching*, as it requires the cooperative management of the nodes in the data center. Many large scale data center services, such as Google and Facebook, make extensive use of cooperative caching.

cooperative
caching

- **Local disk or non-volatile memory.** For client machines, local disk or non-volatile flash memory can serve as backing store when the system runs out of memory. In turn, the local disk serves as a cache for remote disk storage. For example, web browsers store recently fetched web pages in the client file system to avoid the cost of transferring the data again the next time it is used; once cached, the browser only needs to validate with the server whether the page has changed before rendering the web page for the user.

- **Data center disk.** The aggregate disks inside a data center provide enormous storage capacity compared to a computer's local disk, and even relative to the aggregate memory of the data center.

- **Remote data center disk.** Geographically remote disks in a data center are much slower because of wide-area network latencies, but they provide access to even larger storage capacity in aggregate. Many data centers also store a copy of their data on a remote robotic tape system, but since these systems have very high latency (measured in the tens of seconds), they are typically accessed only in the event of a failure.

If caching always worked perfectly, we could provide the illusion of instantaneous access to all the world's data, with the latency (on average) of a first level cache and the size and the cost (on average) of disk storage.

However, there are reasons to be skeptical. Even with temporal and spatial locality, there are thirteen orders of magnitude difference in storage capacity from the first level cache to the stored data of a typical data center; this is the equivalent of the smallest visible dot on this page versus those dots scattered across the pages of a million textbooks just like this one. How can a cache be effective if it can store only a tiny amount of the data that could be stored?

The cost of a cache miss can also be high. There are eight orders of magnitude difference between the latency of the first-level cache and a remote data center disk; that is equivalent to the difference between the shortest latency a human can perceive — roughly one hundred milliseconds — versus one year. How can a cache be effective if the cost of a cache miss is enormous compared to a cache hit?

Exercises

1. A computer system has a 1 KB page size and keeps the page table for each process in main memory. Because the page table entries are usually cached on chip, the average overhead for doing a full page table lookup is 40 ns. To reduce this overhead, the computer has a 32-entry TLB. A TLB lookup requires 1 ns. What TLB hit rate is required to ensure an average virtual address translation time of 2 ns?

9.3 | When caches work and when they don't

How do we know whether a cache will be effective for a given workload? Even the same program will have different cache behavior depending on how it is used.

Suppose you write a program that reads and writes items into a hash table. How well does that interact with caching? It depends on the size of the hash table. If the hash table fits in the first-level cache, once the table is

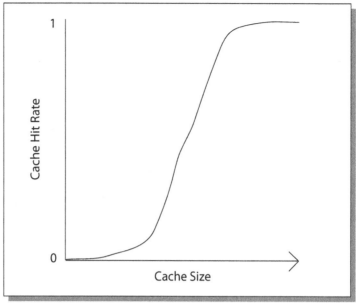

Figure 9.4: Cache hit rate as a function of cache size for a typical program. The knee of the curve is called the working set of the program.

loaded into the cache, each access will be very rapid. If on the other hand, the hash table is too large to store in memory, each lookup may require a disk access.

Thus, it is neither the cache size nor the program behavior, by themselves, that govern the effectiveness of caching, but rather the interaction between the two.

Working set model

A useful graph to consider is the cache hit rate versus the size of the cache. We give an example in Figure 9.4; of course, the precise shape of the graph will vary from program to program.

Regardless of the program, a sufficiently large cache will have a high cache hit rate. In the limit, if the cache can fit all of the program's memory and data, the miss rate will be zero once the data is loaded into the cache. At the other extreme, a sufficiently small cache will have a very low cache hit rate. Anything other than a trivial program will have multiple procedures and multiple data structures; if the cache is sufficiently small, each new instruction and data reference will push out something from the cache that will be used in the near future. For the hash table example, if the size of the cache is much smaller than the size of the hash table, each time we do a lookup, the hash bucket we need will no longer be in the cache.

Thrashing

A closely related concept to the working set is thrashing. A program thrashes if the cache is too small to hold its working set, so that most references are cache misses. Each time there is a cache miss, we need to evict a cache block to make room for the new reference. But the new cache block may in turn be evicted before it is reused.

The word "thrash" dates from the 1960's, when disk drives were as large as washing machines. If a program's working set did not fit in memory, the system would need to shuffle memory pages back and forth to disk. This burst of activity would literally make the disk drive shake violently, making it very obvious to everyone nearby why the system was not performing well.

working set

Most programs will have an inflection point, or knee of the curve, where a critical mass of program data can just barely fit in the cache. This critical mass is called the program's *working set*. As long as the working set can fit in the cache, most references will be a cache hit, and application performance will be good.

The notion of a working set can also apply to user behavior. Consider what happens when you are developing code for a homework assignment. If the files you need fit in memory, compilation will be rapid; if they don't, compilation will be slow as each file is brought in from disk as it is used.

Different programs, and different users, will have working sets of different sizes. Even within the same program, different phases of the program may have different size working sets. For example, the parser for a compiler needs different data in cache than the code generator. In a text editor, the working set shifts when we switch from one page to the next. Users also change their focus from time to time, as when you shift from a programming assignment to a history assignment.

phase change behavior

The result of this *phase change behavior* is that caches will often have bursty miss rates: periods of low cache misses interspersed with periods of high cache misses, as shown in Figure 9.5. Process context switches will also cause bursty cache misses, as the cache discards the working set from the old process and brings in the working set of the new process.

We can combine the graph in Figure 9.4 with the table in Figure 9.3 to see the impact of the size of the working set on computer system performance. A program whose working set fits in the first level cache will run four times faster than one whose working set fits in the second level cache. A program whose working set does not fit in main memory will run a thousand times slower than one who does, assuming it has access to data center memory. It will run a hundred thousand times slower if it needs to go to disk.

Because of the increasing depth and complexity of the memory hier-

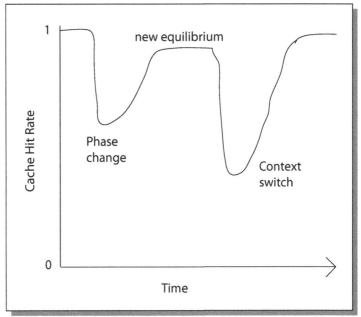

Figure 9.5: Example cache hit rate over time. At a phase change within a process, or due to a context switch between processes, there will be a spike of cache misses before the system settles into a new equilibrium.

archy, an important area of work is the design of algorithms that adapt their working set to the memory hierarchy. One focus has been on algorithms that manage the gap between main memory and disk, but the same principles apply at other levels of the memory hierarchy.

A simple example is how to efficiently sort an array that does not fit in main memory. (Equivalently, we could consider how to sort an array that does not fit in the first level cache.) As shown in Figure 9.6, we can break the problem up into chunks each of which does fit in memory. Once we sort each chunk, we can merge the sorted chunks together efficiently. To sort a chunk that fits in main memory, we can in turn break the problem into sub-chunks that fit in the on-chip cache.

We will discuss later in this chapter what the operating system needs to do when managing memory between programs that in turn adapt their behavior to manage memory.

Zipf model

Although the working set model often describes program and user behavior quite well, it is not always a good fit. For example, consider a *web proxy cache*. A web proxy cache stores frequently accessed web pages to speed web access and reduce network traffic. Web access patterns cause two

web proxy
cache

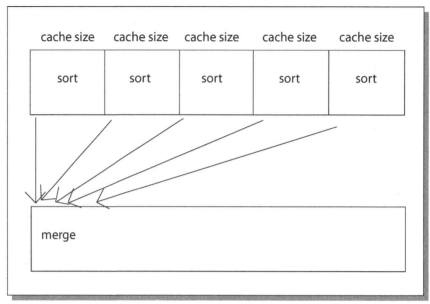

Figure 9.6: Algorithm to sort a large array that does not fit into main memory, by breaking the problem into pieces that do fit into memory.

challenges to a cache designer:

- **New data.** New data is being added to the web at a rapid rate, and the contents of pages changes rapidly. Every time a user accesses a page, the system needs to check whether the page has changed in the meantime.

- **No working set.** Although some web pages are much more popular than others, there is no small subset of web pages that, if cached, give you the bulk of the benefit. Unlike with a working set, even very small caches have some value. Conversely, increasing cache size yields diminishing returns: even very large caches tend to have only modest cache hit rates, as there are an enormous group of pages that are visited from time to time.

Zipf distribution   A useful model for understanding the cache behavior of web access is the *Zipf distribution*. Zipf developed the model to describe the frequency of individual words in a text, but it also applies in a number of other settings.

Suppose we have a set of web pages (or words), and we rank them in order of popularity. Then the frequency users visit a particular web page is (approximately) inversely proportional to its rank:

$$\text{Frequency of visits to the kth most popular page} \propto \frac{1}{k^{\alpha}}$$

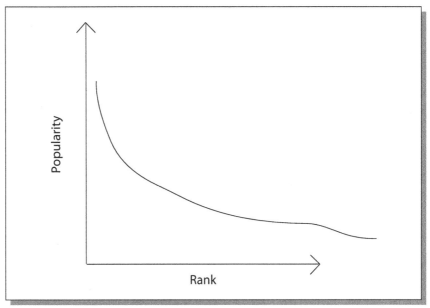

Figure 9.7: Zipf distribution

where α is value between 1 and 2. A Zipf probability distribution is illustrated in Figure 9.7.

The Zipf distribution fits a surprising number of disparate phenomena: the popularity of library books, the population of cities, the distribution of salaries, the size of friend lists in social networks, and the distribution of references in scientific papers. The exact cause of the Zipf distribution in many of these cases is unknown, but they share a theme of popularity in human social networks.

heavy tail   A characteristic of a Zipf curve is a *heavy tail*. Although a significant number of references will be to the most popular items, a substantial portion of references will be to less popular ones. If we redraw Figure 9.4 of the relationship between cache hit rate and cache size, but for a Zipf distribution, we get Figure 9.8. Note that we have rescaled the x axis to be log scale. Rather than a threshold as we see in the working set model, increasing the cache size continues to improve cache hit rates, but with diminishing returns.

Exercises

2. Most modern computer systems choose a page size of 4 KB.

    a) Give a set of reasons why doubling the page size might increase performance.

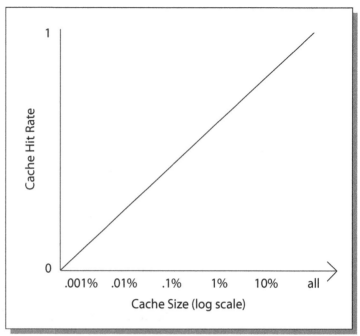

Figure 9.8: Cache hit rate as a function of the percentage of total items that can fit in the cache, on a log scale, for a Zipf distribution.

   b) Give a set of reasons why doubling the page size might decrease
      performance.

9.4 | Memory cache lookup

Now that we have outlined the available technologies for constructing caches, and the usage patterns that lend (or don't lend) themselves to effective caching, we turn to cache design. How do we find whether an item is in the cache, and what do we do when we run out of room in the cache? We answer the first question here, and we defer the second question to the next section.

A memory cache maps a sparse set of addresses to the data values stored at those addresses. You can think of a cache as a giant table with two columns: one for the address and one for the data stored at that address. To exploit spatial locality, each entry in the table will store the values for a block of memory, not just the value for a single memory word. Modern Intel processors cache data in 64 byte chunks. For operating systems, the block size is typically the hardware page size, or 4 KB on an Intel processor.

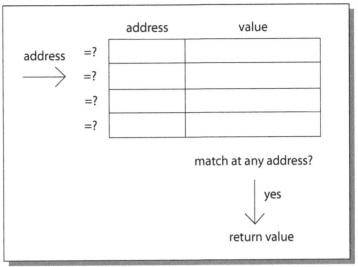

Figure 9.9: Fully associative cache lookup. The cache checks the address against every entry and returns the matching value, if any.

We need to be able to rapidly convert an address to find the corresponding data, while minimizing storage overhead. The options we have for cache lookup are all of the same ones we explored in the previous chapter for address lookup: we can use a linked list, a multi-level tree, or a hash table. Operating systems use each of those techniques in different settings, depending on the size of the cache, its access pattern, and how important it is to have very rapid lookup.

For hardware caches, the design choices are more limited. The latency gap between cache levels is very small, so any added overhead in the lookup procedure can swamp the benefit of the cache. To make lookup faster, hardware caches are often designed to constrain where in the table we might find any specific address. This constraint means that there could be room in one part of the table, but not in another, raising the cache miss rate. There is a tradeoff here: a faster cache lookup needs to be balanced against the cost of increased cache misses.

Three common mechanisms for cache lookup are:

- **Fully associative.** With a fully associative cache, the address can be stored anywhere in the table, and so on a lookup, the system must check the address against all of the entries in the table as illustrated in Figure 9.9. There is a cache hit if any of the table entries match. Because any address can be stored anywhere, this provides the system maximal flexibility when it needs to choose an entry to discard when it runs out of space.

We saw two examples of fully associative caches in the previous

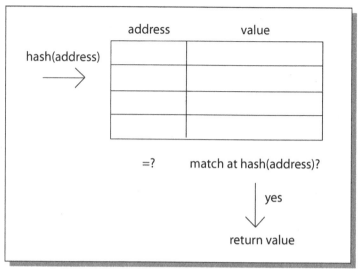

Figure 9.10: Direct mapped cache lookup. The cache hashes the address to determine which location in the table to check. The cache returns the value stored in the entry if it matches the address.

chapter. Until very recently, TLB's were often fully associative — the TLB would check the virtual page against every entry in the TLB in parallel. Likewise, physical memory is a fully associative cache. Any page frame can hold any virtual page, and we can find where each virtual page is stored using a multi-level tree lookup. The set of page tables defines whether there is a match.

A problem with fully associative lookup is the cumulative impact of Moore's Law. As more memory can be packed on chip, caches become larger. We can use some of the added memory to make each table entry larger, but this has a limit depending on the amount of spatial locality in typical applications. Alternately, we can add more table entries, but this means more lookup hardware and comparators. As an example, a 2 MB on-chip cache with 64 byte blocks has 32K cache table entries! Checking each address against every table entry in parallel is not practical.

- **Direct mapped.** With a direct mapped cache, each address can only be stored in one location in the table. Lookup is easy: we hash the address to its entry, as shown in Figure 9.10. There is a cache hit if the address matches that entry and a cache miss otherwise.

A direct mapped caches allows efficient lookup, but it loses much of that advantage in decreased flexibility. If a program happens to need two different addresses that both hash to the same entry, such as the program counter and the stack pointer, the system will thrash.

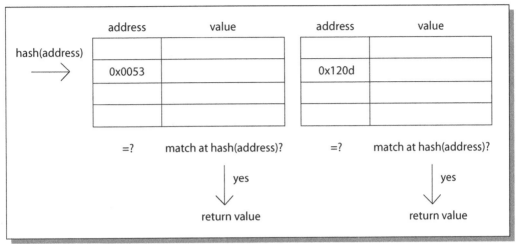

Figure 9.11: Set associative cache lookup. The cache hashes the address to determine which location to check. The cache checks the entry in each table in parallel. It returns the value if any of the entries match the address.

We will first get the instruction; then, oops, we need the stack. Then, oops, we need the instruction again. Then oops, we need the stack again. The programmer will see the program running slowly, with no clue why, as it will depend on which addresses are assigned to which instructions and data. If the programmer inserts a print statement to try to figure out what is going wrong, that might shift the instructions to a different cache block, making the problem disappear!

- **Set associative.** A set associative cache melds the two approaches, allowing a tradeoff of slightly slower lookup than a direct mapped cache in exchange for most of the flexibility of a fully associative cache. With a set associative cache, we replicate the direct mapped table and lookup in each replica in parallel. A k set associative cache has k replicas; a particular address block can be in any of the k replicas. (This is equivalent to a hash table with a bucket size of k.) There is a cache hit if the address matches any of the replicas.

  A set associative cache avoids the problem of thrashing with a direct mapped cache, provided the working set for a given bucket is larger than k. Almost all hardware caches and TLB's today use set associative matching; an 8-way set associative cache structure is common.

Direct mapped and set associative caches pose a design challenge for the operating system. These caches are much more efficient if the working set of the program is spread across the different buckets in the cache. This is easy with a TLB or a virtually addressed cache, as each successive virtual page or cache block will be assigned to a cache bucket. A data structure that

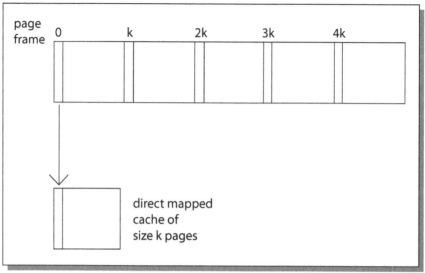

Figure 9.12: When caches are larger than the page size, multiple page frames can map to the same slice of the cache. A process assigned page frames that are separated by exactly the cache size will only use a small portion of the cache. This applies to both set associative and direct mapped caches; the figure assumes a direct mapped cache to simplify the illustration.

straddles a page or cache block boundary will be automatically assigned to two different buckets.

However, the assignment of physical page frames is up to the operating system, and this choice can have a large impact on the performance of a physically addressed cache. To make this concrete, suppose we have a 2 MB physically addressed cache with 8-way set associativity and 4 KB pages; this is typical for a high performance processor. Now suppose the operating system happens to assign page frames in a somewhat odd way, so that an application is given physical page frames that are separated by exactly 256 KB. Perhaps those were the only page frames that were free. What happens?

If the hardware uses the low order bits of the page frame to index the cache, then every page of the current process will map to the same buckets in the cache. We show this in Figure 9.12. Instead of the cache having 2 MB of useful space, the application will only be able to use 32 KB (4 KB pages times the 8-way set associativity). This makes it a lot more likely for the application to thrash.

Even worse, the application would have no way to know this had happened. If by random chance an application ended up with page frames that map to the same cache buckets, its performance will be poor. Then, when the user re-runs the application, the operating system might assign the application a completely different set of page frames, and performance returns to normal.

To make cache behavior more predictable and more effective, operating systems use a concept called *page coloring*. With page coloring, physical page frames are partitioned into sets based on which cache buckets they will use. For example, with a 2 MB 8-way set associative cache and 4 KB pages, there will be 64 separate sets, or colors. The operating system can then assign page frames to spread each application's data across the various colors.

page coloring

Exercises

3. For each of the following statements, indicate whether the statement is true or false, and explain why.

   a) A direct mapped cache can sometimes have a higher hit rate than a fully associative cache (on the same reference pattern).

   b) Adding a cache never hurts performance.

9.5 | Replacement policies

Once we have looked up an address in the cache and found a cache miss, we have a new problem. Which memory block do we choose to replace? Assuming the reference pattern exhibits temporal locality, the new block is likely to be needed in the near future, we need to choose some block of memory to evict from the cache to make room for the new data. Of course, with a direct mapped cache we do not have a choice: there is only one block that can be replaced. In general, however, we will have a choice, and this choice can have a significant impact on the cache hit rate.

As with processor scheduling, there are a number of options for the replacement policy. We caution that there is no single right answer! Many replacement policies are optimal for some workloads and pessimal for others, in terms of the cache hit rate; policies that are good for a working set model will not be good for Zipf workloads.

Policies also vary depending on the setting: hardware caches use a different replacement policy than operating system does in managing main memory as a cache for disk. A hardware cache will often have a limited number of replacement choices, constrained by the set associativity of the cache, and it must make its decisions very rapidly. In the operating system, there is often both more time to make a choice and a much larger number cached items to consider; e.g., with 4 GB of memory, a system will have a million separate 4 KB pages to choose from when deciding which to replace. Even within the operating system, the replacement policy for the file buffer cache is often different than the one used for demand paged virtual memory, depending on what information is easily available about the access pattern.

We first discuss several different replacement policies in the abstract, and then in the next two sections we consider how these concepts are applied to the setting of demand paging memory from disk.

Random

Although it may seem arbitrary, a practical replacement policy is to choose a random block to replace. Particularly for a first-level hardware cache, the system may not have the time to make a more complex decision, and the cost of making the wrong choice can be small if the item is in the next level cache. The bookkeeping cost for more complex policies can be non-trivial: keeping more information about each block requires space that may be better spent on increasing the cache size.

Random's biggest weakness is also its biggest strength. Whatever the access pattern is, Random will not be pessimal — it won't make the worst possible choice, at least, not on average. However, it is also unpredictable, and so it might foil an application that was designed to carefully manage its use of different levels of the cache.

First In First Out (FIFO)

A less arbitrary policy is to evict the cache block or page that has been in memory the longest, that is, First In First Out, or FIFO. Particularly for using memory as a cache for disk, this can seem fair — each program's pages spend a roughly equal amount of time in memory before being evicted.

Unfortunately, FIFO can be the worst possible replacement policy for workloads that happen quite often in practice. Consider a program that cycles through a memory array repeatedly, but where the array is too large to fit in the cache. Many scientific applications do an operation on every element in an array, and then repeat that operation until the data reaches a fixed point. Google's PageRank algorithm for determining which search results to display uses a similar approach. PageRank iterates repeatedly through all pages, estimating the popularity of a page based on the popularity of the pages that refer to it as computed in the previous iteration.

On a repeated scan through memory, FIFO does exactly the wrong thing: it always evicts the block or page that will be needed next. Figure 9.13 illustrates this effect. Note that in this figure, and other similar figures in this figures in this chapter, we show only a small number of cache slots; note that these policies also apply to systems with a very large number of slots.

FIFO															
Reference	A	B	C	D	E	A	B	C	D	E	A	B	C	D	E
1	A				E				D				C		
2		B				A				E				D	
3			C				B				A				E
4				D				C				B			

Figure 9.13: Cache behavior for FIFO for a repeated scan through memory, where the scan is slightly larger than the cache size. Each row represents the contents of a page frame or cache block; each new reference triggers a cache miss.

Optimal cache replacement (MIN)

If FIFO can be pessimal for some workloads, that raises the question: what replacement policy is optimal for minimizing cache misses? The optimal policy, called MIN, is to replace whichever block is used farthest in the future. Equivalently, the worst possible strategy is to replace the block that is used soonest.

As with Shortest Job First, MIN requires knowledge of the future, and so we can't implement it directly. Rather, we can use it as a goal: we want to come up with mechanisms which are effective at predicting which blocks will be used in the near future, so that we can keep those in the cache.

If we were able to predict the future, we could do even better than MIN by prefetching blocks so that they arrive "just in time" — exactly when they are needed. In the best case, this can reduce the number of cache misses to zero. For example, if we observe a program scanning through a file, we can prefetch the blocks of the file into memory. Provided we can read the file into memory fast enough to keep up with the program, the program will always find its data in memory and never have a cache miss.

Least Recently Used (LRU)

One way to predict the future is to look at the past. If programs exhibit temporal locality, the locations they reference in the future are likely to be the same as the ones they have referenced in the recent past.

A replacement policy that captures this effect is to evict the block that has not been used for the longest period of time, or the least recently used (LRU) block. In software, LRU is simple to implement: on every cache hit, you move the block to the front of the list, and on a cache miss, you evict the block at the end of the list. In hardware, keeping a linked list of cached blocks is too complex to implement at high speed; instead, we need to approximate LRU, and we will discuss exactly how in a bit.

Optimality of MIN

The proof that MIN is optimal is a bit involved. If MIN isn't optimal, there must be some alternative optimal replacement policy, which we will call ALT, that has fewer cache misses than MIN on some specific sequence of references. There may be many such alternate policies, so let's focus on the one that differs from MIN at the latest possible point. Consider the first cache replacement where ALT differs from MIN — by definition, ALT must choose a block to replace that is used sooner than the block chosen by MIN.

We construct a new policy, ALT', that is at least as good as ALT, but differs from MIN at a later point and so contradicts the assumption. We construct ALT' to differ from ALT in only one respect: at the first point where ALT differs from MIN, ALT' chooses to evict the block that MIN would have chosen. From that point, the contents of the cache differ between ALT and ALT' only for that one block. ALT contains y, the block referenced farther in the future; ALT' is the same, except it contains x, the block referenced sooner. On subsequent cache misses to other blocks, ALT' mimics ALT, evicting exactly the same blocks that ALT would have evicted.

It is possible that ALT chooses to evict y before the next reference to x or y; in this case, if ALT' chooses to evict x, the contents of the cache for ALT and ALT' are identical. Further, ALT' has the same number of cache misses as ALT, but it differs from MIN at a later point than ALT. This contradicts our assumption above, so we can exclude this case.

Eventually, the system will reference x, the block that ALT chose to evict; by construction, this occurs before the reference to y, the block that ALT' chose to evict. Thus, ALT will have a cache miss, but ALT' will not. ALT will evict some block, q, to make room for x; now ALT and ALT' differ only in that ALT contains y and ALT' contains q. (If ALT evicts y instead, then ALT and ALT' have the same cache contents, but ALT' has fewer misses than ALT, a contradiction.) Finally, when we reach the reference to y, ALT' will take a cache miss. If ALT' evicts q, then it will have the same number of cache misses as ALT, but it will differ from MIN at a point later than ALT, a contradiction.

In some cases, LRU can be optimal, as in the example in Figure 9.14. The table illustrates a reference pattern that exhibits a high degree of temporal locality; when recent references are more likely to be referenced in the near future, LRU can outperform FIFO.

On this particular sequence of references, LRU behaves similarly to the optimal strategy MIN, but that will not always be the case. In fact, LRU can sometimes be the worst possible cache replacement policy. This occurs whenever the least recently used block is the next one to be referenced. A common situation where LRU is pessimal is when the program makes repeated scans through memory, illustrated in Figure 9.15; we saw earlier that FIFO is also pessimal for this reference pattern. The best possible strategy is to replace the most recently referenced block, as this will be used farthest into the future.

LRU

Reference	A	B	A	C	B	D	A	D	E	D	A	E	B	A	C
1	A		+				+				+			+	
2		B			+								+		
3				C					E			+			
4						D		+		+					C

FIFO

Reference	A	B	A	C	B	D	A	D	E	D	A	E	B	A	C
1	A		+				+		E						
2		B			+						A			+	
3				C								+	B		
4						D		+		+					C

MIN

Reference	A	B	A	C	B	D	A	D	E	D	A	E	B	A	C
1	A		+				+				+			+	
2		B			+								+		C
3				C					E			+			
4						D		+		+					

Figure 9.14: Cache behavior for LRU (top), FIFO (middle), and MIN (bottom) for a reference pattern that exhibits temporal locality. Each row represents the contents of a page frame or cache block; + indicates a cache hit. On this reference pattern, LRU is the same as MIN up to the final reference, where MIN can choose to replace any block.

Least Frequently Used (LFU)

Consider again the case of a web proxy cache. Whenever a user accesses a page, it is more likely for that user to access other nearby pages (spatial locality); sometimes, as with a flash crowd, it can be more likely for other users to access the same page (temporal locality). On the surface, Least Recently Used seems like a good fit for this workload.

However, when a user visits a rarely used page, LRU will treat the page as important, even though it is probably just a one-off. When I do a google search for a mountain hut for a stay in Western Iceland, the web pages I visit will not suddenly become more popular than the latest Facebook update from Katy Perry.

A better strategy for references that follow a Zipf distribution is Least Frequently Used (LFU). LFU discards the block that has been used least often; it therefore keeps popular pages, even when less popular pages have been touched more recently.

LRU and LFU both attempt to predict future behavior, and they have

LRU															
Reference	A	B	C	D	E	A	B	C	D	E	A	B	C	D	E
1	A				E				D				C		
2		B				A				E				D	
3			C				B				A				E
4				D				C				B			
MIN															
1	A				+						+		+		
2		B					+					+	C		
3			C					+	D					+	
4				D	E					+					+

Figure 9.15: Cache behavior for LRU (top) and MIN (bottom) for a reference pattern that repeatedly scans through memory. Each row represents the contents of a page frame or cache block; + indicates a cache hit. On this reference pattern, LRU is the same as FIFO, with a cache miss on every reference; the optimal strategy is to replace the most recently used page, as that will be referenced farthest into the future.

complementary strengths. Many systems meld the two approaches to gain the benefits of each. LRU is better at keeping the current working set in memory; once the working set is taken care of, however, LRU will yield diminishing returns. Instead, LFU may be better at predicting what files or memory blocks will be needed in the more distant future, e.g., after the next working set phase change.

Belady's anomaly

Belady's anomaly

Intuitively, it seems like it should always help to add space to a memory cache; being able to store more blocks should always either improve the cache hit rate, or at least, not make the cache hit rate any worse. For many cache replacement strategies, this intuition is true. However, in some cases, adding space to a cache can actually hurt the cache hit rate. This is called *Belady's anomaly*, after the person that discovered it.

First, we note that many of the schemes we have defined can be proven to yield no worse cache behavior with larger cache sizes. For example, with the optimal strategy MIN, if we have a cache of size k blocks, we will keep the next k blocks that will be referenced. If we have a cache of size $k + 1$ blocks, we will keep all of the same blocks as with a k sized cache, plus the additional block that will be the $k + 1$ next reference.

We can make a similar argument for LRU and LFU. For LRU, a cache of size $k + 1$ keeps all of the same blocks as a k sized cache, plus the block

Replacement policy and file size

Our discussion up to now has assumed that all cached items are equal, both in size and in cost to replace. When these assumptions do not hold, however, we may sometimes want to vary the policy from LFU or LFU, that is, to keep some items that are less frequently or less recently used ahead of others that are more frequently or more recently used.

For example, consider a web proxy that caches files to improve web responsiveness. These files may have vastly different sizes. When making room for a new file, we have a choice between evicting one very large web page object or a much larger number of smaller objects. Even if each small file is less frequently used than the large file, it may still make sense to keep the small files. In aggregate they may be more frequently used, and therefore they may have a larger benefit to overall system performance. Likewise, if a cached item is expensive to regenerate, it is more important to keep cached than one that is more easily replaced.

Parallel computing makes the calculus even more complex. The performance of a parallel program depends on its critical path — the minimum sequence of steps for the program to produce its result. Cache misses that occur on the critical path affect the response time while those that occur off the critical path do not. For example, a parallel MapReduce job forks a set of tasks onto processors; each task reads in a file and produces an output. Because MapReduce must wait until all tasks are complete before moving onto the next step, if any file is not cached it is as bad as if all of the needed files were not cached. The cache replacement policy

---

that is referenced farthest in the past. Even if LRU is a lousy replacement policy — if it rarely keeps the blocks that will be used in the near future — it will always do at least as well as a slightly smaller cache also using the same replacement policy. An equivalent argument can be used for LFU.

Some replacement policies, however, do not have this behavior. Instead, the contents of a cache with $k + 1$ blocks may be completely different than the contents of a cache with k blocks. As a result, there cache hit rates may diverge. Among the policies we have discussed, FIFO suffers from Belady's anomaly, and we illustrate that in Figure 9.16.

Exercises

4. Suppose an application is assigned 4 pages of physical memory, and the memory is initially empty. It then references pages in the following sequence:

ACBDBAEFBFAGEFA

a) Show how the system would fault pages into the four frames of physical memory, using the LRU replacement policy.

FIFO (3 slots)

Reference	A	B	C	D	A	B	E	A	B	C	D	E
1	A			D			E					+
2		B			A			+		C		
3			C			B			+		D	

FIFO (4 slots)

	A	B	C	D	A	B	E	A	B	C	D	E
1	A				+		E				D	
2		B				+		A				E
3			C						B			
4				D						C		

Figure 9.16: Cache behavior for FIFO with two different cache sizes, illustrating Belady's anomaly. For this sequence of references, the larger cache suffers ten cache misses, while the smaller cache has one fewer.

b) Show how the system would fault pages into the four frames of physical memory, using the MIN replacement policy.

c) Show how the system would fault pages into the four frames of physical memory, using the clock replacement policy.

9.6 | Case study: memory-mapped files

To illustrate the concepts presented in this chapter, we consider in detail how an operating system can implement *demand paging*. With demand paging, applications can access more memory than is physically present on the machine, by using memory pages as a cache for disk blocks. When the application accesses a missing memory page, it is transparently brought in from disk. We start with the simpler case of a demand paging for a single, memory-mapped file and then extend the discussion to managing multiple processes competing for space in main memory.

As we discussed in Chapter 3, most programs use explicit read/write system calls to perform file I/O. Read/write system calls allow the program to work on a *copy* of file data. The program opens a file and then invokes the system call read to copy chunks of file data into buffers in the program's address space. The program can then use and modify those chunks, without affecting the underlying file. For example, it can convert the file from the disk format into a more convenient in-memory format. To write changes back to the file, the program invokes the system call write to copy the data

demand paging

from the program buffers out to disk. Reading and writing files via system calls is simple to understand and reasonably efficient for small files.

An alternative model for file I/O is to map the file contents into the program's virtual address space. For a *memory-mapped file*, the operating system provides the illusion that the file is a program segment; like any memory segment, the program can directly issue instructions to load and store values to the memory. Unlike file read/write, the load and store instructions do not operate on a copy; they directly access and modify the contents of the file, treating memory as a write-back cache for disk.

memory-
mapped
file

We saw an example of a memory-mapped file in the previous chapter: the program executable image. To start a process, the operating system brings the executable image into memory, and creates page table entries to point to the page frames allocated to the executable. The operating system can start the program executing as soon as the first page frame is initialized, without waiting for the other pages to be brought in from disk. For this, the other page table entries are set to invalid — if the process accesses a page that has not reached memory yet, the hardware traps to the operating system and then waits until the page is available so it can continue to execute. From the program's perspective, there is no difference (except for performance) between whether the executable image is entirely in memory or still mostly on disk.

We can generalize this concept to any file stored on disk, allowing applications to treat any file as part of its virtual address space. File blocks are brought in by the operating system when they are referenced, and modified blocks are copied back to disk, with the bookkeeping done entirely by the operating system.

Advantages

Memory-mapped files offer a number of advantages:

- **Transparency.** The program can operate on the bytes in the file as if they are part of memory; specifically, the program can use a pointer into the file without needing to check if that portion of the file is in memory or not.

- **Zero copy I/O.** The operating system does not need to copy file data from kernel buffers into user memory and back; rather, it just changes the program's page table entry to point to the physical page frame containing that portion of the file. The kernel is responsible for copying data back and forth to disk. We should note that it is possible to implement zero copy I/O for explicit read/write file system calls in certain restricted cases; we will explain how in the next chapter.

- **Pipelining.** The program can start operating on the data in the file as soon as the page tables have been set up; it does not need to wait

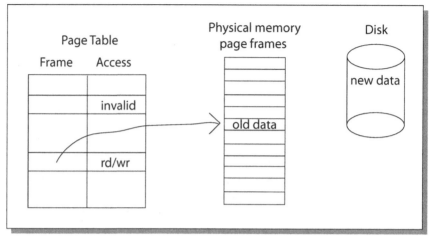

Figure 9.17: Before a page fault, the page table has an invalid entry for the referenced page and the data for the page is stored on disk.

for the entire file to be read into memory. With multiple threads, a program can use explicit read/write calls to pipeline disk I/O, but it needs to manage the pipeline itself.

- **Interprocess communication.** Two or more processes can share information instantaneously through a memory-mapped file without needing to shuffle data back and forth to the kernel or to disk. If the hardware architecture supports it, the page table for the shared segment can also be shared.

- **Large files.** As long as the page table for the file can fit in physical memory, the only limit on the size of a memory-mapped file is the size of the virtual address space. For example, an application may have a giant multi-level tree indexing data spread across a number of disks in a data center. With read/write system calls, the application needs to explicitly manage which parts of the tree are kept in memory and which are on disk; alternatively, with memory-mapped files, the application can leave that bookkeeping to the operating system.

Implementation

To implement memory-mapped files, the operating system provides a system call to map the file into a portion of the virtual address space. In the system call, the kernel initializes a set of page table entries for that region of the virtual address space, setting each entry to invalid. The kernel then returns back to the user process.

When the process issues an instruction that touches an invalid mapped address, a sequence of events occurs, illustrated in Figures 9.17 and 9.18:

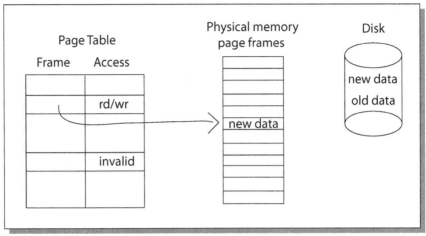

Figure 9.18: After the page fault, the page table has an valid entry for the referenced page with the page frame containing the data that had been stored on disk. The old contents of the page frame are stored on disk and the page table entry that previously pointed to the page frame is set to invalid.

- **TLB miss.** The hardware looks the virtual page up in the TLB, and finds that there is not a valid entry. This triggers a full page table lookup in hardware.

page fault
- **Page table exception.** The hardware walks the multi-level page table and finds the page table entry is invalid. This causes a hardware *page fault* exception trap into the operating system kernel.

- **Convert virtual address to file offset.** In the exception handler, the kernel looks up in its segment table to find the file corresponding to the faulting virtual address and converts the address to a file offset.

- **Disk block read.** The kernel allocates an empty page frame and issues a disk operation to read the required file block into the allocated page frame. While the disk operation is in progress, the processor can be used for running other threads or processes.

- **Disk interrupt.** The disk interrupts the processor when the disk read finishes, and the scheduler resumes the kernel thread handling the page fault exception.

- **Page table update.** The kernel updates the page table entry to point to the page frame allocated for the block and sets the entry to valid.

- **Resume process.** The operating system resumes execution of the process at the instruction that caused the exception.

- **TLB miss.** The TLB still does not contain a valid entry for the page, triggering a full page table lookup.

- **Page table fetch.** The hardware walks the multi-level page table, finds the page table entry valid, and returns the page frame to the processor. The processor loads the TLB with the new translation, evicting a previous TLB entry, and then uses the translation to construct a physical address for the instruction.

To make this work, we need an empty page frame to hold the incoming page from disk. To create an empty page frame, the operating system must:

- **Select a page to evict.** Assuming there is not an empty page of memory already available, the operating system needs to select some page to be replaced. We discuss how to implement this selection in Section 9.6 below.

- **Find page table entries that point to the evicted page.** The operating system then locates the set of page table entries that point to the page that is to be replaced. It can do this with a *core map* — an array of information about each physical page frame, including which page table entries contain pointers to that particular page frame.

core map

- **Set each page table entry to invalid.** The operating system needs to prevent anyone from using the evicted page while the new page is being brought into memory. Because the processor can continue to execute while the disk read is in progress, the page frame may temporarily contain a mixture of bytes from the old and the new page. And because the TLB may cache a copy of the old page table entry, a TLB shootdown is needed to evict the old translation from the TLB.

- **Copy back any changes to the evicted page.** If the evicted page was modified, the contents of the page will need to be copied back to disk before the new page can be brought into memory. Likewise, the contents of modified pages must also be copied back when the application closes the memory-mapped file.

How does the operating system know which pages have been modified? A correct, but inefficient, solution is to simply assume that every page in a memory-mapped file has been modified; if the data hasn't been changed, the operating system will have wasted some work, but the contents of the file won't be affected.

A more efficient solution is for the hardware to keep track of which pages have been modified. Most processor architectures reserve a bit in each page table entry to record whether the page has been modified. This is called a *dirty bit*. The operating system initializes the bit to zero, and the hardware sets the bit automatically when it executes a store instruction for that virtual page. Since the TLB can contain a copy of the page table entry, the TLB also needs a dirty bit per entry. The hardware can ignore the dirty bit if it is set in the TLB, but whenever it goes from zero to one, the

dirty bit

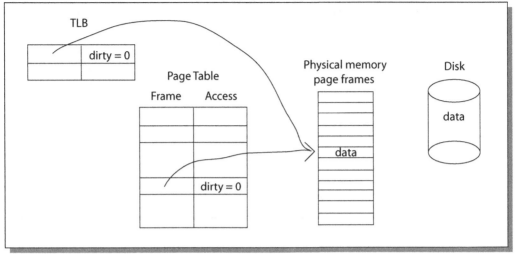

Figure 9.19: When a page is clean, its dirty bit is set to zero in both the TLB and the page table, and the data in memory is the same as the data stored on disk.

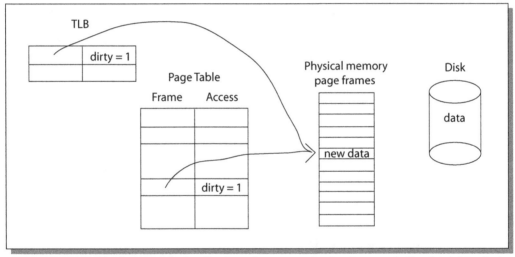

Figure 9.20: On the first store instruction to a clean page, the hardware sets the dirty bit for that page in the TLB and the page table. The contents of the page will differ from what is stored on disk.

hardware needs to copy the bit back to the corresponding page table entry. Figures 9.19 and 9.20 show the state of the TLB, page table, memory and disk before and after the first store instruction to a page.

If there are multiple page table entries pointing at the same physical page frame, the page is dirty (and must be copied back to disk) if *any* of the page tables have the dirty bit set. Normally, of course, a memory-mapped file will have a single page table shared between all of the processes

Emulating a hardware dirty bit in software

Interestingly, hardware support for a dirty bit is not strictly required. The operating system can emulate a hardware dirty bit using page table access permissions. An unmodified page is set to allow only read-only access, even though the program is logically allowed to modified the page. The program can then execute normally. On a store instruction to the page, the hardware will trigger a memory exception. The operating system can then record the fact that the page is dirty, upgrade the page protection to read-write, and restart the process.

To clean a page in the background, the kernel resets the page protection to read-only and does a TLB shootdown. The shootdown removes any translation that allows for read-write access to the page, forcing subsequent store instructions to cause another memory exception.

mapping the file.

Because evicting a dirty page takes more time than evicting a clean page, the operating system can proactively clean pages in the background. A thread runs in the background, looking for pages that are likely candidates for being evicted if they were clean. If the hardware dirty bit is set in the page table entry, the kernel resets the bit in the page table entry and does a TLB shootdown to remove the entry from the TLB (with the old value of the dirty bit). It then copies the page to disk. Of course, the on-chip processor memory cache and write buffers can contain modifications to the page that have not reached main memory; the hardware ensures that the new data reaches main memory before those bytes are copied to the disk interface.

The kernel can then restart the application; it need not wait for the block to reach disk — if the process modifies the page again, the hardware will simply reset the dirty bit, signaling that the block cannot be reclaimed without saving the new set of changes to disk.

Approximating LRU

A further challenge to implementing demand paged memory-mapped files is that the hardware does not keep track of which pages are least recently or least frequently used. Doing so would require the hardware to keep a linked list of every page in memory, and to modify that list on every load and store instruction (and for memory-mapped executable images, every instruction fetch as well). This would be prohibitively expensive. Instead, the hardware maintains a minimal amount of access information per page to allow the operating system to approximate LRU or LFU if it wants to do so.

We should note that explicit read/write file system calls do not have this problem. Each time a process reads or writes a file block, the operating

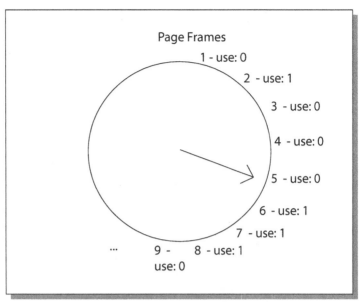

Figure 9.21: The clock algorithm sweeps through each page frame, collecting the current value of the use bit for that page and resetting the use bit to zero. The clock algorithm stops when a sufficient number of unused page frames have been reclaimed.

system can keep track of which blocks are used when. The kernel can use this information to prioritize its cache of file blocks when the system needs to find space for a new block.

use bit   Most processor architectures keep a *use bit* in each page table entry, next to the hardware dirty bit we discussed above. The operating system clears the use bit when the page table entry is initialized; the bit is set in hardware whenever the page table entry is brought into the TLB. As with the dirty bit, a physical page is used if *any* of the page table entries have their use bit set.

The operating system can leverage the use bit in various ways, but a **clock** commonly used approach is the *clock algorithm*, illustrated in Figure 9.21. **algorithm** Periodically, the operating system scans through the core map of physical memory pages. For each page frame, it records the value of the use bit in the page table entries that point to that frame, and then clears their use bits. Because the TLB can have a cached copy of the translation, the operating system also does a shootdown for any page table entry where the use bit is cleared. Note that if the use bit is already zero, the translation cannot be in the TLB. While it is scanning, the kernel can also look for dirty and recently unused pages and flush these out to disk.

Each sweep of the clock algorithm through memory collects one bit of information about page usage; by adjusting the frequency of the clock

Emulating a hardware use bit in software

Hardware support for a use bit is also not strictly required. The operating system kernel can emulate a use bit with page table permissions, in the same way that the kernel can emulate a hardware dirty bit. To collect usage information about a page, the kernel sets the page table entry to be invalid even though the page is in memory and the application has permission to access the page. When the page is accessed, the hardware will trigger an exception and the operating system can record the use of the page. The kernel then changes the permission on the page to allow access, before restarting the process. To collect usage information over time, the operating system can periodically reset the page table entry to invalid and shootdown any cached translations in the TLB.

Many systems use a hybrid approach. In addition to active pages where the hardware collects the use bit, the operating system maintains a pool of unused, clean page frames that are unmapped in any virtual address space, but still contain their old data. When a new page frame is needed, pages in this pool can be used without any further work. However, if the old data is referenced first before the page frame is reused, the page can be pulled out of the pool and mapped back into the virtual address space.

Systems with a software-managed TLB have an even simpler time. Each time there is a TLB miss with a software-managed TLB, there is a trap to the kernel to look up the translation. During the trap, the kernel can update its list of frequently used pages.

---

algorithm, we can collect increasingly fine-grained information about usage, at the cost of increased software overhead. On modern systems with hundreds of thousands and sometimes millions of physical page frames, the overhead of the clock algorithm can be substantial.

not recently used   The policy for what to do with the usage information is up to the operating system kernel. A common policy is called *not recently used*, or k'th chance. If the operating system needs to evict a page, the kernel picks one that has not been used (has not had its use bit set) for the last k sweeps of the clock algorithm. The clock algorithm partitions pages based on how recently they have been used; among page frames in the same k'th chance partition, the operating system can evict pages in FIFO order.

Some systems trigger the clock algorithm only when a page is needed, rather than periodically in the background. Provided some pages have not been accessed since the last sweep, an on-demand clock algorithm will find a page to reclaim. If all pages have been accessed, e.g., if there is a storm of page faults due to phase change behavior, then the system will default to FIFO.

9.7 | Case study: virtual memory

virtual
memory We can generalize on the concept of memory-mapped files, by making *every* memory segment on the system backed by a file on disk. This is called *virtual memory*. Program executables, individual libraries, data, stack and heap segments can all be demand paged to disk. Unlike memory-mapped files, though, process memory is ephemeral: when the process exits, there is no need to write modified data back to disk and we can reclaim the disk space.

The advantage of virtual memory is flexibility. The system can continue to function even though the user has started more processes than can fit in main memory at the same time. The operating system simply makes room for the new processes by paging the memory of idle applications back to disk. Without virtual memory, the user has to do memory management by hand, by closing some applications to make room for others.

All of the mechanisms we've described for memory-mapped files apply when we generalize to virtual memory, with one additional twist. We need to balance the allocation of physical page frames between processes. Unfortunately, this balancing is quite tricky. If we add a few extra page faults to a system, no one will notice. However, a modern disk can handle at most 100 page faults per second, while a modern multi-core processor can execute 10 billion instructions per second. Thus, if page faults are anything but extremely rare, performance will suffer.

Self-paging

One consideration is that the behavior of one process can significantly hurt the performance of other programs running at the same time. For example, suppose we have two processes. One is a normal program, with a working set equal to say, a quarter of physical memory. The other program is greedy; while it can run fine with less memory, it will run faster if it is given more memory. We gave an example of this earlier with the sort program.

Can you design a program to take advantage of the clock algorithm to acquire more than its fair share of memory pages?

We give an example in Figure 9.22, which we'll dub "pig" for obvious reasons. It allocates an array in virtual memory equal in size to physical memory; it then uses multiple threads to cycle through memory, causing each page to be brought in while the other pages remain very recently used.

A normal program sharing memory with the pig will eventually be frozen out of memory and stop making progress. When the pig touches a new page, it triggers a page fault, but all of its pages are recently used because of the background thread. Meanwhile, the normal program will have recently touched many of its pages but there will be some that are less recently used. The clock algorithm will choose those for replacement.

```
static char *workingSet;        // the memory this program wants to acquire
static int soFar;               // how many pages the program has so far
static sthread_t refreshThread;

// this thread touches the pages we have in memory, to keep them recently used
void refresh() {
    int i;

    while (1) {
        // keep every page in memory recently used
        for (i = 0; i < soFar; i += PAGESIZE)
            workingSet[i] = 0;
    }
}

int main (int argc, char **argv) {

    // allocate a giant array
    workingSet = malloc(ARRAYSIZE);
    soFar = 0;

    // create a thread to keep our pages in memory, once they get there
    sthread_create(&refreshThread, refresh, 0);

    // touch every page to bring it into memory
    for (; soFar < ARRAYSIZE; soFar += PAGESIZE)
        workingSet[soFar] = 0;

    // now that everything is in memory, ok to run computation
}
```

Figure 9.22: The "pig" program to greedily acquire memory pages. The implementation assumes we are running on a multi-core computer. When the pig triggers a page fault by touching a new memory page (soFar), the operating system will find all of the pig's pages up to soFar recently used. The operating system will keep these in memory and it will choose pages from the rest of the system to evict.

As time goes on, more and more of the pages will be allocated to the pig. As the number of pages assigned to the normal program drops, it starts experiencing page faults at an increasing frequency. Eventually, the number of pages drops below the working set, at which point the program stops making much progress. Its pages are even less frequently used, making them easier to evict.

Of course, a normal user would probably never run (or write!) a program like this, but a malicious attacker launching a computer virus might use this approach to freeze out the system administrator. Likewise, in a data center setting, a single server can be shared between multiple applications from different users, for example, running in different virtual machines. It is in the interest of any single application to acquire as many physical resources as possible, even if that hurts performance for other users.

self-paging   A widely adopted solution is *self-paging*. With self-paging, each process or user is assigned its fair share of page frames, using the max-min scheduling algorithm we described in Chapter 7. If all of the active processes can fit in memory at the same time, the system does not need to page. As the system starts to page, it evicts the page from whichever process has the most allocated to it. Thus the pig would only be able to allocate its fair share of page frames, and beyond that any page faults it triggers would evict its own pages.

Unfortunately, self-paging comes at a cost in reduced resource utilization. Suppose we have two processes, both of which allocate large amounts of virtual address space. However, the working sets of the two programs can fit in memory at the same time, for example, if one working set takes up 2/3rds of memory and the other takes up 1/3rd. If they cooperate, both can run efficiently because the system has room for both working sets. However, if we need to bulletproof the operating system against malicious programs by self-paging, then each will be assigned half of memory and the larger program will thrash.

Swapping

Another issue is what happens as we increase the workload for a system with virtual memory. If we are running a data center, for example, we can share physical machines among a much larger number of applications each running in a separate virtual machine. To reduce costs, the data center needs to support the maximum number of applications on each server, within some performance constraint.

If the working sets of the applications easily fit in memory, then as page faults occur, the clock algorithm will find lightly used pages — that is, those outside of the working set of any process — to evict to make room for new pages. So far so good. As we keep adding active processes, however, their working sets may no longer fit, even if each process is given their fair share of memory. In this case, the performance of the system will degrade dramatically.

This is illustrated in Figure 9.23, where we plot the system throughput on the y-axis and the number of processes on the x-axis. As we add work to the system, throughput increases as long as there is enough processing capacity and I/O bandwidth. When we reach the point where there are too many tasks to fit entirely in memory, the system starts demand paging. Throughput can continue to improve if there are enough lightly used pages to make room for new tasks, but eventually throughput levels off and then falls off a cliff. In the limit, every instruction will trigger a page fault, meaning that the processor executes at 100 instructions per second, rather than 10 billion instructions per second. Needless to say, the user will think the system is dead even if it is in fact inching forward very slowly.

As we explained in the Chapter 7 discussion on overload control, the only way to achieve good performance in this case is to prevent the overload

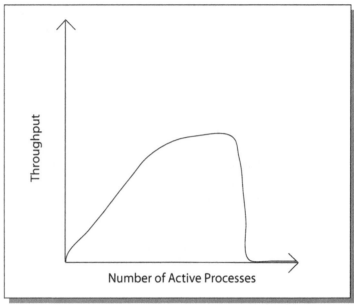

Figure 9.23: System throughput as a function of the number of active processes under a memory constraint. As we add processes, throughput increases until the system begins to demand page. If more demand for memory is added beyond this point, performance will degrade rapidly.

condition from occurring. Both response time and throughput will be better if we prevent additional tasks from starting or if we remove some existing tasks. It is better to completely starve some tasks of their resources, if the alternative, assigning each task their fair share, will drag the system to a halt.

swapping   Evicting an entire process from memory is called *swapping*. When there is too much paging activity, the operating system can prevent a catastrophic degradation in performance by moving *all* of the page frames of a particular process to disk, preventing it from running at all. Although this may seem terribly unfair, the alternative is that *every* process, not just the swapped process, will run much more slowly. By distributing the swapped process' pages to other processes, we can reduce the number of page faults, allowing system performance to recover. Eventually the other tasks will finish, and we can bring the swapped process back into memory.

9.8 | Conclusions and future directions

Caching is central to many areas of computer science: they are used in processor design, file systems, web browsers, web servers, compilers, and kernel memory management, to name a few. To understand these systems, it is important to understand how caches work, and even more importantly, when they fail.

The management of memory in operating systems is a particularly useful case study. Every major commercial operating system includes support for demand paging of memory, using memory as a cache for disk. Often, application memory pages and blocks in the file buffer are allocated from a common pool of memory, where the operating system attempts to keep blocks that are likely to be used in memory and evicting those blocks that are less likely to be used. However, on modern systems, the difference between finding a block in memory and needing to bring it in from disk can be as much as a factor of 100,000. This makes virtual memory paging fragile, acceptable only when used in small doses.

Moving forward, several trends are in progress:

- **Low latency backing store.** Due to the weight and power drain of magnetic disks, many portable devices have moved to solid state persistent storage, such as non-volatile RAM. Current solid state storage devices have significantly lower latency than disk, and even faster devices are likely in the future. Similarly, the move towards data center computing has added a new option to memory management: using DRAM on other nodes in the data center as a low-latency, very high capacity backing store for local memory. Both of these trends reduce the cost of paging, making it relatively more attractive.

- **Variable page sizes.** Many systems use a standard 4 KB page size, but there is nothing fundamental about that choice — it is a tradeoff chosen to balance internal fragmentation, page table overhead, disk latency, the overhead of collecting dirty and usage bits, and application spatial locality. On modern disks, it only takes twice as long to transfer 256 contiguous pages as it does to transfer one, so internally, most operating systems arrange disk transfers to include many blocks at a time. With new technologies such as low latency solid state storage and cluster memory, this balance may shift back towards smaller effective page sizes.

- **Memory aware applications.** The increasing depth and complexity of the memory hierarchy is both a boon and a curse. For many applications, the memory hierarchy delivers reasonable performance without any special effort. However, the wide gulf in performance between the first level cache and main memory, and between main memory and disk, implies that there is a significant performance benefit to tuning applications to the available memory. The poses a particular challenge for operating systems to adapt to applications that are adapting to their physical resources.

Exercises

For convenience, the exercises from the body of the chapter are repeated here, along with several additional problems.

1. A computer system has a 1 KB page size and keeps the page table for each process in main memory. Because the page table entries are usually cached on chip, the average overhead for doing a full page table lookup is 40 ns. To reduce this overhead, the computer has a 32-entry TLB. A TLB lookup requires 1 ns. What TLB hit rate is required to ensure an average virtual address translation time of 2 ns?

2. Most modern computer systems choose a page size of 4 KB.

   a) Give a set of reasons why doubling the page size might increase performance.

   b) Give a set of reasons why doubling the page size might decrease performance.

3. For each of the following statements, indicate whether the statement is true or false, and explain why.

   a) A direct mapped cache can sometimes have a higher hit rate than a fully associative cache (on the same reference pattern).

   b) Adding a cache never hurts performance.

4. Suppose an application is assigned 4 pages of physical memory, and the memory is initially empty. It then references pages in the following sequence:

   ACBDBAEFBFAGEFA

   a) Show how the system would fault pages into the four frames of physical memory, using the LRU replacement policy.

   b) Show how the system would fault pages into the four frames of physical memory, using the MIN replacement policy.

   c) Show how the system would fault pages into the four frames of physical memory, using the clock replacement policy.

5. Consider a computer system running a general-purpose workload with demand paging. The system has two disks, one for demand paging and one for file system operations. Measured utilizations (in terms of time, not space) are:

   For each of the following changes, say what its likely impact will be on processor utilization, and explain why. Is it likely to significantly increase, marginally increase, significantly decrease, marginally decrease, or have no effect on the processor utilization?

Processor utilization	20.0%
Paging Disk	99.7%
File Disk	10.0%
Network	5.0%

a) Get a faster CPU

b) Get a faster paging disk

c) Increase the degree of multiprogramming

6. An operating system with a physically addressed cache uses page coloring to more

a) How many page colors are needed to fully utilize a physically addressed cache, with 1 TB of main memory, an 8 MB cache with 4-way set associativity, and a 4 KB page size?

b) Develop an algebraic formula to compute the number of page colors needed for an arbitrary configuration of cache size, set associativity, and page size.

7. The sequence of virtual pages referenced by a program has length p with n distinct page numbers occurring in it. Let m be the number of page frames that are allocated to the process (all the page frames are initially empty). Let $n > m$.

a) What is the lower bound on the number of page faults?

b) What is the upper bound on the number of page faults?

The lower/upper bound should be for any page replacement policy.

8. You've decided to splurge on a low end netbook for doing your operating systems homework during lectures in your non-computer science classes. The netbook has a single-level TLB and a single-level, physically addressed cache. It also has two levels of page tables, and the operating system does demand paging to disk.

The netbook comes in various configurations, and you want to make sure the configuration you purchase is fast enough to run your applications. To get a handle on this, you decide to measure its cache, TLB and paging performance running your apps in a virtual machine. You discover for your workload:

The TLB is refilled automatically by the hardware on a TLB miss. The page tables are kept in physical memory and are not cached, so looking up a page table entry incurs two memory accesses (one for

Measurement	Value
$P_{CacheMiss}$ = probability of a cache miss	0.01
$P_{TLBmiss}$ = probability of a TLB miss	0.01
P_{fault} = probability of a page fault, given a TLB miss occurs	0.00002
T_{cache} = time to access cache	$1 \, ns = 0.001 \, \mu s$
T_{TLB} = time to access TLB	$1 \, ns = 0.001 \, \mu s$
T_{DRAM} = time to access main memory	$100 \, ns = 0.1 \, \mu s$
T_{disk} = time to transfer a page to/from disk	$10^7 \, ns = 10 \, ms$

each level of the page table). You may assume the operating system keeps a pool of clean pages, so pages do not need to be written back to disk on a page fault.

a) What is the average memory access time (the time for an application program to do one memory reference) on the netbook? Express your answer algebraically and compute the result to two significant digits.

b) The netbook has a few optional performance enhancements:

Item	Specs	Price
Faster disk drive	Transfers a page in 7 ms	$100
500 MB more DRAM	Makes probability of a page fault 0.00001	$100
Faster network card	Allows paging to remote memory.	$100

With the faster network card, the time to access remote memory is 500 ms, and the probability of a remote memory miss (need to go to disk), given there is a page fault is 0.5.

Suppose you have $200. What options should you buy to maximize the performance of the netbook for this workload?

9. On a computer with virtual memory, suppose a program repeatedly scans through a very large array. In other words, if the array is four pages long, its page reference pattern is ABCDABCDABCD...

Sketch a graph showing the paging behavior, for each of the following page replacement algorithms. The y-axis of the graph is the number of page faults per referenced page, varying from 0 to 1; the x-axis is the size of the array being scanned, varying from smaller than physical memory to much larger than physical memory. Label any interesting points on the graph on both the x and y axes.

    a) FIFO

    b) LRU

    c) Clock

    d) MIN

10. Consider two programs, one which exhibits spatial and temporal locality, and the other one exhibits neither. To make the comparison fair, they both use the same total amount of virtual memory — that is, they both touch N distinct virtual pages, among a much larger number of total references.

    Sketch graphs showing the rate of progress (instructions per unit time) of each program as a function of the physical memory available to the program, from 0 to N, assuming the clock algorithm is used for page replacement.

    a) Program exhibiting locality, running by itself

    b) Program exhibiting no locality, running by itself

    c) Program exhibiting locality, running with the program exhibiting no locality (assume both have the same value for N).

    d) Program exhibiting no locality, running with the program exhibiting locality (assume both have the same N).

11. Suppose we are using the clock algorithm to decide page replacement, in its simplest form ("first-chance" replacement, where the clock is only advanced on a page fault and not in the background).

    A crucial issue in the clock algorithm is how many page frames must be considered in order to find a page to replace. Assuming we have a sequence of F page faults in a system with P page frames, let $C(F, P)$ be the number of pages considered for replacement in handling the F page faults (if the clock hand sweeps by a page frame multiple times, it is counted each time).

    a) Give an algebraic formula for the minimum possible value of $C(F, P)$.

    b) Give an algebraic formula for the maximum possible value of $C(F, P)$.

All problems in computer science can be solved by another level of indirection.

David Wheeler

10 Advanced Memory Management

At an abstract level, an operating system provides an execution context for application processes, consisting of limits on privileged instructions, the process' memory regions, a set of system calls, and some way for the operating system to periodically regain control of the processor. By interposing on that interface — most commonly, by catching and transforming system calls or memory references — the operating system can transparently insert new functionality to improve system performance, reliability, and security.

Interposing on system calls is straightforward. The kernel uses a table lookup to determine which routine is called for each specific system call invoked by the application program. Redirecting a system call to a new enhanced routine is as simple as changing the table entry.

A more interesting case is the memory system. Address translation hardware provides an efficient way for the operating system to monitor and gain control on every memory reference to a specific region of memory, while allowing other memory references to continue unaffected. (Equivalently, software-based fault isolation provides many of the same hooks, with different tradeoffs between interposition and execution speed.) This makes address translation a powerful tool for operating systems to introduce new, advanced services to applications. We've already shown how to use address translation for:

- **Protection.** Operating systems use address translation hardware, along with segment and page table permissions, to restrict access by applications to privileged memory locations such as those in the kernel.

- **Fill-on-demand/zero-on-demand.** By setting some page table permissions to invalid, the kernel can start executing a process before all of its code and data has been loaded into memory; the hardware will trap to the kernel if the process references data before it is ready. Similarly, the kernel can zero data and heap pages in the background, relying on page reference faults to catch the first time an application uses an empty page. The kernel can also allocate memory for kernel and user stacks only as needed. By setting unused stack pages as invalid, the kernel needs to allocate those pages only if and when the program executes a deep procedure call chain.

- **Copy-on-write.** Copy-on-write allows multiple processes to have logically separate copies of the same memory region, backed by a single physical copy in memory. Each page in the region is mapped read-only in each process; the operating system makes a physical copy only when (and if) a page is modified.

- **Memory-mapped files.** Disk files can be made part of a process' virtual address space, allowing the process to access the data in the file using normal processor instructions. When a page from a memory-mapped file is first accessed, a protection fault traps to the operating system so that it can bring the page into memory from disk. The first write to a file block can also be caught, marking the block as needing to be written back to disk.

- **Demand paged virtual memory.** The operating system can run programs that use more memory than is physically present on the computer, by catching references to pages that are not physically present and filling them from disk or cluster memory.

In this chapter, we explore how to construct a number of other advanced operating system services by catching and re-interpreting memory references and system calls.

We consider several topics:

- **Zero-copy I/O.** How do we improve the performance of transferring blocks of data between user-level programs and hardware devices?

- **Virtual machines.** How do we execute an operating system on top of another operating system, and how can we use that abstraction to introduce new operating system services?

- **Fault tolerance.** How can we make applications resilient to machine crashes?

- **Security.** How can we contain malicious applications that can exploit unknown faults inside the operating system?

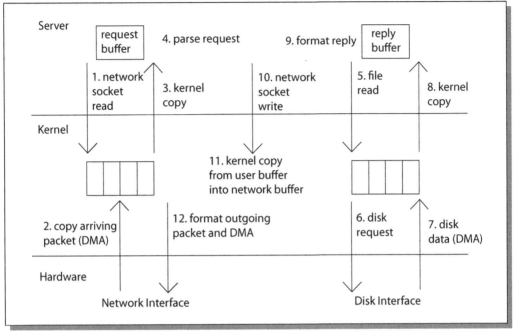

Figure 10.1: A web server gets a request from the network. The server first asks the kernel to copy the requested file from disk or its file buffer into the server's address space. The server then asks the kernel to copy the contents of the file back out to the network.

- **User-level memory management.** How do we give applications control over how their memory is being managed?

10.1 | Zero-copy I/O

A common task for operating systems is to stream data between user-level programs and physical devices such as disks and network hardware. However, this can be very expensive in processing time, if the data is copied as it moves across protection boundaries. A network packet needs to go from the network interface hardware into kernel memory, and then to user-level; the response needs to go from user-level back into kernel memory and then from kernel memory to the network hardware.

Consider the operation of the web server, as pictured in Figure 10.1. Almost all web servers are implemented as user-level programs. This way, the server behavior can be more easily reconfigured, and bugs in the server implementation do not necessarily compromise system security.

A number of steps need to happen for a web server to respond to a web request. For this, let's assume that the connection between the client and server is already established, there is a server thread allocated to each client connection, and we use explicit read/write system calls rather than memory mapped files.

- **Server reads from network.** The server thread calls into the kernel to wait for an arriving request.

- **Packet arrival.** The web request arrives from the network; the network hardware uses DMA to copy the packet data into a kernel buffer.

- **Copy packet data to user-level.** The operating system parses the packet header to determine which user process is to receive the web request. The kernel copies the data into the user-level buffer provided by the server thread and returns to user-level.

- **Server reads file.** The server parses the data in the web request to determine which file is requested. It issues a file read system call back to the kernel, providing a user-level buffer to hold the file contents.

- **Data arrival.** The kernel issues the disk request, and the disk controller copies the data from the disk into a kernel buffer. If the file data is already in the file buffer cache, as will often be the case for popular web requests, this step is skipped.

- **Copy file data to user-level.** The kernel copies the data into the buffer provided by the user process and returns to user-level.

- **Server write to network.** The server turns around and hands the buffer containing the file data back to the kernel to send out to the network.

- **Copy data to kernel.** The kernel copies the data from the user-level buffer into a kernel buffer, formats the packet and issues the request to the network hardware.

- **Data send.** The hardware uses DMA to copy the data from the kernel buffer out to the network.

Although we have illustrated this with a web server, a similar process occurs for any application that streams data in or out of a computer. Examples include a web client, online video or music service, BitTorrent, network file systems, and even a software download. For each of these, data is copied from hardware into the kernel and then into user-space, or vice versa.

We could eliminate the extra copy across the kernel-user boundary by moving each of these applications into the kernel. However, that would be impractical as it would require trusting the applications with the full power of the operating system. Alternately, we could modify the system call interface to allow applications to directly manipulate data stored in a

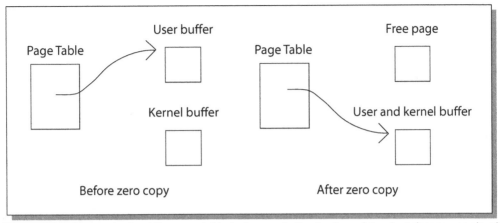

Figure 10.2: The contents of the page table before and after the kernel "copies" data to user-level by swapping the page table entry to point to the kernel buffer.

kernel buffer, without first copying it to user memory. However, this is not a general-purpose solution; it would not work if the application needed to do any work on the buffer as opposed to only transferring it from one hardware device to another.

zero-copy I/O
Instead, two solutions to *zero-copy I/O* are used in practice. Both eliminate the copy across the kernel-user boundary for large blocks of data; for small chunks of data, the extra copy does not impact performance.

The more widely used approach manipulates the process page table to simulate a copy. For this to work, the application must first align its user-level buffer to a page boundary. The user-level buffer is provided to the kernel on a read or write system call, and its alignment and size is up to the application.

The key idea is that a page to page copy from user to kernel space or vice versa can be simulated by changing page table pointers instead of physically copying memory.

For a copy from user-space to the kernel (e.g., on a network or file system write), the kernel changes the permissions on the page table entry for the user-level buffer to prevent it from being modified. The kernel must also *pin* the page to prevent it from being chosen for eviction by the virtual memory manager. In the common case, this is enough — the page will not normally be modified while the I/O request is in progress. If the user program does try to modify the page, the program will trap to the kernel and the kernel can make an explicit copy at that point.

In the other direction, once the data is in the kernel buffer, the operating system can simulate a copy up to user-space by switching the pointer in the page table, as shown in Figure 10.2. The process page table originally pointed to the page frame containing the (empty) user buffer; now it points to the page frame containing the (full) kernel buffer. To the user program, the data appears exactly where it was expected! The kernel can reclaim any physical memory behind the empty buffer.

More recently, some hardware I/O devices have been designed to be able to transfer data to and from virtual addresses, rather than only to and from physical addresses. The kernel hands the virtual address of the user-level buffer to the hardware device. The hardware device, rather than the kernel, walks the multi-level page table to determine which physical page frame to use for the device transfer. When the transfer completes, the data is automatically where it belongs, with no extra work by the kernel. This procedure is a bit more complicated for incoming network packets, as the decision as to which process should receive which packet is determined by the contents of the packet header. The network interface hardware therefore has to parse the incoming packet to deliver the data to the appropriate process.

10.2 | Virtual machines

A virtual machine is a way for a host operating system to run a guest operating system as an application process. The host simulates the behavior of a physical machine so that the guest system behaves as if it was running on real hardware. Virtual machines are widely used on client machines to run applications that are not native to the current version of the operating system. They are also widely used in data centers to allow a single physical machine to be shared between multiple independent uses, each of which can be written as if it has system administrator control over the entire (virtual) machine. For example, multiple web servers, representing different web sites, can be hosted on the same physical machine if they each run inside a separate virtual machine.

Address translation throws a wrinkle into the challenge of implementing a virtual machine, but it also opens up opportunities for efficiencies and new services.

Virtual machine page tables

With virtual machines, we have two sets of page tables, instead of one, as shown in Figure 10.3:

- **Guest physical memory to host physical memory.** The host operating system provides a set of page tables to constrain the execution of the guest operating system kernel. The guest kernel thinks it is running on real, physical memory, but in fact its addresses are virtual. The hardware page table translates each guest operating system memory reference into a physical memory location, after checking that the guest has permission to read or write each location. This way the

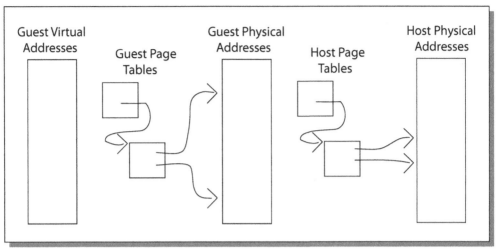

Figure 10.3: A virtual machine typically has two page tables: one to translate from guest process addresses to the guest physical memory, and one to translate from guest physical memory addresses to host physical memory addresses.

host operating system can prevent bugs in the guest operating system from overwriting memory in the host, exactly as if the guest were a normal user-level process.

- **Guest user memory to guest physical memory.** In turn, the guest operating system manages page tables for its guest processes, exactly as if the guest kernel was running on real hardware. Since the guest kernel does not know anything about the physical page frames it has been assigned by the host kernel, these page tables translate from the guest process addresses to the guest operating system kernel addresses.

First, consider what happens when the host operating system transfers control to the guest kernel. Everything works as expected. The guest operating system can read and write its memory, and the hardware page tables provide the illusion that the guest kernel is running directly on physical memory.

Now consider what happens when the guest operating system transfers control to the guest process. The guest kernel is running at user-level, so its attempt to transfer of control is a privileged instruction. Thus, the hardware processor will first trap back to the host. The host kernel can then simulate the transfer instruction, handing control to the user process.

However, what page table should we use in this case? We cannot use the page table as set up by the guest operating system, as the guest operating system thinks it is running in physical memory, but it is actually using virtual addresses. Nor can we use the page table as set up by the host operating system, as that provides would provide permission to the guest

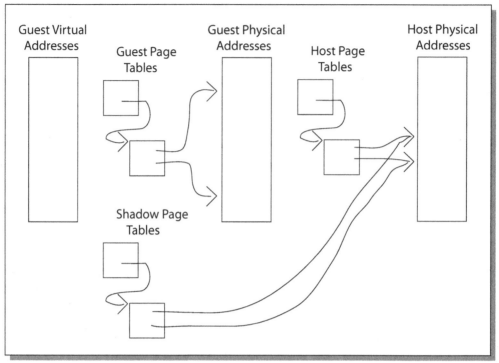

Figure 10.4: To run a guest process, the host operating system constructs a shadow page table consisting of the composition of the contents of the two page tables.

process to access and modify the guest kernel data structures. If we grant access to the guest kernel memory to the guest process, then the behavior of the virtual machine will be compromised.

Instead, we need to construct a composite page table, called a *shadow page table*, that represents the composition of the guest page table and the host page table, as shown in Figure 10.4. When the guest kernel transfers control to a guest process, the host kernel gains control and changes the page table to the shadow version.

To keep the shadow page table up to date, the host operating system needs to keep track of changes that either the guest or the host operating systems make to their page tables. This is easy in the case of the host OS — it can check to see if any shadow page tables need to be updated before it changes a page table entry.

To keep track of changes that the guest operating system makes to its page tables, however, we need to do a bit more work. The host operating system sets the memory of the guest page tables as read-only. This ensures that the guest OS traps to the host every time it attempts to change a page table entry. The host uses this trap to change the both the guest page table and the corresponding shadow page table, before resuming the guest

shadow page table

operating system (with the page table still read-only).

The Intel architecture has recently added direct hardware support for the composition of page tables in virtual machines. Instead of a single page table, the hardware can be set up with two page tables, one for the host and one for the guest operating system. When running a guest process, on a TLB miss, the hardware translates the virtual address to a guest physical page frame using the guest page table, and the hardware then translates the guest physical page frame to the host physical page frame using the host page table. In other words, the TLB contains the composition of the two page tables, exactly as if the host maintained an explicit shadow page table. Of course, if the guest operating system itself hosts a virtual machine as a guest user process, then the guest kernel must construct a shadow page table.

Although this hardware support simplifies the construction of virtual machines, it is not clear if it improves performance. The handling of a TLB miss is slower since two page tables must be consulted instead of one; changes to the guest page table are faster because the host does not need to maintain the shadow page table. It remains to be seen if this tradeoff is useful in practice.

Transparent memory compression

A theme running throughout this book is the difficulty of multiplexing multiplexors. With virtual machines, both the host operating system and the guest operating system are attempting to do the same task: to efficiently multiplex a set of tasks onto a limited amount of memory. Decisions the guest operating system takes to manage its memory may work at cross purposes to the decisions that the host operating system takes to manage its memory.

Efficient use of memory can become especially important in data centers. Often, a single physical machine in a data center is configured to run many virtual machines at the same time. For example, one machine can host many different web sites, each of which is too small to merit a dedicated machine on its own.

To make this work, the system needs enough memory to be able to run many different operating systems at the same time. The host operating system can help by sharing memory between guest kernels, e.g., if it is running two guest kernels with the same executable kernel image. Likewise, the guest operating system can help by sharing memory between guest applications, e.g., if it is running two copies of the same program. However, if different guest kernels both run a copy of the same user process (e.g., both run the Apache web server), or use the same library, the host kernel has no (direct) way to share pages between those two instances.

Another example occurs when a guest process exits. The guest operating system places the page frames for the exiting process on the free list for reallocation to other processes. The contents of any data pages will never be used again; in fact, the guest kernel will need to zero those pages before they are reassigned. However, the host operating system has no (direct) way to know this. Eventually those pages will be evicted by the host, e.g., when they become least recently used. In the meantime, however, the host operating system might have evicted pages from the guest that are still active.

One solution is to more tightly coordinate the guest and host memory managers so that each knows what the other is doing. We discuss this in more detail later in this Chapter.

Commercial virtual machine implementations take a different approach, exploiting hardware address protection to manage the sharing of common pages between virtual machines. These systems run a scavenger in the background that looks for pages that can be shared across virtual machines. Once a common page is identified, the host kernel manipulates the page table pointers to provide the illusion that each guest has its own copy of the page, even though the physical representation is more compact.

There are two cases to consider, shown in Figure 10.5:

- **Multiple copies of the same page.** Two different virtual machines will often have pages with the same contents. An obvious case is zeroed

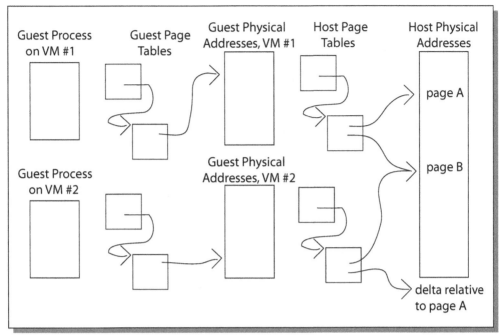

Figure 10.5: When a host kernel runs multiple virtual machines, it can save space by storing a delta to an existing page (page A) and by by using the same physical page frame for multiple copies of the same page (page B).

pages: each kernel keeps a pool of pages that have been zeroed, ready to be allocated to a new process. If each guest operating system were running on its own machine, there would be little cost to keeping this pool at the ready; no one else but the kernel can use that memory. However, when the physical machine is shared between virtual machines, having each guest keep its own pool of zero pages is wasteful.

Instead, the host can allocate a single zero page in physical memory for all of these instances. All pointers to the page will be set read-only, so that any attempt to modify the page will cause a trap to the host kernel; the kernel can then allocate a new (zeroed) physical page for that use, exactly as in copy-on-write. Of course, the guest kernels do not need to tell anyone when they create a zero page, so in the background, the host kernel runs a scavenger to look for zero pages in guest memory. When it finds one, it reclaims the physical page and changes the page table pointers to point at the shared zero page, with read-only permission.

The scavenger can do the same for other shared page frames. The code and data segments for both applications and shared libraries will often be the same or quite similar, even across different operating systems. An application like the Apache web server will not be re-written from scratch for every separate operating system; rather, some OS-specific glue code will be added to match the portable portion of the application to its specific environment.

- **Compression of unused pages.** Even if a page is different, it may be close to some other page in a different virtual machine. For example, different versions of the operating system may differ in only some small respects. This provides an opportunity for the host kernel to introduce a new layer in the memory hierarchy to save space.

Instead of evicting a relatively unused page, the operating system can compress it. If the page is a delta of an existing page, the compressed version may be quite small. The kernel manipulates page table permissions to maintain the illusion that the delta is a real page. The full copy of the page is marked read-only; the delta is marked invalid. If the delta is referenced, it can be re-constituted as a full page more quickly than if it was stored on disk. If the original page is modified, the delta can be re-compressed or evicted, as necessary.

10.3 | Fault tolerance

All systems break. Despite our best efforts, application code can have bugs that cause the process to exit abruptly. Operating system code can have bugs that cause the machine to halt and reboot. Power failures and hardware errors can also cause a system to stop without warning.

Most applications are structured to periodically save user data to disk for just these types of events. When the operating system or application restarts, the program can read the saved data off disk to allow the user to resume their work.

In this section, we take this a step further, to see if we can manage memory to recover application data structures after a failure, and not just user file data.

Checkpoint and restart

One reason we might want to recover application data is when a program takes a long time to run. If a simulation of the future global climate takes a week to compute, we don't want to have to start again from scratch every time there is a power glitch. If enough machines are involved and the computation takes long enough, it is likely that at least one of the machines will encounter a failure sometime during the computation.

Of course, the program could be written to treat its internal data as precious — to periodically save its partial results to a file. To make sure the data is internally consistent, the program would need some natural

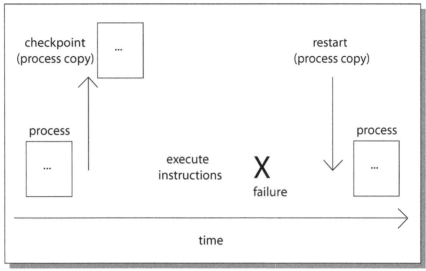

Figure 10.6: By checkpointing the state of a process, we can recover the saved state of the process after a failure by restoring the saved copy.

stopping point; for example, the program can save the predicted climate for 2050 before it moves onto computing the climate in 2051.

A more general approach is to have the operating system use the virtual memory system to provide application recovery as a service. If we can save the state of a process, we can transparently restart it whenever the power fails, exactly where it left off, with the user none the wiser.

To make this work, we first need to suspend each thread executing in the process and save its state — the program counter, stack pointer, and registers to application memory. Once all threads are suspended, we can then store a copy of the contents of the application memory on disk. This is called a *checkpoint* or snaphot, illustrated in Figure 10.6. After a failure, we can resume the execution by restoring the contents of memory from the checkpoint and resuming each of the threads from from exactly the point we stopped them. This is called an application *restart*.

checkpoint

restart

What would happen if we allow threads to continue to run while we are saving the contents of memory to disk? During the copy, we have a race condition: some pages could be saved before being modified by some thread, while others could be saved after being modified by that same thread. When we try to restart the application, its data structures could appear to be corrupted. The behavior of the program might be different than what would have happened if the failure had not occurred.

Fortunately, we can use address translation to minimize the amount of time we need to have the system stalled during a checkpoint. Instead of copying the contents of memory to disk, we can mark the application's pages as copy-on-write. At this point, we can restart the program's threads.

Checkpoints and system calls

An implementation challenge for checkpoint/restart is to correctly handle any system calls that are in process. The state of a program is not only its user-level memory; it also includes the state of any threads that are executing in the kernel and any per-process state maintained by the kernel, such as its open file descriptors. While some operating systems have been designed to allow the kernel state of a process to be captured as part of the checkpoint, it is more common for checkpointing to be supported only at the virtual machine layer. A virtual machine has no state in the kernel except for the contents of its memory and processor registers. If we need to take a checkpoint while a trap handler is in progress, the handler can simply be restarted.

As each page reaches disk, we can reset the protection on that page to read-write. When the program tries to modify a page before it reaches disk, the hardware will take an exception, and the kernel can make a copy of the page — one to be saved to disk and one to be used by the running program.

We can take checkpoints of the operating system itself in the same way. It is easiest to do this if the operating system is running in a virtual machine. The host can take a checkpoint by stopping the virtual machine, saving the processor state, and changing the page table protections (in the host page table) to read-only. The virtual machine is then safe to restart while the host writes the checkpoint to disk in the background.

process migration

Process migration is the ability to take a running program on one system, stop its execution, and resume it on a different machine. Checkpoint and restart provide a basis for transparent process migration. For example, it is now common practice to checkpoint and migrate entire virtual machines inside a data center, as one way to balance load. If one system is hosting two web servers each of which becomes heavily loaded, we can stop one and move it to a different machine so that each can get better performance.

Recoverable virtual memory

Taking a complete checkpoint of a process or a virtual machine is a heavy-weight operation, and so it is only practical to do relatively rarely. We can use copy-on-write page protection to resume the process after starting the checkpoint, but completing the checkpoint will still take considerable time while we copy the contents of memory out to disk.

recoverable virtual memory

Can we provide an application the illusion of persistent memory, so that the contents of memory are restored to a point very soon prior to the failure? The ability to do this is called *recoverable virtual memory*. An example where we might like recoverable virtual memory is in an email client; as you read, reply, and delete email, you don't want your work to be lost if the system crashes.

If we put efficiency aside, recoverable virtual memory is possible. First, we take a checkpoint so that some consistent version of the application's data is on disk. Next, we record an ordered sequence, or *log*, of every update that the application makes to memory. Once the log is written to disk, after a failure, we can recover by reading the checkpoint and applying the changes from the log.

This is exactly how most text editors save their backups, to allow them to recover uncommitted user edits after a machine or application failure. A text editor could repeatedly write an entire copy of the file to a backup, but this would be slow, particularly for a large file. Instead, a text editor will write a version of the file, and then it will append a sequence of every change the user makes to that version. To avoid having to separately write every typed character to disk, the editor will batch changes, e.g., all of the changes the user made in the past 100 milliseconds, and write those to disk as a unit. Even if the very latest batch has not been written to disk, the user can usually recover the state of the file at almost the instant immediately before the machine crash.

A downside of this algorithm for text editors is that it can cause information to be leaked without it being visible in the current version of the file. Text editors sometimes use this same method when the user hits "save" — just append any changes from the previous version, rather than writing a fresh copy of the entire file. This means that the old version of a file can potentially still be recovered from a file. So if you write a memo insulting your boss, and then edit it to tone it down, it is best to save a completely new version of your file before you send it off!

Will this method work for persistent memory? Keeping a log of every change to every memory location in the process would be too slow. We would need to trap on every store instruction and save the value to disk. In other words, we would run at the speed of the trap handler, rather than the speed of the processor.

However, we can come close. When we take a checkpoint, we mark all pages as read-only to ensure that the checkpoint includes a consistent snapshot of the state of the process's memory. Then we trap to the kernel on the first store instruction to each page, to allow the kernel to make a copy-on-write. The kernel resets the page to be read-write so that successive store instructions to the same page can go at full speed, but it can also record the page as having been modified.

We can take an *incremental checkpoint* by stopping the program and saving a copy of any pages that have been modified since the previous checkpoint. Once we change those pages back to read-only, we can restart the program, wait a bit, and take another incremental checkpoint. After a crash, we can recover the most recent memory by reading in the first checkpoint and then applying each of the incremental checkpoints in turn,

log

incremental
checkpoint

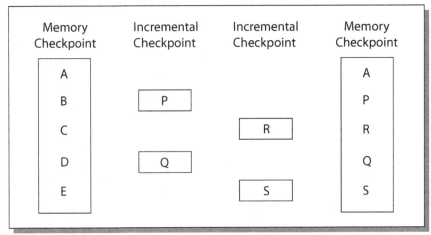

Figure 10.7: The operating system can recover the state of a memory segment after a crash by saving a sequence of incremental checkpoints.

as shown in Figure 10.7.

How much work we lose during a machine crash is a function of how quickly we can completely write an incremental checkpoint to disk. This is governed by the rate at which the application creates new data. To reduce the cost of an incremental checkpoint, applications needing recoverable virtual memory will designate a specific memory segment as persistent. After a crash, that memory will be restored to the latest incremental checkpoint, allowing the program to quickly resume its work.

Deterministic debugging

A key to building reliable systems software is the ability to locate and fix problems when they do occur. Debugging a sequential program is comparatively easy: if you give it the same input, it will execute the same code in the same order, and produce the same output.

Debugging a concurrent program is much harder: the behavior of the program may change depending on the precise scheduling order chosen by the operating system. If the program is correct, the same output should be produced on the same input. If we are debugging a program, however, it is probably not correct. Instead, the precise behavior of the program may vary from run to run depending on which threads are scheduled first.

Debugging an operating system is even harder: not only does the operating system make widespread use of concurrency, but it is hard to tell sometimes what is its "input" and "output."

It turns out, however, that we can use a virtual machine abstraction to provide a repeatable debugging environment for an operating system, and we can in turn use that to provide a repeatable debugging environment for concurrent applications.

It is easiest to see this on a uniprocessor. The execution of an operating system running in a virtual machine can only be affected by three factors: its initial state, the input data provided by its I/O devices, and the precise timing of interrupts.

Because the host kernel mediates each of these for the virtual machine, it can record them and play them back during debugging. As long as the host exactly mimics what it did the first time, the behavior of the guest operating system will be the same and the behavior of all applications running on top of the guest operating system will be the same.

Replaying the input is easy, but how do we replay the precise timing of interrupts? Most modern computer architectures have a counter on the processor to measure the number of instructions executed. The host operating system can use this to measure how many instructions the guest operating system (or guest application) executed between the point where the host gave up control of the processor to the guest, and when control returned back to the kernel due to an interrupt or trap.

To replay the precise timing of an asynchronous interrupt, the host kernel records the guest program counter and the instruction count at the point when the interrupt was delivered to the guest. On replay, the host kernel can set a trap on the page containing the program counter where the next interrupt will be taken. Since the guest might visit the same program counter multiple times, the host kernel uses the instruction count to determine which visit corresponds to the one where the interrupt was delivered. (Some systems make this even easier, by allowing the kernel to request a trap whenever the instruction count reaches a certain value.)

Moreover, if we want to skip ahead to some known good intermediate point, we can take a checkpoint, and play forward the sequence of interrupts and input data from there. This is important as sometimes bugs in operating systems can take weeks to manifest themselves; if we needed to replay everything from boot the debugging process would be much more cumbersome.

Matters are more complex on a multicore system, as the precise behavior of both the guest operating system and the guest applications will depend on the precise ordering of instructions across the different processors. It is an ongoing area of research how best to provide deterministic execution in this setting. Provided that the program being debugged has no race conditions — that is, no access to shared memory outside of a critical section — then its behavior will be deterministic with one more piece of information. In addition to the initial state, inputs, and asynchronous interrupts, we also need to record which thread acquires each critical section in which order. If we replay the threads in that order and deliver interrupts precisely and provide the same device input, the behavior will be the same. Whether this is a practical solution is still an open question.

10.4 | Security

Hardware or software address translation provides a basis for executing untrusted application code, to allow the operating system kernel to protect itself and other applications from malicious or buggy implementations.

A modern smartphone or tablet computer, however, has literally hundreds of thousands of applications. Many or most are completely trustworthy, but others are specifically designed to steal or corrupt local data by exploiting weaknesses in the underlying operating system or the natural human tendency to trust technology. How is a user to know which is which? A similar situation exists for the web: even if most web sites are innocuous, many web sites embed code that exploits known vulnerabilities in the browser defenses.

If we can't limit our exposure to potentially malicious applications, what can we do? One important step is to keep your system software up to date. The malicious code authors recognize this: a recent survey showed that the most likely web sites to contain viruses are those targeted at the most novice users, e.g., screensavers and children's games.

In this section, we discuss whether there are additional ways to use virtual machines to limit the scope of malicious applications.

Suppose you want to download a new application, or visit a new web site. There is some chance it will work as advertised, and there is some chance it will contain a virus. Is there any way to limit the potential of the new software to exploit some unknown vulnerability in your operating system or browser?

One interesting approach is to clone your operating system into a new virtual machine, and run the application in the clone rather than on the native operating system. A virtual machine constructed for the purpose of executing suspect code is called a *virtual machine honeypot*. By using a virtual machine, if the code turns out to be malicious, we can delete the virtual machine and leave the underlying operating system as it was before we attempted to run the application.

virtual machine honeypot

Creating a virtual machine to execute a new application might seem extravagant. However, earlier in this chapter, we discussed various ways to make this more efficient: shadow page tables, memory compression, efficient checkpoint and restart, and copy-on-write. And of course, reinstalling your system after it has become infected with a virus is even slower!

Both researchers and vendors of commercial anti-virus software make extensive use of virtual machine honeypots to detect and understand viruses. For example, a frequent technique is to create an array of virtual machines, each with a different version of the operating system. By loading a potential virus into each one, and then simulating user behavior, we can more easily determine which versions of software are vulnerable and which are not.

A limitation is that we need to be able to tell if the browser or operating system running in the virtual machine honeypot has been corrupted. Often, viruses operate instantly, by attempting to install logging software or scanning the disk for sensitive information such as credit card numbers. There is nothing to keep the virus from lying in wait; this has become more common recently, particularly those designed for military or business espionage.

Another limitation is that the virus might be designed to infect both the guest operating system running in the clone and the host kernel implementing the virtual machine. (In the case of the web, the virus must infect the browser, the guest operating system, and the host.) As long as the system software is kept up to date, the system is vulnerable only if the virus is able to exploit some unknown weakness in the guest operating system and a separate unknown weakness in the host implementation *defense in* of the virtual machine. This provides *defense in depth*, improving security *depth* through multiple layers of protection.

10.5 | User-level memory management

With the increasing sophistication of applications and their runtime systems, most widely used operating systems have introduced hooks for applications to manage their own memory. While the details of the interface differs from system to system, the hooks preserve the role of the kernel in allocating resources between processes and in preventing access to privileged memory. Once a page frame has been assigned to a process, however, the kernel can leave it up to the process to determine what to do with that resource.

Operating systems can provide applications the flexibility to decide:

- **Where to get missing pages.** As we noted in the previous chapter, a modern memory hierarchy is deep and complex: local disk, local non-volatile memory, remote memory inside a data center, or remote disk. By giving applications control, the kernel can keep its own memory hierarchy simple and local, while still allowing sophisticated applications to take advantage of network resources when they are available, even when those resources are on machines running completely different operating systems.

- **Which pages can be accessed.** Many applications such as browsers and databases need to set up their own application-level sandboxes for executing untrusted code. Today this is done with a combination of hardware and software techniques, as we described in Chapter 8. Finer-grained control over page fault handling allows more sophisticated models for managing sharing between regions of untrusted code.

- **Which pages should be evicted.** Often, an application will have better information than the operating system over which pages it will reference in the near future.

Many applications can adapt the size of their working set to the resources provided by the kernel but they will have worse performance whenever there is a mismatch.

- **Garbage collected programs.** Consider a program that does its own garbage collection. When it starts up, it allocates a block of memory in its virtual address space to serve as the heap. Periodically, the program scans through the heap to compact its data structures, freeing up room for additional data structures to be allocated. This causes all pages to appear to be recently used, confounding the kernel's memory manager. By contrast, the application knows that the best page to replace is one that was recently cleaned of application data.

  It is equally confounding to the application. How does the garbage collector know how much memory it should allocate for the heap? Ideally, the garbage collector should use exactly as much memory as the kernel is able to provide, and no more. If the runtime heap is too small, the program must garbage collect, even though more page frames available. If the heap is too large, the kernel will page parts of the heap to disk instead of asking the application to pay the lower overhead of compacting its memory.

- **Databases.** Databases and other data processing systems often manipulate huge data sets that must be streamed from disk into memory. As we noted in Chapter CachingChNum, algorithms for large data sets will be more efficient if they are customized to the amount of available physical memory. If the operating system evicts a page that the database expects to be in memory, these algorithms will run much more slowly.

- **Virtual machines.** A similar issue arises with virtual machines. The guest operating system running inside of a virtual machine thinks it has a set of physical page frames, which it can assign to the virtual pages of applications running in the virtual machine. In reality, however, the page frames in the guest operating system are virtual and can be paged to disk by the host operating system. If the host operating system could tell the guest operating system when it needed to steal a page frame (or donate a page frame), then the guest would know exactly how many page frames were available to be allocated to its applications.

In each of these cases, the performance of a resource manager can be compromised if it runs on top of a virtualized, rather than a physical,

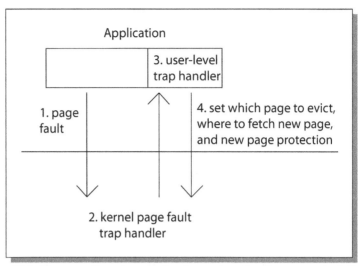

Figure 10.8: The operation of a user-level page handler. On a page fault, the hardware traps to the kernel; if the fault is for a segment with a user-level pager, the kernel passes the fault to the user-level handler to manage. The user-level handler is pinned in memory to avoid recursive faults.

resource. What is needed is for the operating system kernel to communicate how much memory is assigned to a process or virtual machine, to enable the application to do its own memory management. As processes start and complete, the amount of available physical memory will change, and therefore the assignment to each application will change.

To handle these needs, most operating systems provide some level of application control over memory. Two models have emerged:

- **Pinned pages.** A very simple and widely available model is to allow
  pin applications to *pin* virtual memory pages to physical page frames, preventing those pages from being evicted unless absolutely necessary. Once pinned, the application can manage its memory however it sees fit, for example, by explicitly shuffling data back and forth to disk.

- **User-level pagers.** A more general solution is for applications to spec-
  user-level ify a *user-level page handler* for a memory segment. On a page fault
  page handler or protection violation, the kernel trap handler is invoked. Instead of handling the fault itself, the kernel passes control to user-level handler, as in a UNIX signal handler. The user-level handler can then decide how to manage the trap: where to fetch the missing page, what action to take if the application was sandbox, and which page to replace. To avoid infinite recursion, the user-level page handler must itself be stored in pinned memory.

10.6 | Conclusions and future directions

In this chapter, we have argued that address translation provides a powerful tool for operating systems to provide a set of advanced services to applications to improve system performance, reliability, and security. Services such as checkpointing, recoverable memory, deterministic debugging, and honeypots are now widely supported at the virtual machine layer, and we believe that they will come to be standard in most operating systems as well.

Moving forward, it is clear that the demands on the memory management system for advanced services will increase. Not only are memory hierarchies becoming increasingly complex, but the diversity of services provided by the memory management system has added even more complexity.

Operating systems often go through cycles of gradually increasing complexity followed by rapid shifts back towards simplicity. The recent commercial interest in virtual machines may yield a shift back towards simpler memory management, by reducing the need for the kernel to provide every service that any application might need. Processor architectures now directly support user-level page tables. This potentially opens up an entire realm for more sophisticated runtime systems, for those applications that are themselves miniature operating systems, and a concurrent simplification of the kernel. With the right operating system support, applications will be able to set up and manage their own page tables directly, implement their own user-level process abstractions, and provide their own transparent checkpointing and recovery on memory segments.

Exercises

1. This question concerns the operation of shadow page tables for virtual machines, where a guest process is running on top of a guest operating system on top of a host operating system. The architecture uses paged segmentation, with a 32-bit virtual address divided into fields as follows:

   | 4 bit segment number | 12 bit page number | 16 bit offset |

   The guest operating system creates and manages segment and page tables to map the guest virtual addresses to guest physical memory. These tables are as follows (all values in hexadecimal):

   The host operating system creates and manages segment and page tables to map the guest physical memory to host physical memory. These tables are as follows:

Segment Table		Page Table A		Page Table B	
0	Page Table A	0	0002	0	0001
1	Page Table B	1	0006	1	0004
x	(rest invalid)	2	0000	2	0003
		3	0005	x	(rest invalid)
		x	(rest invalid)		

Segment Table		Page Table K	
0	Page Table K	0	BEEF
x	(rest invalid)	1	F000
		2	CAFE
		3	3333
		4	(invalid)
		5	BA11
		6	DEAD
		7	5555
		x	(rest invalid)

a) Find the host physical address corresponding to each of the following guest virtual addresses. Answer "invalid guest virtual address" if the guest virtual address is invalid; answer "invalid guest physical address if the guest virtual address maps to a valid guest physical page frame, but the guest physical page has an invalid virtual address.

    i. 00000000

   ii. 20021111

  iii. 10012222

  iv. 00023333

   v. 10024444

b) Using the information in the tables above, fill in the contents of the shadow segment and page tables for direct execution of the guest process.

c) Assuming that the guest physical memory is contiguous, list three reasons why the host page table might have an invalid entry for a guest physical page frame, with valid entries on either side.

2. Suppose we doing incremental checkpoints on a system with 4 KB pages and a disk capable of transferring data at 10 MB/s.

   a) What is the maximum rate of updates to new pages if every modified page is sent in its entirety to disk on every checkpoint and we require that each checkpoint reach disk before we start the next checkpoint?

   b) Suppose that most pages saved during an incremental checkpoint are only partially modified. Describe how you would design a system to save only the modified portions of each page as part of the checkpoint.

Part IV

Persistent Storage

Memory is the treasury and guardian of all things.
Marcus Tullius Cicero

11 File Systems: Introduction and Overview

Computers must be able to reliably store data. Individuals store family photos, music files, and email folders; programmers store design documents and source files; office workers store spreadsheets, text documents, and presentation slides; and businesses store inventory, orders, and billing records. In fact, for a computer to work at all, it needs to be able to store programs to run and the operating system, itself.

For all of these cases, users demand a lot from their storage systems:

- **Reliability.** A user's data should be safely stored even if a machine's power is turned off or its operating system crashes. In fact, much of this data is so important that users expect and need the data to survive even if the devices used to store it are damaged. For example, many modern storage systems continue to work even if one of the magnetic disks storing the data malfunctions or even if a data center housing some of the system's servers burns down!

- **Large capacity and low cost.** Users and companies store enormous amount of data, so they want to be able to buy high capacity storage for a low cost. For example, it takes about 350 MB to store an hour of CD-quality losslessly encoded music, 4 GB to store an hour-long high-definition home video, and about 1 GB to store 300 digital photos. As a result of these needs, many individuals own 1 TB or more of storage for their personal files. This is an enormous amount: if you printed 1 TB of data as text on paper, you would produce a stack about 20 miles high. In contrast, for less than $100 you can buy 1 TB of storage that fits in a shoebox.

Unit	Binary Bytes	Decimal Bytes
MB	2^{20}	10^6
GB	2^{30}	10^9
TB	2^{40}	10^{12}
PB	2^{50}	10^{15}
EB	2^{60}	10^{18}

- **High performance.** For programs to use data, they must be able to access it, and for programs to use large amounts of data, this access must be fast. For example, users want program start-up to be nearly instantaneous, a business may need to process hundreds or thousands of orders per second, or a server may need to stream a large number of video files to different users.

- **Named data.** Because users store a large amount of data, because some data must last longer than the process that creates it, and because data must be shared across programs, storage systems must provide ways to easily identify data of interest. For example, if you can name a file (e.g., /home/alice/assignments/hw1.txt) you can find the data you want out of the millions of blocks on your disk, you can still find it after you shut down your text editor, and you can use your email program to send the data produced by the text editor to another user.

- **Controlled sharing.** Users need to be able to share stored data, but this sharing needs to be controlled. As one example, you may want to create a design document that everyone in your group can read and write, that people in your department can read but not write, and that people outside of your department cannot access at all. As another example, it is useful for a system to be able to allow anyone to execute a program while only allowing the system administrator to change the program.

Nonvolatile storage and file systems. The contents of a system's main DRAM memory can be lost if there is an operating system crash or power failure. In contrast, *nonvolatile storage* is durable and retains its state across crashes and power outages; nonvolatile storage is also called or *persistent storage* or *stable storage*. Nonvolatile storage can also have much higher capacity and lower cost than the volatile DRAM that forms the bulk of most system's "main memory."

nonvolatile storage

persistent storage

stable storage

However, nonvolatile storage technologies have their own limitations. For example, current nonvolatile storage technologies such as magnetic disks and high-density flash storage do not allow random access to individual words of storage; instead, access must be done in more coarse-grained units — 512, 2048, or more bytes at a time.

Furthermore, these accesses can be much slower than access to DRAM; for example, reading a sector from a magnetic disk may require activating a motor to move a disk arm to a desired track on disk and then waiting for the spinning disk to bring the desired data under the disk head. Because disk accesses involve motors and physical motion, the time to access a random sector on a disk can be around 10 milliseconds. In contrast, DRAM latencies are typically under 100 nanoseconds. This large difference — about five orders of magnitude in the case of spinning disks — drives the operating

Goal	Physical Characteristic	Design Implication
High performance	Large cost to initiate IO access	Organize data placement with *files*, *directories*, *free space bitmap*, and *placement heuristics* so that storage is accessed in large sequential units *Caching* to avoid accessing persistent storage
Named data	Storage has large capacity, survives crashes, and is shared across programs	Support *files* and *directories* with meaningful names
Controlled sharing	Device stores many users' data	Include access-control *metadata* with files
Reliable storage	Crash can occur during update	Use *transactions* to make a set of updates atomic
	Storage devices can fail	Use *redundancy* to detect and correct failures
	Flash memory cells can wear out	Move data to different storage locations to even the wear

Figure 11.1: Characteristics of persistent storage devices affect the design of an operating system's storage abstractions.

system to organize and use persistent storage devices differently than main memory.

File systems are a common operating system abstraction to allow applications to access nonvolatile storage. File systems use a number of techniques to cope with the physical limitations of nonvolatile storage devices and to provide better abstractions to users. For example, Figure 11.1 summarizes how physical characteristics motivate several key aspects of file system design.

- **Performance.** File systems amortize the cost of initiating expensive operations — such as moving a disk arm or erasing a block of solid state memory — by grouping where its placement of data so that such operations access large, sequential ranges of storage.

- **Naming.** File systems group related data together into directories and files and provide human-readable names for them (e.g., /home/ alice/Pictures/summer-vacation/hiking.jpg.) These names for data remain meaningful even after the program that creates the data exits, they help users organize large amounts of storage, and they make it easy for users to use different different programs to create, read, and edit, their data.

- **Controlled sharing.** File systems include metadata about who owns which files and which other users are allowed to read, write, or execute data and program files.

- **Reliability.** File systems use transactions to atomically update multiple blocks of persistent storage, similar to how the operating system uses critical sections atomically update different data structures in memory.

  To further improve reliability, file systems store checksums with data to detect corrupted blocks, and they replicate data across multiple storage devices to recover from hardware failures.

Impact on application writers.   Understanding the reliability and performance properties of storage hardware and file systems is important even if you are not designing a file system from scratch. Because of the fundamental limitations of existing storage devices, the higher-level illusions of reliability and performance provided by the file system are imperfect. An application programmer needs to understand these limitations to avoid having inconsistent data stored on disk or having a program run orders of magnitude slower than expected.

For example, suppose you edit a large document with many embedded images and that your word processor periodically auto-saves the document so that you would not lose too many edits if the machine crashes. If the application uses the file system in a straightforward way, several of unexpected things may happen.

- **Poor performance.** First, although file systems allow existing bytes in a file to be overwritten with new values, they do not allow new bytes to be inserted into the middle of existing bytes. So, even a small update to the file may require rewriting the entire file either from beginning to end or at least from the point of the first insertion to the end. For a multi-megabyte file, each auto-save may end up taking as much as a second.

- **Corrupt file.** Second, if the application simply overwrites the existing file with updated data, an untimely crash can leave the file in an inconsistent state, containing a mishmash of the old and new versions. For example, if a section is cut from one location and pasted in another, after a crash the saved document may end up with copies of the section in both locations, one location, or neither location; or it may end up with a region that is a mix of the old and new text.

- **Lost file.** Third, if instead of overwriting the document file, the application writes updates to a new file, then deletes the original file, and finally moves the new file to the original file's location, an untimely crash can leave the system with no copies of the document at all.

Programs use a range of techniques to deal with these types of issues. For example, some structure their code to take advantage of the detailed semantics of some operating systems. For example, some operating systems guarantee that when a file is renamed and a file with the target name already exists, the target name will always refer to either the old or new file, even after a crash in the middle of the rename operation. In such a case, an implementation can create a new file with the new version of the data and use the rename command to atomically replace the old version with the new one.

Other programs essentially build a miniature file system over the top of the underlying one, structuring their data so that the underlying file system can better meet their performance and reliability requirements.

For example, a word processor might use a sophisticated document format, allowing it to, for example, add and remove embedded images and to always update a document by appending updates to the end of the file.

As another example, a data analysis program might improve its performance by organizing its accesses to input files in a way that ensures that each input file is read only once and that it is read sequentially from its start to its end.

Or, a browser with a 1 GB on-disk cache might create 100 files, each containing 10 MB of data, and group a given web site's objects in a sequential region of a randomly selected file. To do this, the browser would need to keep metadata that maps each cached web site to a region of a file, it would need to keep track of what regions of each file are used and which are free free, it would need to decide where to place a new web site's objects, and it would need to have a strategy for growing or moving a web site's objects as additional objects are fetched.

Roadmap. To get good performance and acceptable reliability, both application writers and operating systems designers must understand how storage devices and file systems work. This chapter and the next three discuss the key issues:

- **API and abstractions.** The rest of this chapter introduces file systems by describing a typical API and set of abstractions, and it provides an overview of the software layers that provide these abstractions.

- **Storage devices.** The characteristics of persistent storage devices strongly influence the design of storage system abstractions and higher level applications. Chapter 12 therefore explores the physical characteristics of common storage devices.

- **Implementing files and directories.** Chapter 13 describes how file systems keep track of data by describing several widely-used approaches to implementing files and directories.

- **Reliable storage.** Although we would like storage to be perfectly reliable, physical devices fall short of that ideal. Chapter 14 describes how storage systems use transactional updates and redundancy to improve reliability.

11.1 | The file system abstraction

Today, almost anyone who uses a computer is familiar with the high-level file system abstraction. File systems provide a way for users to organize their data and to store it for long periods of time. For example, Bob's computer might store a collection of applications such as /Applications/ Calculator and /ProgramFiles/TextEdit and a collection of data files such as /home/Bob/correspondence/letter-to-mom.txt, and /home/Bob/Classes/OS/hw1.txt.

file system

persistent data

named data

More precisely, a *file system* is an operating system abstraction that provides persistent, named data. *Persistent data* is stored until it is explicitly deleted, even if the computer storing it crashes or loses power. *Named data* can be accessed via a human-readable identifier that the file system associates with the file. Having a name allows a file to be accessed even after the program that created it has exited, and allows it to be shared by multiple applications.

There are two key parts to the file system abstraction: files, which define sets of data, and directories, which define names for files.

file

File. A *file* is a named collection of data in a file system. For example, the programs /Applications/Calculator or /ProgramFiles/TextEdit are each files, as are the data /home/Bob/correspondence/letter-to-mom.txt or /home/Bob/Classes/ OS/hw1.txt.

Files provide a higher-level abstraction than the underlying storage device: they let a single, meaningful name refer to an (almost) arbitrarily-sized amount of data. For example /home/Bob/Classes/OS/hw1.txt might be stored on disk in blocks 0x0A713F28, 0xB3CA349A, and 0x33A229B8, but it is much more convenient to refer to the data by its name than by this list of disk addresses.

file metadata

A file's information has two parts, metadata and data. A *file's metadata* is information about the file that is understood and managed by the operating system. For example, a file's metadata typically includes the file's *size*, its *modification time*, its *owner*, and its *security information* such as whether it may be read, written, or executed by the owner or by other users.

file data

A *file's data* can be whatever information a user or application puts in it. From the point of view of the file system, a file's data is just an array of untyped bytes. Applications can use these bytes to store whatever information they want in whatever format they choose. Some data have a simple structure. For example, an ASCII text file contains a sequence of bytes that

Executing "untyped" files

Usually, an operating system treats a file's data as an array of untyped bytes, leaving it up to applications to interpret a file's contents. Occasionally, however, the operating system needs to be able to parse a file's data.

For example, Linux supports a number of different executable file types such as the ELF and a.out binary files and tsch, csh, and perl scripts. You can run any of these files from the command line or using the exec() system call. E.g.,

```
> a.out
Hello world from hello.c compiled by gcc!
> hello.pl
Hello world from hello.pl, a perl script!
> echo "Hello world from /bin/echo, a binary supplied with your system!"
Hello world from /bin/echo, a binary supplied with your system!
```

To execute a file, the operating system must determine whether it is a binary file or a script. If it is the former, the operating system must parse the file to determine where in the target process's memory to load code and data from the file and which instruction to start with. If it is the latter, the operating system must determine which interpreter program it should launch to execute the script.

Linux does this by having executable files begin with a *magic number* that identifies the file's format. For example, ELF binary executables begin with the four bytes 0x7f, 0x45, 0x4c, and 0x46 (the ASCII characters DEL, E, L, and F); once an executable is known to be an ELF file, the ELF standard defines how the operating system should parse the rest of the file to extract and load the program's code and data. Similarly, script files begin with #! followed by the name of the interpreter that should be used to run the script (e.g., a script might begin with \#!/bin/sh to be executed using the Bourne shell or \#!/usr/bin/perl to be executed using the perl interpreter.

Alternative approaches include determining a file's type by its name *extension* — the characters after the last dot (.) in the file's name (e.g., .exe, .pl, or .sh) — or including information about a file's type in its metadata.

---

are interpreted as letters in the English alphabet. Conversely, data structures stored by applications can be arbitrarily complex. For example, a .doc files can contain text, formatting information, and embedded objects and images, an ELF (Executable and Linkable File) files can contain compiled objects and executable code, or a database file can contain the information and indices managed by a relational database.

Directory. Whereas a file contains system-defined metadata and arbitrary **directory** data, directories provide names for files. In particular, a *directory* is a list of human-readable names and a mapping from each name to a specific underlying file or directory. One common metaphor is that a directory is a

---

Multiple data streams

For traditional files, the file's data is a single logical sequence of bytes, and each byte can be identified by its offset from the start of the sequence (e.g., byte 0, byte 999, or byte 12481921 of a file.)

Some file systems support multiple sequences of bytes per file. For example, Apple's MacOS Extended file system supports multiple *forks* per file — a data fork for the file's basic data, a resource fork for storing additional attributes for the file, and multiple named forks for application-defined data. Similarly, Microsoft's NTFS supports *alternate data streams* that are similar to MacOS's named forks.

In these systems, when you open a file to read or write its data, you specify not only the file but also the fork or stream you want.

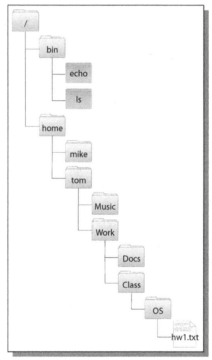

Figure 11.2: Example of a hierarchical organization of files using directories.

folder that contains documents (files) and other folders (directories).

As Figure 11.2 illustrates, because directories can include names of other directories, they can be organized in a hierarchy so that different sets of associated files can be grouped in different directories. So, the directory /bin may include binary applications for your machine while /home/tom (Tom's "home directory") might include Tom's files. If Tom has many files,

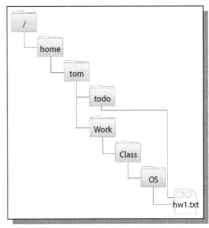

Figure 11.3: Example of a directed acyclic graph directory organization with multiple hard links to a file.

Tom's home directory may include additional directories to group them (e.g., /home/tom/Music and /home/tom/Work.) Each of these directories may have subdirectories (e.g.,/home/tom/Work/Class and /home/tom/Work/Docs) and so on.

path
The string that identifies a file or directory (e.g., /home/tom/Work/Class/OS/hw1.txt or /home/tom) is called a *path*. Here, the symbol / (pronounced *slash*) separates components of the path, and each component represents an entry in a directory. So, hw1.txt is a file in the directory OS; OS is a directory in the directory Work; and so on.

root directory

absolute path
If you think of the directory as a tree, then the root of the tree is a directory called, naturally enough, the *root directory*. Path names such as /bin/ls that begin with / define *absolute paths* that are interpreted relative to the root directory. So, /home refers to the directory called home in the root directory.

relative path

current working directory
Path names such as Work/Class/OS that do not begin with / define *relative paths* that are interpreted by the operating system relative to a process's *current working directory*. So, if a process's current working directory is /home/tom, then the relative path Work/Class/OS is equivalent to the absolute path /home/tom/Work/Class/OS.

home directory
When you log in, your shell's current working directory is set to your *home directory*. Processes can change their current working directory with the chdir(path) system call. So, for example, if you log in and then type cd Work/Class/OS, your current working directory is changed from your home directory to the subdirectory Work/Class/OS in your home directory.

If each file or directory is identified by exactly one path, then the directory hierarchy forms a tree. Occasionally, it is useful to have several different names for the same file or directory. For example, if you are ac-

. and .. and ~

You may sometimes see path names in which directories are named ., .., or ~ . E.g.,

> cd ~/Work/Class/OS
> cd ..
> ./a.out

., .., and ~ are special directory names in Unix. . refers to the *current directory*, .. refers to the *parent directory*, ~ refers to the *current user's home directory*, and *~name* refers to the *home directory of user* name.

So, the first shell command changes the current working directory to be the Work/Class/OS directory in the user's home directory (e.g., /home/tom/Work/Class/OS). The second command changes the current working directory to be the Work/Class directory in the user's home directory (e.g., ~/Work/Class or /home/tom/Work/Class.) The third command executes the program a.out from the current working directory (e.g., ~/Work/Class/a.out or /home/tom/Work/Class/a.out.)

---

tively working on a project, you might find it convenient to have the project appear in both your "todo" directory and a more permanent location (e.g., /home/tom/todo/hw1.txt and /home/tom/Work/Class/OS/hw1.txt as illustrated in Figure 11.3.)

hard link

The mapping between a name and the underlying file is called a *hard link*. If a system system allows multiple hard links to the same file, then the directory hierarchy may no longer be a tree. Most file systems that allow multiple hard links to a file restrict these links to avoid cycles, ensuring that their directory structures form a directed acyclic graph (DAG.) Avoiding cycles can simplify management by, for example, ensuring that recursive traversals of a directory structure terminate or by making it straightforward to use reference counting to garbage collect a file when the last link to it is removed.

In addition to hard links, many systems provide other ways to use multiple names to refer to the same file. See the sidebar for a comparison of hard links, soft links, symbolic links, shortcuts, and aliases.

volume

Volume.   Each instance of a file system manages files and directories for a volume. A *volume* is a collection of physical storage resources that form a logical storage device.

A volume is an abstraction that corresponds to a logical disk. In the simplest case, a volume corresponds to a single physical disk drive. Alternatively, a single physical disk can be partitioned and store multiple volumes or several physical disks can be combined so that a single volume

Hard links, soft links, symbolic links, shortcuts, and aliases

A hard link is a directory mapping from a file name directly to an underlying file. As we will see in Chapter 13, directories will be implemented by storing mappings from *file names* to *file numbers* that uniquely identify each file. When you first create a file (e.g., /a/b), the directory entry you create is a hard link the the new file. If you then use link() to add another hard link to the file (e.g., link("/a/b", "/c/d"),) then both names are equally valid, independent names for the same underlying file. You could, for example, unlink("/a/b"), and /c/d would remain a valid name for the file.

Many systems also support *symbolic links* also known as *soft links*. A symbolic link is a directory mappings from a file name to *another file name*. If a file is opened via a symbolic link, the file system first translates the name in the symbolic link to the target name and then uses the target name to open the file. So, if you create /a/b , create a symbolic link from /c/d/ to /a/b, and then unlink /a/b, the file is no longer accessible and open("/c/d") will fail.

Although the potential for such dangling links is a disadvantage, symbolic links have a number of advantages over hard links. First, systems usually allow symbolic links to directories, not just regular files. Second, a symbolic link can refer to a file stored in a different file system or volume.

Some operating systems such as Microsoft Windows also support *shortcuts*, which appear similar to symbolic links but which are interpreted by the windowing system rather than by the file system. From the file system's point of view, a shortcut is just a regular file. The windowing system, however, treats shortcut files specially: when the shortcut file is selected via the windowing system, the windowing system opens that file, identifies the target file referenced by the shortcut, and acts as if the target file had been selected.

A MacOS file *alias* is similar to a symbolic link but with an added feature: if the target file is moved to have a new path name, the alias can still be used to reference the file.

---

spans multiple physical disks.

A single computer can make use of multiple file systems stored on multiple volumes by mounting multiple volumes in a single logical hierar-

mount   chy. *Mounting* a volume on an existing file system creates a mapping from some path in the existing file system to the root directory of the mounted volume's file system and lets the mounted file system control mappings for all extensions of that path.

For example, suppose a USB drive contains a file system with the directories /Movies and /Backup as shown in Figure 11.4. If Alice plugs that drive into her laptop, the laptop's operating system might mount the USB volume's file system with the path /Volumes/usb1/ as shown in Figure 11.5. Then, if Alice calls open("/Volumes/usb1/Movies/vacation.mov"), she will open the file /Movies/vacation.mov from the file system on the USB drive's volume. If, instead, Bob plugs that drive into his laptop, the laptop's operating system

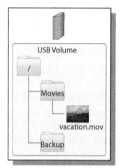

Figure 11.4: This USB disk holds a volume that is the physical storage for a file system.

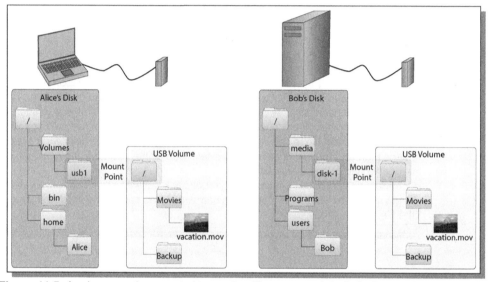

Figure 11.5: A volume can be mounted to another file system to join their directory hierarchies. For example, when the USB drive is connected to Alice's computer, she can access the vacation.mov movie using the path /Volumes/usb1/Movies/vacation.mov, and when the drive is connected to Bob's computer, he can access the movie using the path /media/disk-1/Movies/vacation.mov.

might mount the volume's file system with the path /media/disk-1, and Bob would access the same file using the path /media/disk-1/Movies/vacation.mov.

11.2 | API

For concreteness, Figure 11.6 shows a simple file system API for accessing files and directories.

Creating and deleting files	
create(pathName)	Create a new file with the specified name
link(existingName, newName)	Create a hard link — a new path name that refers to the same underlying file as an existing path name
unlink(pathName)	Remove the specified name for a file from its directory; if that was the only name for the underlying file, then remove the file and free its resources.
mkdir(pathName)	Create a new directory with the specified name
rmdir(pathName)	Remove the directory with the specified name
Open and close	
fileDescriptor = open(pathName)	Prepare the calling process for access to the specified file (e.g., check access permissions and initialize kernel data structures for tracking per-process state of open files)
close(fileDescriptor)	Release resources associated with the specified open file
File access	
read(fileDescriptor, buf, len)	Read len bytes from the process's current position in the open file fileDescriptor and copy the results to a buffer buf in the application's memory
write(fileDescriptor, len, buf)	Write len bytes of data from a buffer buf in the process's memory to the process's current position in the open file fileDescriptor.
seek(fileDescriptor, offset)	Change the process's current position in the open file fileDescriptor to the specified offset
dataPtr = mmap(fileDescriptor, off, len)	Set up a mapping between the data in the file fileDescriptor from off to off + len and an area in the application's virtual memory from dataPtr to dataPtr + len.
munmap(dataPtr, len)	Remove the mapping between the application's virtual memory and a mapped file
fsync(fileDescriptor)	Force to disk all buffered, dirty pages for the file associated with fileDescriptor.

Figure 11.6: A simple API for accessing files.

Creating and deleting files.   Processes create and destroy files with create() and unlink(). Create() does two things: it creates a new file that has initial metadata but no other data, and it creates a name for that file in a directory.

Link() creates a hard link — a new path name for an existing file. After a successful call to link(), there are multiple path names that refer to the same underlying file.

Unlink() removes a name for a file from its directory. If a file has multiple names or links, unlink() only removes the specified name, leaving the file accessible via other names. If the specified name is the last (or only) link to a file, then unlink() also deletes the underlying file and frees its resources.

Mkdir() and rmdir() create and delete directories.

EXAMPLE   **Linking to files v. linking to directories.**

Systems such as Linux support a link() system call, but they do not allow new hard links to be created to a directory. E.g., existingPath must not be a directory. Why does Linux mandate this restriction?

ANSWER   Preventing multiple hard links to a directory prevents cycles, ensuring that the directory structure is always a directed acyclic graph (DAG).

Additionally, allowing hard links to a directory would muddle a directory's parent directory entry (e.g., ".." as discussed in the sidebar on page 490.)

Open and close.   To start accessing a file, a process calls open() to get a *file descriptor* it can use to refer to the open file. *File descriptor* is Unix terminology; in other systems and APIs objects playing similar roles may be called *file handles* or *file streams*.

file descriptor

file handle

file stream

Operating systems require processes to explicitly open() files and access them via file descriptors rather than simply passing the path name to read() and write() calls for two reasons. First, path parsing and permission checking can be done just when a file is opened and need not be repeated on each read or write. Second, when a process opens a file, the operating system creates a data structure that stores information about the process's open file such as the file's ID, whether the process can write or just read the file, and a pointer to the process's current position within the file. The file descriptor can thus be thought of as a reference to the operating system's per-open-file data structure that the operating system will use for managing the process's access to the file.

When an application is done using a file, it calls close(), which releases the open file record in the operating system.

File access.   While a file is open, an application can access the file's data in two ways. First, it can use the traditional procedural interface, making system calls to read() and write() on an open file. Calls to read() and write() start from the process's current file position, and they advance the current file position by the number of bytes successfully read or written. So, a sequence of read() or write() calls moves sequentially through a file. To support random access within a file, the seek() call changes a process's current position for a specified open file.

Modern File Access APIs

The API shown in Figure 11.6 is similar to most widely-used file access APIs, but it is somewhat simplified.

For example, each of the listed calls is similar to a call provided by the Posix interface, but the API shown in Figure 11.6 omits some arguments and options found in Posix. The Posix open() call, for example, includes two additional arguments one to specify various flags such as whether the file should be opened in read-only or read-write mode and the other to specify the access control permissions that should be used if the open() call creates a new file.

In addition, real-world file access APIs are likely to have a number of additional calls. For example, the Microsoft Windows file access API includes dozens of calls including calls to lock and unlock a file, to encrypt and decrypt a file, or to find a file in a directory whose name matches a specific pattern.

Rather than using read() and write() to access a file's data, an application can use mmap() to establish a mapping between a region of the process's virtual memory and some region of the file. Once a file has been mapped, memory loads and stores to that virtual memory region will read and write the file's data either by accessing a shared page from the kernel's file cache, or by triggering a page fault exception that causes the kernel to fetch the desired page of data from the file system into memory. When an application is done with a file, it can call munmap() to remove the mappings.

Finally, the fsync() call is important for reliability. When an application updates a file via a write() or a memory store to a mapped file, the updates are buffered in memory and written back to stable storage at some future time. Fsync() ensures that all pending updates for a file are written to persistent storage before the call returns. Applications use this function for two purposes. First, calling fsync() ensures that updates are durable and will not be lost if there is a crash or power failure. Second, calling fsync() between two updates ensures that the first is written to persistent storage before the second. Note that calling fsync() is not always necessary; the operating system ensures that all updates are made durable by periodically flushing all dirty file blocks to stable storage.

Exercises

1. **Discussion** Suppose a process successfully opens an existing file that has a single hard link to it, but while the process is reading that file, another process unlinks that file. What should happen to subsequent reads by the first process? Should they succeed? Should they fail? Why?

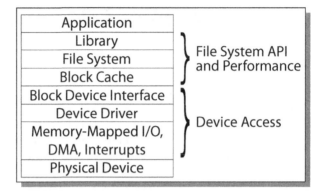

Figure 11.7: Layered abstractions provide access to I/O systems such as storage systems.

2. In Linux, suppose a process successfully opens an existing file that has a single hard link to it, but while the process is reading that file, another process unlinks that file? What happens to subsequent reads by the first process? Do they succeed? Do they fail? (Answer this problem by consulting documentation or by writing a program to test the behavior of the system in this case.)

3. Write a program that creates a new file, writes 100KB to it, flushes the writes, and deletes it. Time how long each of these steps takes.

   Hint You may find the Posix system calls creat(), write(), fflush(), close(), and gettimeofday() useful. See the manual pages for details on how to use these.

4. Consider a text editor that saves a file whenever you click a save button. Suppose that when you press the button, the editor simply (1) animates the button "down" event (e.g., by coloring the button grey), (2) uses the write() system call to write your text to your file, and then (3) animates the button "up" event (e.g., by coloring the button white). What bad thing could happen if a user edits a file, saves it, and then turns off her machine by flipping the power switch (rather than shutting the machine down cleanly)?

11.3 | Software layers

As shown in Figure 11.7, operating systems implement the file system abstraction through a series of software layers. Broadly speaking, these layers have two sets of tasks:

- **API and performance.** The top levels of the software stack — user-level libraries, kernel-level file systems, and the kernel's block cache — provide a convenient API for accessing named files and also work to minimize slow storage accesses via caching, write buffering, and prefetching.

- **Device access.** Lower levels of the software stack provide ways for the operating system to access a wide range of I/O devices. Device drivers hide the details of specific I/O hardware by providing hardware-specific code for each device, and placing that code behind a simpler, more general interfaces that the rest of the operating system can use such as a block device interface. The device drivers execute as normal kernel-level code, using the systems' main processors and memory, but they must interact with the I/O devices. A system's processors and memory communicate with its I/O devices using Memory-Mapped I/O, DMA, and Interrupts.

In the rest of this section, we first talk about the file system API and performance layers. We then discuss device access.

API and performance

The top levels of the file system software stack — divided between application libraries and operating system kernel code — provide the file system API and also provide caching and write buffering to improve performance.

System calls and libraries.   The file system abstraction such as the API shown in Figure 11.6 can be provided by directly by system calls. Alternatively, application libraries can wrap the system calls to add additional functionality such as buffering.

For example, in Linux, applications can access files directly using system calls (e.g., open(), read(), write(), and close().) Alternatively, applications can use the stdio library calls (e.g., fopen(), fread(), fwrite(), and fclose()). The advantage of the latter is that the library includes buffers to aggregate a program's small reads and writes into system calls that access larger blocks, which can reduce overheads. For example, if a program uses the library function fread() to read 1 byte of data, the fread() implementation may use the read() system call to read a larger block of data (e.g., 4 KB) into a buffer maintained by the library in the application's address space. Then, if the process calls fread() again to read another byte, the library just returns the byte from the buffer without needing to do a system call.

Block cache.   Typical storage devices are much slower than a computer's main memory. The operating system's block cache therefore caches recently read blocks, and it buffers recently written blocks so that they can be written back to the storage device at a later time.

In addition to improving performance by caching and write buffering, the block cache serves as a synchronization point: because all requests for a given block go through the block cache, the operating system includes information with each buffer cache entry to, for example, prevent one process from reading a block while another process writes it or to ensure that a given block is only fetched from the storage device once, even if it is simultaneously read by many processes.

Prefetching.   Operating systems use prefetching to improve I/O performance. For example, if a process reads the first two blocks of a file, the operating system may prefetch the next ten blocks.

Such prefetching can have several beneficial effects:

- **Reduced latency.** When predictions are accurate, prefetching can help the latency of future requests because reads can be serviced from main memory rather than from slower storage devices.

- **Reduced device overhead.** Prefetching can help reduce storage device overheads by replacing a large number of small requests with one large one.

- **Improved parallelism.** Some storage devices such as Redundant Arrays of Inexpensive Disks (RAIDs) and Flash drives are able to process multiple requests at once, in parallel. Prefetching provides a way for operating systems to take advantage of available hardware parallelism.

Prefetching, however, must be used with care. Too-aggressive prefetching can cause problems:

- **Cache pressure.** Each prefetched block is stored in the block cache, and it may displace another block from the cache. If the evicted block is needed before the prefetched one is used, prefetching is likely to hurt overall performance.

- **I/O contention.** Prefetch requests consume I/O resources. If other requests have to wait behind prefetch requests, prefetching may hurt overall performance.

- **Wasted effort.** Operating system prefetching is speculative. If the prefetched blocks end up being needed, then prefetching can help performance; otherwise, prefetching may hurt overall performance by wasting memory space, I/O device bandwidth, and CPU cycles.

Device drivers: Common abstractions

device driver   *Device drivers* translate between the high level abstractions implemented by the operating system and the hardware-specific details of I/O devices.

An operating system may have to deal with many different I/O devices. For example, a laptop on a desk might be connected to two keyboards (one internal and one external), a trackpad, a mouse, a wired ethernet, a wireless 802.11 network, a wireless bluetooth network, two disk drives (one internal and one external), a microphone, a speaker, a camera, a printer, a scanner, and a USB thumb drive. And that is just a handful of the literally thousands of devices that could be attached to a computer today. Building an operating system that treats each case separately would be impossibly complex.

Layering helps simplify operating systems by providing common ways to access various classes of devices. For example, for any given operating block device   system, storage device drivers typically implement a standard *block device* interface that allows data to be read or written in fixed-sized blocks (e.g., 512, 2048, or 4096 bytes).

Such a standard interface lets an operating system easily use a wide range of similar devices. A file system implemented to run on top of the standard block device interface can store files on any storage device whose driver implements that interface, be it a Seagate spinning disk drive, an Intel solid state drive, a Western Digital RAID, or an Amazon Simple Block Store volume. These devices all have different internal organizations and control registers, but if each manufacturer provides a device driver that exports the standard interface, the rest of the operating system does not need to be concerned with these per-device details.

Device access

How should an operating system's device drivers communicate with and control a storage device? At first blush, a storage device seems very different from the memory and CPU resources we have discussed so far. For example, a disk drive includes several motors, a sensor for reading data, and an electromagnet for writing data.

Memory mapped I/O.   As Figure 11.8 illustrates, I/O devices are typically connected to an I/O bus that is connected to the system's memory bus. Each I/O device has controller with a set of registers that can be written and read to transmit commands and data to and from the device. For example, a a simple keyboard controller might have one register that can be read to learn the most recent key pressed and another register than can be written to turn the caps-lock light on or off.

To allow I/O control registers to be read and written, systems implement
Memory   memory mapped I/O. *Memory mapped I/O* maps each device's control
mapped I/O

Challenge: Device Driver Reliability

Because device drivers are hardware-specific, they are often written and updated by the hardware manufacturer rather than the operating system's main authors. Furthermore, because there are large numbers of devices — some operating systems support tens of thousands of devices — device driver code may represent a large fraction of an operating system's code.

Unfortunately, bugs in device drivers have the potential to affect more than the device. A device driver usually runs as part of the operating system kernel since kernel routines depend on it and because it needs to access the hardware of its device. However, if the device driver is part of the kernel, then a device driver's bugs have the potential to affect the overall reliability of a system. For example, in 2003 it was reported that drivers caused about 85% of failures in the Windows XP operating system.

To improve reliability, operating systems are increasingly using protection techniques similar to those used to isolate user-level programs to isolate device drivers from the kernel and from each other.

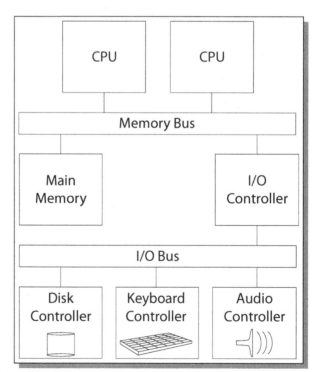

Figure 11.8: I/O devices are attached to the I/O bus, which is attached to the memory bus.

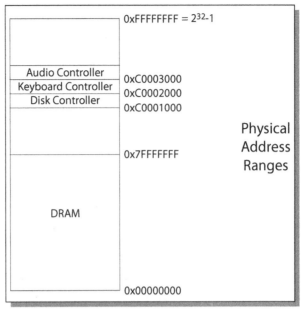

Figure 11.9: Physical address map for a system with 2 GB of DRAM and 3 memory mapped I/O devices.

registers to a range of physical addresses on the memory bus. Reads and writes by the CPU to this physical address range do not go to main memory. Instead, they go to registers on the I/O devices's controllers. Thus, the operating system's keyboard device driver might learn the value of the last key pressed by reading from physical address, say, 0xC00002000.

The hardware maps different devices to different physical address ranges. Figure 11.9 shows the physical address map for a hypothetical system with a 32 bit physical address space capable of addressing 4 GB of physical memory. This system has 2 GB of DRAM in it, consuming physical addresses 0x00000000 (0) to 0x7FFFFFFF (2^{31} - 1). Controllers for each of its three I/O devices are mapped to ranges of addresses in the first few kilobytes above 3 GB. For example, physical addresses from 0xC0001000 to 0xC0001FFF access registers in the disk controller.

DMA. Many I/O devices, including most storage devices, transfer data in bulk. For example, operating systems don't read a word or two from disk, they usually do transfers of at least a few kilobytes at a time. Rather than requiring the CPU to read or write each word of a large transfer, I/O devices can use direct memory access. When using *direct memory access (DMA)*, the I/O device copies a block of data between its own internal memory and the system's main memory.

To set up a DMA transfer, a simple operating system could use memory

direct
memory
access (DMA)

Port mapped I/O

Today, memory mapped I/O is the dominant paradigm for accessing I/O device's control registers. However an older style, *port mapped I/O*, is still sometimes used. Notably, the x86 architecture supports both memory mapped I/O and port mapped I/O.

Port mapped I/O is similar to memory mapped I/O in that instructions read from and write to specified addresses to control I/O devices. There are two differences. First, where memory mapped I/O uses standard memory-access instructions (e.g., load and store) to communicate with devices, port mapped I/O uses distinct I/O instructions. For example, the x86 architecture uses the in and out instructions for port mapped I/O. Second, whereas memory mapped I/O uses the same physical address space as is used for the system's main memory, the address space for port mapped I/O is distinct from the main memory address space.

For example, in x86 I/O can be done using either memory mapped or port mapped I/O, and the low-level assembly code is similar for both cases:

Memory mapped I/O	Port mapped I/O
`MOV register, memAddr // To read` `MOV memAddr, register // To write`	`IN register, portAddr // To read` `OUT portAddr, register // To write`

Port mapped I/O can be useful in architectures with constrained physical memory addresses since I/O devices do not need to consume ranges of physical memory addresses. On the other hand, for systems with sufficiently large physical address spaces, memory mapped I/O can be simpler since no new instructions or address ranges need to be defined and since device drivers can use any standard memory access instructions to access devices. Also, memory mapped I/O provides a more unified model for supporting DMA — direct transfers between I/O devices and main memory.

---

mapped I/O to provide a target physical address, transfer length, and operation code to the device. Then, the device copies data to or from the target address without requiring additional processor involvement.

After setting up a DMA transfer, the operating system must not use the target physical pages for any other purpose until the DMA transfer is done. The operating system therefore "pins" the target pages in memory so that they can not be reused until they are unpinned. For example, a pinned physical page cannot be swapped out to disk and then remapped to some other virtual address.

Interrupts.   The operating system needs to know when I/O devices have completed handling a request or when new external input arrives. One option is *polling*, repeatedly using memory mapped I/O to read a status

polling

Advanced DMA

Although a setting up a device's DMA can be as simple as providing a target physical address and length and then saying "go!", more sophisticated interfaces are increasingly used.

For example rather than giving devices direct access to the machine's physical address space, some systems include an *I/O memory management unit (IOMMU)* that translates device virtual addresses to main memory physical addresses similar to how a processor's TLB translates processor virtual addresses to main memory physical addresses. An IOMMU can provide both protection (e.g., preventing a buggy IO device from overwriting arbitrary memory) and simpler abstractions (e.g., allowing devices to use virtual addresses so that, for example, a long transfer can be made to a range of consecutive virtual pages rather than a collection of physical pages scattered across memory.)

Also, some devices add a level of indirection so that they can interrupt the CPU less often. For example, rather than using memory mapped I/O to set up each DMA request, the CPU and I/O device could share two lists in memory: one list of pending I/O requests and another of completed I/O requests. Then, the CPU could set up dozens of disk requests and only be interrupted when all of them are done.

Sophisticated I/O devices can even be configured to take different actions depending the data they receive. For example, some high performance network interfaces parse incoming packets and direct interrupts to different processors based on the network connection to which a received packet belongs.

---

register on the device. Because I/O devices are often much slower than CPUs and because inputs received by I/O devices may arrive at irregular rates, it us usually better for I/O devices to use interrupts to notify the operating system of important events.

Putting it all together: A simple disk request

When a process issues a system call like read() to read data from disk into the process's memory, the operating system moves the calling thread to a wait queue. Then, the operating system uses memory mapped I/O both to tell the disk to read the requested data and to set up DMA so that the disk can place that data in the kernel's memory. The disk then reads the data and DMAs it into main memory; once that is done, the disk triggers an interrupt. The operating system's interrupt handler then copies the data from the kernel's buffer into the process's address space. Finally, the operating system moves the thread the ready list. When the thread next runs, it will returns from the system call with the data now present in the specified buffer.

Exercises

5. Write a program that times how long it takes to issue 100,000 one-byte writes in each of two ways. First, time how long it takes to use the Posix system calls creat(), write(), and close() directly. Then see how long these writes take if the program uses the stdio library calls (e.g., fopen(), fwrite(), and fclose()) instead. Explain your results.

11.4 | Conclusions and future directions

The file system interface is a stable one, and small variations of interface described here can be found in many operating systems and for many storage devices.

Yet, the file system abstraction is imperfect, and application writers need to use it carefully to get acceptable performance and reliability. For example, if an application write()s a file, the update may not be durable when the write() call returns; application writers often call fsync() to ensure durability of data.

Could better file system APIs simplify programming? For example, if file systems allowed users to update multiple objects atomically, that might simplify many applications that currently must carefully constrain the order that their updates are stored using crude techniques such as using fsync as a barrier between one set of updates and the next.

Could better file system APIs improve performance? For example, one proposed interface allows an application to direct the operating system to transfer a range of bytes from a file to a network connection. Such an interface might, for example, reduce overheads for a movie server that streams movies across a network to clients.

Exercises

For convenience, the exercises from the body of the chapter are repeated here.

1. **Discussion** Suppose a process successfully opens an existing file that has a single hard link to it, but while the process is reading that file, another process unlinks that file. What should happen to subsequent reads by the first process? Should they succeed? Should they fail? Why?

2. In Linux, suppose a process successfully opens an existing file that has a single hard link to it, but while the process is reading that file, another process unlinks that file? What happens to subsequent reads by the first process? Do they succeed? Do they fail? (Answer this

problem by consulting documentation or by writing a program to test the behavior of the system in this case.)

3. Write a program that creates a new file, writes 100KB to it, flushes the writes, and deletes it. Time how long each of these steps takes.

   Hint You may find the Posix system calls creat(), write(), fflush(), close(), and gettimeofday() useful. See the manual pages for details on how to use these.

4. Consider a text editor that saves a file whenever you click a save button. Suppose that when you press the button, the editor simply (1) animates the button "down" event (e.g., by coloring the button grey), (2) uses the write() system call to write your text to your file, and then (3) animates the button "up" event (e.g., by coloring the button white). What bad thing could happen if a user edits a file, saves it, and then turns off her machine by flipping the power switch (rather than shutting the machine down cleanly)?

5. Write a program that times how long it takes to issue 100,000 one-byte writes in each of two ways. First, time how long it takes to use the Posix system calls creat(), write(), and close() directly. Then see how long these writes take if the program uses the stdio library calls (e.g., fopen(), fwrite(), and fclose()) instead. Explain your results.

Memory is the treasury and guardian of all things.
Marcus Tullius Cicero

12 Storage Devices

Although today's persistent storage devices have large capacity and low cost, they have drastically worse performance than volatile DRAM memory.

Not only that, but the characteristics are different and are peculiar to specific persistent storage devices. For example, although programs can access random individual words of DRAM with good performance, programs can only access today's disk and flash storage devices hundreds or thousands of bytes at a time. Furthermore, even if an application restricts itself to supported access sizes (e.g., 2 KB per read or write), if the application accesses pattern is random, the application may be slower by a factor of several hundred than if the application accessed the same amount of data sequentially.

To cope with the limitations and to maximize the performance of storage devices, both file system designers and application writers need to understand the physical characteristics of persistent storage devices.

Roadmap. This chapter discusses two types of persistent storage, *magnetic disks* and *flash memory*. Both are widely used: magnetic disks provide persistent storage for most servers, workstations, and laptops, while flash memory provides persistent storage for most smart phones, tablets, and cameras and for an increasing fraction of laptops.

Figure 12.1: A partially-disassembled magnetic disk drive.

12.1 | Magnetic disk

Magnetic disk is a nonvolatile storage technology that is widely used in laptops, desktops, and servers. Disk drives work by magnetically storing data on a thin metallic film bonded to a glass, ceramic, or aluminum disk that rotates rapidly. Figure 12.1 shows a disk drive without its protective cover, and Figure 12.2 shows a schematic of a disk drive, identifying key components.

platters

surfaces

spindle

Each drive holds one or more *platters*, thin cylinders that hold the magnetic material. Each platter has two *surfaces*, one on each side. When the drive is powered up, the platters are constantly spinning on a *spindle* powered by a *motor*. In 2011, disks commonly spin at 4200–15000 RPM (70–250 revolutions per second.)

head

A disk *head* is the component that reads and writes data by sensing or introducing a magnetic field on a surface. There is one head per surface, and as a surface spins underneath a head, the head reads or writes a sequence of bits along a circle centered on the disk's spindle. As a disk platters spins, it creates a layer of rapidly spinning air, and the disk head floats on that layer, allowing the head to get extremely close to the platter without contacting

head crash

it. A *head crash* occurs when the disk head breaks through this layer with enough force to damage the magnetic surface below; head crashes can be caused by excessive shock such as dropping a running drive.

arm

In order to use the full surface, each head is attached to an *arm*, and all

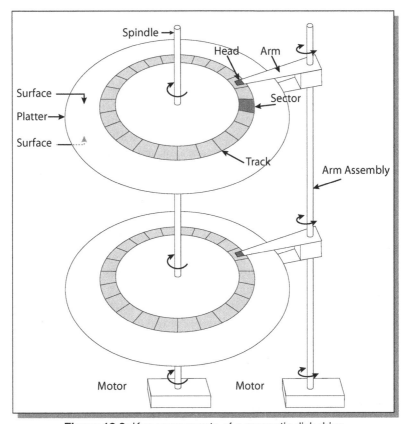

Figure 12.2: Key components of a magnetic disk drive.

arm assembly of a disk's arms are attached to a single *arm assembly* that includes a motor that can move the arms across the surfaces of the platters. Note that an assembly has just one motor, and all of its arms move together.

sectors Data bits are stored in fixed-size *sectors*; typically sectors are 512 bytes. The disk hardware cannot read or write individual bytes or words; instead, it must always read or write at least an entire sector. This means that to change 1 byte in a sector, the operating system must read the old sector, update the byte in memory, and rewrite the entire sector to disk. One reason for this restriction is that the disk encodes each sector with additional error correction code data, allowing it to fix (or at least detect) imperfectly read or written data, which, in turn allows higher density storage and higher bandwidth operation.

track A circle of sectors on a surface is called a *track*. All of the data on a track can be read or written without having to move the disk arm, so reading or writing a sequence of sectors on the same track is much faster than reading or writing sectors on different tracks.

To maximize sequential access speed, logical sector zero on each track is staggered from sector zero on the previous track by an amount corresponding to time it takes the disk to move the head from one track to another or to switch from the head on one surface to the head on another one. This staggering is called *track skewing*.

To increase storage density and disk capacity, disk manufacturers make tracks and sectors as thin and small as possible. If there are imperfections in a sector, then that sector may be unable to reliably store data. Manufacturers therefore include spare sectors distributed across each surface. The disk firmware or the file system's low-level formatting can then use *sector sparing* to remap sectors to use spare sectors instead of faulty sectors. *Slip sparing* helps retain good sequential access performance by remapping all sectors from the bad sector to the next spare, advancing each logical sector in that range by one physical sector on disk.

Disk drives often include a few MB of *buffer memory*, memory that the disk's controller uses to buffer data being read from or written to the disk, for track buffering, and for write acceleration.

Track buffering improves performance by storing sectors that have been read by the disk head but not yet requested by the operating system. In particular, when a disk head moves to a track, it may have to wait for the sector it needs to access to rotate under the disk head. While the disk is waiting, it reads unrequested sectors to its rack buffer so that if the operating system requests those sectors later, they can be returned immediately.

Write acceleration stores data to be written to disk in the disk's buffer memory and acknowledges the writes to the operating system before the data is actually written to the platter; the disk firmware flushes the writes from the track buffer to the platter at some later time. This technique can significantly increase the apparent speed of the disk, but it carries risks — if power is lost before buffered data is safely stored, then data might be lost.

Server drives implementing the SCSI or Fibre Channel interfaces and increasing numbers of commodity drives with the Serial ATA (SATA) interface implement a safer form of write acceleration with *tag command queuing* (TCQ) (also called *native command queuing* (NCQ) for SATA drives.) TCQ allows an operating system to issue multiple concurrent requests to the disk and for the disk to process those requests out of order to optimize scheduling, and it can be configured to only acknowledge write requests when the blocks are safely on the platter.

Disk access and performance

Operating systems send commands to a disk to read or write one or more consecutive sectors. A disk's sectors are identified with *logical block addresses* (LBAs) that specify the surface, track, and sector to be accessed.

To service a request for a sequence of blocks starting at some sector, the disk must first seek to the right track, then wait for the first desired sector to rotate to the head, and then transfer the blocks. So, the time for a disk access is:

$$\text{disk access time} = \text{seek time} + \text{rotation time} + \text{transfer time}$$

seek

- **Seek.** The disk must first *seek* — move its arm over the desired track. To seek, the disk first activates a motor that moves the arm assembly to approximately the right place on disk. Then, as arm stops vibrating from the motion of the seek, the disk begins reading positioning information embedded in the sectors to determine exactly where it

settle

  is and to make fine-grained positioning corrections to *settle* on the desired track. Once the head has settled on the right track, the disk uses signal strength and positioning information to make minute corrections in the arm position to keep the head over the desired track.

  A request's seek time depends on how far the disk arm has to move.

minimum seek time

  A disk's *minimum seek time* is the time it takes for the head to move from one track to an adjacent one. For short seeks, disks typically just "resettle" the head on the new track by updating the target track number in the track-following circuitry. Minimum seek times of 0.3–1.5 ms are typical.

head switch time

  If a disk is reading the tth track on one surface, its *head switch time* is the time it would take to begin reading the tth track on a different surface. Tracks can be less than a micron wide and tracks on different surfaces are not perfectly aligned. So, a head switch between the same tracks on different surfaces has a cost similar to a minimum seek: the disk begins using the sensor on a different head and then resettles the disk on the desired track for that surface.

maximum seek time

  A disk's *maximum seek time* is the time it takes the head to move from the innermost track to the outermost one or vice versa. Maximum seek times are typically over 10 ms and can be over 20 ms.

average seek time

  A disk's *average seek time* is the average across seeks between each possible pair of tracks on a disk. This value is often approximated as the time to seek one third of the way across the disk.

rotational latency

- **Rotate.** Once the disk head has settled on the right track, it must wait for the target sector to rotate under it. This waiting time is called the *rotational latency* . Today, most disks rotate at 4200 RPM to 15,000 RPM (15 ms to 4 ms per rotation), and for many workloads a reasonable estimate of rotational latency is one-half the time for a full rotation — 7.5 ms–2 ms.

  Once a disk head has settled on a new track, most disks immediately begin reading sectors into their buffer memory, regardless of which

---

Beware of "average seek time"

Although the name *average seek time* makes it tempting to use this metric when estimating the time it will take a disk to complete a particular workload, it is often the wrong metric to use. Average seek time — the average across seeks between each possible pair of tracks on disk — was defined this way to make it a well-defined, standard metric, not because it is representative of common workloads.

The definition of average seek time essentially assumes no locality in a workload, so it is very nearly a worst-case scenario. Many workloads access sectors that are likely to be near one another; for example, most operating systems attempt to place files sequentially on disk and to place different files in a directory on the same track or on tracks near one another. For these (common) workloads, the seek times observed may be closer to the disk's minimum seek time than its "average" seek time.

The demise of the cylinder

A *cylinder* on a disk is a set of tracks on different surfaces with the same track index. For example, on a 2-platter drive, the 8th tracks on surfaces 0, 1, 2, and 3 would form the 8th cylinder of the drive.

Some early file systems put related data on different surfaces but in the same cylinder. The idea was that data from the different tracks in the cylinder could be read without a requiring a seek. Once a cylinder was full, the file system would start placing data in one of the adjacent cylinders.

As disk densities have increased, the importance of the cylinder has declined. Today, a disk's tracks can be less than a micron wide. To follow a track at these densities, a controller monitors the signals from a disk's head to control the disk arm assembly's motor to keep the head centered on a track. Furthermore, at these densities, the tracks of a cylinder may not be perfectly aligned. As a result, when a disk switches disk heads, the new head must center itself over the desired track. So, switching heads within a cylinder ends up being similar to a short 1-track seek: the controller chooses the new cylinder/track and the disk head settles over the target track. Today, accessing different tracks within the same cylinder costs about the same as accessing adjoining tracks on the same platter.

---

sectors have been requested. This way, if there is a request for one of the sectors that have already passed under the disk head, the data can be transferred immediately, rather than having to delay the request for nearly a full rotation to reread the data.

- **Transfer.** Once the disk head reaches a desired sector, the disk must transfer the data from the sector to its buffer memory (for reads) or vice versa (for writes) as the sectors rotate underneath the head. Then, for reads, it must transfer the data from its buffer memory to the host's main memory. For writes, the order of the transfers is reversed.

To amortize seek and rotation time, disk requests are often for multiple sequential sectors. The time to transfer one or more sequential sectors from (or to) a surface once the disk head begins reading (or writing) the first sector is the *surface transfer time.*

surface transfer time

On a modern disk, the surface transfer time for a single sector is much smaller than the seek time or rotational latency. For example, disk bandwidths often exceed 100 MB/s, so the surface transfer time for a 512-byte sector is often under 5 microseconds (0.005 ms).

Because a disk's outer tracks have room for more sectors than its inner tracks and because a given disk spins at a constant rate, the surface transfer bandwidth is often higher for the outer tracks than the inner tracks.

For a disk read, once sectors have been transferred to the disk's buffer memory, they must be transferred to the host's memory over some connection such as SATA (serial ATA), SAS (serial attached SCSi), Fibre Channel, or USB (universal serial bus). For writes, the transfer goes in the other direction. The time to transfer data between the host's memory and the disk's buffer is the *host transfer time.* Typical bandwidths range from 60MB/s for USB 2.0 to 2500 MB/s for Fibre Channel-20GFC.

host transfer time

For multi-sector reads, disks pipeline transfers between the surface and disk buffer memory and between buffer memory and host memory; so for large transfers, the total transfer time will be dominated by whichever of these is the bottleneck. Similarly, for writes, disks overlap the host transfer with the seek, rotation, and surface transfer; again, the total transfer time will be dominated by whichever is the bottleneck.

Example: Toshiba MK3254GSY. Figure 12.3 shows some key parameters for a recent 2.5-inch disk drive for laptop computers.

This disk stores 320 GB of data on 2 platters, so it stores 80 GB per surface. The platters spin at 7200 revolutions per minute, which is 8.3 ms per revolution; since each platter's diameter is about 6.3 cm, the outer edge of each platter is moving at about 85 km/hour!

The disk's data sheet indicates an average seek time for the drive of 10.5 ms for reads and 12.0 ms for writes. The seek time for reads and writes differs because the disk starts attempting to read data before the disk arm has completely settled, but it must wait a bit longer before it is safe to write.

When transferring long runs of contiguous sectors, the disk's bandwidth is 54-128 MB/s. The bandwidth is expressed as a range because the disk's outer tracks have more sectors than its inner tracks, so when the disk is

Size	
Platters/Heads	2/4
Capacity	320 GB
Performance	
Spindle speed	7200 RPM
Average seek time read/write	10.5 ms/ 12.0 ms
Maximum seek time	19 ms
Track-to-track seek time	1 ms
Transfer rate (surface to buffer)	54–128 MB/s
Transfer rate (buffer to host)	375 MB/s
Buffer memory	16 MB
Power	
Typical	16.35 W
Idle	11.68 W

Figure 12.3: Hardware specifications for a laptop disk (Toshiba MK3254GSY) manufactured in 2008.

accessing data on its outer tracks, sectors sweep past the disk head at a higher rate.

Once the data is transferred off the platter, the disk can send it to the main memory of the computer at up to 375 MB/s via a SATA (Serial ATA) interface.

Random v. sequential performance.   Given seek and rotational times measured in milliseconds, small accesses to random sectors on disk are much slower than large, sequential accesses.

EXAMPLE   **Random access workload.** For the disk described in Figure 12.3, consider a workload consisting of 500 read requests, each of a randomly chosen sector on disk, assuming requests are serviced in FIFO order. How long will servicing these requests take?

ANSWER   Disk access time is seek time + rotation time + transfer time.

Seek time. Each request requires a seek from a random starting track to a random ending track, so the disk's average seek time of 10.5 ms is a good estimate of the cost of each seek.

Rotation time. Once the disk head settles on the right track, it must wait for the desired sector to rotate under it; since there is no reason to expect the desired sector to be particularly near or far from the disk head when it settles, a reasonable estimate for rotation time is 4.15 ms, one half of the time that it takes a 7200 RPM disk to rotate once.

Transfer time. The disk's surface bandwidth is at least 54 MB/s, so transferring 512 bytes takes at most 9.5 μS (0.0095 ms).

Total time. 10.5 + 4.15 + .0095 = 14.66 ms per request, so 500 requests will take about 7.33 seconds.

EXAMPLE   **Sequential access workload.** For the disk described in Figure 12.3, consider a workload consisting of a read request for 500 sequential sectors on the same track. How long will servicing these requests take?

ANSWER   Disk access time is seek time + rotation time + transfer time.

Seek time. Since we don't know which track we're starting with or which track we're reading from, we'll use the average seek time, 10.5 ms, as an estimate for the seek time.

Rotation time. Since we don't know the position of the disk when the request is issued, a simple and reasonable estimate for the time for the first desired block to rotate to the disk head is 4.15 ms, one half of the time that it takes a 7200 RPM disk to rotate once.

Transfer time. A simple answer is that 500 sectors can be transferred in 4.8 to 2.0 ms, depending on whether they are on the inner or outer tracks.

$$500 \text{ sectors} * 512\frac{\text{bytes}}{\text{sector}} * \frac{\text{second}}{54 * 10^6 \text{bytes}} = 4.8 \text{ ms}$$

$$500 \text{ sectors} * 512\frac{\text{bytes}}{\text{sector}} * \frac{\text{second}}{128 * 10^6 \text{bytes}} = 2 \text{ ms}$$

(Too) simple answer. These three estimates give us a range from

$$10.5 + 4.15 + 2 = 16.7 \text{ ms}$$

to

$$10.5 + 4.15 + 4.8 = 19.5 \text{ ms}$$

More precise answer. However, this simple answer ignores the track buffer. Since the transfer time is a large fraction of the rotation time (about 1/4 to 1/2 of the time for a full rotation), we know that the request covers a significant fraction of a track. This means that there is a good chance that after the seek and settle time, the disk head will be in the middle of the region to be read. In this case, the disk will immediately read some of the track into the track buffer; then it will wait for the first track to rotate around; then it will read the remainder of the desired data.

We can estimate that for the outer track, there is a one in four chance that the initial seek and settle will finish while the head is within the desired range of sectors, and that when that happens, we read an average of $\frac{1}{8}$th of the desired data before we arrive at the first desired sector. So, for the outer track, this overlap will save us $\frac{1}{4} * \frac{1}{8} = \frac{1}{32}$ of a rotation for the average transfer. This effect slightly reduces the average access time: 16.7 ms $- \frac{1}{32} * 8.3$ ms $= 16.4$ ms.

Similarly, for the inner tracks, there is about a one in two chance that the initial seek will settle in the middle of the desired data, saving on average $\frac{1}{2} * \frac{1}{4} = \frac{1}{8}$. This reduces the average access time: 19.5 ms $- \frac{1}{8} * 8.3$ ms $= 18.5$ ms.

So, we estimate that such an access would take between 16.4 ms and 18.5 ms.

Notice that the sequential workload takes vastly less time than the random workload (less than 20 milliseconds v. 5.5 seconds). This orders of magnitude disparity between sequential and random access performance influences many aspects of file system design and use.

Still, even for the 500 sector request, a non-trivial amount of the access time is spent seeking and rotating rather than transferring.

EXAMPLE   **Effective bandwidth.** For the transfer of 500 sequential sectors examined in the previous example, what fraction of the disk's surface bandwidth is realized?

ANSWER   The effective bandwidth ranges from

$$(500 \text{ sectors})(512 \frac{\text{bytes}}{\text{sector}})(\frac{1}{18.5\text{ms}})(\frac{1\text{MB}}{1000000\text{bytes}})(\frac{1000\text{ms}}{\text{s}}) = 13.8\text{MB/s}$$

$$(500 \text{ sectors})(512 \frac{\text{bytes}}{\text{sector}})(\frac{1}{16.4\text{ms}})(\frac{1\text{MB}}{1000000\text{bytes}})(\frac{1000\text{ms}}{\text{s}}) = 15.6 \text{ MB/s}$$

This gives us a range of $\frac{13.8 \text{ MB/s}}{54 \text{ MB/s}} = 26\%$ to $\frac{15.6 \text{ MB/s}}{128 \text{ MB/s}} = 12\%$ of the maximum bandwidth from the inner to the outer tracks.

So, even a fairly large request (500 sectors or 250KB in this case) can incur significant overheads from seek and rotational latency.

EXAMPLE   **Efficient access.** For the disk described in Figure 12.3, how large must a request that begins on a random disk sector be to ensure that the disk gets at least 80% of its advertised maximum surface transfer bandwidth?

ANSWER   When reading a long sequence of logically sequential blocks, the disk will read an entire track, then do a 1 track seek (or a head switch and resettle, which amounts to the same thing) and then read the next track. Notice that track buffering allows the disk to read an entire track in one rotation regardless of which sector the head is over when it settles on the track and starts successfully reading. So, for the outer tracks, it reads for one rotation (8.4 ms) and then does a minimum seek (1 ms).

Thus, to achieve 80% of peak bandwidth after a random seek (10.5 ms), we need to read enough rotations worth of data to ensure that we spend 80% of the total time reading. If x is the number of rotations we will read, then we have

$$0.8 \text{ totalTime} = x \text{ rotationTime}$$
$$0.8(10.5 \text{ ms} + (1 + 8.4)x\text{ms}) = 8.4x \text{ ms}$$
$$x = 9.09$$

We therefore need to read at least 9.09 rotations worth of data to reach an efficiency of 80%. Since each rotation takes 8.4 ms and transfers data at 128 MB/s, 9.09 rotations transfers 9.77 MB of data, or about 19,089 sectors.

Disk scheduling

Because moving the disk arm and waiting for the platter to rotate are so expensive, performance can be significantly improved by optimizing the order in which pending requests are serviced. Disk scheduling can be done by the operating system, by the disk's firmware, or both.

FIFO.   The simplest thing to do is to process requests in first-in-first-out (FIFO) order. Unfortunately, a FIFO scheduler can yield poor performance. For example, a sequence of requests that alternate between the outer and inner tracks of a disk will result in many long seeks.

SPTF/SSTF.   An initially appealing option is to use a greedy scheduler that, given the current position of the disk head and platter, always services the pending request that can be serviced in the minimum amount of time. This approach is called *shortest positioning time first* (SPTF) (or *shortest seek time first* (SSTF) if rotational positioning is not considered.)

shortest
positioning
time first

shortest seek
time first

    SPTF and SSTF have two significant limitations. First, because moving the disk arm and waiting for some rotation time affects the cost of serving subsequent requests, these greedy approaches are not guaranteed to optimize disk performance. Second, these greedy approaches can cause starvation when, for example, a continuous stream of requests to inner tracks prevents requests to outer tracks from ever being serviced.

EXAMPLE   **SPTF is not optimal.** Suppose a disk's head is just inside the middle track of a disk so that seeking to the inside track would cost 9.9 ms while seeking to the outside track would cost 10.1 ms. Assume that for the disk in question, seeking between the outer and inner track costs 15 ms and that a rotation takes 10ms.

Also suppose that the disk has two sets of pending requests. The first set is 1000 requests to read each of the 1000 sectors on the inner track of the disk; the second set is 2000 requests to read each of the 2000 sectors on the outer track of the disk.

Compare the average response time per request for the SPTF schedule (first read the "nearby" inner track and then read the outer track) and the alternative of reading the outer track first and then the inner track.

ANSWER   To service either the outer set of requests, the disk must seek to the appropriate track and then wait for one full rotation while all of the track's data sweeps under the arm. For either set, the average response time for a request in that set will be the delay until the seek completes plus one half the disk's rotation time. Notice that the set is handled second must wait until the first one is completely done before it can start, adding to the response time observed for requests in that set.

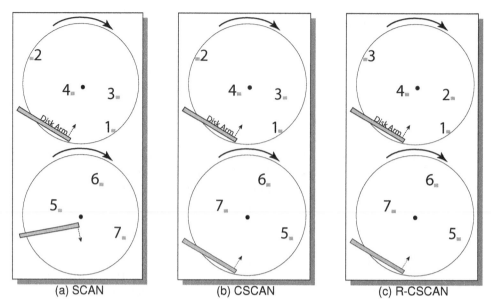

Figure 12.4: Elevator-based scheduling algorithms: (a) SCAN, (b) CSCAN, and (c) R-CSCAN.

Inner first (SPTF): $(1000(9.9+5)+2000(9.9+10+15+5))/3000$ $= 31.6$ ms

Outer first: $(2000(10.1+5)+1000(10.1+10+15+5))/3000$ $= 23.3$ ms

Elevator, SCAN, and CSCAN.   Elevator-based algorithms like SCAN and CSCAN have good performance and also ensure fairness in that no request is forced to wait for an inordinately long time. The basic approach is similar to how an elevator works: when an elevator is going up, it keeps going up until all pending requests to go to floors above it have been satisfied; then, when an elevator is going down, it keeps going down until all pending requests to go to floors below it have been satisfied.

SCAN   The *SCAN* scheduler works in the same way. The disk arm first sweeps from the inner to the outer tracks, servicing all requests that are between the arm's current position and the outer edge of the disk. Then, the arm sweeps from the outer to the inner tracks. Then the process is repeated. Figure 12.4-(a) illustrates the SCAN algorithm travelling from outer-to-inner tracks to service four pending requests and then travelling from inner-to-outer tracks to service three additional requests.

CSCAN   The *CSCAN* (circular SCAN) scheduler is a slight variation on SCAN in which the disk only services requests when the head is traveling in one direction (e.g., from inner tracks to outer ones); when the last request in the direction of travel is reached, the disk immediately seeks to where it started (e.g., the most inner track or the most inner track with a pending request) and services pending requests by moving the head *in the same direction* as the original pass (e.g., from inner tracks to outer ones again.) Figure 12.4-(b) illustrates the CSCAN algorithm travelling from outer-to-inner tracks to service four pending requests and then skipping to the outer track and travelling from outer-to-inner tracks to service three additional requests.

The advantage of CSCAN over SCAN is that if after a pass in one direction, the disk head were to just switch directions (as in SCAN), it will encounter a region of the disk where pending requests are sparse (since this region of the disk was just serviced). Seeking to the opposite side of the disk (as in CSCAN) moves the disk head to an area where pending requests are likely to be denser. In addition, CSCAN is more fair than SCAN in that seeking to the opposite side of the disk allows it to begin servicing the requests that likely been waiting longer than requests near but "just behind" the head.

Rather than pure seek-minimizing SCAN or SCAN, schedulers also take into account rotation time and allow small seeks "in the wrong direction" to avoid extra rotational delays using the rotationally-aware *R-SCAN* or *R-CSCAN* variations. For example, if the disk head is currently over sector 0 of track 0 and there are pending requests at sector 1000 of track 0, sector 500 of track 1, and sector 0 of track 10,000, a R-CSCAN scheduler might service the second request, then the first, and then the third. Figure 12.4-(c) illustrates the R-CSCAN algorithm handling a request on the outer track, then one a few tracks in, then another request on the outer track, and a request near the center on the arm's first sweep. The arm's second sweep is the same as for CSCAN.

R-SCAN

R-CSCAN

EXAMPLE   **Effect of disk scheduling.**

For the disk described in Figure 12.3, consider a workload consisting of 500 read requests, each of a randomly chosen sector on disk, assuming that the disk head is on the outside track and that requests are serviced in CSCAN order from outside to inside. How long will servicing these requests take?

ANSWER   Answering a question like this requires making some educated guesses; different people may come up with different reasonable estimates here.

Seek time. We first note that with 500 pending requests spread randomly across the disk, the average seek from one request to the next will seek 0.2% of the way across the disk. With four surfaces, most of these seeks will also require a head switch. We don't know the exact time for a seek 0.2% of the way across the disk, but we can estimate it by interpolating between the time for a 1 track seek (1 ms) and the time for a 33.3% seek (10.5 ms for reads.) (Disk seek time is not actually linear in distance, but as we will see in a moment, the exact seek time seems unlikely to affect our answer much.)

$$\text{estimated .2\% seek time} = (1 + \frac{.2}{33.3}10.5) \text{ ms}$$
$$= 1.06 \text{ ms}$$

Rotation time. Since we don't know the position of the disk when the seek finishes and since sectors are scattered randomly, a simple and reasonable estimate for the time after the seek finishes for the desired block to rotate to the disk head is 4.15 ms, one half of the time that it takes a 7200 RPM disk to rotate once.

Transfer time. Similar to the example on page 514, transfer time for each sector is at most 0.0095 ms

Total time. 1.06 + 4.15 + .0095 = 5.22 ms per request, so 500 requests will take about 2.6 s. Notice that the time for the SCAN scheduled time is less than half the 7.8 s time for the FIFO-scheduled time for the example on page 514

Exercises

1. **Discussion.** Some high-end disks in the 1980s had multiple disk arm assemblies per disk enclosure in order to allow them to achieve higher performance. Today, high-performance server disks have a single arm assembly per disk enclosure. Why do you think disks so seldom have multiple disk arm assemblies today?

2. How many sectors does a track on the disk described in Figure 12.3 on page 514 have?

3. For the disk in Figure 12.3 on page 514, estimate the distance from the center of one track to the center of the next track.

4. A disk may have multiple surfaces, arms, and heads, but when you issue a read or write, only one head is active at a time. It seems like one could greatly increase disk bandwidth for large requests by reading or writing with all of the heads at the same time. Given the physical characteristics of disks, can you figure out why no one does this?

5. For the disk described in Figure 12.3 on page 514, consider a workload consisting of 500 read requests, each of a randomly chosen sector on disk, assuming that the disk head is on the outside track and that requests are serviced in P-CSCAN order from outside to inside. How long will servicing these requests take?

   Note: Answering this question will require making some estimates.

6. Suppose I have a disk such as the 320GB SATA drive described in Figure 12.9 on page 533 and I have a workload consisting of 10000 reads to sectors randomly scattered across the disk. How long will these 10000 request take (total) assuming the disk services requests in FIFO order?

7. Suppose I have a disk such as the 320GB SATA drive described in Figure 12.9 on page 533 and I have a workload consisting of 10000 reads to 10000 sequential sectors on the outer-most tracks of the disk. How long will these 10000 request take (total) assuming the disk services requests in FIFO order?

8. Suppose I have a disk such as the 320GB SATA drive described in Figure 12.9 on page 533 and I have a workload consisting of 10000 reads to sectors randomly scattered across the disk. How long will these 10000 request take (total) assuming the disk services requests using the SCAN/Elevator algorithm.

9. Suppose I have a disk such as the 320GB SATA drive described in Figure 12.9 on page 533 and I have a workload consisting of 10000 reads to sectors randomly scattered across a 100MB file, where the 100MB file is laid out sequentially on the disk. How long will these 10000 request take (total) assuming the disk services requests using the SCAN/Elevator algorithm?

10. Write a program that creates a 100MB file on your local disk and then measures the time to do each of four things:

    a) **Sequential overwrite.** Overwrite the file with 100MB of new data by writing the file from beginning to end and then calling fsync() (or the equivalent on your platform).

    b) **Random buffered overwrite.** Do the following 50,000 times: choose a 2KB-aligned offset in the file uniformly at random, seek to that location in the file, and write 2KB of data at that position. Then, once all 50,000 writes have been issued, call fsync() (or the equivalent on your platform).

    c) **Random buffered overwrite.** Do the following 50,000 times: choose a 2KB-aligned offset in the file uniformly at random, seek to that location in the file, write 2KB of data at that position, and call fsync() (or the equivalent on your platform) after each individual write.

    d) **Random read.** Do the following 50,000 times: choose a 2KB-aligned offset in the file uniformly at random, seek to that location in the file, and read 2KB of data at that position.

Explain your results.

11. Write a program that creates three files, each of 100MB, and then measures the time to do each of three things:

    a) **fopen()/fwrite().** Open the first file using fopen() and issue 256,000 sequential four-byte writes using fwrite().

    b) **open()/write().** Open the second file using open() and issue 256,000 sequential four-byte writes using write().

    c) **mmap()/store.** Map the third file into your program's memory using mmap() and issue 256,000 sequential four-byte writes by iterating through memory and writing to each successive word of the mapped file.

    Explain your results.

12.2 | Flash storage

Over the past decade, flash storage has become a widely used storage medium. Flash storage is the dominent storage technology for handheld devices from phones to cameras to thumb drives, and it is used in an increasing fraction of laptop computers and machine room servers.

solid state storage   Flash storage is a type of *solid state storage*: it has no moving parts and stores data using electrical circuits. Because it has no moving parts, flash storage can have much better random IO performance than disks, and it can use less power and be less vulnerable to physical damage. On the other hand, flash storage remains significantly more expensive per byte of storage than disks.

Each flash storage element is a floating gate transistor. As Figure 12.5 illustrates, an extra gate in such a transistor "floats" — it is not connected to any circuit. Since the floating gate is entirely surrounded by an insulator, it will hold an electrical charge for months or years without requiring any power. Even though the floating gate is not electrically connected to anything, it can be charged or discharged via electron tunneling by running a sufficiently high-voltage current near it. The floating gate's state of charge affects the transistor's threshold voltage for activation. Thus, the floating gate's state can be detected by applying an intermediate voltage to the transitor's control gate that will only be sufficient to activate the transistor if the floating gate is changed.

In single-level flash storage, the floating gate stores one bit (charge or not charged); in multi-level flash storage, the floating gate stores multiple bits by storing one of several different charge levels.

NOR flash storage is wired to allow individual words to be written and read. NOR flash storage is useful for storing device firmware since it can be

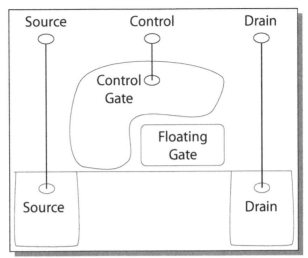

Figure 12.5: A floating gate transistor.

executed in place. NAND flash storage is wired to allow reads and writes of a page at a time, where a page is typically 2 KB to 4 KB. NAND flash is more dense than NOR flash, so NAND is used in the storage systems we will consider.

Flash storage access and performance   Flash storage is accessed using three operations.

- **Erase erasure block.** Before flash memory can be written, it must be erased by setting each cell to a logical "1". Flash memory can only be erased in large units called *erasure blocks*. Today, erasure blocks are often 128 KB to 512 KB. Erasure is a slow operation, usually taking several milliseconds.

  Erasing an erasure block is what gives flash memory its name for its resemblance to the flash of a camera.

- **Write page.** Once erased, NAND flash memory can be written on a page by page basis, where each page is typically 2048-4096 bytes. Writing a page typically takes tens of microseconds.

- **Read page.** NAND flash memory can be read on a page by page basis. Reading a page typically takes tens of microseconds.

erasure blocks appears in the left margin beside the "Erase erasure block" bullet.

flash translation layer appears in the left margin beside the final paragraph.

Notice that to write a page, its entire erasure block must first be erased. This is a challenge both because erasure is slow and because erasure affects a large number of pages. Flash drives implement a *flash translation layer* (FTL) that maps logical flash pages to different physical pages on the flash device. Then, when a single logical page is overwritten, the FTL writes the new version to some free, already-erased physical page and remaps the logical page to that physical page.

Write remapping significantly improves flash performance.

EXAMPLE   **Remapping flash writes.** Consider a flash drive with a 4 KB pages, 512 KB erasure blocks, 3 ms flash times, and 50 μs read-page and write-page times. Suppose writing a page is done with a naive algorithm that reads an entire erasure block, erases it, and writes the modified erasure block. How long would each page write take?

ANSWER   This naive approach would require

$$\frac{512\text{KB/erasure block}}{4\text{KB/page}} * (\text{page read time} + \text{page write time}) + \text{block erase time}$$

$$= 128 * (50 + 50)\mu s + 3\text{ms}$$

$$= 15.8\text{ms per write}$$

Suppose remapping is used and that a flash device always has at least one unused erasure block available for a target workload. How long does an average write take now?

ANSWER   With remapping, the cost of flashing an erasure block is amortized over 512/4 = 128 page writes. This scenario gives a cost of $\frac{3\text{ms}}{128} + 50\mu s = 73.4\mu s$ per write.

In practice, there is likely to be some additional cost per write under the remapping scheme because in order to flash an erasure block to free it for new writes, the firmware may need to garbage collect live pages from that erasure block and copy those live pages to a different erasure block.

Internally, a flash device may have multiple independent data paths that can be accessed in parallel. Therefore, to maximize sustained bandwidth when accessing a flash device, operating systems issue multiple concurrent requests to the device.

Durability.   Normally, flash memory can retain its state for months or years without power. However, over time the high current loads from flashing and writing memory causes the circuits to degrade. Eventually, after a few thousand to a few million program-erase cycles (depending on the type of **wear out**   flash), a given cell may *wear out* and no longer reliably store a bit.

In addition, reading a flash memory cell a large number of times can **read disturb**   cause the surrounding cells' charges to be disturbed. A *read disturb error* **error**   can occur if a location in flash memory is read to many times without the surrounding memory being written.

To improve durability in the face of wear from writes and disturbs from reads, flash devices make use of a number of techniques:

- **Error correcting codes.** Each page has some extra bytes that are used for error correcting codes to protect against bit errors in the page.

- **Bad page and bad erasure block management.** If a page or erasure block has a manufacturing defect or wears out, firmware on the device marks it as bad and stops storing data on it.

- **Wear leveling.** As noted above, rather than overwrite a page in place, the flash translation layer remaps the logical page to a new physical page that has already been erased. This remapping ensures that a hot page that is overwritten repeatedly does not prematurely wear out a particular physical page on the flash device.

wear leveling

Wear leveling moves a flash device's logical pages to different physical pages to ensure that no physical page gets an inordinate number of writes and wears out prematurely. Some wear leveling algorithms also migrate unmodified pages to protect against read disturb errors.

- **Spare pages and erasure blocks.** Flash devices can be manufactured with spare pages and spare erasure blocks in the device. This spare capacity serves two purposes.

  First, it provides extra space for wear leveling: even if the device is logically "full" the wear leveling firmware can copy live pages out of some existing erasure blocks into a spare erasure block, allowing it to flash those existing erasure blocks.

  Second, it allows bad page and bad erasure block management to function without causing the logical size of the device to shrink.

In addition to affecting reliability, wear out affects a flash device's performance over time.

First, as a device wears out, accesses may require additional retries, slowing them. Second, as spare pages and erasure blocks are consumed by bad ones, the wear leveling algorithms have less spare space and have to garbage collect live pages — copying them out of their existing erasure blocks — more frequently.

Example: Intel 710 Series Solid-State Drive   Figure 12.6 shows some key parameters for an Intel 710 Series solid state drive manufactured in 2011. This drive uses multi-level NAND flash to get high storage densities. Normally, multi-level flash is less durable than single-level, but this Intel drive uses sophisticated wear leveling algorithms and a large amount of spare space to provide high durability.

The sequential performance of this drive is very good, with peak sustained read and write bandwidths of 270 MB/s and 210 MB/s respectively. In comparison, a high-end Seagate Cheetah 15K.7 drive manufactured in 2010 spins at 15,000 revolutions per second and provides 122 MB/s to 204 MB/s of sustained bandwidth.

Random read performance is excellent. The latency for a single random 4 KB read is just 75 μs, and when multiple concurrent requests are in flight,

Size	
Capacity	300 GB
Page Size	4KB
Performance	
Bandwidth (Sequential Reads)	270 MB/s
Bandwidth (Sequential Writes)	210 MB/s
Read/Write Latency	75 μs
Random Reads Per Second	38,500
Random Writes Per Second	2,000 (2,400 with 20% space reserve)
Interface	SATA 3 Gb/s
Endurance	
Endurance	1.1 PB (1.5 PB with 20% space reserve)
Power	
Power Consumption Active/Idle	3.7 W / 0.7 W

Figure 12.6: Key parameters for an Intel 710 Series Solid State Drive manufactured in 2011.

the drive can process 38,500 random reads per second — one every 26 μs. This is orders of magnitude better than the random read performance of a spinning disk drive.

Random write performance is also very good, but not as good as random read performance. The latency for a single random 4 KB write is 75 μs; the drive reduces write latency by buffering writes in volatile memory, and it has capacitors that store enough charge to write all buffered updates to flash storage if a power loss occurs.

When multiple concurrent writes are in flight, the drive can process 2,000 random writes writes per second when it is full; if it is less than 80% full, that number rises to 2,400. Random write throughput increases when the drive has more free space because the drive has to garbage collect live pages from erasure blocks less often and because when the drive eventually does do that garbage collection, the erasure blocks are less full.

The drive's is rated for 1.1 PB ($1.1 * 10^{15}$ bytes) of endurance (1.5 PB if it is less than 80% full.) For many workloads, this endurance suffices for years or decades of use. However, solid state drives may not always be a good match for high-bandwidth write streaming. In the extreme, an application constantly streaming writes at 200 MB/s could wear this drive out in 64 days.

EXAMPLE   **Random read workload.** For the solid state disk described in Figure 12.6, consider a workload consisting of 500 read requests, each of a randomly chosen page. How long will servicing these requests take?

ANSWER   The disk can service random read requests at a rate of 38,500 per second, so 500 requests will take 500/38500 = 13 ms. In contrast, for the spinning disk example on page 514, the same 500 requests would take

Technology Affects Interfaces — the TRIM Command

Historically, when a file system deleted a file stored on a spinning disk, all it needed to do was to update the file's metadata and the file system's free space bitmap. It did not need to erase or overwrite the file's data blocks on disk — once the metadata was updated, these blocks could never be referenced, so there was no need to do anything with them.

When such file systems were used with flash drives, users observed that their drives got slower over time. As the amount of free space fell, the drives' flash translation layer was forced to garbage collect erasure blocks more frequently; additionally, each garbage collection pass became more expensive because there were more live pages to copy from old erasure blocks to the new ones.

Notice that this slowing could occur even if the file system appeared to have a large amount of free space. For example, if a file system moves a large file from one range of blocks to another, the storage hardware has no way to know that the pages in the old range are no longer needed unless the file system can tell it so.

The TRIM command was introduced into many popular operating systems between 2009 and 2011 to allow file systems to inform the underlying storage when the file system has stopped using a page of storage. The TRIM command makes the free space known to the file system visible to the underlying storage layer, which can significantly reduce garbage collection overheads and help flash drives retain good performance as they age.

7.33 seconds.

EXAMPLE **Random v. sequential reads.** How does this drive's random read performance compare to its sequential read performance?

ANSWER The effective bandwidth in this case is 500 requests * 4 $\frac{KB}{request}$ / 13 milliseconds = 158 MB/s. The random read bandwidth is thus 158/270 = 59% of the sequential read bandwidth.

EXAMPLE **Random write workload.** For the solid state disk described in Figure 12.6, consider a workload consisting of 500 write requests, each of a randomly chosen page. How long will servicing these requests take?

ANSWER The disk can service random write requests at a rate of 2000 per second (assuming the disk is nearly full), so 500 requests will take 500/2000 = 250 ms.

EXAMPLE **Random v. sequential writes.** How does this random write performance compare to the drive's sequential write performance?

ANSWER   The effective bandwidth in this case is 500 requests * 4 $\frac{KB}{request}$ / 250 milliseconds = 8.2 MB/s. The random write bandwidth is thus 8.2/210 = 3.9% of the sequential write bandwidth.

Exercises

12. Suppose that you have a 256 GB solid state drive that the operating system and drive both support the TRIM command. To evaluate the drive, you do an experiment where you time the system's write performance for random page-sized when the file system is empty compared to its performance when the file system holds 255 GB of data, and you find that write performance is significantly worse in the latter case.

    What is the likely reason for this worse performance as the disk fills despite its support for TRIM?

    What can be done to mitigate this slowdown?

13. 1Suppose you have a flash drive such as the one described in Figure 12.10 on page 535 and you have a workload consisting of 10000 4KB reads to pages randomly scattered across the drive. Assuming that you wait for request i to finish before you issue request $i + 1$, how long will these 10000 request take (total)?

14. Suppose you have a flash drive such as the one described in Figure 12.10 on page 535 and you have a workload consisting of 10000 4KB reads to pages randomly scattered across the drive. Assuming that you issue requests concurrently, using many threads, how long will these 10000 request take (total)?

15. Suppose you have a flash drive such as the one described in Figure 12.10 on page 535 and you have a workload consisting of 10000 4KB writes to pages randomly scattered across the drive. Assuming that you wait for request i to finish before you issue request $i + 1$, how long will these 10000 requests take (total)?

16. Suppose you have a flash drive such as the one described in Figure 12.10 on page 535 and you have a workload consisting of 10000 4KB writes to pages randomly scattered across the drive. Assuming that use a large number of threads to issue many writes concurrently, how long will these 10000 requests take (total)?

17. Suppose you have a flash drive such as the one described in Figure 12.10 on page 535 and you have a workload consisting of 10000 4KB reads to 10000 sequential pages. How long will these 10000 request take (total)?

12.3 | Conclusions and future directions

Today, spinning disk and flash memory dominate storage technologies, and each has sufficient advantages to beat the other for some workloads and environments.

Spinning disk v. flash storage. Spinning disks are often used when capacity is the primary goal. For example, spinning disk is often used for storing media files and home directories. For workloads limited by storage capacity spinning disks can often provide much better capacity per dollar than flash storage. For example, in October 2011, a 2 TB Seagate Barracuda disk targeted at workstations cost about $80 and a 300 GB Intel 320 Series solid state drive targeted at laptops cost about $600, giving the spinning disk about a 50:1 advantage in GB per dollar.

Both spinning disks and flash storage are viable when sequential bandwidth is the goal. In October 2011, flash drives typically have modestly higher per-drive sequential bandwidths than spinning drives, but the spinning drives typically have better sequential bandwidth per dollar spent than flash drives. For example, the same Seagate disk has a sustained bandwidth of 120 MB/s (1.5 MB/s per dollar) while the same Intel SSD has a read/write bandwidth of 270/205 MB/s (about 0.4 MB/s per dollar.)

Flash storage is often used when good random access performance or low power consumption is the goal. For example, flash storage is frequently used in database transaction processing servers, in smart phones, and in laptops. For example, the Seagate described above drive rotates at 5900 RPM, so it takes about 5 ms for a half rotation; even with good scheduling and even if data is confined to a subset of tracks, it would be hard to get more than 200 random I/Os per second from this drive (about 2.5 random I/Os per second per dollar.) Conversely, the Intel SSD can sustain 23,000 random writes and 39,500 random reads per second (about 38 or 66 random writes or reads per second per dollar.)

With respect to power, spinning disks typically consume 10-20W depending on whether it is just spinning or actively reading and writing data, while a flash drive might consume 0.5W-1W when idle and 3-5W when being accessed. Flash drives' power advantage makes them attractive for portable applications such as laptop and smartphone storage.

Flash memory can also have a significant form factor advantage with respect to physical size and weight. Although some flash drives are designed as drop-in replacements for spinning disks and so are similar in size, flash storage can be much smaller than a typical spinning disk. For example, in 2011, a USB flash storage "key" such as the one in Figure 12.7 can store as much as 256 GB in a device that is not much larger than a house key.

Figure 12.8 summarizes these advantages and disadvantages; of course, many systems need to do well on multiple metrics, so system designers may

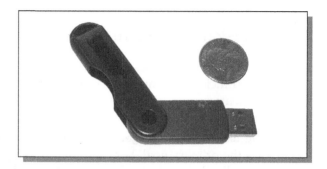

Figure 12.7: In 2011, flash storage "keys" such as this one can store as much as 256 GB in a device that is a few centimeters long, and 1-2 cm wide and tall.

Metric	Spinning Disk	Flash
Capacity/Cost	Excellent	Good
Sequential BW/Cost	Good	Good
Random I/O per Second/Cost	Poor	Good
Power Consumption	Fair	Good
Physical Size	Good	Excellent

Figure 12.8: Relative advantages and disadvantages of spinning disk and flash storage.

need to compromise on some metrics or use combinations of technologies.

Technology trends.   Over the past decades, the cost of storage capacity has fallen rapidly for both spinning disks and solid state storage. Compare the 2 TB disk drive for $80 in 2011 to a 15 MB drive costing $113 in 1984 (or about $246 in 2011 dollars): the cost per byte has improved by a factor of about 400,000 over 27 years — over 50% per year for nearly 3 decades.

Recent rates of improvement for flash storage have been even faster. For example, in 2001, the Adtron S35PC 14 GB flash drive cost $42,000. Today's Intel 320 costs 70 times less for 21 times more capacity, an improvement of about 2x per year over the past decade.

Similar capacity improvements for spinning disk and flash are expected for at least the next few years. Beyond that, there is concern that we will be approaching the physical limits of both magnetic disk and flash storage, so the longer-term future is less certain. (That said, people have worried that disks were approaching their limits several times in the past, and we will not be surprised if the magnetic disk and flash industries continue rapid improvements for quite a few more years.)

In contrast to capacity, performance is likely to improve more slowly for both technologies. For example, a mid-range spinning disk in 1991 might

The first disk drive

Prior to the invention of magnetic disks, magnetic cylinders, called drums, were used for on-line storage. These drums spun on their axes and typically had one head per track. So, there was no seek time to access a block of data; one merely waited for a block to rotate underneath its head.

By using spinning disks instead of drums, the magnetic surface area, and hence the storage capacity, could be increased.

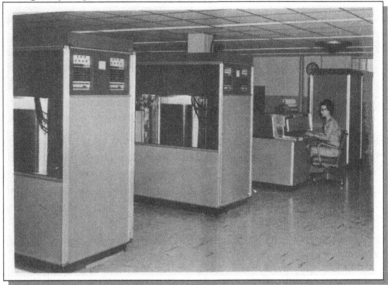

Photo by U. S. Army Red River Arsenal.

The first disk drive, the IBM 350 Disk System (two are shown in the foreground of this photograph), was introduced in 1956 as part of the IBM RAMAC ("Random Access Method of Accounting and Control") 305 computer system. The 350 Disk system stored about 3.3 MB on 50 platters, rotated its platters at 1200 RPM, had an average seek time of 600 ms, and weighed about a ton. The RAMAC 305 computer system with its 350 disk system could be leased for $3,200 per month. Assuming a useful life of 5 years and converting to 2011 dollars, the cost was approximately $1.3 million for the system — about $400,000 per megabyte.

have had a 1.3 MB/s maximum bandwidth and an 17 ms average seek time. Bandwidths have improved by about a factor of 90 in two decades (about 25% per year) while seek times and rotational latencies have only improved by about a factor of two (less than 4% per year.) Bandwidths have improved more quickly than rotational latency and seek times because bandwidth benefits from increasing storage densities, not just increasing rotational rates.

For SSDs, the story is similar, though recent increases in volumes have helped speed the pace of improvements. For example, in 2006 a BitMicro E-Disk flash drive could provide 9,500 to 11,700 random reads per second and 34-44 MB/s sustained bandwidth. Compared to the Intel 320 SSD from 2011, bandwidths have improved by about 40% per year and random access throughput has improved by about 25% per year over the past 5 years.

New technologies.   This is an exciting time for persistent storage. After decades of undisputed reign as the dominant technology for on-line persistent storage, spinning magnetic disks are being displaced flash storage in many application domains, giving both operating system designers and application writers an opportunity to reexamine how to best use storage. Looking forward, many researchers speculate that new technologies may soon be nipping at the heels and even surpassing flash storage.

phase change
memory

For example *phase change memory* (PCM) uses a current to alter the state of chalcogenide glass between amorphous and crystalline forms, which have significantly different electrical resistance and can therefore be used to represent data bits. Although PCM does not yet match the density of flash, researchers speculate that the technology is fundamentally more scalable and will ultimately be able to provide higher storage densities at lower costs. Furthermore, PCM is expected to have much better write performance and endurance than flash.

memristors

As another example, *memristors* are circuit elements whose resistance depends on the amounts and directions of currents that have flowed through them in the past. A number of different memristor constructions are being pursued, and some have quite promising properties. For example, in 2010 Hewlett Packard labs described a prototype memristor constructed of a thin titanium dioxide film with 3 nm by 3 nm storage elements that can switch states in 1 ns. These densities are similar to contemporary flash memory devices and these switching times are similar to contemporary DRAM chips. The devices also have write endurance similar to flash, and extremely long (theoretically unlimited) storage lifetimes. Furthermore, researchers believe that these and others memristors' densities will scale well in the future. For example, in 2009 a design for 3-D stacking of memristors was published in the *Proceedings of National Academy of Sciences* by Dmitri Strukov and R. Stanley Williams of HP Labs.

If technologies such as these pan out as hoped, operating system designers will have opportunities to rethink our abstractions for both volatile and nonvolatile storage: how should we make use of word-addressable, persistent memory with densities exceeding current flash storage devices and with memory access times approaching those of DRAM? What could we do if each core on a 32 core processor chip had access to a few gigabytes of stacked memristor memory?

Size	
Form factor	2.5-inch
Capacity	320 GB
Performance	
Spindle speed	5400 RPM
Average seek time	12.0 ms
Maximum seek time	21 ms
Track-to-track seek time	2 ms
Transfer rate (surface to buffer)	850 Mbit/s (maximum)
Transfer rate (buffer to host)	3 Gbit/s
Buffer memory	8 MB

Figure 12.9: Hardware specifications for a 320GB SATA disk drive.

Exercises

1. **Discussion.** Some high-end disks in the 1980s had multiple disk arm assemblies per disk enclosure in order to allow them to achieve higher performance. Today, high-performance server disks have a single arm assembly per disk enclosure. Why do you think disks so seldom have multiple disk arm assemblies today?

2. How many sectors does a track on the disk described in Figure 12.3 on page 514 have?

3. For the disk in Figure 12.3 on page 514, estimate the distance from the center of one track to the center of the next track.

4. A disk may have multiple surfaces, arms, and heads, but when you issue a read or write, only one head is active at a time. It seems like one could greatly increase disk bandwidth for large requests by reading or writing with all of the heads at the same time. Given the physical characteristics of disks, can you figure out why no one does this?

5. For the disk described in Figure 12.3 on page 514, consider a workload consisting of 500 read requests, each of a randomly chosen sector on disk, assuming that the disk head is on the outside track and that requests are serviced in P-CSCAN order from outside to inside. How long will servicing these requests take?

   Note: Answering this question will require making some estimates.

6. Suppose I have a disk such as the 320GB SATA drive described in Figure 12.9 on page 533 and I have a workload consisting of 10000 reads to sectors randomly scattered across the disk. How long will

these 10000 request take (total) assuming the disk services requests in FIFO order?

7. Suppose I have a disk such as the 320GB SATA drive described in Figure 12.9 on page 533 and I have a workload consisting of 10000 reads to 10000 sequential sectors on the outer-most tracks of the disk. How long will these 10000 request take (total) assuming the disk services requests in FIFO order?

8. Suppose I have a disk such as the 320GB SATA drive described in Figure 12.9 on page 533 and I have a workload consisting of 10000 reads to sectors randomly scattered across the disk. How long will these 10000 request take (total) assuming the disk services requests using the SCAN/Elevator algorithm.

9. Suppose I have a disk such as the 320GB SATA drive described in Figure 12.9 on page 533 and I have a workload consisting of 10000 reads to sectors randomly scattered across a 100MB file, where the 100MB file is laid out sequentially on the disk. How long will these 10000 request take (total) assuming the disk services requests using the SCAN/Elevator algorithm?

10. Write a program that creates a 100MB file on your local disk and then measures the time to do each of four things:

   a) **Sequential overwrite.** Overwrite the file with 100MB of new data by writing the file from beginning to end and then calling fsync() (or the equivalent on your platform).

   b) **Random buffered overwrite.** Do the following 50,000 times: choose a 2KB-aligned offset in the file uniformly at random, seek to that location in the file, and write 2KB of data at that position. Then, once all 50,000 writes have been issued, call fsync() (or the equivalent on your platform).

   c) **Random buffered overwrite.** Do the following 50,000 times: choose a 2KB-aligned offset in the file uniformly at random, seek to that location in the file, write 2KB of data at that position, and call fsync() (or the equivalent on your platform) after each individual write.

   d) **Random read.** Do the following 50,000 times: choose a 2KB-aligned offset in the file uniformly at random, seek to that location in the file, and read 2KB of data at that position.

   Explain your results.

11. Write a program that creates three files, each of 100MB, and then measures the time to do each of three things:

Size	
Usable capacity	2 TB (SLC flash)
Cache Size	64 GB (Battery-backed RAM)
Page Size	4KB
Performance	
Bandwidth (Sequential Reads from flash)	2048 MB/s
Bandwidth (Sequential Writes to flash)	2048 MB/s
Read Latency (cache hit)	15 μs
Read Latency (cache miss)	200 μs
Write Latency	15 μs
Random Reads (sustained from flash)	100,000 per second
Random Writes (sustained to flash)	100,000 per second
Interface	8 Fibre Channel ports with 4Gbit/s per port
Power	
Power Consumption	300 W

Figure 12.10: Key parameters for a hypothetical high-end flash drive in 2011.

a) **fopen()/fwrite().** Open the first file using fopen() and issue 256,000 sequential four-byte writes using fwrite().

b) **open()/write().** Open the second file using open() and issue 256,000 sequential four-byte writes using write().

c) **mmap()/store.** Map the third file into your program's memory using mmap() and issue 256,000 sequential four-byte writes by iterating through memory and writing to each successive word of the mapped file.

Explain your results.

12. Suppose that you have a 256 GB solid state drive that the operating system and drive both support the TRIM command. To evaluate the drive, you do an experiment where you time the system's write performance for random page-sized when the file system is empty compared to its performance when the file system holds 255 GB of data, and you find that write performance is significantly worse in the latter case.

What is the likely reason for this worse performance as the disk fills despite its support for TRIM?

What can be done to mitigate this slowdown?

13. 1Suppose you have a flash drive such as the one described in Figure 12.10 on page 535 and you have a workload consisting of 10000 4KB reads to pages randomly scattered across the drive. Assuming that you wait for request i to finish before you issue request $i + 1$, how long will these 10000 request take (total)?

14. Suppose you have a flash drive such as the one described in Figure 12.10 on page 535 and you have a workload consisting of 10000 4KB reads to pages randomly scattered across the drive. Assuming that you issue requests concurrently, using many threads, how long will these 10000 request take (total)?

15. Suppose you have a flash drive such as the one described in Figure 12.10 on page 535 and you have a workload consisting of 10000 4KB writes to pages randomly scattered across the drive. Assuming that you wait for request i to finish before you issue request $i + 1$, how long will these 10000 requests take (total)?

16. Suppose you have a flash drive such as the one described in Figure 12.10 on page 535 and you have a workload consisting of 10000 4KB writes to pages randomly scattered across the drive. Assuming that use a large number of threads to issue many writes concurrently, how long will these 10000 requests take (total)?

17. Suppose you have a flash drive such as the one described in Figure 12.10 on page 535 and you have a workload consisting of 10000 4KB reads to 10000 sequential pages. How long will these 10000 request take (total)?

What's in a name? That which we call a rose
By any other name would smell as sweet.

Juliet
Romeo and Juliet (II, ii, 1-2)
(Shakespeare)

13 Files and Directories

Recall from Chapter 11 that file systems use directories to provide hierarchically named files, and that each file contains metadata and a sequence of data bytes. However as Chapter 12 discussed, storage devices provide a much lower-level abstraction — large arrays of data blocks. So, to implement a file system, we must solve a translation problem: How do we go from a file name and offset to a block number?

A simple answer is that file systems implement a dictionary that maps keys (file name and offset) to values (block number on a device). We already have many data structures for implementing dictionaries, including hash tables, trees, and skip lists, so perhaps we can just use one of them?

Unfortunately, the answer is not so simple. File system designers face four major challenges that require more elaborate techniques.

- **Performance.** File systems need to provide good performance while coping with the limitations of the underlying storage devices. In practice, this means that file systems strive to ensure good *spatial locality*, where blocks that are accessed together are stored near one another, ideally in sequential storage blocks.

    spatial
    locality

- **Flexibility.** One major purpose of file systems is allowing applications to share data, so file systems must be jacks-of-all-trades. They would be less useful if we had to use one file system for large sequentially-read files, another for small seldom-written files, another for large random-access files, another for short-lived files, and so on.

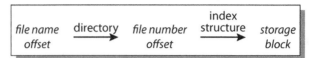

Figure 13.1: File systems map file names and file offsets to storage blocks in two steps. First, they use directories to map names to file numbers. Then they use an index structure such as a persistently-stored tree to find the block that holds the data at any specific offset in that file.

- **Persistence.** File systems must maintain and update both user data and their internal data structures on persistent storage devices so that everything survives operating system crashes and power failures.

- **Reliability.** File systems must be able to store important data for long periods of time, even if machines crash during updates or some of the system's storage hardware malfunctions.

This chapter discusses file systems are organized to meet the first three challenges. Chapter 14 addresses reliability.

13.1 | Implementation overview

FIle systems must map file names and offsets to physical storage blocks in a way that allows efficient access. Although there are many different file systems, most implementations are based on four key ideas: directories, index structures, free space maps, and locality heuristics.

Directories and index structures.   As Figure 13.1 illustrates, file systems map file names and file offsets to specific storage blocks in two steps.

directory   First, they use *directories* to map human-readable file names to file numbers. Directories are often just special files that contain lists of *file name* → *file number* mappings.

Second, once a file name has been translated to a file number, file sys-
index   tems use a persistently stored *index structure* to locate the blocks of the file.
structure   The index structure can be any persistent data structure that maps a file number and offset to a storage block. Often, to efficiently support a wide range of file sizes and access patterns, the index structure is some form of tree.

free space   **Free space maps.**   File systems implement *free space maps* to track which
map   storage blocks are free and which are in use as files grow and shrink. At a minimum, a file system's free space map must allow the file system to find a free block when a file needs to grow, but because spatial locality is important, most modern file systems implement free space maps that allow

Figure 13.2: A directory is a file that contains a collection of *file name* → *file number* mappings.

them to find free blocks near a desired location. For example, many file systems implement free space maps as bitmaps in persistent storage.

Locality heuristics.   Directories and index structures allow file systems to locate desired file data and metadata no matter where they are stored, and free space maps allow them to locate free the space near any location on the persistent storage device. These *mechanisms* allow file systems to employ various *policies* to decide where a given block of a given file should be stored.

locality
heuristics

defragment

These policies are embodied in *locality heuristics* for grouping data to optimize performance. For example, some file systems group each directory's files together but spread different directories to different parts of the storage device. Others periodically *defragment* their storage, rewriting existing files so that each file is stored in sequential storage blocks and so that the storage device has long runs of sequential free space so that new files can be written sequentially. Still others optimize writes over reads and write all data sequentially, whether a given set of writes contains updates to one file or to many different ones.

Implementation details.   In this chapter, we first discuss how directories are implemented. Then, we look at the details of how specific file systems handle the details of placing and finding data in persistent storage by implementing different index structures, free space maps, and locality heuristics.

13.2 | Directories: Naming data

As Figure 13.1 indicates, to access a file, the file system first translates the file's name to its number. For example, the falled called /home/tom/foo.txt might internally known as file 66212871. File systems use directories to store their mappings from human-readable names to internal file numbers, and they organize these directories hierarchically so that users can group related files and directories.

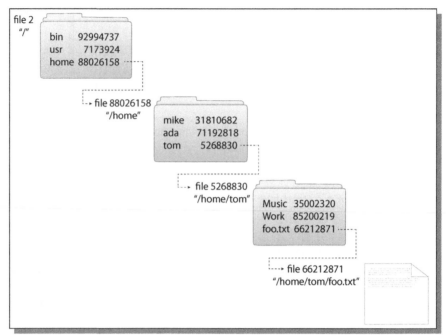

Figure 13.3: Directories can be arranged hierarchically by having one directory contain the *file name* → *file number* mapping for another directory.

Implementing directories in a way that provides hierarchical, name-to-number mappings turns out to be simple: use files to store directories. So, if the system needs to determine a file's number, it can just open up the appropriate directory file and scan through the file name/file number pairs until it finds the right one.

For example, illustrates Figure 13.2 the contents of a single directory file. To open file foo.txt, the file system would scan this directory file, find the foo.txt entry, and see that file foo.txt has file number 66212871.

Of course, if we use files to store the contents of directories such as /home/tom, we still have the problem of finding the directory files, themselves. As Figure 13.3 illustrates, the file number for directory /home/tom can be found by looking up the name tom in the directory /home, and the file number for directory /home can be found by looking up the name home in the root directory /.

Recursive algorithms need a base case — we cannot discover the root directories file number by looking in some other directory. The solution is to agree on the root directory's file number ahead of time. For example, the Unix Fast File System (FFS) and many other Unix and Linux file systems use 2 as the predefined file number for the root directory of a file system.

So, to read file /home/tom/foo.txt in Figure 13.3, we first read the root directory by reading the file with the well known root number 2. In that file, we search for the name home and find that directory /home is stored in file 88026158. By reading file 88026158 and searching for the name tom, we learn that directory /home/tom is stored in file 5268830. Finally, by reading file 5268830 and searching for the name foo.txt, we learn that /home/tom/foo.txt is file number 66212871.

Although looking up a file's number can take several steps, we expect there to be locality (e.g., when one file in a directory is accessed, other files in the directory are often likely to be accessed soon), so we expect that caching will reduce the number of disk accesses needed for most lookups.

Directory API.   If file systems use files to store directory information, can we just use the standard open()/close()/read()/write() API to access them?

No. Directories use a specialized API because they must control the contents of these files. For example, file systems must prevent applications from corrupting the list of *name → file number* mappings, which could prevent the operating system from performing lookups or updates. As another example, the file system should enforce the invariant that each file number in a valid directory entry refers to a file that actually exists.

File systems therefore provide special system calls for modifying directory files. For example, rather than using the standard write() system call to add a new file's entry to a directory, applications use the create() call. By restricting updates, these calls ensure that directory files can always be parsed by the operating system. These calls also bind together the creation or removal of a file and the file's directory entry, so that directory entries always refer to actual files and that all files have at least one directory entry.

In the API described in Figure Overview in Chapter 11, the other calls that modify directory files are mkdir(), link(), unlink(), and rmdir().

So, for example, for the file system illustrated in Figure 13.3, Tom could rename foo.txt to hw1.txt in his home directory by running a process that makes the following two system calls

```
link ( ''foo.txt '',  ''hw1.txt '');
unlink ( ''foo.txt '');
```

Processes can simply read directory files with the standard (read()) call.

EXAMPLE

Reading directories.

It is useful for programs to be able to get a list of all file names in a directory to, for example, recursively traverse a hierarchy from some point. However, the file system API described in Figure Overview in Chapter 11 does not have call specifically for reading directories.

Given just the system call API in that figure, how could a process learn the names of files in the process's current working directory?

ANSWER

Processes can read the contents of directory files using the standard file read() system call used to read the contents of "normal" files.

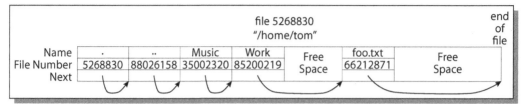

Figure 13.4: A linked list implementation of a directory. This example shows a directory file containing five entries: Music, Work, and foo.txt, along with . (the current directory) and .. (the parent directory.)

> Although operating systems must restrict writes to directory files to ensure invariants on directory structure, they need not restrict applications from reading the contents of directory files (that they have permission to read.) For simplicity, applications would access this function via a standard library that also includes routines for parsing directory files .

Although it is not fundamentally necessary to have dedicated system calls for reading directories, it can be convenient. For example, Linux includes a getdents() ("get directory entries") system call that reads a specified number of directory entries from an open file.

Directory internals.   Many early implementations simply stored linear lists of *file name, file number* pairs in directory files. For example, in the original version of the Linux ext2 file system, each directory file stored a linked list of directory entries as illustrated in Figure 13.4.

Simple lists work fine when the number of directory entries is small, and that was the expected case for many early file systems, but systems occasionally encounter workloads that generate thousands of files in a directory. Once a directory has a few thousand entries, simple list-based directories become sluggish.

To efficiently support directories with many entries, many recent file systems including Linux XFS, Microsoft NTFS, and Oracle ZFS organize a directory's contents as a tree. Similarly, newer versions of ext2 augment the underlying linked list with an additional hash-based structure to speed searches.

For example, Figure 13.5-(a) illustrates a tree-based directory structure similar to the one used in Linux XFS, and Figure 13.5-(b) illustrates how these records are physically arranged in a directory file.

In this example, directory records mapping file names to file numbers are stored in a B+tree that is indexed by the hash of each file's name. To find the file number for a given file name (eg., out2), the file system first computes a hash of the name (e.g., 0x0000c194). It then uses that hash as a key to search for the directory entry in the tree: starting at the B+tree root at a well-known offset in the file (BTREE_ROOT_PTR), and proceeding

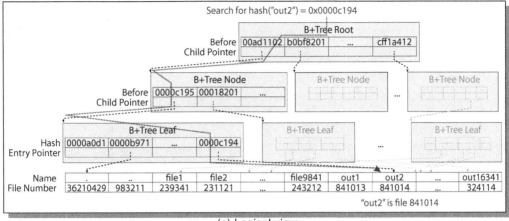

(a) Logical view

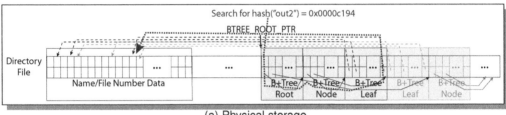

(a) Physical storage

Figure 13.5: Tree-based directory structure similar to the one used in Linux's XFS file system.

through the B+tree's internal nodes to the B+tree's leaf nodes. At each level, a tree node contains an array of *(hash key, file offset)* pairs that each represent a pointer to the child node containing entries with keys smaller than *hash key* but larger than the previous entry's *hash key*, and the file system searches the node for the first entry with a *hash key* value that exceeds the target key, and then it follows the corresponding *file offset* pointer to the correct child node. The *file offset* pointer in the record at the leaf nodes points to the target directory entry.

In the XFS implementation, directory entries are stored in the first part of the directory file. The B+tree's root is at a well-known offset within file (e.g., BTREE_ROOT_PTR). The fixed-size internal and leaf nodes are stored after the root node, and the variable-size directory entries are stored at the start of the file. Starting from the root, each tree node includes pointers to where in the file its children are stored.

Hard and soft links. Many file systems allow a given file to have multiple names. For example, /home/tom/Work/Classes/OS/hw1.txt and /home/tom/todo/hw1.txt may refer to the same file, as Figure 13.6 illustrates.

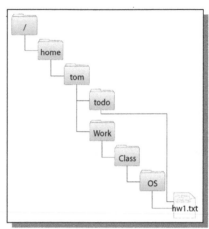

Figure 13.6: Example of a directed acyclic graph directory organization with multiple hard links to a file (figure repeated from Chapter 11)

Figure 13.7: In this directory, the hard links foo.txt and bar.txt and the soft link baz.txt all refer to the same file.

hard link   *Hard links* are multiple file directory entries that map different path names to the same file number. Because a file number can appear in multiple directories, file systems must ensure that a file is only deleted when the last hard link to it has been removed.

To properly implement garbage collection, file systems use reference counts by storing with each file the number of hard links to it. When a file is created, it has a reference count of 1, and each additional hard link made to the file (e.g., link(existingName, newName)) increments its reference count. Conversely, each call to unlink(name) decrements the file's reference count, and when the reference count falls to zero, the underlying file is removed and its resources marked as free.

soft link   Rather than mapping a file name to a file number, *soft links* or *symbolic* **symbolic** *links* are directory entries that map one name to another name.
link

For example, Figure 13.7 shows a directory that contains three names that all refer to the same file. The entries foo.txt and bar.txt are hard links to the same file — number 66212871; baz.txt is a soft link to foo.txt.

Notice that if we remove entry foo.txt from this directory using the unlink() system call, the file can still be opened using the name bar.txt, but if we try to open it with the name baz.txt, the attempt will fail.

EXAMPLE   **File metadata.**

Most file systems store a file's metadata (e.g., a file's access time, owner ID, permissions, and size) in a file header that can be found with the file number. One could imagine storing that metadata in a file's directory entry instead. Why is this seldom done?

ANSWER   In file systems that support hard links, storing file metadata in directory entries would be problematic. For example, whenever a file's attribute like its size changed, all of a file's directory entries would have to be located and updated. As another example, if file metadata were stored in directory entries, it would be hard to maintain a file reference count so that the file's resources are freed when and only when the last hard link to the file is removed.

The venerable Microsoft FAT file system stores file metadata in directory entries, but it does not support hard links.

Exercises

1. Why do we many file systems have separate system calls for removing a regular file (e.g., unlink) and removing a directory (.e.g, rmdir)?

2. In Figure 13.4, suppose we create a new file z.txt and then unlink Work, removing that entry. Draw a figure similar to Figure 13.4 that shows the new contents of the directory.

13.3 | Files: Finding data

Once a file system has translated a file name into a file number using a directory, the file system must be able to find the blocks that belong to that file. In addition to this functional requirement, implementations of files typically target five other goals:

- Support sequential data placement to maximize sequential file acces

- Provide efficient random access to any file block

- Limit overheads to be efficient for small files

- Be scalable to support large files

	FAT	FFS	NTFS	ZFS
Index structure	linked list	tree (fixed, asymmetric)	tree (dynamic)	tree (COW, dynamic)
Index structure granularity	block	block	extent	block
Free space management	FAT array	bitmap (fixed)	bitmap in file (file)	space map (log-structured)
Locality heuristics	defragmentation	block groups reserve space	best fit defragmentation	write-anywhere block groups

Figure 13.8: Summary of key ideas discussed for four common file systems approaches.

- Provide a place to store per-file metadata such as the file's reference count, owner, access control list, size, and access time

File system designers have a great deal of flexibility to meet these goals. Recall from Section 13.1 that

- A file's *index structure* provides a way to locate each block of the file. Index structures are usually some sort of tree for scalability and to support locality.

- A file system's *free space map* provides a way to allocate free blocks to grow a file. When files grow, choosing which free blocks to use is important for providing good locality. A file system's free space map is therefore often implemented as a bitmap so that it is easy to find a desired number of sequential free blocks near a desired location.

- A file system's *locality heuristics* define how a file system groups data in storage to maximize access performance.

Within this framework, the design space for file systems is large. To understand the trade-offs and to understand the workings of common file systems, we will examine four case-study designs that illustrate important implementation techniques and that represent approaches that are in wide use today.

- **FAT.** The Microsoft File Allocation Table (FAT) file system traces its roots to the late 1970s.

   Techniques: The FAT file system uses an extremely simple index structure — a *linked list* — so it is a good place to discuss our discussion of implementation techniques.

   Today: The FAT file system is still widely used in devices like flash memory sticks and digital cameras where simplicity and interoperability are paramount.

- **FFS.** The Unix Fast File System (FFS) was released in the mid 1980s, and it retained many of the data structures in Ritchie and Thompson's original Unix file system from the early 1970s.

  Techniques: FFS uses a *tree-based multilevel index* for its index structure to improve random access efficiency, and it uses a collection of *locality heuristics* to get good spatial locality for a wide range of workloads.

  Today: In Linux, the popular ext2 and ext3 file systems are based on the FFS design.

- **NTFS.** The Microsoft New Technology File System (NTFS) was introduced in the early 1990s as a replacement for the FAT file system.

  Techniques: Like FFS, BTFS uses a tree-based index structure, but the tree is *more flexible than FFS's fixed tree*. Additionally, NTFS optimizes its index structure for sequential file layout by indexing variable-sized *extents* rather than individual blocks.

  Today: NTFS remains the primary file system for Microsoft operating systems such as Windows 7. In addition, the flexible tree and extent techniques are representative of several widely-used file systems such as the Linux ext4, XFS, and Reiser4 file systems, the AIX/Linux Journaled File System (JFS), and the Apple Hierarchical File Systems (HFS and HFS+).

- **COW/ZFS.** Copy on write (COW) file systems update existing data and metadata blocks by writing new versions to free disk blocks. This approach optimizes write performance: because any data or metadata can be written to any free space on disk, the file system can group otherwise random writes into large, sequential group writes.

  To see how these ideas are implemented, we will examine the open-source ZFS, a prominent copy on write file system that was introduced in the early 2000's by Sun Microsystems. ZFS is designed to scale to file systems spanning large numbers of disks, to provide strong data integrity guarantees, and to optimize write performance.

Figure 13.8 summarizes key ideas in these systems that we will detail in the sections that follow.

FAT: Linked list

The Microsoft File Allocation Table (FAT) file system was first implemented in the late 1970s and was the main file system for MS-DOS and early versions of Microsoft Windows. The FAT file system has been enhanced in many ways over the years. Our discussion will focus on the most recent version, FAT-32, which supports volumes with up to 2^{28} blocks and files with up to $2^{32} - 1$ bytes.

Sectors v. pages; blocks v. clusters; extents v. runs

Although storage hardware arranges data in *sectors* (for magnetic disk) or *pages* (for flash), file systems often group together a fixed number of disk sectors or flash pages into a larger allocation unit called a *block*. For example, we might format a file system running on a disk with 512 byte sectors to use 4 KB blocks. Aggregating multiple sectors into a block can reduce the overheads of allocating, tracking, and deallocating blocks, but it may increase space overheads slightly.

FAT and NTFS refer to blocks as *clusters*, but for consistency we will use the term *block* in our discussions.

Finally, some file systems like NTFS, ext4, and btrfs store data in variable-length arrays of contiguous tracks called *extents* in most file systems and *runs* in NTFS. For consistency, we will use the term *extent* in our discussions.

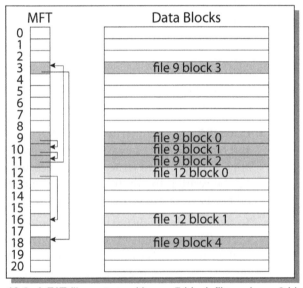

Figure 13.9: A FAT file system with one 5-block file and one 2-block file.

file allocation table**Index structures.** The FAT file system is named for its *file allocation table,* an array of 32-bit entries in a reserved area of the volume. Each file in the system corresponds to a linked list of FAT entries, with each FAT entry containing a pointer to the next FAT entry of the file (or a special "end of file" value). The FAT has one entry for each block in the volume, and the file's blocks are the blocks that correspond to the file's FAT entries: if FAT entry i is the jth FAT entry of a file, then storage block i is the jth data block of the file.

Figure 13.9 illustrates a FAT file system with two files. The first begins at block 9 and contains 5 blocks. The second begins at block 12 and contains 2 blocks.

Directories map file names to file numbers, and in the FAT file system a file's number is the index of the file's first entry in the FAT. So, given a file's number, we can find the first FAT entry and block of a file, and given the first FAT entry, we can find the rest of the file's FAT entries and blocks.

Free space tracking. The FAT is also used for free space tracking. If data block i is free, then FAT[i] contains 0. Thus, the file system can find a free block by scanning through the FAT to find a zeroed entry.

Locality heuristics. Different implementations of FAT may use different allocation strategies, but FAT implementations' allocation strategies are usually simple. For example, some implementations use a *next fit* algorithm that scans sequentially through the FAT starting from the last entry that was allocated and that returns the next free entry found.

Simple allocation strategies like this may fragment a file, spreading the file's blocks across the volume rather than achieving the desired sequential layout. To improve performance, users can run a *defragmentation* tool that reads files from their existing locations and rewrites them to new locations with better spatial locality. The FAT defragmenter in Windows XP, for example, attempts to copy the blocks of each file that is spread across multiple extents to a single, sequential extent that holds all the blocks of a file.

defragment

Discussion The FAT file system is widely used because it is simple and supported by many operating systems. For example, many flash storage USB keys and camera storage cards use the FAT file system, allowing them to be read and written by almost any computer running almost any modern operating system.

Variations of the FAT file system are even used by applications for organizing data within individual files. For example Microsoft .doc files produced by versions of Microsoft Word from 1997 to 2007 are actually compound documents with many internal pieces. The .doc format creates a FAT-like file system within the .doc file to manage the objects in the .doc file.

The FAT file system, however, is limited in many ways. For example,

- **Poor locality.** FAT implementations typically use simple allocation strategies like next fit that can lead to badly fragmented files.

- **Poor random access.** Random access within a file requires sequentially traversing the file's FAT entries until the desired block is reached.

- **Limited file metadata and access control.** The metadata for each file includes information like the file's name, size, and creation time, but it does not include access control information like the file's owner or group ID , so any user can read or write any file stored in a FAT file system.

- **No support for hard links.** FAT represents each file as a linked list of 32-bit entries in the file allocation table. This representation does not include room for any other file metadata, file metadata in stored with directory entries with the file's name. This approach demands that each file be accessed via exactly one directory entry, ruling out multiple hard links to a file.

- **Limitations on volume and file size.** FAT table entries are 32 bits, but the top 4 bits are reserved. So, a FAT volume can have at most 2^{28} blocks. With 4KB blocks, the maximum volume size is limited (e.g., 2^{28} blocks/volume * 2^{12} bytes/block = 2^{40} bytes/volume = 1TB). Block sizes up to 256 KB are supported, but they risk wasting large amounts of disk space due to internal fragmentation.

  Similarly, file sizes are encoded in 32 bits, so no file can be larger than $2^{32} - 1$ bytes (just under 4GB).

- **Lack of support for modern reliability techniques.** Although we will not discuss reliability until Chapter 14, we note here that FAT does not support transactional update techniques that are used in modern file systems to avoid corrupting critical data structures if the computer crashes while writing to storage.

FFS: Fixed tree

The Unix Fast File System (FFS) illustrates important ideas for both indexing a file's blocks so they can be located quickly and for placing data on disk to get good locality.

In particular, FFS's index structure, called a *multilevel index*, is a carefully structured tree that allows FFS to locate any block of a file and that is efficient for both large and small files.

Given the flexibility provided by FFS's multilevel index, FFS employs two locality heuristics — *block group placement* and *reserve space* — that together usually provide good on-disk layout.

Index structures. To keep track of the data blocks that belong to each file, FFS uses a fixed, asymmetric tree called a *multilevel index*, as illustrated in Figure 13.11.

Each file is a tree with fixed-sized data blocks (e.g., 4KB) as its leaves. Each file's tree is rooted at an *inode* that contains the file's metadata (e.g., the file's owner, access control permissions, creation time, last modified time, and whether the file is a directory or not.)

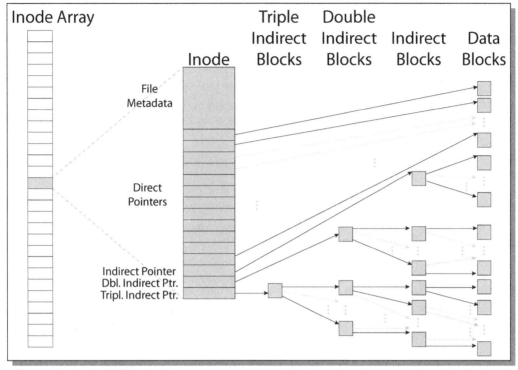

Figure 13.10: An FFS inode is the root of an asymmetric tree whose leaves are the data blocks of a file.

A file's inode (root) also contains array of pointers for locating the file's data blocks (leaves). Some of these pointers point directly to the tree's data leaves and some of them point to internal nodes in the tree. Typically, an inode contains 15 pointers. The first 12 pointers are *direct pointers* that point directly to the first 12 data blocks of a file.

indirect block
The 13th pointer is an *indirect pointer*, which points to an internal node of the tree called an *indirect block*; an indirect block is a regular block of storage that contains an array of direct pointers. So, to read the 13th block of a file, you first read the inode to get the indirect pointer, then you read the indirect block to get the direct pointer, then you read the data block. With 4KB blocks and 4-byte block pointers, an indirect block can contain as many as 1024 direct pointers, which allows for files up to a little over 4MB.

double indirect block
The 14th pointer is a *double indirect pointer*, which points to an internal node of the tree called a *double indirect block*; a double indirect block is an array of indirect pointers, each of which points to an indirect block. With 4KB blocks and 4-byte block pointers, a double indirect block can contain as many as 1024 indirect pointers. So, a double indirect pointer can index as many as $(1024)^2$ data blocks.

Finally, the 15th pointer is a *triple indirect pointer* that points to a *triple*

FFS Access Control

The FFS inode contains information for controlling access to a file. Access control can be specified for three sets of people:

- **User (owner).** The user that owns the file.
- **Group.** The set of people belonging to a specified Unix group. Each Unix group is specified elsewhere as a group name and list of users in that group.
- **Other.** All other users.

Access control is specified in terms of three types of activities:

- **Read.** Read the regular file or directory.
- **Write.** Modify the regular file or directory.
- **Execute.** Execute the regular file or traverse the directory to access files or subdirectories in it.

Each file's inode stores the identities of the file's user (owner) and group as well as 9 basic access control bits to specify read/write/execute permission for the file's user (owner)/group/other. For example, the command ls -ld / shows the access control information for the root directory:

> ls -ld /
drwxr-xr-x 40 root wheel 1428 Feb 2 13:39 /

meaning that the file is a directory (d), owned by the user root the group wheel. The root directory can be read, written, and executed (traversed) by the owner (rwx), and it can be read and executed (traversed) but not written by members of group wheel (r-x) and all other users (r-x).

---

triple indirect block   *indirect block* that contains an array of double indirect pointers. With 4KB blocks and 4-byte block pointers, a triple indirect pointer can index as many as $(1024)^3$ data blocks containing $4KB * 1024^3 = 2^{12} * 2^{30} = 2^{42}$ bytes (4 TB.)

inode array   All of a file system's inodes are located in an *inode array* that is stored in a fixed location on disk. A file's file number, called an *inumber* in FFS, is

inumber   an index into the inode array: to open file (e.g., foo.txt), we look in the file's directory to find its inumber (e.g., 91854), and then look in the appropriate entry of the inode array (e.g., entry 91854) to find its metadata.

FFS's multilevel index has four important characteristics:

- **Tree structure.** Each file is represented as a tree, which allows the file system to efficiently find any block of a file.

- **High degree.** The FFS tree uses internal nodes with many children compared to the binary trees often used for in-memory data structures

Setuid and setgid programs

In addition to the 9 basic access control bits, the FFS inode stores two important additional bits:

- **Setuid.** When this file is executed by any user (with execute permission) it will be executed with the owner's permission. For example, the lprm program allows a user to to remove a job from a printer queue. The print queue is implemented as a directory containing files to be printed, and because we don't want users to be able to remove other users' jobs, this directory is owned by and may only be modified by the root user. So, the lprm program is owned by the root user, can be executed by anyone, and is setuid so that it will execute with root permissions, allowing it to modify the print queue directory.

  E.g.,

  -rwsr-xr-x 1 root root 507674 2010-07-05 12:39 /lusr/bin/lprm*

  Of course, making a program setuid is potentially dangerous. Here, for example, we rely on the lprm program to verify that actual user is deleting his own print jobs, not someone else's. A bug in the lprm program could let one user remove another's printer jobs. Or worse: if the bug allows the attacker to execute malicious code (e.g., via a buffer overflow attack), a bug in lprm could give an attacker total control of the machine.

- **Setgid.** The setguid bit is similar to the setuid bit, execept that the file is executed with the file's group permission. For example, on some machines, sendmail executes as a member of group smmsp so that it can access a mail queue file accessible to group smmsp.

  E.g.,

  -r-xr-sr-x 1 root smmsp 2264923 2011-06-23 14:51 /lusr/opt/sendmail-8.14.4/lib/mail/sendmail*

(i.e., internal nodes have high *degree* or *fan out*). For example, if a file block is 4 KB and a blockID is 4 bytes, then each indirect block can contain pointers to 1024 blocks.

High degree nodes make sense for on-disk data structures where (1) we want to minimize the number of seeks, (2) the cost of reading several kilobytes of sequential data is not much higher than the cost of reading the first byte, and (3) data must be read and written at least a sector at a time.

High degree nodes also improve efficiency for sequential reads and writes — once in indirect block is read, hundreds of data blocks can be read before the next indirect block is needed. Runs between reads of double indirect blocks are even larger.

- **Fixed structure.** The FFS tree has a fixed structure. For a given configuration of FFS, the first set of d pointers always point to the first d blocks of a file; the next pointer is an indirect pointer that points to an indirect block; etc.

  Compared to a dynamic tree that can add layers of indirection above a block as a file grows, the main advantage of the fixed structure is implementation simplicity.

- **Asymmetric.** To efficiently support both large and small files with a fixed tree structure, FFS's tree structure is asymmetric. Rather than putting each data block at the same depth, FFS stores successive groups of blocks at increasing depth so that small files are stored in a small-depth tree, the bulk of medium files are stored in a medium-depth tree, and the bulk of large files are stored in a larger-depth tree. For example, Figure **??** shows a small, 4-block file whose inode includes direct pointers to all of its blocks. Conversely, for the large file shown in Figure 13.11, most of the blocks must be accessed via the triple-indirect pointer.

  In contrast, if we use a fixed-depth tree and want to support reasonably large files, small files would pay high overheads. With triple indirect pointers and 4 KB blocks, storing a 4KB file would consume over 16 KB (the 4KB of data, the small inode, and 3 levels of 4 KB indirect blocks), and reading the file would require reading five blocks to traverse the tree.

The FFS principles are general, and variations on this basic approach have been adopted by many file systems.

EXAMPLE   **FFS variation.**

Suppose BigFS is a variation of FFS that includes in each inode 12 direct, 1 indirect, 1 double indirect, 1 triple indirect, and 1 *quadruple indirect* pointers. Assuming 4KB blocks and 8-byte pointers, what is the maximum file size this index structure can support?

ANSWER   12 direct pointers can index $12 * 4KB = 48KB$

When used as an internal node, each storage block can contain as many as $4KB/block / 8bytes/pointer = 512 pointers/block = 2^9 pointers/block$ pointers.

So, the indirect pointer points to an indirect block with 2^9 pointers, referencing as much as $2^9 blocks * 2^{12} bytes/block = 2^{21} bytes = 2MB$.

Similarly, the double indirect pointer references as much as $2^9 * 2^9 * 2^{12} = 2^{30} bytes = 1GB$, the triple indirect pointer references as much as

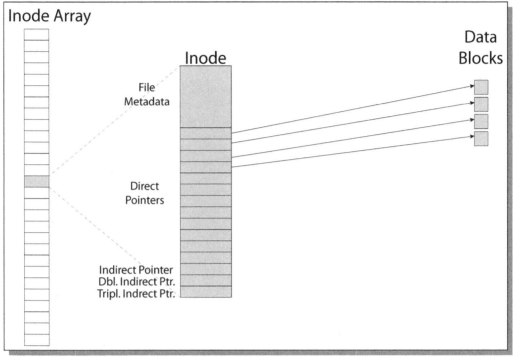

Figure 13.11: A small FFS file whose blocks are all reachable via direct pointers in the inode.

$2^9 * 2^9 * 2^9 * 2^{12} = 2^{39}$bytes $= 512$GB, and the quadruple indirect pointer references as much as $2^9 * 2^9 * 2^9 * 2^9 * 2^{12} = 2^{48}$bytes $= 256$TB. So, BigFS can support files a bit larger than 256.5 TB.

Free space management. FFS's free space management is simple. FFS
bitmap allocates a *bitmap* with one bit per storage block. The ith bit in the bitmap indicates whether the ith block is free or in use. The position of FFS's bitmap is fixed when the file system is formatted, so it is easy to find the part of the bitmap that identifies free blocks near any location of interest.

Locality heuristics.   FFS uses two important locality heuristics to get good performance for many workloads: *block group placement* and *reserved space*.

Block group placement.   FFS block group placement optimizes data placement for common access patterns in which a file's data blocks, a file's data and metadata, and different files from the same directory are accessed together.

Conversely, because everything can not be near everything, FFS lets different directories' files be far from each other.

This placement heuristic has four parts:

Sparse Files

Tree-based index structures like FFS's can support *sparse files* in which one or more ranges of empty space is surrounded by file data. No disk space is consumed by the ranges of empty space.

For example, if we create a new file, write 4 KB at offset 0, seek to offset 2^{30}, and write another 4 KB, an FFS system with 4KB blocks will only consume 16 KB — two data blocks, a double indirect block, and a single indirect block.

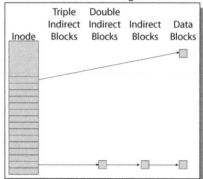

In this case, if we list the *size of the file* using the ls command, we see that the file's size is 1.1 GB. But, if we check the *space consumed by the file*, using the du command, we see that it consumes just 16 KB of storage space.

```
>ls -lgGh sparse.dat
-rwx------ 1 1.1G 2012-01-31 08:45 sparse.dat*
>du -hs sparse.dat
16K sparse.dat
```

If we read from a hole, the file system produces a zero-filled buffer. If we write to a hole, the file system allocates storage blocks for the data and any required indirect blocks.

Similar to efficient support for sparse virtual memory address spaces, efficient support of sparse files is useful for giving applications maximum flexibility in placing data in a file. For example, a database could store its tables starting at the start of its file, store its indices starting at 1 GB into the file, its log starting at 2 GB, and additional metadata starting at 4 GB.

Sparse files have two important limitations. First, not all file systems support them, so an application that relies on sparse file support may not be portable. Second, not all utilities are savvy about handling sparse files, which can lead to unexpected consequences. For example, if I read a sparse file from beginning to end and write each byte to a different file, I will observe runs of zero-filled buffers corresponding to holes and write those zero-filled regions to the new file. The result is a new non-sparse file whose space consumption matches its size.

```
>cat sparse.dat > /tmp/notSparse.dat
>ls -lgGh /tmp/notSparse.dat
-rw-r--r-- 1 1.1G 2012-01-31 08:54 /tmp/notSparse.dat
 >
>du -hs /tmp/notSparse.dat
1.1G /tmp/notSparse.dat
```

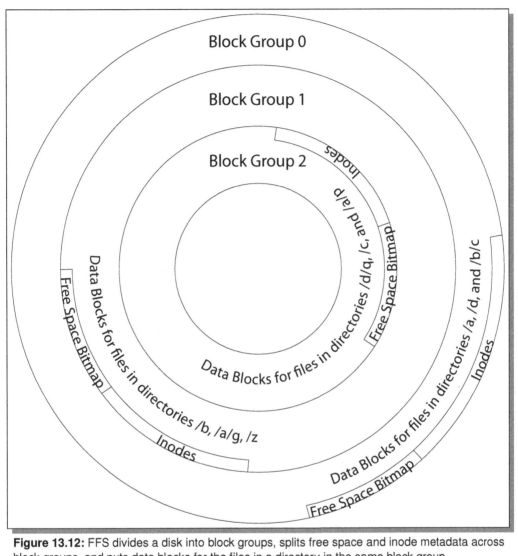

Figure 13.12: FFS divides a disk into block groups, splits free space and inode metadata across block groups, and puts data blocks for the files in a directory in the same block group..

- **Divide disk into block groups.** As Figure 13.12 illustrates, FFS divides a disk in to sets of nearby tracks called *block groups*. The seek time between any blocks in a block group will be small.

block group

- **Distribute metadata.** Earlier multilevel index file systems put the inode array and free space bitmap in a contiguous region of the disk. In such a centralized metadata arrangement, the disk head must often make seeks between a file's data and its metadata.

  In FFS, the inode array and free space bitmap are still conceptually arrays of records, and FFS still stores each array entry at a well-known, easily calculable location, but the array is now split into pieces distributed across the disk. In particular, each block group holds a portion of these metadata structures as Figure 13.12 illustrates,

For example, if a disk has 100 block groups, each block group would store 1% of the file system's inodes and the 1% portion of the bitmap that tracks the status of the data blocks in the block group.

- **Place file in block group.** FFS puts a directory and its files in the same block group: when a new file is created, FFS knows the inumber of the new file's directory, and from that it can determine the range of inumbers in the same block group. FFS chooses an inode from that group if one is free; otherwise, FFS gives up locality and selects an inumber from a different block group.

  In contrast with regular files, when FFS creates a new directory, it chooses an inumber from a different block group. Even though we might expect a subdirectory to have some locality with its parent, putting all subdirectories in the same block group would quickly fill it, thwarting our efforts to get locality within a directory.

  Figure 13.12 illustrates how FFS might groups files from different directories into different block groups.

- **Place data blocks.** Within a block group, FFS uses a first-free heuristic. When a new block of a file is written, FFS writes the block to the first free block in the file's block group.

  Although this heuristic may give up locality in the short term, it does so to improve locality in the long term. In the short term, this heuristic might spread a sequence of writes into small holes near the start of a block group rather than concentrating them to a sequence of contiguous free blocks somewhere else. This short term sacrifice brings long term benefits, however: fragmentation is reduced, the block will tend to have a long run of free space at its end, subsequent writes are more likely to be sequential.

  The intuition is that a given block group will usually have a handful of holes scattered through blocks near the start of the group and a long run of free space at the end of the group. Then, if a new, small file is created, its blocks will likely go to a few of the small holes, which is not ideal, but which is acceptable for a small file. Conversely, if a large file is created and written from beginning to end, it will tend to have the first few blocks scattered through the holes in the early part of the block, but then have the bulk of its data written sequentially at the end of the block group.

  If a block group runs out of free blocks, FFS selects another block group and allocates blocks there using the same heuristic.

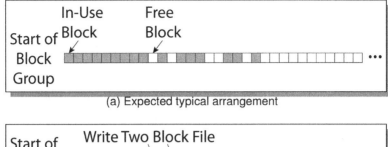

(a) Expected typical arrangement

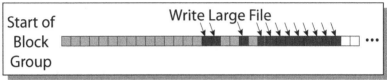

(b) Small files fill holes near start of block group

(c) Large files fill holes near start of block group and then write most data
to a sequential range of blocks

Figure 13.13: FFS's block placement heuristic is to put each new file block in the
first free block in that file's block group

Reserved space.   Although the block group heuristic can be effective, it
relies on there being a significant amount of free space on disk. In particular,
when a disk is nearly full, there is little opportunity for the file system to
optimize locality. For example, if a disk has only a few kilobytes of free
sectors, most block groups will be full, and others will have only a few free
blocks; new writes will have to be scattered more or less randomly around
the disk.

FFS therefore reserves some fraction of the disk's space (e.g., 10%) and
presents a slightly reduced disk size to applications. If the actual free space
on the disk falls below the reserve fraction, FFS treats the disk as full. For
example, if a user's application attempts to write a new block in a file when
all but the reserve space is consumed, that write will fail. When all but the
reserve space is full, the super user's processes will still be able to allocate
new blocks, which is useful for allowing an administrator to log in and
clean things up.

The reserved space approach works well given disk technology trends.
It sacrifices a small amount of disk capacity, a hardware resource that
has been improving rapidly over recent decades, to reduce seek times, a
hardware property that is improving only slowly.

NTFS: Flexible tree with extents

The Microsoft New Technology File System (NTFS), released in 1993, improved on Microsoft's FAT file system with many new features including new index structures to improve performance, more flexible file metadata, improved security, and improved reliability.

We will discuss some of NTFS's reliability features in Chapter 14. Here, we will focus on how NTFS stores data and metadata.

Index structures   Whereas FFS tracks file blocks with a fixed tree, NTFS and many other recent file systems such as Linux ext4 and btrfs track *extents* with *flexible trees*.

extent

- **Extents.** Rather than tracking individual file blocks, NTFS tracks *extents*, variable-sized regions of files that are each stored in a contiguous region on the storage device.

- **Flexible tree and master file table.** Each file in NTFS is represented by a variable-depth tree. The extent pointers for a file with a small number of extents can be stored in a shallow tree, even if the file, itself, is large. Deeper trees are only needed if the file becomes badly fragmented.

**master file
table (MFT)**

**attribute
record**

The roots of these trees are stored in a master file table that is similar to FFS's inode array. NTFS's *master file table (MFT)* stores an array of 1 KB MFT records, each of which stores a sequence of variable-size *attribute records*. NTFS uses attribute records to store both data and metadata — both are just considered attributes of a file.

**resident
attribute**

**nonresident
attribute**

Some attributes can be too large to fit in an MFT record (e.g., a data extent) while some can be small enough to fit (e.g., a file's last modified time). An attribute can therefore be *resident* or *nonresident*. A *resident attribute* stores its contents directly in the MFT record while a *nonresident attribute* stores extent pointers in its MFT record and stores its contents in those extents.

Figure 13.14 illustrates the index structures for a basic NTFS file. Here, the file's MFT record includes a *nonresident data* attribute, which is a sequence of extent pointers, each of which specifies the starting block and length in blocks of an extent of data. Because extents can hold variable numbers of blocks, even a multi-gigabyte file can be represented by one or a few extent pointers in an MFT record, assuming file system fragmentation is kept under control.

If a file is small, the data attribute may be used to store the file's actual contents right in its MFT record as a resident attribute as Figure 13.15 illustrates.

An MFT record has a flexible format that can include range of different attributes. In addition to data attributes, three common metadata attribute types include

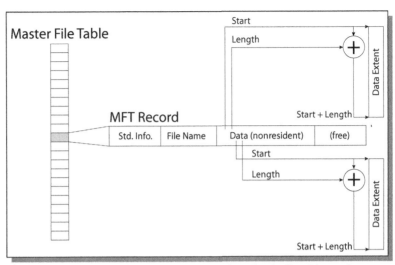

Figure 13.14: NTFS index structures and data for a basic file with two data extents.

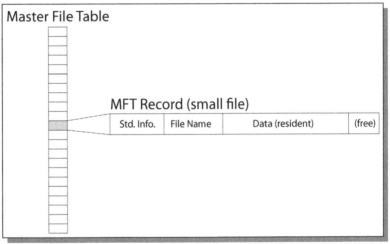

Figure 13.15: A small file's data can be *resident*, meaning that the file's data is stored in its MFT record.

- **Standard information.** This attribute holds standard information needed for all files. Fields include the file's creation time, modification time, access time, owner ID, and security specifier. Also included is a set of flags indicating basic information like whether the file is a read only file, a hidden file, or a system file.

- **File name.** This attribute holds the file's name and the file number of its parent directory. Because a file can have multiple names (e.g., if there are multiple hard links to the file), it may have multiple file

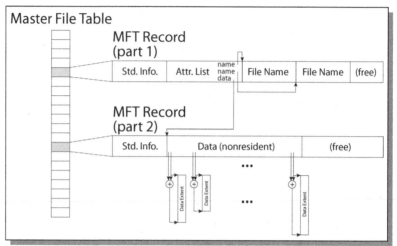

Figure 13.16: Most NTFS files store their attributes in a single MFT record, but a file's attributes can grow to to span multiple MFT records. In those cases, the first MFT record includes an *attribute list* attribute that indicates where to find each attribute record.

name attributes in its MFT record.

- **Attribute list.** Because a file's metadata may include a variable number of variable sized attributes, a file's metadata may be larger than a single MFT record can hold. When this case occurs, NTFS stores the attributes in multiple MFT records and includes an attribute list in the first record. When present, the attribute list indicates which attributes are stored in which MFT records. For example, Figure 13.17 shows MFT records for two files, one whose attributes are contained in a single MFT record and one of whose attributes spans two MFT records.

As Figure **??** illustrates, a file can go through four stages of growth, depending on its size and fragmentation. First, a small file may have its contents included in the MFT record as a resident data attribute. Second, more typically, a file's data lies in a small number of extents tracked by a single nonresident data attribute. Third, occasionally if a file is large and the file system fragmented, a file can have so many extents that the extent pointers will not fit in a single MFT record; in this case, as a file can have multiple nonresident data attributes in multiple MFT records, with the attribute list in the first MFT record indicating which MFT records track which ranges of extents. Fourth and finally, if a file is huge or the file system fragmentation extreme, a file's attribute list can be made nonresident, allowing almost arbitrarily large numbers of MFT records.

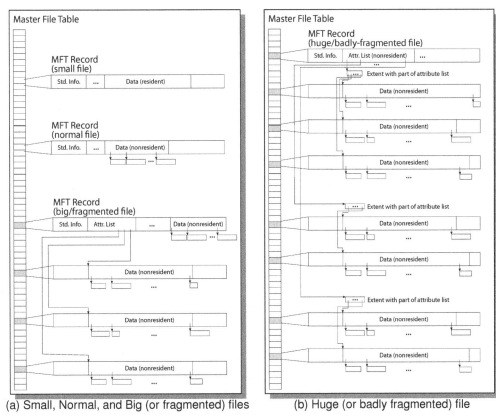

(a) Small, Normal, and Big (or fragmented) files   (b) Huge (or badly fragmented) file

Figure 13.17: An NTFS file's data attribute can be in a *resident data attribute*, in extents tracked by a *single nonresident data attribute*, in extents tracked by *multiple nonresident data attributes* in multiple MFT entries tracked by a *resident attribute list attribute*, or in extents tracked by *multiple nonresident data attributes* stored in multiple MFT entries tracked by a *nonresident attribute list attribute*.

Metadata files   Rather than doing ad-hoc allocation of special regions of disk for file system metadata like free space bitmaps, NTFS stores almost all of its metadata in about a dozen ordinary files with well-known low-numbered file numbers. For example, file number 5 is the root directory, file number 6 is the free space bitmap, and file number 8 contains a list of the volume's bad blocks.

File number 9, called $Secure, contains security and access control information. NTFS has a flexible security model in which a file can be associated with a list of users and groups, with specific access control settings for each listed principal. In early versions of NTFS, such an access control list was stored with each file, but these lists consumed a nontrivial amount of space and many lists had identical contents. So, current implementations of NTFS store each unique access control list once in the special $Secure file, indexed by a fixed-length unique key. Each individual file just stores the appropriate fixed-length key in its MFT record, and NTFS uses a file's security key to find the appropriate access control list in the $Secure file.

Even the master file table, itself, is stored as a file, file number 0, called $MFT. So, we need to find the first entry of the MFT in order to read the MFT! To locate the MFT, the first sector of an NTFS volume includes a pointer to the first entry of the MFT.

Storing the MFT in a file avoids the need to statically allocate all MFT entries as a fixed array in a predetermined location. Instead NTFS starts with a small MFT and grows it as new files are created and new entries are needed.

Locality heuristics.   Most implementations of NTFS use a variation of *best fit* placement, where the system tries to place a newly allocated file in the smallest free region that is large enough to hold it. In NTFS's variation, rather than trying to keep the allocation bitmap for the entire disk in memory, the system caches the allocation status for a smaller region of the disk and searches that region first. If the bitmap cache holds information for areas where writes recently occurred, then writes that occur together in time will tend to be clustered together.

best fit

An important NTFS feature for optimizing its best fit placement is the SetEndOfFile() interface, which allows an application to specify the expected size of a file at creation time. In contrast, file systems like FFS allocate file blocks as they are written, without knowing how large the file will eventually grow.

To avoid having the master file table file ($MFT) become fragmented, NTFS reserves part of the start of the volume (e.g., the first 12.5% of the volume) for MFT expansion. NTFS does not place file blocks in the MFT reserve area until the non-reserved area is full, at which point it halves the size of the MFT reserve area and continues. As the volume continues to fill, NTFS continues to halve the reserve area until it reaches the point where the remaining reserve area is more than half full.

Finally, Microsoft operating systems with NTFS include a defragmentation utility that takes fragmented files and rewrites them to contiguous regions of disk.

Copy on write file systems

copy on write (COW) file system

When updating an existing file, *copy on write (COW) file systems* do not overwrite the existing data or metadata; instead they write new versions to new locations.

COW file systems do this to optimize writes by transforming random I/O updates to sequential ones. For example, when appending a block to a file, a traditional, update-in-place file system might seek to and update its free space bitmap, the file's inode in the inode array, the file's indirect block,

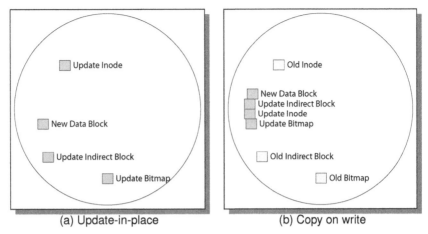

(a) Update-in-place   (b) Copy on write

Figure 13.18: An update-in-place file system updates data and metadata in their existing locations, while a copy on write file system makes new copies of data and metadata whenever they are updated.

and the file's data block. In contrast, a COW file system might just find a sequential run of free space and write the new bitmap, inode, indirect block, and data block there as illustrated in Figure 13.18.

Several technology trends are driving widespread adoption of COW file systems:

- **Small writes are expensive.** Disk performance for large sequential writes is much better than for small random writes. This gap is likely to continue to grow because bandwidth generally improves faster than seek time or rotational latency: increasing storage density can increase bandwidth even if the rotational speed does not increase.

   As a result the benefits of converting small random writes to large sequential ones is large and getting larger.

- **Small writes are especially expensive on RAID.** Redundant arrays of inexpensive disks (RAIDs) are often used to improve storage reliability. However, as we will discuss in the next chapter, updating a single block stored with parity on a RAID requires four disk I/Os: we must read the old data, read the old parity, write the new data, and write the new parity. In contrast, RAIDs are efficient when an entire stripe — all of the blocks sharing the same parity block — are updated at once. In that case, no reads are needed, each new data block is written, and the parity update is amortized across the data blocks in the stripe.

   Widespread use of RAIDs magnifies the benefits of converting random writes to sequential ones.

- **Caches filter reads.**

For many workloads, large DRAM caches can handle essentially all file system reads. But our ability to use DRAM to buffer writes is limited by the need to durably store data soon after it is written.

Thus, the cost of writes often dominates performance, so techniques that optimize write performance are appealing.

- **Widespread adoption of flash storage.**

  Flash storage has two properties that make the COW techniques important. First, in order to write a small (e.g., 4 KB) flash page, one must first clear the large (e.g., 512 KB) erasure block on which it resides. Second, each flash storage element can handle a limited number of write-erase cycles before wearing out, so *wear leveling* — spreading writes evenly across all cells — is important for maximizing flash endurance.

wear leveling

  A flash drive's flash translation layer uses COW techniques to virtualize block addresses, allowing it to present a standard interface to read and write specific logical pages while internally redirecting writes to pages on already-cleared erasure blocks and while moving existing data to new physical pages so that their current erasure blocks can be cleared for future writes.

  Note that a flash drive's flash translation layer operates below the file system — standard update in place or COW file systems are still used over that layer — . But, flash translation layers are constructed using the same basic principles as the COW file systems discussed here.

- **Growing capacity enables versioning.** Large storage capacities make it attractive for file systems to provide interfaces by which users can access old versions of their files.

  Since updates in COW systems do not overwrite old data with new, supporting versioning is relatively straightforward, as we discuss below.

Implementation principles.   Figure 13.19 illustrates the core idea of COW file systems by comparing a traditional file system (FFS in this case) with a COW implementation that uses the same basic index structures.

In the traditional system (Figure 13.19 (a)), a file's indirect nodes and data blocks can be located anywhere on disk, and given a file's inumber, we can find its inode in a fixed location on disk.

In the COW version (Figure 13.19 (b)), we do not want to overwrite inodes in place, so we must make them mobile. A simple way to do that is to store them in a file rather than in a fixed array. Of course that is not quite the end of the story — we still need to be able to find the inode file's inode, called the *root inode*.

root inode

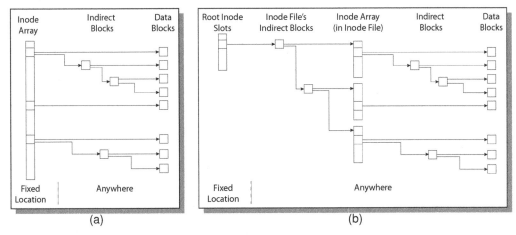

Figure 13.19: (a) A traditional, update-in-place file system (e.g., FFS) and (b) a simple copy-on-write (COW) file system.

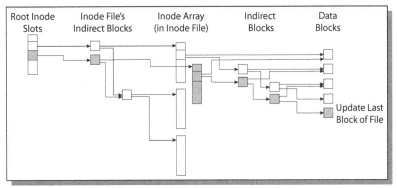

Figure 13.20: In a COW file system, writing a data block causes the system to allocate new blocks for and to write the data block and all nodes on the path from that data block to the root inode.

The simplest thing to do would be to store the root inode in a fixed location. If we did that, then we could find any file's inode by using the root inode to read from a computed offset in the inode file, and from that we could find its blocks.

However, it is useful to make even the root inode copy on write. For example, we do not want to risk losing the root inode if there is a crash while it is being written. A solution is to include a monotonically increasing version number and a checksum in the root inode and to keep a small array of slots for the current and recent root inodes, updating the oldest one when a write occurs. After a crash, we scan all of the slots to identify the newest root inode that has a correct checksum.

In this design, all the file system's contents are stored in a tree rooted

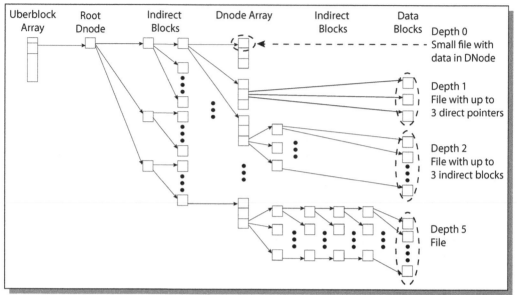

Figure 13.21: ZFS index structures. Note that this diagram is slightly simplified. In reality there are a few more levels of indirection between the uberblock and a file system's root dnode.

in the root inode, when we update a block, we write it — and all of the blocks on the path from it to the root — to new locations. For example, Figure 13.20 shows what happens when one block of a file is updated in our simple COW system.

ZFS index structures.   To better understand how copy on write file systems are implemented, we will look at the open source ZFS file system.

As Figure 13.21 illustrates, the root of a ZFS storage system is called the **uberblock**. ZFS keeps an array of 256 uberblocks in a fixed storage location and rotates successive versions among them. When restarting, ZFS scans the uberblock array and uses the one with a valid checksum that has the highest sequence number.

The current uberblock conceptually includes a pointer to the current root dnode, which holds the dnode array for a ZFS file system. (We say "conceptually" because we are simplifying things a bit here. Once you have read this description, see the sidebar if you want the gory details.)

The basic metadata object in ZFS is called a **dnode**, and it plays a role similar to an inode in FFS or an MFT entry in NTFS: a file is represented by variable-depth tree whose root is a dnode and whose leaves are its data blocks. A dnode has space for three block pointers, and it has a field that specifies the tree's depth: zero indicates that the dnode stores the file's data in it, one means that the pointers are direct pointers to data blocks, two means that the dnode's pointers point to indirect blocks, which point to

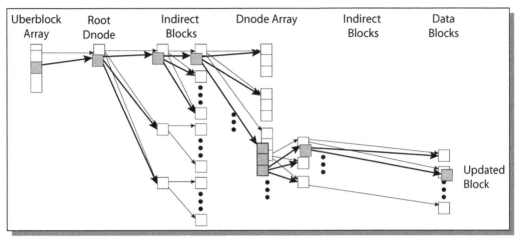

Figure 13.22: Updating a block of a ZFS file

data blocks; three means that the dnode's pointers point to double indirect blocks; and so on up to six levels of indirection.

Data block and indirect block sizes are variable from 512 bytes to 128KB and specified in a file's dnode. Note, however, that even a 128 KB indirect node holds fewer block pointers than you might expect because each block pointer is a 128 byte structure.

ZFS's block pointers are relatively large structures because they include fields to support advanced features like large storage devices, block compression, placing copies of the same block on different storage devices, file system snapshots, and block checksums. Fortunately, we can ignore these details and just treat each block pointer structure as a (rather large) pointer.

Figure 13.22 shows what happens when we update the last block in a 2-level ZFS file. We allocate a new data block and store the new data in it, but that means that we need to update the indirect block that points to it. So, we allocate a new indirect block and store the version with the updated pointer there, but that means we need to update the indirect pointer that points to it. And so on, up through the file's dnode, the indirect blocks that track the dnode array, the root dnode, and the uberblock.

ZFS space map.   ZFS's space maps track free space in a way designed to scale to extremely large storage systems.

One concern the ZFS designers had with bitmaps was that the size of a bitmap grows linearly with storage capacity and can become quite large for large-scale systems. For example, with 4 KB block size, a file server with 1 PB of disk space would have 32 GB of bitmaps.

Large bitmaps affect both a server's memory requirements and the time needed to read the bitmaps on startup. Although one might attempt to cache a subset of the bitmap in memory and only allocate from the

ZFS uberblock, meta-root dnode, and root dnodes

For simplicity, the body of the text describes the uberblock as pointing directly to the file system's root dnode.

In reality, there are a few additional levels of indirection to allow multiple file systems and snapshots to share a ZFS storage pool under a single uberblock. The uberblock has a pointer to a meta-root dnode (called the Meta Object Store dnode in ZFS terminology.) The meta-root dnode tracks the meta-root dnode array. The meta-root dnode array is used by what is essentially a little file system with hierarchical directories that provide mappings from the names of file systems to "files" that store the metadata for each file system, including a pointer to the block where the file system's root dnode is (currently) stored.

So, a more complete picture looks like this:

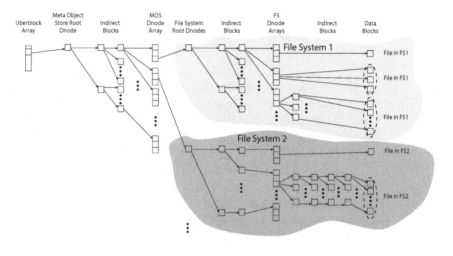

currently-cached subset, we cannot control when blocks are freed. For workloads in which frees have poor locality, caching will be ineffective.

ZFS's space maps use three key ideas to scale to large storage systems:

- **Per block group space maps.** ZFS maintains a space map for each block group, it restricts allocation of new blocks to a subset of block groups at any given time, and it keeps those block groups' space maps in memory.

- **Tree of extents.** Each block group's free space is represented as an AVL tree of extents. The tree allows ZFS to efficiently find a free extent of a desired size, and its search performance does not degrade as the block group becomes full.

- **Log-structured updates.** As noted above, caching a portion of a space map works for allocations but it may not help frees. Therefore, rather than directly updating the on-disk spacemap, ZFS simply appends spacemap updates to a log. When a block group is activated for allocation, ZFS reads in the most recently stored spacemap and then it reads all subsequently logged updates to bring the space map up to date. After applying updates to the in-memory spacemap, ZFS can store the new spacemap to limit the length of its update log.

ZFS locality heuristics. We started the discussion of COW file systems by saying that they are designed to optimize write performance, but the example in Figure 13.22 make it sound like ZFS does a lot of work just to update a block. ZFS does two important things to optimize write behavior:

- **Sequential writes.** Because almost everything in ZFS is mobile, almost all of these updates can be grouped into a single write to a free range of sequential blocks on disk. Only the uberblock needs to go elsewhere. Because sequential writes are much faster than random ones, ZFS and other COW file systems can have excellent write performance even though they write more metadata than update-in-place file systems.

- **Batched updates.** Figure 13.22 shows what happens when we update a single block of a single file, but ZFS does not typically write one update at a time. Instead, ZFS updates several seconds of updates and writes them to disk as a batch. So, updates to a file's dnode and indirect nodes may be amortized over many writes to the file, and updates to the uberblock, root dnode, and the dnode array's indirect blocks may be amortized over writes to many files.

When it is time to write a batch of writes, ZFS needs to decide where to write the new block versions. It proceeds in three steps:

- **Choose a device.** A ZFS storage pool may span multiple devices, so the first step is to choose which device to use. To maximise throughput by spreading load across devices, ZFS uses a variation of round robin with two tweaks. First, to even out space utilization, ZFS biases selection towards devices with large amounts of free space. Second, to maintain good locality for future reads, ZFS places about 512 KB on one device before moving on to the next one.

- **Choose a block group.** ZFS divides each device into several hundred groups of sequential blocks. ZFS's first choice for is to continue to use the block group it used most recently. However, if that group is so full or fragmented that its largest free region is smaller than 128 KB, ZFS selects a new block group.

New block group selection is biased towards groups that have more free space, that are nearer the outer edge of a disk (to improve bandwidth), and that have recently been used to store some data (to limit the range of tracks across which the disk head must seek.)

- **Choose a block within the group.** To maximize opportunities to group writes together, ZFS uses first fit allocation within a block group until the group is nearly full. At that point, it falls back on best fit to maximize space utilization.

Exercises

3. Suppose a variation of FFS includes in each inode 12 direct, 1 indirect, 1 double indirect, 2 triple indirect, and 1 quadruple indirect pointers. Assuming 6 KB blocks and 6-byte pointers

   (a) What is the largest file that can be accessed via direct pointers only?

   (b) To within 1%, what is the maximum file size this index structure can support?

4. On a Unix or Linux system, use the ls -l command to examine various directories. After the first ten characters that define each file's access permissions comes a field that indicates the number of hard links to the file. For example, here we have two files, bar with two links and foo with just one.

   ```
   drwxr-sr-x 2 dahlin prof 4096 2012-02-03 08:37 bar/
   -rw-r--r-- 1 dahlin prof    0 2012-02-03 08:36 foo
   ```

   For directories, what is the smallest number of links you can observe? Why?

   For directories, even though regular users cannot make hard links to directories, you may observe some directories with high link counts. Why?

5. In NTFS, a master file table entry maximises the number of extent pointers it can store by storing extent pointers as a sequence of variable-length records: the first four bits encode the size used to store pointer to the start of the extent and the next four bits encode the size used to store the extent length. To further reduce record size, the extent-start pointer is stored as an offset from the previous extent's pointer, so if we have a 10 block extent starting at block 0x20000 and then a 5 block extent starting at block 0x20050, then the first (absolute) starting address (0x200000) will be stored in three bytes while the

Partitioning, Formatting, and Superblocks

How does an operating system know where to find FFS's inode array, NTFS's MFT, or ZFS's uberblock? How does it know how large these structures are? How does it even know what type of file system is on a disk?

A disk device's space can be divided into multiple *partitions*, each of which appears a separate (smaller) virtual storage device that can be formatted as a separate file system. To partition a disk, an operating system writes a special record (e.g., a master boot record (MBR) or GUID partition table (GPT)) in the first blocks of the disk. This record includes the disk's unique ID, size, and the list of the disk's partitions. Each partition record stores the partition's type (e.g., general file system partition, swap partition, RAID partition, bootable partition), partition ID, partition name, and the partition's starting and ending blocks.

To improve reliability, operating systems store multiple copies of a disk's partition table — often in the first few and last few of a disk's blocks.

Once a disk has been partitioned, the operating system can *format* some or all of the partitions by initializing the partition's blocks according to the requirements of the type of file system being created.

Formatting a file system includes writing a *superblock* that identifies the file system's type and its key parameters such as its type, block size, and inode array or MBR location and size. Again, for reliability, a file system typically stores multiple copies of its superblock at several predefined locations.

Then, when an operating system boots, it can examine a disk to find its partitions, and it can examine each partition to identify and configure its file systems.

second (relative) starting address will be stored in one byte (0x20050 - 0x20000 = 0x50).

An apparent disadvantage of this approach is that seeking to a random offset in a file requires sequentially scanning all of the extent pointers. Given your understanding of NTFS and disk technology trends, explain why this apparent disadvantage may not be a problem in practice.

13.4 | Putting it all together: File and directory access

In Section 13.2 we saw that directories are implemented as files, containing file name to file number mappings, and in Section 13.3 we saw that files are implemented using an index structure — typically a tree of some sort — to track the file's blocks.

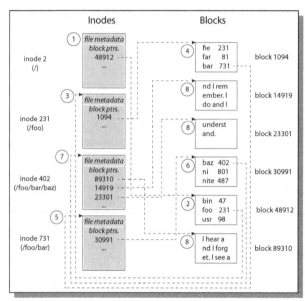

Figure 13.23: The circled numbers identify the steps required to read /foo/bar/baz in the FFS file system.

In this section, we walk through the steps FFS takes to read a file, given that file's name. The steps for the other file systems we have discussed are similar.

Suppose we want to read the file /foo/bar/baz.

First, we must read the root directory / to determine /foo's inumber. Since we already know the root directory's inumber (it is a preagreed number compiled into the kernel, e.g., 2), we open and read file 2's inode in step 1 in Figure 13.23. Recall that FFS stores pieces of the inode array at fixed locations on disk, so given a file's inumber it is easy to find and read the file's inode.

From the root directory's inode, we extract the direct and indirect block pointers to determine which block stores the contents of the root directory (e.g., block 48912 in this example.) We can then read that block of data to get the list of name to inumber mappings in the root directory and discover that directory file /foo has inumber 231 (step 2.)

Now that we know /foo's inumber, in step 3 we can read inode 231 to find where /foo's data blocks are stored — block 1094 in the example. We can then read those blocks of data to get the list of name to inumber mappings in the /foo directory and discover that directory file /foo/bar has inumber 731 (step 4.)

We follow similar steps to read /foo/bar's inode (step 5) and data block 30991 (step 6) to determine /foo/bar/baz inumber 402.

Finally, in step 7 we read /foo/bar/baz's inode (402) and in step 8 we read its data blocks (89310, 14919, and 23301): "I hear and I forget. I see and I remember. I do and I understand."

This may seem like a lot of steps just to read a file. Most of the time, we expect much of this information to be cached so that some steps can be avoided. For example, if the inodes and blocks for / and /foo are cached, then we would skip steps 1 to 4. Also, once file /foo/bar/baz has been opened, the open file data structure in the operating system will include the file's inumber so that individual reads and writes of the file can skip steps 1 to 6 (and step 7 while the inode is cached).

EXAMPLE   **Reading a file.** What would you get if you read the file /foo/fie in the FFS file system illustrated in Figure 13.23?

ANSWER   First we read the root inode (inode 2) and file (block 48912), then /foo's inode (inode 231) and file (block 1094), and then /foo/fie's inode (inode 402 again) and file (blocks 89310, 14919, and 23301 again) — /foo/bar/baz and /foo/fie are hard links to the same file.

Exercises

6. When user tries to write a file, the file system needs to detect if that file is a directory so that it can restrict writes to maintain the directory's internal consistency.

   Given a file's name, how would you design each file system listed below to keep track of whether each file is a regular file or a directory?

   (a) The FAT file system

   (b) FFS

   (c) NTFS

7. Why would it be difficult to add hard links to the FAT file system?

8. For the FFS file system illustrated in Figure 13.23, what reads and writes of inodes and blocks would occur to create a new file /foo/sparse and write blocks 1 and 2,000,000 of that file. Assume that inodes have pointers for 11 direct blocks, 1 indirect block, 1 double-indirect block, and 1 triple indirect block, and assume 4KB blocks with 4-byte block pointers.

13.5 | Conclusions and future directions

We are seeing significant shifts in the technologies and workloads that drive file system design.

On the technologies side, practical solid state storage technologies like flash memory change the constraints around which file systems can be designed. Random access performance that is good both in relative terms compared to sequential access performance and in absolute terms provide opportunities to reconsider many aspects of file system design — directories, file metadata structures, block placement — that have been shaped by the limitations of magnetic disks. Promising future solid state storage technologies like phase change memory or memristors may allow even more dramatic restructuring of file systems to take advantage of their even better performance and their support for fine-grained writes of a few bytes or words.

On the other hand, the limited lifetime and capacity of many solid state technologies may impose new constraints on file system designs. Perhaps we should consider hybrid file systems that, for example, store metadata and the content of small files in solid state storage and the contents of large files on magnetic disks.

Even the venerable spinning disk continues to evolve rapidly, with capacity increases continuing to significantly outpace performance improvements, making it more and more essential to organize file systems to maximize sequential transfers to and from disk.

Workloads are also evolving rapidly, which changes demands on file systems. In servers, the rising popularity of virtual machines and cloud computing pressure operating systems designers to provide better ways to share storage devices with fair and predictable performance despite variable and mixed workloads. At clients, the increasing popularity of apps and specialized compute appliances are providing new ways for organizing storage: rather than having users organize files into directories, apps and appliances often manage their own storage, providing users with a perhaps very different way of identifying stored objects. For example, rather than requiring users to create different directories for different, related sets of photos into different directories, many photo organizing applications provide an interface that groups related photos into events that may or may not reflect where in the file system the events are stored. Perhaps our reliance on directories for naming and locality will need to be rethought in the coming years.

Exercises

1. Why do we many file systems have separate system calls for removing a regular file (e.g., unlink) and removing a directory (.e.g, rmdir)?

2. In Figure 13.4, suppose we create a new file z.txt and then unlink Work, removing that entry. Draw a figure similar to Figure 13.4 that shows the new contents of the directory.

3. Suppose a variation of FFS includes in each inode 12 direct, 1 indirect, 1 double indirect, 2 triple indirect, and 1 quadruple indirect pointers. Assuming 6 KB blocks and 6-byte pointers

   (a) What is the largest file that can be accessed via direct pointers only?

   (b) To within 1%, what is the maximum file size this index structure can support?

4. On a Unix or Linux system, use the ls -l command to examine various directories. After the first ten characters that define each file's access permissions comes a field that indicates the number of hard links to the file. For example, here we have two files, bar with two links and foo with just one.

   drwxr-sr-x 2 dahlin prof 4096 2012-02-03 08:37 bar/
   -rw-r--r-- 1 dahlin prof   0 2012-02-03 08:36 foo

   For directories, what is the smallest number of links you can observe? Why?

   For directories, even though regular users cannot make hard links to directories, you may observe some directories with high link counts. Why?

5. In NTFS, a master file table entry maximises the number of extent pointers it can store by storing extent pointers as a sequence of variable-length records: the first four bits encode the size used to store pointer to the start of the extent and the next four bits encode the size used to store the extent length. To further reduce record size, the extent-start pointer is stored as an offset from the previous extent's pointer, so if we have a 10 block extent starting at block 0x20000 and then a 5 block extent starting at block 0x20050, then the first (absolute) starting address (0x200000) will be stored in three bytes while the second (relative) starting address will be stored in one byte (0x20050 - 0x20000 = 0x50).

   An apparent disadvantage of this approach is that seeking to a random offset in a file requires sequentially scanning all of the extent pointers. Given your understanding of NTFS and disk technology trends, explain why this apparent disadvantage may not be a problem in practice.

6. When user tries to write a file, the file system needs to detect if that file is a directory so that it can restrict writes to maintain the directory's internal consistency.

   Given a file's name, how would you design each file system listed below to keep track of whether each file is a regular file or a directory?

   (a) The FAT file system

   (b) FFS

   (c) NTFS

7. Why would it be difficult to add hard links to the FAT file system?

8. For the FFS file system illustrated in Figure 13.23, what reads and writes of inodes and blocks would occur to create a new file /foo/sparse and write blocks 1 and 2,000,000 of that file. Assume that inodes have pointers for 11 direct blocks, 1 indirect block, 1 double-indirect block, and 1 triple indirect block, and assume 4KB blocks with 4-byte block pointers.

A stitch in time saves nine

English Proverb

14 Reliable Storage

Highly reliable storage is vitally important across a wide range of applications from businesses that need to know that that their billing records are safe to families that have photo albums they would like to last for generations.

So far, we have treated disks and flash as ideal nonvolatile storage: data stored there will remain there forever, until it is overwritten. Physical devices cannot achieve such perfection — they may be defective, they may wear out, or they may be damaged so they may lose some or all of their data.

Unfortunately, the limits of physical devices are not merely abstract concerns. For example, some large organizations have observed annual disk failure rates of 2% to 4%, meaning that an organization with 10,000 disks might expect to see hundreds of failures per year and that important data stored on a single disk by a naive storage system might have more than a 30% chance of disappearing within a decade.

The central question of this chapter is: How can we make a storage system more reliable than the physical devices out of which they are built?

reliable

available

A system is *reliable* if it performs its intended function. Reliability is related to, but different than, availability. A system is *available* if it currently can respond to a request.

In the case of a storage system, the storage system is reliable as long as it continues to store a given piece of data and as long as its components are capable of reading or overwriting that data. We define a storage system's *reliability* as the probability that it will continue to be reliable for some specified period of time. A storage system is available at some moment of

system reliability

583

Figure 14.1: The Voyager "Golden Record," a highly reliable but highly unavailable storage device. Photo Credit: NASA.

system
availability time if a read or write operation could be completed at that time, and we define a storage system's *availability* as the probability that the system will be available at any given moment of time.

To see the difference between reliability and availability, consider the highly reliable but highly unavailable storage device shown in Figure 14.1. In the 1970's, the two Voyager spacecraft sent out of our solar system each included a golden record on which various greetings, diagrams, pictures, natural sounds, and music were encoded, as stated on each record by President Carter, as "a present from a small, distant world, a token of our sounds, our science, our images, our music, our thoughts and our feelings." To protect against erosion, the record is encased in an aluminium and uranium cover. This storage device is highly reliable — it is expected to last for many tens of thousands of years in interstellar space — but it is not highly available (at least, not to us.)

To take a more pedestrian example, suppose a storage system required each data block to be written to a disk on each of 100 different machines physically distributed across 100 different machine rooms spread across the world. Such a system might be highly reliable (since it would take a fairly spectacular catastrophe to wipe out all of the copies of any data that is stored), highly available for reads (since there are 100 different locations to read from), but not highly available for writes (since new writes can not complete if any one of 100 machines is unavailable.)

Two problems.   Broadly speaking, storage systems must deal with two threats to reliability.

- **Operation interruption.** A crash or power failure in the middle of a series of related updates may leave the stored data in an inconsistent state.

  For example, suppose that a user has asked an operating system to move a file from one directory to another:

  > mv drafts/really-important.doc final/really-important.doc

  As we discuss in Chapter 13, such a move may entail many low level operations such as writing the drafts directory file to remove really-important.doc, updating the last-modified time of the drafts directory, growing the final directory's file to include another block of storage to accommodate a new directory entry for really-important.doc, writing the new directory entry to the directory file, updating the file system's free space bitmap to note that the newly allocated block is now in use, and updating the size and last-modfied time of the final directory.

  Suppose that the system's power fails when the updates to the drafts directory are stored in nonvolatile storage but when the updates to the final directory are not; in that case, the file really-important.doc may be lost. Or, suppose that the operating system crashes after updating the drafts and final directories but before updating the file system's free space bitmap; in that case, the file system will still regard the new block in the final directory as free, and it may allocate that block to be part of some other file. The storage device then ends up with a block that belongs to two files, and updates intended for one file may corrupt the contents of the other file.

- **Loss of stored data.** Failures of nonvolatile storage media can cause previously stored data to disappear or be corrupted. Such failures can affect individual blocks, entire storage devices, or even groups of storage devices.

For example, a disk sector may be lost if it is scratched by a particle contaminating the drive enclosure, a flash memory cell might lose its contents when large numbers of reads of nearby cells disturb its charge, a disk drive can fail completely because bearing wear causes the platters to vibrate too much to be successfully read or written, or a set of drives might be lost when a fire in a data center destroys a rack of storage servers.

Two solutions.   Fortunately, system designers have developed two sets of powerful solutions to these problems, and the rest of the chapter discusses them.

- **Transactions for atomic updates.** When a system needs to make several related updates to nonvolatile storage, it may want to ensure that the state is modified atomically: even if a crash occurs the state reflects either all of the updates or none of them. Transactions are a fundamental technique to provide atomic updates of nonvolatile storage

  Transactions are simple to implement and to use, and they often have as good or better performance than ad-hoc approaches. The vast majority of widely-used file systems developed over the past two decades have used transactions internally, and many applications implement transactions of their own to keep their persistent state consistent.

- **Redundancy for media failures.** To cope with data loss and corruption, storage systems use several forms of redundancy such as checksums to detect corrupted storage and replicated storage to recover from lost or corrupted sectors or disks.

  Implementing sufficient redundancy at acceptably low cost can be complex. For example, a widely-used, simple model of RAID (redundant array of inexpensive disk) paints an optimistic picture of reliability that can be off by orders of magnitude. Modern storage systems often make use of multiple levels of checksums (e.g., both in storage device hardware and file system software), sufficient redundancy to survive two or more hardware failures (e.g., keeping 3 copies of a file or two parity disks with a RAID), and rely on software that to detect failures soon after they occur and to repair failures quickly (e.g., background processes that regularly attempt to read all stored data and algorithms that parallelize recovery when a device fails.) Systems that fail to properly use these techniques may be significantly less reliable than expected.

14.1 | Transactions: Atomic updates

When a system makes several updates to nonvolatile storage and a crash occurs, some of those updates may be stored and survive the crash and others may not. Because a crash may occur without warning, storage systems and applications need to be constructed so that no matter when the crash occurs, the system's nonvolatile storage is left in some sensible state.

This problem occurs in many contexts. For example, if a crash occurs while you are installing an update for a suite of applications, upon recovery you would like to be able to use either the old version or the new version, not be confronted with an mismmash of incompatible programs. For example, if you are moving a subdirectory from one location to another when a crash occurs, when you recover you want to see the data in one location or the other; if the subdirectory disappears because of an untimely crash, you will be (justifiably) upset with the operating system designer. Finally, if a bank is moving $100 from Alice's account to Bob's account when a crash occurs, it wants to be certain that upon recovery either the funds are in Alice's account and records show that the transfer is still to be done or that the funds are in Bob's account and the records show that the transfer has occurred.

This problem is quite similar to the critical section problem in concurrency. In both cases, we have several updates to make and we want to avoid having anyone observe the state in an intermediate, inconsistent state. Also, we have no control when other threads might try to access the state in the first case or when a crash might occur in the second — we must develop a structured solution that works for any possible execution. The solution is similar, too; we want to make the set of updates atomic. But, because we are dealing with nonvolatile storage rather than main memory, the techniques for achieving atomicity differ in significant ways.

Transactions extend the concept of atomic updates from memory to stable storage, allowing systems to atomically update multiple persistent data structures.

Ad hoc approaches

Until the mid 1990's many file systems used ad hoc approaches to solving the problem of consistently updating multiple on-disk data structures.

For example, the Unix fast file system (FFS) would carefully control the order that its updates were sent to disk so that if a crash occurred in the middle of a group of updates, a scan of the disk during recovery could identify and repair inconsistent data structures. When creating a new file, for example, FFS would first update the free-inode bitmap to indicate which previously free inode was now in use; after making sure this update was on disk, it would initialize the new file's inode, clearing all of the direct, indirect, double-indirect, and other pointers, setting the file length to 0, setting the file's ownership and access control list, and so on. Finally, once the inode update was safely on disk, the file system would update the directory to contain an entry for the newly created file, mapping the file's name to its inode.

If a system running FFS crashed, then when it rebooted it would use a program called fsck (file system check) to scan all of the file system's metadata (e.g., all inodes, all directories, and all free space bitmaps) to make sure that all metadata items were consistent. If, for example, fsck discovered an inode that was marked as *allocated* in the free-inode bitmap but that did not appear in any directory entry, it could infer that that inode was part of a file in the process of being created (or deleted) when the crash occurred; since the create had not finished or the delete had started, fsck could mark the inode as free, undoing the partially completed create (or completing the partially completed delete.)

Similar logic was used for other file system operations.

This approach of careful ordering of operations with scanning and repair of on-disk data structures was widespread until the 1990's, when it was largely abandoned. In particular, this approach has three significant problems:

1. **Complex reasoning.** Similar to trying to solve the multi-threaded synchronization problem with just atomic loads and stores, this approach requires reasoning carefully about all possible operations and all possible failure scenarios to make sure that it is always possible to recover the system to a consistent state.

2. **Slow updates.** To ensure that updates are stored in an order that allowed the system's state to be analyzed, file systems are forced to insert sync operations or barriers between dependent operations, reducing the amount of pipelining or parallelism in the stream of requests to storage devices.

   For example, in the file creation example above to ensure that the individual updates hit disk in the required order, the system might suffer three full rotations of the disk to update three on-disk data structures even though those data structures may be quite near each other.

3. **Extremely slow recovery.** When a machine reboots after a crash, it has to scan all of its disks for inconsistent metadata structures.

   In the 1970's and 1980s, it was possible to scan the data structures on most servers' disks in a few seconds or a few minutes. However, by the 1990's this scanning could take tens of minutes to a few hours for large servers with many disks, and technology trends indicated that scan times would rapidly grow worse.

fsck Lives

Although few file systems today rely on scanning disks when recovering from a crash, fsck and other similar programs are often still used as an "emergency fix" when on-disk data structures are corrupted for other reasons (e.g., due to software bug or storage device failure).

Although the first two were significant disadvantages of the approach, it was the third that finally made depending on careful ordering and fsck untenable for most file systems. New file systems created since the late 1980's almost invariably use other techniques — primarily various forms of transactions that we discuss in the rest of this section.

Application-level approaches. Although modern file systems often use transactions internally, some standard file system APIs such as the Posix API provide only weaker abstractions, forcing applications to take their own measures if they want to atomically apply a set of updates. Many use application-level transactions, but some continue to use more ad hoc approaches.

For example, suppose that a user has edited several parts of a text file and then wants to save the updated document. The edits may have inserted text at various points in the document, removed text at others, and shifted the remaining text forwards or backwards — even a small insertion or deletion early in the document could ripple through the rest of the file.

If the text editor application were simply to use the updated file in its memory to overwrite the existing file, an untimely crash could leave the file in an incomprehensible state — the operating system and disk schedulers may choose any order to send the updated blocks to nonvolatile storage, so after the crash the file may be an arbitrary mix of old and new blocks, sometimes repeating sections of text, sometimes omitting them entirely.

To avoid this problem, the text editor may take advantage of the semantics of the Posix rename operation, which renames the file called sourceName to be called targetName instead. Posix promises that if a file named targetName already exists, rename's shift from having targetName refer to the old file to having it refer to the new one will be atomic. (This atomicity guarantee may be provided by transactions within the file system or by ad hoc means.)

So, to update an existing file design.txt, the text editor first writes the updates to a new, temporary file such as \#design.txt\#. Then it renames the temporary file to atomically replace the previously stored file.

The transaction abstraction

Transactions provide a way to atomically update multiple pieces of persistent state.

For example, suppose you are updating a web site and you want to replace the current collection of documents in /server/live with a new collection of documents you have created in /development/ready. You don't want users to see intermediate steps when some of the documents have been updated and others have not — they might encounter broken links or encounter new descriptions referencing old pages or vice versa. Transactional file systems like Windows Vista's TxF (Transactional NTFS) provide an API that lets applications apply all of these updates atomically, allowing the programmer to write something like the following pseudo-code:

```
ResultCode publish (){
    transactionID = beginTransaction ();
    foreach file f in /development/ready that is not in /server/live{
        error = move f from /development/ready to /server/live;
        if (error){
            rollbackTransaction (transactionID);
            return ROLLED_BACK;
        }
    }

    foreach file f in /server/live that is not in /development/ready{
        error = delete f;
        if (error){
            rollbackTransaction (transactionID);
            return ROLLED_BACK;
        }
    }

    foreach file f in /development/ready that differs from /server/live{
        error = move f from /development/ready to /server/live;
        if (error){
            rollbackTransaction (transactionID);
            return ROLLED_BACK;
        }
    }
    commitTransaction (transactionID);
    return COMMITTED;
}
```

commit   Notice that a transaction can finish in one of two ways: it can *commit*,
roll back meaning all of its updates occur, or it can *roll back* meaning that none of its updates occur.

Here, if the transaction commits, we are guaranteed that all of the updates will be seen by all subsequent reads, but if it encounters and error and rolls back or crashes without committing or rolling back, no reads outside of the transaction will see any of the updates.

transaction   More precisely, a *transaction* is a way to perform a set of updates while
ACID   providing the following *ACID properties*:
properties

- **Atomicity.** Updates are "all or nothing." If the transaction *commits*, all updates in the transaction take effect. If the transaction *rolls back*, then none of the updates in the transaction have any effect.

  In the website update example above, doing the updates within a transaction guarantees that each of the update is only stored or readable if all of the updates are stored and readable.

- **Consistency.** The transaction moves the system from one legal state to another. A system's invariants on its state can be assumed to hold at the start of a transaction and must hold when the transaction commits.

  In the example above, by using a transaction we can maintain the invariant that every link from one document to another on the server references a valid file.

- **Isolation.** Each transaction appears to execute on its own, and is not affected by other in-progress transactions. Even if multiple transactions execute concurrently, for each pair of transactions T and T', it either appears that T executed entirely before T' or vice versa.

  By executing the web site update in a transaction, we guarantee that each transaction to read from the web site is applied either against the old set of web pages or the new set, not some mix of the two.

  Of course, if each individual read of an object is in its own transaction, then a series of reads to assemble a web page and its included elements could see the old web page and a mix of old and new elements. If web protocols were changed to allow a browser to fetch a page and its elements in a single transaction, then we could guarantee that the user would see either the old page and elements or the new ones.

- **Durability.** A committed transaction's changes to state must survive crashes. Once a transaction is committed, the only way to change the state it produces is with another transaction.

  In our web update example, the system must not return from the commitTransaction() call until all of the transactions updates have been safely stored in persistent storage.

Transactions v. critical sections   The ACID properties are closely related to the properties of critical sections. Critical sections provide a way to update state that is atomic, consistent, and isolated but not durable. Adding the durability requirement significantly changes how we implement atomic updates.

> ### Battling terminology
>
> In operating systems, we use the term *consistency* in two ways. In the context of critical sections and transactions, we use "consistency" to refer to the idea of a system's invariants being maintained (e.g., "are my data structures consistent?") In the context of distributed memory machines and distributed systems, we use "consistency" to refer to the memory model — the order in which updates can become visible to reads (e.g., "are my system's reads at different caches sequentially consistent?").
>
> Where there is potential confusion, we will use the terms *transaction consistency* or *memory model consistency*.

Implementing transactions

The challenge with implementing transaction is that we want a group of related writes to be atomic, but for persistent storage hardware like disks and flash, the atomic operation is a single-sector or single-page write. So, we must devise a way for a group of related writes to take effect when a single-sector write occurs.

If a system simply starts updating data structures in place, then it is vulnerable to a crash in the middle of a set of updates: the system has neither the complete set of old items (to roll back) nor a complete set of new items (to commit), so an untimely crash can force the system to violate atomicity.

intentions Instead, a transactional system can persistently store all of a transaction's *intentions*, the updates that will be made if the transaction commits, in some separate location of persistent storage. Only when all intentions are stored and the transaction commits should the system begin overwriting the target data structures; if the overwrites are interrupted in the middle, then on recovery the system can complete the transaction's updates using the persistently stored intentions.

Redo logging

redo logging A common and very general way to implement transactions is redo logging. *Redo logging* uses a persistent log for recording intentions and executes a transaction in four stages:

1. **Prepare.** Append all planned updates to the log.

   This step can happen all at once, when the transaction begins to commit, or it can happen over time, appending new updates to the log as the transaction executes. What is essential is that all updates are safely stored in the log before proceeding to the next step.

2. **Commit.** Append a commit record to the log, indicating that the transaction has committed.

   Of course a transaction may roll back rather than commit. In this case, a roll-back record may be placed in the log to indicate that the transaction was abandoned. Writing a roll-back record is optional, however, because a transaction will only be regarded as committed if a commit record appears in the log.

3. **Write-back.** Once the commit record is persistent in the log, all of a transactions updates may be written to their target locations, replacing old values with new ones.

4. **Garbage collect.** Once a transaction's write-back completes, its records in the log may be garbage collected.

atomic
commit

The moment in step 2 when the sector containing the commit record is successfully stored is the *atomic commit*: before that moment the transaction may safely be rolled back; after that moment, the transaction must take effect.

Recovery. If a system crashes in the middle of a transaction, it must execute a recovery routine before processing new requests. For redo logging, the recovery routine is simple: scan sequentially through the log, taking the following actions for each type of record:

1. **Update record for a transaction.** Add this record to a list of updates planned for the specified transaction.

2. **Commit record for a transaction.** Write-back all of the transaction's logged updates to their target locations.

3. **Roll-back record for a transaction.** Discard the list of updates planned for the specified transaction.

When the end of the log is reached, the recovery process discards any update records for transactions that do not have commit records in the log.

Example. Consider, for example, a transaction that transfers $100 from Tom's account to Mike's account. Initially, as Figure 14.2-(a) shows, data stored on disk and in the volatile memory cache indicates that Tom's account has $200 and Mike's account has $100.

Then, the cached values are updated and the updates are appended to the nonvolatile log (b). At this point, if the system were to crash, the updates in cache would be lost, the updates for the uncommitted transaction in the log would be discarded, and the system would return to its original state.

Once the updates are safely in the log, the commit record is appended to the log (c). This commit record should be written atomically based on

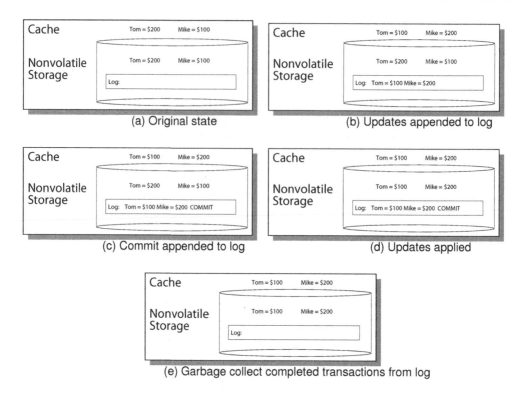

(a) Original state

(b) Updates appended to log

(c) Commit appended to log

(d) Updates applied

(e) Garbage collect completed transactions from log

Figure 14.2: Example transaction with redo logging.

the properties of the underlying hardware (e.g., by making sure it fits on a single disk sector and putting a strong checksum on it). This step is the atomic commit: prior to the successful storage of the commit record, a crash would cause the transaction to roll back; the instant the commit record is persistently stored, the transaction has committed and is guaranteed to be visible to all reads in the future. Even if a crash occurs, the recovery process will see the committed transaction in the log and apply the updates.

Now, the records in persistent storage for Tom and Mike's accounts can be updated (d).

Finally, once Tom and Mike's accounts are updated, the transaction's records in the log may be garbage collected (e).

Implementation details.   A few specific techniques and observations are important for providing good performance and reliability for transactions with redo logs.

- **Logging concurrent transactions.** Although the previous example shows a single transaction, multiple transactions may be executing at once. In these cases, each record in the log must identify the transaction to which it belongs.

- **Asynchronous write-back.** Step 3 of a transaction (*write-back*) can be asynchronous — once the updates and commit are in the log, the writeback can be delayed until it is convenient or efficient to perform it.

  This flexibility yields two advantages. First, the latency from when a transaction calls commit() to when the call returns is minimized: as soon as the commit is appended to the sequential log, the call can return. Second, the throughput for writeback can be improved because the disk scheduler gets to operate on large batches of updates.

  Two things limit the maximum write-back delay, but both are relatively loose constraints. First, larger write-back delays mean that crash recovery may take longer because there may be more updates to read and apply from the log. Second, the log takes space in persistent storage, which may in some cases be constrained.

- **Repeated write-backs are OK.** Some of the updates written back during recovery may already have been written back before the crash occurred. For example, in Figure 14.3 all of the records from the persistent log-head pointer to the volatile one have already been written back, and some of the records between the volatile log-head pointer may have been written back.

  idempotent It is OK to reapply an update from a redo log multiple times because these updates are (and must be) *idempotent* — they have the same effect whether executed once or multiple times. For example, if a log record says "write 42 to each byte of sector 74" then it doesn't matter whether that value is written once, twice, or a hundred times to sector 74.

  Conversely, redo log systems cannot permit non-idempotent records such as "add 42 to each byte in sector 74."

- **Restarting recovery is OK.** What happens if another crash occurs during recovery? When the system restarts, it simply begins recovery again. The same sequence of updates to committed transactions will be discovered in the log, and the same write-backs will be issued. Some of the write-backs may already have finished before the first crash or during some previous, but repeating them causes no problems.

- **Garbage collection constraints.** Once write-back completes and is persistently stored for a committed transaction, its space in the log can be reclaimed.

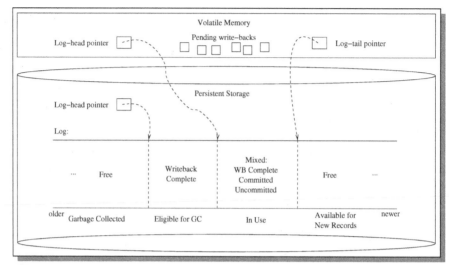

Figure 14.3: Volatile and persistent data structures for a transactional system based on a replay log.

For concreteness, Figure 14.3 illustrates a transaction log with an area of the log that is in use, an area that is no longer needed because it contains only records for transactions whose writebacks have completed, and an area that is free.

In this example system, the system's volatile memory maintains pointers to the head and tail of the log, new transaction records are appended to the tail of the log and cached in volatile memory, a write-back process asynchronously writes pending write-backs for committed transactions to their final locations in persistent storage, and a garbage collection process periodically advances a persistent log-head pointer so that recovery can skip at least some of the transactions whose writebacks are complete.

EXAMPLE   **New writes v. garbage collection.**

Suppose we have a circular log organized like the one in Figure 14.3. We must ensure that new records do not overwrite records that we may read during recovery, so we must ensure that the log-tail does not catch the log-head. But there are two log-heads, one in volatile memory and another in persistent storage. Which log-head represents the barrier that the log-tail must not cross?

ANSWER   The log-tail must not catch the persistent log-head pointer. Even though the records between the persistent and volatile log-heads have already been written back, during crash recovery, the recovery process will begin reading the log from the location indicated by the persistent log-head pointer. As long as the records are intact, recovering from the persistent log-head pointer rather than the volatile one may waste some work, but it will not affect correctness.

- **Ordering is essential.** It is vital to make sure that all of a transaction's updates are on disk in the log before the commit is, that the commit is on disk before any of the write-backs are, and that all of the write-backs are on disk before a transaction's log records are garbage collected.

  In Linux, an application can call sync() or fsync() to tell the operating system to force buffered writes to disk. These calls return only once the updated blocks are safely stored. Within the operating system, a request can be tagged with a BIO_RW_BARRIER tag, which tells the device driver and storage hardware to ensure that all preceding writes and no subsequent ones are stored before the tagged request is.

Isolation and concurrency revisited.   Redo logging provides a mechanism for atomically making multiple updates durable, but if there are concurrent transactions operating on shared state, we must also ensure isolation — each transaction must appear to execute alone, without interference from other transactions.

two-phase
locking

A common way to enforce isolation among transactions is *two-phase locking*, which divides a transaction into two phases. During the *expanding* phase, locks may be acquired but not released. Then, in the *contracting* phase, locks may be released but not acquired. In the case of transactions, because we want isolation and durability, the second phase must wait unti after the transaction commits or rolls back so that no other transaction sees updates that later disappear.

serializability

As we discussed in Chapter 6, two phase locking ensures a strong form of isolation called serializability. *Serializablity* across transactions ensures that the result of any execution of the program is equivalent to an execution in which transactions are processed one at a time in some sequential order. So, even if multiple transactions are executed concurrently, they can only produce results that they could have produced had they been executed one at a time in some order.

Although acquiring multiple locks in arbitrary orders normally risks deadlock, transactions provide a simple solution. If a set of transactions deadlocks, one or more of the transactions can be forced to roll back, release their locks, and restart at some later time.

Performance of redo logging.   It might sound like redo logging will impose a significant performance penalty compared to simply updating data in

Undo logging

Although transactions are often implemented with redo logging in which updates and the commit are written to the log and then the updates are copied to their final locations, transactions can also be implemented with *undo logging*.

To update an object, a transaction first writes the *old* version of the object to the log. It then writes the new version to its final storage location. When the transaction completes, it simply appends *commit* to the log. Conversely, if the transaction rolls back, the updates are undone by writing the old object versions to their storage locations.

The recovery process takes no action for committed transactions it finds in the log, but it undoes uncommitted transactions by rewriting the original object versions stored in the log.

Undo logging allows writes to objects to be sent to their final storage locations when they are generated and requires them to be persistently stored before a transaction is committed. This pattern is similar to update-in-place approaches, so in some cases it may be easier to add undo logging than redo logging to legacy systems. On the other hand, for storage systems like disks whose sequential bandwidth dominates their random I/O performance, undo logging may require more random I/Os before a transaction is committed (hurting latency) and by writing each transaction's updates immediately, it gives up chances to improve disk-head scheduling by writing large numbers of transactions' updates as a batch.

Undo/redo logging stores both the old and new versions of an object in the log. This combination allows updated objects to be written to their final storage locations whenever convenient, whether before or after the transaction is committed. If the transaction rolls back, any modified objects can be restored to the proper state, and if the system crashes, any committed transactions can have their updates redone and any uncommitted transactions can have their updates undone.

---

place: redo logging writes each update twice — first to the log and then to its final storage location.

Things are not as bad as they initially seem. Redo logging can have excellent performance — often better than update in place — especially for small writes. Four factors allow efficient implementations of redo logging:

- **Log updates are sequential.** Because log updates are sequential, appending to the log is fast. With spinning disks, large numbers of updates can be written as a sequential stream without seeks or rotational delay once the write begins. Many high-performance systems dedicate a separate disk for logging so that log appends never require a seek. For flash storage, sequential updates are often significantly faster than random updates, though the advantage is not as pronounced.

- **Writeback is asynchronous.** Because writeback can be delayed until

Multiversion Concurrency Control

An alternative to enforcing transaction isolation with locks is to enforce it with multiversion concurrency control. In *multiversion concurrency control* each write of an object x creates new version of x, the system keeps multiple versions of x and directs each read to a specific version of x. By keeping multiple versions of objects, the system can allow transaction A to read a version of x that has been overwritten by transaction B even if B needs to be serialized after A.

There are various multiversion concurrency control algorithms that ensure serializability. A simple one is multiversion timestamp ordering (MVTO), which processes concurrent transactions, enforces serializability, never blocks a transaction's reads or writes, but which may cause a transaction to roll back if it detects that a read of a later transaction (based on the serializable schedule MVTO is enforcing) was executed before — and therefore did not observe — the write of an earlier transaction (in serialization order.)

MVTO assigns each transaction T a logical timestamp. Then, when T writes an object x, MVTO creates a new version of x labeled with T's timestamp t_T, and when T reads an object y, MVTO returns the version of y, y_v with the highest timestamp that is at most T's timestamp; MVTO also makes note that y_v was read by transaction t_T. Finally, when T attempts to commit, MVTO blocks the commit until all transactions with smaller timestamps have committed or aborted.

MVTO rolls back transaction rather than allowing it to commit in three situations. First, If MVTO aborts any transaction, it removes the object versions written by that transaction and rolls back any transactions that read those versions. Notice that a transaction that reads a version must have a higher timestamp than the one that wrote it, so no committed transactions need to be rolled back.

Second, if a transaction T writes an object that has already been read by a later transaction T' that observed the version immediately prior to T's write, T MVTO rolls back T. It does this because if T were to commit, T''s read must return T's write, but that did not occur.

Third, if MVTO garbage collects old versions and transaction T reads an object for which the last write by an earlier transaction has been garbage collected, then MVTO rolls back T.

some time after a transaction has been committed, transactions using redo logs can have good response time (because the transaction commit only requires appending a commit record to the log) and can have good throughput (because batched writebacks can be scheduled more efficiently than individual or small groups of writes that must occur immediately.)

- **Fewer barriers or synchronous writes are required.** Some systems avoid using transactions by carefully ordering updates to data structures so that they can ensure that if a crash occurs, a recovery process will be able to scan, identify, and repair inconsistent data structures.

<hr/>

Relaxing Isolation

In this book we focus on the strong and relatively simple isolation requirement of serializability: no matter how much concurrency there is, the system must ensure that the results of any execution of the program is equivalent to an execution in which transactions are processed one at a time in some sequence. However, strong isolation requirements sometimes force transactions to block (e.g., when waiting to acquire locks) or roll back (e.g., when fixing a deadlock or encountering a "late write" under multiversion concurrency control).

Relaxing the isolation requirement can allow effectively higher levels of concurrency by reducing the number of cases in which transactions must block or roll back. The cost, of course, is potentially increased complexity in reasoning about concurrent programs, but several relaxed isolation semantics have proven to be sufficiently strong to be widely used.

For example, *snapshot isolation* requires each transaction's reads appear to come from a snapshot of the system's committed data taken when the transaction starts. Each transaction is buffered until the transaction commits, at which point the system checks all of the transaction's updates for *write-write conflicts*. A write-write conflict occurs if transaction T reads an object o from a snapshot at time t_{start} and tries to commit at time t_{commit} but some other transaction T' commits an update to o between T's read at t_{start} and T's attempted commit at t_{commit}. If a write-write conflict is detected for any object being committed by T, T is rolled back.

Snapshot isolation is weaker than serializability because each transaction's reads logically happen at one time and its writes logically happen at another time. This split allows, for example, *write skew anomalies* where one transaction reads object x and updates object y and a concurrent transaction reads object y and updates object x. If there is some constraint between x and y, it may now be violated. For example, if x and y represent the number of hours two managers have assigned you to work on each of two tasks with a constraint that $x + y \leq 40$. Manager 1 could read $x = 15$ and $y = 15$, attempt to assign 10 more hours of work on task x, and verify that $x + y = 25 + 15 \leq 40$. In the mean time manager 2 could read $x = 15$ and $y = 15$, attempt to assign 10 more hours of work on task y, verify that that $x + y = 15 + 25 \leq 40$, and successfully commit the update, setting $y = 25$. Finally, manager 1 could successfully commit its update, setting $x = 25$ and ruining your weekend.

<hr/>

However, these techniques often require large number of barrier or synchronous write operations, which reduce opportunities to pipeline or efficiently schedule updates.

In contrast, transactions need a relatively small number of barriers: one after the updates are logged and before the commit is logged, another after the commit is logged but before the transaction is reported as successful (and before writebacks begin), and one after a transaction's writebacks complete but before the transaction's log entries are garbage collected.

group
commit

- **Group commit.** *Group commit* is often used to further improve transactions' performance. Group commit techniques combine a set of transactions' commits into one log write to amortize the cost of initiating the write (e.g., seek and rotational delays). Group commit techniques can also be used to reduce the number of barrier or sync operations needed to perform a group of transactions.

EXAMPLE

Performance of small-write transactions.

Suppose you have a 1TB disk that rotates once every 10 ms, that has a maximum sustained platter transfer rate of 50 MB/s for inner tracks and 100 MB/s for outer tracks, and that has a 5 ms average seek time, a 0.5 ms minimum seek time, and a 10 ms maximum seek time,.

Consider updating 100 randomly selected 512-byte sectors in place with the total time to first commit the updates to a log; assume that the updates must be ordered for safety (e.g., update i must be on disk before update $i + 1$ is.)

Compare the total time to complete these updates with a simple update in place approach with the cost when using transactions implemented with a redo log.

ANSWER

Using a simple update in place approach, we need to use FIFO scheduling to ensure updates hit the disk in order, so the time for each update is approximately *average seek time + 0.5 rotation time + transfer time = 5 ms + 5 ms + transfer time.* Transfer time will be at most $\frac{512}{50*10^6}$ seconds, which will be negligible compared to the other terms. So, we have *10 ms per request* or *1 s for 100 requests* for update in place.

For transactions, we first append the 100 writes to the log. We will conservatively assume that each update consumes 2 sectors (one for the data and the other for metadata indicating the transaction number, the target sector on disk, etc.) So, assuming that the disk head is at a random location when the request arrives, our time to log the requests is *average seek time + 0.5 rotation time + transfer time = 5 ms + 5 ms + $\frac{200*512}{100*10^6}$ = 10.24 ms.*

Next, we need to append the commit record to the transaction. If the disk hardware supports a barrier instruction to enforce ordering of multiple in-progress requests, the operating system can issue this request along with the 100 writes. Here, we'll be conservative and assume that the system does not issue the commit's write until after the 100 writes in the body of the transaction are in the log. So, we will likely have to wait one full revolution of the disk to finish the commit: *10 ms.*

Finally, we need to write the 100 writes to their target locations on disk. Unlike the case for update in place, ordering does not matter here, so we can schedule them and write them more efficiently. Estimating this time takes engineering judgement, and different people are likely to make different estimates. For this example, we will assume that the disk uses a variant of shortest service time first (SSTF) scheduling in which the scheduler looks at the four requests on the next nearest tracks and picks the one with the shortest predicted seek time + rotational latency from the disk head's current position. Because the scheduler gets to choose from four requests, we will estimate that the average rotational latency will be one forth of a rotation, 2.5 ms; this may be conservative since it ignores the fact that request i will always remove from the four requests being considered the one that would have been rotationally farthest away if it were an option for request $i + 1$. Because we initially have 100 requests and because we are considering the four requests on the nearest tracks, the farthest seek should be around 4% of the way across the disk, and the average one to a member of the group being considered should be around 2%. We will estimate that seeking 2-4% of the way across disk costs twice the minimum seek time: 1 ms.

Putting these estimates for writeback time together, the writebacks of the 100 sectors should take about *estimated scheduled seek time + estimated scheduled rotational latency =1.0 ms + 2.5 ms = 3.5 ms* per request or *350 ms* total.

Adding the logging, commit, and writeback times, we have *10.24 ms + 10 ms + 350 ms = 370.24 ms*. The transactional approach is almost three times faster even though it writes the data twice and even though it provides the stronger atomic-update semantics.

For the same two approaches, compare the response time latency from when a call issuing these requests is issued until that call can safely return because all of the updates are durable.

ANSWER   The time for update in place is the same as above: *1 s*. The time for the transactional approach is the time for the first two steps: logging the updates and then logging the commit: *10.24 ms + 10 ms = 20.24 ms*.

Although small writes using redo logging may actually see performance benefits compared to update in place approaches, large writes may see significant penalties.

EXAMPLE   **Performance of large-write transactions.**

Considering the same disk and approaches as in the example above, compare the total time to for 100 writes, but now assume that each of the 100 writes updates a randomly selected 1 MB range of sequential sectors.

ANSWER   For the update in place approach, the time for each update is approximately *average seek time + 0.5 rotation time + transfer time = 5 ms + 5 ms + transfer time*. We will assume that the bandwidth for an average transfer is 75 MB/s — between the 50 MB/s and 100 MB/s inner and out tracks' transfer rates. So, we estimate the average transfer time to be 100 MB/75 MB/s = 1.333 s, giving a total time of *.005 s + .005 s + 1.333 s = 1.343 s* per request and *134.3 s* for 100 requests.

For the transactional approach, our time will be *time to log updates + time to commit + time to write back*.

For logging the updates, we'll assume a reasonably efficient encoding of metadata that makes the size of the metadata for a 100 MB sequential update negligible compared to the data. So, logging the data will take *seek time + rotational latency + transfer time = 5 ms + 5 ms + 100 * 100 MB/100 MB/s = .005 s + .005 s + 100 s ≈ 100 s*.

Writing the commit adds another 10 ms as in the above example.

Finally, as above, doing the write-backs *estimated scheduled seek time + estimated scheduled latency + transfer time = 1.0 ms + 2.5 ms + 100 MB/75 MB/s*, giving a total of *1.337 s* per request and *133.7 s* for 100 requests.

Adding the data logging, commit, and writeback times together, the transactional approach takes about 233 seconds while the update in place approach takes about 134 seconds. In this case transactions do impose a significant cost, nearly doubling the total time to process these updates.

Now compare the latency from when the call making the 100 writes is issued until it may safely return.

ANSWER   Under the update in place approach, we can only return when everything is written, while under the transactional approach, we can return once the commit is complete. So, we have comparable times: 134 s for update in place and 100 s for transactions.

One way to reduce transaction overheads for large writes is to add a level of indirection: write the large data objects to a free area of the disk, but not in the circular log. Then, the update in the log just needs to be a reference to that data rather than the data itself. Finally, after the transaction commits, perform the writeback by updating a pointer in the original data structure to point to the new data.

Transactions and file systems

File systems must maintain internal consistency when updating multiple data structures. For example, when a file system like FFS creates a new file, it may need to update the file's inode, the free inode bitmap, the parent directory, the parent directory's inode, and the free space bitmap. If a crash occurs in the middle of such a group of updates, the file system could be left in an inconsistent state with, say, the new file's inode allocated and initialized but without an entry in the parent directory.

As discussed in Section 14.1, some early file systems used ad-hoc solutions such as carefully ordering sequences of writes and scanning the disk to detect and repair inconsistencies when restarting after a crash. However, these approaches suffered from complexity, slow updates, and — as disk capacity grew — unacceptably slow crash recovery.

To address these problems, most modern file systems use transactions.

Traditional file systems.   Transactions are added to traditional, update-in-place file systems like FFS and NTFS using either *journaling* or *logging*
.

- **Journaling.** Journaling file systems apply updates to the system's metadata via transactions, but they update the contents of users' files in place.

By protecting metadata updates these systems ensure consistency of their persistent data structures (e.g., updates to inodes, bitmaps, directories, and indirect blocks.) Journaling file systems first write metadata updates to a redo log, then commit them, and finally write them back to their final storage locations.

Updates to the contents of regular (non-directory) files are not logged, they are applied in place. In place updates avoid writing file updates twice, which can be expensive for large updates. On the other hand, updating file contents in place means that journaling file systems provide few guarantees when a program updates a file: if a crash occurs in the middle of the update, the file may end up in an inconsistent state with some blocks but not others updated. If a program using a journaling file system requires atomic multi-block updates, it needs to provide them itself.

- **Logging.** Logging file systems simply include all updates to disk — both metadata and data — in transactions.

Today, journaling file systems are common: Microsoft's NTFS, Apple's HFS+, and Linux's XFS, JFS, and ReiserFS all use journaling; and Linux's ext3 and ext4 use journaling in their default configurations.

Logging file systems are also widely available, at least for Linux. In particular, Linux's ext3 and ext4 file systems can be configured to use either journaling or logging.

Copy on write file systems.   Copy on write file systems like the open source ZFS are designed from the ground up to be transactional. They do not overwrite data in place, and updating the root inode or ZFS uberblock is designed to be an atomic action that commits a set of updates.

For example, suppose we update just a file's data block or just its its indirect blocks, its inode, and the indirect blocks for the inode file, leaving the state as shown in Figure 14.4 (a) or (b). If the system were to crash in such an intermediate state, before the root inode is updated, none of these changes would be included in the file system's tree, and they would have no effect. Only when the root inode is updated as in Figure 14.4 (c) do all of these changes take effect at once.

The implementations of ZFS and other copy on write file systems often add two performance optimizations.

- **Batch updates.** Rather than applying each update individually, ZFS buffers several seconds worth of updates before writing them to stable storage as a single atomic group.

Batching yields two advantages.

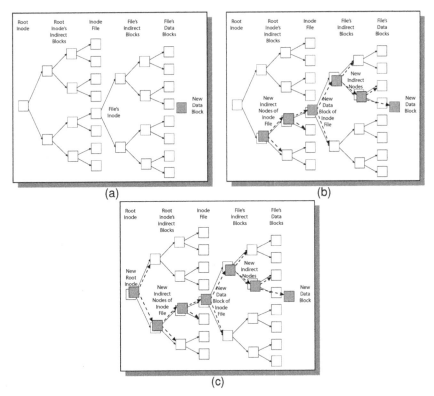

Figure 14.4: In a copy on write file system, intermediate states of an update such as (a) and (b) are not observable; they atomically take effect when the root inode is updated (c).

First, it allows the system to transform large numbers of small, random writes into a few large, sequential writes, which improves performance for most storage devices including individual magnetic disks, RAIDs (Redundant Arrays of Inexpensive Disks), and even some flash storage devices.

Second, not only does batching make writing each block more efficient, it actually reduces how many blocks must be written by coalescing multiple updates of the same indirect blocks and inodes. For example, Figure 14.5 illustrates how updates of inodes and indirect blocks are amortized across updates of multiple data blocks.

- **Intent log.** ZFS typically accumulates several seconds of writes before performing a large batch update, but some applications need immediate assurance that their updates are safely stored on nonvolatile media. For example, when a word processor's user saves a file, the program might call fsync() to tell the file system to make sure the updates are stored on disk. Forcing the user to wait several seconds

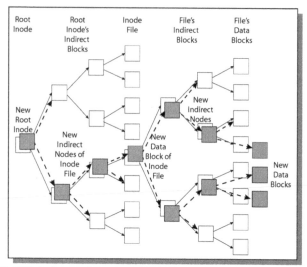

Figure 14.5: With batch updates in a COW file system, updates of inodes and indirect blocks are amortized across updates of multiple data blocks.

to save a file is not acceptable.

ZFS's solution is the ZFS Intent Log (ZIL), which is essentially a redo log. It is implemented as a linked list of ZFS blocks that contain updates that have been forced to disk but whose batch update may not yet have been stored, and it is replayed when the file system is mounted.

ZFS includes several optimizations in the ZIL implementation. First, by default writes are buffered and committed in their batch update without being written to the ZIL; only writes that are explicitly forced to disk are written to the ZIL. Second, the ZIL may reside on a separate, dedicated logging device; this allows us to use a fast device (e.g., flash) for the ZIL and slower, high-capacity devices (e.g., disks) for the main pool; if no separate ZIL device is provided, ZFS uses the main block pool for the ZIL. Finally, the contents of small data writes are included in the ZIL's blocks directly, but the contents of larger writes are written to separate blocks that are referenced by the ZIL; then, the subsequent batch commit can avoid rewriting those large blocks by updating metadata to point to the copies already on disk.

Exercises

1. Suppose that a text editor application uses the rename technique discussed on page 589 for safely saving updates by saving the updated file to a new filed (e.g., #doc.txt# and then calling rename("#doc.txt#",

"doc.txt") to change the name of the updated file from #doc.txt# to doc.txt. Posix rename promises that the update to doc.txt will be atomic — even if a crash occurs,doc.txt will refer to either the old file or the new one. However, Posix does not guarantee that the entire rename operation will be atomic. In particular, Posix allows implementations in which there is a window in which a crash could result in a state where both doc.txt and #doc.txt# refer to the same, new document.

a. How should a text-editing application react if, on startup, it sees both doc.txt and doc.txt and (i) both refer the same file or (ii) each refers to a file with different contents?

b. Why might Posix permit this corner case (where we may end up with two names that refer to the same file) to exist?

c. Explain how an FFS-based file system without transactions could use the "ad hoc" approach discussed in Section 14.1 to ensure that (i) doc.txt always refers to either the old or new file, (ii) the new file is never lost – it is always available as at least one of doc.txt or #doc.txt#, and (iii) there is some window where the new file may be accessed as both doc.txt and #doc.txt#.

d. Section 14.1 discusses three reasons that few modern file systems use the "ad-hoc" approach. However, many text editors still do something like this. Why have the three issues had less effect on applications like text editors than on file systems?

2. Above, we defined two-phase locking for basic mutual exclusion locks. Extend the definition of two-phase locking for systems that use readers-writers locks.

3. Suppose that x and y represent the number of hours two managers have assigned you to work on each of two tasks with a constraint that $x + y \leq 40$. On page 600, we showed that snapshot isolation could allow one transaction to update x and another concurrent transaction to update y in a way that would violate the constraint $x + y \leq 40$. Is such an anomaly possible under serializability? Why or why not?

4. Suppose you have transactional storage system tStore that allows you to read and write fixed-sized 2048-byte blocks of data within transactions, and you run the following code.

```
...
byte b1[2048];   byte b2[2048];
byte b3[2048];   byte b4[2048];

TransID t1 = tStore.beginTransaction();
TransID t2 = tStore.beginTransaction();
TransID t3 = tStore.beginTransaction();
TransID t4 = tStore.beginTransaction();

// Interface is
//      writeBlock(TransID tid, int blockNum, byte buffer[]);
tStore.writeBlock(t1,  1, ALL_ONES);
tStore.writeBlock(t1,  2, ALL_TWOS);
tStore.writeBlock(t2,  3, ALL_THREES);
tStore.writeBlock(t1,  3, ALL_FOURS);
tStore.writeBlock(t1,  2, ALL_FIVES);
tStore.writeBlock(t3,  2, ALL_SIXES);
tStore.writeBlock(t4,  4, ALL_SEVENS);
tStore.readBlock(t2,  1,  b1);
tStore.commit(t3);
tStore.readBlock(t2,  3,  b2);
tStore.commit(t2);
tStore.readBlock(t1,  3,  b3);
tStore.readBlock(t4,  3,  b4);
tStore.commit(t1);

// At this point, the system crashes
```

The system crashes at the point indicated above.

Assume that ALL_ONES, ALL_TWOS, etc. are each arrays of 2048 bytes with the indicated value. Assume that when the program is started, all blocks in the tStore have the value ALL_ZEROS.

Just before the system crashes, what is the value of b1 and what is the value of b2?

a) In the program above, just before the system crashes, what is the value of b3 and what is the value of b4?

b) Suppose that after the program above runs and crashes at the indicated point. After the system restarts and completes recovery and all write-backs, what are the values stored in each of blocks 1, 2, 3, 4, and 5 of the tStore?

14.2 Error detection and correction

Because data storage hardware is imperfect, storage systems must be designed to detect and correct errors. Storage systems take a layered approach:

- Storage hardware detects many failures with checksums and device-level checks, and it corrects small corruptions with error correcting codes

- Storage systems include redundancy using RAID architectures to reconstruct data lost by individual devices

- Many recent file systems include additional end-to-end correctness checks

These techniques are essential. Essentially all persistent storage devices include internal redundancy to achieve high storage densities with acceptable error rates, but the limits of this internal redundancy are significant enough that it is difficult to imagine designing a storage system for important data without additional redundancy for error correction, and it is hard to think of a significant file system developed in the last decade that does not include higher-level checksums.

Though essential and widespread, there are significant pitfalls in designing and using these techniques. In our discussions, we will point out issues that, if not handled carefully, can drastically reduce reliability.

The rest of this section examines error detection and correction for persistent storage, starting with the individual storage devices, then examining how RAID replication helps tolerate failures by individual storage devices, and finally looking at the end-to-end error detection in many recent file systems.

Storage device failures and mitigation

Storage hardware pushes the limits of physics, material sciences, and manufacturing processes to maximize storage capacity and performance. These aggressive designs leave little margin for error, so manufacturing defects, contamination, or wear can cause stored bits to be lost.

Individual spinning disks and flash storage devices exhibit two types of failure. First, isolated disk sectors or flash pages can lose existing data or degrade to the point where they cannot store new data. Second, an entire device can fail, preventing access to all of its sectors or pages. We discuss each of these in turn to understand the problems higher level techniques need to deal with.

Sector and page failures

sector failure

page failure

Disk *sector failures* occur when data on one or more individual sectors of a disk are lost, but the rest of the disk continues to operate correctly. Flash *page failures* are the equivalent for flash pages.

Storage devices use two techniques to mitigate sector or page failures: error correcting codes and remapping.

> ### What causes sector or page failures?
>
> For spinning disks, permanent sector failures can be caused by a range of faults such as pits in the magnetic coating where a contaminant flaked off the surface, scratches in the coating where a contaminant was dragged across the surface by the head, or smears of machine oil across some sectors of a disk surface.
>
> *Transient sector faults*, where a sector's stored data is corrupted but where new data can be successfully written to and read from the sector, can be caused by factors such as write interference where writes to one track disturb bits stored on nearby tracks and "high fly writes" where the disk head gets too far from the surface, producing magnetic fields too weak to be accurately read.
>
> For flash storage, permanent page failures can be caused by manufacturing defects or by wear-out when a page experience a large number of write/erase cycles.
>
> Transient flash storage failures can be caused by write disturb errors where charging one bit also causes a nearby bit to be charged, read disturb errors where repeatedly reading one page changes values stored on a nearby page, over-programming errors where too high a voltage is used to write a cell, which may cause incorrect reads or writes, and data retention error where charge may leak out of or into a flash cell over time, changing its value; wear-out from repeated write/erase cycles can make devices more susceptible to data retention errors.

error correcting codes

Mitigation: Error correcting codes. *Error correcting codes* deal with failures when some of the bits in a sector or page are corrupted. When the device stores data, it encodes the data with additional redundancy. Then, if a small number of bits are corrupted in a sector or page being read, the hardware automatically corrects the error, and the read successfully completes. If the damage is more extensive, then with high likelihood the read fails and returns an error code; being told that the device has lost data is not a perfect solution, but it is better than having the device silently return the wrong data.

Manufacturers balance storage space overheads against error correction capabilities to achieve acceptable advertised sector or page failure rate, typically expressed as the expected number of bits that can be read before encountering an unreadable sector or page. In 2011, advertised disk and flash *nonrecoverable read error* rates typically range between one sector or page per 10^{14} to 10^{16} bits read. The nonrecoverable read error rate is sometimes called the *bit error rate*.

nonrecoverable read error

bit error rate

Mitigation: Remapping   Disks and flash are manufactured with some number of spare sectors or pages so that they can continue to function despite some number of permanent sector or page failures by remapping failed sectors or pages to good ones. Before shipping hardware to users, manufacturers scan devices to remap bad sectors or pages caused by manufacturing defects. Later, if additional permanent failures are detected, the operating system or device firmware can remap the failed sectors or pages to good ones.

Pitfalls. Although devices' nonrecoverable read rate specifications are helpful, designers must avoid a number of common pitfalls:

- **Assuming that nonrecoverable read error rates are negligible.** Storage devices' advertised error rates sound impressive, but with the large capacities of today's storage, these error rates are non-negligible. For example, if you completely read a 2 TB disk with a bit error rate of 1 sector per 10^{14} bits, there may be more than a 10% chance of encountering at least one error.

- **Assuming nonrecoverable read error rates are constant.** Although a device may specify a single number as its unrecoverable read error rate, many factors can affect the rate at which such errors manifest. A given device's actual bit error rate may depend on its load (e.g., some faults may be caused by device activity), its age (e.g., some faults may become more likely as a device ages), or even its specific workload (e.g., faults in some sectors or pages may be caused by reads or writes to nearby sectors or pages.)

- **Assuming independent failures.** Errors may be correlated in time or space: finding an error in one sector may make it more likely that you will find one in a nearby sector or that you will to find a fault in another sector soon.

- **Assuming uniform error rates.** The relative contributions of different causes of nonrecoverable read errors can vary across models and different generations or production runs of the same model. For example, one model of disk drive might have many of its sector read errors caused by contaminants damaging its recording surfaces while another model might have most of its errors caused by write interference where writes to one track perturb data stored on nearby tracks. The first might see its error rate rise over time, while the second might have an error rate that increases as its write/read ratio increases.

Failure rates can even vary across different individual devices. If you deploy several outwardly identical disks, some may exhibit tens of nonrecoverable read errors in a year, while others operate flawlessly.

EXAMPLE **Unrecoverable read errors.**

| **What causes whole-device failures?** |

Disk failures can be caused by a range of faults such as a disk head being damaged, a capacitor failure or power surge that damages the electronics, or mechanical wear-out that makes it difficult for the head to stay centered over a track.

Common causes of flash device failures include wear-out, when enough individual pages fail that the device runs out of spare pages to use for remapping, and failures of the device's electronics such as having a capacitor fail.

Suppose that the nearly-full 500 GB disk on your laptop has just stopped working. Fortunately, you have a recent, full backup on a 500 GB USB drive with an unrecoverable read error rate of 1 sector per 10^{14} bits read. Estimate the probability of successfully reading the entire USB backup disk when restoring your data to a replacement laptop disk.

ANSWER   We need to read 500 GB, so the expected number of failures is 500 GB $*$ $\frac{8*10^9\text{bits}}{\text{GB}} * \frac{1\text{error}}{10^{14}\text{bits}} = 0.04$. The probability of encountering at least one failure might be a bit lower than that (since we may encounter multiple failures as we scan the entire disk), but there appears to be a chance of at least a few percent that the restoration will not be fully successful.

We can approach the problem in a slightly different way by interpreting the unrecoverable read rate as meaning that each bit has a 10^{-14} chance of being wrong and that failures are independent (both somewhat dubious assumptions, but probably OK for a ballpark estimate). Then each bit has a $1\text{-}10^{-14}$ chance of being correct, and the chance of reading all bits successfully is $P_S = (1 - 10^{-14})^{8*500*10^9} = 0.9608$. Under this calculation, we estimate that there is slightly less than a 4% chance of encountering a failure during the full-disk read of the backup disk.

As noted in the sidebar, these calculations ignore some important factors, so the results may not be precise. But, even if they are off by as much as an order of magnitude, then it is still reasonable to conclude that the rate of nonrecoverable read errors is likely to be non-negligible.

Note that the impact of a small number of lost sectors may be modest (e.g., the backup software succeeds in restoring all but a file or two) or it may be severe (e.g., no data is restored.) For example, if the sector failure corrupts the root directory, a significant fraction of the data may be lost.

Device failures

disk device failure, flash device failure   *Full disk or flash drive failures* are when a device stops being able to service reads or writes to all sectors.

When a whole device fails, the host computer's device driver will detect the failure, and reads and writes to the device will return error codes rather than, for example, returning incorrect data. This explicit failure notification is important because it reduces the amount of cross-device redundancy needed to correct failures.

annual failure rate

mean time before failure (MTTF)

Full device failure rates are typically characterized by an *annual failure rate*, the fraction of disks expected to fail each year, or by a *mean time before failure (MTTF)* which is the inverse of the specified constant annual failure rate. In 2011, specified annual failure rates (or MTTFs) for spinning disks typically range from 0.5% ($1.7*10^6$ hours) to 0.9% ($1*10^6$ hours); specified failure rates for flash solid state drives are similar.

Systems with many storage devices expect to encounter frequent failures. For example,

Pitfalls. Storage system designers must consider several pitfalls when considering advertised device failure rates.

- **Relying on advertised failure rates.** Studies across several large collections of spinning disks have found significantly variability in failure rates. In these studies, many systems experienced failure rates of 2%, 4%, or higher despite advertised failure rates of under 1%.

  Some of the discrepency may be due to different definitions of "failure" by manufacturers and users, some may be due to challenging field conditions, and some may be due to the limitations of the accelerated-aging and predictive techniques used by manufacturers to estimate MTTF.

- **Assuming uncorrelated failures.** Evidence from deployed systems suggests that when one fault occurs, other nearby devices are more likely to fail soon. Many factors can cause such correlation. For example, manufacturing irregularities can cause a batch of disks to be substandard, and an organization that purchases many disks from the same vendor at the same time may find themselves installing a batch of disks likely to fail in similar ways. As another example, disks in the same machine or rack may be of a similar age, may experience similar environmental stress and workloads, and may wear out at a similar time.

- **Confusing a device's MTTF with its useful life.** If a device has an MTTF of one million or more hours, it does not mean that it is expected to last for 100 years or more. Disks are designed to be operated for some finite lifetime, perhaps 5 years. A disk's advertised annual failure rate (i.e., 1/MTTF) applies during the disk's intended service life. As that lifetime is approached, failure rates may rise as the device wears out.

- **Assuming constant failure rates.** A device may have different failure rates over its lifetime. Some devices exhibit *infant mortality*, where their failure rate may be higher than normal during their first few

infant mortality

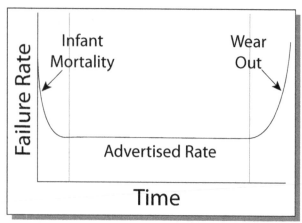

Figure 14.6: Bathtub model of device lifetimes

weeks of use as latent manufacturing defects are exposed. Others exhibit *wear out*, where their failure rate begins to rise after some years.

wear out

A simple model for understanding infant mortality and wear out is the *bathtub model* illustrated in Figure 14.6.

bathtub model

- **Ignoring warning signs.** Some device failures happen without warning, but others are preceded by increasing rates of non-fatal anomalies. Many storage devices implement the *SMART (Self-Monitoring, Analysis, and Reporting Technology)* interface, which provides a way for the operating system to monitor events that may be useful in predicting failures such as read errors, sector remappings, inaccurate seek attempts, or failures to spin up to the target speed.

SMART (Self-Monitoring, Analysis, and Reporting Technology)

- **Assuming devices behave identically.** Different device models or even different generations of the same model may have significantly different failure behaviors. One generation might exhibit significantly higher failure rates than expected and the next might exhibit significantly lower rates.

EXAMPLE **Disk failures in large systems.**

Suppose you have a departmental file server with 100 disks, each with an estimated MTTF of $1.5 * 10^6$ hours. Estimate the expected time until one of those disks fails. For simplicity, assume that each disk has a constant failure rate and that disks fail independently.

ANSWER If each disk has a MTTF of $1.5 * 10^6$ hours, then 100 disks fail at a 100 times greater rate, giving us a MTTF of $1.5 * 10^4$ hours. So, although the annual failure rate of a single disk is $\frac{1\,\text{failure}}{1.5*10^6\,\text{hours}} * 24\frac{\text{hours}}{\text{day}} * 365\frac{\text{days}}{\text{year}} =$

$0.00585 \frac{\text{failures}}{\text{year}}$, the annual failure rate of the 100-disk system is 0.585 = 58.5%.

EXAMPLE **Pitfalls.**

Given the pitfalls discussed above, is this calculation above likely to overestimate or underestimate the failure rate of the system?

ANSWER Of the factors listed above, the pitfall of *relying on advertised failure rates* seems most significant, and it could lead us to significantly *underestimate* the failure rate of the system.

This solution does *assume constant failure rates*. If the disks are very new or very old, they may suffer higher failure rates than expected, which might cause us to *underestimate* the failure rate of the system.

Because we are only interested in the average rate, the *correlation* pitfall is not particularly relevant to our analysis.

RAID: Multi-disk redundancy for error correction

Given the limits of physical storage devices, storage systems use additional techniques to get acceptable end-to-end reliability. In particular, rather than trying to engineer perfectly reliable (and extremely expensive) storage devices, storage systems use Redundant Arrays of Inexpensive Disks (RAIDs) so that a partial or total failure of one device will not cause data to be lost.

Basic RAIDs

RAID

A *Redundant Array of Inexpensive Disks (RAID)* is a system that spreads data redundantly across multiple disks in order to tolerate individual disk failures. Note that the term RAID traditionally refers to redundant *disks*, and for simplicity we will discuss RAID in the context of disks. The principles, however, apply equally well to other storage devices like flash drives.

Figures 14.7 and 14.8 illustrate two common RAID architectures: mirroring and rotating parity.

mirroring

RAID 1

- **Mirroring.** In RAIDs with *mirroring* (also called *RAID 1*), the system writes each block of data to two disks and can read any block of data from either disk as Figure 14.7 illustrates. If one of the disks suffers a sector or whole-disk failure, no data is lost because the data can still be read from the other disk.

rotating
parity

RAID 5

- **Rotating parity.** In RAIDs with *rotating parity* (also called *RAID 5*), the system reduces replication overheads by storing several blocks of data on several disks and protecting those blocks with one redundant block stored on yet another disk as Figure 14.8 illustrates.

In particular, this approach uses groups of G disks, and writes each of $G - 1$ blocks of data to a different disk and 1 block of parity to the

---

The exponential distribution

When — as in the example — device failures events occur at a constant rate, the number of failure events in a fixed time period can be mathematically modelled as a Poisson process, and the interarrival time between failure events follows an exponential distribution.

The exponential distribution is *memoryless*—since the rate of failure events is constant across time, then the expected time to the next failure event is the same — no matter what the current time and no matter how long it has been since the last failure. So, if a device has an annual failure rate of 0.5 and thus a mean time to failure of 2 years, and we've been operating the device without a failure for a year, the expected time from the current time to the next failure is still 2 years.

So, if random variable T represents the time between failures and has an exponential distribution with λ representing the average number of failure events per unit of time, then the probability density function $f_T t$ is:

$$f_T(t) = \begin{cases} \lambda e^{-\lambda t} & \text{if } t \geq 0 \\ 0 & \text{if } t < 0 \end{cases}$$

and the mean time to failure is $MTTF = \frac{1}{\lambda}$.

Exponential distributions have a number of convenient mathematical properties. For example, because the failure rate is constant, the mean time to failure is the inverse of the failure rate; this is why it is easy to convert between MTTF and annual failure rates in storage specifications. Also, if the expected number of failures is given for one duration (e.g., 0.1 failures per year), it can easily be converted to the expected number for a different duration (e.g., 0.0003 failures per day). Finally, if we have k independent failure processes with rates of $\lambda_1, \lambda_2, \ldots, \lambda_k$, then the aggregate failure function — the rate at which failures of any of the k kinds occurs — is

$$\lambda_{tot} = \lambda_1 + \lambda_2 + \ldots + \lambda_k$$

and the mean time to the next failure of any kind is $MTTF_{tot} = \frac{1}{\lambda_{tot}}$. For example, if we have 100 disks, each with a $MTTF_{disk} = 1.5 * 10^6$ hours or, equivalently, each failing at a rate of 0.00585 failures per year, then the overall 100-disk system suffers failures at a rate of $100 * 0.00585 = 0.585$ failures per year or, equivalently, the 100-disk system has $MTTF_{100disks} = 1.5 * 10^4$ hours.

Warning. Because the exponential distribution is so mathematically convenient, is tempting to use it even when it is not appropriate. Remember that failures in real systems may be correlated (i.e., they are not independent) and may vary over time (i.e., they are not constant).

---

remaining disk. Each bit of the parity block is produced by computing the exclusive-or of the corresponding bits of the data blocks:

$$parity = data_0 \oplus data_1 \oplus \ldots \oplus data_{G-1}$$

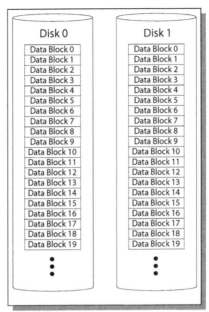

Figure 14.7: RAID 1 with mirroring.

	Disk 0	Disk 1	Disk 2	Disk 3	Disk 4
Stripe 0	Strip (0,0) Parity (0,0,0) Parity (1,0,0) Parity (2,0,0) Parity (3,0,0)	Strip (1,0) Data Block 0 Data Block 1 Data Block 2 Data Block 3	Strip (2,0) Data Block 4 Data Block 5 Data Block 6 Data Block 7	Strip (3,0) Data Block 8 Data Block 9 Data Block 10 Data Block 11	Strip (4,0) Data Block 12 Data Block 13 Data Block 14 Data Block 15
Stripe 1	Strip (0,1) Data Block 16 Data Block 17 Data Block 18 Data Block 19	Strip (1,1) Parity (0,1,1) Parity (1,1,1) Parity (2,1,1) Parity (3,1,1)	Strip (2,1) Data Block 20 Data Block 21 Data Block 22 Data Block 23	Strip (3,1) Data Block 24 Data Block 25 Data Block 26 Data Block 27	Strip (4,1) Data Block 28 Data Block 29 Data Block 30 Data Block 31
Stripe 2	Strip (0,2) Data Block 32 Data Block 33 Data Block 34 Data Block 35	Strip (1,2) Data Block 36 Data Block 37 Data Block 38 Data Block 39	Strip (2,2) Parity (0,2,2) Parity (1,2,2) Parity (2,2,2) Parity (3,2,2)	Strip (3,2) Data Block 40 Data Block 41 Data Block 42 Data Block 43	Strip (4,2) Data Block 44 Data Block 45 Data Block 46 Data Block 46

Figure 14.8: RAID 5 with rotating parity.

If one of the disks suffers a sector or whole-disk failure, lost data blocks can be reconstructed using the corresponding data and parity blocks from the other disks. Note that because the system already knows which disk has failed, parity is sufficient for error correction, not just error detection. For example, if the disk containing block $data_0$ fails, the block can be constructed by computing the exclusive-or of the parity block and the remaining data blocks:

$$data_0 = parity \oplus data_1 \oplus \ldots \oplus data_{G-1}$$

To maximize performance, rotating parity RAIDs carefully organize their data layout by rotating parity and striping data to balance parallelism and sequential access:

- **Rotating parity.** Because the parity for a given set of blocks must be updated each time any of the data blocks are updated, the average parity block tends to be accessed more often than the average data block. To balance load, rather than having $G - 1$ disks store only data blocks and 1 disk store only parity blocks, each disk dedicates $\frac{1}{G}$th of its space to parity and is responsible for storing $\frac{1}{G}$th of the parity blocks and $\frac{G-1}{G}$ of the data blocks.

strip

stripe

- **Striping data.** To balance parallelism versus sequential-access efficiency, a *strip* of several sequential blocks is placed on one disk before shifting to another disk for the next strip. A set of $G - 1$ data strips and their parity strip is called a *stripe*.

  By striping data, requests larger than a block but smaller than a strip require require just one disk to seek and then read or write the full sequential run of data rather than requiring multiple disks to seek and then read smaller sequential runs. Conversely, the RAID can service more widely spaced requests in parallel.

Combining rotating parity and striping, we have the arrangement shown in Figure 14.8.

EXAMPLE   **Updating a RAID with rotating parity.** For the rotating parity RAID in Figure 14.8, suppose you update data block 21. What disk I/O operations must occur?

ANSWER   The challenge is that we must not only update data block 21, we must also update the corresponding parity block. Since data block 21 is block 1 of its strip and the strip is part of stripe 1, we need to update parity block 1 of the parity strip for stripe 1 (*Parity (1,1,1)* in the figure.)

It takes 4 I/O operations to update both the data and parity. First we read the old data D_{21} and parity $P_{1,1,1}$ and "remove" the old data from the parity calculation $P_{tmp} = P_{1,1,1} \oplus D_{21}$. Then we can compute the new parity from the new data $P'_{1,1,1} = P_{tmp} \oplus D'_{21}$. Finally we can write the new data D'_{21} and parity $P'_{1,1,1}$ to disks 2 and 1, respectively.

RAIDs with rotating parity have high overheads for small writes. Their overheads are far smaller for reads and for full-stripe writes.

Atomic update of data and parity

A challenge in implementing RAID is atomically updating both the data and the parity (or both data blocks in a RAID with mirroring.)

Consider what would happen if the RAID system in Figure 14.8 crashes in the middle updating block 21, after updating the data block on disk 2 but before updating the parity block on disk 1. Now, if disk 2 fails, the system will reconstruct the wrong (old) data for block 21.

The situation may be even worse if a write to a mirrored RAID is interrupted. Because reads can be serviced by either disk, reads of the inconsistent block may sometimes return the new value and sometimes return the old one.

Solutions. Three solutions and one non-solution are commonly used to solve (or not) the atomic update problem.

- **Nonvolatile write buffer.** Hardware RAID systems often include a battery-backed write buffer. An update is removed from the write buffer only once it is safely on disk. The RAID's startup procedures ensure that any data in the write buffer is written to disk after a crash or power outage.

- **Transactional update.** RAID systems can use transactions to atomically update both the data block and the parity block. For example, Oracle's RAID-Z integrates RAID striping with the ZFS file system to avoid overwriting data in place and to atomically update data and parity.

- **Recovery scan.** After a crash, the system can scan all of the blocks in the system and update any inconsistent parity blocks. Note that until that scan is complete, some parity blocks may be inconsistent, and incorrect data may be reconstructed if a disk fails. The Linux md (multiple device) software RAID driver uses this approach.

- **Cross your fingers.** Some software and hardware RAID implementations do not ensure that the data and parity blocks are in sync after a crash. *Caveat emptor.*

Recovery. In either RAID arrangement, if a disk suffers a sector failure, the disk reports an error when there is an attempt to read the sector and, if necessary, remaps the damaged sector to a spare one. Then, the RAID system reconstructs the lost sector from the other disk(s) and rewrites it to the original disk.

If a disk suffers a whole-disk failure, an operator replaces the failed disk, and the RAID system reconstructs all of the disk's data from the other disk(s) and rewrites the data to the replacement disk. The average time from when a disk fails until it has been replaced and rewritten is called the

mean time to repair/MTTR

mean time to repair (MTTR).

RAID Levels

An early paper on RAIDs, http://dl.acm.org/citation.cfm?id=50214"A Case for Redundant Arrays of Inexpensive Disks (RAID)," by David Patterson, Garth Gibson, and Randy Katz described a range of possible RAID organizations and named them RAID 0, RAID 1, RAID 2, RAID 3, RAID 4, and RAID 5. Several of these RAID levels were intended to illustrate key concepts rather than for real-world deployment.

Today, three of these variants are in wide use:

- **RAID 0—JBOD.** RAID level 0 spreads data across multiple disk without redundancy. Any disk failure results in data loss. For this reason, the term RAID is somewhat misleading, and this organization is often referred to as JBOD—Just a Bunch Of Disks.

- **RAID 1—Mirroring.** RAID level 1 mirrors identical data to two disks.

- **RAID 5—Rotating Parity.** RAID level 5 stripes data across G disks. $G - 1$ of the disks in a stripe store $G - 1$ different blocks of data and the remaining disk stores a parity block. The role of storing the parity block for different data blocks is rotated among the disks to balance load.

Subsequent to the "Case for RAID" paper, new organizations emerged, and many of them were named in the same spirit. Some of these names have become fairly standard.

- **RAID 6—Dual Redundancy.** RAID level 6 is similar to RAID level 5, but instead of one parity block per group, two redundant blocks are stored. These blocks are generated using erasure codes such as Reed Solomon codes that allow reconstruction of all of the original data as long as at most two disks fail.

- **RAID 10 and RAID 50—Nested RAID.** RAID 10 and RAID 50 were originally called RAID 1+0 and RAID 5+0. They simply combine RAID 0 with RAID 1 or RAID 5. For example, a RAID 10 system mirrors pairs of disks for redundancy (RAID 1), treats each pair of mirrored disks as a single reliable logical disk, and then stripes data non-redundantly across these logical disks (RAID 0).

Many other RAID levels have been proposed. In some cases, these new "levels" have more to do with marketing than technology ("Our company's RAID 99+ is much better than your company's puny RAID 14"). In any event, we regard the particular nomenclature used to describe exotic RAID organizations as relatively unimportant; our discussion focuses on mirroring (RAID 1), rotating parity (RAID 5), and dual redundancy (RAID 6). Other organizations can be analyzed using principles from these approaches.

RAID reliability

A RAID with one redundant disk per group (e.g., mirroring or rotating parity RAIDs) can lose data in three ways: two full disk failures, a full disk failure and one or more sector failures on other disks, and overlapping sector failures on multiple disks. The expected time until one of these events occurs is called the *mean time to data loss* (MTTDL.)

mean time to
data loss

MTTDL

Two full-disk failures. If two disks fail, the system will be unable to reconstruct the missing data.

To get a sense of how serious a problem this might be, suppose that a system has N disks with one parity block per G blocks, and suppose that disks fail independently with a mean time to failure of $MTTF$ and a mean time to replace a failed disk and recover its data of $MTTR$.

Then, when the system is operating properly, the expected time until the first failure is $MTTF/N$. Assuming $MTTR \ll MTTF$, there is essentially a race to replace the disk and reconstruct its data before a second disk fails. We lose this race and hit the second failure before the repair is done with probability $\frac{MTTF/(G-1)}{MTTR}$, giving us a mean time to data loss from multiple full-disk failures of

$$MTTDL_{two-full-disk} = \frac{MTTF^2}{N(G-1)MTTR}$$

EXAMPLE

Mean time to double-disk failure.

Suppose you have 100 disks organized into groups of 10, with one disk storing a parity block per nine disks storing data blocks. Assuming that disk failures are independent and the per-disk mean time to failure is 10^6 hours and assuming that the mean time to repair a failed disk is 10 hours, estimate the expected mean time to data loss due to a double-disk failure.

ANSWER

Because failures are assumed to occur independently and at a constant rate, we can use the equation above:

$$MTTDL_{two-full-disk} = \frac{MTTF^2}{N(G-1)MTTR}$$
$$= \frac{(10^6 \text{hours})^2}{(10^2)(9)(10 \text{hours})}$$
$$\approx 10^8 \text{hours}$$

So, assuming independent failures at the expected rate and assuming no other sources of data loss, this organization appears to have raised the mean time to data loss from about 100 years (for a single disk) to about 10,000 years (for 90 disks worth of data and 10 disks worth of parity).

One full-disk failure and a sector failure. If one or more disks suffer sector failures and another disk suffers a full-disk failure, the RAID system can not recover all of its data. Assuming independent failures that arrive at a constant rate, we can estimate probability of data loss over some interval as the probability of suffering a disk failure times the probability that we will fail to read all data needed to reconstruct the lost disk's data:

$$P_{lostDataFromDiskAndSector} = P_{DiskFailure} \cdot P_{RecoveryError}$$

$$P_{lostDataFromDiskAndSector} = \frac{N}{MTTF} \cdot P_{fail\_recovery\_read}$$

If this gives us the probability of losing data over some period of time or equivalently the rate of data-loss failures, then inverting this equation gives us the mean time to data loss (MTTDL). Thus, we can estimate the mean time to data loss from this failure mode based on the expected time between full disk failures divided by the odds of failing to read all data needed to reconstruct the lost disk's data.

$$MTTDL_{disk+sector} = \frac{MTTF}{N} \cdot \frac{1}{P_{fail\_recovery\_read}}$$

EXAMPLE   **Mean time to failed disk and failed sector.** Assuming that during recovery, latent sector errors are discovered at a rate of 1 per 10^{15} bits read and assuming that the mean time to failure for each of 100 1 TB disks organized into groups of 10 is 10^6 hours, what is the expected mean time to data loss due to full-disk failure combined with a sector failure?

ANSWER

$$MTTDL_{disk+sector} = \frac{MTTF}{N} \cdot \frac{1}{P_{fail\_recovery\_read}}$$

$$= \frac{10^6}{100} \cdot \frac{1}{P_{fail\_recovery\_read}}$$

To estimate $P_{fail\_recovery\_read}$ we will assume that each bit fails independently and is successfully read with probability $(1/(1 - 10^{-15}))$. Then the probability of reading 1 TB from each of 9 disks is

$$P_{succeed\_recovery\_read} = P_{succeed\_bit\_read}^{numberofbits}$$

$$= (1 - 10^{-15}))^{9 \text{ disks} \cdot 10^{12} \frac{bytes}{disk} *8 \frac{bits}{byte}}$$

$$\approx 0.93$$

So, there is roughly a 93% chance that recovery will succeed and a 7% chance that recovery will fail. We then have

$$MTTDL_{disk+sector} = \frac{10^6}{100} \cdot \frac{1}{.07} = 1.4 \cdot 10^5 hours$$

Notice that this rate of data loss is much higher than the rate from double disk failures calculated above. Of course, the relative contributions of each failure mode will depend on disks' MTTF, size, and bit error rates as well as the system's MTTR.

Failure of two sectors sharing a redundant sector. In principle, it is also possible to lose data because the corresponding sectors fail on different disks. However, with billions of distinct sectors on each disk and small numbers of latent failures per disk, this failure mode is likely to be a negligible risk for most systems.

Overall data loss rate. If we assume independent failures and constant failure rates, then we can add the failure rates from the two significant failure modes to estimate the combined failure rate:

$$
\begin{aligned}
FailureRate_{indep+const} &= FailureRate_{two-full-disk} + FailureRate_{disk+sector} \\
&= \frac{1}{MTTDL_{two-full-disk}} + \frac{1}{MTTDL_{disk+sector}} \\
&= \frac{N(G-1)MTTR}{MTTF^2} + \frac{N \cdot P_{fail\_recovery\_read}}{MTTF} \\
&= \frac{N}{MTTF}(\frac{MTTR(G-1)}{MTTF} + P_{fail\_recovery\_read})
\end{aligned}
$$

The total failure rate is thus the rate that the first disk fails times the rate that either a second disk in the group fails before the repair is completed or a sector error is encountered when the disks are being read to rebuild the lost disk.

We label the above $FailureRate_{indep+const}$ to emphasize the strong assumptions of independent failures and constant failure rates. As noted above, failures are likely to be correlated in many environments and failure rates of some devices may increase over time. Both of these factors may result significantly higher failure rates than expected.

EXAMPLE　**Combined failure rate.** For the system described in the previous examples (100 disks, rotating parity with a group size of 10, mean time to failure of 10^6 hours, mean time to repair of 10 hours, and nonrecoverable read error rate of one sector per 10^{15} bits) assuming that all failures are independent, estimate the MTTDL when both double-disk and single-disk-and-sector failures are considered.

ANSWER

$$FailureRate_{indep+const} = \frac{N}{MTTF}\left(\frac{MTTR(G-1)}{MTTF} + P_{fail\_recovery\_read}\right)$$

$$= \frac{100 \text{ disks}}{10^6} \text{ hours}\left(\frac{10 \text{ hours}}{10^6 \text{ hours}} + 0.0694\right)$$

$$= \frac{1}{10^4 \text{ hours}}\left(\frac{1}{10^4} + 0.0694\right)$$

$$= \frac{1}{10^4 \text{ hours}}(0.0695)$$

$$= 6.95 \cdot 10^{-6} \frac{\text{failures}}{\text{hour}}$$

$$=$$

Inverting the failure rate gives the mean time to data loss:

$$MTTDL_{const+indep} = \frac{1}{FailureRate_{indep+const}}$$

$$= 1.44 \cdot 10^5 \frac{\text{hours}}{\text{failure}}$$

$$= 16.4 \frac{\text{years}}{\text{failure}}$$

Two things in the example above are worth special note. First, for these parameters, the dominant cause of data loss is likely to be a single disk failure combined with a nonrecoverable read error during recovery. Second, for these parameters and this configuration, the resulting 6% chance of losing data per year may be unacceptable for many environments. As a result, systems use various techniques to improve the MTTDL in RAID systems.

Improving RAID reliability

What can be done to further improve reliability? Broadly speaking, we can do three things: (1) increase redundancy, (2) reduce nonrecoverable read error rates, and (3) reduce mean time to repair. All of these approaches, in various combinations, are used in practice.

Here are some common approaches:

Increasing redundancy with more redundant disks.   Rather than having a single redundant block per group (e.g., using two mirrored disks or using one parity disk for each stripe) systems can use double redundancy (e.g., three disk replicas or two error correction disks for each stripe.) In some cases, systems may use even more redundancy. For example, the Google File System (GFS) is designed to provide highly reliable and available storage across thousands of disks; by default GFS stores each data block on three different disks.

dual
redundancy
array
     A *dual redundancy array* ensures that data can be reconstructed despite

any two failures in a stripe by generating two redundant blocks using erasure codes such as Reed Solomon codes. This approach is sometimes **RAID 6** called *RAID 6*.

A system with dual redundancy can be much more reliable than a simple single redundancy RAID. With dual redundancy, the most likely data loss scenarios are (a) three full-disk failures or (b) a double-disk failure combined with one or more nonrecoverable read errors.

If we optimistically assume that failures are independent and occur at a constant rate, a system with two redundant disks per stripe has a potentially low combined data loss rate:

$$FailureRate_{dual+indep+const} = \frac{N}{MTTF} \times \frac{MTTR(G-1)}{MTTF} \times (\frac{MTTR(G-2)}{MTTF} + P_{fail\_recovery\_read})$$

This data loss rate is nearly $\frac{MTTF}{MTTR(G-1)}$ times better than the single-parity data loss rate; for disks with MTTFs of over one million hours, MTTRs of under 10 hours, and groups sizes of ten or fewer disks, double parity improves the estimated rate by about a factor of 10,000.

We emphasize, however, that the above equation almost certainly underestimates the likely data loss rate for real systems, which may suffer correlated failures, varying failure rates, higher failure rates than advertised, and so on.

Reducing nonrecoverable read error rates with scrubbing. A storage device's sector-level error rates are typically expressed as a single *nonrecoverable read rates*, suggesting that the rate is constant. The reality is more complex. Depending on the device, errors may accumulate over time and heavier workloads may increase the rate that errors accumulate.

An important technique for reducing a disk's nonrecoverable read rate **scrubbing** is *scrubbing*: periodically reading the entire contents of a disk, detecting sectors with unrecoverable read errors, reconstructing the lost data from the remaining disks in the RAID array, and attempting to write and read the reconstructed data to and from the suspect sector. If writes and reads succeed, then the error was caused by a transient fault, and the disk continues to use the sector, but if the sector cannot be successfully accessed, the error is permanent, and the system remaps that sector to a spare and writes the reconstructed data there.

Reducing nonrecoverable read error rates with more reliable disks. Different disk models promise significantly different nonrecoverable read error rates. In particular, in 2011, many disks aimed at laptops and personal computers claim unrecoverable read error rates of one per 10^{14} bits read, while disks aimed at enterprise servers often have lower storage densities but can promis unrecoverable read error rates of one per 10^{16} bits read. This two order of magnitude improvement greatly reduces the probability that a RAID system loses data from a combination of a full disk failure and a nonrecoverable read error during recovery.

Reducing mean time to repair with hot spares.   Some systems include "hot spare" disk drives that are idle, but plugged into a server so that if one of the server's disks fails, the hot spare can be automatically activated to replace the lost disk.

Note that even with hot spares, the mean time to repair a disk is limited by the time it takes to write the reconstructed data to it, and this time is often measured in hours. For example, if we have a 1 TB disk and can write at 100 MB/s, the mean time to repair for the disk will be at least 10^4 seconds—about 3 hours. In practice, repair time may be even larger if the bandwidth achieved is less than assumed here.

Reducing mean time to repair with declustering.   Disks with hundreds of gigabytes to a few terabytes can take hours to fully write with reconstructed data. *Declustering* splits reconstruction of a failed disk across multiple disks. Declustering thus allows parallel reconstruction, thus speeding up reconstruction and reducing MTTR.

declustering

For example, the Hadoop File System (HDFS) is a cluster file system that writes each data block to three out of potentially hundreds or thousands of disks. It chooses the three disks for each block more or less randomly. If one disk fails, it rereplicates the lost blocks approximately randomly across the remaining disks. If we have N disks each with a bandwidth of B, total reconstruction bandwidth can approach $\frac{N}{2}B$; for example, if there are 1000 disks with 100 MB/s bandwidths, reconstruction bandwidth can theoretically approach 500 GB/s, allowing rereplication of a 1 TB disk's data in a few seconds.

In practice, rereplication will be slower than this for at least three reasons. First, resources other than the disk (e.g., the network) may bottleneck recovery. Second, the system may throttle recovery speed to avoid starving user requests. Third, if a server crashes and its disks become inaccessible, the system may delay starting recovery — hoping that the server will soon recover — to avoid imposing extra load on the system.

Pitfalls

When constructing a reliable storage system, it is not enough to plug provide enough redundancy to tolerate a target number of failures. We also need to consider how failures are likely to occur (e.g., they may be corre-lated) and what it takes to correct them (e.g., successfully reading a lot of other data.) More specifically, be aware of the following pitfalls:

- **Assuming uncorrelated failures..** It is easy to get gaudy MTTDL num-bers by adding a redundant device or two and multiplying the de-vices' MTTFs. But the simple equation on page 621 only applies when failures are uncorrelated. Even a 1% chance of correlated failures dra-matically changes the estimate. Unfortunately, it is often difficult to estimate correlation rates *a priori*, so designers must sometimes just add a significant safety margin and hope that it is enough.

- **Ignoring the risk from latent errors..** It is not uncommon to see anal-yses of RAID reliability that considers full device failures but not nonrecoverable read failures. As we have seen above, nonrecoverable read errors can dramatically reduce the probability of successfully recovering data after a disk failure.

- **Not implementing scrubbing..** Periodically scrubbing disks to detect and correct latent errors can significantly reduce the risk of data loss. Although it can be difficult to predict the appropriate scrubbing frequency *a priori*, a system that uses scrubbing can monitor the rate at which noncorrectable read errors are found and corrected and use the measured rate to adjust the scrubbing frequency.

- **Not having a backup..** The techniques discussed in this section can protect a system against many, but not all, faults. For example, a widespread correlated failure (e.g., a building burning down), an operator error (e.g., "rm -r *"), or a software bug could corrupt or delete data stored across any number of redundant devices.

backup

A *backup* system provides storage that is separate from a system's main storage. Ideally, the separation is both physical and logical.

physical
separation

Physical separation means that backup storage devices are in different locations than the primary storage devices. For example, some sys-tems achieve physical separation by copying data to tape and storing the tapes in a different building than the main storage servers. Other systems achieve physical separation by storing data to remote disk arrays such as those provided by cloud backup and disaster recovery services.

logical
separation

Logical separation means that the interface to the backup system is restricted to prevent premature deletion of data. For example, some backup systems provide an interface that allows a user to read *but not write* old versions of a file (e.g, the file as it existed one hour, two hours, four hours, one day, one week, one month, and one year ago.)

Modeling Real Systems

The equations in the main text for estimating a system's mean time to data loss are only applicable if failure rates are constant and if failures are uncorrelated. Unfortunately, empirical studies often observe correlation among full-disk failures, among sector-level failures, and between sector-level and full-disk failures, and they frequently find failure rates that vary significantly with disks' ages. Unfortunately, if failure rates vary over time or failures are correlated, the the failure arrival distribution is no longer described by an exponential distribution, and the math quickly gets difficult.

One solution is to use randomized simulation to estimate the probability of data loss over some duration of interest. For example, we might want to estimate the probability of losing data over 10 years for a 1000-disk system organized in groups of 10 disks with rotating parity.

To do this, our simulation would track which disks are functioning normally, which have latent sector errors, and which have suffered full disk failures. The transitions between states could be based on measurement studies or field data on key factors like (a) the rate that disks suffer full disk failures (possibly dependent on the disks' ages, the number of recent full disk failures, or the number of individual sector failures a disk has had), (b) the rate at which sector failures arise (possibly dependent on the age of the disk, workload of the disk, and recent frequency of sector failures), (c) the repair time when a disk fails, and (d) the expected time for scrubbing to detect and repair a sector error.

To estimate the probability of data loss, we would repeatedly simulate the system for a decade and count the number of times the system enters a state in which data is lost (i.e., a group has two full disk failures or has both a full disk failure and a sector failure on another disk.)

Software integrity checks

Although storage devices include sector- or page-level checksums to detect data corruption, many recent file systems have included additional, higher-level, checksums and other integrity checks on their data.

These checks can catch a range of errors that hardware-level checksums can miss. For example, they can detect *wild writes* or *lost writes* where a bug in the operating system software, device driver software, or device firmware misdirects a write to the wrong block or page or fails to complete an intended write. They can also detect rare *ECC false negatives* when the hardware-level error correcting codes fail to detect a multi-bit corruption.

When a software integrity check fails on a block read or during latent-error scrubbing, the system reconstructs the lost or corrupted block using the redundant storage in the RAID.

Two examples of software integrity checks used today are *block integrity metadata* and *file system fingerprints*.

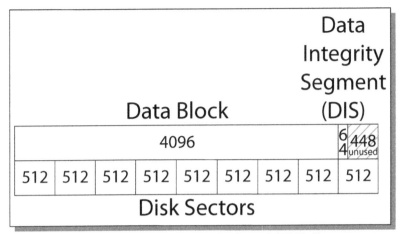

Figure 14.9: To improve reliability Network Appliance's WAFL file system stores a 64 byte data integrity segment (DIS) with each 4 KB data block.

Block integrity metadata. Some file systems, like Network Appliance's WAFL file system, include *block integrity metadata* that allows the software to validate the results of each block it reads.

block
integrity
metadata

As Figure 14.9 illustrates, WAFL stores a 64 byte *data integrity segment* (DIS) with each 4 KB data block. The DIS contains a checksum of the data block, the identity of the data block (e.g., the ID of the file to which it belongs and the block's offset in that file), and a checksum of the DIS, itself.

Then, when a block is read, the system performs three checks. First, it checks the DIS's checksum. Second, it verifies that the data in the block corresponds to the checksum in the block's data integrity segment. Third, it verifies that the identity in the block's DIS corresponds to the file block it was intending to read. If all of these checks pass, the file system can be confident it is returning the correct data; if not, the file system can reconstruct the necessary data from redundant disks in the RAID.

File system fingerprints. Some file systems, like Oracle's ZFS, include *file system fingerprints* that provide a checksum across the entire file system in a way that allows efficient checks and updates when individual blocks are read and written.

file system
fingerprint

As illustrated in Figure 14.10 (a), all of ZFS's data structures are arranged in a tree of blocks with a root node called the uberblock. At each internal node of the tree, each reference to a child node includes both a pointer to and a checksum of the child. Thus, the reference to any subtree includes a checksum that covers all of that subtree's contents, and the uberblock holds a checksum that covers the entire file system.

When ZFS reads data (i.e., leaves of the tree) or metadata (i.e., internal nodes of the tree), it follows the pointers down the tree to find the right

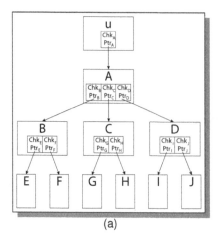
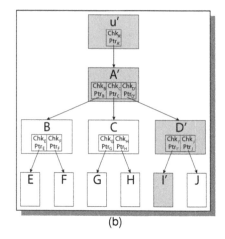

(a)   (b)

Figure 14.10: (a) ZFS stores all data in a Merkle tree so that each node of the tree includes both a pointer to and a checksum of each of its children (Chk and Ptr in the figure). On an update (b) all nodes from the updated block (I') to the root (u') are updated to reflect the new pointer and checksum values.

Layers Upon Layers Upon Layers

In this chapter we focus on error detection and correction at three levels: the individual storage devices (e.g., disks and flash), storage architectures (e.g., RAID), and file systems.

Today, storage systems with important data often include not just these layers, but additional ones. Enterprise and cloud storage systems distribute data across several geographically-distributed sites and may include high-level checksums on that geographically-replicated data. Within a site, they may replicate data across multiple servers using what is effectively a distributed file system. At each server, the distributed file system may store data using a local file system that includes file-system-level checksums on the locally-stored data. And, invariably, the local server will use storage devices that detect and sometimes correct low-level errors.

Although we do not discuss cross-machine and geographic replication in any detail, the principles described in this chapter also apply to these systems.

---

block to read, computing a checksum of each internal or leaf block and comparing it to the checksum stored with the block reference. Similarly, as Figure 14.10 (b) illustrates, when ZFS writes a block, it updates the references from the updated block to the uberblock so that each includes both the new checksum and (since ZFS never updates data structures in place) new block pointer.

Exercises

5. Go to an on-line site that sells hard disk drives, and find the largest capacity disk you can buy for less than $200. Now, track down the spec sheet for the disk and, given the disk's specified bit error rate (or unrecoverable read rate), estimate the probability of encountering an error if you read every sector on the disk once.

6. Suppose we define a RAID's *access cost* as the number disk accesses divided by the number of data blocks read or written. For each of following configurations and workloads, what is the access cost?

   a) Workload: a series of random 1-block writes
      Configuration: mirroring

   b) Workload: a series of random 1-block writes
      Configuration: distributed parity

   c) Workload: a series of random 1-block reads
      Configuration: mirroring

   d) Workload: a series of random 1-block reads
      Configuration: distributed parity

   e) Workload: a series of random 1-block reads
      Configuration: distributed parity with group size G and one failed disk

   f) Workload: a long sequential write
      Configuration: mirroring

   g) Workload: a long sequential write
      Configuration: distributed parity with a group size of G

7. Suppose that an engineer who has not taken this class tries to create a disk array with dual-redundancy but instead of using an appropriate error correcting code such as Reed Soloman, the engineer simply stores a copy of each parity block on two disks. e.g.,

   Give an example of how a two-disk failure can cause a stripe to lose data in such a system. Explain why data cannot be reconstructed in that case.

8. Some RAID systems improve reliability with intra-disk redundancy to protect against nonrecoverable read failures. For example, each individual disk on such a system might reserve one 4KB parity block

in every 32 KB extent and then store 28KB (7 4KB blocks) of data and 4 KB (1 4KB block) of parity in each extent.

In this arrangement, each data block is protected by two parity blocks: one interdisk parity block on a different disk and on intradisk parity block on the same disk.

This approach may reduce a disk's effective nonrecoverable read error rate because if one block in an extent is lost, it can be recovered from the remaining sectors and parity on the disk. Of course, if multiple blocks in the same extent are lost, the system must rely on redundancy from other disks.

    a) Assuming that a disk's nonrecoverable read errors are independent and occur at a rate of one lost 512 byte sector per 10^{15} bits read, what is the effective nonrecoverable read error rate if the operating system stores one parity block per seven data blocks on the disk?

       Hint: You may find the bc or dc arbitrary-precision calculators useful. These programs are standard in many Unix, Linux, and OSX distributions. See the man pages for instructions.

    b) Why is the above likely to significantly overstate the impact of intra-disk redundancy?

9. Many RAID implementations allow on-line repair in which the system continues to operate after a disk failure, while a new empty disk is inserted to replaced the failed disk, and while regenerating and copying data to the new disk.

Sketch a design for a 2-disk, mirrored RAID that allows the system to remain on-line during reconstruction, while still ensuring that when the data copying is done, the new disk is properly reconstructed (i.e., it is an exact copy of other disk.)

In particular, specify (1) what is done by a recovery thread, (2) what is done on a read during recovery, and (3) what is done on a write during recovery. Also explain why your system will operate correctly even if a crash occurs in the middle of reconstruction.

10. Suppose you are willing to sacrifice no more than 1% of a disk's bandwidth to scrubbing. What is maximum frequency at which you could scrub a 1 TB disk with 100 MB/s bandwidth?

11. Suppose a 3 TB disk in a mirrored RAID system crashes. Assuming the disks used in the system can sustain 100MB/s sequential bandwidth, what is the minimum mean time to repair that can be achieved? Why might a system be configured to perform recovery slower than this?

14.3 | Conclusion and future directions

Although individual storage devices include internal error correcting codes, additional redundancy for error detection and correction is often needed to provide acceptably reliable storage. In fact, today, it is seldom acceptable to store valuable data on a single device without some form of RAID-style redundancy. By the same token, many if not most file systems designed over the past decade have included software error checking to catch data corruption and loss occurrences that are not detectable by device-level hardware checks.

Increasingly now and in the future, systems go beyond just replicating data across multiple disks on a single server to distributed replication across multiple servers. Sometimes these replicas are configured to protect data even if significant physical disasters occur.

For example, Amazon's Simple Storage Service (S3) is a cloud storage service that allows customers to pay a monthly fee to store data on servers run by Amazon. As of when this paragraph was written (January 2012), Amazon stated that the system was "designed to provide 99.999999999% durability ... of objects over a given year." To provide such high reliability, Amazon must protect against disasters like a data center being destroyed in a fire. Amazon S3 therefore stores data at multiple data centers, it works to quickly repair lost redundancy, and it periodically scans stored data to verify its integrity via software checksums.

Exercises

1. Suppose that a text editor application uses the rename technique discussed on page 589 for safely saving updates by saving the updated file to a new filed (e.g., #doc.txt# and then calling rename("#doc.txt#", "doc.txt") to change the name of the updated file from #doc.txt# to doc.txt. Posix rename promises that the update to doc.txt will be atomic — even if a crash occurs,doc.txt will refer to either the old file or the new one. However, Posix does not guarantee that the entire rename operation will be atomic. In particular, Posix allows implementations in which there is a window in which a crash could result in a state where both doc.txt and #doc.txt# refer to the same, new document.

   a. How should a text-editing application react if, on startup, it sees both doc.txt and doc.txt and (i) both refer the same file or (ii) each refers to a file with different contents?

   b. Why might Posix permit this corner case (where we may end up with two names that refer to the same file) to exist?

   c. Explain how an FFS-based file system without transactions could use the "ad hoc" approach discussed in Section 14.1 to ensure that (i) doc.txt always refers to either the old or new file, (ii) the new file is never lost – it is always available as at least one of doc.txt or #doc.txt#, and (iii) there is some window where the new file may be accessed as both doc.txt and #doc.txt#.

   d. Section 14.1 discusses three reasons that few modern file systems use the "ad-hoc" approach. However, many text editors still do something like this. Why have the three issues had less effect on applications like text editors than on file systems?

2. Above, we defined two-phase locking for basic mutual exclusion locks. Extend the definition of two-phase locking for systems that use readers-writers locks.

3. Suppose that x and y represent the number of hours two managers have assigned you to work on each of two tasks with a constraint that $x + y \le 40$. On page 600, we showed that snapshot isolation could allow one transaction to update x and another concurrent transaction to update y in a way that would violate the constraint $x + y \le 40$. Is such an anomaly possible under serializability? Why or why not?

4. Suppose you have transactional storage system tStore that allows you to read and write fixed-sized 2048-byte blocks of data within transactions, and you run the following code.

```
. . .
byte b1[2048];   byte b2[2048];
byte b3[2048];   byte b4[2048];

TransID t1 = tStore.beginTransaction();
TransID t2 = tStore.beginTransaction();
TransID t3 = tStore.beginTransaction();
TransID t4 = tStore.beginTransaction();

// Interface is
//     writeBlock(TransID tid, int blockNum, byte buffer[]);
tStore.writeBlock(t1, 1, ALL_ONES);
tStore.writeBlock(t1, 2, ALL_TWOS);
tStore.writeBlock(t2, 3, ALL_THREES);
tStore.writeBlock(t1, 3, ALL_FOURS);
tStore.writeBlock(t1, 2, ALL_FIVES);
tStore.writeBlock(t3, 2, ALL_SIXES);
tStore.writeBlock(t4, 4, ALL_SEVENS);
tStore.readBlock(t2, 1, b1);
tStore.commit(t3);
tStore.readBlock(t2, 3, b2);
tStore.commit(t2);
tStore.readBlock(t1, 3, b3);
tStore.readBlock(t4, 3, b4);
tStore.commit(t1);

// At this point, the system crashes
```

The system crashes at the point indicated above.

Assume that ALL_ONES, ALL_TWOS, etc. are each arrays of 2048 bytes with the indicated value. Assume that when the program is started, all blocks in the tStore have the value ALL_ZEROS.

Just before the system crashes, what is the value of b1 and what is the value of b2?

a) In the program above, just before the system crashes, what is the value of b3 and what is the value of b4?

b) Suppose that after the program above runs and crashes at the indicated point. After the system restarts and completes recovery and all write-backs, what are the values stored in each of blocks 1, 2, 3, 4, and 5 of the tStore?

5. Go to an on-line site that sells hard disk drives, and find the largest capacity disk you can buy for less than $200. Now, track down the spec sheet for the disk and, given the disk's specified bit error rate (or unrecoverable read rate), estimate the probability of encountering an error if you read every sector on the disk once.

6. Suppose we define a RAID's *access cost* as the number disk accesses divided by the number of data blocks read or written. For each of following configurations and workloads, what is the access cost?

a) Workload: a series of random 1-block writes
   Configuration: mirroring

b) Workload: a series of random 1-block writes
   Configuration: distributed parity

c) Workload: a series of random 1-block reads
   Configuration: mirroring

d) Workload: a series of random 1-block reads
   Configuration: distributed parity

e) Workload: a series of random 1-block reads
   Configuration: distributed parity with group size G and one failed disk

f) Workload: a long sequential write
   Configuration: mirroring

g) Workload: a long sequential write
   Configuration: distributed parity with a group size of G

7. Suppose that an engineer who has not taken this class tries to create a disk array with dual-redundancy but instead of using an appropriate

error correcting code such as Reed Soloman, the engineer simply stores a copy of each parity block on two disks. e.g.,

| data0 | data1 | data2 | data3 | parity | parity |

Give an example of how a two-disk failure can cause a stripe to lose data in such a system. Explain why data cannot be reconstructed in that case.

8. Some RAID systems improve reliability with intra-disk redundancy to protect against nonrecoverable read failures. For example, each individual disk on such a system might reserve one 4KB parity block in every 32 KB extent and then store 28KB (7 4KB blocks) of data and 4 KB (1 4KB block) of parity in each extent.

   In this arrangement, each data block is protected by two parity blocks: one interdisk parity block on a different disk and on intradisk parity block on the same disk.

   This approach may reduce a disk's effective nonrecoverable read error rate because if one block in an extent is lost, it can be recovered from the remaining sectors and parity on the disk. Of course, if multiple blocks in the same extent are lost, the system must rely on redundancy from other disks.

   a) Assuming that a disk's nonrecoverable read errors are independent and occur at a rate of one lost 512 byte sector per 10^{15} bits read, what is the effective nonrecoverable read error rate if the operating system stores one parity block per seven data blocks on the disk?

      Hint: You may find the bc or dc arbitrary-precision calculators useful. These programs are standard in many Unix, Linux, and OSX distributions. See the man pages for instructions.

   b) Why is the above likely to significantly overstate the impact of intra-disk redundancy?

9. Many RAID implementations allow on-line repair in which the system continues to operate after a disk failure, while a new empty disk is inserted to replaced the failed disk, and while regenerating and copying data to the new disk.

   Sketch a design for a 2-disk, mirrored RAID that allows the system to remain on-line during reconstruction, while still ensuring that when the data copying is done, the new disk is properly reconstructed (i.e., it is an exact copy of other disk.)

   In particular, specify (1) what is done by a recovery thread, (2) what is done on a read during recovery, and (3) what is done on a write

Size	
Platters/Heads	2/4
Capacity	320 GB
Performance	
Spindle speed	7200 RPM
Average seek time read/write	10.5 ms/ 12.0 ms
Maximum seek time	19 ms
Track-to-track seek time	1 ms
Transfer rate (surface to buffer)	54–128 MB/s
Transfer rate (buffer to host)	375 MB/s
Buffer memory	16 MB
Reliability	
Nonrecoverable read errors per sectors read	1 sector per 10^{14}
MTBF	600,000 hours
Product life	5 years or 20,000 power-on hours
Power	
Typical	16.35 W
Idle	11.68 W

Figure 14.11: Disk specification

during recovery. Also explain why your system will operate correctly even if a crash occurs in the middle of reconstruction.

10. Suppose you are willing to sacrifice no more than 1% of a disk's bandwidth to scrubbing. What is maximum frequency at which you could scrub a 1 TB disk with 100 MB/s bandwidth?

11. Suppose a 3 TB disk in a mirrored RAID system crashes. Assuming the disks used in the system can sustain 100MB/s sequential bandwidth, what is the minimum mean time to repair that can be achieved? Why might a system be configured to perform recovery slower than this?

12. Suppose I have a disk such as the one described in Figure 14.11 and a workload consisting of a continuous stream of updates to random blocks of the disk.

    Assume that the disk scheduler uses the SCAN/Elevator algorithm.

    (a.) What is the throughput in number of requests per second if the application issues one request at a time and waits until the block is safely stored on disk before issuing the next request?

    (b.) What is the throughput in number of requests per second if the application buffers 100 MB of writes, issues those 100 MB worth of writes to disk as a batch, and waits until those writes are safely on disk before issuing the next 100 MB batch of requests?

Suppose that we must ensure that – even in the event of a crash – the ith update can be observed by a read after crash recovery only if all updates that preceded the ith update can be read after the crash. That is, we have a FIFO property for updates – the i+1'st update cannot "finish" until the ith update finishes. (1) Design an approach to get good performance for this workload. (2) Explain why your design ensures FIFO even if crashes occur. (3) Estimate your approach's throughput in number of requests per second. (For comparison with the previous part of the problem, your solution should not require significantly more than 100MB of main-memory buffer space.)

- (c.) Design an approach to get good performance for this workload. (Be sure to explain how writes, reads, and crash recovery work.)

- (d.) Explain why your design ensures FIFO even if crashes occur.

- (e.) Estimate your approach's throughput in number of requests per second.

Part V

Index and References

Index

References

Keith Adams and Ole Agesen. A comparison of software and hardware techniques for x86 virtualization. In *Proceedings of the 12th International conference on Architectural Support for Programming Languages and Operating Systems*, ASPLOS-XII, pages 2–13, 2006.

Thomas E. Anderson, Brian N. Bershad, Edward D. Lazowska, and Henry M. Levy. Scheduler activations: effective kernel support for the user-level management of parallelism. *ACM Trans. Comput. Syst.*, 10(1):53–79, February 1992.

Thomas E. Anderson, Henry M. Levy, Brian N. Bershad, and Edward D. Lazowska. The interaction of architecture and operating system design. In *Proceedings of the fourth International conference on Architectural Support for Programming Languages and Operating Systems*, ASPLOS-IV, pages 108–120, 1991.

Andrew W. Appel and Kai Li. Virtual memory primitives for user programs. In *Proceedings of the fourth International conference on Architectural Support for Programming Languages and Operating Systems*, ASPLOS-IV, pages 96–107, 1991.

Amittai Aviram, Shu-Chun Weng, Sen Hu, and Bryan Ford. Efficient system-enforced deterministic parallelism. In *Proceedings of the 9th USENIX conference on Operating Systems Design and Implementation*, OSDI'10, pages 1–16, 2010.

Özalp Babaoglu and William Joy. Converting a swap-based system to do paging in an architecture lacking page-referenced bits. In *Proceedings of the eighth ACM Symposium on Operating Systems Principles*, SOSP '81, pages 78–86, 1981.

David Bacon, Joshua Bloch, Jeff Bogda, Cliff Click, Paul Haahr, Doug Lea, Tom May, Jan-Willem Maessen, Jeremy Manson, John D. Mitchell, Kelvin Nilsen, Bill Pugh, and Emin Gun Sirer. The "double-checked locking is broken" declaration. *http://www.cs.umd.edu/~pugh/java/memoryModel/DoubleCheckedLocking.html*.

Gaurav Banga, Peter Druschel, and Jeffrey C. Mogul. Resource containers: a new facility for resource management in server systems. In *Proceedings of the third USENIX symposium on Operating Systems Design and Implementation*, OSDI '99, pages 45–58, 1999.

Paul Barham, Boris Dragovic, Keir Fraser, Steven Hand, Tim Harris, Alex Ho, Rolf Neugebauer, Ian Pratt, and Andrew Warfield. Xen and the art of virtualization. In *Proceedings of the nineteenth ACM Symposium on Operating Systems Principles*, SOSP '03, pages 164–177, 2003.

Joel F. Bartlett. A nonstop kernel. In *Proceedings of the eighth ACM Symposium on Operating Systems Principles*, SOSP '81, pages 22–29, 1981.

Andrew Baumann, Paul Barham, Pierre-Evariste Dagand, Tim Harris, Rebecca Isaacs, Simon Peter, Timothy Roscoe, Adrian Schüpbach, and Akhilesh Singhania. The multikernel: a new OS architecture for scalable multicore systems. In *Proceedings of the 22nd ACM Symposium on Operating Systems Principles*, SOSP '09, pages 29–44, 2009.

A. Bensoussan, C. T. Clingen, and R. C. Daley. The multics virtual memory: concepts and design. *Commun. ACM*, 15(5):308–318, May 1972.

Tom Bergan, Nicholas Hunt, Luis Ceze, and Steven D. Gribble. Deterministic process groups in dOS. In *Proceedings of the 9th USENIX conference on Operating Systems Design and Implementation*, OSDI'10, pages 1–16, 2010.

B. N. Bershad, S. Savage, P. Pardyak, E. G. Sirer, M. E. Fiuczynski, D. Becker, C. Chambers, and S. Eggers. Extensibility safety and performance in the SPIN operating system. In *Proceedings of the fifteenth ACM Symposium on Operating Systems Principles*, SOSP '95, pages 267–283, 1995.

Brian N. Bershad, Thomas E. Anderson, Edward D. Lazowska, and Henry M. Levy. Lightweight remote procedure call. *ACM Trans. Comput. Syst.*, 8(1):37–55, February 1990.

Brian N. Bershad, Thomas E. Anderson, Edward D. Lazowska, and Henry M. Levy. User-level interprocess communication for shared memory multiprocessors. *ACM Trans. Comput. Syst.*, 9(2):175–198, May 1991.

Andrew Birrell. An introduction to programming with threads. Technical Report 35, Digital Equipment Corporation Systems Research Center, 1991.

Andrew D. Birrell and Bruce Jay Nelson. Implementing remote procedure calls. *ACM Trans. Comput. Syst.*, 2(1):39–59, February 1984.

Silas Boyd-Wickizer, Austin T. Clements, Yandong Mao, Aleksey Pesterev, M. Frans Kaashoek, Robert Morris, and Nickolai Zeldovich. An analysis of Linux scalability to many cores. In *Proceedings of the 9th USENIX conference on Operating Systems Design and Implementation*, OSDI'10, pages 1–8, 2010.

Lee Breslau, Pei Cao, Li Fan, Graham Phillips, and Scott Shenker. Web caching and Zipf-like distributions: evidence and implications. In *INFOCOM*, pages 126–134, 1999.

Thomas C. Bressoud and Fred B. Schneider. Hypervisor-based fault tolerance. *ACM Trans. Comput. Syst.*, 14(1):80–107, February 1996.

Sergey Brin and Lawrence Page. The anatomy of a large-scale hypertextual web search engine. In *Proceedings of the seventh International conference on the World Wide Web*, WWW7, pages 107–117, 1998.

Max Bruning. Zfs on-disk data walk (or: Where's my data?). In *OpenSolaris Developer Conference*, 2008.

Edouard Bugnion, Scott Devine, Kinshuk Govil, and Mendel Rosenblum. Disco: running commodity operating systems on scalable multiprocessors. *ACM Trans. Comput. Syst.*, 15(4):412–447, November 1997.

Brian Carrier. *File System Forensic Analysis*. Addison Wesley Professional, 2005.

Miguel Castro, Manuel Costa, Jean-Philippe Martin, Marcus Peinado, Periklis Akritidis, Austin Donnelly, Paul Barham, and Richard Black. Fast byte-granularity software fault isolation. In *Proceedings of the 22nd ACM Symposium on Operating Systems Principles*, SOSP '09, pages 45–58, 2009.

J. Chapin, M. Rosenblum, S. Devine, T. Lahiri, D. Teodosiu, and A. Gupta. Hive: fault containment for shared-memory multiprocessors. In *Proceedings of the fifteenth ACM Symposium on Operating Systems Principles*, SOSP '95, pages 12–25, 1995.

Jeffrey S. Chase, Henry M. Levy, Michael J. Feeley, and Edward D. Lazowska. Sharing and protection in a single-address-space operating system. *ACM Trans. Comput. Syst.*, 12(4):271–307, November 1994.

J. Bradley Chen and Brian N. Bershad. The impact of operating system structure on memory system performance. In *Proceedings of the fourteenth ACM Symposium on Operating Systems Principles*, SOSP '93, pages 120–133, 1993.

Peter M. Chen and Brian D. Noble. When virtual is better than real. In *Proceedings of the Eighth Workshop on Hot Topics in Operating Systems*, HOTOS '01, 2001.

David Cheriton. The V distributed system. *Commun. ACM*, 31(3):314–333, March 1988.

David R. Cheriton and Kenneth J. Duda. A caching model of operating system kernel functionality. In *Proceedings of the 1st USENIX conference on Operating Systems Design and Implementation*, OSDI '94, 1994.

David D. Clark. The structuring of systems using upcalls. In *Proceedings of the tenth ACM Symposium on Operating Systems Principles*, SOSP '85, pages 171–180, 1985.

Jeremy Condit, Edmund B. Nightingale, Christopher Frost, Engin Ipek, Benjamin Lee, Doug Burger, and Derrick Coetzee. Better I/O through byte-addressable, persistent memory. In *Proceedings of the 22nd ACM Symposium on Operating Systems Principles*, SOSP '09, pages 133–146, 2009.

Fernando J. Corbató. On building systems that will fail. *Commun. ACM*, 34(9):72–81, September 1991.

Fernando J. Corbató and Victor A. Vyssotsky. Introduction and overview of the Multics system. *AFIPS Fall Joint Computer Conference*, 27(1):185–196, 1965.

R. J. Creasy. The origin of the VM/370 time-sharing system. *IBM J. Res. Dev.*, 25(5):483–490, September 1981.

Michael D. Dahlin, Randolph Y. Wang, Thomas E. Anderson, and David A. Patterson. Cooperative caching: using remote client memory to improve file system performance. In *Proceedings of the 1st USENIX conference on Operating Systems Design and Implementation*, OSDI '94, 1994.

Robert C. Daley and Jack B. Dennis. Virtual memory, processes, and sharing in Multics. *Commun. ACM*, 11(5):306–312, May 1968.

Wiebren de Jonge, M. Frans Kaashoek, and Wilson C. Hsieh. The logical disk: a new approach to improving file systems. In *Proceedings of the fourteenth ACM Symposium on Operating Systems Principles*, SOSP '93, pages 15–28, 1993.

Jeffrey Dean and Sanjay Ghemawat. MapReduce: simplified data processing on large clusters. In *Proceedings of the 6th conference on Symposium on Opearting Systems Design & Implementation*, OSDI'04, pages 10–10, 2004.

Peter J. Denning. The working set model for program behavior. *Commun. ACM*, 11(5):323–333, May 1968.

P.J. Denning. Working sets past and present. *Software Engineering, IEEE Transactions on*, SE-6(1):64 – 84, jan. 1980.

Jack B. Dennis. Segmentation and the design of multiprogrammed computer systems. *J. ACM*, 12(4):589–602, October 1965.

Jack B. Dennis and Earl C. Van Horn. Programming semantics for multiprogrammed computations. *Commun. ACM*, 9(3):143–155, March 1966.

E. W. Dijkstra. Solution of a problem in concurrent programming control. *Commun. ACM*, 8(9):569–, September 1965.

Edsger W. Dijkstra. The structure of the "THE"-multiprogramming system. *Commun. ACM*, 11(5):341–346, May 1968.

Mihai Dobrescu, Norbert Egi, Katerina Argyraki, Byung-Gon Chun, Kevin Fall, Gianluca Iannaccone, Allan Knies, Maziar Manesh, and Sylvia Ratnasamy. Routebricks: exploiting parallelism to scale software routers. In *Proceedings of the 22nd ACM Symposium on Operating Systems Principles*, SOSP '09, pages 15–28, 2009.

Alan Donovan, Robert Muth, Brad Chen, and David Sehr. Portable Native Client executables. Technical report, Google, 2012.

Fred Douglis and John Ousterhout. Transparent process migration: design alternatives and the sprite implementation. *Softw. Pract. Exper.*, 21(8):757–785, July 1991.

Richard P. Draves, Brian N. Bershad, Richard F. Rashid, and Randall W. Dean. Using continuations to implement thread management and communication in operating systems. In *Proceedings of the thirteenth ACM Symposium on Operating Systems Principles*, SOSP '91, pages 122–136, 1991.

Peter Druschel and Larry L. Peterson. Fbufs: a high-bandwidth cross-domain transfer facility. *SIGOPS Oper. Syst. Rev.*, 27(5):189–202, December 1993.

George W. Dunlap, Samuel T. King, Sukru Cinar, Murtaza A. Basrai, and Peter M. Chen. ReVirt: enabling intrusion analysis through virtual-machine logging and replay. *SIGOPS Oper. Syst. Rev.*, 36(SI):211–224, December 2002.

Petros Efstathopoulos, Maxwell Krohn, Steve VanDeBogart, Cliff Frey, David Ziegler, Eddie Kohler, David Mazières, Frans Kaashoek, and Robert Morris. Labels and event processes in the Asbestos operating system. In *Proceedings of the twentieth ACM Symposium on Operating Systems Principles*, SOSP '05, pages 17–30, 2005.

D. R. Engler, M. F. Kaashoek, and J. O'Toole, Jr. Exokernel: an operating system architecture for application-level resource management. In *Proceedings of the fifteenth ACM Symposium on Operating Systems Principles*, SOSP '95, pages 251–266, 1995.

Dawson Engler, David Yu Chen, Seth Hallem, Andy Chou, and Benjamin Chelf. Bugs as deviant behavior: a general approach to inferring errors in systems code. In *Proceedings of the eighteenth ACM Symposium on Operating Systems Principles*, SOSP '01, pages 57–72, 2001.

R. S. Fabry. Capability-based addressing. *Commun. ACM*, 17(7):403–412, July 1974.

Jason Flinn and M. Satyanarayanan. Energy-aware adaptation for mobile applications. In *Proceedings of the seventeenth ACM Symposium on Operating Systems Principles*, SOSP '99, pages 48–63, 1999.

Christopher Frost, Mike Mammarella, Eddie Kohler, Andrew de los Reyes, Shant Hovsepian, Andrew Matsuoka, and Lei Zhang. Generalized file system dependencies. In *Proceedings of twenty-first ACM Symposium on Operating Systems Principles*, SOSP '07, pages 307–320, 2007.

Gregory R. Ganger, Marshall Kirk McKusick, Craig A. N. Soules, and Yale N. Patt. Soft updates: a solution to the metadata update problem in file systems. *ACM Trans. Comput. Syst.*, 18(2):127–153, May 2000.

Simson Garfinkel and Gene Spafford. *Practical Unix and Internet security (2nd ed.)*. O'Reilly & Associates, Inc., 1996.

Tal Garfinkel, Ben Pfaff, Jim Chow, Mendel Rosenblum, and Dan Boneh. Terra: a virtual machine-based platform for trusted computing. In *Proceedings of the nineteenth ACM Symposium on Operating Systems Principles*, SOSP '03, pages 193–206, 2003.

Kirk Glerum, Kinshuman Kinshumann, Steve Greenberg, Gabriel Aul, Vince Orgovan, Greg Nichols, David Grant, Gretchen Loihle, and Galen Hunt. Debugging in the (very) large: ten years of implementation and experience. In *Proceedings of the 22nd ACM Symposium on Operating Systems Principles*, SOSP '09, pages 103–116, 2009.

R.P. Goldberg. Survey of virtual machine research. *IEEE Computer*, 7(6):34–45, June 1974.

Kinshuk Govil, Dan Teodosiu, Yongqiang Huang, and Mendel Rosenblum. Cellular Disco: resource management using virtual clusters on shared-memory multiprocessors. In *Proceedings of the seventeenth ACM Symposium on Operating Systems Principles*, SOSP '99, pages 154–169, 1999.

Jim Gray. The transaction concept: virtues and limitations (invited paper). In *Proceedings of the seventh International conference on Very Large Data Bases*, VLDB '81, pages 144–154, 1981.

Jim Gray. Why do computers stop and what can be done about it? Technical Report TR-85.7, HP Labs, 1985.

Jim Gray, Paul McJones, Mike Blasgen, Bruce Lindsay, Raymond Lorie, Tom Price, Franco Putzolu, and Irving Traiger. The recovery manager of the System R database manager. *ACM Comput. Surv.*, 13(2):223–242, June 1981.

Jim Gray and Andreas Reuter. *Transaction Processing: Concepts and Techniques*. Morgan Kaufmann, 1993.

Jim Gray and Daniel P. Siewiorek. High-availability computer systems. *Computer*, 24(9):39–48, September 1991.

Diwaker Gupta, Sangmin Lee, Michael Vrable, Stefan Savage, Alex C. Snoeren, George Varghese, Geoffrey M. Voelker, and Amin Vahdat. Difference engine: harnessing memory redundancy in virtual machines. In *Proceedings of the 8th USENIX conference on Operating Systems Design and Implementation*, OSDI'08, pages 309–322, 2008.

Hadoop. http://hadoop.apache.org.

Steven M. Hand. Self-paging in the Nemesis operating system. In *Proceedings of the third USENIX Symposium on Operating Systems Design and Implementation*, OSDI '99, pages 73–86, 1999.

Per Brinch Hansen. The nucleus of a multiprogramming system. *Commun. ACM*, 13(4):238–241, April 1970.

Mor Harchol-Balter and Allen B. Downey. Exploiting process lifetime distributions for dynamic load balancing. In *Proceedings of the fifteenth ACM Symposium on Operating Systems Principles*, SOSP '95, pages 236–, 1995.

Kieran Harty and David R. Cheriton. Application-controlled physical memory using external page-cache management. In *Proceedings of the fifth International conference on Architectural Support for Programming Languages and Operating Systems*, ASPLOS-V, pages 187–197, 1992.

Rober Haskin, Yoni Malachi, and Gregory Chan. Recovery management in QuickSilver. *ACM Trans. Comput. Syst.*, 6(1):82–108, February 1988.

John L. Hennessy and David A. Patterson. *Computer Architecture - A Quantitative Approach (5. ed.)*. Morgan Kaufmann, 2012.

Maurice Herlihy. Wait-free synchronization. *ACM Trans. Program. Lang. Syst.*, 13(1):124–149, January 1991.

Maurice Herlihy and Nir Shavit. *The Art of Multiprocessor Programming*. Morgan Kaufmann, 2008.

Dave Hitz, James Lau, and Michael Malcolm. File system design for an NFS file server appliance. Technical Report 3002, Network Appliance, 1995.

C. A. R Hoare. Monitors: An operating system structuring concept. *Communications of the ACM*, 17:549–557, 1974.

Charles Antony Richard Hoare. The emperor's old clothes. *Commun. ACM*, 24(2):75–83, February 1981.

Thomas R. Horsley and William C. Lynch. Pilot: A software engineering case study. In *Proceedings of the 4th International conference on Software engineering*, ICSE '79, pages 94–99, 1979.

Raj Jain. *The Art of Computer Systems Performance Analysis*. John Wiley & Sons, 1991.

Paul A. Karger, Mary Ellen Zurko, Douglas W. Bonin, Andrew H. Mason, and Clifford E. Kahn. A retrospective on the VAX VMM security kernel. *IEEE Trans. Softw. Eng.*, 17(11):1147–1165, November 1991.

Yousef A. Khalidi and Michael N. Nelson. Extensible file systems in spring. In *Proceedings of the fourteenth ACM Symposium on Operating Systems Principles*, SOSP '93, pages 1–14, 1993.

Gerwin Klein, Kevin Elphinstone, Gernot Heiser, June Andronick, David Cock, Philip Derrin, Dhammika Elkaduwe, Kai Engelhardt, Rafal Kolanski, Michael Norrish, Thomas Sewell, Harvey Tuch, and Simon Winwood. sel4: formal verification of an OS kernel. In *Proceedings of the ACM SIGOPS 22nd Symposium on Operating Systems Principles*, SOSP '09, pages 207–220, 2009.

L. Kleinrock and R. R. Muntz. Processor sharing queueing models of mixed scheduling disciplines for time shared system. *J. ACM*, 19(3):464–482, July 1972.

Leonard Kleinrock. *Queueing Systems, Volume II: Computer Applications.* Wiley Interscience, 1976.

H. T. Kung and John T. Robinson. On optimistic methods for concurrency control. *ACM Trans. Database Syst.*, 6(2):213–226, June 1981.

Leslie Lamport. A fast mutual exclusion algorithm. *ACM Trans. Comput. Syst.*, 5(1):1–11, January 1987.

B. W. Lampson. Hints for computer system design. *IEEE Softw.*, 1(1):11–28, January 1984.

Butler Lampson and Howard Sturgis. Crash recovery in a distributed data storage system. Technical report, Xerox Palo Alto Research Center, 1979.

Butler W. Lampson and David D. Redell. Experience with processes and monitors in Mesa. *Commun. ACM*, 23(2):105–117, February 1980.

Butler W. Lampson and Howard E. Sturgis. Reflections on an operating system design. *Commun. ACM*, 19(5):251–265, May 1976.

James Larus and Galen Hunt. The Singularity system. *Commun. ACM*, 53(8):72–79, August 2010.

Hugh C. Lauer and Roger M. Needham. On the duality of operating system structures. In *Operating Systems Review*, pages 3–19, 1979.

Edward D. Lazowska, John Zahorjan, G. Scott Graham, and Kenneth C. Sevcik. *Quantitative system performance: computer system analysis using queueing network models.* Prentice-Hall, Inc., 1984.

Will E. Leland, Murad S. Taqqu, Walter Willinger, and Daniel V. Wilson. On the self-similar nature of Ethernet traffic (extended version). *IEEE/ACM Trans. Netw.*, 2(1):1–15, February 1994.

N. G. Leveson and C. S. Turner. An investigation of the Therac-25 accidents. *Computer*, 26(7):18–41, July 1993.

H. M. Levy and P. H. Lipman. Virtual memory management in the VAX/VMS operating system. *Computer*, 15(3):35–41, March 1982.

J. Liedtke. On micro-kernel construction. In *Proceedings of the fifteenth ACM Symposium on Operating Systems Principles*, SOSP '95, pages 237–250, 1995.

John Lions. *Lions' Commentary on UNIX 6th Edition, with Source Code.* Peer-to-Peer Communications, 1996.

J. S. Liptay. Structural aspects of the System/360 model 85: ii the cache. *IBM Syst. J.*, 7(1):15–21, March 1968.

David E. Lowell, Subhachandra Chandra, and Peter M. Chen. Exploring failure transparency and the limits of generic recovery. In *Proceedings of the 4th conference on Symposium on Operating Systems Design and Implementation*, OSDI'00, pages 20–20, 2000.

David E. Lowell and Peter M. Chen. Free transactions with Rio Vista. In *Proceedings of the sixteenth ACM Symposium on Operating Systems Principles*, SOSP '97, pages 92–101, 1997.

P. McKenney. Is parallel programming hard, and, if so, what can be done about it? http://kernel.org/pub/linux/kernel/people/paulmck/perfbook/perfbook.2011.05.30a.pdf.

Paul E. McKenney, Dipankar Sarma, Andrea Arcangeli, Andi Kleen, Orran Krieger, and Rusty Russell. Read-copy update. In *Ottawa Linux Symposium*, pages 338–367, June 2002.

Marshall K. McKusick, William N. Joy, Samuel J. Leffler, and Robert S. Fabry. A fast file system for UNIX. *ACM Trans. Comput. Syst.*, 2(3):181–197, August 1984.

Marshall Kirk McKusick, Keith Bostic, Michael J. Karels, and John S. Quarterman. *The design and implementation of the 4.4BSD operating system.* Addison Wesley Longman Publishing Co., Inc., 1996.

Scott Meyers and Andrei Alexandrescu. C++ and the perils of double-checked locking. *Dr. Dobbs Journal*, 2004.

Jeffrey C. Mogul and K. K. Ramakrishnan. Eliminating receive livelock in an interrupt-driven kernel. *ACM Trans. Comput. Syst.*, 15(3):217–252, August 1997.

Jeffrey C. Mogul, Richard F. Rashid, and Michael J. Accetta. The packet filter: An efficient mechanism for user-level network code. In *In the Proceedings of the eleventh ACM Symposium on Operating Systems Principles*, pages 39–51, 1987.

C. Mohan, Don Haderle, Bruce Lindsay, Hamid Pirahesh, and Peter Schwarz. ARIES: a transaction recovery method supporting fine-granularity locking and partial rollbacks using write-ahead logging. *ACM Trans. Database Syst.*, 17(1):94–162, March 1992.

Gordon E. Moore. Cramming more components onto integrated circuits. *Electronics*, 38(8):114âĂŞ–117, 1965.

Madanlal Musuvathi, Shaz Qadeer, Thomas Ball, Gerard Basler, Piramanayagam Arumuga Nainar, and Iulian Neamtiu. Finding and reproducing Heisenbugs in concurrent programs. In *Proceedings of the 8th USENIX conference on Operating Systems Design and Implementation*, OSDI'08, pages 267–280, 2008.

George C. Necula and Peter Lee. Safe kernel extensions without run-time checking. In *Proceedings of the second USENIX Symposium on Operating Systems Design and Implementation*, OSDI '96, pages 229–243, 1996.

Edmund B. Nightingale, Kaushik Veeraraghavan, Peter M. Chen, and Jason Flinn. Rethink the sync. *ACM Trans. Comput. Syst.*, 26(3):6:1–6:26, September 2008.

Elliott I. Organick. *The Multics system: an examination of its structure*. MIT Press, 1972.

Steven Osman, Dinesh Subhraveti, Gong Su, and Jason Nieh. The design and implementation of Zap: a system for migrating computing environments. In *Proceedings of the fifth USENIX Symposium on Operating Systems Design and Implementation*, OSDI '02, pages 361–376, 2002.

John Ousterhout. Scheduling techniques for concurrent systems. In *Proceedings of Third International Conference on Distributed Computing Systems*, pages 22–âĂŤ30, 1982.

John Ousterhout. Why aren't operating systems getting faster as fast as hardware? In *Proceedings USENIX Conference*, pages 247–256, 1990.

Vivek S. Pai, Peter Druschel, and Willy Zwaenepoel. Flash: an efficient and portable web server. In *Proceedings of the annual conference on USENIX Annual Technical Conference*, ATEC '99, pages 15–15, 1999.

Vivek S. Pai, Peter Druschel, and Willy Zwaenepoel. IO-lite: a unified I/O buffering and caching system. In *Proceedings of the third USENIX Symposium on Operating Systems Design and Implementation*, OSDI '99, pages 15–28, 1999.

David A. Patterson, Garth Gibson, and Randy H. Katz. A case for redundant arrays of inexpensive disks (RAID). In *Proceedings of the 1988 ACM SIGMOD International conference on Management of Data*, SIGMOD '88, pages 109–116, 1988.

L. Peterson, N. Hutchinson, S. O'Malley, and M. Abbott. RPC in the x-Kernel: evaluating new design techniques. In *Proceedings of the twelfth ACM Symposium on Operating Systems Principles*, SOSP '89, pages 91–101, 1989.

Jonathan Pincus and Brandon Baker. Beyond stack smashing: recent advances in exploiting buffer overruns. *IEEE Security and Privacy*, 2(4):20–27, July 2004.

Eduardo Pinheiro, Wolf-Dietrich Weber, and Luiz André Barroso. Failure trends in a large disk drive population. In *Proceedings of the 5th USENIX conference on File and Storage Technologies*, FAST '07, pages 2–2, 2007.

Vijayan Prabhakaran, Lakshmi N. Bairavasundaram, Nitin Agrawal, Haryadi S. Gunawi, Andrea C. Arpaci-Dusseau, and Remzi H. Arpaci-Dusseau. IRON file systems. In *Proceedings of the twentieth ACM Symposium on Operating Systems Principles*, SOSP '05, pages 206–220, 2005.

Richard Rashid, Robert Baron, Alessandro Forin, David Golub, Michael Jones, Daniel Julin, Douglas Orr, and Richard Sanzi. Mach: A foundation for open systems. In *Proceedings of the Second Workshop on Workstation Operating Systems(WWOS2)*, 1989.

Richard F. Rashid, Avadis Tevanian, Michael Young, David B. Golub, Robert V. Baron, David L. Black, William J. Bolosky, and Jonathan Chew. Machine-independent virtual memory management for paged uniprocessor and multiprocessor architectures. *IEEE Trans. Computers*, 37(8):896–907, 1988.

E.S. Raymond. *The Cathedral and the Bazaar: Musings On Linux And Open Source By An Accidental Revolutionary*. O'Reilly Series. O'Reilly, 2001.

David D. Redell, Yogen K. Dalal, Thomas R. Horsley, Hugh C. Lauer, William C. Lynch, Paul R. McJones, Hal G. Murray, and Stephen C. Purcell. Pilot: an operating system for a personal computer. *Commun. ACM*, 23(2):81–92, February 1980.

Dennis M. Ritchie and Ken Thompson. The UNIX time-sharing system. *Commun. ACM*, 17(7):365–375, July 1974.

Mendel Rosenblum and John K. Ousterhout. The design and implementation of a log-structured file system. *ACM Trans. Comput. Syst.*, 10(1):26–52, February 1992.

Chris Ruemmler and John Wilkes. An introduction to disk drive modeling. *Computer*, 27(3):17–28, March 1994.

J. H. Saltzer, D. P. Reed, and D. D. Clark. End-to-end arguments in system design. *ACM Trans. Comput. Syst.*, 2(4):277–288, November 1984.

Jerome H. Saltzer. Protection and the control of information sharing in Multics. *Commun. ACM*, 17(7):388–402, July 1974.

M. Satyanarayanan, Henry H. Mashburn, Puneet Kumar, David C. Steere, and James J. Kistler. Lightweight recoverable virtual memory. *ACM Trans. Comput. Syst.*, 12(1):33–57, February 1994.

Stefan Savage, Michael Burrows, Greg Nelson, Patrick Sobalvarro, and Thomas Anderson. Eraser: a dynamic data race detector for multithreaded programs. *ACM Trans. Comput. Syst.*, 15(4):391–411, November 1997.

Bianca Schroeder and Garth A. Gibson. Disk failures in the real world: what does an mttf of 1,000,000 hours mean to you? In *Proceedings of the 5th USENIX conference on File and Storage Technologies*, FAST '07, 2007.

Bianca Schroeder and Mor Harchol-Balter. Web servers under overload: How scheduling can help. *ACM Trans. Internet Technol.*, 6(1):20–52, February 2006.

Michael D. Schroeder, David D. Clark, and Jerome H. Saltzer. The Multics kernel design project. In *Proceedings of the sixth ACM Symposium on Operating Systems Principles*, SOSP '77, pages 43–56, 1977.

Michael D. Schroeder and Jerome H. Saltzer. A hardware architecture for implementing protection rings. *Commun. ACM*, 15(3):157–170, March 1972.

D. P. Siewiorek. Architecture of fault-tolerant computers. *Computer*, 17(8):9–18, August 1984.

E. H. Spafford. Crisis and aftermath. *Commun. ACM*, 32(6):678–687, June 1989.

Structured Query Language (SQL). http://en.wikipedia.org/wiki/SQL.

Michael Stonebraker. Operating system support for database management. *Commun. ACM*, 24(7):412–418, July 1981.

Michael M. Swift, Muthukaruppan Annamalai, Brian N. Bershad, and Henry M. Levy. Recovering device drivers. *ACM Trans. Comput. Syst.*, 24(4):333–360, November 2006.

K. Thompson. Unix implementation. *Bell System Technical Journal*, 57:1931–1946, 1978.

Ken Thompson. Reflections on trusting trust. *Commun. ACM*, 27(8):761–763, August 1984.

Joost S. M. Verhofstad. Recovery techniques for database systems. *ACM Comput. Surv.*, 10(2):167–195, June 1978.

Michael Vrable, Justin Ma, Jay Chen, David Moore, Erik Vandekieft, Alex C. Snoeren, Geoffrey M. Voelker, and Stefan Savage. Scalability, fidelity, and containment in the Potemkin virtual honeyfarm. In *Proceedings of the twentieth ACM Symposium on Operating Systems Principles*, SOSP '05, pages 148–162, 2005.

Robert Wahbe, Steven Lucco, Thomas E. Anderson, and Susan L. Graham. Efficient software-based fault isolation. In *Proceedings of the fourteenth ACM Symposium on Operating Systems Principles*, SOSP '93, pages 203–216, 1993.

Carl A. Waldspurger. Memory resource management in VMware ESX server. *SIGOPS Oper. Syst. Rev.*, 36(SI):181–194, December 2002.

Andrew Whitaker, Marianne Shaw, and Steven D. Gribble. Scale and performance in the Denali isolation kernel. In *Proceedings of the fifth USENIX Symposium on Operating Systems Design and Implementation*, OSDI '02, pages 195–209, 2002.

J. Wilkes, R. Golding, C. Staelin, and T. Sullivan. The HP AutoRAID hierarchical storage system. In *Proceedings of the fifteenth ACM Symposium on Operating Systems Principles*, SOSP '95, pages 96–108, 1995.

Alec Wolman, M. Voelker, Nitin Sharma, Neal Cardwell, Anna Karlin, and Henry M. Levy. On the scale and performance of cooperative web proxy caching. In *Proceedings of the seventeenth ACM Symposium on Operating Systems Principles*, SOSP '99, pages 16–31, 1999.

W. Wulf, E. Cohen, W. Corwin, A. Jones, R. Levin, C. Pierson, and F. Pollack. Hydra: the kernel of a multiprocessor operating system. *Commun. ACM*, 17(6):337–345, June 1974.

Bennet Yee, David Sehr, Gregory Dardyk, J. Bradley Chen, Robert Muth, Tavis Ormandy, Shiki Okasaka, Neha Narula, and Nicholas Fullagar. Native Client: a sandbox for portable, untrusted x86 native code. In *Proceedings of the 2009 30th IEEE Symposium on Security and Privacy*, SP '09, pages 79–93, 2009.

Nickolai Zeldovich, Silas Boyd-Wickizer, Eddie Kohler, and David Mazières. Making information flow explicit in HiStar. *Commun. ACM*, 54(11):93–101, November 2011.